Theories and Applications of Counseling and Psychotherapy

I dedicate this textbook to Jackie Ginter. If truth be told, I would have accomplished very few—more likely none—of my professional achievements without the undying support, vital assistance, insightful opinions, and love that Jackie provided me over the last 43 years of our relationship. Years ago I read in The Bhagavad-Gita: Krishna's Counsel in Time of War (Vyasa, 1986) a passage (repeated below) that relates to clear thinking, strong passion, and inactivity that can comingle in a manner to bring about a "dark inertia." Jackie has always been there to share her views concerning how I could successfully overcome any such problematic dark inertia.

Lucidity addicts one to joy,

and passions to actions,

but dark inertia obscures knowledge

and addicts one to negligence.

Earl J. Ginter

*For my parents, Nepal Chandra and Amita Rai Sircar, who believed in their daughters'
educational and professional advancements, which belief I transmit to
my granddaughters Josephine Amita, Simone Sangitha, and Katherine Swati.*

Gargi Roysircar

*To my brilliant doctoral program advisors, Wayne Antenen and Abraham Tesser, and my highly talented
and creative psychotherapy mentors and teachers: Harry Bates, Insoo Berg, Warren C. Bonney,
Steve de Shazer, Helen Kramer, Elizabeth Sheerer, Peter Sherrard, and Elwyn Zimmerman.*

Lawrence H. Gerstein

Sara Miller McCune founded SAGE Publishing in 1965 to support the dissemination of usable knowledge and educate a global community. SAGE publishes more than 1000 journals and over 800 new books each year, spanning a wide range of subject areas. Our growing selection of library products includes archives, data, case studies and video. SAGE remains majority owned by our founder and after her lifetime will become owned by a charitable trust that secures the company's continued independence.

Los Angeles | London | New Delhi | Singapore | Washington DC | Melbourne

Theories and Applications of Counseling and Psychotherapy

Relevance Across Cultures and Settings

Earl J. Ginter

University of Georgia

Gargi Roysircar

Antioch University New England

Lawrence H. Gerstein

Ball State University

Los Angeles | London | New Delhi
Singapore | Washington DC | Melbourne

FOR INFORMATION:

SAGE Publications, Inc.
2455 Teller Road
Thousand Oaks, California 91320
E-mail: order@sagepub.com

SAGE Publications Ltd.
1 Oliver's Yard
55 City Road
London EC1Y 1SP
United Kingdom

SAGE Publications India Pvt. Ltd.
B 1/I 1 Mohan Cooperative Industrial Area
Mathura Road, New Delhi 110 044
India

SAGE Publications Asia-Pacific Pte. Ltd.
3 Church Street
#10–04 Samsung Hub
Singapore 049483

Acquisitions Editor: Abbie Rickard
Content Development Editor: Emma Newsom
Editorial Assistant: Jennifer Cline
Marketing Manager: Susannah Goldes
Production Editor: Veronica Stapleton Hooper
Copy Editor: Colleen Brennan
Typesetter: C&M Digitals (P) Ltd.
Proofreader: Dennis W. Webb
Indexer: Jean Casalegno
Cover Designer: Michael Dubowe
Cover Art: Lawrence H. Gerstein and John Melvin

Printed in the United States of America

Library of Congress Cataloging-in-Publication Data

Names: Ginter, Earl J., 1950- author. | Roysircar Sodowsky, Gargi, author. | Gerstein, Lawrence H., author.

Title: Theories and applications of counseling and psychotherapy : relevance across cultures and settings / Earl J. Ginter, The University of Georgia, Gargi Roysircar, Antioch New England Graduate School, Lawrence H. Gerstein, Ball State University.

Description: Thousand Oaks : SAGE, [2019] | Includes bibliographical references and index.

Identifiers: LCCN 2017053991 | ISBN 9781412967594 (pbk. : acid-free paper)

Subjects: LCSH: Counseling—Philosophy. | Psychotherapy—Philosophy.

Classification: LCC BF636.6 .G56 2019 | DDC 158.301—dc23
LC record available at https://lccn.loc.gov/2017053991

This book is printed on acid-free paper.

SFI label applies to text stock

18 19 20 21 22 10 9 8 7 6 5 4 3 2 1

BRIEF CONTENTS

DETAILED CONTENTS

FOREWORD

What is the purpose of this book? Unlike most books presenting major theories of counseling and psychotherapy, this text focuses on preparing the reader (most likely a student) to arrive at a self-constructed theoretical model to follow. In fact, Chapter 15, the final chapter, is devoted to guidelines and procedures to follow to accomplish this goal. This is a unique and a challenging effort on the part of the authors.

My first impression of the text was its comprehensiveness. In fact, I use the term *encyclopedic* to describe it. Let me go on to describe some of the major features of the text in addition to the 12 major theories that are presented.

In Chapter 1, the authors present a brief but important history of the development of the terms *counseling* and *psychotherapy* to describe the practices that identified them. They conclude that what were quite different emphases in the beginning in treating mental and emotional illness have become less clear and overlapping today. Chapter 1 also deals with the attributes used to judge the soundness of a theory, terminology, target audience, foci of the 12 theory chapters, and seeing the big picture, such as the fundamental nature of reality and human existence.

Also in Chapter 1, the authors describe a unique feature of this text. It is what they call moving beyond words through the use of creative forms of expression such as eye-catching symbols or visual illusions, works by painters and sculptors, segments of poems, and musical lyrics that convey insight and tell a story.

Chapter 2 is especially valuable because it focuses on the development of the counselor and psychologist as a person and the professional associations and ethical and legal requirements, such as licensure and certification, for counselors and psychologists.

The following theoretical positions are presented in Chapters 3 through 14: psychoanalysis, Adlerian, existential, client- or person-centered, gestalt, behavioral, cognitive-behavioral, reality, feminist, postmodern, family systems, and multicultural. Each theory is comprehensively described with respect to the following: biographical background on the major originator(s) of a theory, basic theoretical concepts and assumptions, components of the therapeutic process (e.g., role of counselor or psychotherapist and client, nature of the therapeutic relationship, how goals are established, therapeutic techniques that are commonly linked with the approach, theoretical explanation for client change), unique ethical concerns, research support for the theory's approach, critique of strengths and identification of shortcomings, relevance to current mental health delivery systems (e.g., how the approach is suited for systems that rely on managed care time limits, use of the approach in mental health settings, client populations generally served), an example of how the theoretical approach covered might be applied when working with actual clients (including the role of multiculturalism), the role of social justice, summary comments by the chapter's author(s), and recommended publications.

The authors made a concerted effort to describe each of the theories and approaches in a manner that offers a "balanced, deliberate, and judicious coverage of the various theoretical approaches." My evaluation of their effort to do so exceeded my expectations.

According to the authors, this textbook was designed to provide a comprehensive overview of those therapeutic approaches that emerged from what was to become a multitheoretical system whose origin could be traced to the late 1800s. This textbook was also designed for readers who seek an introduction to the world of therapy, especially those enrolled in introductory undergraduate courses offered through counselor education, psychology, social work, and criminal justice programs. Further, this textbook is appropriate for advanced curriculums, which reacquaint students with previously studied theories. This reviewer fully agrees with the recommended users of the text and is unequivocal in his recommendation!

George M. Gazda, EdD

Research Professor of Education, Emeritus

College of Education, University of Georgia

Past President of American Counseling Association

Past President of American Psychological Association Division 17 (Society of Counseling Psychology)

PREFACE

The decision to write this textbook began when Lawrence (Larry) Gerstein, who had just published the ***Handbook for Social Justice in Counseling Psychology: Leadership, Vision, and Action,*** was approached by Kassie Graves of SAGE Publications and asked if he would consider co-authoring a theories of counseling and psychotherapy textbook. After Larry agreed to take on the proposed project he subsequently contacted Earl Ginter and Gargi Roysircar and invited them to participate. Before the writing phase of this collaborative effort started the three authors decided that a critical first step was to compile a list of strengths and weaknesses found in various theory textbooks that were used in psychology and counseling programs. In addition to the weaknesses and strengths the authors were personally aware of in a number of existing textbooks, they approached veteran teachers of theory courses at several universities to elicit what these professors considered to represent common problematic features and inherent assets of the textbooks they had adopted for use in their theory course(s). The authors pooled their own and the consulted professors' assessment of negative and positive qualities. A larger number of weaknesses than strengths were identified that everyone agreed posed problems that hindered, to varying degrees, what students needed to learn by the end of an academic term. The authors of this textbook made a concerted effort to avoid and/or address the weaknesses uncovered while also incorporating the strengths identified.

Goals for this Textbook

The authors believe they have written a textbook that offers both upper level undergraduates and beginning graduate students in counseling and psychology a comprehensive, readily attainable examination of essential theories that support and guide the therapeutic approaches relied upon by practitioners. The authors also believe that persons pursuing a career in another of the mental health fields, for example, social work, psychiatric nursing, criminal justice, paraprofessional jobs focused on alcohol and substance abuse, and so forth would find this textbook invaluable for broadening their understanding of how certain treatment approaches might interface with their treatment responsibilities.

The optimum depth and width of coverage that characterize this textbook, believed by the authors to be necessary for a theory course, was accomplished using a style of presentation that would appeal to present day students. The authors purposely sought clarity of content by avoiding the use of needless jargon that might make a topic area needlessly difficult, if not unintelligible, for readers who were new to the field. The primary aim was to expose readers to enough specialized terminology to allow them to differentiate among the various approaches to therapy and to comprehend the unique contributions made by each of the theories to the practice of therapy. (The term "therapy" is used throughout this textbook to refer to the wide array of existing mental health practices.) Whenever technical terms, and concepts tied to those terms, were introduced in one chapter they were used in a consistent manner throughout the remainder of this textbook. In addition to these characteristics, there are several other special features of this textbook that should be emphasized.

Features of this Textbook

Guides for Summarizing the Various Theories

The authors included an ongoing student exercise that is explained at the end of Chapter 1 and concludes in Chapter 15. This exercise prepares students to write six specific summaries for each of the theory chapters by utilizing a template provided at the end of Chapter 1. The exact procedure students are to follow was illustrated via a completed template that corresponded to six critical elements that are covered in each of the twelve theory chapters. In Chapter 15, students receive further instructions that outline the steps to take and the questions to answer so they can correctly utilize their personal summaries to isolate those aspects of the various theories that they find most helpful to create their own personal theoretical approach to counseling or psychotherapy.

Professional Organizations, Ethical Codes, Stresses Encountered, and Self-Care

The content found in Chapter 2 is especially valuable for readers to consider since it focuses on the development of the person as a professional and it reviews important features of two prominent associations (i.e., American Counseling Association and American Psychological Association) in the mental health field. The chapter also covers ethical and legal requirements associated with professional practice, licensure and certification, and the issue of self-care to prevent the kind of burnout associated with the exhaustion of physical, emotional, and motivational resources that can result from prolonged exposure to stress.

Authors' Use of Cultural Artifacts

A unique feature of this textbook resulted from the authors deciding to explain certain theoretical concepts or intervention strategies by incorporating dialogues and characters from movies and TV shows, paintings, drawings, quotations, poems, short stories, lyrics, news articles, photographs, or comics. The authors have found in their own classes that such an approach heightens students' attention to and interest in a textbook's content even when that content can prove a challenge to those unfamiliar with the various theories. For example, the well-known painting by Edvard Munch, "The Scream," portrays a strong felt experience without using a single word (see Figure 1). The image created by Munch resonates with viewers of his painting, an image that immediately communicates the horrible anguish felt by the depicted figure. The quality of certain images, such as this one, have the power to persist and retain their effect long after a student moves on to consider something else. Without a doubt Munch's painting can be relied on to convey the type of potentially life changing experience often referred to by existential therapists. If one looks carefully at "The Scream" one begins to see the high-pitched wail of someone who realizes he or she is nothing more than a speck in an immense universe that is bone-chilling cold and uncaring. A universe that does not provide any ready-made, universally applicable reason for living. According to existential theory, this represents the turning point where a client can either give in to the overwhelming pain, grief, and anger associated with such a horrifying realization or the client can seize the situation as an opportunity to create his or her own meaningful purpose and reason for living.

Focus on Multicultural and Social Justice Issues

Multicultural and social justice principles and therapeutic strategies were also incorporated by the authors throughout this textbook. This was done to help students understand the interaction between diversity, social justice, and how to conceptualize, assess, and intervene with clients from various racial and ethnic backgrounds. In addition, the textbook features two client cases for each of the theory chapters. One case is introduced once and not used elsewhere in the textbook, and the other one is a multicultural client case (i.e., the case of Miguel Sanchez) that is reintroduced in each of the twelve theory chapters to illustrate how different therapists, operating from different therapeutic approaches, are likely to conceptualize and approach the same case. The repeated use of the latter client case serves to educate students about how the same exact client can receive treatment using a different theoretically based approach. The case of Miguel Sanchez allowed the authors to explicitly demonstrate how each theory motivates a therapist's actions and thoughts during therapy sessions and guides the therapist in ways to gauge the degree of progress made by a client and when it is appropriate to terminate therapy. Returning repeatedly to the Miguel Sanchez case also enables students to acquire a fuller understanding of how various theoretical approaches function toward solving clients' problems which lies at the heart of comprehending more completely the different forms of therapy practiced today.

Practice Implications

Additionally, each theory chapter also informs students about how the marketplace perceives a particular theory (e.g., whether it receives insurance reimbursement), the type of service delivery setting where it is applied (e.g., private practice, community mental health centers, psychiatric hospitals, health care settings), populations it serves (e.g., children, youth, adults, couples, families, groups), type and severity of presenting problems it handles well, whether it is adapted for short term treatment, and if certification in the approach is offered. Each

▼ FIGURE P.1

Edvard Munch's Painting
The Scream

theory chapter includes current research on the effectiveness of the theory's applications which serves to indicate the strengths and limitations of using a particular approach with certain presenting problems (e.g., clients diagnosed with various *DSM* disorders).

Special Ethical Considerations Highlighted

Furthermore, the authors integrated into each of the twelve theory chapters those ethical considerations that are especially tied to a specific theoretical approach. For example, the possible ethical ramifications of countertransference situations where the psychoanalytic therapist's own formative family dynamics are re-created and distorts how the client is perceived by the therapist.

Finally, even though differences in the organization and content can be found among the chapters due to the structural nature of certain theories, each theory chapter was arranged in a definite and consistent pattern of presentation. This uniform organization allows for easier comparison and discussion of different theories. Critical thinking questions appear at the end of each theory chapter and are designed to deepen students' understanding of important theoretical components. Boxes are inserted in each chapter that highlight certain remarks made by the originator(s) of a theory. These "quotation boxes" give a voice to the various theorists/therapists and provide a brief glimpse into how these provocative thinkers view(ed) the world.

Hoped for Outcome

The Indian philosopher and polymath Rabindranath Tagore stated that "we think that we think clearly, but that is only because we don't think clearly" (p. 14, as cited in Popova, 2015). The authors hope that they have proved all readers of this textbook the tools to think clearly about what they have read. The authors strove to cover the theories in a manner that would enable a reader to successfully walk the precarious length of the razor's edge that divides two requirements for thinking clearly: maintaining an open mind to each theory's position and ascertaining the true contribution made by each theory to present day therapy practice. To facilitate a successful journey of learning for both new and seasoned students the authors sought to provide a balanced, deliberate, and judicious coverage of the various theoretical approaches covered. This called for each author to keep his or her theoretical biases at bay, but in the end it is up to each of the readers to decide if the authors were successful at avoiding the adverse effects that can accompany unchecked theoretical favoritism.

Reference

Popova, M. (2015, November 29). Force of impact. *The New York Times Book Review*, p.14.

Instructor and Companion Resources

Instructor Resources include a **Test Bank** with a diverse range of pre-written options as well as the opportunity to edit any question and/or insert personalized questions to effectively assess students' progress and understanding. Editable, chapter-specific **PowerPoint®** **slides** offer complete flexibility for creating a multimedia presentation for the course. (http://study.sagepub.com/ginter)

Student Resources provide a personalized approach to help students accomplish their coursework goals in an easy-to-use learning environment. That includes online **Learning Objectives** to study and reinforce the most important material, and **Multimedia** content that appeals to diverse learners. (http://study.sagepub.com/ginter)

ACKNOWLEDGMENTS

I am extremely thankful and proud of my three sons Matthew E. Ginter, Michael J. Ginter, and Mark D. Ginter for their art work that was included in this textbook. I want to especially recognize Garrison Bickerstaff, a longtime friend, whose linguistic expertise concerning the use, structure, and psychology of the English language proved to be invaluable in completing the chapters I wrote. There are no words I can call upon to capture the sort of gratitude that I harbor toward George M. Gazda for agreeing to review this textbook and write its foreword. I would be remiss if I did not mention the names of various individuals I encountered and interacted with over the years that significantly broadened my worldview of what does and does not define the theory and practice of counseling and psychotherapy. Their influence reverberates throughout the pages of this textbook. The names of those who helped to forge me as a theorist and practitioner are Ahmed M. Abdel-Khalek, Wayne Antenen, Lois Bergen, Warren Bonney, Jerold Bozarth, John Dagley, Robert L. Dingman, Albert Ellis, Erik Homburger Erikson, Robert Erk, George M. Gazda, Lawrence (Larry) Gerstein, Brian A. Glaser, Ann Shanks Glauser, Roger D. Herring, Thomas (Tom) H. Hohenshil, Arthur (Andy) M. Horne, Don C. Locke, Dubi Lufi, J. B. Martin, F. G. Miller, Norman (Norm) Presse, Bert O. Richmond, Keith Runyon, Joseph J. Scalise, and Pansy and E. Paul Torrance. In addition to the aforementioned individuals, I also want to acknowledge the important contributions made by Jeffrey Cornelius White and Matthew E. Lemberger, co-writers of the person-centered theory chapter in this textbook and Chad Luke and Frederick Redekop, co-writers of the behavioral theory chapter. I want to thank four members of SAGE Publications, Kassie Graves, who first proposed this textbook; Nathan Davidson, who provided sage advice to overcome a publication hurdle; Abbie Rickard, whose persistence and support proved inspiring; and Veronica Stapleton Hooper, whose efforts led to the conclusion of this ten-year project. Finally, I want to recognize Larry Gerstein's contributions toward completing the publication of this textbook. Even though Larry and I are long-standing professional colleagues, more importantly, I view Larry as a member of my own family—a brother whom I have always been able to call upon when needed. At one point during the writing phase of this project, for unexpected reasons, I experienced an unshakable form of frustration that caused me to seriously consider to stop working on this textbook. Larry reminded me of my decades-long interest in writing a theory textbook that would clearly communicate to interested parties, especially those new to the mental health field, the importance of developing a clear understanding of how various theories provide the support necessary for current day counseling and psychotherapy practice. Several years ago I summed up my explanation for why theory fulfills a critical role when I stated that *therapy cannot exist without theory.* I still believe this to be true.

—Earl J. Ginter

I want to thank my advisees, research assistants, and alumni psychologists, and members of the Department of Clinical Psychology at Antioch University New England who read and discussed the chapters and leaning objectives I wrote for this book and gave me feedback. As true scholar-practitioners, they helped me to ground my theoretical and research leanings in the realness of case-based clinical conceptualizations, assessment, and treatment. I am grateful that they requested readability and a straightforward writing style. My students returned the mentoring and editing I provided for their dissertations and doctoral scholarship.

—Gargi Roysircar

This project seemed to take an eternity to complete. I am extremely thankful to my wife, Dawa Lhamo; Earl Ginter's wife, Jackie Ginter; and my department chair, Sharon Bowman, for their continuous and strong support throughout the process of working on this book. I also want to thank Jeffrey Cornelius White and Matthew E. Lemberger for writing the initial draft of the *Person-Centered Theory* chapter and Chad Luke and Frederick Redekop for their draft of the *Behavioral Theory* chapter. I am appreciative as well to the many individuals that helped with gathering literature that I found useful when writing various sections of the chapters including Yamini Bellare, Alyssa Brown, Kelly Picard Clougher, Jessica Collins, Erin Davis, Mona Ghosheh, Joel Hartong, Ashley Hutchison, Matthew Jackson, Claire Kubiesa, Nicholas A. Lee, David Martin, Donald Nicholas, Gerald Novack, Michael O'Heron, Juno Park, Erin L. Sadler, Nehad Sandozi, Kyle P. Stepler, Holly Tenbrink, Rich Usdowski, Andy Walsh, Laila E. N. Sayyah, and Stefanía Ægisdóttir.

Since the inception of this book, I have worked with three different Acquisitions Editors at SAGE Publications, Kassie Graves, Nathan Davidson, and Abbie Rickard. Without your patience, commitment, and support for this project it would not have been completed. And for that, I am grateful. I am also appreciative of the excellent work performed by our Copy Editor, Colleen Brennan. My very good friend and go-to talented graphic designer, John Melvin, was responsible for accurately translating my vision for this book's front cover into an art form, and for this, I am very grateful!

Finally, it has been 39 years since Earl Ginter and I first met as classmates in the doctoral program at the University of Georgia. Since then, we have been extremely close friends and, at times, collaborators on professional projects. This book stretched us to the max, but as always we had each other's back for which I am deeply appreciative. And, as always, Earl amazed me with the depth of his knowledge in counseling and psychology, and also the arts and movies. Luv ya Earl!

—Lawrence H. Gerstein

ABOUT THE AUTHORS

Earl J. Ginter, PhD, LMFT, LPC is Professor Emeritus at The University of Georgia. Earlier in his career he worked at Nicholls State University as a counselor, teacher, and researcher. He also has more than 38 years of experience working as a private practitioner. Before he retired on April 1, 2016, he served as the Director for the Division of Academic Enhancement at the University of Georgia. This academic unit worked with approximately 10,000 undergraduate, graduate, and international students each year offering them an array of skill-building services, academic courses designed to meet students' academic concerns, and counseling services which included treating dissertation anxiety. Ginter was also responsible for managing the Division's four federally funded TRiO programs for low-income and first-generation students; operation of the Division's learning center, peer tutoring program, satellite and outreach services; and a special program developed to increase retention and graduation rates at the university. The special retention/graduation program was utilized by 10 academic schools/colleges at the University of Georgia. Other professional experiences include having served as the editor for both the *Journal of Mental Health Counseling* and the *Journal of Counseling & Development*. The latter is the flagship journal of the American Counseling Association with approximately 55,000 subscribers. In addition, he served as the contributing editor for *National Association of Rehabilitation Professionals in the Private Sector* and the associate editor of the theory section of the *Journal of Mental Health Counseling*. Ginter has authored or coauthored numerous publications including journal articles, monographs, book chapters, and books, e.g., *Group Counseling and Group Psychotherapy: Theory and Application* by George M. Gazda, Earl J. Ginter, and Arthur M. Horne. Ginter's publications have focused on issues that comprise the theoretical and practice aspects of counseling and marriage and family therapy. His research and assessment interests pertain to the application of developmental-based approaches to working with individuals, couples, families, and groups.

Gargi Roysircar received her doctorate in educational psychology with emphasis in counseling psychology at Texas Tech University. She is the Founding Director of the Antioch Multicultural Center for Research and Practice at Antioch University New England and Professor of Clinical Psychology. She conducts research on disaster outreach in international settings, the effects of acculturation and enculturation on immigrant mental health, multicultural competencies in practice and assessment, and training graduate students in culturally informed practice. She has authored more than 100 journal articles and chapters on these topics, with her most recent publications in *Traumatology, Counselling Psychology Quarterly, Professional Psychology: Research and Practice, The Journal of Black Psychology, Journal of Muslim Mental Health, Journal of Career Development,* and *The Oxford Handbook of Social Class in Counseling.*

Dr. Roysircar has participated in mental health counseling in earthquake-destroyed Haiti, tsunami-affected fishing communities in Southern India; Hurricanes Katrina and Rita-affected communities and first responders in the United States Gulf Coast; and in Southern African orphanages that serve HIV/AIDS-infected and affected children and women. She has provided psychoeducation in flood-ravaged Villahermosa, Tabasco, Mexico. Dr. Roysircar trains her counseling teams in disaster trauma, culture-centered skills specific to a community disaster, and in clinician self-care and resilience. She is a grantee of the American Psychological Foundation for her research on her disaster mental health assessment and services.

In 2001, Dr. Roysircar was elected as the first Asian president of the Association for Multicultural Counseling and Development, and was appointed as the first woman and first Asian editor of the *Journal of Multicultural Counseling and Development* from 2004–2011. Her awards include the 2002 Extended Research Award of the American Counseling Association (ACA) as well as ACA's 2007 Research Award. Her co-authored books are *Multicultural Assessment in Counseling and Clinical Psychology, Handbook of Social Justice in Counseling Psychology,* and the Spanish translation of *Multicultural Counseling Competencies (2003),* having previously co-authored this book in English. Her instrument, the Multicultural Counseling Inventory (MCI), is the most frequently cited instrument among published self-report multicultural competency scales. Her article (Sodowsky et al., 1998), which uses the MCI instrument, was ranked over the past decades among 25 most cited articles of the *Journal of Counseling Psychology.* Dr. Roysircar is ranked in productivity ratings of authors in 5 multicultural psychology journals. She is a fellow of the American Psychological Association (APA) and served on the APA Taskforce Re-envisioning the Multicultural Guidelines for the 21st Century, adopted by APA in August 2017 and titled Multicultural guidelines: An ecological approach to context, identity, and intersectionality. Dr. Roysircar was the recipient of the 2017 Division 35 Psychology of Women Strickland Daniel Mentoring Award. Dr. Roysircar's 44-year teaching career has been spent in three countries across three continents.

Lawrence H. Gerstein earned a B.B.A. in public administration and a Ph.D. in counseling and social psychology. He is a Ball State University George and Frances Ball Distinguished Professor of Psychology and Director of the Center for Peace and Conflict Studies, Fulbright Scholar, and a fellow of the American Psychological Association. Professor Gerstein is a co-editor of the *Journal for Social Action in Counseling and Psychology* and an editorial board member for the *Journal of Counseling Psychology.* He has published more than 100 scholarly articles and three books including the *International Handbook of Cross-Cultural Counseling* and the *Handbook for Social Justice in Counseling Psychology*. He is known for his research on cross-cultural methodology, nonviolence, social justice, emotions, and sports for youth development. Professor Gerstein has received more than two million dollars in funding including four U.S. State Department grants and one U.S. Institute of Peace grant. He has performed conflict prevention and resolution work and/or research with adults, children, and youth in the U.S.A, Jordan, Pakistan, Tajikistan, China, Hong Kong, Korea, Indonesia, Israel, Taiwan, and Burma. He has also trained Iraqi young leaders in social entrepreneurship.

CHAPTER 1

INTRODUCTION
AND OVERVIEW

wo key terms found in the title of this textbook are *psychotherapy* and *counseling*. In the traditional sense of the term, *psychotherapy* was used to identify professionals who were trained to deal with serious mental or emotional disorders primarily through some form of psychological treatment; these professionals included clinically trained psychiatrists, clinical psychologists, and psychiatric social workers. The term *counseling* was used to identify professionals who worked with others to help them accomplish various outcomes, such as establishing vocational or career goals, learning needed skills (e.g., parenting), promoting changes that would allow them to overcome obstacles in academic and work settings, and assisting with less disruptive mental health–related issues. Psychotherapy and counseling started to acquire definite forms toward the end of the 1800s and the beginning of the 1900s, but after more than

After reading this chapter, each student should be able to:

1. Compare the similarities and differences between the concepts "psychotherapy" and "counseling."

2. Sketch the history of contemporary therapy and theory.

3. Appraise therapy's relationship to theory.

4. Critique attributes used to judge the soundness of a theory.

5. Evaluate the strategies to assess the effectiveness of therapy.

6. Explain the authors' approach to writing this textbook.

100 years, the distinctions between the two had weakened considerably, and the crossover between each territory of work caused the distinctiveness of the two practice areas to disappear essentially. Even though the areas of psychotherapy and counseling are relatively recent, development from a historical perspective, including interest in promoting mental health, dates back eons. Because of such early occurrences, it is correct to state that psychotherapy and counseling have a long past but a short history.

Throughout history many notable occurrences have clearly represented forward thinking in the providing of mental health assistance. One example of such forward thinking occurred with the Muslim scholar Abu Zayd Ahmad ibn Sahl al-Balkhi, who wrote *Sustenance for Body and Soul,* a thesis that addressed what constitutes mental health, why various forms of mental illness occur, and procedures that would enable a suffering person to gain mental health.

Al-Balkhi provided a surprisingly contemporary view of what would be recognizable today as a form of cognitive therapy. Haque (2004) summarized al-Balkhi's basic treatment approach in these words, "He suggested that just as a healthy person keeps some drugs and First Aid medicine nearby for unexpected physical emergencies, he should also keep *healthy thoughts and feelings in his mind* [italics added] for unexpected emotional outbursts" (p. 362). Like many others, al-Balkhi understood that from time to time, everyone experiences the pain and disappointment that is associated with life's inevitable misfortunes, but al-Balkhi differed from others because he gave us a means to prevent such misfortunes from escalating into mental illness. His message was simple: We need to maintain a realistic and balanced perspective whenever we encounter the serrated edges of life.

In *Sustenance for Body and Soul,* al-Balkhi distinguished between neuroses and psychoses and also explained the interaction of physiological mechanisms that led to psychosomatic illnesses. Furthermore, al-Balkhi designated four diagnostic categories with connections to identifiable symptoms: (1) anger and aggression, (2) anxiety and fear (i.e., phobias), (3) obsession (i.e., obsessive-compulsive disorders), and (4) sadness and depression (Badri, 2013; Edson & Savage-Smith, 2004; Pickren, 2014). Al-Balkhi wrote extensively about this last diagnostic category. He asserted that disturbances in the area of sadness and depression take one of three forms (Haque, 2004). One form is normal depression that represents a *normal reaction* to daily life's struggles. Another form, *reactive depression*, originates from outside the person, for instance, when a person fails to fulfill a very important personal goal or when an individual suffers a significant loss of property or personal status. The, final type, *endogenous depression*, originates within the person and is marked by symptoms of incessant distress, profound unhappiness, and significant withdrawal from daily activities. Al-Balkhi believed endogenous depression has a strong body connection that requires a combination of medical and cognitive and/or affective-based treatment.

Clearly an interest in mental illness and its treatment can be traced back through human history, which predates al-Balkhi by centuries. The lay psychoanalyst Sudhir Kakar (1991), for example, showed that India's earliest societies practiced shamanistic healing rituals that were applied to both physical and psychological problems. While we (the authors of this textbook) earnestly believe that the roots of psychotherapy and counseling extend deep into humanity's past, we also believe such prophetic thinkers as al-Balkhi were more the exception than the rule in terms of explaining key causes and viable treatments for mental illness. Such thinkers were often simply the victim of being in the wrong place at the wrong time.

The Start of Contemporary Therapy and Theory

Although various historical documents and practices of ancient cultures might seem synonymous with contemporary mental health practice, not until the 19th century did a persistent and significant shift in understanding mental disorders occur. This type of understanding, which had authentic focus, depth, and scope, had found its right time and place. In contrast to earlier times, we only have to look back approximately 200 years to appreciate the magnitude of this major shift in thinking. During the 18th century, the hospital-prison called Bedlam was regarded by the social vanguard of England as imbued with high amusement value and well worth the penny fee charged to enter this human zoo, so visitors could safely observe the mysteriously acting inmates who were placed on public display (Pickren, 2014). The 19th century marked the dividing line between rare and fleeting occurrences of humane treatment of people with mental illness and an explosion of widespread and sustained efforts to develop comprehensive approaches to help these people. The second half of this remarkable century is especially notable for a series of events that led to what we know today as psychotherapy.

During the 19th century, a cadre of European healers and theorists emerged with a strong disdain for how mental problems had previously been handled and conceptualized. One measure of the fundamental change in approach to mental illness was the rise of the term *alienist* (an archaic term generally attributed to early practitioners of psychiatry). These professionals were called *alienists* because of the generally held opinion that those who suffered from mental disorders were basically alienated from themselves and from others. The term *alienist* can still be found in works of fiction, such as Caleb Carr's 1994 crime novel, *The Alienist,* in which the author used the term to contextualize the story shortly after the turn of the century.

Establishing a Foundation for New Theories and Therapies

The original group of "psychological" healers and theorists who are covered in this textbook can be thought of as frame-breakers. These individuals departed from the theoretical frameworks and approaches to treat mental disorders that dominated during their time. They accomplished this departure by presenting new discoveries and revolutionary ideas that provided the requisite support to make important advances in theory and practice. Two such frame-breakers who departed from the prominent, unquestioned beliefs of 19th century were Jean-Martin Charcot and Sigmund Freud. Charcot was a renowned French neurologist who established the first neurology clinic at the Pitié-Salpêtrière Hospital, Paris, France. The existence of this hospital allowed for the removal and isolation from society those individuals who were suffering from mental illness. Charcot used the controversial procedure of hypnosis to study and manipulate symptoms of hysteria, which was a common mental disorder in the late 1800s and was considered to be confined solely to women until Charcot argued otherwise (see Figure 1.1). During Charcot's time, hysteria manifested in an array of conditions, including amnesia that was limited to forgetting specific events; emotional outbursts that could change rapidly and unpredictably; overdramatic displays of behavior and narcissistic monologues; and displays of anxiety or depression that were converted into some form of pseudo-illness, such as paralysis that did not match any known patterns of genuine paralysis (Oxford University, 1971).

Upon learning of Charcot's work, Sigmund Freud traveled to Paris to observe and study his work. These pioneers not only significantly contributed to what would become contemporary forms of therapy, but their efforts eventually led to new methods of conceptualizing and treating mental disorders. This process did not progress easily or without complications. Such difficulties were reflected in Freud's years of concerted efforts to establish what was to become psychoanalysis. Although Freud's effort would eventually garner him worldwide recognition, he initially received considerable resistance and experienced years of isolation from Vienna's medical establishment. This was the case even among those professionals who were initially attracted to Freud's new treatment approach and became affiliated with him, for example, Carl Jung and Alfred Adler, among others, who eventually broke with Freud because of disagreements. These disagreements were often rooted in a difference of theoretical opinion, but in some cases they led to acrimony and a partisan type of contentious quarreling that persisted for decades between members of each theoretical camp (e.g., Jungian and Adlerian practitioners).

Freud tended to categorize such departures and the resulting therapeutic approaches as misdirection that at best added little significance to the understanding of or treatment

Nineteenth Century Photographs of Women Diagnosed With Hysteria

Source: Photographs from *Iconographie Photographique de la Salpêtrière*.

of mental disturbance; at worse, he felt these departures led to theoretical dead ends. In fact, the stories that surround the creation of psychoanalysis or the reasons for Carl Jung's break with Sigmund Freud have all the necessary ingredients to portray great literary or cinematic drama. (To appreciate the true nature of these stories of conflict or contrast of character, read Jean-Paul Sartre's screenplay *The Freud Scenario* [1984/2013], portions of which were used by the film director John Huston for his 1962 movie *Freud*, or watch David Cronenberg's 2011 movie *A Dangerous Method*, which vividly portrays the intense relationship that developed between Carl Jung and Sigmund Freud.) The various streams of thinking that led to the current forms of therapy represent fascinating endeavors that cannot be appreciated by reading a brief summary of a particular theory.

Therapy's Relationship to Theory

Since contemporary therapy's roots can be traced to the late 19th and early 20th century, one would assume sufficient time has elapsed for a single theory to arise that can explain the etiology and best means to treat mental disorders. However, a single explanation for why mental disorders occur has not emerged, nor has a single, best therapeutic approach emerged. In fact, Corsini and Wedding (2000) asserted that the term *therapy* cannot be defined to everyone's satisfaction because the word itself lacks the necessary exactness. These editors added that it is probable that more than 400 different therapies exist. Is it possible to tally what we cannot define? When these two seemingly contrary assertions are simultaneously considered, one may experience the sensation of having fallen into a bottomless pit.

The authors of this textbook acknowledge the inherent difficulties in determining what should and should not be included in a representative list of therapeutic approaches, but we also feel that the task is feasible. Our starting point does not consider all of what might fall within the realm of the term *therapy*; the approach we take starts with the following question. Of the present therapies, which are the most likely to be encountered by today's clients? The answer is tied to what might be referred to as "major approaches," which is a much more manageable number than the hundreds of "therapies" identified by some professionals.

Furthermore, we believe that to start the discussion by delineating the various types of available treatments is placing the proverbial carriage before the horse because all three authors of this textbook agree with the following statement: *Therapy cannot exist without theory*. This statement is consistent with the position held by Murray Bowen, a well-known family therapy practitioner who foremost regarded himself as a theorist: "Therapy and theory are part of the same fabric" (see Gladding, 2002, p. 127). Thus, before the widely used therapies can be understood, we must momentarily sidestep the issue of what is and is not therapy and focus our attention on determining what constitutes a viable major theory of therapy (keeping in mind that each major theoretical approach defines what is and is not therapy).

Each theory provides a therapist with a set of interconnected ideas that possess enough explanatory power to enable a therapist to hypothesize causes for a client's problem. Theory provides a springboard from which to decide the therapeutic course to take so that specific theory-forged techniques can be strategically enacted in ways to achieve a meaningful closure to the therapeutic process. A theory is a road map of sorts that gives direction from the start to the end of therapy.

Even though we have significantly reduced the number of theories that will be covered in this textbook by narrowing our focus, it should be obvious at this point that having more than one major theory to consider means that the psychological territory presented by any one client can be traversed by using a number of different theoretical maps. In fact, the particular map selected by a therapist will determine to a large extent whether a client is perceived, for instance, as suffering from a mental disorder or in the midst of a developmental challenge, and if the client is even diagnosed as experiencing a mental disorder, and whether an appropriate diagnostic label should be applied.

This process can be illustrated by contrasting the *Diagnostic and Statistical Manual of Mental Disorders* (*DSM*) with the theoretical positions known as psychoanalysis and reality therapy. The fifth edition of the *DSM* (*DSM-5*, 2014) uses the term *psychosis* but not *neurosis* even though psychoanalysis relies upon a diagnostic continuum that includes the term *neurotic* (McWilliams, 2011), which is a term used in the 2015 version of the *International Classification of Diseases* (*ICD*) of the World Health Organization. Furthermore, although the *DSM*'s current and previous editions have recognized schizophrenia as a form of mental illness, William Glasser, who created reality therapy, rejected this assertion. Glasser shares company with several other prominent thinkers who also criticized the value or purpose of certain labels, such as Michel Foucault, who wrote *Madness and Civilization*. (Foucault argued that the label "madness" has been misused throughout history by powerful groups to isolate society's outcasts, misfits, and deviants; the label was used to "imprison" society's undesirables while the groups responsible maintained, at best, only a tepid interest in treating genuine mental illnesses.)

Finally, the map analogy also serves to remind us that whatever theoretical chart we ultimately decide to rely upon, we should avoid becoming so enamored of a particular map that we mistake it for the actual territory; in other words, no map (or label) can capture the complete complexity and subtle nature of any client. The map analogy also helps us to remember that just like printed or GPS-generated road maps, maps can lose accuracy when they are not updated to reflect changes. Similarly, a therapist's theoretical map's accuracy is likely to change over time in light of new findings and advances in the field.

Certain qualities typically characterize the major theories presented in this textbook; these qualities include robust concepts, consistency of treatment outcomes, and good applicability for the range of problems that individuals confront today, including a range from the relatively common relationship problems that can wreak havoc on a family's day-to-day existence to the less frequent but significant disturbances rendered by psychoses. Regrettably, instances have occurred in which a so-called theoretically based approach used to treat mental illness has not been adequately tested to determine the soundness of its conceptually derived assumptions, degree of outcome certainty, or level of treatment applicability—even in modern times. One case in point is the *transorbital lobotomy*, which is a form of psychosurgery that was introduced by Dr. Walter Freeman. The procedure was used as a remedy for conditions, such as aggressive tendencies, mild learning difficulties, delinquency, schizophrenia, postnatal depression, and unruliness—applications that could not be unequivocally justified.

Freeman was a psychiatrist with no formal surgical training who created the procedure commonly referred to as the "ice pick lobotomy" because of the surgery instrument used, an orbitoclast, which resembled an ice pick. Freedman would insert an orbitoclast above a patient's eyeball, hammer it through the bone of the orbit into the frontal lobe (an area of the brain associated with the control and regulation of behavior and various abilities associated with executive functioning such as planning and retrieving memories), and move the orbitoclast in a manner to sever brain tissue. He then performed the same surgical procedure on the opposite frontal lobe.

Considering that Freedman did not conduct animal studies to ascertain the effects of a transorbital lobotomy, nor was he interested in doing so, he essentially introduced an extremely invasive procedure that was based on personally held beliefs that lacked evidence of validity. In addition, as evidence shows, the outcomes of this form of psychosurgery were not always predictable; scores of patients died, and others (such as President John F. Kennedy's sister, Rosemary Kennedy) became incapacitated for life.

Amazingly, Freeman performed 2,500 transorbital lobotomies in 23 states at 55 different psychiatric hospitals. One of Freeman's patients, Howard Dully, was misdiagnosed by Freeman as suffering from schizophrenia (Dully & Fleming, 2008; National Public Radio, 2014). Other medical and psychiatric professionals, who had seen Dully prior to Dr. Freeman, had not detected a mental disorder. Based on available information, Dully was most likely reacting to both the death of his mother and the remarriage of his father a year later to a woman who had rejected Dully as a stepson (he described his stepmother as a person who "hated me").

Freeman performed a transorbital lobotomy on Dully at 12 years of age in 1960, years after the procedure had been discredited and replaced with breakthroughs in pharmacological treatments, such as the introduction of the antipsychotic drug chlorpromazine (brand name Thorazine). Dully described coming out of the surgery feeling as if he had been "zombified." Figure 1.2 shows Freeman performing Dully's psychosurgery. Specifically, Freeman is demonstrating the procedure he used to perform a transorbital lobotomy.

Attributes Used to Judge the Soundness of a Theory

What qualities make a particular major theory solid and strong? In addition to the need for factually based assumptions, reliable outcomes, and wide applicability, referential integrity is also extremely important to judging whether a theory is sound. Although no major theory completely fulfills all these qualities to the fullest degree, a major theory should be sufficiently strong in each area to justify its status as representing a major theory. These four qualities are defined and illustrated with references to psychoanalytic theory.

- *Structural Integrity:* Components of the theory are complete, coherent, and internally consistent. Structural integrity provides the conceptual glue that binds ideas and assumptions to form a unified whole. Such an explanation can be illustrated through Freud's theory of the dynamic unconscious. According to Freud, disturbing desires, feelings, and thoughts may be made to disappear from awareness through a mental process he termed *repression*, but he also asserted that what was repressed is likely to have a dynamic nature; that is, repressed experiences will continue to affect a person's behavior in various ways, such as when psychological symptoms develop. Freud spent decades forming a tightly constructed and elaborate theory of mental functioning that was based on his concept of the dynamic unconscious.

- *Explanatory Power:* The extent to which a theory can effectively explain the subject matter it encompasses (i.e., explanatory power) provides explanations for a wide array of mental processes and behaviors. Freudian *defense mechanisms* can be thought of as habitual strategies that are unconsciously activated for the purpose of distorting reality to protect us from any anxiety-provoking desires, feelings, or thoughts. If these occurrences were not controlled (which prevents us from consciously dwelling on them), our benignant self-image would reveal a repugnant brutish self.

- *Therapeutic Scope:* This quality specifically pertains to the degree that a theory's concepts and techniques are relevant for treating a range of mental disorders. Whereas Freud focused on treating conditions that fell under the umbrella term *neuroses* (e.g., anxiety disorders and dissociative disorders), contemporary versions of psychoanalysis have been developed that are designed to treat *borderline personality disorders* (serious conditions marked by unstable moods, behaviors, and relationships that are problematic) and psychoses (e.g., schizophrenia).

- *Referential Integrity:* This quality hinges upon establishing a correspondence between what the theory claims and what has been termed *bias-free objective reality*. Thus, regardless of how well Freud's theory explains human problems, holds together conceptually, or can be widely applied, ultimately the theory must be shown to match real-life situations; that is, reasonable proof for the existence of dynamic unconscious processes must be provided. One means for testing the quality of referential integrity is through

▼ FIGURE 1.2

Dr. Walter Freeman Performs a Lobotomy Using the "Ice Pick" Instrument He Created

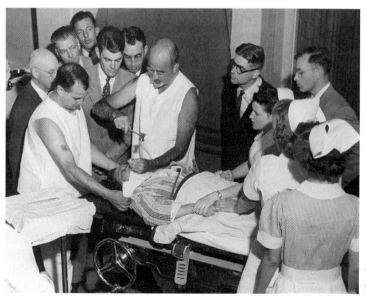

empirical investigations. For example, in 2012, university-based researchers reported that empirical support had been found for the psychoanalytic assertion that a connection exists between unconscious conflicts and the conscious symptoms experienced by individuals diagnosed with an anxiety disorder (University of Michigan Health System, 2012).

These four qualities are closely related and even though they influence each other, each quality introduces an aspect about theories that none of the others fully addresses.

Interestingly, pseudoscientific approaches to therapy continued to appear despite the establishment of standards to judge the soundness of such newly introduced "therapeutic approaches." In the book *Alternative Psychotherapies: Evaluating Unconventional Mental Health Treatments*, Mercer (2014) critiques various regression therapies along with other questionable therapies. According to Mercer, regression therapies focus on having someone drop back to an earlier time in their lives (literally becoming their former adolescent or child self again) that supposedly positions the person to overcome deeply disturbing early experiences. Mercer discussed how *adultomorphism* (the belief that infants and children share adult characteristics) can cloud the thinking of regression advocates, some of whom have asserted that birth itself is traumatic enough to cause psychological problems. Mercer referred to evidence that infants experience neither agitation nor distress during birth; nor do they make a physical effort to escape the experience. In fact, an infant's movement is inhibited by a paralysis reflex. Mercer further stated that "certainly an experience resembling birth would be agonizing for an adult, with fully developed, unbending skeleton, tight tendons, and fully formed skull, but the soft bones and malleable skull of the newborn ease the passage" (Mercer, 2014, p. 51). Mercer has reviewed a number of alternative therapies (e.g., energy therapies such as qigong and reiki; holding and attachment therapies; and *le packing*, which treats autistic children by tightly wrapping them in wet, chilled sheets for up to 6 hours) and has cogently argued that these alternative therapies are not in accordance with scientific views and lack sufficient evidentiary support for claims made by their advocates.

Assessing Effectiveness

Historically, theorists and researchers were curious about the effectiveness of therapy, with the earliest studies appearing in the literature in the 1920s (Lambert, 2011). Luminaries such as Sigmund Freud observed clients carefully and recorded notes about similarities and differences in patterns in clients' behaviors and their responses to treatment. Through qualitative methods reported by groups such as the Berlin Psychoanalytic Institute (Fenichel, 1930), various conceptualizations or diagnoses about individuals' psychological functioning were formed, and specific intervention strategies were introduced and employed. In addition, successful prototypical cases were shared with relevant professional communities as evidence of the effectiveness of psychotherapy.

In the late 1940s, Carl Rogers, founder of the client-centered (person-centered) approach, introduced the new technology of audiotaping of therapy sessions, which allowed Rogers and others to review the interactions between a therapist and client.

From this innovation (i.e., the utilization of systematic procedures to capture and assess clients' behaviors during a therapy session), an interest increased in tracking client–therapist interactions from the first session through the point of therapy's termination (Rogers & Dymond, 1954). Such attention also contributed directly to a new way of educating and supervising aspiring therapists who were interested in learning client-centered therapy. Like Freud and his colleagues, Rogers and his followers relied on a qualitative method to extract themes that they noticed in the audiotapes, and they modified their theories and strategies accordingly and also shared their case examples with the professional community.

In the 1950s, a quantitative procedure was employed to investigate the effectiveness of therapy. Since then, a growing number of researchers have relied on a randomized control design to investigate the process and outcome of various therapy approaches. Hans Eysenck, a highly recognized scholar, reviewed many outcome studies and reported that therapy is not beneficial and potentially even harmful (Eysenck, 1952, 1961, 1966). Based on their review of the literature, other investigators arrived at a different conclusion and stated that therapy is effective (Bergin, 1971; Luborsky, Singer, & Luborsky, 1975). In addition, in a seminal meta-analysis of the effectiveness of psychotherapy, two other researchers found strong support for the effectiveness of therapy (Smith & Glass, 1977). Finally, since the 1970s, other individuals have argued that certain theoretically inspired approaches are best suited for certain types of client problems. On the other hand, Wampold et al. (1997) conducted a meta-analysis investigation and concluded that no evidence supports the claim that some forms of therapy are better than others.

Other scholars found interesting results that have brought us to a much deeper level of understanding of what exactly contributes to the effectiveness of therapy. This realization was accomplished by changing the focus from comparing various approaches to investigating the specific characteristics of three components of successful therapeutic outcomes; that is, the characteristics associated with the therapist, the client, and how the intervention approach is applied. Researchers found that regardless of the particular therapy approach, the effective therapist is aligned with other effective practitioners and appears to display what the researchers called common factors that are curative in nature (Norcross, 2002). Some of the common factors that were linked to effective therapists include exhibiting warmth, showing respect, possessing a capacity for empathy, displaying unconditional positive regard, presenting themselves in a genuine manner, and offering the client encouragement. Common factors associated with clients believed to be linked with successful outcomes include attributes such as having hope, being motivated, having a social support system in place, and having an expectation for a positive outcome due to participating in therapy. Common factors reported to be tied to positive outcomes of the therapy process are factors such as establishing a positive working alliance (the connection between the therapist and the client), agreement on treatment goals, and agreement on tasks to be employed during therapy (Horvath & Bedi, 2002; Wampold, 2001).

Various professional organizations also have made concerted efforts to address factors that surround therapy's effectiveness. One such professional organization is the American Psychological Association (APA). The debate about the effectiveness of therapy reached a new level in 1995 when APA introduced the concept of empirically validated treatment (Task Force on Promotion and Dissemination, 1995). The APA Task Force on Promotion and Dissemination of Psychological Procedures was charged with identifying scientifically validated therapy approaches for specific problems, as determined by a particular mental disorder diagnosis (Garfield, 1996). In time, approximately 50 of more than 500 treatment approaches were considered effective (Wampold, 2010). As a result of strong criticism about the exclusionary nature of what was considered "validated" treatments (as if no other interventions had any validity), in 1998, the task force agreed to change the validated treatments label to "empirically supported treatments" (ESTs). It is interesting that, since 1996, the task force has not updated its report of ESTs (Wampold, 2010).

More recently, in 2006, another APA task force (i.e., Task Force on Evidence-Based Practice) was formed to once again focus, in part, on the effectiveness of therapy. This committee defined what was termed *evidence-based practice* (EBP) in therapy as "the integration of the best available research with clinical expertise in the context of patient characteristics, culture, and preferences" (American Psychological Association, 2006, p. 273). Evidence for the efficacy of an intervention as defined earlier resulted in a designation of a treatment as an EBP (e.g., De Los Reyes & Kazdin, 2008). This task force defined best available research as scientific findings that were connected to assessment and intervention strategies for specific client problems and populations. Whereas the more recent EBP policy of the APA did not endorse ESTs (Wampold, 2010), the APA's Division of Clinical Psychology has identified what it considers to be the best research evidence available for effective approaches of therapy given a specific client problem, and this group of professionals has made the information that it gathered available at http://www.div12.org/psychological-treatments.

Still, EBP and EST are not the same constructs. EBP is a much more comprehensive construct (APA, 2006) that is not confined solely to the profession of psychology. In fact, the original definition and practice of EBP was introduced by the Evidence-Based Medicine Working Group (Sackett, Straus, Richardson, Rosenberg, & Haynes, 2000), and, eventually, an official definition of EBP was endorsed by the Institute of Medicine (Institute of Medicine, 2001). In recent years, other health care disciplines (e.g., medicine, nursing, public health, physical, speech, and occupational therapy) also have endorsed the paradigm of evidence-based practice.

Along with the best available research, the EBP approach to determining effectiveness also stresses the importance of clinical expertise (e.g., competencies such as assessment, diagnosis, case formulation, forming and maintaining the therapeutic relationship, treatment planning, clinical decision making, self-reflection) in the promotion of positive outcomes in therapy (APA, 2006). As mentioned earlier, client characteristics (e.g., presentation and severity of problem, personality traits, developmental functioning, gender, race, ethnicity, social class, gender identity, disability status, sexual orientation) and the client's culture (e.g., values, beliefs, understanding of health and illness, help-seeking behaviors, expectations about therapy) are critical components of EBP as well (APA, 2006).

Since therapeutic approaches were first conceptualized and put into practice during the late 19th century, much has changed, including judging what is and is not an effective application of theory. Today, therapists are required to obtain a complex understanding of human behavior and develop a keen ability to employ interventions that are suitable and appropriate for a particular individual's present and ongoing concerns. Although it is difficult to predict the direction that the study of therapy's effectiveness will take in the future, Ivey and Zalaquett (2011) argued that the effectiveness of various theory-derived therapies should be examined in ways that consider the link between psychological functioning and new discoveries taking place in modern neuroscience that have led to a greater understanding of the role that the nervous system plays in all forms of disease, which also includes mental illnesses.

The Authors' Approach to Writing This Textbook

Terminology

In writing this book, we sought clarity over relying on unnecessary terminology and, when possible, avoided using jargon in ways that might make a topic area needlessly difficult, if not unintelligible, for readers who are new to the field. Using specialized words or expressions to explain other specialized words or expressions does little more than create a theoretical quagmire that muddles understanding and drowns readers in enough confusion to extinguish their interest. Our primary aim in writing this textbook was to expose readers to the amount of conceptual terminology that would both allow them to differentiate among various theoretical approaches to therapy and grasp the unique contribution made by each of these approaches to the practice of therapy. In addition, we sought to use terminology in a consistent manner throughout the textbook when referring to practitioners and the client recipients of what practitioners have to offer. Thus, a decision was made to use the terms *therapist* and *therapy* (or *psychotherapist* and *psychotherapy*) and *client* in a generic manner throughout this textbook rather than alternating between terms, such as *client* or *patient*; *counselor, psychologist, psychiatrist, social worker*, or *therapist* (or its synonym *psychotherapist*); and *counseling, psychology, psychiatry, social work*. (Exceptions to this decision occur when, for the sake of clarity, another term is deemed more appropriate, such as in Chapter 2, where professional counseling and counseling psychology are discussed.)

As mentioned at the beginning of this chapter, the terms *psychotherapy* and *counseling* were originally used to differentiate forms of treatment. For example, therapy was used to indicate the use of a long-term treatment approach designed to assist a person overcoming some form of a serious psychological disorder by fostering changes in the person's personality. Counseling was used to define short-term treatments that were much less intrusive in nature and sought a solution for what were generally thought of as everyday sorts of problems or concerns, such as the selection of a meaningful career path. As alluded to earlier, over time the distinctions that once existed began to blur when therapists developed and utilized short-term applications of their approaches, and counselors started to work with the full range of problem situations, including various mental disorders. One factor that contributed significantly to this melding of therapy and counseling was the contribution made by Carl Rogers. Rogers's client-centered approach was adopted by many counselors in training and is a good example of the movement toward the growing similarity of clients' needs. In 1962, Eugene T. Gendlin reported on how he had adapted Rogers's approach to assist individuals who suffered from schizophrenia. Eventually, the approach originally developed by Rogers was being used to treat a number of serious concerns, such as depression, alcohol abuse, cognitive dysfunction, and personality disorders.

Target Audiences

This textbook was designed to provide a comprehensive overview of those therapeutic approaches that emerged from what was to become a multitheoretical system whose origin could be traced back to the late 1800s. This textbook was also designed for readers who seek an introduction to the world of therapy, especially those enrolled in introductory undergraduate courses offered through counselor education, psychology, social work, and criminal justice departments or programs. Further, this textbook is appropriate for advanced curriculums, which reacquaint students with previously studied theories. In addition, certain paraprofessionals who have earned bachelor's degrees and plan to complete a training program that will certify them to work in mental health, for example, as a paraprofessional substance abuse counselor, may benefit from this textbook. Many such trained paraprofessionals will also find this textbook suitable for their area of practice, broadening their understanding of how certain treatment approaches might interface with their treatment responsibilities, such as family therapy, which can make an invaluable contribution to the healing process for family members adversely affected by a family member's addiction. In addition, to the aforementioned audiences, numerous training programs exist outside the United States, programs that expect their students to be familiar with the theoretical approaches in this textbook. We believe the information contained in subsequent chapters can help such students in training to obtain a general foundation of knowledge that they can build upon as they advance in their specific areas of expertise. Even though differences exist in the training programs found among different countries and the theories and strategies employed in the therapeutic relationship, globalization is a force that affects much more than the exchange of consumable goods and has increasingly affected intangibles, such as ideas, world views, and other aspects of different cultures that are increasingly being "imported" and "exported" around the world. Such exchanges include important aspects of what comprises the ingredients for effective therapy. Bergin, Bigham, Ginter, and Scalise (2013), for instance, used stratified random sampling of marriage and family therapy practitioners who resided in either the United States or Canada and found an exceptionally high degree of similarity in the responses given by participants in both countries to more than 350 survey items that measured six categories of performance: the practice of systematic therapy; assessing, hypothesizing, and diagnosis; designing and conducting treatment; evaluating ongoing process and terminating treatment; managing crisis situations; and maintaining ethical, legal, and professional services. The globalization of knowledge is helping to spread and shape what therapy is today and what therapy will become in the future.

Foci of the 12 Theory Chapters

In addition to the current chapter, Chapter 2 covers topics such as the therapist as a person and a professional, and Chapter 15 summarizes commonalities and practice-related considerations. Other than Chapters 1, 2, and 15, the majority of chapters are devoted to examining the various theoretical foundations that support contemporary forms of therapy. Furthermore, the 12 theories or approaches reviewed were christened with names that are now widely known—psychoanalysis, Adlerian, existential, client-centered, gestalt, behavioral, cognitive-behavioral, reality, feminist, family systems, multicultural, and postmodern. Various other descriptors are also found throughout this textbook, including the identification of Albert Ellis's form of therapy as "rational-emotive behavior therapy," which can be logically paired with several other versions of what has generally become known as cognitive-behavioral approaches to therapy.

The theories covered in this book span three centuries from the late 1800s to the present. Even though differences in the organization and content can be found among the 12 chapters of this textbook, each theory chapter was structured to encourage comparisons of theories. We used a rubric that organized each chapter into sections that provide the following information about a theoretical approach: biographical background on major proponent(s), basic theoretical concepts and assumptions, components of the therapeutic process (e.g., role of therapist and client, nature of the therapeutic relationship, how goals are established, therapeutic techniques that are commonly linked with the approach), theoretical explanation for client change, the role that assessment plays in therapy, unique ethical concerns, research support for a theory's approach, relevance to current mental health delivery systems (e.g., how the approach is suited for systems that rely on managed care, time limits, evidence to support its use of the approach in various mental health settings), critique of strengths and identification of shortcomings, client populations generally served, and an example of how the theoretical approach covered might be applied when working with actual clients.

In addition to devoting an entire chapter to examining multiculturalism's role in today's therapies, all other theory chapters also contain a multicultural section that specifically calls attention to how multiculturalism interplays with the theory that is being reviewed. Another theoretical aspect that is emphasized is how each theoretical position considers the role of social justice.

Finally, each of the 12 chapters closes with summary comments and critical thinking questions related to the chapter's content. Also, some recommended publications or websites are provided to enable the reader to acquire additional information and understanding of the key topics covered in each chapter. Each chapter concludes with a list of the resources that were consulted and cited in that chapter.

Connecting the Dots: Seeing the Big Picture

Each theory molds and shapes the therapeutic approach that it has given birth to since each theory determines how a therapist is to explore a client's problem through maintaining a distinctive style of focus; helps to explain the reason why a therapist relying upon a certain theoretical approach would tackle a client's problem quite differently from a therapist relying on another theoretical position; motivates a therapist's actions and thoughts during therapy sessions and guides the therapist in ways to gauge the degree of progress made and when it is appropriate to terminate therapy; and provides the necessary raw material to construct and test the accuracy of hypotheses. Thus, an understanding of how various theoretical approaches function toward solving clients' problems lies at the heart of understanding more fully the different forms of therapy practiced today.

An important aspect of every theory that deserves recognition is the philosophical position represented by a theory concerning the *fundamental nature of reality and human existence.* The latter raises a critical question related to whether human existence encompasses the attribute of free will. Specifically, to what degree can humans willfully affect who they become during the course of their lives? If humans lack a sufficient degree of free will, then attempting therapeutic change becomes futile because the power to act without the constraint of fate is impossible, and any changes thought to be the result of free will are an illusion.

Concerning the issue of free will's role in affecting change, Carl Rogers (1951) stated:

> I have yet to find the individual who, when he examines his situation deeply, and feels that he perceives it clearly, deliberately chooses dependence. Deliberately chooses to have the integrated direction of himself undertaken by another. When all the elements are clearly perceived, the balance seems invariably in the direction of the painful but ultimately rewarding path of self-actualization or growth. (p. 490)

The power for humans to pursue their unique personal potential and actively construct who they will become without the constraints of fate is the meaning of *free will.* In addition to Carl Rogers's humanistic approach, which stresses a client's dignity and worth and capacity for self-realization, existentialism is another theoretical perspective that also highlights the central role of free will in therapeutic change.

Created by Viktor Frankl, logotherapy (*logos* is Greek for "meaning") rests upon his belief that humans are free to search for a meaningful life (Devoe, 2012). Frankl is best known for his book *Man's Search for Meaning,* in which he outlines his existential position, a position that even the atrocities he encountered in a Nazi concentration camp were unable to alter. By the end of World War II, Frankl had survived a literal hell on earth. Later, he used his concentration camp experiences to further support the importance of free will to facilitate important therapeutic shifts in a client's life.

One of existentialism's strongest advocates was Jean-Paul Sartre, whose work titled *Being and Nothingness* carefully presents the philosophical basis for this framework using terms such as *anguish, essence, existence,* and *responsibility.* The root phrase that best captures what Sartre was trying to communicate to the world is "Existence precedes essence." Sartre meant that a person's *existence* is a given, an outcome of birth, but that the person we ultimately become is ideally sculpted through meaningful choices we make to reach our potential, which Sartre called *essence.* Choice is an inescapable quality of living according to Sartre, for even if we consciously decide not to make a meaningful choice, we have still made a choice. Relying upon happenstance rather than our free will to self-determine our essence eventually leads to living a life driven by basic urges or one driven by radically conforming to others' expectations of who we should become. No matter how much we give in to our impulses or try to conform, any happiness that results is fleeting and leaves in its wake a sense of dread and lingering unhappiness. Personal happiness comes with assuming the responsibility that accompanies our becoming aware that we are meant to be the "incontestable author" of our own lives (Sartre, 1956/1974, p. 552).

Providing Greater Understanding by Moving Beyond Words

In keeping with our goal to write with clarity about complex theoretical perspectives and applications, we make use of other creative forms of expression, such as eye-catching symbols or visual illusions, works by painters and sculptors, segments of poems or musical lyrics that convey vivid images or elicit emotional reactions, portions of stage plays, snippets of scenes from movies, photographic images that tell a story, and so forth. There are instances when the proverb "A picture is worth a thousand words" is true with regard to students who are genuinely grasping the meaning of an abstract or even some generic idea generated by a particular theoretical position. An example of how "moving beyond words" can be used to facilitate understanding is provided next by juxtaposing a technical definition for existential anguish with a widely recognized painting by Edvard Munch.

Sartre (1956/1974) defines the term *anguish* this way:

> The reflective apprehension of the Self as freedom, the realization that a nothingness slips between my Self and my past and future so that nothing relieves me from the necessity of continually choosing myself and nothing guarantees the validity of the values which I choose. Fear is of something in the world, anguish is anguish before myself. (p. 547)

The essential meaning and relationship of this term to other key existential concepts would likely pose a challenge for anyone who lacks a general understanding of Sartre's form of existentialism, but what the experience of anguish means for one who experiences the dread that marks its presence is indubitably conveyed by Edvard Munch's painting *The Scream*. Chant (2003) wrote that Munch's famous painting was inspired by a personal experience, which Munch recorded in his journal in 1892. The journal entry read as follows:

> I was walking along the road with two friends. The sun was setting. I felt a breath of melancholy–Suddenly the sky turned blood-red. I stopped, and leaned against the railing, deathly tired–Looking out across the flaming clouds that hung like blood and a sword over the blue-black fjord and town. My friends walked on–I stood there trembling with fear. And I sensed a great, infinite scream pass through nature. (n.p.)

▼ FIGURE 1.3
Munch's Painting *The Scream*

Munch's painting (Figure 1.3) portrays a felt experience without using a single word. It creates a powerful image that resonates with us by immediately communicating the horrible anguish felt by the depicted figure. Munch's creation has the power to linger long after we look away; this is an image that, once it is seen, cannot be "unseen" by the viewer. By contrast, at this point in the chapter, the exact wording used earlier to define *anguish* has probably already disappeared from the reader's mind. Certain images, such as the one created by Munch, have the power to persist and retain their effect long after the image's creator is gone. In addition, such powerful images can morph and find new expression in some alternate form. An example of such staying power coupled with the ability to change over time from one image into another is provided by Chant (2003), who referenced the intimidating mask worn by the two killers in Wesley "Wes" Craven's 1996 horror movie *Scream* (Figure 1.4). The mask worn in the movie seems to personify the existential notion of anguish, but in addition to taking on the qualities of being human anguish, the wearer of the mask in *Scream* carries a knife that possesses the potential power to threaten others with death or what might more appropriately be called existential nonexistence.

Source: The Scream (or The Cry) by Edvard Munch. Wikimedia Commons.

Reappearing Case Study Used in Each Theoretical Chapter

Another way we, the authors, have been able to instill a greater appreciation of each theoretical area covered in this textbook is through the provision of case studies that highlight several key components of a particular theoretical approach. The case illustration found at the end of each theory chapter is based on the Case of Miguel Sanchez box on page 17.

▼ FIGURE 1.4
Mask used in the Movie *Scream*

It should be noted that in some chapters new story elements are introduced into the Sanchez case information for the purpose of better illustrating the type of strategies relied on by a therapist who is affiliated with the theoretical model discussed in the specific chapter. This reexamination of the same case in each of the theory chapters is intended to enable a reader of this textbook to ascertain genuine differences and similarities among various therapeutic approaches.

In addition to returning to the Sanchez case study in each of the 12 theory chapters, each of these chapters begins with a unique case not found in any of the other chapters. These unique cases embrace several different forms. For example, a case may represent an amalgamation of cases that the chapter's author(s)

Source: Konrad, C. and Woods, C. (Producer), & Craven, W. (Director). (1996). Scream [Motion Picture]. USA: Woods Entertainment.

THE CASE OF MIGUEL SANCHEZ

Miguel Sanchez is a 14-year-old Mexican American male who emigrated from Mexico City to South Los Angeles with his family 6 years ago. His guidance counselor, Mrs. Torres, refers Miguel to receive psychological services and assessment. Mrs. Torres cites a decrease in Miguel's school attendance, a shift in gravitation toward a negative peer group, and potential substance abuse as reasons for her referral. Mrs. Torres reports her being particularly concerned about Miguel's recent negative behavior because he has a history of being a bright student who has been involved with various student organizations. Mrs. Torres calls a local community mental health agency and requests that Miguel be matched with a male clinician, preferably Hispanic. Miguel's mother, Mrs. Sanchez, agrees that it might be in her son's best interest to engage in psychological services and leaves a message at the agency that she would like to schedule an appointment.

Dr. Ramirez is assigned to the case and contacts Mrs. Sanchez to schedule an initial assessment. Dr. Ramirez explains on the phone how he initially works with a new client and their family by discussing his theoretical orientation, the client's right to confidentiality, cancellation policy, sliding scale to receive reduced fee services, and how he may work collaboratively with the school and other providers. Mrs. Sanchez confirms that she has recently noticed a negative change in her son and agrees to bring him to see Dr. Ramirez in the following week.

After the initial session, Dr. Ramirez could not help but wonder if the Sanchez family situation were more complicated than they originally presented. The Sanchez family spent the first session focusing on behaviors and expectations; however, Dr. Ramirez left the session feeling as if there might be underlying unresolved issues. He made a mental note to further explore how acculturation may be affecting the Sanchez family.

In the following session, Dr. Ramirez helps to initiate a conversation between mother and son as to how their experiences of moving to the United States might be different as well as how it might be similar. During this session Mrs. Sanchez tearfully explains how she feels that her son is losing his heritage by wearing baggy clothes, listening to rap music, and refusing to participate in familial and cultural activities that he once enjoyed. In defense, Miguel loudly tells his mother that she embarrasses him because of the traditional clothing that she chooses to wear and by her refusing to learn to read or write in English.

Miguel is noticeably agitated when the conversation moves to his decreased connection to his Mexican heritage. Miguel attempts to explain to his mother, in Spanish, that the only people that he can truly relate to are his new friends. A heated discussion then ensues about Mrs. Sanchez's view of Miguel's new friends' criminal mentality and lack of morals. Miguel shouts, "At least they give me respect" and storms out of the room. Dr. Ramirez is left with Mrs. Sanchez as she sobs in the room with her hands held over her face.

had experienced in a private practice setting, or the case may take a more hypothetical form such as when a chapter's author explores how the progenitor of a certain approach might have worked with a client or situation that has been spawned by the author's imagination (such cases are found in the following chapters: psychoanalysis, Adlerian, gestalt, reality/choice, and family therapy). Regardless of the source of these unique cases, they all serve to provide another illustration of how the variety of theoretically oriented therapists would handle a therapeutic situation.

At this point we hope that the current chapter piques the interest of the readers in a field of study and practice that has fascinated us throughout our careers. The theories covered in this textbook offer a wide range of therapeutic formulas designed to provide a therapist with the requisite structure and strategies to effectively work with a large array of client concerns, ranging from individuals interested in achieving personal growth to persons who are experiencing the serious ramification of a mental disorder.

Further, we hope that upon reaching the end of this textbook, a reader will become aware of how the theories explored within its pages share divergent characteristics but also certain commonalities. One such commonality is that these theories offer much more than what is solely associated with processes that occur within the confines of a therapy room's four walls. These are theories that have general implications for how we are to live, love, and work. Such wide-ranging implications help to explain why Carl Rogers moved from calling his approach "client-centered" to "person-centered" once he realized that his theoretical position offered transformative possibilities beyond what was taking place in traditional therapy settings (Rogers, 1980). Similar to Carl Rogers, the researcher B. F. Skinner, whose theory was deterministically driven rather than free will driven, also believed that his theory of operant conditioning had implications well beyond what was being applied in and outside his research laboratory; this belief prompted Skinner to write *Walden Two*, a novel that describes how behaviorism can serve as a blueprint for building a modern-day utopia (Skinner, 1962). The point is that the 12 theoretical areas covered in this textbook have much to offer anyone who is willing to immerse himself or herself in what is presented. We believe such immersion coupled with an open mind will allow the reader to reach the end of the last chapter having abstracted from this textbook what will be of greatest benefit in terms of how that reader chooses to live, love, and work in ways that are both meaningful and satisfying.

Ongoing Exercise That Concludes in Chapter 15

By this textbook's conclusion, readers should be able to express clearly what they believe are the elements that would comprise their own personal theoretical approach to therapy. In Chapter 15 we provide a method to achieve this important end goal. Table 1.1 is an example of how such a comparison method is intended to work. Specifically, the six rows in Table 1.1 depict how a reader might have responded when writing a comparison summary (e.g., "1. Theoretical perspective used to understand basic human nature") for each of the four theoretical approaches (i.e., feminist therapy, postmodern therapy, marriage and family therapy, and multicultural/cross-cultural therapy) selected to illustrate how a reader can establish similarities and dissimilarities among theories.

After writing summary statements across all "Six Areas of Comparison" found in Table 1.1 for the four theoretical approaches listed across the top of the table, the reader will have filled 24 cells. The contents of these 24 cells reveal the prominent differences and similarities among the four theoretical approaches. As the reader looks across each row of written summary statements, a means for the reader to review six key points in which the listed theories diverge or converge with one another is presented.

The concluding exercise found in Chapter 15 expects readers of this textbook to isolate from their own written summaries for each of the theoretical chapters read what they consider most meaningful to them for the purpose of constructing their own unique theoretical position. Furthermore, in Chapter 15 a number of important concepts are explained (e.g., syncretism, technique matching, theoretical frames, and common factors) that readers will be required to consider in light of the summaries they wrote. The information in Chapter 15 creates a structure for readers to achieve a critical assessment of the various theories in this textbook, the type of assessment that is necessary before a reader can clearly state what comprises his or her personal theory.

Four Therapies Juxtaposed on Six Areas

Six Areas of Comparison	Feminist Therapy	Postmodern Therapy (Narrative Therapy)	Marriage and Family Therapy	Multicultural/ Cross-Cultural Therapy
1. **Theoretical perspective used to understand basic human nature**	The interplay of male and female perspectives, biological differences, and social expectations related to gender	Personal "stories" are what define an individual's or group's understanding of reality and the role they play in that reality	The family represents the fulcrum to understand individuals and various groupings of family members	Factors, such as racial and ethnic diversity, sexual orientation, disabilities, classism, and the history of marginalized groups
2. **Mental events, processes, or other attributes focused on**	Prejudice in favor of or against one gender in a way considered to be unfair and detrimental to mental health	Cognitively humans are driven to make meaning of the experiences encountered in their lives	What occurs within and between individuals is related to family dynamics	Factors that contribute to beliefs (positive, negative, or unbiased) about other individuals and groups
3. **General explanation given for client problems**	Thinking that reflects inherent privilege that leads to systemic gender inequalities within a society or culture	The way clients have interpreted and "written out" the events in their lives can create personal problems	Dysfunctional family systems originate in many possible ways, but all have a disruptive impact on family relationships	Attitudes, judgments, and behaviors reflect prejudice, stereotyping, and discrimination
4. **Emphasis placed on client's past, present, or future**	Depends on the particular form of feminist therapy referred to because theoretical views overlap and differ	Full range because the past, present, and future can all contribute to the deconstruction and reconstruction of a meaningful narrative	The full range of time periods is utilized, but focus depends largely on the specific family therapy utilized	Full range referred to but can differ as a result of the particular theoretical position and a client's worldview
5. **The role that free agency plays in therapeutic change**	Self-determination is a key aspect of feminist-oriented therapies in uncovering possible solutions for client concerns	Individuals, couples, and families possess the ability to rescript their lives through reinterpreting events in their lives	Depends on the particular approach referred to because theoretical views differ concerning amount of free agency possessed	In general, the degree of free agency believed to exist allows for changes in the self, others, and systems to occur
6. **Theoretical developments**	Other forms include Marxist feminism, radical feminism, ecofeminism, erotic feminism, and lesbian feminism	Postmodern theory encompasses several conceptually important additions that continue to remain influential, such as hyper-reality	Encompasses earlier approaches and newer approaches that operate from a systems perspective	Theoretical developments include cultural identity development theory, integrative life pattern model, and feminist therapy

Table 1.2 is a summary format that readers should use to collect the information they will need to complete the concluding exercise. Readers should photocopy, scan, or create their own version of the guide in Table 1.2 and use it to write summaries for each of the theoretical chapters they complete. Finally, users of this textbook are strongly encouraged to review those pages near the end of Chapter 15, which concern the final exercise discussed here. In reviewing those pages, readers will notice that the concluding exercise has three parts (and subparts) to complete. The last part, Part III, requires readers to write a detailed description of their own personal theoretical position. Their description must also incorporate what they learned by completing Parts I and II, including an explanation of how the knowledge gained from these two parts helped them construct their own unique theoretical approach to therapy.

Guide for Summarizing the 12 Areas

Name of Theoretical Approach Reviewed: _____	
The 12 Areas	Summary Statement for the Corresponding Area (Areas 1–12)
Area 1: Philosophy concerning basic human nature	
Area 2: Role of therapist	
Area 3: Key concepts	
Area 4: Goals of therapy	
Area 5: Therapeutic relationship described	
Area 6: Techniques of therapy	
Area 7: Applications of the approach	
Area 8: Multicultural considerations	
Area 9: Social justice consideration	
Area 10: General contributions to the field	
Area 11: General limitations	
Area 12: General strengths	

CHAPTER 2

COUNSELOR ROLE AND FUNCTIONS, PROFESSIONAL ETHICS, STRESS, AND SELF-CARE

Introduction

In this chapter, *counselors* refers to practitioners in the distinct fields of *professional counseling* (i.e., professional counselors) and *counseling psychology* (i.e., counseling psychologists), which represent different professions; possess a different history of development; in most instances, have different professional organizations; and have separate accreditation bodies. Professional counseling and counseling psychology have different orientations to training and deliver education at different graduate levels and for a different number of years. The two professions have different licenses for practice and third-party/insurance payers. Because professional counselors and counseling psychologists have distinct identities and may even be competitive or adversarial with each other over professional standing issues and resources, the professions are addressed separately in this chapter.

A Brief History of Professional Counseling

The American Counseling Association (ACA) is the largest organization devoted to providing counseling services (Gladding, 2009). Initially, ACA was known as the American Personnel and Guidance Association (APGA; Ginter, 2002). Established in 1952 by a loose constellation of organizations, APGA was primarily "concerned with vocational guidance and other personnel activities" (Harold, 1985, p. 4). ACA has grown from its "guidance" infancy into a multifaceted profession of approximately 55,000 members and 20 chartered divisions (American Counseling Association, 2017; Cashwell, 2010). The State of Virginia passed the first counselor licensure law in 1976, followed by all 49 other states, Washington, D.C., and Puerto Rico. Professional counselors now bill private health insurance, and the U.S. Department of Veterans Affairs (VA) recently ruled that professional counselors can work in VA hospitals. There are about 635,000 counselors who work in a variety of settings, and this number is "expected to grow much faster than the average for all occupations through 2016" (Bureau of Labor Statistics, 2010–2011, p. 209).

Counselor Education and Accreditation. Accreditation was a latecomer to the counseling profession, but in 1981 the Council for the Accreditation of Counseling and Related Programs (CACREP) was established (Hollis & Dodson, 2001). CACREP is now an independent organization recognized by the Council for Higher Education Accreditation to accredit the master's degree in eight counseling specialties (e.g., school counseling, clinical mental health counseling, addictions counseling) and doctoral programs in counselor

After reading this chapter, each student should be able to:

1. Differentiate between professional counseling and counseling psychology by comparing their developmental history, professional organization, accreditation bodies, identities, and training.

2. Evaluate one's own personal motivation, values, and responsibilities as a counselor to better understand professional ethics.

3. Articulate the rationale and importance of informed consent and record keeping.

4. Describe the differences and similarities between the ACA Code of Ethics and the APA Ethical Principles and Code of Conduct with regard to confidentiality, multiple roles, and competence.

5. Recall ethical decision making when given examples of possible ethical dilemmas.

6. Describe the definition of subjective and professional well-being and the risks of professional burnout.

7. Identify the importance of self-care and its seven domains, and give examples of self-care for each.

education. Although counselor accreditation is voluntary for counseling programs, the CACREP accreditation requirements serve as the foundation for most state licensure laws (Remley & Herlihy, 2015).

Because ACA has delegated accreditation responsibility to CACREP, this has created an identity issue for professional counselors. There has been an informal opinion within the counseling field that CACREP accreditation should be dropped in favor of ACA accreditation. Although some counseling professionals would like to see the change for clarity purposes, CACREP will likely remain the accrediting organization (Cashwell, 2010).

Licensure and Certification. In the United States, professional counselors must become licensed to receive insurance reimbursement. To attain licensure, professional counselors must graduate from a master's-level counseling program, be supervised by a licensed professional for the period of time specified by the licensure board, and pass the licensure board's examination (e.g., National Clinical Mental Health Counselor Examination, National Counselor Examination, Certified Rehabilitation Counselor Examination). Licensure requirements are set by the individual state or territory and may vary considerably, making it difficult for a counselor who relocates from state to state. The professional counselor may have to take a second state examination, accrue more hours of supervision, and possibly complete additional coursework, as required by a particular state licensing body (Remley & Herlihy, 2015). The American Association of State Counseling Boards (AASCB) currently represents an effort to centralize disparate state licensure requirements (AASCB, 2017; Cashwell, 2010).

Another complication regarding vagaries in counselor licensure lies in the various licensure names and acronyms. Names for licensed counselor vary among states, for example, Licensed Professional Counselor (LPC), Licensed Mental Health Counselor (LMHC), Licensed Clinical Mental Health Counselor (LCMHC), or Licensed Clinical Professional Counselor (LCPC). Furthermore, some states have a two-tiered licensure system, meaning initial licensure is given (1) at the completion of a master's degree and/ or upon passing the state examination and (2) accumulation of the required supervised hours of counseling practice. Because the first tier is limited, professional counselors must continue to be supervised by a counselor holding the higher tier license. Some states require the higher tiered license to bill health insurance. Most states have not instituted a tier system, but as the field matures, it may become more common.

National certification is a voluntary credential, second in importance and function to state licensure. National certification is the purview of the National Board for Certified Counselors (NBCC), a separate credentialing organization overseeing national certification in a variety of specialty areas, including mental health counseling and school counseling, and others (NBCC, 2016). The coexistence of state licensure and national certification may be confusing to professionals outside the counseling field.

NBCC offers several credentials, most notably the National Certified Counselor and the Certified Clinical Mental Health Counselor. For certification, a counselor must earn a master's degree and then pass the National Counselor Examination for Licensure and Certification to become certified as a National Certified Counselor or the National Clinical Mental Health Counselor Examination for certification as a Certified Clinical

Mental Health Counselor. These examinations have also been adopted by numerous states as their licensure examination (National Board for Certified Counselors, 2017).

Some counseling professionals have questioned the validity of a national certification because national certification does not provide counselors the vehicle to bill health insurance or supervise beginning counselors (Weinrach & Thomas, 1993). Remley (1995) contended that a license ought to be for general practice, whereas national certification ought to acknowledge specialty areas. The field has moved toward Remley's model although arguments regarding certifications' necessity persist.

A Brief History of Counseling Psychology

Counseling psychologists are doctorate-level psychologists (PhD, PsyD, or EdD) who have received general education in the core areas of psychology, specialized training in interventions and treatments, and extensive supervised practice and have completed a dissertation in the field of psychology. Counseling psychologists, in contrast to clinical psychologists, focus on the adaptive functioning of individuals in their personal and interpersonal lives across the life span. In particular, counseling psychologists focus on emotional, social, vocational, developmental, organizational, and health-related adaptation problems. The settings in which their education, research, or application of therapy occur include colleges and universities, local hospitals, veterans hospitals, community clinics, and private practices.

Although both clinical and counseling psychologists provide psychotherapy, they differ in the means they utilize to deliver treatment. When the two subfields were developed, clinical psychologists focused on the care of the ill or bedridden. (The term *clinical* derives from the Greek word *kline*, which means bed.) Counseling psychologists focused on consultation with those who were generally well. (*Counsel* comes from the Latin word *consulere*, which means to consult, advise, or deliberate.) Currently, clinical psychologists typically use more assessment and treatment methods linked to psychopathology than do counseling psychologists, who use more developmental and prevention methods.

Counseling psychology as a formal discipline in the United States is about 100 years old, being launched by the movements of mental hygiene (1920s), vocational guidance (1940s), and psychometrics (1940s). Its professional affiliation with the American Psychological Association (APA) started in 1946, with the founding of the Personnel and Guidance Psychology Division, Division 17 of APA. Division 17 subsequently had two name changes: Counseling Psychology and, since 2002, Society of Counseling Psychology. Division 17 has evolved beyond one organization and includes collaborative relations with the Council of Counseling Psychology Training Programs (CCPTP) and the Association of Counseling Center Training Agencies (ACCTA). Both of these organizations are strong forces within professional psychology and university-based accredited bodies.

The 1980s were wrought with societal changes in the field of psychology in the United States. National training conferences as well as groups and task forces (e.g., Task Force on the Scope and Criteria for Accreditation of the APA) proposed a shift in pedagogy, expanding curricula to include diversity issues, consultation, policy formation, supervision, and program development. Psychology was written into Medicare statutes, which ultimately intensified battles between medicine/psychiatry and psychology. Ethical complaints about dual relationships (i.e., sexual relationships with clients), diversity, and HIV/AIDS status became obvious. Also, for the first time, attention was given to the distressed psychologist because it was naive and dangerous to ignore the stressors counseling psychologists faced in their work and personal lives.

APA's Evidence-Based Policy. Counseling psychology's parent body, APA, has been compelled to remain current. At the turn of this century, APA responded to two different pressures: (1) the increasing force of government funding agencies and managed care companies to verify the utility and necessity of psychotherapeutic interventions and (2) additional forces as from the practitioners of psychology (cf. Fox, 1995; Lichtenberg, Goodyear, & Genther, 2008; Roysircar, 2009b). Levant (APA, 2005) officially endorsed a policy statement advocating the use of evidence-based practice (EBP) as a means for delivering quality and cost-effective treatment for mental disorders (Council for Training in Evidence-Based Behavioral Practice, 2008). As defined by APA (APA, 2005), "Evidence-based practice in psychology is the integration of the best available research with clinical expertise in the context of patient characteristics, culture, and preferences" (p. 271). The EBP process thus integrates the best available evidence with regard to practitioners' expertise, empirical research, and scholarship with the cultural and economic conditions, needs, values, and preferences of clients who are served and affected (Council for Training in Evidence-Based Behavioral Practice, 2008). Types of research evidence to support decision making in practice include clinical observation, qualitative research, systematic case studies, single-case experimental designs, public health and ethnographic research, process-outcome studies, studies of interventions as they are delivered in naturalistic settings (effectiveness research), basic psychological and health science, and meta-analysis (APA Presidential Task Force on Evidence-Based Practice, 2006). Experimental studies are read critically with regard to the constitution of experimental and control groups, methodology, threats to validity, and effect sizes (Wampold & Bhati, 2004). When drawing conclusions used for making decisions, psychologists ask whether a study's methods and findings justify causal explanations, particularly as applied in a local context (Shedler, 2015). In evaluating the evidence used in clinical decision making, psychologists pay particular attention to issues related to social justice and cultural relevance, view evidence as ecologically or systemically embedded as well as historical, and evaluate it accordingly (APA, 2017).

The Council for Counseling Psychology Training Programs Competency Benchmarks for Doctoral Training. The benchmark training document (For a comprehensive review, see Fouad et al., 2009.) outlines the necessary competencies that counseling psychology students must have when they enter practicum, internship, and finally doctoral-level practice. It is believed that these three developmental levels are necessary for trainees to become effective and competent psychologists.

Overall, counseling psychology students must have foundational competencies that are apparent in their behavior and comportment, reflecting the ethics, integrity, values, and responsibility of the profession. Students must have professional as well as personal self-awareness and reflexivity. They must have skills to reflect on professional practice (reflection-on-action). Students are expected to problem-solve, think critically, and have intellectual curiosity and flexibility. Self-assessment involves determining one's knowledge of core competencies. Self-care involves attending to one's well-being and personal health to ensure effective functioning as a professional.

Practicum-Level Skills. Students who do doctoral practicum training for two to three years must have a basic understanding of (a) research, including methodology and procedures for collecting data and conducting analysis; (b) development across the life span; and (c) biological and cognitive–affective bases of behavior. Also, students must relate meaningfully and effectively with individuals, groups, and/or communities. They must have interpersonal skills such as the ability to listen and be empathic with others, show respect for and interest in others' experiences and cultures, and demonstrate knowledge and awareness of various aspects of their own diversity and their attitudes about diverse others. Emotional maturity and effective expressive skills are essential. Students must have a basic understanding of the APA Ethical Principles and Code of Conduct (APA, 2002, including 2010 and 2016 amendments). They must have the ability to comply with regulations and, at the same time, make autonomous judgment within an organization's management and leadership. In addition, they must be capable of working in interdisciplinary teams.

In addition to being able to administrate and score traditional assessment instruments, students must be knowledgeable of assessment practices stemming from a basic understanding of the theoretical, contextual, and scientific bases of test construction and interviewing. Assessment mastery should result in formulating diagnoses, linking assessment and intervention, and effectively writing reports and notes. Finally, supervision is crucial for practicum students. Therefore, they must have a basic understanding of the expectations of supervision and process of supervision, interpersonal skills of communication and openness to feedback, and the awareness of the need to be truthful, respectful, and straightforward in their communication with their supervisor.

Managed Care Demands

The evolution of professional counseling and counseling psychology has changed with the increase in managed care. Previously, counseling psychologists' professional roles were equally divided between academician (40.2%) and clinical practitioner (39.7%), with less self-report for administrator (14.1%) and other work (6.0%) (Lichtenberg et al., 2008). Counseling psychologists have now begun to move from the relative security of salaried, academic, or administrative positions to work as independent, fee-for-service professionals. Professional counselors are also in private practice. So counseling psychologists and professional counselors need to deal with managed care, for which they were not prepared by their prevention-, developmental-, and academic-focused training programs.

Managed care began in 1929 (National Council on Disability, 2013), but it did not begin to have a broad impact on health care delivery until health care costs skyrocketed. Managed care organizations' increasing focus on improving the quality of care is one of the major trends shaping the delivery of mental health services. There is an interest in rewarding therapists for quality performance. The Centers for Medicare and Medicaid Services for the retired/elderly (i.e., Medicare) and indigent populations (i.e., Medicaid) are working with at least several states to implement pay-for-performance (or quality-based purchasing) Medicaid programs. (For more information, visit https://www.ced.org/blog/entry/top-healthcare-stories-for-2016-pay-for-performance.)

Quality performance might be measured, for instance, by client satisfaction, symptom reduction, and indexing the client's subsequent health care usage. As a result, there has been increasing emphasis on medically necessary treatments, reducing services overall, and restricting reimbursement rates. The cost of health care and the fact that millions of people have no health insurance create a problem for health care providers whose goal is it to ensure access to care and also contradicts professional counseling's and counseling psychology's multicultural and social justice advocacy. An added concern harbored by professional counselors and counseling psychologists pertains to ethical issues related to working with managed care organizations, a concern that further complicates clinical practice. This concern relates to how professional ethical codes and managed care policies do not always agree with one another, creating ethical challenges for mental health providers. Furthermore, practicum students may be afforded fewer training opportunities as managed care directs who can provide treatment to clientele. Moreover, with budgetary cuts being made across the mental health sector (e.g., community mental health centers, hospitals, jails, residential treatment), training opportunities for students will continue to dwindle while there is an increased enrollment of students in professional counseling and professional psychology training programs.

Professional Ethics

Professional counselors and counseling psychologists must abide by professional ethical guidelines that are designed to ensure beneficence to clients. Ethical dilemmas with clients are frequently due to the paradoxical nature of a counselor's personal or community life and professional practice. (Note. The term *counselor[s]* is used to indicate that a section's information applies to both professional counselors and counseling psychologists.) This chapter examines counselors' role and functions as well as their encounters with stressful ethical dilemmas. Ethical decision making helps counselors maintain ethical practice and relieves them of inner conflicts, while their practice of self-care enhances their well-being so that they meet the demands of a challenging profession. To effectively help their clients, counselors need to have an understanding of their personal motivation for pursuing this profession, as well as the values and responsibilities inherent in being a counselor.

Personal Motivation of a Counselor

Counselors have an obligation to be aware of their own issues in life, such as their personal motivation for becoming counselors. If counselors fail to bring awareness to their personal needs, they may obstruct client progress as counseling shifts from meeting the client's needs to meeting the counselor's needs. For example, counselors may be motivated to pursue work in a helping profession because of a need to be appreciated by others; a need to nurture, save, or protect others; or a need to feel powerful. Counselors need to be aware of these personal needs, so that these needs do not assume priority over the client's well-being. Progress in counseling can be impeded if counselors use their clients to fulfill their own needs, even if unconsciously.

Values and Responsibility of a Counselor

Counselors must take an honest look at their professional identity, personal identity, and personal life to gain self-awareness of the influence of their needs, goals, job stress, impairment, personality traits, personal dynamics, countertransference, the importance of self-care, and the challenge in balancing life roles (Corey, Corey, & Callanan, 2007). Counselors must examine any unresolved conflicts that may show up in the therapy room, as well as their personal reactions to the client. Counselors must also make every effort to balance stress and self-care to avoid work burnout (Roysircar, 2008).

Research has discredited the previous notion that counselors can keep their personal values out of the therapeutic environment (Richards, Rector, & Tjeltveit, 1999). Research has also revealed that counselors' values affect every phase of the counseling relationship, such as assessment strategies, goals, intervention techniques, and evaluation of therapeutic techniques (Roysircar, Arredondo, Fuertes, Ponterotto, & Toporek, 2003; Roysircar, Dobbins, & Malloy, 2009). Finally, many value conflicts can occur regarding gender identity, sexual orientation and behavior, abortion, religiosity and spirituality, and end-of-life decisions. Counselors must consider the role of personal influence in their practice, even their unconscious, implicit, and subtle biases.

Informed Consent

Counselors have the ethical responsibility to talk to their clients about their rights, so that their clients have enough information to render informed choices about entering and continuing in the counselor–client relationship (Corey et al., 2007). Many clients do not realize that they have rights, especially those in crisis who unquestioningly accept whatever the counselor says or does. The purpose of informed consent is to improve the probability that the client will become educated, involved, and willing to participate in counseling. Informed consent documents should clearly outline the counselor's twofold responsibility: to protect other individuals from potentially dangerous clients and to protect clients from themselves with respect to self-harm and suicide (refer to Laura Brown Psychotherapy Information Disclosure Statement, http://www.drlaurabrown.com/media/PsychotherapyConsentForm.pdf; Fisher & Oransky, 2008; Pope & Vasquez, 2016). Clients should be informed of all risks, benefits, and alternatives to the proposed treatment. However, counselors should observe a balance between providing too much professional information at the start of therapy, thus scaring off or confusing clients, and informing too little. It can be detrimental to clients' mental health to overwhelm them with information at the start of therapy.

Record Keeping

Counselors also have a prominent responsibility to keep adequate records on their clients. Record keeping serves multiple purposes: It helps to structure quality care, decrease liability exposure, and fulfill requirements for reimbursement (Rivas-Vasquez, Blais, Rey, & Rivas-Vasquez, 2001). Records can also serve as a counselor's defense against a malpractice claim or an ethical violation charge. Record keeping is especially helpful when clients are transferred to new counselors. Counselors are legally and ethically obligated to maintain client records in a secure fashion and to protect their clients' confidentiality.

ACA Code of Ethics

The ACA recently published a revised code of ethical guidelines (i.e., the Code of Ethics; ACA, 2014). There are nine sections in the Code of Ethics that provide ethical guidance on topics ranging from the counseling relationship to distance counseling, technology, and social media. The 2014 Code of Ethics also clarifies the ethical responsibilities of the ACA.

Among other objectives, the Code of Ethics stipulates the ethical obligations of ACA members, assists members in constructing a course of ethical action, establishes expectations of professional counselor conduct, and serves as the foundation for processing ethical complaints made against ACA members. Thus, the primary purpose of the ACA Code of Ethics is to protect the welfare of clients by detailing what is in their best interest. Three guidelines of the Code of Ethics—confidentiality, multiple role relationships, and competence—are discussed next.

Confidentiality

Confidentiality refers to respecting and safeguarding the client's right to privacy (ACA, 2014). As a rule, professional counselors are not permitted to disclose confidential communications to a third party unless they obtain permission from the client or are mandated by law to do so. Confidentiality is related to one of the fundamental guidelines in the Code of Ethics, that is, fidelity, which entails honoring commitments to and trust in the therapeutic relationship (ACA, 2014). Honoring a client's privacy means that a professional counselor is protecting the integrity of the client–counselor relationship. The guideline of confidentiality is covered in sections A and B of the ACA Code of Ethics.

Section A. Section A outlines the counseling relationship and refers to confidentiality in several areas: (a) safeguarding documentation of clients and ensuring that all documentation accurately reflects client progress, (b) discussing limitations to confidentiality for mandated clients (such as those referred by the law enforcement or judicial system), and (c) obtaining the client's consent before engaging in advocacy efforts on behalf of a client (ACA, 2014).

Section B. Section B focuses exclusively on confidentiality and privacy in the therapeutic relationship. As trust is the foundation of the counseling relationship, professional counselors should communicate the parameters of confidentiality and privacy in a culturally competent manner because multicultural clients may not be familiar with the notion of professional counselor confidentiality. Section B highlights (a) respecting client rights (e.g., having an awareness of and sensitivity to cultural meanings of privacy, inquiring about private information from clients only when therapeutically useful, obtaining consent when disclosing information); (b) knowing exceptions to confidentiality (e.g., disclosing to protect others or clients from harm, end-of-life issues, contagious life-threatening diseases, court-ordered disclosure); (c) sharing information with others (e.g., disclosing client information to training supervisors, subordinates, interdisciplinary team members, third-party payers, and protecting information of deceased clients); (d) understanding confidentiality differences in group, family, and couples therapies; (e) recognizing that certain clients lack capacity to give consent (e.g., minors or the elderly with cognitive difficulties, responsibilities of confidentiality to parents of minor children); (f) utilizing records and documentation (e.g., seeking permission to record information in session, providing client access to records, and seeking permission to transfer records to third parties); and (g) doing case consultation (ACA, 2014).

Section D, G, and H. Section D (relationships with other professionals), section G (research and publication), and section H (distance counseling, technology, and social media) in the ACA Code of Ethics also touch on issues of confidentiality (ACA, 2014). Section D outlines the importance of professional counselors clarifying role expectations and the boundaries of confidentiality with their coworkers when obligated by law to serve in judicial proceedings. Section G outlines the importance of keeping information about research participants confidential and the procedures implemented to protect participant privacy. Last, section H outlines the limitations of maintaining the confidentiality of electronic transmissions and records.

An Illustration of Confidentiality. An illustration of confidentiality includes treating a client in the VA health care system. Client records are available to all professional counselors and medical professionals in the form of electronic medical records. Professional counselors must explain to clients that relevant professionals engaged in their mental and medical health care can view their records. Professional counselors should explain about the client-centered system of VA hospitals and how an interdisciplinary team uses access to records to provide collaborative care to the client. Clients with symptoms of paranoia may have difficulty understanding and accepting electronic medical records. Professional counselors should take precaution with these clients and spend extra time outlining the benefits of an electronic medical record system. Professional counselors should also explain security measures set in place (e.g., the security setting on the electronic medical records that provides an alert when staff members without authorized access try to view a client's record).

Multiple Role Relationships

Another principle in the ACA Code of Ethics is multiple role relationships, also known as dual relationships. This refers to any situation where multiple roles exist between a professional counselor and a client in counseling. Another way of saying this is that a professional counselor enters into a dual relationship whenever the professional counselor has another, significantly different association with a student, client, or a supervisee (Herlihy & Corey, 2006). Multiple role relationships also include offering counseling to a relative or a friend's relative, socializing with clients, becoming emotionally or sexually involved with a client (or former client), combining the roles of counselor and supervisor, having a business association with a client, loaning money to a client, or borrowing money from a client (Corey et al., 2007). Professional counselors also could serve different roles when providing assessment services, psychological consultation to courts, or switching from individual therapy to couples therapy with a client.

In some cases, multiple role relationships cannot be avoided and professional counselors need to manage rather than avoid these relationships (Herlihy & Corey, 2006). An example where multiple role relationships may be unavoidable is in isolated rural settings, where the local minister, merchant, beautician, banker, pharmacist, and mechanic might all be the clients of one professional counselor. In this setting, the professional counselor may have to engage in several multiple role relationships. (This situation is addressed further when discussing the APA Ethical Principles and Code of Conduct later in this section.)

Boundary Crossing Versus Boundary Violation. Related to multiple role relationships are boundary crossings and violations, which refer to any departure from the traditional forms of counseling. Boundary violations refer to when professional counselors exploit their clients, whereas boundary crossing may involve clinically effective interventions like home-visits, receiving gifts, nonsexual touch, self-disclosure, or bartering for services (Gutheil & Gabbard, 1993; Zur, 2015). Sexual relationships with clients are considered the most severe of all boundary violations because they involve a betrayal of trust and an abuse of power that can have disastrous effects on clients (Simon, 1998). Figure 2.1, while exaggerated, does point to behaviors that can lead to a boundary violation.

Boundary crossings are not prohibited by the ACA Code of Ethics. Several examples of boundary crossings from evidence-based treatment plans include going for a walk with a client suffering from depression, flying in a plane with a client who suffers from a phobia of planes, or going to a coffee shop or mall with a person who tends to avoid crowds (Zur, 2015). Other activities may include attending a wedding, lending a book, or attending a client performance in a show.

Section A. Section A outlines several aspects of multiple role relationships. Section A prohibits noncounseling roles and relationships with current clients, their romantic partners, or family members (ACA, 2014). This prohibition also extends to electronic interactions. Professional counselors should not counsel clients with whom they have had a previous relationship such as a friendship or who are family members. Last, professional counselors should address any role changes in the professional relationship with clients and obtain informed consent from the client to continue therapy (ACA, 2014). Examples of professional counselor role changes include (a) changing from one-on-one to couples therapy or vice versa, (b) changing from an evaluative role to a professional counselor role or vice versa, and (c) changing from a professional counselor to a mediator role or vice versa (Kitchener, 1988; Kocet, 2006; Reamer, 1998, as cited in Pugh, 2007).

▼ FIGURE 2.1
Problematic Behaviors

Source: © 2006, Harry Bliss. Used with permission of Pippin Properties, Inc.

An Illustration of Multiple Role Relationships. An illustration of a multiple role relationship includes a professional counselor who switches from providing individual therapy for a client to providing couples counseling to the client and his wife. In this situation, the wife attends one session with the client and requests that they attend couples therapy to work on their relationship. The professional counselor should obtain informed consent from the client, in the absence of his wife, to switch from providing individual therapy to couples counseling. The professional counselor should outline the changing nature of the therapeutic relationship and give the client the opportunity to accept or reject the professional counselor's new role in couples therapy.

Professional Counselor Competence

A third principle in the ACA Code of Ethics is counselor competence. This refers to practicing in a competent and ethical manner (ACA, 2014). Competence is an ethical as well as legal concept because a lack of competence is a significant contributing factor in harm done to clients, and incompetent professional counselors are vulnerable to malpractice suits (Corey et al., 2007). Professional counselors need to demonstrate competence with the many forms of diversity, including gender, age, race, ethnicity, socioeconomic status, sexual orientation, religiosity and spirituality, physical ability, and educational status (Roysircar et al., 2009). Thus, multicultural competence is a necessary prerequisite to providing effective therapy. Multicultural counseling competency refers to "having good self-awareness of attitudes and worldviews into which the counselor has been socialized, in addition to recognizing and being sensitive to a client's worldview and attitudes" (Roysircar, 2003, p. 18). This multicultural counseling competencies framework suggests that professional counselors must have knowledge of the client's culture, while also understanding their own background, biases, and values.

APA Ethical Principles of Psychologists and Code of Conduct

Members of APA are expected to comply with the Ethical Principles of Psychologists and Code of Conduct (American Psychological Association, 2016). Numerous ethical dilemmas of counseling psychologists are the result of disparities in what is ethically expected in the profession and what is conceivable when counseling psychologists balance their personal or community life with professional practice. The APA general principles, five in number, guide psychologists to the highest ethical aspirations of the profession. These are Principle A: Beneficence and Non-maleficence; Principle B: Fidelity and Responsibility; Principle C: Integrity; Principle D: Justice; and Principle E: Respect for People's Rights and Dignity. For instance, Principle E encourages counseling psychologists to be aware that special protections may be necessary to protect the welfare and rights of persons or communities. In addition, counseling psychologists try to prevent the influence of biases in their work, and they do not knowingly take part in or condone activities of others based upon prejudice. Although biases and prejudices are common in all persons, they become unethical when counseling psychologists do not attempt to prevent their effects.

The APA ethical standards, on the other hand, represent organizational obligations and form the basis for imposing sanctions on psychologists. Select standards are explained here with the example of a White counseling psychologist working with a Black client. Although there are no specific ethics for conducting counseling with consideration for the dynamics of mixed racial dyads, Standard 2.01 Boundaries of Competence states, (a) Psychologists provide services "with populations and in areas only within the boundaries of their competence, based on their education, training, supervised experience, consultation, study or professional experience" (APA, 2016; p. 4). The second criterion of Standard 2.01 states, (b) Where scientific or professional knowledge in the discipline of psychology establishes that an understanding of factors associated with "race, ethnicity, culture . . . or socioeconomic status is essential for effective implementation of their services . . . psychologists have or [should] obtain the training, experience, consultation or supervision necessary to ensure the competence of their services, or they make appropriate referrals" (APA, 2016; p. 5). Much of the discussion on mixed racial dyads is that White counseling psychologists who have not understood their own racial identity may not know whether or not the services they provide are helpful or effective. Consequently, developing one's racial identity is a precursor to being aware of whether Standard 2.01 is being followed when providing therapy for people with various racial, ethnic, and cultural backgrounds.

Counseling psychologists could place an appropriate referral for any potential Black American client to ensure they follow Standard 3.04 Avoiding Harm, which details that (a) "Psychologists take reasonable steps to avoid harming their clients . . . and to minimize harm where it is foreseeable and unavoidable" (APA, 2016; p. 6). However, counseling psychologists who may refer out their Black clients may avoid, refuse, or repress the need to gain competence in treating Black Americans because the process involves difficult self-reflection about their racial identity, biases, and socialization in privilege. Prolonged difficulty with this professional developmental task may fall under Standard 3.01 Unfair Discrimination, which stipulates that, "in their work-related activities, psychologists do not engage in unfair discrimination based on . . . race, ethnicity, culture . . . or socioeconomic status" (APA, 2016; p. 6).

Confidentiality

Confidentiality is viewed as particularly important for gaining and maintaining the trust of a client, as well as allowing a client to be forthcoming in counseling. The APA ethical Standard 4.01 stipulates that a psychologist engages in measures to protect the confidential information of all clients, while acknowledging the contradiction that confidentiality may be regulated outside of the profession by local laws, federal laws, and institutional rules. Even though the client has the freedom to disclose information about his treatment, it is not permissible for the counseling psychologist to do so (Nagy, 2011). Werth, Hastings, and Riding-Malon (2010) stated, however, that citizens of small towns may be aware when clients' cars are parked in front of a counseling psychologist's office or may see them walk in, and so in settings where everyone knows everyone, confidentiality is limited.

Many people hold a stigma about psychological help, making confidentiality even more important to both the client and the counseling psychologist. Helbok (2003) argued that residents in rural areas might be hesitant to enter group therapy because they may know other group members. The counseling psychologist should be particularly mindful of where she has acquired information when participating in social conversations within one's local community to avoid a breach of confidentiality of information learned within therapy.

A referral source, such as a school administrator or a minister, may wish to be apprised of the progress of a person whom he referred to a counseling psychologist, although the standard of confidentiality does not allow such communication without the informed consent in writing of the client. A challenge occurs since a counseling psychologist risks alienating sources of referrals and the potential loss of referrals (Helbok, 2003). A counseling psychologist cannot change either a community's culture or the professional code of ethics, which places the counseling psychologist in a double bind ("damned if you do, damned if you don't"), which is a professional stressor.

Multiple Role Relationships

The topic of multiple relationships is addressed by Standard 3.05 and is frequently discussed in the clinical practice literature. All definitions of multiple role relationships first necessitate that a counseling psychologist be in a professional relationship with a client. The first kind of multiple role relationship happens when the counseling psychologist is involved with the same client in another role such as being a client's neighbor. The second kind happens when a counseling psychologist has an association with a person closely tied to a client, such as a relative of the client who works at the school served by the psychologist. Third, a counseling psychologist can promise to be involved in a future relationship with a client or an individual with whom that client is closely associated, such as playing on a basketball team at the invitation of the client who serves as the team coach (APA, 2002; Schank & Skovholt, 2006; Zur, 2015).

Nonsexual multiple role relationships can differ in complexity and take on a variety of forms (Pugh, 2007). An example would be a counseling psychologist engaging in a relationship whose sole aim is to attain benefits such as material goods, for example, by purchasing groceries from a client's store, the only grocery store in the counseling psychologist's neighborhood. A counseling psychologist may fulfill the needs of a client through altruistic acts (Pope & Vasquez, 2016; Sonne, 2006; Zur, 2015), such as helping a stranded client whose ride has not shown up. Counseling psychologists and their current or former clients may connect through happenstance, for example, by running into each other at a café or standing in line together at the bank.

Multiple role relationships are proscribed when such associations present a risk to the counseling psychologist's objectivity, helpfulness to clients, and effective clinical judgment (Hargrove, 1986). Counseling psychologists experience an increased probability of inner struggles because of dilemmas in multiple role relationships, a major professional stressor.

There are times when a counseling psychologist may recognize that a multiple role relationship dilemma has occurred unexpectedly and that it will probably cause harm (Younggren & Gottlieb, 2004). Should this occur, "the psychologist takes reasonable steps to resolve it with due regard for the best interests of the affected person and maximal compliance with the ethics code" (APA, 2002, p. 6). Other situations may arise whereby, because of legal or institutional requirements, the counseling psychologist is obligated to assume various roles (e.g., expert witness) as part of legal proceedings. In these cases, it is recommended that the counseling psychologist be open about the limits of confidentiality and her obligations. At the beginning and during the process of counseling, psychologists must be clear with their clients about such obligations (APA, 2002; Nagy 2011; Pope & Vasquez, 2016). There may be a tendency in some clients to seek psychological services from a person they know. In communities where outsiders are not trusted, a counseling psychologist's involvement with her community is beneficial to establishing trust (Schank & Skovholt, 1997). As such, multiple role relationships can be challenging to prevent if the counseling psychologist wants to build a client base in her community.

A counseling psychologist may encounter a situation where he assists a client who is a child and attending the same class as the counseling psychologist's child, and a situation where this child's mother is employed as the check-out person at a drive-through coffee shop often visited by the counseling psychologist (Campbell & Gordon, 2003). Evaluating the potential affect of these situations on the counseling relationship would be essential prior to the psychologist agreeing to see the child in counseling (Sonne, 2006). As Erickson (2001) noted, the burden of making the correct decision about multiple role relationships is on the counseling psychologist rather than the client. Therapist–client interactions also may change considerably over time. For instance, relationships that at the onset of counseling were not perceived to be harmful may change. A counseling psychologist must be cognizant of all multiple role relationships to guard against possible harm (Erickson, 2001; Gottlieb, 1993; Kitchener, 1988; Nagy, 2011). This is a heavy work-related and personal burden for the counseling psychologist.

Competence

In situations where a counseling psychologist is asked to help a client for whom no other counseling is available, APA Standard 2.01 notes (d) that counseling psychologists may offer services to ensure that treatment is not denied. The counseling psychologist, however, must make an effort to obtain the needed competence through, for example, engaging in literature reviews, consultation, or other strategies (Barnett, Behnke, Rosenthal, & Koocher, 2007). For instance, consider a counseling psychologist who has expertise in couples counseling. If this person is the only mental health professional available in her community and is asked to work with a 6-year-old child, the counseling psychologist would need to determine whether it is ethically feasible to help the child or whether the child should be referred to the nearest counseling psychologist 120 miles away, which carries the risk of the child not securing the needed treatment (Sobel, 1992).

Thus, the APA ethical standards for maintaining and practicing according to one's expertise can be challenging for counseling psychologists in particular settings. For instance, counseling psychologists might need to work as a generalist, instead of employing their skills to engage in a specific form of practice (Helbok, 2003). Even though trained as a generalist and practicing so, a counseling psychologist may need to make a decision about whether to offer services that might be at the boundary of his expertise (Schank & Skovholt, 2006). To further complicate the situation, the necessary training to obtain competence may be far away. Additionally, if a counseling psychologist is isolated in his practice, there is a greater probability that his judgment will be compromised. Without obtaining feedback from colleagues, the counseling psychologist may be inclined to minimize complicated ethical situations and deliver services beyond his expertise and lack awareness that this is occurring (Helbok, 2003).

A further complication involves the fact that expertise is not operationalized clearly in the APA code of conduct (Helbok, 2003). The code fails to stipulate the number of clients or years of preparation a counseling psychologist must accumulate with a particular disorder or treatment to be deemed competent. APA's *Dictionary of Psychology* defines *competence*, in part, as "one's developed repertoire of skills, especially as it is applied to a task or set of tasks" (VandenBos, 2007, p. 204). This definition, however, does not elucidate or quantify how a person might know when a counseling psychologist has achieved the appropriate level of competence. Because the degree of competence is not clearly stipulated, it is likely to result in varied interpretations and to contribute to the ambiguity when faced with ethical challenges. For instance, a counseling psychologist may be promoted to a leadership position early in her career by becoming director of mental health services in a hospital. Obtaining this promotion can generate anxiety for the novice counseling psychologist who may view herself as unprepared to assume a senior administrative position. This counseling psychologist may be the sole provider or one of a few counseling psychologists in the locale with the necessary qualifications.

Some possible strategies to address challenges involving competencies have been offered (Schank & Skovholt, 2006). First, counseling psychologists may use distance learning tools such as Internet resources, webinars, and consultation by telephone to obtain support and knowledge if they are not able to acquire the appropriate expertise through continuing education. Second, a counseling psychologist may tell the client at the onset of counseling of his concerns about treating the client and express the potential of needing to refer the client to another provider, should their interventions not appear to be effective. A counseling psychologist would employ general counseling strategies to help the client and, at the same time, try to acquire further information about the client's initial presenting concerns and other issues for which the counseling psychologist thinks he is not appropriately prepared. Third, some individuals may be willing to drive a long distance to obtain the most appropriate mental health care that is available (Barnett, Baker, Elman, & Schoener, 2007; Nagy, 2011; Pope & Vasquez, 2016; Schank & Skovholt, 2006).

Ethical Decision Making: Professional Counselors and Counseling Psychologists

When therapists experience complicated ethical dilemmas, they also are required to undertake a process of ethical decision making, consulting available resources (e.g., the ACA Code of

Ethics, the APA Ethical Principles and Code of Conduct) as needed. These professional codes, however, are not intended to be the framework for ethical reasoning. It is critical to mention that the ACA Code of Ethics tends to be reactive rather than proactive. This means that the ACA Code of Ethics is not a preventive measure, and many counselors consult the Code of Ethics after an ethical dilemma has occurred. The APA Ethical Principles are aspirations and are not intended to offer solutions to ethical dilemmas. Practitioners who rigidly follow the APA ethical standards and principles are likely to miss the complex nature of ethical issues (Ridley, Liddle, Hill, & Li, 2001). Counselors must recognize that there may be some gray area in many situations with client problems that are not easily solved by looking through professional ethical guidelines. Counselors must use an active, deliberative, and creative approach that involves consultation (Corey et al., 2007; Ridley et al., 2001).

Steps in Ethical Decision Making

The first step in addressing an ethical violation is for the therapist to be aware that she behaved in an unethical manner. Barnett, Behnke, Rosenthal, & Koocher (2007) suggested that a counselor first ask a number of questions: "Will doing this be helpful to my client?" "Will this action likely harm anyone?" and "Have I allowed my judgment to become impaired as a result of inadequate attention to my own care or needs?" (p. 8). Barnett et al. also stated that, when faced with ethical challenges, the therapist should review local and state laws, as well as the policies and procedures of relevant organizations where the therapist works. Lastly, they encourage therapists to consult with peers who have expertise in the specific challenge.

Nagy (2011) suggested ethical decisions should be based on behavior that would result in the most good or lead to happiness for the greatest number of people. This viewpoint is tied to the outcome of one's behaviors. A therapist evaluates a particular circumstance and avoids a one-size-fits-all strategy to making decisions. The therapist must consider the negative consequences that could emerge in the worst case scenario. Even if the negative consequence is not likely to occur, a therapist maintains awareness of the potential risks and works to avoid bringing harm to the client.

Ridley et al. (2001) noted that a therapist's process of decision making is linked to whether the ethical problem is likely to occur or whether it has been already experienced. Depending on the point of entry, the actions that a therapist must take may vary. Ridley et al. (2001) delineated four components of effective decision-making models. First, the decision-making process must be thorough and consider all relevant aspects of the dilemma. Next, the process must be clear, logical, and based in firm and widely embraced knowledge. Third, the decision-making process must be relevant to the dilemma at hand and easily followed. Lastly, the process must involve all stakeholders when generating solutions to the ethical dilemma. Ridley et al. claimed that decision-making strategies that do not encompass the four elements just mentioned are apt to lead a professional toward poor ethical choices.

Therapists should do their best to solve ethical dilemmas relying on open and direct dialogue with all relevant individuals. Many benefits to the process of therapy can emerge from including the client in the process of ethical decision making (Corey et al., 2007). Clients benefit the most from ethical situations when therapists monitor their own ethics. Therapists can do this by challenging their own thoughts and applying the ethical guidelines to their own actions. They might ask themselves, for example, "What does the ACA Code of Ethics have to say about my actions?" and "Am I behaving in such a way that I have the best interest of my client as a priority?" Numerous violations of ethics are not noticed because only the therapists who commit the violation are aware of it. Therapists must practice with integrity and honesty to achieve what is in the best interest of the individuals they serve.

Section I of the ACA Code of Ethics (resolving ethical issues) references the ACA Policy and Procedures for Processing Complaints of Ethical Violations (ACA, 2014). This section highlights that the ethical decision-making process includes the generation of possible courses of action, deliberation of benefits and risks, and the selection of an objective decision derived from the welfare and context of all parties involved. It also highlights what to do in case of suspected violations with other therapists (try to resolve the issues informally with the assistance of other counselors, if feasible), procedures for reporting ethical violations that are not resolved properly, unfair discrimination against respondents and complainants, and cooperation with professional ethics committees.

Code of Ethics Versus the Law

One major challenge for counselors is when conflicts occur between the law and the professional code of ethics, where the values of the counselor may come into play. Conflict may occur between codes of ethics and the law regarding advertising services, clients' right of access to their own files, and confidentiality. One potential conflict between codes of ethics and the law involves counseling minors, for example, counseling children or adolescents in school settings. More specifically, parents may have a legal right to content disclosed in counseling sessions, whereas the school counselor tries to maintain confidentiality with the minor. In an ethical dilemma where adhering to one's professional code of ethics may result in disobeying the law, it may be necessary to obtain legal advice or contact one's state licensing board for consultation (Corey et al., 2007).

Online Counseling

Another area where ethical issues may arise is in online counseling. Telehealth (electronic consultation between counselors and clients) or online counseling can benefit clients because a greater number of people can receive services, especially those with physical disabilities or those who live in rural areas. However, with telehealth, inaccurate diagnoses or ineffective treatment may be given (due to lack of behavioral cues), confidentiality and privacy cannot be guaranteed, and transference and countertransference may be difficult to address (Corey et al., 2007). Counselors must weigh the pros and cons for the client before engaging in online counseling to provide the best care possible for the client.

Therapist Well-Being and Burnout

Well-Being

The *APA Dictionary of Psychology* defines *well-being* as "a state of happiness, contentment, low levels of distress, overall good physical and mental health or outlook, or good quality of life" (VandenBos, 2007, p. 996). In specific, mental health is composed of subjective and functional well-being (Ambler, 2008). Subjective well-being is composed of states of internal emotional well-being that are evaluated by an individual's explanation of positive and negative opinions that the person possesses about his experiences in life. Functional well-being is the level at which an individual is functioning socially and psychologically. (Note. The generic term *therapist[s]* is used to delineate that a section's information applies to all mental health practitioners.)

Subjective Well-Being. Subjective well-being is characterized as positive associations with others, purpose in life, personal growth, autonomy, environmental mastery, and self-acceptance (Cummins, 2013). Social well-being is included in subjective well-being, meaning that individuals experience a feeling of belonging to their communities and believe they make meaningful contributions to society. They find social interactions meaningful. Consistent with these observations, the goal of the theory of well-being posited by Seligman (2011) includes improving the degree of thriving in a person's life and in her world by utilizing engagement, positive emotions, relationships, meaning making, and achievement (called PERMA in short). Cummins (2013) conceptualized subjective well-being as a relatively stable dynamic, which sustains homeostasis through internal and external buffering mechanisms (see also Diener & Lucas, 1999); however, it is thought that significant stress can overpower such buffers (Cummins, 2013).

Professional Well-Functioning. A related concept, applied to features of one's professional functioning, is "the enduring quality in one's professional functioning over time and in the face of professional and personal stressors" (Coster & Schwebel, 1997, p. 5). Well-functioning is the opposite of impairment (e.g., a well-functioning therapist is the opposite of an impaired therapist or one who is experiencing burnout).

Turning to another aspect of well-functioning, therapists who claimed to acquire support through personal counseling (either in the present or past) and supervision from professionals disclosed more experiences of personal growth than did their coworkers who did not obtain these supports (Linley & Joseph, 2007). Moreover, experiencing strong personal relationships and the support of peers apart from work were critical aspects in therapists' continuing to function well (Coster & Schwebel, 1997). A balance between professional and personal activities (e.g., taking time with friends and family and participating in recreational activities) is critical to maintaining well-functioning (Coster & Schwebel, 1997). Lastly, therapists who reported strong therapeutic alliances with their clients and a strong feeling of coherence (as opposed to disintegration and inner conflicts) experienced fewer negative changes than their colleagues and were less likely to experience burnout (Linley & Joseph, 2007).

According to Rath and Harter (2010), well-being is affected by five factors that differentiate between a life of flourishing and a life of suffering. The first factor is *career well-being*, which is a person's satisfaction with the responsibilities of daily life, both nonvocational and vocational task behaviors. The second factor, *social well-being*, has to do with the existence and strength of love and social relationships in a person's life. The third factor, *financial well-being*, pertains to money management skills. The fourth factor, *physical well-being*, is the state of an individual's health along with the adequacy of a person's energy that allows him to fulfill goals (see also Coster & Schwebel, 1997), while the fifth factor is community well-being.

Rath and Harter (2010) argued that out of the five components of well-being, career well-being has the most influence on a person's overall well-being. Similarly, Warr (1999) stated that the well-being linked to work affects context or overall well-being. It is important to find enjoyment and meaning in one's career. Persons who were not engaged at work displayed a significant likelihood for developing depression (Rath & Harter, 2010). Warr (1999) claimed that the degree of demands on the job influences the well-being tied to work. When a person experiences extremely high or low demands at work, job-specific well-being is thought to decrease.

Social well-being contributes to one's career well-being as well as health (Rath & Harter, 2010). Friends are apt to influence exercise and eating habits, as well as harmful behaviors such as smoking. Experiencing positive social interactions during stressful circumstances can help individuals to cope more effectively, and time spent in social activities can enhance the likelihood of enjoying one's day (Rath & Harter, 2010; for research on professional functioning/well-functioning as being opposite of impairment, see Coster & Schwebel, 1997; Keyes, 2003; Linley & Joseph, 2007).

Burnout of Human Service Providers

When therapists do not experience a sense of well-being, they might be experiencing burnout. A clear explanation of burnout is

> physical, emotional, or mental exhaustion, especially in one's job or career, accompanied by decreased motivation, lowered performance, and negative attitudes towards oneself and others. It results from performing at a high level until stress and tension, especially from extreme and prolonged physical or mental exertion or an overburdening workload, take their toll. . . . Burnout is most often observed in professionals who work closely with people (e.g., social workers, teachers, correctional officers) in service-oriented vocations and experience high levels of stress. It can be particularly acute in therapists or counselors doing trauma work, who feel overwhelmed by the cumulative secondary trauma of witnessing the effects. (VandenBos, 2007, p. 140)

Maslach, Schaufeli, and Leiter (2001) further noted that burnout engenders three components. When *emotional exhaustion* occurs, a therapist is apt to feel devoid of resources and extremely strained, both physically and emotionally. When *cynicism* occurs, a therapist presents depersonalization, "a negative, callous, or excessively detached response to various aspects of the job" (p. 399). Lastly, when *full-blown burnout* occurs, a therapist feels devoid of personal accomplishments and ineffective.

Burned-out employees appear to have less efficacy and seem to be less productive at work (Maslach et al., 2001). These employees seem to be less committed to their work and less satisfied. In mental health services, these are potential causes of harm to clients, especially as a therapist may be the only provider in her community.

Isolation at work is strongly connected to developing burnout (Maslach et al., 2001). A therapist must have colleagues with whom to share experiences and seek guidance. Receiving support from supervisors is important; therefore, the therapist needs to receive frequent or adequate supervision.

Therapists are expected to be "super human," to remain professional, objective, and without flaws. Therapists are entrusted with protecting the well-being of their clients, but it is not always apparent how a therapist's well-being is to be preserved. When caring for others, it is essential that therapists take care of themselves (Roysircar, 2009a; Shallcross, 2011; Skovholt, 2001; Smith & Moss, 2009).

Burnout can lead to a therapist's terminating his position and leaving clients with no services. More often the outcome of therapist burnout is decreased quality of work. When therapists underperform, clients suffer (Maslach & Goldberg, 1998).

Maslach and Goldberg (1998) identified aspects of the job or workplace that contribute to the development of burnout. First, the job site fosters an imbalance in the demands on a therapist and the resources available to the person to assist in meeting her demands (see also Bowman & Roysircar, 2010). Next, the stressors at work are chronic, without any relief. Finally, the job site is plagued by conflict that can occur in many different ways. For example, there can be conflict between colleagues, clients, or even among the various demands placed on the particular therapist.

A therapist may have unique personal or sociocultural characteristics, and he may have challenges adjusting to a community and may feel excluded (Cohen, 1993). For instance, if adult residents of a community are older than a therapist, the residents may not take the professional seriously. The same perceived low credibility might be experienced by women in professional roles. Being of a culture or race that is not familiar to residents in a therapist's place of residence can result in the therapist experiencing prejudice. Therapists' attitudes to such issues as racial and religious bigotry, domestic violence, and substance abuse are likely to vary from those of some clients, and these value differences with clients may be stressful for therapists (Kersting, 2003).

The varied and high levels of stress in a therapist's work have been discussed so far. What follows is a delineation of how therapists can integrate self-care practices into their daily life that can help them with stress management and in pursuing fulfilling careers.

What Is Self-Care?

Self-care is a multidimensional concept in which aspects of physical and psychological well-being are interdependent and result in a sense of fulfillment and an enhanced quality of life (Roysircar, 2008). Self-care includes being knowledgeable about emotional traumas, their sources, and how to address them; possessing loving relationships; exercising regularly; having a healthy diet; receiving massages; engaging in mindfulness/meditation, counseling, and adequate leisure; having companionship when involved in leisure activities; and enjoying simple pleasures like hiking, humor, conversations, music, shared play, storytelling, reading, and singing (Roysircar, 2008).

Individuals undertake self-care to promote, ensure, and/or restore physical and psychological health; to prevent, manage, or recover from injury, disease, or trauma; or to fulfill a sense of well-being. Ideally, self-care is pursued in seven functional domains: emotional, physical, intellectual, social, relational, spiritual, and safety/security (Roysircar, 2008).

Physical Self-Care

Physical self-care includes fitness, nutrition, preventive medical care, and early intervention and treatment (Cameron & Leventhal, 2003). The positive association between emotional well-being and physical activity is widely acknowledged. Regular exercise can help to reduce depression, contribute to successful aging, reduce stress, and improve self-concept and body image, among other benefits.

Fitness is not just about structured activity in a gym; it includes almost anything that gets the body moving, from dancing, walking, to playing sports. The nutritional aspects of self-care include eating regular meals that limit sugar and fat and include a variety of fruits, vegetables, proteins, and grains. It's also important to avoid excessive drinking of alcohol and the use of tobacco or illegal substances.

When therapists are caught up in clinical work, they might not get enough sleep or eat fresh fruits and vegetables. Therapists may put off going to a doctor when not feeling well. Preventive medical care and getting the treatment one needs are key components of physical self-care.

Emotional Self-Care

Emotional self-care pertains to the identification, acceptance, and expression of a range of feelings (Roysircar, 2008). Research clearly demonstrates a link between emotions and health (Fredrickson, 2000). Such findings underscore the importance of understanding and addressing one's feelings. When doing clinical work, a therapist will likely encounter people and situations that cause feelings of anxiety, fear, anger, stress, and insecurity in clients and communities. These repeated negative feelings can be transferred to a therapist as vicarious trauma, which is harmful to the therapist's health if not effectively addressed through therapy sought by the therapist.

Practicing self-confident behaviors is one way of exercising emotional self-care. A therapist communicates feelings in an honest, frank, and direct way, while maintaining respect for others (Roysircar, 2008). The therapist establishes physical, cognitive, emotional, and religious or spiritual boundaries that define who he is and help control his life (Cloud & Townsend, 1992). It is also important to give oneself permission to be average. Perfectionism can be a roadblock to progress and can contribute to feelings of insecurity (Roysircar, 2009a).

Seeking counseling or psychotherapy also can be an extremely helpful self-care strategy, whether a therapist is dealing with anger, depression, or other negative feelings, or needs help finding and maintaining the balance and focus she desires. When looking at self-care from a prevention point of view, the major focus of a counseling agency or practice is to prevent burdening its staff therapists with one member's unresolved personal problems. A counseling practice's emphasis is to make energetic and satisfying contributions amid the unpredictability, chaos, and stresses involved in counseling work and, thereby, adding to the spirit of humor, stability, good cheer, and mutual respect among its counseling staff (Roysircar, 2009a).

Therapists cannot work effectively to establish a resilient society if they are always carrying their own emotional baggage. Training programs for graduate therapy students must incorporate opportunities for students, faculty, and clinic staff members to acquire the skills to end inflicting their dysfunctional behaviors on others along with helping them to learn the skills to interrupt others' inappropriate behaviors. The beliefs, feelings, behaviors, and perceptions of therapists, despite their commitment to client and community recovery and resilience, are still frequently shaped by a couple of the worst aspects of a machine-dependent culture—powerlessness and hopelessness (Roysircar, 2009a).

Key personal characteristics of therapists are that they like people; build friendships and trust easily; possess a sense of humor; are good listeners; help people to believe in themselves; allow others to take credit; are hard workers; are mature, self-disciplined, and capable of setting limits; do not easily get discouraged; possess a grounded sense of personal vision and social identity or identities; are open to new ideas and are flexible; are courageous even in the face of fear and stress; and are honest. These essential therapist attributes can be threatened when therapists experience burnout, personal neglect, or spiritual despair. Counseling agencies or practices must consult with and monitor staff therapists on their self-care (Roysircar, 2009a).

Related to emotional self-care, *emotional intelligence* involves personal and social competence. Personal competence refers to accurate self-assessment, emotional awareness, self-control, self-confidence, trustworthiness, adaptability, conscientiousness, drive for achievement, innovation, commitment, optimism, and initiative. Social competence refers to how one handles relationships through empathic understanding and helping others, a service orientation, appreciation of diversity, and political awareness. It also includes social adeptness, such as the ability to communicate openly and convincingly, influence others, manage conflict, initiate and manage change, lead and inspire others, build relationships, cooperate, collaborate, and work with groups (Roysircar, 2008).

Spiritual Self-Care

Spiritual self-care addresses the ongoing search for meaning and understanding in life and what may extend beyond. Fostering spiritual self-care involves exploring and expressing beliefs and values that are shaped by experience. Spirituality may be manifested through religion, but religion and spirituality are not synonymous (McCormick, 1994). Spirituality also may be expressed through connections to nature and the environment and may be characterized as an individual sense of purpose. Spiritual self-care can be facilitated in numerous ways from simply watching the sunrise to becoming active in organized religion or other spiritual communities.

Intellectual Self-Care

Intellectual self-care is about engaging regularly in critical thinking and inquiry to expand knowledge and stimulate the mind. At its most basic level, intellectual self-care involves an abiding interest in ideas, learning, thinking, and creativity (Roysircar, 2008). Intelligence is a multifaceted and well-studied area of psychology. Many of the connotations and constructs of intelligence have remained intertwined with the techniques developed to measure intelligence. Cognitive abilities include reasoning, imagination, judgment, and adaptability. Additionally, cognitive intelligence includes verbal and performance abilities. Likewise, crystallized intelligence is the ability to utilize facts, and fluid intelligence is the capacity to solve novel problems creatively.

In 1983, a theory of multiple intelligences was advanced by Howard Gardner to provide practical definitions of intelligence that pair cognitive skills with culturally valued activities. These types of intelligences include verbal, mathematical/logical, musical, spatial, kinesthetic/body control, intrapersonal (self-understanding), and interpersonal (social understanding).

Social Self-Care

Social self-care pertains to the regular, emotional investment in relationships outside of the immediate family (Roysircar, 2008). It includes establishing, nurturing, and expanding social networks and friendships through community involvement, group affiliation, and contribution to collective causes. Friendships may provide emotional support, companionship, reciprocity, and assistance in problem solving.

Often the rigors of clinical work limit the time therapists have to take care of themselves socially. However, studies have demonstrated the importance of doing so. For example, the Harvard Medical School's Nurses' Health Study of 2001 revealed that friendships among women play a critical role in improving health and quality of life. The study concluded that lacking at least one good confidante was as detrimental to a woman's health as was obesity or smoking (Hu et al., 2001). Whether a therapist is male or female, friendships and fulfilling social activities are an important part of a balanced life. Putting effort into social self-care can result in personal and professional relationships that can last a lifetime.

Relational Self-Care

Relational self-care pertains to the establishment, development, and strengthening of relationships with spouses, partners, children, parents, and extended family (Roysircar, 2008). Research shows that daily interaction among family members impacts a person's overall health status (Bylund & Duck, 2004). Maintaining family ties is at the core of relational self-care. Relational self-care takes on added importance given that people expect to live longer lives, are reinforced for their healthy habits, and improve their health when they report high degrees of familial emotional support, mediated by the perception that one has a person to consult when one is in need or sick (Ross & Mirowsky, 2002).

Safety and Security Self-Care

Self-care for safety and security involves personal, environmental, and financial planning. It includes taking precautions to feel safe and comfortable in one's home and community (Roysircar, 2008). Understanding personal finances, obtaining health insurance, and taking steps to ensure a comfortable financial future are critical yet often overlooked aspects of self-care. Too often, safety and security issues are only addressed when a threat, breach of safety, or trauma occurs. Planning ahead can alleviate some of the stress of an actual traumatic event and will help a therapist rest more easily, knowing that he is prepared.

Table 2.1 provides therapists a means to integrate into their lives daily self-care homework activities. Activities are listed for each of the seven domains of self-care covered in this chapter.

According to Roysircar (2008), self-care is a multidimensional concept in which psychological and physical well-being aspects are interdependent and lead to an enhanced quality of life and a sense of fulfillment. The following lists provide therapists a means to integrate into their lives *daily self-care homework activities*. Choosing homework activities from the lists below serves to allow therapists to practice stress management to avoid burnout. Homework activities are listed for each of the seven domains of self-care proposed by Roysircar (2008).

▼ TABLE 2.1

Self-Care Homework Activities

Suggestions for Practice as Homework
Physical Self-Care • Take a walk. • Go bowling. • Go dancing. • Play games. • Swim. • Run with a friend. • Get a massage. (Massages can improve blood circulation, increase the delivery of oxygen, and help stretch connective tissues.) • If you smoke, discuss ways to quit with your health care professional. • Keep alcohol, caffeine, and processed foods to a minimum. • Never use anyone else's prescription medications. • Schedule a checkup with your physician. • Be sure to get regular checkups. • Watch a movie.
Emotional Self-Care • Build and maintain supportive relationships (talk to trusted friends and family). • Celebrate your successes, unique strengths, and unique talents. • Use creative outlets to express your feelings (drawing, painting, sewing, cooking, playing music). • Practice humor. • Meditate and use other relaxation techniques such as mindfulness. • Schedule regular getaways and vacations, making them long enough or frequent enough to enable you to relax.

Suggestions for Practice as Homework

Spiritual Self-Care

- Notice what you find uplifting, noble, or creative, and do more of these activities.
- Pray and/or meditate spiritually.
- Worship with others.
- Read books and listen to music that you find inspirational.
- Join conversations and dialogues you find meaningful.
- Visit places of natural beauty or attend performing arts (e.g., ballet, music performance, opera, theater, and film or theatrical musicals).

Intellectual Self-Care

- Given that intelligence is a broad construct, there are numerous activities for meeting intellectual needs, such as occupational or career development, awareness of current events, creative arts participation, and involvement in a reading club.

Social Self-Care

- Spend time with friends talking, sharing feelings, and sharing experiences.
- When possible, avoid negative people who do not have your best interests at heart.
- Join a group or chat group in a local organization.
- Join local and state counseling or psychology associations.
- Join city committees.
- Organize community events for your area.
- Participate in potluck gatherings.

Relational Self-Care

- Schedule date nights or time alone with your significant other, even if you must limit it during "crunch times."
- Spend quality time with children and, if needed, seek advice on how to help them understand when you must take time for work responsibilities.
- Stay in contact with family even if it is via email or text messages when time is limited.

Safety and Security Self-Care

- Write a living will.
- Live within your means and save money monthly.
- Start a savings bank account and place important documents in a bank safety box.
- Have a getaway plan in case of a disaster.
- Develop an emergency storage of first aid, including prescription medications; extra clothes; toiletries; canned, freeze-dried, and packaged foods and other groceries; gasoline, electric generator, and natural-burning fuel.
- Keep cash on hand.
- Develop a shelter in your home in case of a tornado or hurricane.
- Have available flashlights, candles, matchsticks, and a weather radio for emergencies.

Self-Care Plan

Writing or maintaining a journal is a common method for processing thoughts and emotions and tracking and changing behavior (Roysircar, 2008). The Self-Care Tracker (Table 2.2) is intended to help therapists create and monitor their own self-care plan. This form can be used to help therapists ensure that activities in each of the seven domains of self-care are included, that they can identify any gaps, and track their own progress. The bottom of the form provides space for journaling personal comments.

Self-Care Tracker

Self-Care Domain	Activity (List)	Week						
		Place a check or an X on days the self-care activity was performed, and rate the extent to which this activity was practiced. Rating Scale: 4 = Did the most, 3 = Did a good amount, 2 = Did less, and 1 = Did the least.						
		Sun	Mon	Tues	Wed	Thurs	Fri	Sat
1. Physical								
2. Emotional								
3. Spiritual								
4. Intellectual								
5. Social								
6. Relational								
7. Safety/Security								
Daily Totals								
Weekly Grand Total								
Journal:								

Source: Adapted with permission from Roysircar (2008).

CHAPTER REVIEW

SUMMARY AND COMMENTARY ▶▶

Professional counselors, counseling psychologists, and other mental health practitioners are expected to follow their respective ethical codes. Many of the ethical dilemmas of therapists are due to disparities in what is ethically expected by a profession and what is plausible within one's work. Ethical guidelines that are especially problematic include concerns for confidentiality, multiple relationships, and competence, which have been discussed in the chapter along with examples and vignettes. The ethics codes do not provide ready-made solutions to ethical dilemmas. Therapists need to consider a number of models that exist beyond the ethics codes and serve to elucidate approaches to ethical decision making. Ethical decision-making methods range in intricacy from considering various factors causing an ethical dilemma to step-by-step decision trees.

When assisting others, it is essential that therapists also take proper care of themselves. When a therapist is perhaps the only provider or one of a handful of therapists to help people in a small locale and the surrounding area, numerous complex ethical dilemmas may arise related to confidentiality, multiple roles, and competence. The stress of ethical quandaries with clients, the lack of social and professional support, and other aspects of a specific counseling setting can result in decreased therapist well-being and professional burnout.

Well-being is a multidimensional construct that is affected by many variables. A person's context, physical health, finances, and social support can all contribute to his overall functioning. Well-being at work is particularly important because we spend many hours in our place of employment. Burnout happens because of chronic stress and other negative features of a person's workplace. Burnout can lead to decreased productivity, lowered work efficacy, and hostility toward clients (Maslach et al., 2001; Roysircar, 2009a; Shallcross, 2011; Skovholt, 2001; Smith & Moss, 2009; VandenBos, 2007).

Stress is a huge factor in counseling and psychotherapy practice. The daily challenges and stressors of work with clients quickly add up. Therapists may not be sure how to decrease their stress levels or may say they do not have the time to do so. Integrating self-care practices into one's daily life can help to manage the ups and downs of clinical work and ensure that therapists establish good habits that contribute to their success as therapists and active human beings. Self-care practices that contribute to accomplishing these objectives were delineated in the chapter.

CRITICAL THINKING QUESTIONS ▶▶

1. Which areas of competence are therapists accountable for?
2. Discuss the ethical dilemmas of a therapist involved in dual or multiple relationships.
3. Would you consider ethical decisions based on the particular case, or would you rely on the same rule in all circumstances? Discuss both of your arguments.
4. When you experience an ethical quandary, what strategies will you use to solve it? Identify three strategies that you would use most often (e.g., consult a colleague, discuss the dilemma with the client, review the ethical guidelines).
5. What types of ethical dilemmas do rural and small town therapists experience?
6. What are the different dimensions of therapist well-being?
7. What are the different dimensions of therapist burnout?
8. As a student, how do you practice self-care in your daily life?
9. What have you learned about therapist confidentiality? Give an example of confidentiality that may be broken by a therapist.

SUGGESTED READINGS: IMPORTANT PRIMARY SOURCES ▶▶

Cameron, L. D., & Leventhal, H. (2003). *The self-regulation of health and illness behavior.* London, UK: Routledge.

Corey, G., Corey, M. S., & Callanan, P. (2007). *Issues and ethics in the helping professions* (7th ed.). Belmont, CA: Thomson Brooks/Cole.

Nagy, T. F. (2011). *Essential ethics for psychologists: A primer for understanding and mastering core issues.* Washington, DC: American Psychological Association.

Remley, T. P., Jr., & Herlihy, B. (2015). *Ethical, legal, and professional issues in counseling* (5th ed.). Boston, MA: Pearson.

Schank, J. A., & Skovholt, T. M. (2006). *Ethical practice in small communities: Challenges and rewards for psychologists.* Washington, DC: American Psychological Association.

Seligman, M. E. P. (2011). *Flourish: A visionary new understanding of happiness and well-being.* New York, NY: Free Press.

PSYCHOANALYTIC THEORY

Introduction

This chapter provides an overview of psychoanalytic theory and practice and includes other areas of interest intended to provide the reader a broader and more thorough understanding of Sigmund Freud's impact on counseling and psychotherapy (i.e., historical information provided later is based on publications by Gay [1989] and Ernst Freud, Lucie Freud, & Grubrich-Simitis [1978]). The chapter focuses on the interacting mental components called *id, ego,* and *superego* and how these components contribute to our experience of anxiety and conflict; motivational processes such as life drives, which push us to take action; various defense mechanisms designed to protect us from ourselves; and the Oedipal reaction, which predicts that a child will eventually desire the full attention of one parent while simultaneously excluding the other parent entirely from the triadic relationship. Freud's unique ability to penetrate the depths of self-imposed ignorance to retrieve pieces of the human puzzle (e.g., as the Oedipal reaction) and figure out how the various pieces fit together to account for human behavior was a mammoth achievement. This achievement spans three centuries of mental health treatment and continues to influence other fields such as art, history, religion, anthropology, and philosophy. Although sometimes difficult to detect or understand, Freud's views have brought about subtle but significant changes in the way many people view their world.

In addition, the chapter touches on the work of other theorists, whose ideas functioned either as theoretical tributaries that flowed into and strengthened mainstream Freudian theory or as streams of thought that meandered away from mainstream Freudian theory. Whereas many of these attempts to branch out and away from Freud's theoretical approach eventually dried up, some did not, and several of these became major psychodynamic positions alongside Freud's (e.g., object relations theory). Very few of these early psychodynamic departures from Freud, such as the theoretical framework proposed by Alfred Adler, were vibrant enough to stand alone and to offer an alternative to Freudian theory and practice.

LEARNING OBJECTIVES

After reading this chapter, each student should be able to:

1. Discuss the case of William S.

2. Summarize the historical context of psychoanalytic theory.

3. Evaluate Sigmund Freud's contribution.

4. Critique the basic concepts of psychoanalytic theory.

5. Assess the therapeutic process of psychoanalytic theory.

6. Explain deviations from Freudian theory and therapy.

7. Appraise the benefits and limitations of psychoanalytic theory with respect to multiculturalism and social justice (e.g., working with diverse populations).

8. Describe the relevance of psychoanalytic theory to the current-day practice of counseling.

Historical Context

Freud's father, Jacob (Jakob) Kallamon Freud (1815–1896), married his third wife, Amalie Nathanson (1835–1930), in 1855. A year later, on May 6, 1856, Sigmund was born in Pribor, in the former Czech Republic. Sigmund was the eldest of Amalie and Jacob's eight children. Both parents exposed Sigmund early to Jewish religion and traditions but avoided an orthodox religious approach. As a result, Sigmund Freud displayed a nonreligious

WHEN THE PAST OVERTAKES THE PRESENT: THE CASE OF WILLIAM S.

William enters therapy reporting he suffers from both depression and an inexplicable sense of guilt. William states his professional life has not gone well for several years but that things changed for him after he "got a big break." William explained that he had written a number of plays while he was "killing time teaching" in a speech department at a small state college in south Louisiana. During the past six years he submitted almost one play per year to everyone he thought might be interested in financially backing such a production. Even though his own department head expressed an interest in staging one of his plays, this never materialized due to college budget cuts.

This was the "last straw," according to William, and as a result he gave up writing. It was after marrying a fellow academic who was "much older than I am that I felt the urge to write plays again—when growing up, I remember being encouraged to write and to be as creative as possible." William also recalled he resumed writing around the time his father was informed he had pancreatic cancer. Reviewing these events, William states he now finds it very odd that he felt energized and was able to focus on writing a new play when his father was so ill.

William went on to discuss what the "big break" was that changed his life. Because of his interest in history, William decided to try something different and write a play based on an actual historical event. After several months of searching through old documents, William found what he considered the perfect story on which to base a dramatic play. "Once I came across this wonderful story, it was as if the play wrote itself. It seemed to me that I had been carrying the play around inside me for years—I just didn't know it."

The play was divided into several acts and told the story of a young prince named Cronos, whose uncle was rumored to have murdered the prince's father. Cronos's uncle subsequently married his mother for the sole purpose of gaining control of the throne. The prince starts to believe the rumor after a shadowy figure visits his bedroom late one night. The shadowy intruder reveals it is the spirit of his dead father, and it pleads with the prince to seek revenge because without revenge the dead father will be forced to walk the earth as a spirit forever. Determined to kill his uncle, the prince decides he can only succeed if his uncle does not view him as a genuine threat. Cronos pretends he has gone insane because of his father's death.

A subplot of the play involves a young princess, Rhea, who was to marry the young prince in the spring. On receiving the news the prince has gone mad, the princess decides to travel to his castle. On seeing the princess in the company of his uncle, the prince decides he must continue to act insane. When the two are brought together by the uncle, the prince unexpectedly acts in a contemptuous manner followed by an angry outburst of filthy language directed toward the princess. Convinced of his madness, the princess leaves the room. The next day, the young princess is discovered floating face down in a pond near the castle after having drowned herself. Hearing of the princess's death, the prince begins to doubt his plan and wonders whether the princess's death was punishment from God for his murderous plan. His hesitation is short lived, and his motivation to seek revenge reemerges after he overhears a conversation that seems to suggest his mother and uncle conspired to kill the king, his father. Before the prince carries out the murder, he speaks to the audience and shares what he has learned about life and death: Men and women are little more than puppets whose strings Destiny pulls to achieve its goal, even if this goal results in a disastrous end for Destiny's puppets and the entire kingdom in which they exist.

After providing the therapist a synopsis of his play, William elaborated on the play's funding and the preparations made to take the play to an off-Broadway location for a trial run. If the play was profitable it would allow William's wife to quit her "dead-end" job and enable them to make several purchases they would not have made otherwise. After a long pause, the therapist asked, "What did your father think of this success?" The client looked down to the floor and said, "The day my play was financed for production off-Broadway, I went to tell him the good news. Knocking on his door and not hearing a response, I opened my father's bedroom door and discovered he had died. My father had fallen and was lying face down on the floor. My first thought when I saw him lying on the floor was 'Dad has a halo over his head.' When I looked again, I saw the halo was nothing more than a puddle of blood." The client began to weep.

Case Discussion—Near the end of this chapter, a psychoanalytic hypothesis is provided for William's depression and guilt reaction, as is the psychoanalytic oriented diagnosis that would dictate treatment.

perspective of the world, and yet his self-proclaimed identity was unalterably Jewish. The 1857 economic crisis devastated the family business, and when Sigmund was 4 years old, the family moved to Vienna, Austria, where Sigmund began his formal education. Freud was a superior student known for his meticulous approach to learning, quickness of comprehension, and breadth of interests. See Figure 3.1 for a depiction of Freud.

The young Freud enjoyed the universal appeal of classic literature such as Sophocles's *The Oedipus Plays* and found himself intrigued by the power of historical events to sway the flow of human destiny. The young Freud was also fascinated by the symbolic underpinnings of words and images and curious enough about languages other than his native German to learn French, English, Italian, and Spanish. Such academic interests served Freud well when he later pulled from his cache of knowledge to illustrate important concepts: *slips of the tongue* that possessed special meanings in light of their spoken situational contexts; *dream symbols* that revealed hidden aspects of the mind; and the early familial drama termed the *Oedipus complex* from which a child's enduring personality was a by-product—a crystallized identity that helped to propel the male child toward adult status.

Although Freud's adult career path was influenced by the classism and prejudices of the time (emancipation for Jews living in Vienna came in 1848), Freud's motivation to achieve important discoveries proved to be the strongest force determining his future. Freud took a prolonged path to the practice of medicine while enrolled at the University of Vienna. It was typical to take final exams within five years, but Freud studied an additional three more years. This led relatives and associates of Freud to think he had become an intellectual vagrant who shunned "real world" work. Contributing further to this perception were the economic difficulties that his family endured in part to support Freud's education.

After completing his final exams, he spent several years working at the Vienna General Hospital to hone his skills and obtain practical experiences. After fulfilling the necessary requirements, Freud was accepted as a university lecturer for neuropathology in 1895. During these years, Freud displayed a voracious appetite for learning, even if it meant going beyond the Viennese circle of medicine. Freud received a small grant to travel to France to work at Pitié-Salpêtrière Hospital in order to study advances in Parisian medicine. Once in Paris, Freud attended Jean-Martin Charcot's medical demonstrations. He learned that Charcot believed hysteria was a condition that affected both sexes, represented a true mental condition and not a sham illness, and was a mental condition that could be created by implanting a thought via hypnotic suggestion. Charcot also believed that hypnosis allowed for a better understanding of hysteria but was useless as a treatment because symptom elimination through hypnotic suggestion eventually failed to prevent the return of symptoms.

Freud married Martha Bernays following a 4-year engagement, and he also established a private practice. The couple had their first child in 1887. Freud's practice grew quickly with most appointments taken by patients

▼ FIGURE 3.1
Freud's Portrait

SMETEK/Science Photo Library/Getty Images

who suffered from various nervous diseases. Frustrated with typically prescribed treatments—cold baths, massages, and the Faradic method of electrotherapy—Freud began to experiment with the use of hypnosis but became dissatisfied with his ability to effectively use the technique, even after traveling to Nancy, France, to seek the help of experts. Despite his efforts to master the technique, he was dissatisfied with the treatment's effectiveness.

Interestingly, prior to Freud's encounter with Charcot, the eminent Viennese doctor Josef Breuer had discussed with Freud his successful use of hypnosis to treat hysteria. Freud recalled this exchange after his return from Nancy, recalling that Breuer stated that when he asked a patient to trace a symptom back to its origin and then allowed the patient to release any lingering emotions tied to this actual past event, the result was symptom removal.

Freud sought Breuer's advice, and their professional relationship grew stronger over time. Their professional collaboration concluded in 1895 with their seminal work *Studies on Hysteria*, which documented their findings supporting the use of hypnotic-induced cathartic treatment. Breuer and Freud soon withdrew from collaborating as a result of growing theoretical differences concerning the origin of hysteria. However, the foundation for what was to become psychoanalysis was now securely in place. It remained to Freud to build on this foundation.

In addition to these collaborative efforts and developing his own clinical approach to treating hysteria, Freud discovered that his personal memories provided some of the richest raw material to understand human nature. Freud turned his analytic eye on himself during mid-life when he experienced psychosomatic symptoms along with persistent and irrational fears. Coinciding with this period of self-analysis was Freud's concerted effort to probe dreams for clues. Eventually Freud's exploration of his own mental landscape resulted in a profound insight that he was convinced had significant general repercussions. Specifically, Freud discovered that as a child he harbored strong negative feelings for his father. These feelings were strong enough to require repression's activation because the feelings fueled hostile urges. This hostility had a strong emotional counterpoint that complemented the negative feelings. In other words, counteracting Freud's feelings toward his father was his strong desire to be the sole recipient of his mother's affection.

Freud's inner journey produced the uncomfortable realization that these early, heavily laden emotional events played out during childhood had significantly contributed to shaping his adult personality. Furthermore, Freud realized certain events during one's adult life (e.g., death of a parent) could trigger a return to the original conflict situation as evidenced by his own neurotic symptoms. One of Freud's greatest discoveries was that shadowy memories inhabiting a realm beneath consciousness often retained enough emotional power to create and energize an ongoing neurotic reaction.

In 1923, Freud was diagnosed with cancer and endured 33 operations during the remaining years of his life. The second of these operations was a radical procedure to remove the upper palate and lower jaw on one side. These areas were then fitted with prosthetic devices that contributed to a series of health-related problems. Not wanting anything to interfere with his clarity of thinking and his daily regime of working, which often allowed for only 6 hours of sleep, Freud avoided strong medications, relying instead on mild pain relievers such as Bayer aspirin. Also confronting Freud late in his life was the growing power of Nazi Germany. At one Nazi event, psychoanalytic publications were collected and burned while the following proclamation was read: "Against the soul-destroying glorification of the instinctual life, for the nobility of the human soul! I consign to the flames the writings of the school of Sigmund Freud." The Nazis' treatment of Jews continued to worsen. The Nazis took control of Vienna during the Anschluss on March 12, 1938. On March 15, a group of thugs entered Freud's dwelling. After the robbers stole 6,000 schillings, Freud appeared and silently confronted the robbers, and they left. When Freud's daughter Anna informed him of the amount of money stolen, Freud commented that "he had never been paid so much for a single visit" (Jones, 1957, p. 219).

While determined to remain defiant, Freud changed his mind about leaving Vienna after the Schutzstaffel (SS) invaded his home and removed his daughter for several hours. Influential friends and various dignitaries concerned about the unfolding events taking place in Austria worked collectively to relocate Freud to England. He was warmly welcomed. After settling in his new home, Freud received a number of notable figures interested in meeting the father of psychoanalysis, including the Spanish surrealist painter Salvador Dalí, who drew Freud's likeness during his visit. Freud died on September 23, 1939.

Sigmund Freud's Contribution

Approximately 70 years after Freud's death, Michael Hart's book *The 100: A Ranking of the Most Influential Persons in History* ranked Freud 32nd. According to Hart,

> of the [all the] individuals who have inhabited the world, less than one in a million is listed in a large biographical dictionary. Of the perhaps twenty thousand individuals whose achievements have merited mention in biographical dictionaries, only about *one-half* of one percent are included on my list. Thus, every person on this list, in my opinion, is one of the truly monumental figures of history. (1987, p. 30)

In 2014, John Cloud listed only three mental health theorists in his chapter on social sciences for the publication *Great Scientists*. In their order of appearance were the following names: Sigmund Freud, Albert Ellis (creator of rational emotive behavior therapy), and Marsha Linehan (creator of dialectical behavior therapy). Cloud wrote the following about Freud: "Prolific, influential, misunderstood . . . he forever changed the way we see the mind in action" (p. 83).

Although opinions of Freud's achievements in psychotherapy and other fields with applied psychoanalytic concepts vary, Freud inarguably was a prominent figure in the 21st century whose impact continues. Freud was a prolific writer whose efforts spanned approximately 50 years and whose numerous publications encompass a variety of topics. The term *metapsychology* was applied by Freud to aspects of his work that offered comprehensive, basic explanations for psychological, social, and historical events. Although the metapsychology approach offered Freud an opportunity to systematically apply various psychoanalytic concepts, it is important to note that the approach also relies upon a speculative type of logic that can lead to conclusions that do not neatly conform to empirical methods used to test hypotheses. For example, Freud's concept of a death drive, while possibly true and logical from a psychoanalytic perspective, does not lend itself to empirical testing.

The breadth and style of Freud's writings often led to a number of memorable assertions that impart a type of wisdom that seems to transcend time and place. As a result, these statements have been inserted into conversations and the published works of others since Freud first penned or said them (see Table 3.1 for a sample).

Although the full extent of Sigmund Freud's contribution to therapy is difficult to assess, it is not difficult to claim that Freud's efforts at theory construction established much of the theoretical and practice agenda that was to follow. In the decades after the publication of *The Interpretation of Dreams* in 1900 (Freud, 1900/1953), up until the 1960s, Freudian theory grew until it marked many aspects of the therapeutic landscape for both individual and group therapy.

Even a cursory review of psychoanalytic theory's history would reveal that there are three fundamental theoretical tenets necessary and sufficient to define a theory as psychoanalytic-oriented or a version of such (this includes various theories referred to as *psychodynamic*).

The first, and foremost, tenet is the existence of a *dynamic unconscious* resulting in various aspects of the mind clashing with one another, thus generating anxiety (e.g., hidden sexual fears conflicting with moral beliefs of right and wrong). It is the specific manner in which Freud described the qualifier *dynamic* that set Freud's conceptualization of the unconscious apart from precursors to psychoanalysis such as those presented by the philosophers Spinoza and Nietzsche, who also wrote about the unconscious. Freud's unconscious is always active and allows the individual no escape; even sleep does not provide a means for the person to avoid its influence. In fact, Freud saw dreams as largely composed of forgotten experiences that had been

▼ TABLE 3.1

Quotable Sigmund Freud

- The interpretation of dreams is the royal road to a knowledge of the unconscious activities of the mind. –Freud (1900) *The Interpretation of Dreams*
- Our hysterical patients suffer from reminiscences. –Freud (1910) *Five Lectures on Psychoanalysis*
- Men have gained control over the forces of nature to such an extent that with their help they could have no difficulty in exterminating one another to the last man. They know this, and hence comes a large part of their current unrest, their unhappiness and their mood of anxiety. –Freud (1930) *Civilization and Its Discontents*
- It almost looks as if analysis were the third of those "impossible" professions in which one can be quite sure of unsatisfying results. The other two, much older-established, are the bringing-up of children and the government of nations. –Freud (1937) *Analysis Terminable and Interminable*
- The poets and philosophers before me discovered the unconscious; what I discovered was the scientific method by which the unconscious can be studied. –Lionel Trilling (1957) *The Liberal Imagination*
- The great question . . . which I have not been able to answer, despite my thirty years of research into the feminine soul, is "What does a woman want?" –Ernest Jones (1955) *Life and Work of Sigmund Freud*, Vol. 2
- *To love and to work* [= mental health]. –Erik H. Erikson (1963) *Childhood and Society*
- Sometimes a cigar is just a cigar. –Anonymous

Source: Kaplan, 2002 (pp. 607–608).

pushed to the dark recesses of the mind. These forgotten memories still retain enough emotional power to allow them to partially enter consciousness through the disguised content of dreams.

Second is the tenet that an adult personality materializes only after a series of *developmental stages* have unfolded and are dealt with by the child. According to Freud, the best possible outcome waiting for the child who successfully travels the full distance of these stages is the acquisition of mature adult love and the ability to do productive work. Basically, the child's task is to successfully adapt to the changing course of interpersonal expectations represented by the various stages identified by Freud. Failing to do so results in nonadaptive reactions toward others taking hold. These nonadaptive reactions can range from a relatively simple behavioral pattern that undermines an adult's ability to get along with others in certain situations to a highly vibrant dysfunctional set of reactions that becomes strongly rooted in the final adult personality. This latter outcome is likely to have a pervasive negative impact on much of the person's life.

Third is the tenet that during the course of therapy the client will eventually respond to the therapist as if the therapist was a significant person from the past, as if therapy has created "small cracks" in the boundary that separates the client's past and present, allowing forgotten memories to slowly ooze into consciousness. Freud termed this particular repetitive pattern of thinking and behaving that symbolically mirrors an early traumatic event a *transference reaction,* and Freud contended it was a necessary occurrence if lasting change is to occur. While effectively dealing with transference was the best avenue toward accomplishing transformation of the client's personality, this was not an easy therapeutic task because, paradoxically, the client would strongly resist such transformation.

In conclusion, before a therapeutic approach can be considered to represent a true psychoanalytic (psychodynamic) approach it must possess at a minimum three essential theoretical ingredients: *dynamic unconscious, stages of development,* and *transference reactions.*

Basic Concepts

Human Nature

Some claim that Freud's view of human nature is narrow in scope and too simplistic to capture the essential truth about humans. However, his view is actually multifaceted and encompassing. Freud essentially saw humans as divided between unconscious biological qualities that are tied to sensual, physical, or carnal forces and largely conscious mental qualities that are tied to various intellectual forces. Thus, while humans can be described partly in terms of their animalistic heritage, this was not the whole story for Freud. Humans can also be described in terms of actions that show an acute mental discernment and keen practical sense that is capable of curtailing or even altering animalistic tendencies through *sublimation* (A. Freud, 1937/1966), which occurs, for example, when a taboo sexual desire is redirected in such a way that it becomes socially acceptable. A series of paintings (i.e., *Danaë and the Shower of Gold*) by the 16th-century painter Titian depict the rape of a woman by the god Zeus. In these paintings Zeus is symbolically represented by a golden shower of coins that fall between Danaë's legs and impregnate her.

Of the two human qualities—animalistic and rational—Freud elevated the ability to think rationally to a superior position and expressed the following words to summarize his view: "Where id was there shall ego be." Despite his belief in the ultimate power of rational thinking, Freud saw firsthand the difficulties imposed on his clients when the person struggled with conflicting forces and how difficult such conflicts were to overcome, even when the level of rational thinking was enhanced through therapy and utilized to alter the balance of forces. Interestingly, what is true of individuals can be extended to humans collectively. Freud viewed World War I as irrefutable evidence that even the rational capabilities of humans can be overwhelmed by ancient, primordial aspects of the mind to the potential detriment of humankind.

Dynamic Unconscious

Freud's clinical experiences led him to initially view the mind as relying on three mental processes that are essentially linear and layered (Freud, 1915/1957). He termed the three processes the *unconscious*, the *preconscious*, and the *conscious*. Similar to a large iceberg floating in the ocean, the conscious lies above water and is visible to an observer, the preconscious lies just below the waterline and, although faint, is still visible and accessible. Finally, the unconscious is too far below the surface to be easily seen or accessible. This third and hidden level comprises the vast majority of the iceberg.

The term *preconscious* refers to memory traces that are retrievable. The *conscious* refers to the actual perception of both inner and outer states of reality. Obviously, Freud was most interested in the *unconscious* because this involves aspects of one's life blocked from easy recall. Activating unconscious processes to obtain glimpses of unconscious content requires special effort or the use of some type of memory aid such as hypnosis. This *topographical description* of the mind soon proved to be problematic. Additional clinical findings did not fit with Freud's initial conceptualization, and he realized a more elaborate interactive system of mental structures was required. Specifically, he posited it is not only primitive, innate impulses being blocked from awareness but also various experiences encountered during the span of one's life.

Due to the principles Freud used to govern his pursuit of correct inferences, he was forced to conclude that an additional mental operation remained to be identified and incorporated into what was to become a structural model of the mind. Freud's conclusion was based on his belief that it is not logical to have unconscious material embedded in one of the other processes, such as the preconscious or the conscious. Freud encountered clients who experienced unconscious guilt, which led to inconsistencies when he applied his initial topographical model of the mind. For example, throughout childhood it is very likely that a child's father expresses on numerous occasions his definition of right and wrong behavior, as well as the logical consequences for violating standards of conduct. Freud was forced to consider how a parent's publically expressed views on moral conduct could take up residence in the child's unconscious. Pondering such inconsistencies led Freud to what is known as the *structural hypothesis* of the mind, which can be summarized by defining its three components: id, ego, and superego (Freud, 1923/1961). Finally, although it is tempting to link these three mental constructs with certain areas of the brain, this was not Freud's intention as neurology was still far from being an exact science.

Structural Hypothesis of Mind

At birth we are close to being pure *id*, which is completely unconscious and remains so throughout our life. We mentally enter the world as a swirling batch of primordial forms of various drives, which certainly have a biological foundation. These drives are unlearned and emotionally fueled by the overriding goal of personal survival. The id's drives differ from animal instincts because drives are malleable and over time encompass more objects, but Freud believed the id could not be responsible for reshaping its own drives since reshaping required repeated expression of its drives combined with pressures introduced by the real world. Thus, a mental structure must exist that straddles the world of drives and the outer would of reality. This structure is the ego.

The *ego* has mostly conscious aspects, but also preconscious and unconscious aspects. It is the mental structure capable of learning about the real world through sensory probes designed to gather pertinent information. Over time the ego becomes increasingly cognitive oriented and skilled at arriving at conclusions, judgments, inferences, and methods that include creative approaches to effectively solve problems. Most important from the standpoint of the id, it is the ego that is responsible for "testing the waters of reality" to satisfy the demands of the id while simultaneously adding to the ego's repertoire of adaptive tactics.

Finally, the maturing child is confronted with certain expectations expressed by parents and certain others throughout life. Internalized, such expectations have the power to become strong motivators for one's actions, and even a force that collides with id urges. Expectations can take two forms referred to as the *conscience*, which reflects the moral component of personality, and the *ego-ideal*, which represents the aspirations that parents and other significant others hold for the person. Together these two components define what constitutes the *superego*. Similar to the ego, the superego has conscious, preconscious, and unconscious aspects. The superego can call upon the ego to fulfill or pursue either set of expectations, and the ego can be self-activated to serve as a mediator when id urges and superego expectations clash.

Drives

As alluded to earlier, while many forms of life display ready-made patterns of behavior (i.e., instincts) when exposed to certain environmental cues, this is not what is meant by the term *instinct* when it appears in psychoanalytic literature. In fact, Freud did not use this term. When his publications were translated into other languages such as English, Freud's (1915/1957) term *treib* (i.e., drive) was translated as if he had written the term *instinkt* (i.e., instinct). This substitution had the effect of distorting and animalizing Freud's original meaning. In Freud's view, a drive encompassed two worlds: the somatic and the mental, and each drive could be characterized by its source, aim, and object. For example, an oral drive's source, or somatic origin, might take the form of painful sensations or the sense of weakness sometimes experienced when we have gone too long without eating. Obviously, the aim is to fulfil, to bring an end to the hunger, and finally, the object of the oral drive is whatever satisfies the felt hunger (e.g., mother's breast or a bottle of formula). Finally, the difference between an instinct and a Freudian drive becomes remarkably clear when one realizes drives are flexible and do not pertain to fixed relationships; in fact, drives can mutate over time as a result of the developmental stages all humans pass through as they become mature adults.

Anxiety

Everyone has experienced distress or a sense of mental uneasiness caused by misfortune, fear, or danger. At other times anxiety seems to be tied to an earnest but intense desire to succeed at a very important task, such as earning a high score on an examination for admission to college or graduate school. Finally, we can also recall times when we experienced a state of apprehension without being able to provide an acceptable reason for such a state of mind. Obviously, life experiences inform us that anxiety possesses a range of intensity and can be a reaction to many sources.

From a psychoanalytic perspective, anxiety is a fundamental concept with a broad application. Freud's (1926/1959) publication of *Inhibitions, Symptoms and Anxiety* provided his final explanation concerning the role of anxiety in mental life. He believed anxiety is typically a reaction of the ego, and the feeling of anxiety itself is a *signal* that a threat exists. Although fear and anxiety may feel as if they are one in the same, there is a key difference between these two common experiences. Fear is what occurs when confronted with a real danger, and the sensation of fear lessens when we flee the danger or when the danger no longer exists. Anxiety results from something internal that we cannot run from or totally avoid in the future because anxiety is literally part of the human condition.

Essentially, anxiety represents a psychic signal that is triggered within the ego. This occurs because the ego is primarily responsible for blocking what is starting to emerge from the id. Thus, the chain of tactical events is the following: (1) An id impulse is on the verge of becoming readily apparent, (2) the ego experiences anxiety as a result, and (3) the ego subsequently relies upon one or more ego-defense mechanisms to quash expression of the id impulse and quench anxiety's uprising. This effective blocking of id material from unadulterated expression reestablishes an acceptable level of mental quiescence. Defense mechanisms assume a form that may be called a *lying-truth* because deceit is used to corral an unpleasant reality—the cognitive-behavioral peculiarity of all defense mechanisms is they serve to trick the trickster.

Ego-Defense Mechanisms

Individuals are capable of avoiding real and even chimerical dangers via defense mechanisms and are capable of lessening the intensity of any drive pushing for fulfillment (A. Freud, 1937/1966). Keeping in mind there is no consensus concerning a definitive listing of all the possible defense mechanisms to counter manifestations of anxiety, Ginter and Glauser (2008) presented a categorization scheme that calls attention to the level of problem-solving sophistication. Because their scheme is intended to provide a rough measure of ego functioning (and measure of reality contact), it requires a therapist to factor in the influence of age when identifying a client's general level of thinking or cognitive maturity. For example, it may be developmentally acceptable for a young child to act out when told it's time for bed, but it would be developmentally unacceptable for a 16-year-old to react in the same manner when told to go to bed.

At the highest level of developmental sophistication, a person's reactions reflect two things: (1) an adequate awareness of consensus-based reality and (2) reliance on an appropriate problem-solving approach. Freud would place these responses in the category of behaviors typical of someone who is relatively healthy. For example, the person functioning at this level consistently displays a nonhostile sense of humor, even when humor is used to reduce felt anxiety. In this case the use of humor reduces the level of tension, and its aim is not to hurt anyone. A person who operates from this sphere of behavior typically accepts himself or herself, frequently approaches difficult situations from a problem-centered type of focus, and is appropriately spontaneous and interested in others' feelings and thoughts (Table 3.2). Finally, it should be noted that despite examples where sublimation is cited in the literature as a defense mechanism, in truth it is not. Even though some writers have viewed sublimation as a form of reaction formation, Freud viewed sublimation as a means for a drive to convert its aim toward something socially acceptable. In some cases, the end result of sublimation would even garner praise. For example, rather than leading to the repression of some drive due to the signal of anxiety, sublimation allows sexual urges to be redirected over time, resulting in an accomplished artist widely recognized for her nude paintings, or aggressive urges to be redirected, eventually resulting in a gifted surgeon widely known

▼ TABLE 3.2

Levels of Developmental Sophistication

High Level of Developmental Sophistication
Sublimation, anticipation, self-assertion, group affiliation, altruism, self-observation, and humor
Growing Conflict and Anxiety Results in the Ego Activating Some Form of Defensive Action
Low-Minor Level of Developmental Sophistication Intellectualization, rationalization, help-rejecting complaining, passive aggressive, reaction formation, undoing, apathetic withdrawal, acting out, displacement, projection, and repression
Low-Major Level of Developmental Sophistication Denial, splitting of self-image/image of others, idealization, devaluation, omnipotence, delusional projection, autistic fantasy, psychotic distortion, psychotic denial

for her skillful use of a scalpel to save lives. Sublimation short-circuits the usual element of repression that is a part of all defense mechanisms.

Defense Mechanism Defined by Category. The *low-major level* of developmental sophistication encompasses reactions that lie at the opposite extreme, reactions that exemplify an obvious disregard for facts and adequate problem-solving steps. These reactions largely are driven by fantasy-derived id-based urges. Furthermore, the displayed behavior is largely incongruent with the person's expected level of cognitive and/or emotional development.

Compared to the *low-major level* of defense mechanisms, the *low-minor level* of defense mechanisms can sometimes be difficult to detect when first encountered. This is because the low-minor level of defense mechanisms better incorporates elements of reality, but the true nature of these defense mechanisms is eventually revealed because they are part of a repetitive pattern of behavior that is ineffective and detectable by a trained therapist. To paraphrase Freud: If you cannot do something, give up. The mark of poor mental health is trying the same ineffective solution over and over with no foreseeable end in sight.

Specific Examples and Definitions: Low-Minor Level Defense Mechanism

- *Rationalization:* emphasizing abstract matters and giving little, if any, consideration to emotions
- *Help-rejecting complaining:* vacillating between (a) providing what is necessary to help another complete a task or to satisfy another's need and (b) not providing assistance while expressing dissatisfaction, pain, uneasiness, resentment, and so forth
- *Passive aggressive:* displaying hostility through passive actions such as remaining unyielding, displaying a headstrong reaction, procrastinating, reacting via the silent treatment, displaying ill-humor, or maintaining an offended mood
- *Reaction formation:* acting or saying the direct opposite of what a repressed impulse seeks
- *Undoing:* attempting to reverse a psychologically unacceptable action by literally doing its opposite ("doing its opposite" often more than once)
- *Apathetic withdrawal:* becoming detached from objects and displaying a lack of interest or concern for things that typically elicit passion, emotion, or excitement
- *Acting out:* displaying immature, inappropriate behavior sustained by repressed impulses and/or thoughts
- *Displacement:* relocating an emotion or thought from its original point of focus to another point of focus, such as an object, person, or situation not originally associated with the emotion or thought
- *Projection:* attributing to another person one's own intolerable emotion or thought (e.g., guilt, stupidity, laziness, lack of concentration) or viewing some aspect of external reality as embodying this intolerable emotion or thought
- *Repression:* in its pure form, removing from consciousness (and preventing reentry) disagreeable and anxiety-provoking memories, thoughts, feelings, or impulses (Note: It is important to recognize that repression is an essential part of

all the defense mechanisms. No defense mechanism can flourish without repression's contribution. Although repression is a vital component of all the defense mechanisms it can also stand alone.)

Specific Examples and Definitions: Low-Major Level Defense Mechanism

- *Denial:* controlling anxiety by literally disowning or refusing to acknowledge certain thoughts, feelings, or facts that cannot be consciously tolerated
- *Splitting of self-image or image of others:* occurs when various parts that comprise the self or another person is poorly organized or cognitively fragmented. The process blocks these separated aspects from forming a unified image or impression of a whole person
- *Idealization:* holding another person in too great esteem or expecting too much of another
- *Devaluation:* having an unrealistic reduction of the true value inherent in another person, object, or situation
- *Omnipotence:* attributing very great or unlimited authority or power to one's self or another person or thing
- *Delusional projection:* an obviously false belief attributed to another person or object. This belief is resistant to change even when the person is confronted with facts that counter the false belief.
- *Autistic fantasy:* imagining or summoning images that fulfill a psychological need while simultaneously impairing communication and increasing emotional detachment
- *Psychotic distortion:* experiencing elements of the psyche—images, knowledge, sounds heard, and so forth—to such an altered degree that the person's contact with reality is obviously impaired
- *Psychotic denial:* disowning thoughts, feelings, or facts to such a degree that the lack of contact with reality can prove life-threatening

Personality: Stages of Development

Personality refers to a complex system that encompasses both unseen dynamic functions that organize various processes to mediate reactions to perceived inner and outer reality and those publically displayed qualities that mark the person as distinct from others. According to Freud, a number of factors account for the qualities and peculiarities of a person. In addition to innate biological components, the historical litany of interactions (the way others interact with the child and the way the child interacts with others) can prove to be a major determinant of the child's adult personality. Freud also asserted that around age 5, personality's complex system of interacting components coalesces and largely crystallizes.

Freud proposed there are distinct stages of human development with each contributing to the final adult personality assumed. One's own identity and the way an adult person interacts with others, especially the opposite gender, starts with the oral stage and continues through the stages labeled anal, phallic, latency, and genital (Freud 1953b; 1905/1926/1959).

Each developmental stage has ramifications for who the child becomes later in life and for the type of interactional pattern activated when interpersonal conflict is experienced with, for example, a stranger, coworker, acquaintance, friend, or family member. These interactional patterns indirectly serve as a gauge indicative of the degree the person, as a child, successfully confronted the challenges posed at each stage of development. The less successful the child is, the greater the level of fixation will be, which essentially means the child maintains an immature attachment to a source of satisfaction or even some object positively or negatively associated with a source of satisfaction. Finally, as one would expect, the child's biological parents (or surrogate parents) often play a prominent role in the child's life and, as a result, are positioned to contribute directly to the child's eventual personality.

Also, the stages of development demonstrate how both life and death drives target different areas of the body to find expression as the child develops; in some instances, both sets of drives intertwine to achieve a common goal. Therefore, a review of the developmental expectations embedded in each of Freud's stages can shed light on why certain dysfunctional patterns remain a fixture of later adult interactions.

Oral Stage. At this stage, the infant primarily seeks survival through oral gratification. When a newborn enters the world, the neonate starts life with several reflex actions (Ginter & Glauser, 2008) that do not require learning or, it appears, conscious thought as we know it. An example is the *startle reflex,* which becomes evident when a loud noise causes the infant's arms to shoot out, followed by what appears to be an attempt to embrace and cling with its fingers. Other reflexes playing a central role include the *rooting reflex* (touching the right cheek, or left, causes the infant's head to turn toward the point of touch) and the *sucking reflex,* which is designed to automatically draw nourishment from the mother's breast. At this stage, sucking and later biting provide meaningful expressions of the life and death drives, respectively. Finally, it is important to recognize that both sucking and biting are pleasurable activities for the infant. Appropriate curtailing of biting contributes positively to ego development.

According to Freud, the child will develop a certain response pattern to parental attempts to fulfill its oral needs (attempts that are not likely to be perfect but are likely to lean toward the direction of either underfeeding or overfeeding). If parents consistently overfeed or underfeed, the child's response pattern will strengthen over time and possibly assume a form that continues into adult life (referred to as an *oral personality*). For example, overfeeding may result in a personality too trusting, gullible, and overly optimistic. Underfeeding may result in a personality that is untrusting, envious, and doubting of self-value. Finally, because pleasure can also be derived from biting, the end result of "biting the feeder" may be an adult personality that continues to "bite others" through excessive use of sarcasm, profanity, or verbal bullying.

Anal Stage. At about 2 years of age (keeping in mind stages do not start and stop at precise ages and may even overlap in terms of age), the child discovers pleasure centers around expulsion or retention of bodily waste. Toilet training is typically imposed at this stage. Again, the efforts and reactions of the parents and child prove critical to further personality development. Toilet training results in the child realizing that certain behaviors result in praise, whereas other behaviors result in parental displeasure, disgust, and even anger. It should not be overlooked that this stage starts at a time often referred to as the "terrible twos," a time when a higher level of thinking occurs before the child has obtained the corresponding language to express what is being thought (Ginter & Glauser, 2008). Thus, parents who are attempting to have the child control a pleasurable urge can expect to be repeatedly frustrated before the child is toilet trained, especially in light of the child's level of thinking, which is more advanced than the child's ability to use language to express wants and needs.

Parents typically expect (and convey in subtle and not so subtle ways) that the child will achieve total success with what could very well be the first important task assigned to the child by the parents. Again, if certain types of interactions between the parents and child are consistently enacted, the child is likely to experience certain personality outcomes. The best outcomes are associated with mastery over urges that do in fact require discretionary fulfillment, satisfaction from accomplishing a very important task that only "grown-up children can do," and the budding sense of pride that emerges from the child's ability to control the delivery of something of value (feces) for both parents.

The conflict confronting the child at this stage is pleasing parents over the desire to seek uncensored pleasure through the expulsion of feces. Any resulting anal fixation that results from the parent–child struggle at this point in the child's development typically takes one of two forms. The *anal-retentive personality* is said to result from the child retaining feces to defy parental attempts to control a pleasurable urge (Freud, 1926/1959). Frequently this personality is characterized in the adult by attributes such as regularity, orderliness, thriftiness, and stubbornness. If this child's resulting personality attributes fall at the extreme, as an adult the person might act in an aggressive or destructive manner in response to another's accomplishment (e.g., job promotion), especially if the accomplishment results in a lot of attention for the other person (e.g., the promotion is covered in the local newspaper). Although the *anal-expulsive personality* can also display aggressive behaviors, this type of fixation is more likely to take the form of displaying inconsistent or irregular behavior. For example, persons with anal-expulsive personality may sometimes be overly expressive and allow their feelings to pour out at an inappropriate time or location. This personality type also approaches work situations in a manner that can be best described as unorganized and messy. Finally, in extreme manifestations the person might display a level of nonconformity consistent with refusing to follow established rules, customs, etiquette, morality, or laws.

Phallic Stage. Around age 5, both male and female children find masturbation especially pleasurable as the child's genitalia become the new focal point for the life drives (and the child's aggressive urges). A desirable outcome at this stage is for the child to identify strongly with one parent over the other (which implies this is the stage when the superego takes definite form, as incorporating a parent's qualities includes incorporating that parent's moral sense of right and wrong conduct). Identity development is one of several important concepts brought to the forefront by Freud, and even though there have been different explanations offered after Freud to account for various factors contributing to identity formation, Freud's clinical work and self-analysis led him to call attention to a child's desire for special parental attention as the primary factor contributing to the formation of one's identity. Finally, Freud was convinced that failing to adequately confront the demands imposed on the child at this stage largely accounted for the basis of the neurotic conditions he encountered in therapy.

This stage invokes a different conflict scenario for males and females at this juncture in their life. The male Oedipus complex or reaction occurs when the feelings of the son become energized to a new level and focused on obtaining the mother's full attention. The male's desire to consume all of his mother's attention is accompanied by an equally strong desire to exclude the father (and others in the family such as siblings) completely from receiving any attention from the mother. Soon after these thoughts occur, the child becomes fearful because he believes the powerful all-knowing father may have "heard his thoughts" and realized his son wants to wish him away from the family. Because the life and death drives can become intertwined at an unconscious level, one may conclude that the male child develops the fear that his father will destroy the focal point of his bodily derived pleasure at this stage—his penis. This is known as *castration anxiety*, and it serves to motivate the child to identify with the father. In identifying with the aggressor, the male child has called on a defensive tactic that protects him from harm. In other words, "If I am like father, he won't hurt me because it would be like hurting himself."

Freud theorized a different set of factors contributed to females identifying with their mother. While somewhat less satisfied with his explanation, one can conclude there is a different set of factors contributing to females identifying with their mother. While girls may view the lack of a penis (classically referred to as "penis envy") as something that devalues females, in truth it is not the actual lack of a penis that is important but rather what it represents in many societies and cultures. Specifically, it is more appropriate to think of penis envy as a culturally inspired symbol for the discriminatory and prejudicial beliefs and practices directed toward women in general.

It should be pointed out that one critical power possessed by females that is not shared by males is the potential to create through giving birth. This dormant ability in the young female can be a powerful factor contributing to her identity formation. This special creative ability is often reinforced during the early years of a female's life through play, as when a girl plays with and cares for a doll.

Similar to his beliefs about the male child, Freud believed female children were interested in gaining the attention of the opposite-sex parent. The primary way this can be accomplished in most families is for the female to enhance her feminine behaviors so she becomes, in the eyes of her father, "Daddy's special little girl." In addition, the female child unconsciously begins to realize that it is unrealistic to assume she can replace the mother (Mother is capable of having children, the child is not) to obtain all of father's attention, but by identifying with the mother (who is the recognized love object of the father) will garner her more attention from the father than not identifying with the mother. Finally, because the mother is perceived as less of a threatening figure than the father, there is always the potential that the mother–daughter conflict will not be completely resolved at this stage and, as a result, periodically it may reemerge in various forms through the remainder of their lives, especially during the teen years.

Latency Stage. What follows the stage during which personality is formed is a period that begins around age 6 and is marked by children becoming focused on interacting with peers of their own gender and developing and mastering skills that will prove helpful in the future (skills that can be used to better sublimate various id drives). These interests continue until the next stage commences when sexual urges jump to the forefront again during the onset of puberty (which now takes place much earlier than it occurred during Freud's time). It is assumed that, during the latency stage, and until puberty starts, urges of a sexual nature are mostly but not entirely repressed or sublimated (Figure 3.2).

Genital Stage. This final stage is associated with the expression of a healthy adult personality. At this stage the person is assumed to have satisfactorily resolved the male or female Oedipal reaction, which means the person is capable of possessing and displaying a level of development that allows for mature sexuality and true intimacy. Such a person is not self-focused but rather maintains a reasonable balance between seeking from and providing sexual pleasure to one's partner. It should be noted that this description provides the ideal outcome. Most individuals are prevented from achieving this level of healthy adult personality by disruptive past events occurring at earlier stages. The greater these disruptions are, the greater is their impact and the more likely the person will display a neurotic character at this final stage.

The Therapeutic Process

Freud's approach to working with clients was much more flexible and open-ended than his writings about therapeutic procedures suggest. Freud became well aware of how his theory and approach to therapy could be modified by others and even significantly altered in ways he thought incongruent with his hard-earned discoveries and insights into human nature. Even leaders in the psychoanalytic movement, most notably Carl Jung and Alfred Adler, left to create their own theoretically based treatments. These departures were not always amicable. Freud (1914/1959) wrote the following about Alfred Adler's theory: "It is actually nothing else but psycho-analytic knowledge, which the author extracted from all the sources open to him during ten years of work in common and has now labelled as his own by changing the terminology of it" (p. 342). In responding to such allegations, Adler (1956) indicated it was true that he had learned a considerable amount from his association with the psychoanalytic movement, but Adler clarified his meaning by stating "I profited from his [Freud's] mistakes" (p. 358).

This exchange between Freud and Adler, and the comments of some historians, may generate a belief that Freud was dogmatic—an arrogant theorist who provided no room for others to question or contribute—but such a belief would be incorrect. Having traveled a long and arduous road, often alone in the early years, to give birth to a theory that was vehemently rejected by the professional establishment when first proposed, Freud was sensitive to any situation in which someone claimed allegiance to psychoanalysis while misrepresenting key concepts of the theory. Eventual acceptance of his work, coupled with the rapid growth of psychoanalysis in the early 1900s as a means to treat mental disorders, prompted Freud to provide an outline of therapeutic practice that was precise and offered a standard to follow. Freud felt to do otherwise would inadvertently invite others to confound with errors the treatment approach (and theory) it took him years to develop.

Illustration of Partial Repression or Sublimation (Drawn by a Pubescent Male, Age 11)

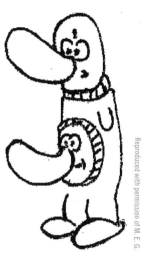

Reproduced with permission of M. E. G.

Assessment

Freud adopted a certain frame of mind while listening to the client, which he described in the following manner: The technique . . . is a very simple one. It disclaims the use of any special aids, even of note taking, . . . and simply consists in making no effort to concentrate the attention on anything in particular, and in maintaining in regard to all that one hears the same measure of calm, quite attentiveness—of 'evenly-hovering attention' "(as cited in Ellman, 1991, p.154)". Giovacchini (1977) later described Freud's approach as a "nondirective attitude" that excluded any sort of systematic gathering of personal history.

For Freud, initial sessions represented a form of trial analysis—a period of time to ascertain whether individuals possessed sufficient ego strength to adapt to situations, call upon personal resources, acquire needed stability from a sound identity, and initiate efficacious action when required. Unsuitable candidates for therapy possessed inadequate ego strength as evidenced by poor emotional control, an overly defensive posture, a wavering type of personal identity that is poorly suited to serve as a stabilizing anchor during difficult times, unrealistic career and/or life expectations, and ongoing difficulty mastering necessary life skills.

Over time, several psychoanalysts developed formal assessment tools or developed specific types of questions to gauge a potential client's ego strength. For example, Bellak's (1989) *Ego Function Assessment* proved to be a reliable and valid measure of ego functions. Akhtar (1995) suggested using verbal probes intended to elicit descriptions of important others such as parents, siblings, schoolmates, teachers, supervisors, and intimate others. The following descriptions probably indicate a weakened, diminished, or damaged ego structure, which suggests the person may be a poor candidate for psychoanalytic treatment.

1. The potential client focuses exclusively on personal feelings associated with the other person who is typically described in one-dimensional terms.

   - Therapist's probe: "Please describe your mother."
   - Response to probe: "I hate her. I was treated badly for years. I could smell the regret she encased me in from the moment I woke up until I fell asleep at night."

2. The potential client provides a distorted account of the other's actions that are frequently described in emotionally incongruent terms.

   - Response to probe: "She never displayed any interest in what I was doing or who my friends were. She was always uncaring and very distant, but I have to say she was always a good caring wife and very loving toward other family members."

3. The potential client believes the other person's motives are inevitably tied back to him or her. In addition, the person possesses a poor ability to deconstruct and then reconstruct the mistaken perception into a more accurate depiction of motives.

   - Response to probe: "Just to avoid having to speak to me, my mother would donate huge amounts of her time to help out at church." [In truth, the mother donated a reasonable amount of time to her family's church and found the experience to be very uplifting.]

Goals

The general aim of Freudian therapy is to focus on what plagues the client at an unconscious level and make it consciously meaningful. One expected outcome is that, in the process of bringing into awareness hidden material relevant to the client's problem, various ego functions will be strengthened. Thus, the enhancement of the client's cognitive abilities, especially those abilities required to effectively find a solution for future challenges confronting the client, is a major goal. In addition to these cognitive gains, the client can expect to develop a higher level of frustration tolerance, enabling that client to interact with difficult others more appropriately. Finally, clients should expect that the magnitude of personality or character change to occur is dependent on factors such as the degree the client is consciously motivated to change and the overall length of time spent in therapy, because the length of therapy correlates positively with the depth of unconscious exploration accomplished by the client.

Therapist's Role

The perception that the psychoanalytic therapist hides behind a persona that exudes a stoic kind of distance is inaccurate. The therapist can be expected to avoid making judgments concerning the client's expressed emotions or behaviors and to stay within established therapeutic boundaries while communicating warmth and interest toward the client. The therapist will likely share little, if any, personal information with the client for an important reason. Parsimonious self-disclosure allows the therapist to create a blank screen personality. Because the therapist's expressed personality is void of much content, the client will begin to fill in the empty space with projections tied to past and present events. Maintaining a blank facade facilitates the occurrence of transference reactions. Finally, the therapist is expected to be generally comfortable with enacting the role of an expert. Embracing such a role during therapist–client interactions is an accurate portrayal of the therapist's level of special training, clinical experience, and knowledge of psychoanalytic theory and procedures. Even more important, when the therapist genuinely accepts the role of the expert in the relationship, it causes the client's superego to automatically project a certain degree of authority onto the therapist. That authority, if used skillfully and ethically by the therapist, will facilitate progress in the early stages of therapy and, later, helps foster transference reactions. However, it is important for the therapist to remember that near the end of successful therapy, when ego functions have strengthened significantly and certain id influences have weakened, the therapist must wean the client from any residual dependency on the therapist that lingers from early superego projections. One characteristic of mental health is the balance of mature dependence on and independence from others, and this includes both the client and the therapist.

Client's Role

In the beginning, the therapist will review with the client what psychoanalysis is and, moreover, what it is not. The therapist will also discuss what the client can expect to happen if success is achieved, such as incorporating positive changes into the client's life, as well as replacing various defense mechanisms with effective methods to confront interpersonal conflict and anxiety. The client is told of the importance of the fundamental rule (i.e., free association) and that if it is performed properly, the result is a steady stream of seemingly unconnected ideas, feelings, and sensations, but that in truth this steady outpouring of words provides the therapist with invaluable raw material to search for and find unconscious nuggets from the past.

The meaning and implications of structured therapy sessions is also covered. The client is expected to follow certain ground rules, such as arriving to sessions on time and ending the sessions on time. Incidents of violating the agreed-upon structure are viewed as having special psychological implications, which will be subsequently explored by the therapist. The structure imposed on therapy is an important contributor to the overall therapeutic endeavor and the ultimate success of therapy because structure provides a healthy consistency and interpersonal balance that clients may lack in their current life (or rarely experienced earlier in life).

Finally, it is essential to remember that while the therapist is working to expose and weaken certain unconscious factors, the therapist is also focused on replacing faulty ego defenses with more mature and effective ways of handling problems. During the transition process, the client may be susceptible to poor judgment involving decisions of a personal nature, such as making a proposal of marriage or purchasing a first house. Because unconscious forces stirred up in therapy have not been fully explored, confronted, or put to rest, it is sensible from a therapeutic standpoint to assume any important decision suddenly being contemplated by a client deserves careful consideration by the therapist. It is for this reason that therapists may require the client to discuss any major decision being considered during the course of treatment. The purpose of such a discussion is to prevent the client from making an id-driven decision that the client later regrets.

Techniques and Strategies

The Talking Cure: Free Association. A common technique used in various forms is free association, which seems easy to carry out but typically proves more difficult than initially believed by clients. For example, outside of sharing an insight with the therapist or discussing a certain issue or other matter with the therapist, Freud expected the client to maintain a state of free association. This concept means that the client must produce an ongoing flow of words unfiltered by the ego and uncensored by the superego (a process whose level of difficulty is tied directly to a client's level of resistance toward "looking within"). Rather than aiming to have a client provide a well thought out depiction of early experiences, the client is instructed to simply talk without consideration of the typical restraints imposed upon speaking. The client must not to be concerned with occurrences of grammatical errors, slang, cursing, illogical statements, mispronounced words, clichés, or any other departure from what commonly governs speaking. Far from leading the therapist away from the cause for the client's affliction, the seemingly nonsensical gibberish spoken actually provides an abundance of information that eventually leads the therapist to key causal factors. Paradoxically, given the opportunity, many clients will speak in a manner that serves to keep certain aspects of their problem hidden, but in the topsy-turvy atmosphere of the therapy room where speaking is turned on its head, the resulting flow of words allows the therapist to glimpse, and over time to clearly see, what lies below the surface of consciousness.

Dreams. Freud (1900/1953) considered dreams to be the royal road to the unconscious because he believed repression is less effective during sleep as is the ego's ability to maintain a distinct border between awareness and unconscious impulses, desires, and urges. Freud further explained that the dream story we recall upon awakening is a result of secondary revision. Once awake, the ego again assumes control and automatically alters the dream when we try to recall it. The ego works to "make sense" of the bizarre sequence created by filling in gaps and creating a storyline to hold the various parts of the dream together. The ego is activated to reconfigure what was created while dreaming for the purpose of better disguising, and not clarifying, the contents of the dream. This disguising helps to prevent awareness of the dream's actual meaning.

Even though the ego is not fully functioning while we sleep, it can still rely upon a process termed *dream work*, whose purpose is to obscure the id's wish fulfilling purpose (i.e., if the id is denied satisfaction in reality, it will seek satisfaction through the fantasy world of dreams). On those occasions when dream work starts to fail and unconscious material is on the verge of entering awareness, the person's ego is activated to awaken the person. The person often refers to such episodes as "having a nightmare." Two other terms introduced by Freud were *latent meaning* (the true meaning of the dream) and *manifest meaning* (the fragmented images and verbal elements that make up the dream), with the latter being provided via the dream work process.

According to Freud, dreams can frequently be tied back to some object, situation, or person encountered during the day (termed *day residue*). Day residue is stored during the day and retrieved from memory that night. For example, a person may dream of someone met for the first time because of a singular characteristic or feature associated with an important other. The portions of day residue selected to become part of a dream are those that have an unconscious link to some past occurrence in the client's life. According to Freud, dream work relies upon certain tools to disguise the true meaning of a dream: displacement, condensation or overdetermination, and symbols. An example of *displacement* is when a person encountered that day is used to represent a person from the dreamer's past. An example of *condensation* or *overdetermination* is when a person in a dream is used to represent two or more persons from the dreamer's past. This helps to explain why a single person in a dream might change hair color, clothes, or even age several times during the course of the dream. Finally, Freud recognized *individual symbols* (frequently tied to aspects of the dreamer's culture) that require the use of free association to ferret out their meaning and *universal symbols*, which appear to have a general meaning shared by many people across cultures. The following is a list of examples of universal symbols.

- Birth—pond, lake, water, certain hidden objects (e.g., wrapped gift)
- Breast—any round fruit
- Children—small animals, small creatures, toy representing an animal or person
- Death—going on a long trip, skeleton
- Erection—finger pointing, anything that can be enlarged or expanded (e.g., an umbrella)

- Female genitalia—cave, jar, box, flower, bag, purse, mouth
- Male genitalia—elongated vegetables, tree, pole, walking stick, sword, serpent, ax with a long handle, sausage-shaped food, suit tie
- Male sexual symbol—wild animal (bear, wolf), mythical creatures (e.g., were-wolf, vampire, centaur)
- Parent—king, queen, enforcer of laws, boss, supervisor, chief, overseer, teacher
- Sexual intercourse—something (e.g., train) or someone going into a tunnel or cave, riding a horse, climbing (e.g., going up steps or rungs of a ladder)

Finally, it should be kept in mind that certain universal symbols have a primordial quality that makes them supra-universal in nature, such as water representing birth, whereas other symbols considered universal are less representative of the overall human experience. For example, in western cultures it is the color black that symbolizes death whereas in India it is just as likely that death is symbolized by the color white.

Evidence suggests that many practitioners of psychoanalysis find dream interpretation to be much more difficult to master and utilize than implied by Freud's description of the process. Furthermore, the particular psychoanalytic approach relied upon obviously alters the meaning garnered from the same dream. For example, Mitchell (1988) has discussed how the same dream will be analyzed differently by therapists depending on their theoretical orientation. This can be illustrated by using a classic drive perspective, ego psychology, object relations, and self-psychology approach to psychodynamic dream interpretation. Let's assume that an adult female client reports the following dream: "I had a vivid dream last night. In my dream, a person—a male whose face kept changing during the dream—stole a special box of mine in which I kept things that I felt were part of me. The box contained drawing materials and a photograph of me as a child with a red heart drawn on it. I woke up, once the theft occurred in my dream, with a terrible sense of having lost something."

Adopting a *drive* perspective, the dream seems to reveal a sexual encounter, possibly the loss of the person's virginity, since boxes or containers are universal symbols representing the womb that, in turn, represents one aspect of a woman's creative potential. (Following up with having the person free associate to the dream's elements will clarify the possible meaning of individualized symbols and check the therapist's reliance on what appears to be a universal symbol.) An *ego* interpretation might reveal that the dreamer's early curiosity and creative urges were "boxed up" and never allowed to fully develop because the parents nurtured only certain aspects of achievement, causing the client's raw creative ability to hibernate. The stolen box itself and the changing figure, from an *object relations* perspective, may be interpreted to mean the dreamer perceives that close relationships are ultimately untrustworthy. By allowing herself to become close to a male, she makes herself vulnerable to having the male hurt her by taking or using for himself what she cherishes or creates. This perspective, formed very early in life by this client, has resulted in the client's inability to see males as complex beings with a wide range of motives. Finally, from the *self-psychology* perspective, the dream may be symbolic of a self-love that was hindered from fully developing into an ability to create an empathic adult-to-adult love relationship because of certain innate potentialities not being accepted by her parents. Her parents only "reflected" back qualities consistent with their image of what comprised "a pretty little girl," not qualities associated with being a mature, independent woman.

Interpretation. Delivering full-blown interpretations are typically the exception rather than the rule. The general aim of interpretations is not to deliver a ready-made insight to the client; rather the point of interpretation is to enable the client to focus on certain material revealed during the process of therapy and to have the client consider the implications of some remark made (or even what a prolonged silence might represent). The best interpretations are expressed in ways that are slightly ahead of where the client is in his or her understanding of how various factors contribute to personal problems.

The quality of, and responsibility for, rendering interpretations will change over the course of therapy. For instance, near the end of successful therapy, interpretations are likely to possess a less definitive hypothetical quality and often can be more accurately described as a means to reinforce insights already achieved by the client. In addition, one sign of significant movement toward health is that the client begins to offer accurate interpretations for his or her own actions.

Overcoming Resistance. Resistance is best thought of as representing any behavioral or cognitive pattern employed to prevent the unfettered expression of unconscious components that contribute to the reason the client entered therapy. The concept of resistance implies that the client is inclined to hold back from the therapist certain thoughts, images, feelings, sensations, abilities, desires, fantasies, remembered actions, and so forth, to block progress. Resistance is a form of unconscious obstruction that negatively impacts on the recovery of important unconscious aspects of the client's current life difficulties. Overcoming instances of resistance through persistent effort allows for a key element of therapy, the *transference reaction*, to fully arise. It is the transference reaction that provides the therapist with what is needed to bring about significant change in the neurotic's personality or character.

Transference Reactions—The Dance Between Client and Therapist. The importance of the relationship between the therapist and the client was recognized very early by Freud, primarily through his discovery of the phenomenon of transference (Freud, 1905/1953a; 1912/1958; 1915/1958). The transference of feelings from the client's childhood onto the therapist provides a powerful avenue for the exploration of the origins of the client's current difficulties. Transference reactions result in the client freely projecting hidden fears and wishes as well as relationship issues from previous developmental stages.

Freud also considered the reverse of this process, that is, for the analyst to project any of his or her feelings onto the client (i.e., *countertransference*). When countertransference occurred, Freud believed it had to be corrected immediately; otherwise, therapy would be adversely affected.

Ginter and Bonney (1993a, 1993b) have argued there is evidence to suggest Freud failed to completely recognize certain aspects of the therapeutic potential of unconscious communication. Further theoretical developments made by Klein and others led to a change in how transference and countertransference were viewed and confronted in therapy.

Klein (1946) coined the term *projective identification* and defined it as "a combination of splitting off parts of the self and projecting them onto another person" (p. 108). It was as if portions of the self—that is, feelings and/or images—that were associated with anxiety were psychologically cut from one's mind and placed elsewhere. Klein (1957) later expanded the concept to include "the feeling of identification with other people, because one has attributed qualities or attitudes of one's own to them" (p. 311). As a result of this elaboration, the processes of identification and projection began to represent different sides of the same psychological coin.

Klein's expansion of the concept was significant because it allowed theorists to broaden the concept to include the reactions of the person who is the recipient of these projections (St. Clair, 1986); that is, the recipient can also "identify" with what has been projected. Thus, what starts as an intrapsychic event ends with being an interpersonal event that psychologically involves both individuals (Kernberg, 1984; Scharff, 1989). Simply stated, projective identification occurs when one person, via primarily unconscious processes, elicits a certain behavior, thought, and/or feeling in someone else. That person unknowingly accepts and responds to the projection. This codetermination of behaviors was recognized by Wachtel (1977):

> The signals we emit to other people constitute a powerful force field. The shy person does many (sometimes almost invisible) things to make it difficult for another person to stay open to him very long. Even a well-intentioned person is likely . . . to help confirm his views that others aren't really very interested. (p. 52)

Zinner and Shapiro (1989) argued that there are many events discussed in the professional literature that represent instances of projective identification: scapegoating, irrational role assignments, symbiotic relationships, family projection processes, and so forth. According to these authors, such labels depict events that have common features that denote the occurrence of projective-identification:

- The subject perceives the object as if the object contained elements of the subject's personality.
- The subject can evoke behaviors or feelings in the objects that conform to the subject's perceptions.
- The subject can experience vicariously the activity and feelings of the object.
- The participants in close relationships are often in collusion with one another to sustain mutual projections—that is, to support one another's defensive operations and to provide experiences through which the other can participate vicariously. (p. 114)

Instances of projective identification sometimes define the most significant content of interactions. For example, many dysfunctional parent–child relationships rest on a foundation of projective identification. The child who becomes the family scapegoat may be the recipient of "bad" projections. Unacceptable parts of the self are made to "disappear" from the parent's psyche and are "recognized only as qualities of the child." Zinner and Shapiro (1989) suggested that psychological pain can be externalized by a parent and manifested in the scapegoated child.

The child's psychological acceptance of the projected element (e.g., "stupidity") can even be manifested in the child's own contribution to the projected role (e.g., "I am stupid and deserve to be punished"). The child's psychological acceptance of the projected role allows the parent to more easily transfer bad elements *onto* and *into* the child. This process, once entrenched, may partly account for the abused child's love for the abusive parent, who may be viewed as correct in treating the child harshly because the parent seems to lack the bad quality the child possesses. In extreme cases, the child can become the object of severe physical and psychological abuse. The pathological aim in cases of severe abuse is to destroy and not take back the projected elements ("You are a worthless child and I wish you were dead!").

According to Ginter and Bonney (1993b), a transference reaction induced by a projective identification process significantly differs from the transference reaction as conceptualized by Freud. By way of Freud's conceptualizations, one would assume a client simply projects his or her past emotional attachments to the therapist (counter-transference occurs when the therapist is the initiator of a projection). In classic psychoanalytic theory (drive theory), the recipient of the projection becomes a parental figure or another significant other from the past while the projection represents previous emotional attachments. In such a situation, skillful therapeutic interpretations made during a series of sessions will eventually alter the projecting member's behavior.

Ginter and Bonney (1993b) have argued that transference reactions resulting from a projective-identification process start as an intrapsychic event that has the potential to alter the behavior, thoughts, and perceptions of both the client initiating the process and the therapist. The recipient of this type of transference interaction will enact a special role dictated primarily by the initiator's unconscious projections.

Psychological boundaries between the person projecting and the recipient become amorphous and are distorted in such a dramatic and profound fashion that distinctions become blurred, boundaries collapse, and a special type of unity occurs. Such a manifestation of transference that represents a complex of mental, emotional, and social mechanisms was termed a *Mobius interaction* by Ginter and Bonney, although several terms have been applied to psychologically based events of this type (e.g., scapegoating). As the term *countertransference* now lacks exactness, and because the type of transference under discussion is analogous to a geometric shape called the Mobius strip (appearing to have two sides but actually having one, so that what is seen by one's own eyes as a boundary does not exist), Ginter and Bonney (1993a, 1993b) elected to use the term *Mobius interaction* to help differentiate among the types of transference reactions possible (Figure 3.3).

▼ FIGURE 3.3

Visual Depiction of the Classic Two-Sided Freudian Transference Reaction and the One-Sided Countertransference Reaction, i.e., Möbius Reaction

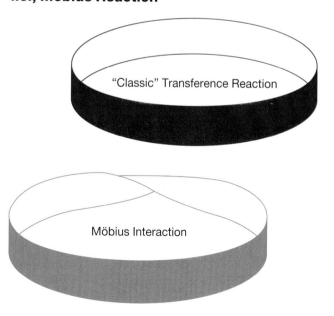

"Classic" Transference Reaction

Möbius Interaction

Compared to the classic type of transference reaction (and countertransference reaction) hypothesized by Freud (1912/1958), Ginter and Bonney (1993a) are careful to point out that the power of a Mobius interaction should not be underestimated. Prior to effective confrontation of the Mobius interaction itself, the therapist must isolate factors related to his or her own contributory role (Colson, 1985). Leary (1957) illustrated the level of difficulty involved in identifying one's own contribution to maintaining a client's dysfunctional behavior:

> The more extreme and rigid the person, the greater the person's interpersonal "pull"—that is, the stronger his or her ability to shape the relationship with others. The withdrawn catatonic, the irretrievable criminal, the compulsively flirtatious charmer can inevitably provoke the expected response from a better balanced "other." The flexible person can pull a greater variety of responses from others, depending on his or her conscious or unconscious motives at the moment. He can get others to like him, take care of him, obey him, lead him, envy him, and so on. The "sick" person has a narrow range of interpersonal tactics, but these are generally quite powerful in their effect. (p. 126)

Because the transference reaction labeled a Mobius interaction can be found to reside at the core of the psychoanalytic method, allowing the repressed dynamic relationship from the past to surface and play out again is critical. Using "both sides" of the transference reaction as suggested by Ginter and Bonney allows for the past traumatic relationship to be worked through, permitting the client to relive the event in a manner that allows for healthy resolution rather than a replication of the neurotic outcome that has come to dominate the client's life prior to entering therapy. Such resolution also sets the stage for the client to learn skills that he or she can apply in situations outside of therapy, an application of skills that will serve to reinforce the positive changes achieved in therapy.

Process of Change. Through the use of prescribed psychoanalytic techniques, the therapist provides an atmosphere of safety in which clients can explore the meaning of their symptoms, especially in light of their personal histories. Over time, the psychoanalytic process fosters significant and powerful insights into how a person's early family environment has led to current dysfunctional symptoms. Unlike the immature and often unpremeditated impulse-driven client who started therapy, the client has broken free of past psychological burdens and displays the type of ego-based thinking associated with mental health.

Beyond Freud

Group Therapy

A number of Freud's techniques and intervention strategies are used in psychoanalytic group therapy. Free association has been applied to group therapy by Wolf and Schwartz (1962) and was referred to as the *go-around technique*. Each member was instructed to look at other members and say, without filtering thoughts or emotions, the first thing that came to mind. Obviously, the technique was used in groups to provide greater access to each member's unconscious mind and thus repressed memories. In a similar fashion,

Foulkes (1964) used the term *free-floating discussion* or *free group association*. However, beyond such applications, it is essential to keep in mind that a particular group therapist's psychodynamic orientation will affect the therapist's use of well-established techniques.

In responding to the possible meaning of a dream reported by a member of group therapy, the therapist could focus attention only on the group member reporting the dream, but it could also be judged more appropriate by the therapist to relate the latent content of the dream to something occurring within the group as a whole. For example, something that may have prompted the dreamer to have this particular dream is the unconscious realization that others in the group do not appreciate the dreamer's genuinely "creative and insightful contributions." Whether the therapist should focus at any given time on an individual member, the group as a whole, or even himself or herself has generated considerable discussion. It can be argued that overreliance on any single type of therapeutic focus probably inhibits full use of the inherent advantages provided in group therapy.

Although group therapy can take on different formats and lengths of duration, there is an advantage to providing long-term ongoing group therapy, but it should be noted that a danger is posed. The group dynamic of this type of therapeutic approach introduces the possibility of group addiction, that is, "group analysis interminable" with resulting loss of independence and self-reliance and the subtle but eventual formation of a psychologically encapsulated group. This suggests there is an advantage to the open-group format where individuals leave when goals and objectives are met and new members are introduced.

Finally, it is also important to note that brief formats have been increasingly introduced and utilized in both individual and group psychoanalysis (Bauer & Kobos, 1987). For example, Sifneos (1987) used a type of confrontational-supportive approach and limited sessions to 12 to 15 meetings. Confrontation, clarification, and interpretation are directed toward a common theme (e.g., specific Oedipal issues) rather than a wide range of issues. Finally, such an approach, when applied to group therapy, would seem to lend itself better to groups that are more homogenous than heterogeneous simply because of the narrow focus.

Deviations From Freudian Theory and Therapy

Early associates of Freud, such as Alfred Adler, Carl Jung, and Otto Rank developed divergent theories leading to new types of therapies. Other theorists, more inspired by Freud's ideas than opposed to them, brought attention to themes not fully developed by Freud. Erich Fromm and Karen Homey drew attention to both cultural and interpersonal factors comprising human existence. The latter theme, interpersonal factors, has come to play a central role in contemporary psychoanalytic formulations and is not necessarily seen today as representing a significant departure from Freudian theory. Rather, this theme is seen as part of the logical evolution of Freud's intrapsychic theory (Alonso & Rutan, 1984; Ginter & Bonney, 1993a, 1993b).

Anna Freud, Erik Erikson, and Heinz Hartmann were able to combine earlier psychoanalytic notions such as the id with an ever-expanding role for the ego. "Conflict-free" ego functions that were adaptive in nature were discussed. The ego's defense measures were eventually seen not only as maladaptive attempts to cope with reality but also as a means of dealing with everyday events while remaining "more within the limits of the normal" rather than the pathological (A. Freud, 1937/1966, p. 50). Erikson deserves special recognition for extending Freud's view of human development to cover the entire life span of humans. Erikson's (1950a) theory of human development had universal appeal to both psychoanalytic and nonpsychoanalytic thinkers.

Finally, Carl Jung is noteworthy for introducing a number of interesting concepts and changes to therapy. For example, Jung introduced a logical extension of free association when he developed a word association test in which the client was instructed to respond to a list of 100 words. Essentially, the client was to report his or her first reaction to a given word on the list. Jung's word association tests often revealed important dimensions of the client's personality. Jung is also recognized for introducing the concept known as *synchronicity*, which is an event that occurs and has a special meaning in relation to another event, but neither has a direct causal link to the other. Jung believed that paying attention to such occurrences during therapy had the potential to positively influence the psychological growth of both the client and the therapist.

Table 3.3 gives additional information pertaining to Jung's contributions.

Contemporary Investigations:
Moving Beyond Freud's Methodology

In recent years, researchers have started to move beyond earlier used methods of gathering support for psychoanalysis, venturing into and making significant strides in conceptual research, outcome research, process research, and developmental research (Person, Cooper, & Gabbard, 2005). For example, Greenspan and Shanker (2005) report that research efforts have provided a means to construct a developmental framework for depth psychology. According to Greenspan and Shanker, the following empirically based stages (representing the child's sequential mental development) have been isolated and provide clear direction for further study:

- Perceive, attend and regulate, and move.
- Form relationships and develop the capacity for sustained intimacy.
- Learn to interact, read social/emotional cues, and express a wide range of emotions.
- Form a sense of self that involves many different emotional feelings, expressions, and interaction patterns.
- Construct a sense of self that integrates different emotional polarities (e.g., love and hate).
- Regulate mood, behavior, and impulses, and engage in ongoing social coregulation.
- Create internal representations of a sense of self, feelings, and wishes, as well as impersonal ideas.
- Categorize internal representations in terms of reality versus fantasy (as a basis for reality testing), sense of self and others (self and object representations), different wishes and feelings, modifications of wishes and feelings (defenses and coping capacities), and use of these for judgment, peer relationships, and a range of higher level self-observing and reflective capacities. (Greenspan & Shanker, 2005, p. 339)

The Red Book

Source: The original uploader was Ekabhishek at English Wikipedia - http://jezebel.com/5361680/ does-carl-jung-still-matter, Public Domain, https://commons .wikimedia.org/w/index .php?curid=16405551.

Carl Gustav Jung (1875–1961). By August 1914, Carl Jung had curtailed all correspondence with Freud, withdrew as president of the International Psychoanalytic Association and later as a member, and resigned his teaching position at the University of Zurich. These changes were followed by a concerted focus on practicing therapy; conducting theoretically inspired research; training future therapists; and studying areas such as mythologies and ritualistic ceremonies, cultural approaches to death, shamanistic practices, and the ways in which neurotics and psychotics see and interact with their environments. In Jung's autobiography *Memories, Dreams, Reflections*, he mentioned that the primary inspiration for much of his theory and therapy practice could be traced to an unpublished manuscript that Jung commonly referred to as the *Red Book*. The *Red Book* records a self-experiment that was conducted by Jung and lasted from 1913 to 1930, which was a period of time during which he relied upon a special technique to access the deepest level of his psyche, which later he referred to as *active imagination*. The *Red Book* was postumously published in 2009 and provides a detailed record of Jung's looking deep into his mind's eye where he encountered several principal entities—an elderly man of wisdom, a young woman figure, and a large black snake. In recording these episodes, Jung used calligraphy and numerous drawings to capture the fantastic images that he was confronted with during his inner exploration, for example, a multi-legged crocodile creature, Christ on the cross, mystical trees, winged figures, numerous mandalas, and vividly colored mosaics that capture a dazzling array of crystalline images.

According to Corbett (2009), scholars have used a range of descriptors to summarize what they believe the book represents, descriptors such as "a creative illness, a descent into the underworld, a bout with insanity, a narcissistic self-deification, a transcendence, a midlife breakdown and an inner disturbance mirroring the upheaval of World War I" (n. p.). Even though Jung considered the work to be a magnum opus, it was never published during his lifetime because of his belief that the *Red Book* could generate a strong negative reaction, as suggested when he wrote, "to the superficial observer, the work would seem like madness" (Jung, 2009, p. 215). But to dismiss this particular work because Jung might have descended into a period of mental illness would be tantamount to asserting that all of Vincent van Gogh's paintings are of no intrinsic value because his mental illness affected what he painted. The question of Jung's mental condition during the *Red Book*'s creation is irrelevant since we know that it served as a fountainhead from which Jung repeatedly pulled inspiration over his lifetime to build his theory.

One concept that firmly emerged from Jung's sequence of imaginative episodes of inner exploration was how he conceptualized the archetype. Jung (1964) addressed the fact that the concept was often misunderstood when he wrote, "My views about the [archetypes] have been constantly criticized by people who lack a sufficient knowledge of the psychology of dreams and of mythology. The term 'archetype' is often misunderstood as meaning certain definite mythological images or motifs. But these are nothing more than conscious representations; it would be absurd to assume that such variable representations could be inherited. The archetype is a tendency to form such representations of a motif—representations that can vary a great deal in detail without losing their basic pattern" (p. 67). For example, the archetype generally described as the Wise Old Man may appear in a dream as Merlin the wizard of Arthurian legend. During his professional career, Jung wrote about the possible embedded themes of several universal archetypes (e.g., Divine Child, Father, Hero, Mother, Trickster) and how these themes could be used to uncover important truths that, if accepted by the client, offered an avenue for growth and achievement of the ultimate Jungian goal of individuation, which, in other words, is the psychological ideal that represents an integrated and balanced self.

Appropriate Client Populations

Considering the amount of opposition Freud's approach has received for decades, why does it persist as a form of treatment? Although a scholarly review of Freud's work will reveal flaws, this is outweighed by those aspects of his work that can be empirically shown to contribute to the therapy's effectiveness. A review of the historical events surrounding Freud's efforts would support his use of a careful, methodical approach, but this approach also restricted him to a fairly narrow range of disorders (essentially hysteria and anxiety neurosis). Interestingly, a widely held false assumption is that Freud believed psychoanalysis could never be adapted for use with other conditions such as schizophrenia. In fact, it was during a lecture in 1904 that Freud (1905/1953a) stated,

Psychosis, states of confusion and deeply rooted . . . depression are . . . not suitable for psychoanalysis; as least not for the method as it has been practiced up to the present. I do not regard it as . . . impossible that by suitable changes in the method we may succeed in advancing it beyond these hindrances—and so be able to initiate a psychotherapy of the psychoses. (p. 258)

Freud's comments proved prophetic. Only a few years after Freud's lecture, William A. White (see D'Amore & Eckburg, 1976) and Edward Kempf (1919) modified psychoanalysis to use it to treat schizophrenia. Today psychodynamic therapy is best thought of as being applicable to a wide range of client concerns and disorders. In addition, contemporary psychoanalytic researchers such as Jonathan Shedler (2010) are making a concerted effort to empirically study the effectiveness of psychoanalytic-based treatments and to disperse their findings in ways to reach a spectrum of professionals.

Multiculturalism and Social Justice

Multiculturalism

Although some psychoanalytic theorists maintained a multicultural perspective in their writings, for example, Erikson (1950b), who wrote about childhood in two American Indian tribes, multiculturalism as a primary consideration lagged somewhat behind other psychoanalytic interests. (The same is historically true of other major therapeutic approaches.) Obviously, clients may leave therapy if certain cultural issues are avoided, and certainly if their cultural background is frequently misinterpreted, especially if there are negative connotations attached to these misinterpretations. "[Although] this is not to suggest that a successful therapeutic relationship can only be achieved with someone of similar ethnic or cultural background or that minority patients can only be treated by therapist of the same minority group," it does suggest that it is important to be culturally sensitive (Serrano & Ruiz, 1991, p. 325).

Robinson and Ginter (1999) called attention to the profound effects of racism and its permeation of U.S. society. In reviewing the role that culture and ethnicity play in working with clients, Robinson (1999) concluded that a guiding principle is that therapists "must avoid the attribution of certain occupations, attitudes, and experiences to their clients due to the visibility of their race, gender, and other identities. Making judgments about people's humanity and its quality due to established criteria is to rely on tired but extremely powerful discourses steeped in oppression" (p. 77).

In current psychoanalytic circles, just as in therapy in general, greater attention is being devoted to how cultural factors play a role in therapy. Multicultural awareness and competencies better enable therapists to handle the challenging interplay of culture, ethnicity, and the transference reaction. Therapists should expect to find that cultural or ethnic factors, in at least some cases, serve as a key or core component of a client's transference reactions (Comas-Diaz & Minrath, 1985; Tang & Gardner, 1999). Such transference reactions can only be therapeutically filtered and distilled via the psychoanalytic therapy process if they are first recognized for what they are and not mistaken for something else. As pointed out by Brantley (1983), cultural sensitivity allows the therapist to consider the significance of cultural and ethnic aspects of a client as well as to bring to the forefront his or her own thoughts and behaviors related to racism (i.e., countertransference).

Furthermore, psychoanalysis has significantly benefited whenever therapists and researchers have applied its approach while relying upon their own unique cultural perspective. For example, Eizirik and de Armesto (2005) provide a synopsis of psychoanalysis's successful growth in recent years throughout Latin America. This movement essentially began in Argentina, has displayed rapid growth in Brazil in recent years, and has spread to Mexico, Venezuela, Uruguay, Chile, Peru, and Colombia. Contributions are being made to both theory and practice in each of these locations, especially Argentina, where recent theoretical and practice developments have focused on the following:

> Theory of ideals, the ego ideal, the work on the negative, the transgenerational, the not-representable, narcissism, the metapsychological understanding of psychoses, and the pathologies of impulsiveness. They cast a different light with which to see the previous concepts. (Eizirik & de Armesto, 2005, p. 440)

Several psychoanalysts have made important contributions that embody a Latin American perspective, such as Angel Garma (e.g., therapy process, psychosomatic conditions, and dreams), Heinrich Racker (e.g., countertransference's manifestations and as an "instrument" that can be used to understand a client's mind), David Liberman (e.g., communication styles between the client and therapist), Ignacio Matte Blanco (differential forms of logic found between unconscious and conscious functions), and Willy and Madeleine Baranger (the special dynamic field—bipersonal unconscious fantasy environment established during each analysis).

Social Justice

Without any doubt Freud can be described as an independent thinker who was unyielding to prejudice, straightforward in his presentations of psychoanalytic concepts, and rebellious toward any authority, control, or tradition whose inherent goal was to maintain the status quo. These are the traits one would expect to find in a person who values social justice. Far from being politically unaware or socially disengaged as some critics accused, Freud exhibited an attitude of progressive social responsibility that positively affected the lives of many disfranchised inhabitants of Vienna and elsewhere.

An early misguided criticism of psychoanalysis—fueled in part by anti-Semitic beliefs about Jews and money—was the assertion that psychoanalysis was only available to members of the upper and wealthy classes because lower socioeconomic classes lacked the financial resources and the amount of spare time needed to pursue this form of treatment. In truth, Freud held a very egalitarian view toward psychoanalysis in terms of whom he trained to use it and for whom it should be made available as a treatment. In fact, many of the prominent psychoanalytic thinkers of Freud's time, including Helene Deutsch, Erik Erikson, Erich Fromm, and Wilhelm Reich, believed that mental health care should be universally available. Freud captured the essence of this shared belief when he stated that "the poor man should have just as much right to assistance for his mind as he now has to life-saving help offered by surgery" (Danto, 2005, p. 17). Freud believed so strongly in the idea of free clinics that he addressed the issue at the Fifth International Psychoanalytic

Congress held in 1918. As a result of the combined effort of Freud and others, by 1938 there were a total of ten psychoanalytic free clinics operating across seven countries.

Freud personally helped to fund the *Ambulatorium* (free clinic founded in Vienna) and was known to have sent letters to others requesting support for these clinics. According to evidence uncovered (Columbia University Press, 2005), these clinics provided indiscriminate, culturally sensitive assistance for a wide array of clients, including "students, artists, craftsmen, laborers, factory workers, office clerks, unemployed people, farmers, domestic servants, and public school teachers" (p. 1). The therapist staffing these clinics essentially had two goals in mind: (1) to provide effective treatment for every individual seeking help and (2) to eventually achieve a critical mass of cured clients whose positive effect would inevitably permeate the whole of society (Danto, 2005). Although this second transformational goal fell short of being fulfilled, it is clear many of those seeking help at the clinics benefited, as did the psychoanalytic profession itself. In this later instance, the therapeutic work conducted at these clinics led to psychoanalysts developing new forms of treatments, such as task-centered and short-term formats and new ways to conceptualize the nature of psychosis, human sexuality, and childhood depression.

Finally, although the spread of Nazism through Europe proved to be a serious setback for this phase of the psychoanalytic movement, Nazi tactics ultimately failed to entirely quench the movement's pursuit of social justice. In addition, one can find contemporary manifestations of social justice in psychoanalysis. Two examples are the organization Psychoanalysts for Peace and Justice, which was established in 2003 by Stephen Soldz for the purpose of shedding light on the Iraq war and other social issues, and the online journal *Human Relations, Authority, and Justice: Experiences and Critiques,* founded by Robert M. Young of the United Kingdom and Toma Tomov of Bulgaria. The journal promotes the application of psychoanalytic principles to various cultural, institutional, and political processes to better understand the underlying dynamics of these areas.

Limitations and Criticisms of Psychoanalysis

Kubie (1953) stated the following in relation to psychoanalytic theory and practice:

> In general, they [the limitations] can be summarized by saying that the basic design of the process of analysis has essential scientific validity, but that the difficulties of recording and reproducing primary observations, the consequent difficulty in deriving the basic conceptual structure, the difficulties in examining with equal ease the circular relationship from unconscious to conscious and from conscious to unconscious, the difficulties in appraising quantitatively the multiplicity of variables, and finally the difficulty of estimating those things which increase and those which decrease the precision of its hypotheses and the validity of its predictions are among the basic scientific problems which remain to be solved. (pp. 143–144)

In spite of these challenges, the scientific validity of psychoanalysis has been tested. Fisher and Greenberg (1977) analyzed the findings of nearly 2,000 reports across an array of disciplines. They abstracted data based only on procedures that could be replicated, thus excluding case study data. They found support for certain personality types, such as oral and anal; tension reduction due to dreaming; and aspects of the Oedipal reaction as it pertained to males. Specifically, in relation to groups, researchers have studied splitting, self-representations, boundary phenomena, and countertransference (Greene, Rosenkrantz, & Muth, 1985, 1986); effects of early child–caregiver interactions on subsequent adult behavior (Kilmann et al., 1999); treatment approaches with introjection clients (Blatt, 1992); transference reactions (Burrows, 1981a, 1981b; Chance, 1952; Klein, 1977); and group-as-a-whole transference (MacKenzie, 2001; MacKenzie, Dies, Coché, Rutan, & Stone, 1987). Again, support was found for psychoanalytic concepts.

Contemporary Research Support

The literature on the efficacy and effectiveness of psychoanalytic-based treatment (specifically, results of meta-analysis), however, strongly indicates that this approach is effective and efficacious for a wide range of psychological disorders. Abbass, Hancock, Henderson, and Kisely (2006), for example, examined 12 studies that included 23 random-control trials. They found that patients who were exposed to psychodynamic treatment showed significant improvement in general symptoms. They also discovered that the improvement *effect size* (see note at paragraph's end) was .97 at posttreatment and 1.51 at follow-up. Similarly, de Maat et al. (2013) completed a meta-analysis of 13 pre/post cohort studies and one randomized controlled trial and found, across all measures, an initial pre/post treatment effect size of 1.27 and a follow-up effect size of 1.46 for those who had received psychoanalysis. These results suggest that the psychodynamic approach is effective and that its effect lasts beyond the completion of therapy. Messer and Abbass (2010) also conducted a meta-analysis investigation comparing seven studies on the treatment outcome of psychodynamic therapy for general client symptoms. A within-group effect size of .91 was found attesting to the effectiveness of the approach. (Note. *Effect size* has also been referred to by the name *treatment effect*. Probably for most readers of this textbook, the latter term possesses a readily understandable meaning that the former lacks. In fact, the actual number associated with an effect size does provide a means to assess the extent to which clients improved when a particular treatment was applied. Based on Cohen's [1988] early work in the area of effect sizes and the subsequent work completed by Sawilowsky [2009], who expanded upon Cohen's work, one may assume that the effect sizes listed below can be used to gauge the degree to which a therapeutic effect occurred. The various qualitative descriptors Sawilowsky advocated to gauge how much a particular therapy helped clients are provided next, along with various corresponding effect size examples: .01 = very small, .20 = small, .50 = medium, .80 = large, 1.20 = very large, and 2.00 = huge.)

In addition to the evidence just highlighted, it has been reported that psychodynamic therapy is effective in reducing somatic and general psychiatric symptoms (Abbass, Kisely, & Kroenke, 2009), improving interpersonal functioning (Messer & Abbass, 2010), and treating anxiety disorders (Keefe, McCarthy, Dinger, Zilcha-Mano, & Barber, 2014). It seems beneficial when treating complex mental disorders (Leichsenring & Rabung, 2008). Additionally, preliminary findings suggest psychoanalytic therapy may be successful at treating anxiety and depression in children (Göttken, White, Klein, & von Klitzing, 2014; Weitkamp et al., 2014). Therefore, it appears psychoanalytic-based treatment is effective for a wide range of mental disorders.

In addition, there is evidence that supports the conclusion that there are no significant differences between psychoanalytic-based and other forms of therapy. In yet another meta-analysis, Leichsenring and Leibing (2003) compared 14 studies of psychodynamic treatment and 11 investigations of cognitive-behavioral therapy (CBT). The results revealed that the approaches did not differ in their effectiveness. More recent meta-analytic studies have yielded similar results. Gerber et al. (2011) examined 63 comparisons between psychodynamic and other forms of therapy, including CBT, supportive therapy, behavioral therapy, family therapy, group therapy, and medication alone. They found that 75% of the examined comparisons were not significant. Even when differences were significant, psychodynamic therapy was found to be either superior (10%) or inferior (16%) to other forms of therapy.

Gerber et al. (2011) further analyzed the data by reselecting the studies to be included in the analyses based on the quality of the project's research design. Among the 39 selected higher quality studies, it was discovered that there were no significant differences in 72% of the comparisons. Their results suggested that psychoanalytic-based treatment was generally equivalent to other forms of therapy in the improvement of psychological symptoms.

The effectiveness of short-term psychoanalytic-based therapy has been investigated as well. Leichsenring, Rabung, and Leibing (2004) conducted a meta-analysis study on the efficacy of this form of treatment. The researchers concluded that short-term psychodynamic therapy was effective for treating psychiatric disorders. Another meta-analysis study also examined the effectiveness of short-term psychodynamic psychotherapy with somatic symptom disorders (Abbass et al., 2009). Results yielded significant effects and suggested this treatment was effective in reducing clients' somatic symptoms and improving their social functioning.

Bachrach, Galatzer-Levy, Skolnikoff, and Waldron (1991), in comparison, reviewed six systematic studies that examined the effectiveness of long-term psychodynamic therapy. The investigators found there was a meaningful improvement for clients in the range of 60% to 90%. A more recent meta-analysis by Leichsenring and Rabung (2008) examined the effectiveness of long-term psychodynamic therapy. This was defined as a minimum of 1 year of therapy or a minimum of 50 therapy sessions. It was discovered that the improvement *effect size* ranged from .78 to 1.98 in 14 studies. Additionally, in eight studies, Leichsenring and Rabung (2008) found the effect size for long-term psychodynamic as compared to other forms of short-term therapy (e.g., CBT, cognitive-analytic therapy, dialectical behavioral therapy, family therapy, supportive therapy, short-term psychodynamic therapy, and psychiatric treatment as usual) was 1.8 for overall treatment outcomes. Based on all these findings, Leichsenring and Rabung (2008) concluded that long-term psychodynamic therapy was effective and that it was potentially more effective than other forms of short-term therapy. Most recently, Leichsenring, Abbass, Luyten, Hilsenroth, and Rabung (2013) reassessed meta-analytic findings supporting the efficacy of long-term psychodynamic psychotherapy and found that its use did, indeed, lead to significant improvements for those with complex mental disorders.

Shedler (2010) helps lay to rest the widely held opinion that psychoanalytic-based approaches are ineffective and are nothing more than relics of a time past that deserve to be relegated to psychology's historical dustbin. Shedler reported the following findings in an article published in the *American Psychologist*.

- Psychodynamic therapy lessens symptoms as effectively as newer, more targeted therapies.
- A meta-analysis study of 160 published psychodynamic studies that represented a considerable range of mental disorders also included randomized controlled trials and studies that evaluated the same clients before and after treatment. This meta-analysis study uncovered an effect size of 0.97. For the sake of comparison, Shedler also reported on a recent meta-analysis of 33 rigorously conducted studies of CBT for depression and anxiety, which found an effect size of 0.68.
- The meta-analysis study reporting the 0.97 effect size for psychodynamic studies also reported on follow-up data gathered 9 months after treatment had ended. The effect size moved from 0.97 to 1.51. Similarly, six other meta-analyses reporting the results of follow-up assessments all showed increases. Thus, it was concluded that clients who underwent psychodynamic therapy continued to make substantial gains after therapy had ended. (Shedler speculated that these increases were due to psychodynamic treatments focusing attention on unconscious or underlying patterns that affect many areas in a client's life.)

In conclusion, this research suggests that both long-term and short-term psychoanalytic-based treatments are effective in reducing a host of symptoms associated with mental disorders and improving social functioning.

Relevance of Psychoanalytic Theory

The influence of psychoanalytic-based treatment on the practice of counseling has been extensive and tied to the long history and tradition of psychoanalysis. For example, the International Psychoanalytical Association (IPA), founded in 1910, has had a great influence on the field of counseling. The IPA is actively involved in publishing psychoanalytic literature, training psychoanalysts, and promoting psychoanalytic therapy. Psychoanalytic training institutes are located widely throughout the United States and elsewhere. To become a psychoanalyst certified by the IPA, a person must be trained at one of IPA's constituent organizations. There is no restriction, however, to calling oneself a psychoanalyst. Various training programs are offered by the IPA, including child and adolescent psychoanalytic psychotherapy training, adult psychoanalytic psychotherapy training, a fellowship program, a psychoanalytic education program, and a doctoral-level psychology internship program. Some of these programs are accredited, for example, by the Accreditation Council for Continuing Medical Education and the American Psychological Association to provide continuing education credit.

Psychoanalytic-based treatment can be found in a host of settings such as psychiatric hospitals, private practices, community mental health centers, substance abuse clinics, social service agencies, and the military (e.g., Bradshaw, Roseborough, Pahwa, & Jordan, 2009; Brunstetter, 1998; Steinberg et al., 2004). This approach has been employed with a wide variety of clients, including children, adolescents, adults, couples, and families. Persons presenting with a broad range of problems (e.g., depressive disorders, anxiety disorders, anorexia nervosa, posttraumatic stress disorder, somatoform disorder, bulimia nervosa, borderline personality disorders, substance-related disorders, psychosis, neurosis) may benefit from psychoanalytic-based therapy (Leichsenring, 2005). Individual, couple, family, and group psychoanalytic-based treatment is available. This approach also has been adapted to supervision theory and practice (e.g., Bernard & Goodyear, 2009).

Typically, psychoanalytic-based therapy is long term, but it also has been adapted for short-term treatment. Insurance providers will reimburse for this form of therapy depending on the criteria outlined in the insurance policy. Self-pay insurance plans are available in many clinical settings as well. Because of its popularity among psychiatrists, aspects of the psychodynamic approach were reflected in the first two versions of the American Psychiatric Association's *Diagnostic and Statistical Manual of Mental Disorders* (*DSM*). This focus disappeared with the publication of the third edition (*DSM-III*) and its emphasis on symptom-based diagnosis (Mayes & Horwitz, 2005). The symptom-based emphasis of the *DSM-III, DSM-IV, DSM-IV-TR,* and *DSM-V,* however, seems to have facilitated the publication of the *Psychodynamic Diagnostic Manual* (*PDM*), which considers individuals' deep- and surface-level characteristics (PDM Task Force, 2006).

Special Ethical Considerations

Even though Freud was often drawn to larger issues surrounding societal views about what constituted right and wrong behavior, he did discuss various "rules" intended to govern practice and wrote about "wild" psychoanalysis, that is, the unethical application of psychoanalytic concepts by untrained professionals. Although a number of clarifications written or spoken by Freud contributed to today's ethical codes, only a few of the therapy's unique characteristics contributing to contemporary ethical practice are highlighted here.

In addition to informing the client about what typically can be expected to occur during the course of treatment (a step that is especially important in the case of brief therapy since imparting specific information about key concepts and explaining the importance of confronting resistance will expedite achievement of therapy goals), a contemporary therapist is responsible for establishing rules about fee amount and the consequences of nonpayment, coming late to an appointment, failing to cancel an appointment 24 hours in advance when the client had ample occasions to do so, and so forth. Although such rules may seem to be confined solely to the business side of therapy, they also serve another function as some rule violations create a venue for therapeutic focus. For example, if forgetting an appointment represents a true instance of psychological resistance to therapy, the incident most likely requires attention to prevent therapeutic stalling. Finally, considering the pivotal role that *transference* plays in psychoanalysis, it should not be a surprise to find the ethical emphasis placed on safeguarding both the client and therapist from the type of interpersonal maelstroms that can be created and energized by transference reactions. One of the available codes of ethics, *Principles and Standards of Ethics for Psychoanalysts* (American Psychoanalytic Association, 2007), contains statements intended to help practitioners avoid the type of harmful situations that can result when past emotions, especially those experienced in childhood, are allowed to take on nontherapeutic expression. Paraphrased portions of this ethical code are presented next to illustrate the importance placed on not yielding to transference reactions.

- It is unethical for a psychoanalyst to use the transference relationship to solicit clients, students, or supervisees into treatment or to obtain testimonials from current or former clients, or the parents or guardians of current or former clients.
- Physical touching is not typically regarded as a technique of value in treatment. If touching occurs between the client and the psychoanalyst, regardless of who initiated the touching, the event should alert the psychoanalyst to the potential for misunderstanding by the client and the psychoanalyst. Potential harm to the future course of treatment should be considered.
- Marriage between a psychoanalyst and a current or former client, or between a psychoanalyst and a parent or guardian of a current or former client, is to be avoided.

Application: Psychoanalytic Theory

WHEN THE PAST OVERTAKES THE PRESENT: RETURNING TO THE CASE OF WILLIAM S.

The case presented at the beginning of this chapter was a thinly veiled version of William Shakespeare's *Hamlet*. In *An Outline of Psycho-Analysis* Freud (1940/1949) stated,

> Hamlet's delay in acting out his plan for revenge can be explained by the Oedipus complex, stating that the prince came to grief over the task of punishing someone else for what coincided with the substance of his own Oedipus wish—whereupon the general lack of understanding on part of the literary world showed how ready is the mass of mankind to hold fast to its infantile repressions. (p. 75)

Kahn (2002) elaborated on Freud's comments by adding that, typical of an Oedipus situation, Hamlet was ambivalent toward his mother. This ambivalence was displayed by his movement between tender feelings of attachment for her and anger against her in an attempt to unconsciously join with his father. In addition, believing his mother had betrayed his father, Hamlet's earlier repressed desire for his mother and death urge toward his father was reactivated and served to invigorate his movement toward murder. Finally, one of several puzzles encountered when watching the play is what prompts Hamlet's reaction toward the woman he loves and promises to wed? Kahn speculated it may have resulted from a displacement of his ambivalence toward his mother, and possibly even a symbolic rejection of his "first love in life" (mother). Hamlet was rejected not only by his mother to stay with his father when Hamlet was 5 years old, but again by his mother for a new lover, who successfully completed the Oedipal act of murdering his father, an act that Hamlet could only fantasize about as a child.

Interestingly, historical evidence suggests that William Shakespeare was the first-born son of John Shakespeare and Mary Arden. John Shakespeare died in 1601, around the time the play *Hamlet* was produced. One is tempted to speculate that the many ambiguities found in *Hamlet* were in fact due to a reawakening of an Oedipus reaction between William Shakespeare and his father. The reawakening of this past son–father conflict found creative expression in the form of a widely known play that has universal appeal. Kahn concluded that the conflict played out by Hamlet on stage represented a form of *repetitive compulsion* experienced by the author of Hamlet (i.e., William S.) and would have been treated as such in therapy (as would the fictitious character William S. introduced in the opening of this chapter if he had been real).

▼ FIGURE 3.4

Self-Portrait on the Borderline Between Mexico and the United States, by Frida Kahlo

Archivart/Alamy Stock Photo

The Case of Miguel Sanchez

Even before Freud's death, adherents to psychoanalytic theory began to refine certain features and methods of practice that clearly departed from the theoretical beliefs and standards of practice that were established by Freud. However, despite such differences, when these various advances are examined closely in terms of their essential components, many of these psychoanalytic advances can accurately be categorized as discoveries that remained true to the three imperative assumptions that Freud had originally formulated. (1) Mental processes exist that are not readily apparent, which possess a dynamic nature capable of influencing our thoughts and behaviors in apparently illogical or even absurd ways. (2) The interplay of early developmental milestones and early relationships often provides the content of and structure for one's mature personality, that is, the set of emotional qualities, ways of behaving, and the host of other attributes that make an individual different from other people. (3) Childhood feelings and desires reemerge that are capable of altering one's perception of another person in such a manner as to foster highly subjective interactions; such incidents of misperception are especially likely to involve others who fulfill significant roles in our adult lives (Gazda, Ginter, & Horne, 2001; Ginter & Bonney, 1993a).

In terms of the previous comments, the case example that is presented is a snippet from a series of sessions with Miguel. Miguel's school principal stipulates that Miguel may continue to attend school if he sees the therapist who is recommended by the school counselor; also, the school counselor must receive a monthly report that verifies Miguel's attendance in therapy. Finally, no additional "disrespectful exchanges" may occur between Miguel and any of the school's teachers. Miguel has agreed to meet weekly with the therapist until school ends (a duration of 20 sessions).

Session Segment

Therapist Hola. (Hello.)

Miguel Hola.

Therapist Miguel, the last time we met we were talking about how much you like the art class you're taking at school, and I got to thinking about how one of the drawings you brought in—its images and colors—reminded me of a painting by Frida Kahlo. Have you heard of her?

Miguel No.

Therapist She was a very famous painter. [The therapist hands Miguel a photograph of Kahlo's painting (see Figure 3.4).]

Therapist What do you think?

Miguel	Hmm. It's interesting. You were thinking about my drawing of the U.S. factory where Mexican women are working. I used the same colors of Mexico's flag that the woman is holding—green, white, red—to color the *ilegales* (illegal immigrants) walking to the factory. The blue skull in the photo looks like the *Día de los Muertos* (Day of the Dead) mask I used for the factory boss's face. Yeah, the colors are very much the same. [Miguel places the photograph on the side table next to his chair without further comment. During the first half of the session, Miguel glances several times at the photograph. Observing his glances, the therapist returned to the topic of the photograph.]
Therapist	Miguel, I think it's interesting you didn't have much to say about Kahlo's painting, but you keep glancing at it on the table.
Miguel	It means nothing. Just looking.
Therapist	Nothing?
Miguel	The woman in the painting—she reminds me of *mi madre*—my mother. The woman in the painting is stuck between Mexico and the U.S. She's here in the U.S., but hangs onto her old ways and beliefs. She wanted a better life for her kids, but she fears her kids are becoming gringos (people from the United States). Sometimes when she looks at me, I'm sure she just sees a stranger.
Therapist	There's no anger in your voice.
Miguel	Qué? (What?)
Therapist	During our first couple of sessions, you kept repeating how angry you were toward your mother. While I sensed you were angry then, I've come to believe it is much more complicated, more involved than what people at your school say. I'm just guessing, but to me your anger seems misplaced, and it sometimes bubbles up and spills over into your life, causing problems. Like what happened with Mr. Smith, your teacher—you said that afterward even you didn't understand why you reacted as you did.
Miguel	Yeah. Hmm. [After sitting quietly for a while, Miguel starts talking again.] You know why my mother left Mexico? It was because of *el jefe de familia* (the father of our family). After having four kids, my father started a second family. My oldest brother said he referred to his second family as *mi casita* (my little house). It wasn't long before he left us, I was about 6 years old, all I remember is how much my mother was sad back then. I guess he left because he couldn't earn enough to support two families. [Miguel sits quietly for a couple of minutes.] It's not that I was angry at her so much or angry about her need to stay Mexican—I can understand that. I was angry because she made it too easy for my father by clinging to what Mexicans say makes a good mother. *Una madre abnegada que llevaba su cruz.* (A self-sacrificing mother who bore her cross.)
Therapist	Why do you think it took so long for you to get around to talking about this?
Miguel	Talk about it! I hate thinking about it!

Therapist	Yes. That's it. [Long pause] There's something I want you to think about before we meet again. Think about how you reacted to Mr. Smith when he said, "Illegals are not wanted in the U.S."
Miguel	Yes.
Therapist	Will you think about this before we meet again?
Miguel	I guess it's like you said before: "Conflicts we have today are sometimes just old conflicts dressed in new clothes." I think I'm starting to get what you meant about how things we aren't even aware of can affect how we act and feel about things sometimes. [After sitting quietly for a moment, Miguel starts talking again.] Yes, I'll think about what you said before I come back.

Even though the approach taken by the therapist represents a brief version of psychoanalytic therapy, in the beginning the therapist devoted the time to build a trusting relationship with Miguel and to explain how his approach to therapy was informed by psychoanalytic theory. The therapist explained in everyday language the three key assumptions that are discussed at the beginning of this section, even using relevant cultural examples to make the assumptions understandable for Miguel. This brief exchange between the therapist and client calls attention to why transference reactions (Ginter & Bonney, 1993a) are important to understand in general, not just as an occurrence between a therapist and client, because such subjective reactions are prevalent in everyday human existence and sometimes are capable of creating interpersonal conflict. This phenomenon was identified by Miguel when he repeated Dr. Ramirez's comment, "Conflicts we have today are sometimes just old conflicts dressed in new clothes." Finally, several authors (e.g., Moncayo, 1998; Santisteban, Mena, & Abalo, 2013) have addressed difficulties that pertain to contemporary applications of psychoanalytic theory and various multicultural factors that require consideration in association with a psychoanalytic approach. For example, the importance of a therapist's having bilingual skills is made evident by the clinical observation in which sometimes clients will automatically switch from speaking English to their native language to create a linguistic defense mechanism, whose aim is to prevent a conflictual memory from being revealed.

CHAPTER REVIEW

SUMMARY AND COMMENTARY ▶▶

Since 1895, numerous individuals (some better informed about psychoanalysis than others) have claimed Freud's theory was dead only to discover later the theoretical zombie has risen again. In the 21st century, the field of neuroscience is uncovering some of the strongest evidence for psychoanalytic theory. Solms (2005) reported that researchers have found hard evidence for the following: unconscious processing, a connection between repression and neurotic symptoms (implying the unconscious has a dynamic quality), the equivalent of the pleasure principle aimed at producing wish-fulfilling outcomes, and four drive-like mechanisms (apparently linked to various minor systems and subcomponents). The four drive-like mechanisms have been described by Solms in the following manner:

- Seeking system: also referred to as the reward, wanting, and curiosity-interest-expectancy system (representing a subcomponent of the pleasure-lust system)
- Anger-rage system: system governing anger but not predatory aggression, which is monitored by the seeking system (i.e., "male dominance" behavior)
- Panic system: also referred to as the "separation-distress" system, which is linked to complex social drives that oversee the mother–infant connection and human bonding
- Fear-anxiety system: system linked to unconscious memory (p. 543)

Solms states that although terminology differs between what Freud used and what neuroscientists rely upon today, there exists a remarkable similarity between the seeking system and Freud's conception of sexuality (i.e., Freud's libidinal drive).

To summarize, even though psychoanalytic theory and therapy have received extensive, prolonged scrutiny since their introduction (e.g., Cohen & Nagel, 1934; Nagel, 1959; Vaughan, 1997), the accumulation of evidence supports the use of psychoanalysis. Although other approaches may possess advantages over psychoanalytic-based therapies because of the unique factors surrounding a particular client or mental disorder, in general, it can be concluded that psychoanalytic therapy, as with other major treatment approaches, has proven to be a valuable treatment modality (Ginter, 1988).

I (the author of this chapter, Earl J. Ginter) maintained a private practice for approximately 38 years during which time my approach was often informed by psychodynamic concepts. Three beliefs I held throughout those years are that Freud started a practice-based revolution that is far from over, many present-day practitioners unknowingly owe much to Freud's persistence and accomplishments, and there remains much for us to still learn from psychoanalysis—all that learning requires is to maintain an open attitude. Table 3.4 provides a brief overview of key aspects of current psychoanalytic-derived therapies.

▼ TABLE 3.4

Brief Overview of Current Therapy Practice

Variable	Current Application
Type of service delivery setting	Private practice Clinic Military Legal setting Psychiatric hospital Substance abuse clinic Mental health agency Mental health consultation to K–12 schools Management consultation
Population	Child Teen Adult Couple Family Group Organization
Type of presenting problems	Wide range
Severity of presenting problems	Wide range
Adapted for short-term approach	Yes
Length of treatment	Brief to long term
Ability to receive reimbursement	Insurance companies will reimburse with appropriate *DSM* diagnosis.
Certification in approach	The National Association for the Advancement of Psychoanalysis offers certification as a Nationally Certified Psychoanalyst (NCPsyA). In addition, other educational bodies (e.g., the Academy of Clinical and Applied Psychoanalysis) offer psychoanalytic postgraduate certificate programs.
Training in educational programs	More than 70 U.S. and international training institutes offer training in psychoanalytic theory and therapy. The Vermont Graduate School of Psychoanalysis offers a Doctor of Psychoanalysis degree (i.e., PsyaD). In addition, many graduate programs include psychoanalytic theory and therapy in various courses.
Location	Urban Rural Suburban
Type of delivery system	HMO PPO Fee for service
Credential	Various forms of credentialing are available, such as the Fellow of the International Psychoanalytic Association (i.e., FIPA) issued by the International Psychoanalytical Association.
Practitioners	Professionals Paraprofessionals
Fit with *DSM* diagnoses	No (Refer to Nancy Williams's *Psychoanalytic Diagnosis* [2nd ed.]. New York, NY: Guilford Press.)

CRITICAL THINKING QUESTIONS ▶▶

1. List two examples of a transference reaction that could occur outside the context of ongoing therapy. Also, explain what factors would contribute to the first incident listed having a positive outcome for those involved, and explain what factors would contribute to the remaining incident having a negative outcome for those involved.

2. Explain how each concept listed below could theoretically impact the event that follows it.

- Unconscious forces and career selection
- An Oedipal reaction and one's religious beliefs
- Life and death drives and cultural attitudes toward death
- Transference reactions and mate selection

SUGGESTED READINGS: IMPORTANT PRIMARY SOURCES ▶▶

Books

Danto, E. A. (2005). *Freud's free clinics: Psychoanalysis and social justice, 1918-1938*. New York, NY: Columbia University Press.

Freud, A. (1966). *The writings of Anna Freud: Vol. 2. The ego and the mechanisms of defense* (C. Baines, Trans.). New York, NY: International Universities Press. (Original work published 1937)

Freud, S. (1953). The interpretation of dreams. In J. Strachey (Ed. & Trans.), *The standard edition of the complete psychological works of Sigmund Freud* (Vols. 4 & 5). London, UK: Hogarth Press. (Original work published 1900)

Gabbard, G.O., Litowitz, B.E., & Williams, P. (2012). *Textbook of psychoanalysis* (2nd ed.). Washington, DC: American Psychiatric Publishing.

Journals

Contemporary Psychoanalysis

International Journal of Psychoanalysis

Neuropsychoanalysis

Psychoanalytic Quarterly

Psychoanalytic Social Work

Websites

APA Division of Psychoanalysis: www.division39.org

Freud Archives: Sigmund Freud Collection (Library of Congress): https://www.loc.gov/item/prn-17-005

Psychodynamic Diagnostic Manual: www.pdm1.org

ADLERIAN THEORY

Individual Psychology: An Introduction

In an attempt to clarify the relationship between Sigmund Freud's theory and subsequent theories that appeared and drew the interest of scholars, writers sometimes used categorical labels that unintentionally deemphasized the extent of existing differences. One label in particular, "neo-Freudian," introduced during the early 1940s created a sort of theoretical fly-paper that some in the field found difficult to escape. The prefix *neo-* was used to imply something recent, modified, or revived but failed to communicate the width and depth of theorists such as Alfred Adler who acquired an extensive knowledge of Freud's explanation for reality only to later denounce it. Adler actively worked for the remainder of his life to construct a new science of mental states and processes. Interestingly, even Erik Erikson who wholeheartedly embraced Freud's ideas was not viewed as "psychoanalytic enough" by close followers of Freud. In 1950, when Erikson released *Childhood and Society,* he hoped Anna Freud (Erikson's therapist during his training) would appreciate his expansion of her father's theory. Instead she viewed Erikson as a "renegade," whose book was a nonevent (Bloland, 2005, p. 136).

What does this mean? It means Adler was his own person, and as such, he deserves recognition for his unique contributions to advancing our understanding of the human condition. Adler saw in humans something that was irrepressible and strong, and it was this strength, not fragility, that he wanted to harness and release during therapy. Adler referred to his explanation as *individual psychology* to convey a clear message that each person represents an indivisible, one holistic self, whose mental functions are cooperating, not competing (John C. Dagley, personal communication, October 19, 2011). In a number of ways it was Adler, and not Freud, who provided the prototypical structure for carrying out face-to-face psychotherapy and counseling as we know it today.

Alfred Adler: Inside and Outside the *Inner Circle*

Intellectuals from the arts and sciences and other figures viewed as the spokespersons of their time were eventually drawn to Freud's theory. Whereas an accurate and complete accounting of those with direct access to Freud would be very difficult to compile, it is easy to identify the much smaller and well-known group of individuals close to Freud. Members of this tight knit group of early 20th-century radical thinkers were referred to as Freud's *inner circle,* and Alfred Adler was one of these radical thinkers. The problem with radical thinkers is that they often make poor followers because their very nature is to

LEARNING OBJECTIVES

After reading this chapter, each student should be able to:

1. Diagnose the case of "The Man of a Thousand Faces."

2. Argue that Adler was either inside or outside the "inner circle."

3. Defend the Adlerian theoretical approach.

4. Describe the major concepts of Adlerian theory.

5. Create a plan to employ Adlerian therapeutic approaches to address your responses to the Table 4.3 worksheet.

6. Defend the assumption that Adlerian theory is committed to social justice and multiculturalism (e.g., working with diverse populations).

7. Assess the effectiveness of the Adlerian theory in assisting Mrs. Sanchez.

HYPOTHETICAL CASE STUDY: THE "MAN OF A THOUSAND FACES" ENTERS THERAPY WITH ALFRED ADLER

Lon Chaney entered the room wearing dark sunglasses and, after an exchange of introductions, sat in a chair across from Adler, who then prompted him to begin. Chaney said, "Hazel, my wife, is very concerned about me. I've been feeling different for a while and it worries her. I have been a very active person all my life. I have a good physique and enjoy doing physical kinds of things, but my stamina and concentration have been off [long pause]. I'm having a big problem with memorizing my lines for an upcoming movie [long pause]. I was first attracted to Hazel because she is also an active person like me. I met her years ago while she was a dancer on tour. It was Hazel who convinced me to go to see a doctor I've known for years. He's really more of a friend than my doctor — we've hunted and fished together. I trust him and know he'll always give me good advice [pauses]. It boils down to this. A few weeks before I saw him about my fatigue and lack of focus, I had told him about a special movie project when we were out fishing together. He made a house call. After a complete physical exam, he said he couldn't find anything wrong with me, but what he said next startled me. He said if he had to guess, he would say my symptoms were somehow tied to the upcoming movie where I have to speak on camera for the first time. He also said I should see you, Dr. Adler. I have done vaudeville, worked in theater, and completed well over 150 silent films. It just seems peculiar that my first 'talkie' could put things all a kilter."

Chaney went on to elaborate about his film career (see Figure 4.1) during which time he made four remarks that Adler believed would be pertinent to understanding how Chaney approached life: "Between pictures there is no Lon Chaney"; "My whole career has been devoted to keeping people from knowing me"; "I don't feel comfortable being photographed as myself"; and "I want to remind people that the lowest types of humanity may have within them the capacity for supreme self-sacrifice. The dwarfed, misshapen beggar of the streets may have the noblest of ideals." When Chaney stopped speaking, Adler stated that there was a commonsense cause for his symptoms and

a practical solution that they would work together to find. Adler further explained that it was necessary for him to assess the situation thoroughly, which would involve asking questions about memories of various interactions, family relationships, possibly what he dreamt about, important goals, and other types of questions that would allow both of them to develop a clearer understanding of what solution best fit Chaney's situation.

Biographical Source: Basinger (1999).

CASE DISCUSSION

Near the end of this chapter, additional information collected from Lon Chaney is reviewed in terms of how it might be used to gain a mutual understanding of Chaney's aims, general approach to life, and the difficulties he experienced that motivated him to seek therapy with Adler. The ending discussion reviews how an Adlerian therapist's gained knowledge might be used to assist Chaney.

question authority—even when that authority is Sigmund Freud. Adler's eventual break from the inner circle represented an early and significant departure from this group. Carefully reviewed in light of what is known today, we discover that similar to shadows, much of the early criticism directed toward Adler by Freud and others disappears once an objective light is shined in its direction. (See Ansbacher & Ansbacher, 1970 and Manaster et al., 1977 for biographical information cited in this section.)

Although he unquestionably was very interested in hearing Freud's opinions, Adler remained an independent thinker who became increasingly vocal about his own ideas. Once he was outside the circle of Freudian acolytes, Adler wrote approximately 300 books, articles, and other publications that served multiple purposes and included offering alternatives to what Adler believed were Freud's mistakes. Adler's theory and approach to therapy represents a unique non-Freudian method that foreshadowed many of the later developments in the field.

To better understand the person who stood up and rejected Freud's truth as fiction requires us to go back to February 7, 1870, to the town of Penzig, Austria, where Adler was born the third of six children in a middle-class Jewish family. Although anti-Semitism existed in Adler's early life its effect was much less memorable than that of the health-related issues that played a central role in his early development. He is known to have suffered from rickets, which is characterized by softening of the bones. The resulting low activity level resulting from this condition appears to have added to his body weight at the time. He also suffered from spasms of the upper part of the larynx, between the vocal cords, which affected his breathing and the sound of his voice. Around age 4, he experienced a bout of pneumonia severe enough to bring him to the brink of death.

The combined impact of three things—the illnesses mentioned, his near accidental death on two occasions, and the death of a sibling (whom Adler slept next to during the night)—created a critical mass that led to a sustained reaction that propelled Adler forward and marked the remainder of his life. Specifically, these events resulted in a person who felt driven to subdue, overcome, defeat, or even crush any obstacle creating a sense of inferiority. For example, his keen sense of confronting rather than avoiding a perceived weakness probably accounts for Adler's intense interest in

▼ FIGURE 4.2

Alfred Adler

Source: Ixitixel at German Wikipedia [Public domain], via Wikimedia Commons.

music and being able to achieve "a strong dependable voice and a good gift for delivery" (Manaster, Painter, Deutsch, & Overholt, 1977, p. 10) despite his early vocal difficulties. It may also account for his early interest in becoming a medical doctor, because he encountered physicians at an early age and understood they fought against illnesses that weaken humanity.

Far from a stellar student when he began, Adler persisted and eventually excelled in school. He later entered the Vienna Medical School and graduated in 1895. Despite the fact that records from this time are spotty and incomplete, it appears one physician, Hermann Nothnagel, influenced Adler. Specifically, this physician's general attitude concerning patient care was expressed in an oft repeated medical fiat of his: "The physician must always look at the patient as a whole, not as an isolated organ or an isolated ailment . . . the emotional influence of the physician on the patient must be taken into account" (Manaster et al., 1977, p. 10). A final experience that seems to have cemented Adler's approach to working with others occurred after he graduated from medical school and started a practice in Vienna close to the Prater, a large park equipped with recreational devices, games, and refreshments. Patients from the Prater often depended upon some physical skill or ability to earn a living, such as acrobats. He discovered a basic similarity between a number of his patients from the Prater and himself. Like Adler, many were confronted early in their lives with one or more physical weaknesses that they fought to overcome, gradually turning a weakness into a strength and eventually into a means to earn a living.

Adler met Timofeyewna Epstein at a meeting organized by socialists. Both were drawn to socialism's cooperative approach to solving society's problems. The couple married in 1897, and the first of four children was born to the couple a year later. In 1898, Adler began practicing as an ophthalmologist but later decided to pursue a practice in general medicine, eventually settling on psychiatry. His initial interest in psychiatry started with Freud's theory of dreams. In 1902, Adler accepted Freud's invitation to join Freud's inner circle, which met on a regular basis. He remained a member for 9 years as the group expanded from its original four members. Toward the end of those 9 years, Adler had become one of two coeditors of the psychoanalytic journal on which Freud served as editor in chief, and Adler had assumed the presidency of the Vienna branch of the International Psychoanalytic Association.

Adler left the Vienna Psychoanalytic Society in 1911 along with 9 others, leaving the original group with 14 members. Reconciliation efforts failed and Adler's group formed the Society for Free Psychoanalytic Research or Investigation (soon renamed Society for Individual Psychology). In 1914, the *Journal for Individual Psychology* was created. Even though Adler gave credit to Freud for drawing his attention to the importance of early childhood and unconscious factors, it was clear that Adler earnestly rejected the central role played by the unconscious, as well as drive-fueled motives and the position that civilization simply represents a psychic compromise between mental phenomena. These differences created such an extraordinary divide between Freud's followers and those attracted to Adler's position that the divide between the two groups could never be bridged. The resulting imbroglio only became more complicated and bitter over time. Freud was to later comment about two movements that emerged from psychoanalysis; the second referred to Adler's departure.

The other (originated by Alfred Adler in Vienna) reproduced many factors from psychoanalysis under other names—regression, for instance, appeared in a sexualized version as the "masculine protest." But in other respects it turned away from the unconscious and the sexual instincts, and endeavored to trace back the development of character and of the neuroses to the "will to power," which by means of overcompensation strives to check the dangers arising from "organ inferiority." Neither of these movements, with other systematic structures, had any permanent influence on psychoanalysis. In the case of Adler's theories it soon became clear that they had very little in common with psychoanalysis, which they were designed to replace. (Freud, 1922/1959, pp. 123–124)

World War I interrupted developments in the new movement when Adler was called to active duty. During the years he served as a physician in the Austro-Hungarian army, Adler concluded that we should not only seek to find cures for mental illness but to find ways to prevent its occurrence in order to better society at large. This conclusion logically led to his increased focus on societal issues after the war. For example, in 1922 he established the first child guidance clinics in Vienna. Before the end of the decade, Adler had witnessed the creation of 32 such clinics devoted to improving education. During this period, Adler's influence was growing in both Europe and America. In 1929, he was appointed a visiting professor at Columbia University in New York City and, in 1932, to first chair at the Long Island Medical College.

By 1934, fascists had imposed their extreme right-wing views on the Austrian Republic, and one of their first official acts was to close all of Adler's progressive clinics. One year later, Adler and Timofeyewna left Vienna to settle in the United States, a trip made easier due to the close ties Adler had with various academics and others, ties established mainly through the lectures he gave at Harvard, Brown, and several schools in California. In fact, at one of his lectures, 2,500 applications to attend were turned down because of space limitations. Consistent with what Adler advocated, since he perceived his ability to speak in English as "weak," he scheduled lessons and continued practicing until he felt confident about his ability to speak in English during lectures.

Adler continued to travel abroad to lecture and participate in meetings. It was during a trip to Aberdeen, Scotland, in 1937 when he died from a heart attack on May 28 on route to a hospital. The power of individual psychology was strong enough to continue long after Adler's untimely demise.

Individual psychology was championed by a number of talented, exceedingly bright professionals before and after 1937, including but not limited to Alexandra Adler and Kurt A. Adler, the children of Alfred Adler (both of whom were psychiatrists); Paul Rom, a psychotherapist and editor for *Individual Psychology Newsletter;* Heinz Ansbacher and Rowena Ansbacher, editor and associate editor, respectively, for *Journal of Individual Psychology;* Rudolf Dreikurs who became widely known for applying Adler's theory to child behavior; and Antony M. Bruck, a psychologist who taught Adlerian theory and therapy in North America, South America, and Europe. Adler's theory appealed to many people in part because of its optimism. After World War I, Freud saw darkness waiting at the end of the tunnel for humanity and felt it necessary to introduce the death drive. Adler saw light at the end of the tunnel for humanity in the form of a spirit of equality and self-actualization.

The Adlerian Approach: Individual Psychology

Adler's name for his theoretical approach, *individual psychology,* was intended to convey the central role that a holistic perspective played in understanding others' thoughts, feelings, and actions. Adler's comment that he had gained from his early association with Freud (i.e., "I profited from his mistakes") is revealing. He was essentially announcing to past and current associates that he aimed to upend the widely accepted approach of psychoanalysis as the means to obtain the truth about neuroses—truth which was supposed to be buried in the rambling, disjointed stories constructed by clients through free association. Adler was determined in his effort to replace *analysis* with *synthesis,* and this was no simple task considering the early foothold obtained by Freud and other psychoanalytic writers and practitioners.

For Adler the starting point with a client was always the person, as an indivisible organic entity whose natural setting was the interpersonal world. Undoubtedly, Adler affected a different means to conceptualize clients' thoughts, behaviors, and feelings. He believed a real understanding of the human condition always required placing clients in front of the backdrop of the community in which they lived on a daily basis.

Adler strongly believed in a *teleological world* of final causes or purposes. Behind the thin veneer of fashionable (as well as unfashionable) behavior, and available to all of us, is a powerful motivational component that can energize us to discover and then embrace our unique purpose in life. To Adler, being human meant that all of us have the potential to overcome biological, environmental, and imaginary constraints so we can rely on self-determination to create a world of our own making. Whether that world is meant to be heaven, hell, or somewhere between the two extremes is for the most part up to us. (Although no human is either innately good or bad, any of us could fall on either side of the good–bad equation depending largely on how we decide to live.)

An important reoccurring theme of Adler's was that it is neither the past nor the present that owns us (unless we allow one or both to dictate who we are); we are meant by our nature to strive and overcome any bondage imposed by time. Finally, whereas psychoanalytic theory had its sights firmly trained on the past, Adler's conceptualization of time's role in our life meant that individuals are intended to straddle both their past and present time while looking steadfast toward the future. Life's answer did not inhabit the past, but was always to be found rooted in our future through our intentions.

What makes individual psychology so unique is the contribution it provides to solving client problems. First, Adler's work foreshadowed much of the theory, research, and therapeutic applications to come. Second, Adler's approach was firmly anchored to real-world situations and everyday problems that challenge all of us as individuals and as members of larger groups, whether a dyad or a nation. Third, the emphasis Adler placed on ***inter***personal rather than ***intra***personal existence as the

▼ TABLE 4.1

Quotable Alfred Adler

- The unity of the personality is generally overlooked by most schools of psychology; or it does not receive in their hands the attention it deserves.
- What is truly remarkable about our psychic life is that it is our points of view which decide the direction we take, and not the facts themselves.
- What is the basis of differentiating between useful and useless manifestations of striving for superiority? The Answer is interest in the community.
- Psychology means to understand the scheme of apperception [a non S-R process of assimilation] by which the child acts and by which he reacts to stimuli, to understand how he regards certain stimuli, how he responds to them, and how he uses them for his own purposes.
- It is the [person's] general attitude toward life which is the basis of all dreams.
- The psychic life of [people] is determined by [their] goals.
- The hardest thing for human beings to do is to know themselves and to change themselves.
- The three great challenges of life: love, work, and society.

Sources: Adler (1927/1954, 1930/1968).

ultimate point of entry for therapists to understand clients and the worlds they create for themselves was a critical change. In fact, Freud's seemingly formidable drive-based theory failed to build a rampart strong enough to fortify psychoanalysis against the growing onslaught of theorists, similar to Adler, who chose to elevate the importance of interpersonal factors. Table 4.1 represents a sample of comments made by Adler. These quotes are intended to add a more personal dimension to Adler's work and should provide the reader a better sense of what he hoped to communicate to the rest of us.

Major Concepts

A novice to Adlerian theory may initially find Adler's style of writing less than clear. Interestingly, the lack of clarity experienced by the reader probably resides with the reader, rather than resulting from Adler's ability to explain his theory. The difficulty encountered reading Adler's *Understanding Human Nature,* for example, can be explained largely as a result of Adler's holistic perspective, which caused him at times to rely upon an interwoven type of presentation that can entangle a reader. In such instances, Adler is just being true to his holistic theory that humans must be approached and presented as a single entity rather than as a sum of individual parts.

Adler's views simply do not lend themselves to a series of simple factoids or theoretical elements abstracted from something larger. Once a human is reduced to parts, any attempted discussion on those parts will always fall short of describing what it means to be human. Although Adler's theoretical writings cover many facets of human nature, it would be incorrect to assume Adlerian concepts can be meaningfully discussed as if they were independent building blocks to understand others. In a sense, there are no building blocks.

The holistic quality that permeates all of Adler's theory can be illustrated by the qualities of a jigsaw puzzle. Imagine in front of you a completely assembled jigsaw puzzle that pictures a finished diamond with many cut facets. To better understand what constitutes this diamond, a psychoanalytic oriented person would pull apart the picture of the diamond, carefully study each jigsaw piece, and reassemble the pieces based on the understanding of how a diamond should look as a result of investigating the qualities restricted to each jigsaw piece. In contrast, an Adlerian oriented person would not bother to disassemble the picture but simply study the assembled picture to understand how a whole diamond with many facets should look.

Adler firmly believed that the therapy approach most in alignment with reality must involve a collaborative relationship if a therapist hopes to expand the client's field of understanding of the situation and effectively awaken a client's innate healing potential. Without question, a piecemeal approach to working with clients was to be avoided. Adler remained true to the earlier advice given to him by Hermann Nothnagel. If paraphrased in terms of therapy it would read: A therapist must always look at the client as a whole, not as an isolated organ or an isolated ailment or mental disorder. In a similar fashion, the various Adlerian concepts discussed next are best understood by approaching them as a unit of interlocked facets that represent a single thing—a human.

Human Nature

Alfred Adler (1927/1954) wrote, "The understanding of human nature seems to us indispensable to every [person] and the study of its science, the most important activity of the human mind" (p. 224). Whether it was to be Adler or someone else who would facilitate such a universal level of understanding is beside the point. Adler truly believed that if enough members of various cultures around the world genuinely understood human nature, this global understanding would provide a literal worldview that fostered healthy social cohesion capable of forming a type of social loyalty that would go far in preventing many of the everyday—and not so everyday—problems that have plagued humans for countless ages.

Adler also emphasized other characteristics of humanness, such as mind over body, primacy of future time to understand personal destiny, the importance of parental and sibling dynamics on personality, the qualities of good and bad being tied to choices made, and human existence being neither determined nor totally free of surrounding influences. Concerning the last facet listed, Adler believed we possess what might be termed *good-enough freedom* to make important decisions that can literally propel us toward a future that is framed by our personal goals. Essentially, it is the choices we make that create the road map for our future. Furthermore, all living organisms are characterized by movement, and in the case of humans, this movement is directional and not chaotic or random. Being human means one is incapable of standing still (unless mental illness is interfering with our potential). Even more important is that this inability to stand still is purposeful and—whether we are aware or not—tied to an attempt to answer the question "Who am I and how do I move beyond my current state to manifest the person I am meant to be?"

Adler acknowledged that Hans Vaihinger's notion of fictional finalism meaningfully contributed to his theory of human nature and typically guided his work with clients. Fictional finalism is a derivative of Vaihinger's doctrine that human phenomena are guided not only by mechanical forces but follow a trajectory toward certain goals capable of supporting self-realization. Interestingly, to be counted as a genuine instance of self-realization for Adler, it had to be a state that nourished both the individual and members of the individual's social sphere. Adler believed strongly in the importance of positive forms of connectedness to others. Although Harry Stack Sullivan and other early interpersonal theorists disagreed with Adler on many issues, both Sullivan and Adler agreed that it is the social facet of human existence that represents the be-all and end-all to theory and practice.

Social Interest

Decades ago Adler introduced the term *Gemeinschaftsgefuhl,* which was meant to capture the full range of social interests that he believed were critical to fostering mental health. *Gemeinschaftsgefuhl* was a combination of two German words: *Gemeinschaft* which means "community" or "neighborship," and *Gefühl,* which means "feeling." When Adler used this word he was referring to a "sense of fellowship in the human community" or "social feeling" (Alfred Adler, 1927/1954, p. 38). Other meanings for *Gemeinschaftsgefuhl* include unity, social belonging, being equal, and social interest. The last meaning, social interest, gained popularity and use over the years.

Gemeinschaftsgefuhl is what makes it possible for us to overcome unhealthy detachment and move toward wider types of social involvement, including social activism. It is the facet of our external (and internal) world that helps make us more resilient and capable of facing the myriad problems and challenges that confront us during our lives—especially earth-shattering events like the combination of a tsunami and the failure of several nuclear reactors experienced by Japan in 2011. The strong social unity felt in Japan helped prevent looting, encouraged workers to return to the reactors to prevent an even greater disaster, and started many on a path toward recovery and healing. For contrast, think about the near collapse of the U.S. monetary system during the first decade of this century; it is clear that ubiquitous greed played a role. Without a doubt, the rapacious desire for wealth displayed a few years ago was 180 degrees removed from *Gemeinschaftsgefuhl.*

It is a lack of *Gemeinschaftsgefuhl* that makes the sociopath such a danger to individuals and the larger society. Although *Gemeinschaftsgefuhl* is certainly tied to living empathically, it goes well beyond what is typically considered empathy's territory. According to Adler, we are exposed to multiple dimensions of how social interest can manifest. In fact, there appears to be at least five important areas that pose tasks for all of us to complete if we are to experience a healthy state of existence. Specifically, the five task areas involve establishing a relationship with (1) those with whom we have familial ties (e.g., parental figures and siblings), (2) members of our work environment, (3) a sexual partner, (4) ourselves, and (5) something beyond our immediate existence—a chance to reach beyond (Sweeney, 1998). Area five pertains to things such as finding a self-sustaining purpose to guide one, identifying life affirming goals, discovering one's reason for existing at this time and place in the universe, and even establishing meaningfulness in an oppressive environment. The last item listed is important to consider. Obviously, not all humans on the planet are provided with a neat, orderly array of Pollyanna-type options to select from on their way to self-actualize. While very difficult, it is still possible to establish a meaningful socially conscious existence in an oppressive environment. Such meaningfulness took place during October 1966 at Berkeley, California, when Stokely Carmichael gave a speech titled "Black Power." A small portion of his speech follows:

> We are not going to wait for white people to sanction Black power. We're tired of waiting; every time black people move in this country, they're forced to defend their position before they move. It's time that the people who are supposed to be defending their position do that. That's white people. They ought to start defending themselves as to why they have oppressed and exploited us.

In the same speech Carmichael (1966) stated,

> We cannot have white people working in the black community, and we mean it on a *psychological ground* [emphasis added]. The fact is that all black people often question whether or not they are equal to whites, because every time they start to do something, white people are around showing them how to do it. If we are going to eliminate that for the generation that comes after us, then black people must be seen in positions of *power* [emphasis added].

There are many instances where the healthy thing to do is resist a larger social force. Although Carmichael's form of social interest may not conjure up the images of ethereal beauty we like to associate with self-actualization, Adler's idea of *Gemeinschaftsgefuhl* can take many healthy forms.

Regrettably, when enough people in a society wield sufficient power to significantly confine, restrict, or narrow *Gemeinschaftsgefuhl* expression, the outcome is eventually counterproductive, even to those in positions of power. Such situations can lead to large-scale economic exploitation, unfair class designations, a pervasive level of societal tension, religious conflict and misunderstanding, and even hostility between various societal groups, regions, or nations. One subtle outcome of such socially toxic environments can be found in how words are sometimes used. Some words that originally had a strong negative meaning are used in ways that are misleading. Take the word *war*, whose archaic meaning was indisputably negative—its meaning implied battles that would result in the loss of many lives and various atrocities being committed (e.g., during a series of Russo-Turkish wars, soldiers performed anal sex on the dying in order to experience the resulting rectal spasm that coincided with death).

In contrast to the original meaning for war, when used in a phrase such as a "fare war" among airlines, what might be negative for the airlines has a positive meaning for potential passengers. Nor does a phrase such as the "war on drugs" sound terrible to many Americans. But what if the airlines cut the amount spent on safety procedures to make up for any losses due to the fare war? Or what if it is an 18-year-old family member who faces prison time for possessing a drug that some areas of the country currently allow to be purchased and/or carried on one's person without penalty? It seems the more we veer from acting in ways congruent with *Gemeinschaftsgefuhl*, the more likely we are to contribute to an increase in societal problems instead of a reduction.

Conscious and Unconscious Mental Activity

Adler asserted that various mental activities designated as conscious and unconscious are actually in concert with one another, that the mind represents the unison of processes that are naturally structured to work together rather than at odds with one another. The mind does not purposely struggle against itself to hide certain mental processes from awareness, nor are emotionally loaded memories automatically relegated to some shadowy region of the mind only to be heard from again in the repressed form of repetitive and self-defeating behaviors. Alfred Adler (1930/1968) stated, "Upon deeper inspection there appears no contrast between the conscious and the unconscious, that both cooperate for a higher purpose" (p. 341). In fact, Adler broke with Freud because Adler believed "in the equality or democracy of drives. Adler did not believe the id—with its primary emphasis on the sex drive—was the basic moving force in behavior [or was] any more powerful or influential than any other drive. Adler opposed the view that humans are composed of competing drives" (John C. Dagley, personal communication, October 19, 2011).

Adler noted that although a person's mind could register ambivalence, it was not the type of conflict where different parts of the mind—conscious and unconscious—were in disagreement or struggled for supremacy. Adler viewed such explanations as a false dichotomizing of the human experience because mental functions operated in unison. In truth, rather than conflicting feelings or thoughts, a sense of ambivalence was basically a state of indecisiveness as to what direction or course of action one should take to accomplish an important goal. Thus, according to Adler, the sensation often called mental conflict is caused by stalling in making a decision from among alternatives.

It is the high level of freedom that each person possesses that sets the stage for these alternatives to become bothersome in the first place. Of course, confounding the picture is the realization there is the possibility of selecting the wrong alternative. Interestingly, the possibility of going back or forward in time, prior to or after a person makes an important decision, has served as a story plot for several movies, including Woody Allen's *Midnight in Paris* (Aronson, Tenenbaum, Roures, & Allen, 2011). The story's protagonist, Gil Pender, an unfulfilled Hollywood screenwriter, travels to Paris in 2010 with his extremely materialistic fiancée, Inez. Each midnight Gil travels back in time to the 1920s where he encounters Ernest Hemingway, Gertrude Stein, and an array of other famous creative personalities. Through these midnight experiences Gil comes to realize that all time periods, even the purportedly exciting 1920s, can become monotonous and unfulfilling for those who live then. More important is Gil's insight that his lack of personal fulfillment is due to his failure to develop his abilities and character as they were meant to be. After the profound realization that he had previously chosen the wrong alternatives in life, Gil returns to 2010 where he jettisons his current job and relationship with Inez in order to pursue the life of a serious writer. The high degree of personal freedom that each person has to select from a wide range of alternatives can make life difficult.

Clearly, Adler did not accept the psychoanalytic unconscious as humankind's prime mover, nor does he believe it is some type of stimulus–response dynamic. For Adler, any form of stimulus–response reductionism would always fall short of providing a complete explanation as to why a person feels pulled or pushed to act.

Polarities: The First and Last Steps

Adler's concept of polarities further clarifies the role and importance of an individual's decisions. It is rare for a single decision to have the power to transport any decision maker immediately to the point he needs to be in life. End goals represent a successive series of decisions that may require weeks, months, or possibly years to achieve, but regardless of the duration or the exact number of decisions required, once a person has identified a specific starting point as important, then the decisions that follow share a commonality. This commonality forms the trajectory for future decisions that enable a person to successfully arrive at the much sought after goal or end point. Understanding the connection between the start and finish often proves helpful in situations when a client is derailed from a beneficial path that is now blocked. A therapist should keep in mind that decisions already made by the client can be used to reconstruct the trajectory to better understand what the person hoped to achieve and the true meaning of what is currently hindering the person from reaching the intended goal.

The starting point for the goal-oriented trajectory that the person was following until a problem arose can generally be conceptualized in terms of a perceived inferiority. At the same time, the end point can be viewed as a means to obtain a state of superiority over the originally perceived weakness. Adler described the end point of such polarities as success, completion, and even a "felt minus" moving toward a "perceived plus" (North American Society of Adlerian Psychology, 2011). The word most often used by Adler to describe arriving at one's goal was *superiority*. To correctly understand what Adler meant by the term *superiority*, we must return to Adler's concept of *Gemeinschaftsgefuhl*. Adler was not advocating power over others when he applied the term *superiority*, but rather an achievement in the sense of mastery or competence. Table 4.2 provides examples of what may be various starting points and their corresponding end points.

A male considered by others to be physically weak as an adolescent might become a champion bodybuilder. Whether the final goal coincides with sound mental health and

▼ TABLE 4.2

Goal-Oriented Trajectories: Starting Points and End Points

Start Point	End Point
Sickly	Bodybuilder
Disparagement	Esteem
Unrestrained	Disciplined
Sight Impairment	Artistic Painting
Unschooled	Intellectual
Isolation	Social Expansion
Dull	Witty
Distracted	Focused
Naive	Worldly
Shy	Stage Actor
Ignorance	Wisdom

an appropriate reaction to the original perception of weakness can be determined by looking through the lens of *Gemeinschaftsgefuhl*. The point can be illustrated by referring to an advertisement frequently printed in 1950s–1960s comic books that depicted a bodybuilder kicking sand in the face of a "98-pound weakling" (the paid announcement promised the adolescent reader he would be able to "kick sand at bullies by becoming strong too—for the low price of . . ."). Despite having overcome prior feelings of physical weakness, the bodybuilder would certainly have failed the litmus test of possessing adequate social interest. In this instance, rather than healthy goal attainment, we have an example of someone who has achieved a neurotic goal. For comparison purposes, take the example of *sight impairment* found in Table 4.2. The end point in this instance is *artistic painting*. Such an artistic goal is beautifully illustrated by the work of David A. Kontra. Kontra's painting *Iron Man* (based on the song of the same name by Black Sabbath) appears in Figure 4.3. Kontra is an African American who is legally blind because his visual field is less than 20 degrees diameter (10 degrees radius), which prevents him from seeing the whole canvas at any given moment, forcing Kontra to lean toward the canvas as he paints one section at a time. The resulting whole scene painted in *Iron Man* has the power to easily stir up feelings and thoughts the longer we study the figures depicted in

▼ FIGURE 4.3

Iron Man

Source: Reproduced with permission of E. J. Ginter.

the foreground, all of whom appear to be frantically running from the gigantic iron man figure dominating the background. Kontra's *Iron Man* provides an example of healthy goal achievement that exemplifies the type of social connectedness implied by Adler's theory. Each person who pauses to enjoy *Iron Man,* including those reading this chapter, literally help to contribute to a necessary quality required for the artist's end goal to be completed. In other words, taking time to appreciate this artist's work serves to create a meaningful social connection between the viewer and the artist in which both parties give and receive something in return. Specifically, for the artist, the presence of interested viewers confirms for him that he has genuinely achieved his goal.

Style of Life

According to Adler, style of life is essentially the combination of outer and inner characteristics of a person that contribute to the person being a distinct, independent, and self-contained entity, as well as the impression the person makes upon others. Style of life represents the way we seek to act and think in a manner that is consistent with our view of the world. It represents our own unique private logic that informs our actions.

According to Adler, each person's style of life is formed early (most likely before age 5), starting with the multitude of tasks a child has to master to move beyond childhood. Over time, one's style of life becomes a psychological magnet of sorts that pulls toward the person those things (knowledge, skills, and relationships) that will better prepare the person to achieve important goals. We are attracted to gathering those things we believe will lead to a significant end point. What starts as a means to overcome natural infant inferiority changes over time—developmentally, this will to power moves beyond the seeking of personally meaningful goals and becomes a striving that involves the common good.

Creative Self. What makes a style of life anything more than a mechanistic occurrence of events where A leads to B, and B leads to C, ad infinitum? The answer lies in Adler's discussion of a creative self, which left no doubt that individual psychology was a new category of theory and not a recasting of behaviorism or psychoanalysis cloaked in different terminology as some critics have claimed. So what made Adler's creative self such a powerful ingredient? Ansbacher's (1977) answer was that there are three malleable forces in a person's life: heredity, environment, and a creative quality that allows for a staggering number of possible outcomes.

The transformative power of the creative self operates in a way to form a personality that is unified, dynamic, and stands to a large degree independent from others in how the person goes about constructing her life. Whenever we are part of a group, it is our creative side that enables us to think the thoughts that differ from those of other members and thus contribute a qualitative solution rather than a quantitative addition of being just one more member of a group. It is our creative nature that mirrors the very essence of what makes each person among the billions of Earth's inhabitants different from one another.

Toward the end of Adler's life (he died in 1937), a radical form of behaviorism was taking hold in the United States, which eschewed the study of esoteric topics, such as unconscious processes, consciousness, and mind, and its proponents' new image for humanity was a world of automatons who lack active intelligence or free existence. Adler's concept of the creative self foreshadowed later humanistic thinkers such as Rogers and Maslow, because his concept emphasized the belief that persons could be masters of their fate. Adler's position has been referred to as *soft determinism*, which means that although human actions are not totally independent of external events, free will always enters the picture. This view is beautifully illustrated in the 1969 rock opera *Tommy* by the Who. Tommy, the main character, is referred to as this "deaf, dumb, and blind kid" who, through a sense of touch, becomes a "pinball wizard" and achieves the status of a guru. Tommy's Adlerian triumph is recognized as he sings "I'm free and freedom tastes of reality."

Human Development

Owing to a deep appreciation of the social cauldron, Adler realized parents singularly and together create much of the early developmental soup that gels to become a child's style of life. Adler was keenly interested in calling attention to various early dynamics within the family that had the power to contribute significantly to a child's style of life. More than any major therapist of his time, Adler called attention to the importance of understanding and helping young children and teenagers.

The term *family constellation* has been used to refer to the sum total of relationships at the family level. This includes familial patterns of interacting, roles played by family members, ages of each person, number of parents and children living together, birth order of each parent and their children, culture the family identifies with, and so forth.

Early Predisposing Experiences That Contribute to One's Personality. In addition to birth order, Adler focused on three experiences he believed deserves special attention as they pertain to children: disabilities, neglect, and pampering. Adler discovered that many prominent individuals began life with some sort of *infirmity*, but due to a loving home environment that encouraged independence and healthy social interactions these people transformed the actual weakness into strength. In other cases families reinforce, often unknowingly, the notion that there is something wrong. This type of treatment lowers the child's self-esteem and results in an indelible identity tied to being less than others. According to Adler, overprotection and trying to prevent the child from failing in life is psychologically more crippling than any physical disability in terms of the child's future goals and social interests.

In cases of pampering, it is as if the child's motivation is killed through too much sugar—often without the parents recognizing their contribution to preventing the child from achieving his or her potential. According to Adler, the pampered child represents a potential danger for society because these individuals develop weak social feelings. Today, these are the individuals who are tagged with the popular catch-all label "narcissistic." According to Adler, they are the despots of the world who enjoy power over others and who inflict damage on society in direct portion to their level of power.

Finally, the neglected child is one who responds to her world of quiet or blatant abuse by developing a lack of trust or interest in others. She soon adopts the stance that others are potential enemies. The neglected child sometimes has a need for revenge that can manifest itself directly or in less obvious but still very detrimental ways. For example, a financial advisor who steals money may believe it is justified since the world cannot be trusted or does not care about him.

Birth Order in the Family and Its Contribution to One's Personality

Considering the importance of others in shaping our personality, Adler considered how birth order might affect a child. Adler believed that the positioning of children in the family as first, middle, or last born, can have just as powerful an effect as being born an only child (Alexandra Adler, 1938).

First-Born or Only Child. The child typically enters the family as the focus of attention. As a result of this redistribution of familial attention, even the father and mother's previous pattern of interactions as a couple is altered. The first-born is the "prince" or "princess" of the family. If the parents have a second child, the first-born may experience a sense of being dethroned from her favored position. Another redistribution of attention is experienced by the first-born as unexpected and hurtful. This experience may cause the first-born to display for the remainder of his life behaviors and concerns that suggest feelings and thoughts of insecurity or even animosity toward those who garner attention.

For example, the coworker who is dethroned in life is a difficult person to work with for no reason apparent to the new hire. Adler suggested that as adults, first-born children may become past oriented since in the past they were the center of attention. In addition, depending on experiences that unfold after being dethroned, the child could follow a path that prevents the development of full social interest. Adler advocated for parents to prepare the child well before the arrival of another child, deflating as much as possible the perspective that a rival has been brought into the family. The advantage of being a first-born or only child is a motivation to achieve and excel in life to a large extent because of the early parental attention and parental expectations. The only child differs in that she never encounters sibling rivalry and in some form retains her "royal" position, with both advantages and disadvantages, throughout life. For example, an only child possesses a high need to achieve and a strong desire to control situations, which is accompanied by a low need for affiliation.

Second or Middle Child. Adler believed these children are better adjusted and capable of interacting with others—they are the socially adept in the world. We should also expect the child to develop a competitive attitude toward the first-born and older children in the family. Rebelliousness is not an uncommon trait, nor is it uncommon for these children as adults to express envy of others. The second-born desires to assume the older child's special status and will attempt to gain an advantage over the special-status child if the opportunity arises.

Youngest Child. Next to the first-born, the youngest was thought by Adler to be the most likely to develop a neurotic personality. This is the person labeled the "baby of the family"—a label that can be carried well into adulthood where the adult individual is still referred to as the "baby" whenever taking part in family gatherings. The danger for the last-born is to be "babied" to the point that the person experiences a continuous state of pampering, which denies him many opportunities to meet life's challenges and develop the requisite skills to be successful on his own. Youngest children may also possess high degrees of self-esteem and develop good interpersonal skills that get them what they want in life, causing them to be seen by some as mostly concerned about their own welfare.

Although we can certainly relate to varying degrees about the pressure we feel to excel and lead the way, or the need experienced as a second-born to "dethrone" the oldest sibling to obtain parental attention, or being called the "baby of the family," in truth, research findings for birth order have been debated for years.

Therapy

The atmospheric quality of the client's current social life, coupled with understanding the client's goals and frustrations, informed Adler where to begin therapy, but such knowledge only created a rough framework. According to Adler, the specifics of the process—such as what therapy tools are needed—depend largely on what unfolds along the way. What can be expected with absolute certainty is that the unique nature of each client's case requires the therapist to remain creative and flexible throughout the therapeutic process and to be ready to pull from a wide range of techniques as needed.

Goal of Therapy

Adlerian-based goals generally fall into one of two categories (Alexandra Adler, 1938): (1) change within the stock of skills associated with the style of life (e.g., developing more effective ways to handle social conflict) and (2) structural change to the style of life itself (i.e., personality change). Most client changes fall somewhere between these two categories. Before a client can be helped, it is necessary to discover why there is a misalignment between the client's actions and meaningful direction in the person's life. One can expect that clients, prior to entering therapy, experienced a sense of nonfulfillment and discouragement seeping into their everyday life. This sense of nonfulfillment and discouragement eventually pools into a static existence where achievement motivation has essentially come to a standstill.

Because the specificity of goals is seen as critically important, it is not unusual for Adlerians to use a contract to record goals so they can be expressed in a clear and precise manner. If needed, the contract might also clarify exactly what the therapist and the client are responsible for in moving toward meeting the agreed upon goals. Beyond the two general categories of goals mentioned earlier, goals developed in therapy can be expressed in a seemingly infinite variety of client concerns such as those found in Table 4.3.

Therapist's Role

At the moment of contact with the client, the therapist begins to establish a relationship with the client in which mutual trust and respect permeate their interactions. Time is devoted to explaining that the client–therapist relationship will be "50–50," so collaboration is of primary importance. Dreikurs (1967/1973) elaborated on the importance of collaborative goal setting when he stated that whatever the goal is, both the client and the therapist must agree that the needed change can be achieved.

The therapist also will hone in on displays of social interests on the part of the client, because such displays provide a common ground on which the therapist and client can meet. Instances of such client behavior create an opportunity for the therapist to convey the importance of social interest to healthy functioning.

It is important to realize collaboration is not seen or used as a technique. The collaborative attitude displayed by the therapist reflects the therapist's belief that clients are

▼ TABLE 4.3

Possible Therapy Goals

• Cultivate greater empathy and interests in others. • Change self-defeating behavior to wise action. • Find a meaningful purpose in life. • Overcome my stifling comfort zone. • Expand my interpersonal space to involve more people. • Discover who I am. • Learn how to realize a long-time daydream. • Discover and apply my talents in new and satisfying ways.	• Connect rather than compete with others. • Build life goals based on my competencies rather than what other people say I should do. • Expand my avenues for creative expression. • Learn to embrace what life has to offer. • Develop healthy ways to interact with my family. • Learn socially healthy ways to confront intolerance. • Break free of the fear that hinders my living. • Become more like the old me that was productive and happy.

masters of their own lives and possess the ability to change. For this reason the therapist responds in ways that denote the client is viewed as the one responsible for her life. For example, even though the Adlerian therapist has acquired the requisite training and experience to interpret various aspects of what is uncovered about the client, the therapist will avoid taking responsibility away from the client, as when a therapist responds with dogmatic statements or adopts the role of an expert. This is why an Adlerian interpretation is introduced to the client with phrases such as the following:

"Could it be _____?"

"I have a thought, but tell me if I am wrong."

"I just had a thought I will share. You tell me if it helps explain _____."

"Is it possible that the feeling you just described reflects _____?"

Finally, even how the therapist is physically positioned in relation to the client conveys the collaborative nature of the relationship. "Adler sat 'knee-to-knee' with his clients, in a simple, human exchange, rather than taking a position behind and outside of the person's visible range" during therapy (John C. Dagley, personal communication, October 19, 2011).

Client's Role

As mentioned previously, a critical quality of the client's role emphasized during sessions is responsibility. Although a dimension in all forms of therapy, responsibility acquires its own distinctive form in Adlerian therapy. Adler recognized that a desire to change and a fear of change can cancel one another out just as they frequently do for most people outside of therapy. Adler claimed, "The neurotic style represents a 'yes-but' manner of approach. Because of their logic neurotics say 'yes' to various tasks which confront them and in saying 'but' they stress all the obstacles preventing them from going ahead" (Alexandra Adler, 1938, p. 7). Individuals entering therapy often feel powerless to determine appropriate action because of perceived restraints. Adlerians believe it is important for the client to assume the responsibility that comes with freedom. Accepting responsibility is associated with increases in client resilience, adaptability, and buoyancy to rise above the problems of life and meet head on the challenges that strengthen us.

The 1-2-3-4 of Therapy

Adlerian therapy requires the therapist to be vigilant from the start. The way the client enters the therapy room, what words the client selects, where the client sits, what mannerisms the client uses, how the client is dressed—these impressions must form a united view of the client in the mind of the therapist. Thus, at first blush the therapist seeks to obtain an impression of the client's style of life. Rather than diagnosing a disease or disorder, the therapist is looking for system failure—what is it about the person's style of life that faltered to such an extent that the person now finds himself entangled in a troublesome situation? Adler conceptualized the process and outcome of therapy to be captured within a four-phase sequence: relationship building, exploration, insight, and action.

Therapeutic Relationship. Although it seems paradoxical, clients who seek therapy are expected to show resistance or what many Adlerians refer to as *safeguarding* (Jones & Lyddon, 2003). This tendency toward self-deception lies waiting among the symptoms described by the client, and it can take on a multitude of forms, all with the single purpose of protecting the client from certain therapist requests or from unpleasant realizations (i.e., inferiority feelings). This is just one of several reasons for the therapist to focus on creating the therapeutic relationship advocated by Adler.

Because the client is experiencing a state of discouragement rather than being psychologically sick, the Adlerian relationship entails creating a bond of encouragement. (Although Adlerians understand that *DSM* symptoms are used to identify and report disorders to a third party, for Adlerians the real value of symptoms is what the symptoms say about the client's attempt to find a solution. Symptoms are the remnants of failed solutions.) *Encouragement* requires the therapist to maintain focused listening, respond in ways that are empathic, and convey a genuine respect for, and confidence in, the client's ability to find solutions. Encouragement is singularly important to the therapeutic process.

According to Dinkmeyer and Sperry (1999), the therapy process that was derived from Adler's position entails looking for and finding a client's strengths and assets that are brought to the forefront of what is discussed. Interestingly, maintaining such a focus—finding strengths and value in others—seems to be increasingly difficult to achieve in what might be called today's "mistake-centered culture." Regrettably, today's electro-culture has elevated the conveyors of the current mistake-centered world to a new level. For example, cell phone cameras provide a means of capturing the ludicrous, bizarre, or dehumanizing and the forwarding of the captured images to what constitutes a worldwide audience of electronic voyeurs can lead to devastating results, such as when the unwanted exposure by an internet bully leads to what might be termed e-suicide.

Exploration. Adlerian assessment uncovers signifiers of poorly developed social interests, mistaken notions about the self and the surrounding world, a style of life built on a faulty foundation of nostalgia, and early family mishaps or traditions that misdirected early choices. Assessment enables the therapist to perceive the client as a three-dimensional person with a problem unique to whom the person is.

Adler found that asking about early memories is a very useful means to understanding a client's personality in both individual and group sessions, because these early memories provide valuable snapshots of the client's style of life. For example, when someone known by one of the authors of this text was asked to recall an early memory, the person reported the following incident that took place approximately 55 years earlier in his life.

> I was sitting at a window of our second story apartment, looking out at the neighborhood store, which was situated at an intersection. I remember seeing a mother with two children. The older child seemed to be my age and he

was arguing with his mother. The mother seemed to instruct the child he was to remain at the corner as she crossed the street to go into the store with the younger child. I left my position at the window to go into another room. After a few minutes I heard the siren of a police car and I returned to the window where I discovered the child my age had been run over by a large truck. The mother had dropped her grocery bag, and items had scattered everywhere on the street. What immediately caught my attention was the milk from the shattered milk bottle: Glaring white milk was intermingling with the bright red blood on the street. The colors mixing were a powerful image that sticks with me to this day. The mother stood by the body with her head turned upward. She was screaming as the young child next to her sobbed uncontrollably. Transfixed by the horrible image of a child crushed by the tires of a delivery truck I thought: *He should have listened and not tried to cross the street.*

For Adlerians, the accuracy of this reported incident is less important than what it tells us about the person because the stories we recall are very likely significant contributors to our particular style of life. In the case of the person who told this particular story, his style of life is marked by a high degree of cautiousness that often prevents him from making up his mind quickly. He tends to dwell on possible negative outcomes that could occur from making a decision. Once he is mentally prepared for the "worst case scenario," he then takes action, feeling he is prepared for the impending disaster.

Having the client report dreams can serve a useful purpose throughout the therapeutic process. Similar to the useful information generated by probing early memories, dreams allow a therapist to assess a client's style of life as well as measure changes as therapy progresses. There is emphasis placed on the personal meaning of dreams over universal symbols because what might appear to have absolute meaning may not.

It is not unusual for Adlerians to use a structured set of questions that are best completed in a session. Table 4.4 provides a form that utilizes an Adlerian approach to assessment.

Insight: Therapist's and Client's. In the next phase, the therapist concentrates on helping the client achieve an understanding of various relationships that will shed light on and help solve the client's reason for becoming discouraged. Because insight is immeasurably more meaningful and useful when reached by the client, the therapist's understanding of the client's situation is used as a guide to create the therapeutic environment necessary for the client to achieve insight. Confrontation enters the picture at this point since the client is still invested in protecting an erroneous view of self that is reinforced by a fear of change. The therapist often contends with the faulty belief that somehow someone or something (e.g., bad luck, punishment for something done, cosmic fate) is responsible for the client's discouragement.

The therapist uses various techniques to both overcome resistance and increase client understanding (*resistance* is a means of protecting oneself against inferiority feelings). For example, the client might say, "Others are always taking advantage of me at work and not giving me the credit I am due." In this example, the client's comment is an attempt to protect her self-esteem by clinging to an inflated self-importance. In such

A Structured Exploration: Using the A—Worksheet

Name _____ Date _____

Age _____ Place of birth _____

Level of education _____

Occupation _____

Occupation of parents _____

Reply to the following 13 sections.

1. Identify the member of your family who displays(ed) the *greatest amount* of each characteristic listed below in the box. Do not forget to include yourself (indicate by using the word *me*). Keep in mind you are to use the descriptor you believe best identifies the family member. For example, if a person had "two mothers," using a person's name would clarify who is being referred to whereas the word *mom* would not.

_____ a. Complaining		_____ n. Submissiveness
_____ b. Sharing		_____ o. Sadness
_____ c. Blaming		_____ p. Joy
_____ d. Creativity		_____ q. Sympathy
_____ e. Anxiety		_____ r. Empathy
_____ f. Determination		_____ s. Ambition
_____ g. Giving up		_____ t. Jealousy
_____ h. Supportiveness		_____ u. Playfulness
_____ i. Helplessness		_____ v. Raw talent
_____ j. Anger		_____ w. Envy
_____ k. Love		_____ x. Moodiness
_____ l. Fear		_____ y. Immaturity
_____ m. Cheerfulness		_____ z. Modesty

2. Describe what you see as your purpose in life.

   _____

   _____

3. In what situation are you most likely to feel discouraged?

   _____

   _____

4. List and briefly describe at least two important beliefs that guide your actions.

   _____

   _____

(Continued)

(Continued)

5. Using what is listed in the box below, compare yourself to the other sibling(s) in your family. Rate yourself on the 26 areas listed below, using the scale provided. (If you are an *only child,* please compare yourself to your peers.)

1	2	3	4	5	6	7
Low			Medium			High

_____ a. Sense of control

_____ b. Social skills

_____ c. Sense of worth

_____ d. Sense of humor

_____ e. Level of talent

_____ f. Ability to manage stress

_____ g. Meaningfulness derived from school

_____ h. Meaningfulness derived from work

_____ i. Ability to love

_____ j. Ambition

_____ k. Need for solitude

_____ l. Social interest

_____ m. Empathetic ability

_____ n. Sense of being connected to all of humanity

_____ o. Ability to form strong friendships

_____ p. Degree I am self-directed

_____ q. Degree I feel inadequate

_____ r. Attention seeking

_____ s. *Desire* to overcome obstacles in my life

_____ t. Leadership skills

_____ u. *Ability* to overcome obstacles in my life

_____ v. Participation skills

_____ w. Social activism

_____ x. Degree I am unique

_____ y. Able to effectively interact with members of diverse groups (e.g., gender, ethnicity, sexual identity, disabilities, economic status, and ages)

_____ z. Able to effectively interact with members of groups with beliefs that differ from my own (e.g., religion, politics, or philosophy of life)

6. In what type of situations does it become difficult to follow your beliefs?

_____

_____

7. I experience a sense of belongingness when I _____? (Finish the sentence.)

_____

8. My typical approach to problems that obstruct or hinder my progress is to _____? (Finish the sentence.)

_____

9. When I daydream, I daydream about _____? (Finish the sentence.)

_____

10. Briefly describe your earliest three memories of a parent and name the parent.

_____

instances, the therapist would not respond to the comment's surface meaning but would respond in a way meant to prevent resistance from completing its mission of self-protection.

Adler thought it important to avoid terminology and to speak to clients as clearly and transparently as possible. When a client who had previously undergone psychoanalysis concluded his problem evolved out of an unresolved Oedipal complex, Adler confronted this claim with, "Look here, what do you want of the old lady?" (Ansbacher, 1977, p. 68). What is the client to say in response to such a straightforward comment by a therapist? To reject the remark is to play cat and mouse where client engages in a game-like relationship, but to answer truthfully is to be one step closer to achieving successful termination.

Action-Infused Reorientation. The framework of client understanding is tested in the final phase. Somewhat amorphous at first, through therapist and client collaboration the newly developed cognitive framework created through an accumulation of understandings soon provides the client a detailed blueprint for taking action to reconstruct a meaningful style of life.

Adler never thought client insight or just attending therapy sessions was enough. The client's insight had to be brought back into the client's world. Because time between sessions should be used to help the client advance toward meeting established therapeutic goals, homework assignments are invaluable. The intent of Adlerian homework is not to create challenges but rather to reinforce or complement what is being achieved through therapeutic collaboration. Therefore, the homework is constructed with a high probability for success, which provides an opportunity during a follow-up session to further encourage a client's inherent strengths and even discuss ways to make these strengths more effective. Finally, Adlerian reparation essentially means that errors and perceived deficiencies are replaced by a renewed, vibrant, and convincing style of life that replaces neurotic, self-serving, interpersonal interest with genuine social interest.

Therapeutic Techniques and Procedures

Adlerian techniques are more than just a skilled way of interacting with a client. They should be seen as logical extensions of Adler's philosophical view of the world (Ansbacher & Ansbacher, 1956; Sweeney, 1998; Watts, 2003; Watts, Peluso, & Lewis, 2008).

The Question. When a client raised a health concern in therapy, Adler would determine whether the client suffered from a psychological or physically centered problem since each requires a different approach. Adler did this by asking a question: "What would you do if you were well?" If a client said something such as "I believe I could finally sleep through the night without tossing and turning due to pain," Adler suspected a physiological component. If a client said something such as "I would be capable of getting along better with my coworkers," then Adler suspected the reported illness disguised a psychologically embedded tactic to protect self-esteem.

Acting "As If." This action is intended to have the client try an action that the client believes likely to fail. As the client is reluctant to try the action, the therapist will ask the client to "act as if" the action will be successful.

Client	"I loathe speaking with my boss about a project. I'd like to propose something that I believe would draw new business."
Therapist	"You are uncomfortable in situations where you must defend an action, but you need to step up to the challenge. Set up a meeting with your boss next week and speak to her *as if* you were certain about your proposal's success. We will take a little time now so we look at ways you might prepare for this responsibility."

In this example, the client has been given an assignment to complete. After completing the "acting as if" assignment in a real-world setting, the outcome will be explored in therapy (keeping in mind that the therapist believes the client is ready to try this action). A successful outcome will be built upon, but even outcomes viewed as less than stellar can be reviewed in ways to strengthen the client's confidence for the next action assigned to be carried out.

Prescribing the Symptom. Adler introduced this technique, which also has been called "anti-suggestion" by Adlerians. It is widely used in marriage and family therapy where it is called "paradoxical intention." It is implemented when a client is unrealistically focused on a problem behavior he wants to avoid but seems unable to do so. Adler would instruct the client to purposely do the behavior the client is concerned about. Increasing a particular behavior is intended to cause the client to perceive it in a different light. Specifically, by increasing the level of repetition, the client comes to realize he is controlling the action rather than the action controlling him. This places the client in a position where in the future he has to choose to either accept the consequences of acting this way or change.

Avoiding the Tar Baby. When the therapist senses a client is stalling, it is likely that the inner voice of the client is saying something to avoid responsibility, for example, "If I'm so inept and irresponsible with my life that I wound up in therapy. How can I ever believe I possess the strength to conquer my problem?" The phrase used to describe a therapist falling prey to such manipulation is "touching and sticking to the tar baby." This can be avoided by the therapist staying on task, that is, encouraging and assisting the client in developing more realistic steps that will lead to success rather than looking to the end goal without knowing how to get there (which generates anxiety and a self-protective mode of responding). Breaking homework assignments into smaller steps is one way to do this.

Catching Oneself. Even if a client genuinely commits to change with the aim of satisfying a goal that was collaboratively established, it does not mean the client will not revert back to previous forms of faulty thinking and behavior. The therapist can actually use such slippage to elevate the client rather than allow the client to wallow in discouragement. The therapist essentially does this by putting a positive spin on the event by teaching the client how to look for early signs of future slippage and use these signs as a cue for the client to apply tactics that will prevent previous forms of faulty thinking and behavior from taking hold and manifesting full force. Each time the client applies these tactics, the client strengthens the skills needed to move forward in therapy.

Spitting in the Client's Soup. Once the therapist understands the reasons for certain counterproductive behavior, the therapist is able to make the behavior "less tasty" for the client by revealing the true motive behind the behavior. This causes the client to realize the therapist will see the particular behavior as a means of torpedoing progress inside and outside of therapy. Just the thought of the therapist understanding this leaves a "bad taste" and a reluctance to fall back on a counterproductive behavior.

Push-Button Technique. The therapist has a client recall in detail a past experience of feeling pleasant, in control, and free of worries. Once the client has a clear image of the past situation, the client is asked to concentrate on the thoughts and feelings associated with the image with eyes shut. Following this accomplishment, the therapist has the client imagine an unpleasant past event in detail. After the client successfully creates both images, the therapist can have the client practice juxtaposing the early pleasant image onto the unpleasant one. The procedure establishes that the client has the ability to break free of unpleasant thoughts by shifting the mind's focus. The technique encourages and inspires the client to assume personal responsibility for negative, self-defeating thinking.

Process of Change

Adlerian therapy leads to clients abandoning their original life-defining goals that were based on factors such as self-limiting assumptions and misguided motives or faulty ideals. Clients' abilities to initiate meaningful personal change in their lives emerges when they alter their personal direction and embrace what is required for them to live a fuller life. Change means that clients redirect their focus toward achieving life-defining goals that are genuinely meaningful, unique, and prosocial in nature.

Research Support

According to Alexandra Adler (1938), her father prescribed Adlerian therapy for individuals who were *unable to help themselves* (p. 82). The comment reveals important information concerning Adler's perspective, and a search of the literature provides support for the therapy's effectiveness and several of Adler's theoretical conceptualizations. As far back as 1977, a seminal article by Mary Smith and Gene Glass provided evidence to support the effectiveness of Adlerian therapy in terms of statistically integrated effect sizes (an effect size is also referred to as a treatment effect; in 2009 Sawilowsky proposed the following scale for interpreting the strength of a reported treatment effect: .01 = very small, .20 = small, .50 = medium, .80 = large, 1.20 = very large, and 2.00 = huge). In their 1977 article, Smith and Glass reported the following effect sizes (treatment effects): .71 for Adlerian, .76 for behavior modification, .63 for client-centered, .48 for eclectic, .26 for gestalt, .59 for psychodynamic, and .77 for rational-emotive therapy. In addition, the positive findings of several research studies (i.e., Amerikaner, Elliot, & Swank, 1988; Burnett, 1988; Herrington, Matheny, Curlette, McCarthy, & Penick, 2005; Johansen, 2005; Manaster et al., 1977; Newton & Mansager, 1986; Perkins-Dock, 2005; Shlien, Mosak, & Dreikurs, 1962; Zarski, Sweeney, & Barcikowski, 1977) are reported next to provide a sample of the types of studies that exist in support of Adler's position. The previously mentioned researchers found support for the following: Time-limited Adlerian therapy resulted in clients reporting their real selves were closer to what they considered to be their ideal selves at the point of termination; Adlerian parenting programs were found to be effective; a healthy style of life is tied to less anxiety; the expected style of life descriptors associated with being a priest was confirmed; and Adler's early recollections were found to accurately predict career choice.

When Murdock (2009) summarized findings for Adler's social interest concept, she found it to be positively correlated to age of the person, altruism, marital adjustment, belief in religion, trustworthiness, vigor, and volunteerism. In addition, she found that social interest was negatively correlated to depression, hostility, narcissism, and the status of having committed a felony. Interestingly, the area that has been researched the most—birth order—has proven to be problematic in terms of obtaining consistent results. However, it is important to note that thousands of professional journal articles and other articles in the public media have been published on the construct of birth order.

Systematic Training for Effective Parenting (STEP), which is rooted in Adlerian psychology, is a skills-based approach to teaching parents how to avoid problems that can arise from reliance on an autocratic parenting style. The U.S. Department of Health and Human Services (2010) reviewed several published STEP studies and found a number of significant and positive outcomes for parents who received STEP training, such as the following: (a) Mothers of 3- and 4-year-olds rated their children more positively. (b) Parents were potentially less likely to physically abuse their children. (c) Parents of 3- to 16-year-old children who were receiving mental health services showed improvement in the areas of problem solving, communication, emotional responsiveness, and behavior control. Furthermore, 38% of the

STEP participants moved from a clinical range in family functioning to a healthy range, whereas only 12% of the comparison group's parents did so. (d) Parents of infants and toddlers showed a decline in parenting stress. Also, one subgroup of mothers (those recruited from a drug treatment program) experienced decreased stress toward how they felt about themselves. (e) Parents exposed to a mildly stressful teaching situation demonstrated improved parent–infant interaction during the situation.

Researchers also have conducted Adlerian play therapy (AdPT) with preschoolers (Dillman-Taylor & Bratton, 2014) and other elementary school students (Meany-Walen, Bratton, & Kottman, 2014). Dillman-Taylor and Bratton (2014) determined that 4-year-olds lack the conceptual development to express thoughts and feelings through words, so this type of therapy could be beneficial to implement into treatment protocols within an appropriate developmental framework. Meany-Walen et al. (2014) found that AdPT significantly reduced disruptive behavior in elementary school students. An additional benefit of AdPT was that teachers who worked with students receiving the treatments also reported a significant reduction in stress.

Additionally, researchers recently have incorporated Adlerian therapy into family therapy (Fennell & Fishel, 1998; Pfefferle & Mansager, 2014; Sperry, 2011). Sperry discussed working with "borderline families," or a combination of severe personality traits expressed in family members. Sperry introduced effective suggestions for therapists to use while conducting Adlerian therapy with this population: Therapists should be able to maintain effective control, teach on how to set limits, help clients to simplify their actions and activities, strengthen boundaries, and help them to take appropriate risks while experiencing emotional pain. Researchers are beginning to see the benefits of implementing Adlerian strategies in their family therapy sessions.

One strength of Adlerian therapy is that there are several instruments with solid psychometric properties that are based on this approach. These measures include Crandall's (1991) Social Interest Scale; Sulliman's (1973) Social Interest Scale; Campbell, White, and Stewart's (1991) Psychological Birth Order Inventory; the Basic Adlerian Scales for Interpersonal Success—Adult Form (Wheeler, Kern, & Curlette, 1993); and the Encouragement Scale (Dagley, Evans, & Taylor, 1992).

Finally, it should be noted that other investigators have explored the possible benefits of integrating cognitive, constructivist, psychoanalytic-based, and systems perspectives with contemporary Adlerian therapy. One possible benefit from this integration is the greater use of time in therapy as a result of increased structure. The flexibility inherent in Adlerian therapy allows for an integration of a variety of methods, which in turn facilitates employing the approach with a diverse clientele (Watts, 2003). In addition, according to Watts and Shulman (2003), because Adlerian therapy is better able to therapeutically adapt to the unique needs of a client, therapists using this approach are less likely to force-fit a client into some readymade form of treatment compared with some approaches. Overall, despite the research cited in this section, the support for the use of Adlerian therapy is relatively limited compared to some other approaches.

Individual Psychology and Social Justice

It is evident from Adler's writings and lectures that he was keenly aware of the damage inflicted on society by male dominance throughout the ages. Early in his career he began to speak out against the lopsided status of the sexes and the alleged inferiority of women. Using historical evidence he pointed to the prior existence of matriarchies where women, especially mothers, played a prominent role in society. He compared such historical events with laws in the early 1900s undertaken to ensure that a deceased's personal estate (e.g., money, valuables, securities, and chattel) and real estate (land and buildings) were passed on to a male descendant, even if the male was a distant relative, rather than a female from the immediate family. An example of this is found in the striking dramatic subplot explored in Jane Austen's *Pride and Prejudice*.

Alfred Adler (1927/1954) concluded that male dominance was literally no more than an artifact of man's creation and not inherently natural, stating "there is no justification for the differentiation of 'manly' and 'womanly' character traits" (p. 107). As a partial means to correct for what Adler termed *masculine privilege*, he advocated for coeducation, starting at the first rung of education's ladder, because he was convinced that such a learning environment would eventually put aside many of the fallacious opinions held about women.

The extent that Adler was committed to social justice went well beyond writing about and speaking out against various forms of oppression. Concern for treating neurosis (Alfred Adler, 1935) and preventing delinquency through the creation of free child guidance clinics in various schools and areas around Vienna was a tangible commitment to improving society for both adults and children. In addition, Adler was known to hold weekly lectures in the People's Institute of Vienna auditorium, where attendees of both sexes as well as a range of ages heard Adler speak on various topics, including those related to creating positive societal changes.

After reviewing the Adlerian literature, Watts (2003) concluded, "Adler campaigned for social equality of women, contributed much to the understanding of gender issues, spoke against the marginalization of minority groups, and specifically predicted the black power and women's liberation movements" (p. 29). Watts also uncovered that during the Supreme Court's landmark decision for the plaintiffs in *Brown v. Board of Education*, a team of social scientists led by Kenneth B. Clark used Adlerian theory to argue against the separate-but-equal doctrine that moved the Court to find for the plaintiffs. Adler's commitment to social justice continues into this century at various programs and institutes currently using an Adlerian training model, such as the Adler School of Professional Psychology located in Chicago and founded by Rudolf Dreikurs. The institute's mission statement includes three interconnected components: producing socially responsible practitioners, community engagement, and social justice.

Multicultural Perspective

Although it may appear that Adlerian theory and therapy have limited application, there is cultural evidence to the contrary. Johansen (2005) argued that the basic foundational elements of individual psychology are applicable for those who follow the Islamic faith, but Johansen believed its application is less clear for clients who identify with cultures that strongly adhere to a collective view of behavior. On the other hand, Perkins-Dock (2005, p. 235) argued that careful consideration of certain core components of individual psychology—such as the importance of wholeness and unity over the fragmentation of reality, social interest in the group, family constellation, goals emerging from collaborative efforts, and applying interventions that respect the unique situation—can be adapted without much difficulty to meet Johansen's concern of applicability. Furthermore, if we zero in on Carl Rogers's core conditions, we uncover important similarities in Rogers's approach and Adler's concept of social interest (Watts et al., 2008). These similarities and other humanistic qualities of the two approaches would seem to provide support to claim that Adler's approach could be adapted and used in those cultures where Rogers's approach has proven useful (Gerstein, Heppner, Ægisdóttir, Leung, & Norsworthy, 2009).

Finally, whereas Adler seemed to adhere to the prevailing psychiatric view of his time concerning homosexuality, in truth his views are more complicated than one might initially suspect. When a social worker contacted Adler to obtain his opinion about a gay client, Adler asked if the client was happy. Receiving the answer "yes," Adler essentially stated that homosexuality in this case was a nonissue (Manaster et al., 1977). Considering this particular response, it appears that other aspects of Adler's views may have superseded even the widely held view of the time concerning what was generally considered to be a perversion of normality.

It appears safe to conclude that a strength of Adlerian therapy is its emphasis on multiculturalism. This focus is inherent in the theory. Arciniega and Newlon (1999) reported, for instance, that due to its understanding of clients in a sociocultural context, its focus on social justice, and its acknowledgment of the collective spirit, Adlerian therapy is an approach that has the uppermost potential to correct for issues of multicultural injustice. By stressing the importance of social context, Adlerian therapy can be used with a variety of clients. Adlerian therapists actively explore their clients' role in the social environment. This creates a natural space for the concepts of age, ethnicity, lifestyle, and gender to be discussed. When Adlerian therapy is practiced as intended by Adler, it is believed few if any issues from a multicultural perspective emerge as a hindrance to treatment effectiveness. As a result, Adlerian therapy can be effectively utilized with a diverse clientele (Carlson & Carlson, 2000; Ivey, Ivey, & D'Andrea, 2011; Watts & Pietrzak, 2000; Watts, Trusty, & Lim, 1996).

Relevance of the Adlerian Approach

Adlerian therapy's strong focus on concepts such as self-esteem and social interest allows it to be useful in various settings, such as private practices, social service agencies, clinics, and educational and health care facilities (Ambrason, 2007; Dinkmeyer, McKay, & Dinkmeyer, 2008; Dinkmeyer & Sperry, 1987; Prout & Brown, 2007; Sweeney, 1998; Ziomek-Daigle, McMahon, & Paisley, 2008). Psychiatric hospitals and the military also have found Adlerian therapy to be helpful. Many veterans and inpatients in psychiatric hospitals have low self-esteem and lack a sense of belonging (Blackburn, O'Connell, & Richman, 1984; Croake & Myers, 1985). The Adlerian approach fosters a sense of belonging and promotes competence in these individuals (Milliren, Evans, & Newbauer, n.d.). Additionally, the Adlerian approach has been used in child, youth, adult, parent–child, marital, family, group, correctional, and rehabilitation counseling (Ambrason, 2007; Carlson, Watts, & Maniacci, 2006; Dinkmeyer et al., 2008; Emener, Richard, & Bosworth, 2009; Ferguson, 2010; Prout & Brown, 2007; Sweeney, 1998; Ziomek-Daigle et al., 2008). Adlerian therapists work with clients presenting with a range of issues and who differ greatly in the severity of their concerns. Adlerian therapy has been found to be helpful with a broad spectrum of issues because of its focus on individuals' lifestyles. This approach highlights how faulty interpretations of life events may lead to difficulty in functioning. During therapy, clients give new meaning to these life events, which in turn improves their mental health (Ansbacher, 1974). This approach also focuses on social connectedness and how we may form more healthy relationships that lead to an increased sense of security and worthiness (Alfred Adler, 1927/1954).

Adlerian therapy is considered to be a psychoeducational approach that is both present and future oriented as well as brief in nature (Watts, 2000). Scholars argue whether Adlerian therapy was truly intended to be a brief approach (Watts, 2000). According to Watts (2000), Adler was a proponent of time-limited therapy during which clients are educated about their lifestyle and how such a style relates to their life tasks. Due to the therapy's time-limited focus, insurance providers may reimburse for Adlerian therapy if an appropriate diagnosis from the American Psychological Association's *Diagnostic and Statistical Manual of Mental Disorders* (*DSM*) is provided (Corsini & Wedding, 2010). Many proponents of Adlerian therapy, however, do not support labeling clients based on the *DSM* criteria. They contend that a *DSM* diagnosis fails to highlight the movement in an individual's life, focusing instead on static descriptions of an individual's functioning (Corsini & Wedding, 2010; Maniacci, 2002). Numerous clinical settings offer Adlerian therapy for clients that pay for services themselves. In such cases, it is not crucial to generate a diagnosis based on the *DSM* criteria because insurance providers are not involved in the payment process.

Training of Adlerian Therapists. One measure of Adlerian therapy's continued relevancy is indicated by the many individuals who have sought and continue to seek training in this very practical and especially socially applicable form of therapy. Alfred Adler's initial interests in training others has continued to this day, and along the way, training has become truly international in scope with training sites spread across the globe. The first group of Adler's students came to the United States from Europe and established centers in New York City, San Francisco, and Chicago. The next group of students sprang up in Minneapolis, Boise, Victoria, BC (Canada), South Carolina, and Tampa, Florida. Today, many institutes in Lithuania, Austria, the United Kingdom, Germany, and North America provide training in Adlerian therapy. Institutes in New York, Chicago, Minneapolis, Berkeley, San Francisco, St. Louis, Fort Wayne (Indiana), and Vancouver, BC (Canada), for example, offer a certification in Adlerian therapy. Although many universities offer courses in Adlerian therapy, Bowie State University features a master's degree with an Adlerian curriculum and the Adler School of Professional Psychology in Chicago offers a doctoral program in clinical psychology (Corsini & Wedding, 2010). Professionals practicing Adlerian therapy also have an opportunity to receive a Certification of Professional Studies in Adlerian Psychology from the Idaho Society of Individual Psychology (ISIP). Additionally, the North American

Society of Adlerian Psychology offers a diplomate in Adlerian psychology. This is the highest professional recognition endorsed by this organization for members who demonstrate the greatest level of professional accomplishment in and contribution to Adlerian psychology. Achieving this status can occur through counseling and psychotherapy, clinical practice, education, parent education, theory, research, or organizational leadership (NASAP, n.d.). Along with mental health professionals, paraprofessionals such as the clergy employ Adlerian techniques in their work with the community (Hester, 1987).

Special Ethical Considerations

Working with families provides a unique challenge to informed consent, which requires the Adlerian therapist to provide enough information about the typical duration, benefits, risks, and alternatives to an Adlerian approach to enable family members to make a reasoned judgment concerning whether or not they should enter therapy. In situations where young children will participate in the therapy process, it is important for the Adlerian therapist to not solely rely on the parents granting consent for the child to participate. The therapist should take the time needed to explain the process in lay terms and seek willing participation. More problematic are situations where the therapist will work with a family only if all available members agree to participate. Such a requirement can cause certain family members to coerce a reluctant or disinterested family member into participating. Such issues are important to consider and address at the beginning of therapy.

Criticisms of the Adlerian Approach

Compared to psychoanalytic, behavioral, and client- or person-centered approaches, Adlerians have not added substantially to the body of empirical research examining its theoretical tenets or its applications. More research is needed to validate its constructs, and more rigorous outcome studies are required.

As with all the theorists covered in this textbook, there are times when Adler was wrong or when he spoke with certainty about a topic that required a more tentative tone. However, when the whole of his work is considered, it is safe to say that any degree of wrongheadedness that filtered into his theory is outweighed by its positive contributions. In fact, it is difficult to accept as true remarks such as "the Adlerian approach is based mainly on a commonsense, perhaps even simplistic, view of human behavior as opposed to having a research-based foundation" (Peterson & Nisenholz, 1999, p. 186). In truth the approach is not void of empirical research, and Adler's views can be glimpsed in other psychodynamic therapies, client- or person-centered therapy, existential therapy, rational-emotive behavior therapy, cognitive therapy, reality therapy, constructivist and social constructivist approaches, and solution-focused marriage and family therapy (e.g., the "magic question" used by solution-focused therapists can be traced back to Adler). In fact, Richard Watts (2003) provided a logically sound and comprehensive presentation in *Adlerian, Cognitive, and Constructivist Therapies* of how the Adlerian approach intersects with both cognitive and constructivist approaches of today. It seems more appropriate to assert that the greatest weakness of individual psychology is that it failed to obtain the widespread recognition Adler deserves.

Application: Adlerian Theory

REVISITING THE HYPOTHETICAL CASE OF LON CHANEY, SR.

Note: Only the portion of Adler's case notes he viewed as most salient to the case are reported here.

ANALYSIS PHASE OF THERAPY

Early recollections. Two early recollections stand out: (1) Chaney recalled that both of his deaf-mute parents' faces expressed great pleasure when he "entered the room after stuffing my pants and shirt with crumpled newspaper to create the appearance of a neighbor who was always angry about something. My parents' enjoyment peaked when I mimicked his walk," and (2) Chaney remembered someone coming into his father's barber shop saying "Dummy Frank, I need a haircut and shave." The man appeared to be embarrassed when he realized Chaney was seated there. Even more important was the reaction of Chaney's father, who could read lips better than Chaney. Chaney could tell the remark bothered his father even though his reaction was too subtle for others to notice. Chaney thought at the time that no one should be treated that way just because the person is different.

Birth order/family atmosphere. Chaney reported that his parents "deserved a great deal of credit for just getting up in the morning rather than give up on life. They found one another, fell in love, had five children, and lived as normal a life as possible." Chaney said there were other people in the community without any disabilities who were much less capable of dealing with life than his parents. Chaney's memory reveals parents who loved their children. Chaney was the second of five children, and the oldest was John.

Mother's illness. When Chaney was about 10 years old, his mother developed inflammatory rheumatism, which resulted in the young Chaney dropping out of school to take care of his mother and the other siblings. Chaney recalled the hardship resulted in him taking the "lead among the children." Chaney was highly successful in this new role as caretaker because of two unique characteristics: a "very competitive nature" and a "great ability to pantomime the actions of other people." Chaney discovered he could tell a story depicting different emotions and actions by gesturing with his hands, arms, legs, body, head, or face. Chaney recalls he could easily elicit laughter from family members during one of his "shows," but even more important, Chaney's special talent served as a way for his bedridden mother to keep up with events in the community. For 3 years, Chaney assumed the responsibility of taking care of the family while his father worked.

Reoccurring dream. Chaney reported a reoccurring dream that was prevalent when he first started acting in movies. This dream had reappeared recently. The dream always depicted a movie that Chaney had been selected to star in as a "deformed person ridiculed and laughed at by society." Upon awakening it was not unusual for him to experience a feeling of anger that "gradually changed into a sense of disappointment or fear."

Career path, marriages, and other contributing factors. Chaney reported his pantomime ability grew and eventually led to seeking a career in theater where he met his first wife, a singer by the name of Cleva Creighton. Their child, Creighton Chaney, was born in 1906. Marital discord was present from the start and increased over time. In April 1913, after the Chaney family had settled in California, Cleva went to the Majestic Theater where Chaney worked and attempted suicide by ingesting mercury biochloride. The attempt failed, but the chemical destroyed her singing voice. The malicious gossip resulting from the suicide attempt forced Chaney to quit his theater job and find employment in silent films. While Chaney was building a reputation for playing character parts in silent films, he married Hazel Hastings, who had worked as a chorus girl at the Majestic Theater. The couple obtained custody of Chaney's 10-year-old son, who had been placed in a facility that provided housing for "children of divorce and disaster."

A silent film role in 1919, *The Miracle Man,* received wide public attention, and its success resulted in Chaney being casted in a series of important roles (e.g., *The Phantom of the Opera*). The role of the phantom, as with several others, required Chaney to transform himself into a grotesque character, but a character that Chaney claims to have "always portrayed as one genuinely deserving of a sympathetic response from the movie goers."

Tentative conclusions. The following attributes and interests combined to form Chaney's unique personality:

- High need for achievement
- Competitive to the point of self-sacrifice
- Affiliation needs based on knowing and trusting others
- High level of artistic skills
- Strong sense of responsibility and self-confidence
- Appreciation of reading and writing
- High interest in physical activities, such as camping, fishing, and hiking
- Athletic appearance
- Mature and disciplined approach to life
- Strong empathic nature
- Self-esteem enhanced by public popularity but not dependent upon it
- Healthy masculine identity that allows a broad range of skills, including those associated with females (e.g., knitting, sewing, and use of makeup)

Fulfilling the adult role imposed on him at age 10 allowed Chaney to psychologically remove the older brother from the "familial throne," whom Chaney had viewed as the favored son until that time. Basically, his mother's illness provided Chaney an opportunity to redirect his competitive focus away from his older brother John and toward the world in general.

LATTER PHASES OF THERAPY

Critical insight and action taken by client. Chaney's reoccurring dream happened again and during our discussion of his dream, Chaney realized that his life was driven by a desire to show the world that even people with weakness, like his parents, could achieve their dreams given a chance. Chaney also made the connection between his early experiences and his final career choice and why it had proven so successful. In the session that followed, Chaney accomplished a major breakthrough when he understood that he harbored an irrational fear tied to talking in the upcoming movie because it placed him on the side of those who had taunted and mocked his parents. Near the end of the same session, Adler created a homework assignment for Chaney: "I want you to practice the entire script for your talkie and have it memorized in two weeks at which time you will see me again. At that session you are to go through your parts as I read out loud the corresponding comments of the other actors." . . . As I expected, Chaney was able to memorize the script and successfully play the three different characters he was assigned to play. He created a unique and convincing voice for each of these characters. At this point, Chaney was ready to terminate therapy.

Follow-up notation. Chaney starred successfully in his first talkie playing the three different roles we went over—for each, Chaney used a different and convincing voice. Interestingly, advertisement for the film billed Chaney as the "Man of a Thousand Voices."

The Case of Miguel Sanchez

Based on the material that has been covered in this chapter, Adler's approach was clearly family oriented in terms of both theory and therapy. In addition, a number of strong adherents (e.g., Heinz and Rowena Ansbacher, Rudolf Dreikurs, Richard E. Watts) expanded upon Adler's body of work by adding substantially to his approach's applicability, including application to family-related issues, such as those that were experienced by Miguel and Mrs. Sanchez.

Adler constructed a therapeutic approach that was delivered in a fashion that required careful consideration of the unique nature of each client's situation as well as of the inherent and also unique contributions of family members who were affected by and were affecting the problem at issue; in other words, the overall family atmosphere is an important consideration. Adlerian therapists are trained to pay close attention to how and what the client is communicating and to take the time necessary to fully understand all dimensions of the problem being discussed.

The previously listed qualities as well as others, such as the genuine respect afforded to clients, contribute substantively to Adlerian therapy's effectiveness in treating a wide variety of problems and individuals. The importance of displaying respect toward clients cannot be overstated, especially as it would apply to Miguel and Mrs. Sanchez since a widely held value in Mexican culture is *respeto* (respect). Adler embodied both the qualities of a consummate professional and a true egalitarian who believed firmly in the principle that all people are equal and deserve equal rights and opportunities. He also understood that what was seen as "good, valuable, and important" in terms of a woman's cultural role was often devalued in male-oriented cultures. John Sommers-Flanagan and Rita Sommers-Flanagan (2004) cited a remark attributed to Alfred Adler by J. B. Miller:

> It is frequently overlooked that a girl comes into the world with a prejudice sounding in her ears which is designed only to rob her of her belief in her own value, to shatter belief in her own value, to shatter her self-confidence and destroy her hope of ever doing anything of worthwhile, if this prejudice is constantly strengthened, if a girl sees again and again how women are given servile role to play, it is not hard to understand how she loses courage, fails to face her obligations, and sinks back from the solutions of her life's problems. (p. 106)

According to Perkins-Dock (2005), four Adlerian propositions that underpin the approach's multicultural strength are the role of social interest, importance of family atmosphere, effect of the multigenerational legacies, and the flexibility of therapeutic strategies that are implemented (p. 235). The aforementioned strengths possessed by the Adlerian approach would certainly come into play while assisting both Miguel and Mrs. Sanchez.

In discussing the situation with Mrs. Sanchez, the therapist comprehends that clearly identified suggestions as to what Mrs. Sanchez is struggling with are needed, and the therapist explores such possibilities with her.

Session Segment

Therapist Why do you think Mrs. Torres (i.e., school counselor) suggested you contact our counseling center to provide assistance?

Mrs. Sanchez She said I need some help in building up—learning ways to interact with my son to reduce *agitación* (turmoil). She's right. Mrs. Torres is a friend to the family who was very helpful to my oldest son—getting him to go to the *colegio comunitario* (community college) near our home. That is why we came to this country—for a better life.

Therapist You have sacrificed a lot to come to the United States. Based on what you have told me, you have overcome a lot to get to where you are today. And the current situation can be made much better. I agree with Mrs. Torres there are things you can learn to change what is happening for you and your son. [Pauses for a few seconds] I noticed that after your son left to go to the waiting room, you said, in a very low voice, that you felt *pisado* (stepped on)—as if you were nothing.

Mrs. Sanchez Yes, I felt that way.

Therapist Respect is important to everyone. For you and for your son. who also indicated he felt a lack of respect. It sounds like one goal of coming here is that both you and your son can agree that there's a need for respect. This can be done by communicating expectations and what is called logical consequences for not following through.

Mrs. Sanchez I tried to punish him, but that led to even more *agitación*.

Therapist Yes, that can be the result of trying to punish what we see as unacceptable.

Mrs. Sanchez So what do I do?

Therapist I run a program for my clients that I call a parent study group. The parents who attend have similar problems to yours. Over the years Mrs. Torres has recommended that a number of parents take my parent study group, and all who participated have found it to be very helpful.

Mrs. Sanchez Will Miguel go also?

Therapist No, the focus is helping parents develop skills. But I will continue to work with both of you and discuss with him what we've discussed. He will need to be told about how expectations and the logical consequences that follow fit together.

Mrs. Sanchez Yes, I want to try this. I trusted Mrs. Torres when she told me to come here, and I think I know a parent who came here and attended your parent group.

Therapist I'll describe what you can expect to occur at these training sessions. What you learn in the group and what you apply from these training sessions has been shown to reduce the turmoil that hinders families. Specifically, I cover topics such as communication, decision making, family meetings, developing confidence, encouragement, understanding behavior, use of emotions, and developing responsibility (see Ellison, 2009; Newlon, Borboas, & Arciniega, 1986). For example, encouragement is different from giving praise when a child has done a good job. Encouragement is given regardless of what a child has accomplished since it is intended to communicate respect for the child's existing abilities–I might say something like, "I can tell you put in a lot of effort and worked hard on this school project." Do you have any questions?

Mrs. Sanchez Yes, does it take place here at the counseling center and when?

CHAPTER REVIEW

SUMMARY AND COMMENTARY ▶▶

Over the span of my career, I (the author of this chapter) have encountered several professionals with Adlerian ties—Keith Runyon, John C. Dagley, Jon Carlson, Richard Watts, and Tom Sweeney—and with each of these individuals I have been struck by their passion for an approach that contributes significantly to therapeutic practice and yet is still an approach that is sorely underrated. Certainly, Adler should be given credit for being one of the first in the field to bring social aspects of human nature to the forefront as they pertain to human potential. He should also be recognized for the attention he paid to social justice issues such as feminism, racism, and classism, all of which remain important concerns regardless of the gains made in each of these areas. Finally, Adler offered us many compelling and pragmatic concepts such as the inferiority–superiority dynamic that can energize and move us to action, the power of family dynamics to leave its mark on our personality, the notion of a psychologically based style of life that forms early and yet is capable of making each one of us unique among billions of others, the immensely positive effects of humanistic collaboration, and the assertion that people should be viewed and treated as whole entities with teleological direction rather than disembodied fragments. All of these thoughts retain a high pragmatic value for today's practitioners.

Considering all the profound issues confronting the world today, it is critical for us to remember that Adler's concept of social interest applies to more than *kith* (acquaintances) and *kin* (relatives) as it also entails *ken* (knowledge, understanding, and vision). In the 21st century, it is clear that Adler's mission of developing a healthy community now expands to the world at large. It behooves all of us to use our individual freedom and creativity to mold the best possible future for all of us and those who follow. Table 4.5 provides an overall summary of several key areas pertaining to Adlerian therapy as it is currently practiced.

▼ TABLE 4.5

Brief Overview of Current Therapy Practice

Variable	Current Application
Type of service delivery setting	Private practice Schools Clinic Psychiatric hospital Health care setting Substance abuse clinic Military Social service agency

Variable	Current Application
Population	Child Teen Adult Couple Family Group Organization
Type of presenting problems	Wide range of presenting problems
Severity of presenting problems	Wide range of severity of presenting problems
Adapted for short-term approach	Yes
Length of treatment	Brief to long term
Ability to receive reimbursement	Insurance companies will reimburse with appropriate *DSM* diagnosis.
Certification in approach	Certification of Professional Studies in Adlerian Psychology by the Idaho Society of Individual Psychology
Training in educational programs	Many graduate programs offer courses in Adlerian psychology. Bowie State College offers a master's degree with an Adlerian curriculum. The Adler School of Professional Psychology in Chicago offers a doctoral program in clinical psychology.
Location	Urban Rural Suburban
Type of delivery system	HMO PPO Fee for service
Credential	Diplomate in Adlerian psychology by the North American Society of Adlerian Psychology
Practitioners	Professionals Paraprofessionals
Fit with *DSM* diagnoses	No

CRITICAL THINKING QUESTIONS ▶▶

1. Freud was not an Adlerian and Adler was not a Freudian. Explain the following assertion: Adler was not an Adlerian.

2. How are selfish goals similar to and different from defense mechanisms?

3. According to Adler's theory, should we expect a mature, psychologically healthy adult to possess equal amounts of social interest and self-interest? Justify your answer.

SUGGESTED READINGS: IMPORTANT PRIMARY SOURCES ▶▶

Books

Adler, A. [Alfred]. (1954). *Understanding human nature* (W. B. Wolfe, Trans.). New York, NY: Fawcett Premier. (Original work published 1927)

Carlson, J., Watts, R. E., & Maniacci, M. (2006). *Adlerian therapy: Theory and practice.* Washington, DC: American Psychological Association.

Watts, R. E. (2003). *Adlerian, cognitive, and constructivist therapies: An integrative dialogue.* New York, NY: Springer.

Journals

Journal of Individual Psychology

Websites

Idaho Society of Individual Psychology (ISIP): http://adleridaho.org

Journal of Individual Psychology: https://utpress.utexas.edu/journals/journal-of-individual-psychology

North American Society of Adlerian Psychology: www.alfredadler.org

CHAPTER 5

EXISTENTIAL THEORY

Introduction

The author Eric Maisel (2009) stated the following:

> Why aren't we offered an existential training? Because one of society's unacknowledged goals is to minimize existential thought. A company making widgets doesn't want you to wonder about the meaningfulness of its widget. It wants you to be attracted to the widget's design and buy two of them. A Broadway producer wants you to tap your feet; a police officer wants you to obey; a politician wants you to vote for her; a clergyman wants you to opt for his religion. None of them are likely to invite you to step back and ponder the meaning of their product, policy, or ideology. You are supposed to buy, to agree, and not to think too hard about anything. That is what society wants and believes it needs from you. (pp. 45–46)

Maisel asserted that even though individuals naturally possess the ability to maximize their existential thinking, societies are inherently prone to minimize any thinking that affirms individuality and results in a questioning attitude. Even though humans are capable of breaking free from the herd mentality that keeps them in check, too often the fear of being ostracized by others prevents them from moving beyond a life of passive acceptance in which they are prone to being led and controlled.

Maisel's advice is to take a leap of faith and avoid the easy route of seeking meaning for one's existence by accepting ready-made answers to the question "Why do I exist?" The responsibility for uncovering the meaning for one's own existence resides with the person who is seeking such meaning and with no one else. Maisel recommended that everyone should *make meaning* for their existence, that is, find the answer for their own unique reason or purpose for why they exist. Once individuals achieve meaning, they move from being a faint representation of their true self to become their true self, which is evident through their authenticity. This far-reaching change essentially means that these individuals are no longer the same persons. Existential-oriented persons are experiencing something genuinely new, a meaningful life that is driven by awakened potentialities (Ginter & Glauser, 2010; Walsh & McElwain, 2002). The intrinsic nature of this transformative experience was captured in words uttered by the fictional character created by Lewis Carroll (Figure 5.1). Alice states, "It's no use going back to yesterday, because I was a different person then" (Carroll, 1898, p. 84).

▼ FIGURE 5.1

Alice in Wonderland

Source: Robinson (1907) for Alice's Adventures in Wonderland by Lewis Carroll.

TO BE OR NOT TO BE: THE CASE OF JUAN

Juan is a 22-year-old second-generation Jamaican who grew up in New York with his older sister and mother. His mother, who is dying of breast cancer, shows little affection toward him, while his older sister frequently looks out for him and is supportive. Juan does not know his father. During the summers in his childhood, Juan was usually in Jamaica, spending time with his family members and experiencing his cultural and familial roots.

Currently, Juan still lives with his mother at home and is employed as a substitute teacher at the local junior high school. Juan sought therapy because his depression was becoming more intense since his recent attempt at suicide. He feels socially isolated, lacks a support system, and has few conversations at his school. Juan noted that he has difficulty finding motivation in the morning, even after a good night's sleep. He reported that his biggest challenge is determining his personal identity and purpose in the world.

A common theme in Juan's life centers on what it means to be Jamaican. The role of Jamaican males is quite clear in Juan's culture: They are sexually experienced, powerful, and macho. Juan is dark skinned and overweight. He reported having difficulty talking with women and that he is a virgin. He also claimed to be a "nerd." He enjoys writing fantasy stories and hopes one day to be a "Jamaican J. R. R. Tolkien." Throughout much of his life, he has been criticized by his peers, colleagues, other family members, and even strangers, on occasion, for his weight, dark skin, hobbies, and not being "Jamaican enough." Juan's belief that he fails to meet the expectations of others makes him feel inadequate and hopeless.

Further, Juan reported that he often dwells on the reality of the *fuku*, a curse placed on people who disobeyed the Dominican Republic dictator, Rafael Trujillo. Although Juan claimed the curse was placed on his family three generations earlier, he said that the *fuku* is thought to influence one's entire family intergenerationally. As a result, he

▼ FIGURE 5.2

"To be, or not to be: That is the question . . ."

Source: Sarah-Bernhardt (Hamlet)/Lafayette-photo- London.

obsesses on the thought that he is eventually doomed. Juan continues to contemplate suicide, although he claims he will not follow through because of the negative impact it would have on his sister. The therapist noted that twice, during the session, Juan quoted a line from a William Shakespeare play, that is, the part of Hamlet's soliloquy that states, "To be, or not to be: That is the question." The therapist correctly interprets this phrase to mean "Is it better to live or die?" (Figure 5.2). The therapist tentatively concludes that Juan is experiencing an existential crisis.

Case Discussion. Near the end of this chapter the case of Juan will be discussed in greater detail to illustrate how existential therapy can be applied to Juan's situation.

Note. This case is based in large part on a case published in Roysircar and Pignatiello (2015).

This chapter discusses the history and main premises of existentialism and its major constructs. Existential therapy, therapy techniques, multicultural and social justice concerns about existentialism, ethical considerations, research support, and relevance to current practice are also discussed. Therapy wrapped around an existential perspective is applied to two cases that illustrate this approach's unique contributions.

Key Players of Existentialism

Viktor Frankl

Viktor Frankl (1905–1997) was born in Vienna, Austria, to a Jewish family involved in the civil service (Frankl, 2008; Redsand, 2006). Early in his life he became interested in psychology. He wrote a paper for the final exam in *Gymnasium* on the psychology of philosophical thinking. In 1923, Frankl began to study medicine at the University of Vienna. Later, he specialized in psychiatry and neurology, focusing on depression and suicide. While in medical school, Frankl worked in the university clinic and arranged cost-free therapy clinics for youth in Vienna and six other cities. He made available a stress management program to assist students when they were to obtain their academic grades. During his service at the university clinic, not a single student committed suicide. In 1930, Frankl received his doctorate in medicine and continued his training in neurology. Frankl's early development in the 1920s was affected by his contacts with Alfred Adler and Sigmund Freud. Although he was more influenced by Adler's concept of social interest, he would later diverge from both Freud's and Adler's teachings.

Viktor Emil Frankl

Source: Prof. Dr. Franz Vesely Viktor-Frankl-Archiv.

From 1933 to 1937, Frankl led the "suicide pavilion" of the Vienna General Hospital; that is, he treated thousands of women disposed to suicide ("Viktor Frankl," 2014). Then, in 1938, with the Nazi takeover of Austria, Frankl, who was a Jew, was forbidden to treat "Aryan" patients. In 1940 Frankl moved to the Rothschild Hospital, the only hospital in Vienna that continued to admit Jews. He rendered many inaccurate diagnoses of his patients to bypass the new policies requiring that the mentally ill be euthanized. At this time, Frankl started writing the document, "The Doctor and the Soul."

On September 25, 1942, Frankl and his wife and parents were relocated to the Theresienstadt concentration camp (Figure 5.4, At the camp, Frankl was assigned to labor details. He also was asked to create a special unit to assist new arrivals who were experiencing grief and shock. In response, he established a suicide watch unit and all warnings of suicide were shared with him. Frankl had a post in the psychiatric care unit, led the neurological clinic in block B IV, and developed and maintained a camp mental care service for individuals who were sick and who were weary of life. Frankl also gave presentations titled "Body and Soul," "Sleep and Its Disturbances," "Medical Care of the Soul," "How I Keep My Nerves Healthy," "Psychology of Mountaineering," "Social Psychotherapy," and "Existential Problems in Psychotherapy." To preserve feeling worthy in dismal conditions, Frankl would often march outside and give a lecture to an imaginary group of people on "Psychotherapeutic Experiences in a Concentration Camp." He thought that by deeply experiencing the suffering reflectively—that is, by talking about it and naming it—he would end it. According to Frankl (1975), the opposite of thinking reflectively is *dereflection*, which occurs when a person shifts his focus away from himself and concentrates on a topic that does not provoke anxiety.

FIGURE 5.4

Prisoners in a Nazi Concentration Camp

Source: Record Group 111: Records of the Office of the Chief Signal Officer, 1860–1985.

On October 19, 1944, Frankl was relocated to the Auschwitz concentration camp, where his document "The Doctor and the Soul" was found and destroyed. During subsequent transportations to camps, Frankl reconstructed his manuscript on stolen pieces of paper. He was relocated to Türkheim, a concentration camp connected to Dachau. He arrived at this camp on October 25, 1944, where he spent 6 months and 2 days as a laborer. His wife had been moved to the Bergen-Belsen concentration camp, where she was killed. Frankl's father died from pulmonary edema, pneumonia, and starvation in the Theresienstadt camp, and his mother was relocated to Auschwitz from Theresienstadt and also killed there. Frankl was liberated from the camp by Americans troops on April 27, 1945.

Although nearly broken and very much alone, Frankl assumed the directorship of the Vienna Polyclinic of Neurology, a role he held for 25 years. In 1946, he re-created and published "The Doctor and the Soul," which led to a position at the University of Vienna Medical School. In 1945, he dictated another book, his world-famous publication, translated as *Saying Yes to Life in Spite of Everything: A Psychologist Experiences the Concentration Camp*, also recognized in English as *Man's Search for Meaning* (1959/2006). In this publication, Frankl discussed the life of an ordinary concentration camp prisoner through the lens of a psychiatrist. In 1948, he earned a PhD in philosophy. His dissertation, "The Unconscious God," was an investigation of the connection between psychology and religion.

Frankl's Logotherapy

Because of his own and others' suffering while in the concentration camps, Frankl concluded that even in the most daunting, dehumanizing, and painful situations, life has potential meaning, and as a result, even suffering can be meaningful (Gurman & Messer, 2003). This observation was the foundation for Frankl's logotherapy (Frankl, 2008). Frankl's observation is apparent in this description of an experience he had while at Auschwitz:

> We stumbled on in the darkness, over big stones and through large puddles, along the one road leading from the camp. The accompanying guards kept shouting at us and driving us with the butts of their rifles. Anyone with very sore feet supported himself on his neighbor's arm. Hardly a word was spoken; the icy wind did not encourage talk. Hiding his mouth behind his upturned collar, the man marching next to me whispered suddenly: "If our wives could see us now! I do hope they are better off in their camps and don't know what is happening to us."

That brought thoughts of my own wife to mind. And as we stumbled on for miles, slipping on icy spots, supporting each other time and again, dragging one another up and onward, nothing was said, but we both knew: each of us was thinking of his wife. Occasionally I looked at the sky, where the stars were fading and the pink light of the morning was beginning to spread behind a dark bank of clouds. But my mind clung to my wife's image, imagining it with an uncanny acuteness. . . .

A thought transfixed me: . . . The truth—that love is the ultimate and the highest goal to which man can aspire. Then I grasped the meaning of the greatest secret: The salvation of man is through love and in love . . . In a position of utter desolation, when man cannot express himself in positive action, when his only achievement may consist in enduring his sufferings in the right way—an honorable way—in such a position man can, through loving contemplation of the image he carries of his beloved, achieve fulfillment. (Frankl, 1959/2006, pp. 35–36)

Frankl (1959/2006) also observed,

If a prisoner felt that he could no longer endure the realities of camp life, he found a way out in his mental life—an invaluable opportunity to dwell in the spiritual domain, the one that the SS were unable to destroy. Spiritual life strengthened the prisoner, helped him adapt, and thereby improved his chances of survival. (p. 123)

Logotherapy (Gurman & Messer, 2003; Lukas, 2014) is viewed as the third Viennese school of psychotherapy after Freud's psychoanalysis and Adler's individual psychology. It is an existential approach or analysis that emphasizes a will to meaning as compared to Freud's drive for pleasure or Adler's principle of will to power. Instead of pleasure or power, Frankl's logotherapy is guided by the assumption that it is the motivation to find a meaning in one's life that acts as the primary, most powerful driving force for individuals. Logotherapy explores the spirit at the center of a person for resources of healing, and it does not analyze psychopathology (Fabry, Bulka, & Sahakian, 1996).

Logotherapy's aim is to help the client seek meaning (*logos* = meaning). In religious circles, the Greek word *logos* is typically translated as the "word" or "will" of God (Frankl, 2004). However, in the sense used by Frankl, it can be seen as that which provides reason for being. The name itself, logotherapy, means treatment through meaning. Within this framework, to Frankl, existential neurosis was identical to a crisis of meaninglessness (Frankl, 1967). Frankl presented the concept "Sunday neurosis," which refers to a type of depression resulting from a feeling of emptiness when the work week has ended. Sunday neurosis emerges from an existential vacuum, which is characterized by the subjective state of boredom and apathy. Whereas Sunday neurosis is a passing frustration, existential neurosis is a long-term experience of meaninglessness.

The basic assumptions of logotherapy (Frankl, 1959/2006, 1967) are that (a) life has meaning in all circumstances, (b) individuals possess a will to meaning, and (c) individuals possess freedom in all circumstances to activate the will to meaning and to seek meaning. Although individuals can experience sickness in the mind and body, their spirit or *noetic* core remains healthy. Access to the healthy core, however, can be obstructed. The characteristics of the spirit or noetic dimension include authenticity, responsibility to others, choices, creativity, values, will to meaning, self-transcendence, love, ideals, and conscience. The use of the word *spirit* is not meant to imply either religious or spiritual. Instead, from Frankl's perspective, the spirit is the will of the human being. Thus, the focus of logotherapy is on the search for meaning, which is not really the search for God, although it could be for a particular person's quest (Beckett, 1982). Frankl warned against affluence, hedonism, and materialism because he saw these as barriers to the search for meaning (May & Yalom, 1995; Schneider, 2011).

In 1947, Frankl married for a second time. His wife was a practicing Catholic, but the spouses respected one another's religious backgrounds and attended church and synagogue. They also observed Christmas and Hanukkah. Frankl and his second wife had one daughter, Gabriele, who later became a child psychologist. Frankl taught seminars, lectured around the world, and was awarded 29 honorary doctorate degrees. Frankl passed away on September 2, 1997, of heart failure (Redsand, 2006).

Rollo Reese May

Rollo May (1909–1994) was born in the small town of Ada, Ohio. His childhood was quite difficult. His parents had a problematic marriage and eventually divorced. May was one of six children, and his mother frequently left all the children to "take care" of herself. His sister suffered from schizophrenia, and he bore a lot of child care responsibility. After staying briefly at Michigan State University, where he was requested to leave because of his connection to a radical student magazine, he attended Oberlin College in Ohio. At Oberlin, May earned his bachelor's degree in English (see Figure 5.5). After he graduated, May taught college English in Greece for 3 years. During this period, May also spent time as a roving artist and studied for a short period with Alfred Adler.

▼ FIGURE 5.5

Rollo May

Hulton Archive/Getty Images

When he returned to the United States, May entered the Union Theological Seminary in New York City, where he developed a friendship with one of his teachers, Paul Tillich. Tillich was an existentialist theologian, and his work had a profound influence on May's thinking. May received his bachelor's degree in divinity in 1938 and practiced ministry for a few years.

Diagnosed with tuberculosis in 1942, May spent 3 years in a hospital. This was likely an important turning point in his life. Faced with possible death, May occupied his time with reading. Along with the other literature he read, May read the work of Søren Kierkegaard, whose publications contributed to inspiring the existential movement in Europe. It was Kierkegaard's writings that motivated May to develop his own theory.

May studied psychoanalysis at William Alanson White Institute in New York City, one of the most prominent and respected psychoanalytic training centers. There he met Harry Stack Sullivan, who developed an interpersonal theory focused on social factors that impacted human development, and Erich Fromm, who developed a culture-based theory focused on the search for meaning. Both Sullivan and Fromm had become critics of Freud's libido concept. May attended Columbia University in New York, where in 1949 he earned the first PhD in therapy psychology awarded by Columbia. In 1958, May coedited the book *Existence*, which introduced European existentialists and existential psychology to the United States. May was a founder and a faculty member of Saybrook Institute in San Francisco, whose mission was to provide an innovative learner-centered educational environment devoted to humanistic psychology and research; currently, Saybrook University houses the Rollo May Research Center. May spent his final years in Tiburon on the San Francisco Bay. He passed away in October 1994 at the age of 85.

May's Existentialism

Rollo May is the best known American existential psychologist. May wanted to reconcile existential psychology with Freud's psychoanalysis. He used the construct ego but understood it as self-consciousness or self-awareness and also tied it to motivation (May, 1953). May employed traditional existential concepts in a slightly different way than the Europeans, and he created new words for some of existentialism's old ideas. *Destiny*, for instance, is basically similar to "thrownness" combined with "fallenness" (Heidegger's *Dasein*). It is an aspect of our lives that is determined for us, our inherent raw materials, for the task of establishing our lives. The word *courage* is another example. May utilized this word more frequently than the traditional existential concept of authenticity, which meant facing one's anxiety and rising above it (May, 1994).

May also was the only existential psychologist who discussed specific "stages," but not in the Freudian sense of development (Boeree, 2006; May, 1981). May's stages are as follows:

- *Innocence* is the pre-egoic, pre-self-conscious stage of an infant. The innocent stage is premoral, meaning neither good nor bad. The innocent is only doing what a person must do. However, an innocent does have a certain amount of will in that there is a drive to fulfill a person's needs.
- *Rebellion* is the childhood and adolescent stage of forming an ego. This self-consciousness occurs as a result of a contrast with adults. The rebellious adolescent or child wishes for freedom but does not have a complete understanding of the responsibility that freedom carries.
- *Ordinary* is the stage associated with the normal adult ego, noncreative, conventional, and taking no risks. Ordinary adults learn to be responsible, but they experience it as too demanding and thus pursue refuge in conformity.
- *Creative* represents the stage of the authentic adult who has moved past the ego to the existential stage of self-actualizing. This is the individual who, accepting her destiny, faces anxiety with courage (see Boeree, 2006). May defined anxiety as "the apprehension cued off by a threat to some value which the individual holds essential to his existence as a self" (May, 1967, p. 72). May's use of anxiety includes fear of death or "nothingness."

Love and Will. A number of May's unique observations appear in his book *Love and Will* (May, 1969). In his attempt to reconcile Freud and the existentialists, May looked to motivation. His most basic motivational construct was called the *daimonic* (Diamond, 1996), which represents the complete system of motives and varies for each person. It is composed of a collection of specific motives termed *daimons,* a word derived from the Greek language and means "little gods." Although American readers tended to interpret it to mean "demon," a negative connotation, May contended a daimon could be good or bad. Daimons include lower needs such as sex and food, and higher needs such as the need for love. Basically, May claimed a daimon is anything that can absorb the individual as a compulsion, a situation he labeled as a "daimonic possession" (Diamond, 1996). When the balance among daimons is disturbed, they should be viewed as "evil," as the phrase "daimonic possession" implies. For Rollo May, one of the most essential daimons is *eros* (May, 1969), which represents love (not sex). In Greek mythology, eros was depicted as a minor god represented by a young man. May perceived love as the need individuals have to "become one" with someone else, and he referred to an ancient Greek story by Aristophanes (May, 1981, 1991). According to Aristophanes's story, people were originally four-legged, four-armed, two-headed creatures. When they became a little too prideful, the gods split them in two, male and female, and cursed them with the never-ending desire to recover their missing half. Like any daimon, eros is good until it takes over the personality and people become obsessed with it (May, 1981, 1991).

Another critical concept for May was *will,* which was different from how Frankl explained will as striving to find a meaning in suffering. According to May, will is the ability to organize oneself to achieve one's goals. This definition of will is basically the same as what is associated with reality-testing and ego, with its own supply of energy (May, 1969), as discussed in ego psychology. May posited that will is also a daimon that can possess a person in negative ways. Another explanation of will is the capacity to make wishes come true (Diamond, 1996). Wishes are thought to be manifestations of daimons and playful imaginings of possibilities (Sodowsky & Sodowsky, 1997). However, wishes require will to make them occur. Therefore, out of an individual's relative source of wishes for love and the will to realize such a wish, three personality types emerge (Boeree, 2006; May, 1969).

- *Neo-Puritan* is all will and no love. This personality type has incredible self-discipline and can cause things to happen, but this type does not have wishes. This type of an individual becomes a perfectionistic.
- *Infantile* is all wishes and no will. Individuals who are considered to be this personality type are filled with desires and dreams, yet they lack the self-discipline to make anything of their desires and dreams. These persons become dependent. They love, but their love has little meaning.
- *Creative* is the type of individual that May recommended people strive for and become. He claimed an individual's task is to unite will and love, which might be opposing motivations, but represents a healthy type of personality (Boeree, 2006; May, 1969).

May's last publication was *The Cry for Myth* (1991), in which he argued that a major problem in the 20th century was individuals' loss of values. All the diverse values resulted in people doubting all values. As Nietzsche stated, if God is dead (i.e., absolutes are gone), then anything is permitted. May claimed that individuals must establish their own values, each individually. Because this is difficult, individuals require help from tales and myths presented to them (Roysircar, Clarke, Love, Thomas, & Aufiero, 2010). *Myths* are stories that assist people in making sense of their lives; they are guiding narratives (Roysircar et al., 2010). May's assumption about myths is similar in some respects to Carl Jung's archetypes. However, myths can be unconscious and conscious, personal and collective. Many unhelpful myths, however, focus on the magical granting of a person's wishes (a view consistent with the *infantile* personality). Other myths ensure success in exchange for self-sacrifice and hard work (believed by the *neo-Puritan*). Many relativistic stories of modern times argue that valuelessness is, in and of itself, the best value. Instead, May posited that individuals should be actively engaged in establishing new myths accompanied by values that support individuals' efforts at making the best of life (May, 1991).

Irvin Yalom

Another prominent American existentialist is Irvin Yalom (born 1931). Yalom was born in Washington, D.C., to Jewish immigrant parents from Russia who ran a grocery store (see Figure 5.6). Yalom occupied much of his childhood time reading books in his home above the grocery store and in a local library. He earned a bachelor's degree from George Washington University and a doctor of medicine degree from Boston University School of Medicine. He completed his medical internship at Mount Sinai Hospital in New York and his residency at the Phipps Clinic of Johns Hopkins Hospital in Baltimore. His medical training ended in 1960. After 2 years of serving in the army at Tripler General Hospital in Honolulu, Yalom started his academic career at Stanford University. During the 1970s at Stanford, Yalom produced a number of his most important and lasting contributions by teaching about group therapy and creating his model of existential therapy. His writings on existential psychology revolve around what he called the "four givens" of the human experience: meaninglessness, isolation, freedom, and mortality. Yalom discussed ways in which the individual can respond to these crucial givens in either a dysfunctional or functional fashion.

▼ FIGURE 5.6

Irvin D. Yalom

By Haemmerli (Own work) [CC BY-SA 4.0 (https://creativecommons .org/licenses/by-sa/4.0)], via Wikimedia Commons.

At present, Yalom is Professor Emeritus of Psychiatry at Stanford University and the author of many highly acclaimed textbooks such as *Existential Psychotherapy* and *The Theory and Practice of Group Psychotherapy*. He also has written novels connected to therapy (*Lying on the Couch, When Nietzsche Wept, The Schopenhauer Cure*) as well as short story collections (*Love's Executioner, Momma and the Meaning of Life*). Yalom coauthored the nonfiction *Every Day Gets a Little Closer* with a client. This book has two distinct voices that examine the same therapy experience in alternating sections. Yalom's publications have been adopted as college textbooks and standard texts for counseling and psychology students.

Table 5.1 lists some Frankl, May, and Yalom quotes.

Quotable Viktor Frankl, Rollo May, and Irvin Yalom

Viktor Frankl

- Striving to find meaning in one's life is the primary motivational force. . . . (Frankl, 2014, p. 92)
- Only when the emotions work in terms of values can the individual feel pure joy. (Frankl, 1986, p. 40)
- Human freedom is not a freedom from but freedom to. (Frankl, 1988, p. 16)

Rollo May

- Freedom is . . . our capacity to mold ourselves. (May, 1953, p. 138)
- Memory is not just the imprint of the past time upon us; it is the keeper of what is meaningful for our deepest hopes and fears. (May, 1953, p. 220)
- The past has meaning as it lights up the present, and the future as it makes the present richer and more profound. (May, 1953, p. 227)
- Hate is not the opposite of love; apathy is. (May, 1969, p. 29)
- Depression is the inability to construct a future. (May, 1969, p. 243)
- Neither Kierkegaard nor Nietzsche had the slightest interest in starting a movement—or a New system, a thought which would indeed have offended them. Both proclaimed, in Nietzsche's phrase, "Follow not me, but you." (May, 1983, p. 76)

Irvin Yalom

- One might think of "life" as a symphony in which each life is assigned some instrumental part to play. (Yalom, 1980, p. 424)
- The world's indifference can be transcended by rebellion, a prideful rebellion against one's condition. (Yalom, 1980, p. 427)
- Creativity overlaps with altruism in that many search to be creative in order to improve the condition of the world, to discover beauty, not only for its own sake but for the pleasure of others. (Yalom, 1980, p. 436)
- The more one focuses on oneself, for example in sexual relationships, the less is one's ultimate satisfaction. If one watches oneself, is concerned primarily with one's own arousal and release, one is likely to suffer sexual dysfunction. (Yalom, 1980, p. 440)

Sources: Frankl, V. E. (1986). *The doctor and the soul* (3rd ed.). New York, NY: Vintage Books; Frankl, V. E. (1988). *The will to meaning: Foundations and applications of psychotherapy.* New York, NY: Penguin Books; Frankl, V. E. (2014). *Man's search for meaning* (H. Pisano, Trans.). Boston, MA: Beacon Press. (Original work published 1959); May, R., (1953). *Man's search for himself.* New York, NY: W. W. Norton & Company; May, R., (1969). *Love and will.* New York, NY: Norton & Company; May, R. (1983). *The discovery of being: Writings in existential psychology.* New York, NY: W. W. Norton & Company; and Yalom, I. D. (1980). *Existential psychotherapy.* New York, NY: Basic Books.

Historical Context

The roots of existential thought can be traced back several centuries. The word *existentialism* comes from the Latin term *ex-sistere*, literally meaning "to stand out" or "to emerge" (May, 1983, p. 50). It was not until the mid-19th century, however, that existentialism was recognized as its own school of thought in Europe. Søren Kierkegaard's "concept of dread" shone the spotlight on the concepts of freedom, experiential reflection, and responsibility. He called for a movement away from an externalized, mechanized existence to one centered on the individual and personal experience. The only way to do this, Kierkegaard argued, is to grapple with ourselves and face the crises stemming from intellectual, emotional, and physical imprisonment. Only then can consciousness expand and deepen, and true freedom be experienced. Around the same time, Friedrich Nietzsche lamented the devitalization of culture due to the dominance of rationalist-linear thinking (what he called *Apollonian* living) over emotional-spontaneous living (or *Dionysian* living).

In the early 20th century, two schools of thought—behaviorism, which took a mechanistic perspective of human functioning, and Freud's psychoanalysis, which championed an intrapsychic form of determinism—were coming into their own. Martin Heidegger, expanding on Kierkegaard's emphasis on the individual and echoing Nietzsche's commentary on the need for a balanced Apollonian and Dionysian living, put forth a philosophy of being, termed "being-in-the-world" or *Dasein*. This was a critique of the development in Europe of a separation of inner from outer or subjective from objective, which was mirrored in the concurrent developments of behaviorism and psychoanalysis. Heidegger asserted that humans possessed subjective selves that were simultaneously separated from and connected to the outside world (Schneider, 2011).

By the mid-20th century, a number of European psychoanalysts (e.g., Ludwig Binswanger) broke from traditional Freudian thinking, alleging that its schematic/structural approach (id, ego, and superego interfaced with child development and parental figures) was inadequate to appreciate the unique experiences of each particular client. This group of "existential analysts," however, was scattered, and did not agree on very much, other than one basic point: that an analyst must approach each client from a phenomenological standpoint. As Ludwig Binswanger put it, "There is not one space and time only, but as many spaces and times as there are subjects" (quoted in Yalom, 1980, p. 17).

Meanwhile, across the Atlantic, by the mid-20th century a number of Americans working in abnormal and interpersonal psychology had grown sufficiently uncomfortable with the narrow frame of behaviorism and psychoanalysis. This discomfort warranted a distinctly new line of thinking. They spoke of important qualities that make people human beings, such as choice, love, creativity, self-awareness, and human potential. Sometimes called the "third force" in psychology (Yalom, 1980, p. 18), the school of humanistic psychology developed in the United States. Humanistic psychology grew more or less independently, at least until the late 1950s, from the European existentialists. Irvin Yalom, one of the most prolific and highly regarded players in modern existentialism in the United States, concedes that even today, existentialism and humanism have a "hazy relationship," although "they share many tenets" (Yalom, 1980, p. 20).

Basic Concepts of Existential Therapy

This section introduces constructs utilized by current existential therapists in the United States. Overall, existentialism's focus is on constructs that represent the shared commonness of all human beings that make them human. Clemmont Vontress (1985), a current African American existentialist, put this view of humanity best when he noted, "All who live must die; those who must die should live cooperatively and supportively with others" (p. 208). Existential therapists assert that all humans are free and in control of their own destinies, placing the majority of the responsibility for change on the individual client. Existential therapists attempt to help individuals to become self-aware to increase their freedom and responsibility. The philosophy of self-awareness has been around since the times of Ancient Greece when Socrates encouraged individuals to know themselves. Existentialists also focus on the ways in which clients form their identities and find relatedness through relationships. Emphasis is placed on both the person's individual identity and how this person understands personhood by relating to others and nature. Other important concepts within existentialism include meaning-making, life, death, and anxiety (Wolff, 1950).

Franz Kafka's "The Metamorphosis"

Freedom, Responsibility, and Self-Awareness

According to Irving Yalom (1980), personal freedom comes from a lack of constraints or external control. Humans are not born into a predetermined world but rather have the ability to create their own lives. Individuals, therefore, are considered entirely responsible for their own choices, choices that include not only actions taken and decisions made but also inaction and indecisions, because not acting and not making decisions are choices by default. This freedom to make one's own choices assigns responsibility for the resulting consequences, both positive and negative, to the individual.

Freedom does not make life easy. Sartre (1943/ 1969), a European existential philosopher, wrote that people are "doomed to freedom," because the recognition of the options people truly have provokes in them a feeling of groundlessness. However, to avoid responsibility for their freedom, Sartre claimed, is to live in "bad faith" and to be inauthentic.

Likewise, an individual is accountable for his own level of self-awareness; this, too, is a choice with consequences. It is only through self-awareness and acceptance of responsibility that people are able to live more freely in the world. Ignorance may allow individuals, who seek the safety of structure and conformity, to avoid having feelings of dread or taking responsibility, but it also leaves them without control of their own destiny.

Identity, Aloneness, and Relatedness

Existentialists believe that all people are trying to find their individual identity. Each person has a core, a self that is truer and deeper than an identity defined by another individual. The realization that one is not fulfilling her full potential leads to existential guilt. The person's awareness of this guilt can occur through self-reflection and can be resolved by the individual taking responsibility for herself (Yalom, 1980).

In addition, existentialists believe that human beings, despite their relatedness to others, are essentially alone in the world, which is a paradox of life. People experience birth, life's events, and death individually (Yalom, 1980). This isolation is believed to be an essential human condition, one from which people can gain meaning for their lives. Simultaneously, humans desire to connect with others, have relationships, and be part of a greater whole. This is a contradiction with one's sense of individuality that can result in existential conflict (Yalom, 1980). Vontress (1985) further noted the contradiction that people have a responsibility not only to themselves but also to others and to nature.

The pivotal role that identity, aloneness, and relatedness play in our lives was captured by Franz Kafka in his novella "The Metamorphosis." The main character,

Gregor Samsa, wakes up one morning to discover that he has been transformed into a giant insect (Figure 5.7). One can interpret Kafka's story as a message concerning the alienation that confronts all of humanity because Gregor, before the transformation, is depicted as being alienated from his family, work, and life in general. He walks through life as a mindless automaton. After the metamorphosis, Gregor becomes more human than those around him. Over time he becomes more independent and finds meaning in the music that his sister plays on a violin. He becomes mesmerized by the music. Gregor's metamorphosis has allowed him to symbolically peel away the veneer of an inauthentic existence to reveal the potential that lies within everyone. In the end, the other characters in the story remain stagnant, which becomes clear after Gregor's death when his sister, father, and mother return to living painfully ordinary, meaningless lives that are void of true authenticity.

Meaning-Making

Another critical theme in existentialism is *meaning-making*. Existentialists believe that humans often strive to find meaning in their lives. This may include finding their reason for being in the world or discovering what gives their life purpose. Examining meaning within one's life during therapy can lead to revamping one's belief and value system. Lack of meaning or meaninglessness can result in experiences of hollowness and emptiness, or a condition that Frankl (1996) called *existential vacuum*. Meaninglessness, along with other inevitable aspects of existence, such as dread and doubt, can lead to living a restricted existence. As with other aspects of existentialism, people are responsible for their own meaning-making.

Life, Death, and Anxiety

Yalom (1980) explained existential anxiety as the apprehension that emerges because of the *givens of existence*—that is, freedom, death, isolation, and meaninglessness. According to Rollo May (1969), people live life (accompanied with freedom and relationships) experiencing anxiety just as they face death (accompanied by meaninglessness and isolation) experiencing anxiety. Fears about death, even those that are repressed, can create a sense of urgency, desperation, or gravity that, if unaltered, can cause distress or dysfunction. Yalom (1980) described this particular existential conflict as "the tension between the awareness of the inevitability of death and the wish to continue to be" (p. 8). By accepting that one will die at some point (i.e., having a sense of nonbeing), a person will be able to live more fully in the present.

Existentialists distinguish between normal and neurotic anxiety, considering anxiety normal if it is a common response to a stressful situation and neurotic if it is excessive, compulsive, or an unusual response to the actual context of the situation. Normal anxiety can be useful because it can act as a motivator, whereas neurotic anxiety can actually inhibit the individual.

The Therapeutic Process

Existential psychology provides the therapist with a particular orientation to living; some refer to it a philosophical stance or a worldview. At the core is the existentialist contention that essence, or a person's reality of life, follows existence. Reality is created by, and does not exist apart from, an individual's existence (Sartre, 1943/1969). Essence highlights the importance of individuals' idiosyncratic experiences, an important factor to consider during the therapy process. Therapists practicing existential therapy address a person's individuality as well as universality.

Goals

As in other forms of therapy, when starting existential therapy a client is likely to have targeted one or more goals that are tied to any number of concerns, but one primary goal that is common to this particular therapeutic approach is to improve the client's self-awareness, which will increase the client's personal freedom and responsibility. A therapist can be expected to challenge any boundaries that are hindering clients from accepting responsibility and to help clients recognize that they have choices. During sessions, a therapist also would help clients to appreciate their personal uniqueness and define their own identity based on their uniqueness rather than having them rely on others to define their identity for them. The therapist would be especially interested in assisting clients to find meaning and purpose in life and in assisting clients to build on their personal strengths in ways that enable them to harness their anxiety so that it is useful rather than immobilizing.

Therapist's Role

The role of the therapist is crucial, and he must show "empathic availability" toward the client (Walsh & Lantz, 2007, p. 35). In other words, the therapist must be present and compassionate. Next, the therapist must allow clients to share their emotions and talk about their experiences. This process is likely to be painful for clients, requiring the therapist to provide support and empathy during this difficult phase of self-disclosure. A therapist also needs to assist clients in acknowledging the fact that each person is alone in the world and that each person must search for explanations of self from within instead of relying on other individuals' definitions. In addition, a therapist could encourage clients to document their experiences and discover their unique identity through their own words. In such a situation, the therapist should not provide any specific guidelines but rather increase clients' freedom through allowing them to find their own.

Client's Role

According to existential writers, an individual's healthy core is situated in the noetic or spirit dimension (Batthyány, 2016; Wong, 2014), and that is where a cure or solution will be found. There, the fighting back strength of the spirit must be activated and channeled toward current life situations in order to accomplish the desired change that is life-giving or healing. Recognizing that individuals are spirit enables clients to become aware that their possessions can be removed from them, but their spirit cannot be taken. Clients may have permitted other individuals to define their identity, instead of defining it for themselves. An example of this is called the "bandwagon effect," which occurs when a growing number of people do something simply because others are doing it. (This dynamic helps to explain the spontaneous nature of fads.) When clients allow others to define them, they experience a life of inauthenticity. When this happens, a client's beliefs about self and self-esteem are derived from the opinions of others. Existential therapy can be intense at times, and to fulfill their role in the therapeutic process, clients are to "[hold] up the problem experience so that it may be seen, remembered, and reexperienced" (Walsh & Lantz, 2007, p. 28).

Mastering one's own identity means clients must create and accept their own definition of what constitutes their identity. This requires a person to recognize that she can make her own choices. In accepting herself for who she is, she would be able to live more authentically; that is, she would be able to appreciate and celebrate the elements that make her a unique being. She would also need to recognize the consequences of this alternative view of herself, as increased freedom comes with increased responsibility (Walsh & Lantz, 2007). Thereafter, she is responsible for the choices she makes because she has not been coerced; she is no longer a member of the herd. Roberts and Yeager (2009) found writing and journaling to be an effective means of exploring identity and finding meaning in life.

If the therapeutic process works as expected, clients will credit their pain for positive changes that have emerged. Once clients have discovered a deeper comprehension and acceptance of their true self, they realize and appreciate the opportunities offered by the pain of "identity conflict" within their lives. Clients will also develop through authenticity a greater ability to recognize the suffering that other persons have experienced through living their own pain of having an existence defined by others. Finally, rather than forget the pain that inauthentic living brings with it, it is important for clients to "honor" their pain; that is, it is the pain of living a false identity that has pushed them to find a meaningful life.

Existential therapists view clients as individuals who are unique in myriad ways. Furthermore, individuals experience their uniqueness during acts of creativity and in relationships formed. Perhaps the sculpture a client created is not a masterpiece, but the sculpture is uniquely the client's. Recognizing one's unique qualities and abilities and meaningfully applying such assets helps one to maintain a steady sense of authenticity.

Therapeutic Change

Change occurs by transcending past limitations, working toward worthwhile goals, and connecting to other people. It is through such positive involvements that clients acquire fulfillment in their lives and achieve meaning (Schneider, 2011). Existential therapists assert that individuals are capable of changing their attitude. When experiencing unavoidable suffering, for example, clients can discover meaning in the situation by examining it differently (Frankl, 1959/2006). For example, finding meaning could involve having the person courageously understanding and accepting what cannot be changed (Frankl, 1988). If clients have difficulty comprehending what currently gives them meaning, an existential therapist could have such clients list domains in which they wish to find meaning (Basescu, 1963). This often leads to the client gaining enough momentum to start the change process.

Sharing their emotional experiences with the therapist allows clients to display their feelings externally instead of keeping them inside. Sharing of this nature also typically improves the client–therapist relationship. Additionally, this process can result in naming emotions, which normalizes them and allows them to be more easily mastered, which is an important step toward therapeutic change. Dereflection, on the other hand, occurs when clients are simply pushing aside emotions of inner conflict while misunderstanding that their therapist will help them to push aside emotions as an aspect of their treatment (Frankl, 1975).

Once change is accomplished, clients must assume responsibility for themselves and their own continued progress. Clients are made independent of the therapist through the therapist assisting them to discover their "guidance" within themselves (Guttmann, 1996).

Assessment

The therapist assesses four components of human existence (May & Yalom, 1995; Roysircar & Mayo, 2012; Schneider, 2011; Sodowsky & Sodowsky, 1997): the physical (*Umwelt*), the intrapersonal self or the psychological (*Eigenwelt*), the social (*Mitwelt*), and the spiritual (*überwelt*). Clients have created their personal attitude based on their particular understanding of their experiences in each of these components or dimensions of human existence. Specifically, their orientation toward the world is derived from these four dimensions, which also accounts for clients' perception of reality. Interwoven or nested, the four components are believed to offer a complex "ecological force field" that influences everyone's existence (Roysircar & Mayo, 2012).

Assessing Four Components of Human Existence

A thorough assessment of a client's situation involves asking questions related to each of the four components.

1. Physical Dimension (*Umwelt*). Assessment of clients' physical dimension seeks answers to the following questions: How do clients relate to the "givens" of the natural world and their environment? This includes their attitudes toward their body, material possessions, the concrete surroundings in which they find themselves, the weather and the climate, their own bodily needs, the bodies of other individuals, illness and health, and their own mortality (Roysircar & Mayo, 2012). Using an existential framework, Kluckhohn (1956) asked questions about people's worldview orientation, such as how they view human nature (good, bad, or a mixture of both), natural phenomena and the supernatural (a blessing to be prayed for, fearful and overpowering, able to be controlled), and time (past, present, future, infinite). The struggle clients have in the physical dimension is basically between the search for domination over natural laws and elements (as in sports or technology) and the need to accept the confines of natural boundaries (as in old age or ecological systems). If individuals strive for physical security through wealth and health, the therapist evaluates for clients' gradual disillusionment and realization that this form of security can only be short lived. Clients' awareness of such limitations can lead to a big release of tension, which is viewed as a positive outcome in existential therapy (May & Yalom, 1995; Roysircar & Mayo, 2012; Schneider, 2011; Sodowsky & Sodowsky, 1997).

2. Social Dimension (*Mitwelt*). Individuals relate to other people as they navigate the social world around them. This dimension includes individuals' response to

the culture they reside in, the race and class they belong to, and the groups they are not affiliated with in life. Attitudes evaluated here range from hate to love and from competition to cooperation. Some individuals wish to withdraw as much as possible from the world of other people. Other individuals strive for public acceptance by adhering to the fashions and rules of the time. Clients' interpersonal interactions can be understood in terms of rejection versus acceptance or isolation versus belonging (May & Yalom, 1995; Roysircar & Mayo, 2012; Schneider, 2011; Sodowsky & Sodowsky, 1997). Kluckhohn's (1956) worldview question for this dimension is, How do people view relationships (individualistic/independent, dependent, interdependent, etc.)?

3. Psychological/Individual Dimension (*Eigenwelt*). People relate to themselves and, as a result, establish a personal world. Therapists evaluate clients' perceptions about their own character, past experiences, and future possibilities. Contradictions that are uncovered are evaluated with respect to personal weaknesses and strengths. Therapists evaluate if clients are searching for a feeling of being substantial, a sense of identity, and possessing a solid self. Many clients seek therapy in reaction to situations that have challenged them with contrary evidence and thrust them into a state of disintegration or confusion. In looking at this component, passivity/activity is a critical polarity to address to uncover impediments to personal growth. Self-affirmation and resolution are linked with activity, and yielding and surrender are associated with passivity (May & Yalom, 1995; Roysircar & Mayo, 2012; Schneider, 2011; Sodowsky & Sodowsky, 1997). Kluckhohn's (1956) worldview question for this dimension is, How do clients view activity (problem-solving, resignation, quiet non-confrontation)? The paradox is that while the therapist assesses whether clients are searching for and finding meaning in their personal identity, the therapist also assesses whether clients can give up their sense of self-importance. Experiencing the final dissolution of self that accompanies personal loss and the realization of death may activate confusion and anxiety for clients who are self-centered and possess a lot of self-pride (May & Yalom, 1995; Roysircar & Mayo; 2012; Schneider, 2011; Sodowsky & Sodowsky, 1997).

Additional assessment can be accomplished by using the Personal Orientation Inventory (Shostrom, 1964). This inventory provides scores of relative time competence with regard to the here and now (i.e., time competence), relative other- and inner-directedness (i.e., inner directed), and 10 additional subscales that discriminate among those who are self-actualized, normal, and non-self-actualized. Means for the three states of existence provide support for the inventory's validity. The mean for self-actualized individuals has been found to be above the mean for the norm, and the mean for non-self-actualized individuals has been found to be below the mean for the norm.

4. Spiritual Dimension (*Überwelt*). Individuals establish a sense of what makes an ideal world, a philosophical outlook to relate to the unknown, or an ideology, to put all the pieces of the puzzle together for themselves and thus find meaning. For some individuals, this is accomplished by adhering to religion or some other

prescriptive worldview, whereas for other individuals it involves discovering or attributing meaning in a more personal or secular way. Therapists assess for this spiritual dimension because they can apply their clients' values and belief systems to solve the contradictions that must be confronted in therapy—contradictions that are tied to the tension between absurdity and purpose and between despair and hope. People establish their values when searching for something that matters to them to live or die for, something that might even have universal and ultimate validity (e.g., risking one's life to help a stranger; May & Yalom, 1995; Roysircar & Mayo, 2012; Schneider, 2011; Sodowsky & Sodowsky, 1997). Thus, therapists assess clients' belief system that "provides an implicit frame of reference for interpretation of the world and its experiences" (Ibrahim, Roysircar-Sodowsky, & Ohnishi, 2001, p. 445).

Tomkins (1965) operationalized two worldview dimensions: the humanist and normative orientations. Therapists can assess these two orientations of their clients by using the Modified Polarity Scale (de St. Aubin, 1996), a measure of worldview. The scale assesses beliefs about politics, human nature, child rearing, human relationships, and the nature of reality. It also measures an individual's humanism and normativism (Frey & Roysircar, 2004). The *humanist* orientation is existential in nature and represents maintaining a view of reality as being self-constructed, complex, and evolving and human beings as active, creative, thinking, and loving. Preferred cognitive styles are constructivism and rationalism, and values include creativity, open-mindedness, and equal opportunity for all. The humanist worldview is followed by people drawn to an individualistic culture with democratic, societal structures. The *normative* orientation is assessed as the opposite of existentialism because it views reality as stable and preexisting, separate from humankind; and human beings are viewed as meeting their potential through conformity to set values, norms, and that which is predetermined. Preferred cognitive styles are objectivism and realism; and values, such as, courtesy, self-discipline, and respect for the socially worthy (Roysircar-Sodowsky & Frey, 2003). In their assessment of the normative worldview, therapists can identify clients who come from group-oriented cultures with hierarchical societal structures and with whom existential therapy may not be effective. However, people from group-oriented cultures who adhere to hierarchy and collective action can also, as individuals, lead a private contemplative life, as noted in Asian cultures.

Therapists, when assessing worldviews, can also assess for locus of control and attribution style. They can ask questions such as the following: What are my (therapist) and client's locus of control (internal or external)? How do the therapist and client attribute responsibility for happiness and sorrow, success and failure (to oneself, others, luck, randomness)? Is there a match between therapist and client on perceived control and attribution? Overall, existential assessment using the worldview framework asks questions on values, feelings, and reasoning and is less concerned with the diagnosis of psychopathology. Research findings on existential measures, *Purpose of Life,* including its Spanish version, *Meanings of Meaningfulness of Life,* and *Meaning and Automatic Stereotyping* are reported in Batthyány (2016).

Existential Analytic Diagnosis

There are several steps involved in conducting an existential analytic diagnosis (Bartuska, Buchsbaumer, Mehta, Pawlowsky, & Wiesnagrotzki, 2008). The steps can be performed in any order, but an accurate assessment requires each step to be examined at least once. Step 1 in the existential analytic process is gaining a three-dimensional, structural view of human nature (*Eigenwelt, Mitwelt,* and *Umwelt*). Step 2 aims to determine where the blocks are in the client's existentiality: at the input, process, or output level. The therapist uses the client's report of how he handles various life situations and the state of the therapeutic relationship in conjunction with the level of existential block to determine the degree of disturbance. The degree of disturbance in existentiality helps predict the severity of the existing disorder. Step 3 identifies the specific suffering of the client by examining the client's motivations for therapy, subjective understanding of and attitudes toward the disorder uncovered, and expectations for therapy. In addition, step three requires professional assessment of the disorder's specific elements and causes. Step 4 lays the groundwork for existential analytic therapy using personal existential analysis to determine the client's personal resources and personal dynamics. Step 5 in evaluating the client is a professional assessment by the therapist, based on the professional observations and knowledge of the immediate client needs to assist with the improvement of his life, creating the therapeutic plan (Bartuska et al., 2008). Step 6 requires an assessment of the therapist's own personality, competencies, personal sense of responsibility, motivation, and the purpose and meaning of therapy, along with the client's symptoms, personality, and problems to ensure both parties are protected, secure, and ready for therapy (La Roche, 2013; Roysircar & Pignatiello, 2011; Tummala-Narra, 2016). Simultaneously, the therapist makes a second diagnosis based on current diagnostic schemata to ensure there are no blind spots or errors. This assessment offers the therapist a view of the entirety of the client's diagnosis and the extent and scope of what is required therapeutically.

Techniques and Strategies

Existential-oriented therapists make use of a wide variety of techniques and strategies because existential psychology is more of a meta-theory and thus espouses few specific strategies and techniques. This is a common criticism of existential theory and its practice (Schneider, 2011). Existentialist therapists such as Yalom (1980) firmly believe that inflexible obedience to specific therapy techniques is overly authoritarian, possibly obscures a comprehension of the client, undercuts authenticity, and results in short-lived instead of enduring outcomes. Further, proponents argue that technique should be selected based on understanding of the client, not the other way around (Spinelli, 2006) such as when a theory dictates what to use.

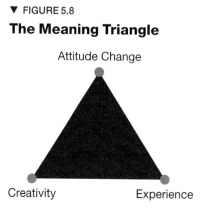

▼ FIGURE 5.8

The Meaning Triangle

Attitude Change

Creativity   Experience

The Meaning Triangle. A meaning triangle is an effective means to illustrate to clients (individuals and groups) three aspects of establishing meaning in one's life, which are creativity, experiencing, and change of attitude (see Figure 5.8). In *creativity,* individuals find meaning by contributing to the world through self-expression; they can use their talents in different ways and through different kinds of involvements, for example, through occupational work or various forms of art. In *experiencing,* people connect with the world through culture, nature, relationships, and interactions with the environment and other individuals. Any of these points of connection can serve as an avenue to establish meaning. In *change of attitude,* even if individuals are unable to modify a circumstance or situation, they can continue to decide on their attitude toward an unchangeable condition; this is frequently accomplished through a self-transcending method of discovering meaning, especially in cases where suffering is unavoidable (Breitbart & Masterson, 2016; Frankl, 1959/2006; Hwang, 2017; Wong 2010).

There are basically two levels of meaning in life. *Ultimate meaning* which people can never reach completely, but on occasion catch a glimpse of what it embodies. *Meaning of the moment* consists of the answers people constantly have to questions posed by life (Fabry, Bulka, & Sahakian, 1996). Logotherapy teaches clients that people cannot pose life questions, that is, "why" questions. Instead, therapists posit that life is the questioner (Guttmann, 1996). According to existentialists, individuals respond to life by listening with judgment to a moment's meaning and then arriving at responsible decisions within their available range of freedom. Furthermore, Frankl (1967, 1988) believed an individual's choices are guided by her values, which are associated with the voice of her conscience.

Given that life is dynamic, individuals are constantly faced with aspects of the tragic triad: unavoidable suffering, guilt, and death. Therefore, typically the most effective way to discover a meaning, particularly in a situation that is not amenable to change, is to modify one's attitude (Frankl, 1959/2006, 1967, 1988). A new meaning will frequently emerge for a client using this strategy. Existentialists believe that meaning cannot be given; it must be discovered by the client. The first pathway to finding meaning is to make clients realize that they are not victims of circumstances. A client might have symptoms, but the client (i.e., the client's spirit) is not the symptoms (Frankl, 1959/2006, 1967, 1988).

Socratic Dialogue. One of the main strategies used by existential therapists is *Socratic dialogue,* in which the therapist and the client collaboratively attempt to discover a meaning in life (Yalom, 1980). The technique is also called the Socratic-therapeutic method and often takes the form of an exploratory discussion to isolate the thoughts, beliefs, and values that pertain to what the person does and the kind of choices the person makes during a typical day. Such an exploratory discussion is intended to ferret out information that is used to establish meaning.

Paradoxical Intention. Another important logotherapy tool is paradoxical intention, which basically instructs clients to "embrace" what frightens them the most. Effectively applied, this technique causes what once was frightening to no longer be a problem (Frankl, 1959/2006). For example, a person experiencing anticipatory anxiety over some future event (e.g., she is required to give a speech) may fear she will not be able to get a good night's sleep and as a result of this fear she cannot fall asleep. This is a situation where she hinders her ability to fall sleep because she is trying too hard (i.e., hyper-intend) to go to sleep. In such a situation a logotherapist could use paradoxical intention to magnify the upsetting symptom. The therapist would tell the person to go to bed and purposefully try to keep awake, instructing her not to shut her eyes. This strategy is expected to reduce her fear of not falling asleep, which was responsible for keeping the person up in the first place, thus permitting the client to fall asleep in a suitable period of time (Guttmann, 1996). The following is an example of paradoxical intention given by Frankl (1988) himself. Once, an older general practitioner consulted with Frankl about his severe depression. He was unable to stop grieving the death of his wife 2 years previously and whom he had loved more than anything else. Frankl did not tell him anything, but rather confronted the man with a question: What would have happened if the doctor had died first and his wife had survived him? The doctor reported that his wife would have had a terrible time and that she would have suffered a lot. In response, Frankl answered that she had been spared such suffering and that it was the doctor who had spared his wife this terrible suffering, and now, he had to experience it by living and mourning her. The doctor did not utter a word but shook Frankl's hand and calmly left his office (Frankl, 1988).

Existential therapy does not use a specific set of techniques or interventions, thus allowing the opportunity for an individualized experience in therapy. In fact, logotherapy can be used in conjunction with interventions from other approaches, as long as issues of meaninglessness and identity are addressed.

Multiculturalism and Social Justice

Existentialism may not be effective with some multicultural clients. For example, certain religious, spiritual clients may not wish to give up their beliefs in supernatural curses, blessings, or in predestination or fate (e.g., *fuku* for Jamaicans, *karma* in Hinduism; Roysircar & Pignatiello, 2015). Such perspectives of destiny differ with Rollo May's perspective of establishing one's destiny and the concepts of self-determinism and freedom (Roysircar, 2012). Using a therapeutic strategy to honor spiritualism, for example, may contribute to developing multicultural clients' inner self (Afrocentric spiritness, Hindu *atma*; Roysircar, 2012; Roysircar & Pignatiello, 2011; Roysircar, Thompson, & Boudreau, 2017), whereas trying to get a Latino client to forego *espiritsmo* may impede this client's bicultural identity development, such as in the case of Juan, whose difficulties were described at the beginning of this chapter. The latter action would reveal the therapist's bias favoring assimilation to the culture of European Americans. Modifications in existential therapy are possible and could be orchestrated to allow clients to accept supernatural powers and recognize that they have choices of spiritually guided rituals to remove evil spirits and use existential therapy to regain control of their lives.

In addition, Hispanics are more inclined to value and rely on social support (Gonzales, German, & Fabritt, 2012; Padilla & Salgado de Snyder, 1985), and the Chinese have been shown to have an interdependent self-construal (Leong & Lee, 2006). Thus, some multicultural clients from collectivistic cultures may strongly wish to be in social relationships and to have positive family dynamics. Like Juan, their presenting problem may be that they are not good at social interactions and that they want to address this culture-specific interpersonal deficit. Their goal may be to connect with people and resist the existential notion that one is ultimately alone and must seek autonomy. Such clients may have trouble conceiving self-determination when they operate in the context of natural support systems, ingroup hierarchies, and strict gender roles regardless of how restrictive these social mores might appear to an existential therapist (Comas-Díaz, 2012). On the other hand, the interaction of abusive microsystems in the client's life (family, peers, the dominant group, one's own ethnic group, place of worship) make for a life of persecution, as in Juan's case. The need to connect with social units and social persecution is an existential paradox that the therapist needs to illuminate. Therefore, an existential therapist's understanding of family characteristics and structural relationships within a collectivistic culture is critical for therapy utilization by and retention of minority clients (Roysircar, 2009). Finally, for Chinese clients, for example, interdependent self-construal is an important consideration, but it must be handled in such a way that it does not undermine the basic existential tenet of individual uniqueness.

Racial and ethnic minorities are members of the larger society that has discriminated and oppressed them for their nationality, ethnicity, culture, color, language, and gender-role behaviors (Sue & Sue, 2015). These constraints provide realistic boundaries to available choices for minority clients. Whereas other persons in the dominant culture might have the freedom to make specific choices, some minority individuals may not (Young, 1990). For instance, a minority client who is poor may not be able to make choices to make his life better because other lower order (basic) needs (e.g., food, physical comfort, emotional safety, and protection from harassment) have not been met. Furthermore, less educated, low-income, and psychologically unsophisticated clients may desire more direction from an existential therapist; that is, they may want the therapist to simply tell them the solution to their problems. Such needs cannot be ignored when conducting therapy with existentially less privileged clients.

In situations of oppression a therapist can ask the oppressed client questions and make statements that do not make the client responsible for the oppression (see Roysircar & Pignatiello, 2015). For example, the therapist can say, "the one thing the oppressor can't take away from you is the way you choose to respond to what the oppressor does to you. Everyone possesses the immutable freedom to choose one's attitude in any given circumstance. You cannot control what happens to you, but you can control your attitude toward what happens to you, and in that you will be mastering change rather than allowing it to master you."

Internalized marginalization refers to a person accepting societal discriminatory attitudes, which communicate that one's own cultural group, and thus oneself, is subhuman, inferior, incapable, or a burden on society. Sartre (1943/1969) and Yalom (1980), as explained by Roysircar and Pignatiello (2015), would not view internalized marginalization to be a real constraint on a person's freedom. Rather, they would think that people are responsible for their psychological responses to adversities. May (1969) wrote, "A person can meet anxiety to the extent that his values are stronger than the threat" (p. 17). Traditional existentialists imply that an oppressed individual should come to recognize her "responsibility" for internalized marginalization, regardless of systemic oppression. This therapy judgment, however, can be considered "blaming the victim." Friedman (1962), a moderate existentialist, in contrast, takes a tempered approach:

Kierkegaard once remarked that one cannot judge another person, for no one knows how much of his action is suffering—a compulsion he must bear—and how much is temptation—a matter about which he has some real choice. This is not a theoretical question of "free will" versus "determinism," but a concrete question of the resources of a particular situation. Probably even he himself will not know afterward to what extent he was able to respond to the situation with the spontaneity of the whole person and to what extent his action was the product of fragmentary and conditioned responses. (p. 287)

Thus, Friedman (1962) might suggest that in most cases the individual does not actually have the internal resources, and hence freedom of choice, to rid himself of internalized marginalization. Rather, an existential therapist might suggest that freedom from the obstacle of hopelessness along with the actualization of freedom through the awareness of the external root of oppression is one *goal* of existential therapy, not a personal responsibility (Friedman, 1962). Taking the responsibility for internalized marginalization would be empowering only if the person were actually free (i.e., possessed the resources to overcome forced constraints) to do so (Fanon, 1967; Sodowsky & Sodowsky, 1991). Roysircar (2009) wrote, "Therapists who have not experienced oppression to the degree that many ethnic minority persons have could perceive racism-induced anxiety as residing within the individual. Resultantly, such therapists may erroneously suggest personal responsibility or accountability. Thus, the most effective methods of dealing with racism may not be intrapersonally based" (p. 82). With their emphasis on personal responsibility, existential therapists should be particularly aware of the negative parameters of this construct.

Ethical Considerations

A client like Juan may find that his existence leads to boredom and eventually suicide. He discusses with the therapist his impulse to move to an imagined form of life that is imbued with what ought to be and what is pleasurable. This concept of the afterlife, attained as a natural development of life, has not been addressed by existentialists, who focus instead on how to live authentically in the here and now. An existentialist might say that the challenge of relationships interfacing with one's ultimate aloneness is what is causing Juan's anxiety.

In existential therapy, the ethical is what is universal, and the goal of an ethical life is to reconcile the individual or the particular situation with the universal. Ethical action is acting only on that principle, and taking one's life is not a universal prescription. When something is universally right, people must just do it, such as having the courage to live and love. The ethical therapist connects the individual to the universal and relates the self to others, nature, and the environment. A therapist lives within the universal frame.

A religious life (*Überwelt*) is different from an ethical life. The ethical life is one of reconciliation with the universal (*Umwelt*). In faith, the individual is higher than the universal. Individuals determine on their own their relation to the absolute (i.e., God) and not by their relation to the universal. According to Frankl (1967, 1988), the paradox between connection to the universal and connection to the absolute or ultimate can also be expressed by saying that there is an absolute duty toward God.

People who choose the subjective path of faith over other paths instantly comprehend the entire dialectical difficulty because they must spend a long time to find God in some sensory way like seeing or feeling God. They must comprehend this dialectical quandary in the entirety of its pain since they need to turn to God at the precise moment they take such a path because each moment they are without God is wasted (see Beckett, 1982; Frankl, 1967, 1988). However, many therapists do not function in the realm of faith. If clients bring up spiritual issues in their contemplation of suicide, as in the case of Juan, existential therapists instead will refer to the existential vacuum and despair, depression, guilt, shame, anger, or neurotic anxiety that underlies the client's thought of taking his own life.

Existentialism has an assortment of tenets and beliefs, but it does not include a detailed code of ethics. It is left to each individual to work that out within the tenets of the existential thought system. That gives individuals a wealth of latitude, and some people may reach spurious notions of right and wrong. The idea that you create what you are by your actions can give a person a good moral base. However, existentialism is hard for many people to interpret, and this results in few people being able to use its principles as ethical guidelines. This ambiguity in interpretation makes it difficult to translate existential principles into ethical guidelines.

Evaluating Existential Theory

Research Support

Although existential therapy has a long tradition, there is a dearth of empirical studies directly investigating its therapeutic efficacy or effectiveness (Elliott, Greenberg, & Lietaer, 2004; Keshen, 2006). The lack of research support for this approach may speak less about its therapeutic utility and more about the difficulty of designing outcome studies to test assumptions and strategies linked with this form of therapy. The very idea of quantifying constructs is at odds with the assumptions of existentialism and existential therapy (Keshen, 2006). Because existentialists highly value subjective experience, this therapeutic approach is rather heterogeneous, experiential, and free form. By its very nature, existential therapy does not lend itself to manualized treatments necessary for randomized controlled trials. As a result, direct support for this approach is limited (Keshen, 2006).

As Elliot and colleagues (2004) stated, however, "Experiential therapies are part of the tradition of humanistic psychology, with the major sub-approaches being person-centered, gestalt, and existential (others include psychodrama and emotion-focused therapy). Originally designated as humanistic or third-force therapies, these therapies have recently begun to be grouped together under the experiential umbrella" (p. 493). Favorable research support has been reported for process-experiential therapy, an approach with a framework that relies heavily on existential therapy. For example, in their meta-analysis, Elliott and colleagues (2004) claimed that uncontrolled, pre/post test studies of process-experiential therapy had elicited an effect size of .86. When compared against nontherapy controls, this approach appeared to have a similar effect size (.78). When compared to cognitive-behavioral or other types of therapy, however, Elliot et al. reported the overall process-experiential effect sizes were nonsignificant (.11 and .4, respectively). Process-experiential therapy does seem to be efficacious for anxiety, depression, and trauma or abuse (Elliot et al., 2004). Directly extrapolating the efficacy of process-experiential therapy to existential therapy remains troublesome, however, given the eclectic nature of both forms of intervention.

Although formalized existential techniques and accompanying protocols are theoretically not available, various interventions linked with this approach have shown promise. For instance, supportive-expressive group therapy has been found to be efficacious in increasing overall and existential well-being for persons with primary breast cancer (Classen & Spiegel, 2011). Dignity therapy also has been shown to be efficacious in improving overall quality of life, sense of dignity, and existential well-being in dying hospice patients (Chochinov et al., 2011).

Limitations and Criticisms of Existentialism

The 19th- and 20th-century European existentialists never really coalesced into a cohesive ideological school, and many of these thinkers were virtually unknown to their counterparts in the United States. Other than Binswanger and Frankl, European existentialist thinkers remain little known in the United States. American existentialist thinkers tend to be more optimistic than their European counterparts. Existential therapy is individualistic in its orientation and often fails to recognize the impact of larger and powerful systems that influence the individual client. Bronfenbrenner and Ceci (1994) described four systems: *macrosystem* (e.g., cultural and societal beliefs that impact an individual), *exosystem* (e.g., parent loses job, which has an indirect but important financial impact on other individuals in a family), *mesosystem* (e.g., relationship that an individual's family has with school teachers), and *microsystem* (e.g., the individual's relationship with her parents). Thus, the significance of the family as a support or abuse system at the microsystemic level may be neglected in existentialism. When emphasizing the universal, existentialists overlook change brought about by time, how time makes things relative, and how time helps to give perspectives. Existential therapy uses constructs and language that embody Western values and abstractions that may not be understood easily by less formally educated clients for whom English is a second language. Overall, existentialism is a product of European and European American philosophies and may need to be culturally adapted for use with ethnic minority clients.

Relevance to Current Practice

 As May and Yalom (1995) stated, "Existential psychotherapy is *not* a comprehensive psychotherapeutic system; it is a frame of reference—a paradigm by which one views and understands a client's suffering in a particular manner" (p. 278). In this sense, existential therapy is relevant but must be incorporated into other forms of therapy. An existential therapist may use various techniques from other approaches as long as he thinks and acts from an existential frame of reference (May & Yalom, 1995). As such, therapists may employ existential strategies in a variety of therapy settings with different types of clients to address a wide range of presenting problems or to treat persons displaying a variety of *DSM* diagnoses at all levels of severity. Existential therapy is most likely best suited, however, to persons interested in meaning-making (Park, 2010; Wong, 2010), facing illness (e.g., Classen & Spiegel, 2011), experiencing end-of-life issues (e.g., Chochinov et al., 2011), coping with tragedy (e.g., Frankl, 1959/2006), engaged in career decision making (Cohen, 2003), or other concerns related to the four so-called givens of life (i.e., death, freedom, isolation, meaninglessness; Yalom, 1980).

Assuming the appropriate *DSM* diagnoses and proper documentation, third-party payers will reimburse therapists for providing existential therapy. Such reimbursement may be more likely for treatment of mood, anxiety, and adjustment disorders. If third-party payment criteria become increasingly based on providing objective outcomes in behavioral terms, reimbursement for existential treatment may become more difficult. As practice continues to be regulated by third-party payers, existential therapists might need to capitalize on existential techniques linked to evidenced-based outcomes (e.g., Chochinov et al., 2011; Classen & Spiegel, 2011) and evidenced-based techniques associated with other approaches. To be eligible for insurance reimbursement, existential therapists will need to continue to develop frameworks amenable to scientific study and short-term treatment (e.g., Chochinov et al., 2011; Classen & Spiegel, 2011; Wong, 2010).

In terms of training, "the spirit of existential psychotherapy has never supported the formation of specific institutes because it deals with the presuppositions underlying therapy of any kind" (May & Yalom, 1995, p. 271). Some societies and training programs, however, have been developed around the globe. For example, the Society for Existential Analysis (SEA) in London, the International Society for Existential Psychology and Psychotherapy (ISEPP) based out of Canada, the Existential-Humanistic Institute in San Francisco, and the Boulder Psychotherapy Institute in Colorado are organizations devoted to advancing existential therapy.

Although existentialism has been traditionally a Western philosophy, it also has been integrated with some Eastern perspectives. One good example of this is the Zhi Mian International Institute of Existential-Humanistic Psychology. Most of the organizations mentioned thus far have some form of education and training, such as professional conferences, workshops, books, journals, and newsletters. The *International Journal of Existential Psychology and Psychotherapy* is the official publication of ISEPP, and *Existential Analysis* is the official publication of SEA. Although ISEPP and SEA have no known credentialing process, some organizations do host certification programs. Both the Existential-Humanistic Institute and Boulder Psychotherapy Institute, for example, offer certification programs in existential therapy. Moreover, the College of Arts and Sciences at Seattle University offers a terminal master's degree program in existential-phenomenological therapeutic psychology.

RETURNING TO THE CASE OF JUAN

Although Juan is fairly self-aware, spending a lot of time pondering his own situation, he has not taken responsibility for his own choices or accepted his own freedom, rendering him unable to control his destiny. Perhaps his utilization of the *fuku* is a way to avoid this freedom by placing responsibility on an external source beyond his control. Additionally, Juan is struggling with his own identity, hampering him from an authentic existence and resulting in his feeling guilt. He is uncertain about his purpose in life; he experiences meaninglessness and thus has a restricted existence. Last, Juan's anxiety to live and die has immobilized him, and his belief in *fuku* does not permit him to live in the moment.

Despite his uncertainties, it would seem problematic and multiculturally unethical to hold Juan responsible for his self- and social-alienation. Rather than fostering a sense of responsibility for his alienation, the therapist's task would be to first assist Juan in clarifying the extent of his capability at this point in time. Then, the therapist should encourage him to embrace the responsibility for the freedom to take action based on this capability.

If Juan, with the collaboration of his therapist, determines that he is capable (i.e., has the freedom) to walk to the gym doors tomorrow, it may be empowering for him to accept responsibility for his decision to do so (or not). Whether Juan decides to visit or not visit the gym is less critical; what is critical is that he experiences a sense of control for his actions and in his life. When free will is viewed in this way—as a relative goal guided by both internal *and* external resources—existential therapy appears less at odds with multicultural psychology and is an empowering and hopeful form of therapy.

A therapist would also want to work with Juan to challenge boundaries that are hindering him from accepting responsibility and to help him recognize that he has choices. Juan would need to see that he is responsible for writing his destiny rather than leaving it to the *fuku*. Furthermore, a therapist could help Juan to value his unique bicultural life as a Jamaican American and to describe his own identity instead of relying on other individuals to define it for him. Juan could be helped to see he does not have to be either Jamaican or "un-Jamaican," and to accept an ethnic identity that integrates elements of both in order to help him be comfortable with his true self and to live more authentically. A therapist would also want to assist him in finding purpose and meaning in life and in harnessing his anxiety so that it is useful rather than immobilizing. Juan would need to be comfortable with his eventual nonbeing to have a more productive life and maximize on his development in the immediate moment, thereby preventing the precipitation of meaninglessness, despair, and the occurrence of suicidal thoughts.

INTERVENTION

One intervention that could be used in conjunction with other interventions to help Juan targets the issues of meaninglessness and identity. This intervention is based on Walsh and Lantz's (2007) four principles of intervention: holding, telling, mastering, and honoring.

Juan is experiencing conflict because he has permitted others to define his identity for him instead of defining it for himself. This situation has led to him living inauthentically. Many of Juan's beliefs and his self-esteem are derived from others' opinions. The first stage of the intervention strategy would require Juan to "hold" the experience, that is, to "[hold] up the problem experience so that it may be seen, remembered, and re-experienced" (Walsh & Lantz, 2007, p. 28). In Juan's case, he may have many recollections of experiencing discrimination because he did not fit stereotypical ideals for Jamaican males, such as when others judged him based on his weight, color, and unique hobbies. Holding these experiences

Points in discussion
MC who Benefits

(Continued)

would likely be hard for Juan as they are about painful emotions, which need to be empathically recognized by the therapist. The role of the therapist is crucial here, and she must show "empathic availability" toward Juan (Walsh & Lantz, 2007, p. 35). In other words, the therapist must be present and compassionate.

Next, the therapist would allow Juan to share his emotions and experiences. Again, this process could be painful for Juan, requiring that the therapist provide support and empathy during this difficult phase of self-disclosure. Sharing these emotional experiences would allow him to externalize the feelings instead of keeping them inside; this, in turn, would improve the connection he has with the therapist. Additionally, this process would result in naming his emotions, an accomplishment that normalizes the emotions and allows them to be mastered more easily. Juan has kept numerous painful emotions to himself and has been unable to share his experience with anyone because of his lack of social support and the fear of social stigma.

The mastering stage of this intervention process would involve Juan establishing and accepting his own perspective about his identity. A therapist would also need to assist Juan in acknowledging the realization that he is alone in this world so that he may seek definitions of himself from inside instead of relying on other persons to define him. He would need to begin to question the validity of his previous values, beliefs, and assumptions about himself and to confront the notion that his identity must be derived from the expectations of other individuals. In addition, he could begin to challenge the idea that he must fit the stereotypical characteristics of a Jamaican male in order to identify as such, and work to incorporate and accept the aspects of himself that he has selected. In coming to accept himself for who he is, he would be able to live more authentically; that is, he would be able to appreciate and celebrate the elements that make him a unique being. He would also need to recognize the consequences of this alternative view of self, because increased freedom comes with increased responsibility (Walsh & Lantz, 2007). The view of himself as bicultural would require him to function adaptively in different contexts of two cultures (e.g., Jamaican spiritual beliefs; male gender role in the United States). Negotiation between two cultures—one's ethnic minority culture and the European American dominant culture—is challenging.

In addition, a therapist could encourage Juan to write down his experiences and investigate his own identity through his own words. The therapist would not want to provide Juan with any particular guidelines, but instead increase his freedom through permitting him to find his own guidelines. As writing is already something that Juan greatly enjoys and would like to do as a profession, authoring and then sharing his words with the therapist or others could be used to help strengthen his identity as a writer and to help him connect with others. He may learn to embrace the idea that he can be both a writer and a Jamaican, and that neither of those needs to be defined by others. Furthermore, writing may help Juan to embrace this unacceptable part of himself from the past and offer more meaning in life.

The final stage would involve Juan embracing his pain. Once Juan has discovered greater acceptance and understanding of his true self, he may appreciate the chances offered by the identity conflict within his life. Juan will have a greater recognition of the pain other persons have experienced through having been discriminated against or from living existences defined by others. Juan's writing, perhaps even publishing it, could be utilized as a way to reach out to others and assist them in overcoming their pain.

Another intervention could modify existential therapy to allow Juan to accept his belief in supernatural powers. The therapist can discuss how Juan could offset the evil of *fuku* with a spiritual counter spell involving the positive spirit *zafa*. Keeping in mind May's (1983) suggestion that myths are simply stories that assist individuals to make meaning of their lives, that they're guiding narratives, Juan could be asked to come up with a myth that counteracts the *fuku*. Juan might tell the story of a mongoose that has golden lion eyes and an absolute black coat that emerged right before he (Juan) intended to jump from a bridge and led him with songs toward life and not death. The therapist and Juan can conclude that the magical mongoose served as Juan's *zafa* and the invention of the myth helped him to regain control of his life.

In delivering therapeutic services to multicultural individuals, therapists must possess multicultural competence in self- and other-awareness, knowledge, and skills (Roysircar, Arredondo, Fuertes, Ponterotto, & Toporek, 2003). It is crucial for therapy interventions to target the needs of multicultural clients to increase their effectiveness and not result in harm. Existential therapy acts as an efficient cross-cultural strategy for providing therapy to persons like Juan, a second-generation Jamaican male, as it emphasizes the experience of being human instead of specific strategies that might be European American biased (see Roysircar & Mayo, 2012). Juan may be helped to accept his identity through the reflective process of holding, telling, mastering, and honoring, as described by Walsh and Lantz (2007), with the incorporation of his love of writing. Although existentialism may prove to be effective for multicultural clients, it still has limitations and may require modification.

Returning to the Multicultural Case of the Sanchez Family

Existential therapists hold certain assumptions that are congruent with the values of Latinos and their collectivistic culture. For example, present-day existential practitioners value the concepts of holism, integration, and complementarity (Messer & Gurman, 2011). They emphasize an individual's multidimensional experience occurring in the physical, social, psychological, and spiritual domains. They value various facets of their clients' psychological selves, including affect, spirituality, and culture. These principles are particularly useful in therapy with Latinos, whose cognitive styles tend to be context interdependent. That is, in Latino ethnic psychology, the belief is that perception, judgment, and behaviors are guided by their connection to contexts and that it is essential for Latinos to build competence across contexts (Comas-Díaz, 2006). By viewing themselves as a component of their surrounding context, Latinos underscore well-roundedness, mind–body connection, and holism (Comas-Díaz, 2006), which is in keeping with existential therapy's goal of integrating polarities. Miguel and his mother's polar interface with U.S. society, either through assimilation (in Miguel's behaviors) or separation (in Miguel's mother's behaviors), is a relational conflict ripe for existential questioning.

Existential psychology's focus on the therapy relationship and emphasis on the client's unique world of experience suggest that it will be an effective method for working with Miguel and his mother. Latinos are relationship oriented, and they will be responsive to a therapist for whom the therapeutic alliance is essential to client change. All aspects of a client's experience, including past, present, unconscious, and conscious, are meaningful to therapists operating from a perspective that matches existential psychology. Therefore, Dr. Ramirez is likely to view Miguel's experience of his childhood in Mexico, his immigration to the United States, and his current challenges at home and at school as unique and essential to the therapeutic process.

The process of existential therapy often entails a dialogue between the therapist and client (Truscott, 2010). Using existential questioning, specifically, an existential therapist elicits self-awareness in his or her client with hopes of learning about his or her values, struggles, and anxieties (Truscott, 2010).

Despite the convergence of values between existential theory and the Latino culture, there are aspects of this therapeutic approach that should be tailored to properly fit the cultural needs of the Sanchez family. One principle of existential therapy that should be modified is the concept of meaninglessness. Existentialists maintain the belief that life is filled with meaninglessness and that humans must create their own meaning in their individual ways. Existentialism also proposes that all individuals are ultimately alone in this world and wish to be connected with others, which is the concept of *Mitwelt*. Therefore, when addressing meaninglessness with Miguel, Dr. Ramirez encourages him to search for meaning in his life in relation to other people. This may include dedication to his mother, student groups, teams, or other entities that tend to underscore context interdependence.

Interventions

When working with the Sanchez family, Dr. Ramirez will utilize three interventions that stem from existential theory: empathic mirroring, confrontation, and paradoxical intention. Empathic mirroring is an existential therapeutic technique designed to strengthen the "I–Thou" therapeutic relationship. When existential clinicians employ empathic mirroring, they reflect their clients' nuanced manifestations that are present in the therapy room. Empathic mirroring is often implemented in the form of verbal invitations, which are ways to invoke a client's in-session enactments. A common example of a verbal invitation is when a therapist tells his client, "Stay with that feeling for a few moments." This could be a particularly useful strategy when working with the Sanchez family because it is designed to foster an affective connection, an authenticity that is commonly sought after by Latinos in therapy (Comas-Díaz, 2006).

Different from empathic mirroring, confrontation is a way to directly let clients know when they are engaging in discrepant, disingenuous, or harmful behavioral patterns. However, this intervention needs to be implemented gradually. Typically, existential therapists do not use confrontation with their clients until a strong therapeutic alliance has been established. Once Dr. Ramirez has established rapport with Miguel and his mother, he can progressively utilize confrontations in order to help them discover therapeutic insight.

Another commonly used intervention is paradoxical intention. When existential practitioners employ this technique, they give their clients advice that theoretically does not appear to be logical, but can actually be quite effective. For example, Frankl once worked with a client who was suffering from severe writer's cramp. By using paradoxical intention, he advised his client to write as illegibly as possible. At first, the client was resistant, but when he actually tried to write sloppily, he was unable to do so. Within days, the client's writer's cramp had subsided. This method tends to be particularly useful when dealing with clients who suffer from anxiety because suggested paradoxes often allow the individual to relinquish control and, thus, free themselves of anxiety. To use paradoxical intent as an existential therapy method, Dr. Ramirez incorporates *Sabiduria*, a key facet of Latino ethnic psychology. *Sabiduria* refers to an appreciation of life's paradoxes that perceives setbacks as opportunities for personal and spiritual growth (Comas-Díaz, 2006). One tool used to foster *Sabiduria* in Hispanic culture is the integration of *dichos*, Spanish proverbs that have deep-rooted meanings. These proverbs can be especially useful in helping Hispanic clients conceptualize life's paradoxes. One commonly used *dicho* is "El que canta, sus males espanta" (He who sings scares his sorrow away; Comas-Díaz, 2006, p. 443). This phrase highlights the value of embracing a positive outlook on life, even when one encounters hardships. In therapy, the inclusion of sabiduria and *dichos* will provide Miguel opportunities to learn to tolerate the ambiguous and often paradoxical nature of adolescence. Because these proverbs are designed to give individuals an appreciation for paradoxes that occur in life, referring to them may be an effective way to address any anxiety-related issues in therapy sessions with Miguel and his mother. In addition, these culturally focused techniques will help bridge the mother–son acculturation gap that is negatively affecting the Sanchez family. By learning about how *Sabiduria* and *dichos* are applicable in his life, Miguel may become more attuned to his own culture, which will help appease Mrs. Sanchez's concerns about the possibility that her son is alienating himself from his cultural heritage.

Because the relationship, as opposed to technical factors, is the core facilitative condition in existential therapy, and because authenticity is the central component to change, existential therapists must be truly present as genuine persons and be ready to act in a respectful and genuine manner (Schneider & May 1995; Truscott, 2010). Thus, Dr. Ramirez must have reflected upon his own biases, developed cultural awareness of and sensitivity for the cultural-specific challenges Miguel may be experiencing, such as the process of acculturation, potential racism, and issues of class and privilege. To further strengthen the therapeutic alliance, Dr. Ramirez may also choose to conduct therapy in Miguel and his mother's dominant language (Altarriba & Santiago-Rivera, 1994). Moreover, the fact that Dr. Ramirez and Miguel are both male and have been ethnically matched further increases their chances of developing an authentic therapeutic relationship and also increases the likelihood of positive outcomes (Lakes, López, & Garro, 2006). Dr. Ramirez is likely to know that, although family treatment is culturally congruent for many Latinos because of their collectivistic culture, this is a group stereotype that often fails to address individual needs (Lakes et al., 2006). Thus, Dr. Ramirez is likely to implement interventions that both support the autonomy and personal development of his adolescent client and also preserve mutuality and interconnectedness with his family.

Existential Questioning in Individual Therapy. As a process of self-reflection, existential questioning is used to promote authenticity and assist Miguel in creatively exploring and solidifying his cultural identity and his self-identity. Through a specific series of questions, traditionally used in times of transition, Miguel is asked to explore his personal history (Brent, 1998). Additionally, he is asked to explore his heritage and "demonstrate possibilities and, from these, choose the possibilities he judges to be most authentic (uniquely his own) for future appropriation" (Brent, 1998, p. 11).

Dr. Ramirez will use change tasks when appropriate. Change tasks are used in as much as they emerge out of a deep comprehension of the client's unique experience. Change tasks are typically utilized to "hold up a mirror" for the client and as a result create an openness for self-confrontation (Truscott, 2010). For example, Dr. Ramirez might say, "When you say you *can't* do something, aren't you really saying you *won't* do it?" (see Brent, 1998). Of course, change tasks will be employed in a culturally sensitive manner.

This brief individual therapy will include five phases of questions (based on Brent, 1998) that Miguel will be asked to reflect on at different times during therapy.

1. What personal message is contained in my disquietude? Am I living according to beliefs and values that are my own?
2. Am I willing to consider that an awareness of my heritage and sense of destiny may open possibilities in my present dilemma?
3. What resources from my heritage and personal history are essential for a sense of wholeness and purpose? What possibilities have I closed off due to their anxiety-producing quality?

4. What few uncustomary and meaningful activities am I prepared to initiate that will draw on my newfound sense of heritage and destiny? How will I continue to hold myself open, so as to recognize those few interests that are truly my own?

5. How will I draw on my accomplishments in therapy to persevere in authenticity?

A Family Intervention. In existential therapy, a family developmental challenge happens if the developmental progression needs of a single family member challenges the speed of the total family developmental progression (Lantz, 1993). Some family members, such as Miguel's mother, may respond to a developmental challenge, such as acculturation, with avoidance, anger, and cultural separation. It is quite clear that Mrs. Sanchez is distressed over her son's choices and feels that he is losing his heritage by wearing baggy clothes, listening to rap music, and refusing to participate in familial and cultural activities that he once enjoyed. Subsequently, the relationship between Miguel and his mother is strained. Because existential questioning can be used to illuminate one's unique worldview of cultural adaptation, it may very well be a meaningful way for Miguel and his mother to gain an understanding of, and develop compassion for, the different ways in which they have each dealt with the process of acculturation.

In attending to the relationship between Miguel and his mother, Dr. Ramirez may elicit a therapeutic conversation, at times in their native language, by asking Miguel and his mother to engage in the following two tasks: (1) Draw a "psychological map" of where you are in the center of the universe. Indicate the people who are closest to you and the people that are most distant from you. (2) Draw "a totem pole of the important people in your life. Put the weakest person at the bottom and put the most powerful person on the top. Be sure to include yourself and anyone in the community or elsewhere who is very important to you" (Kohatsu, Concepcion, & Perez, 2010, p. 346). The second task may provide further information regarding Miguel's relationship with his mother and may also serve as a segue to learning more about Miguel's friendships outside of the home.

Dr. Ramirez may also ask Mrs. Sanchez, specifically, the following questions/probes (Kohatsu et al., 2010): "(1) What types of things make you feel important? (2) What types of things make you feel that you are living life to the fullest? (3) If you "fit in" at home and in your community, tell me what a normal day would be like. (4) What type of normal day are you striving for? Each community has certain images of a successful person. In what ways would your community judge you to be successful or unsuccessful?" (p. 344). Whatever conversation may ensue will be met with opportunities to explore resistance and to revisit the ways in which Mrs. Sanchez may deter herself from fuller personal and interpersonal access (Schneider, 2011). More importantly, the hope is that through a therapeutic conversation, Dr. Ramirez will be able to assist both Miguel and his mother in their quest to actualize their cultural and life meanings and, ultimately, obtain harmony in their personal and familial lives (Schneider, 2011).

Dr. Ramirez also needs to consider adjusting the number of therapy sessions to accommodate the Sanchez family's financial needs. Traditional existential therapy is intensive and long term, usually consisting of biweekly sessions for multiple years. Because of changes to managed care, this frequency and duration of sessions may not be available at the local community mental health center.

CHAPTER REVIEW

SUMMARY AND COMMENTARY ▶▶

Logotherapy is considered a philosophy of life (Basescu, 1963) and, as a result, it can be utilized in all professions and all walks of life. Currently, it is used by therapists, educators, ministers, and business managers (cf. Brent, 1998, Chochinov et al., 2011; Classen & Spiegel, 2011; Cohen, 2003; Fabry et al., 1996; Lantz, 1993; Roysircar-Sodowsky & Frey, 2003; van Deurzen & Hanaway, 2012; Walsh & Lantz, 2007; Wicks, Parsons, & Capps, 1993). People can rely on it in their day-to-day existence, when interacting with family members, colleagues, or friends. Individuals can read Viktor Frankl's (1959/2006) book *Man's Search for Meaning* about his experience during the Holocaust. The book offers a valuable, experience-based introduction to the assumptions that guide logotherapy and is a great vehicle for people to start to utilize logotherapy in their lives, along with treatment. According to May (1981, 1983), individuals' acceptance of their lives and where they are today is a result of their previous choices, and their future will be shaped by their current choices. Each day individuals have numerous possibilities from which to select within their range of freedom. They must select the most responsible alternative and render the best choice, not only for themselves, but also for individuals in their life (Sodowsky & Sodowsky, 1997). The result of taking an existential journey is twofold: meaning fulfillment and authentic happiness. Table 5.2 provides an overview of current existential practice.

▼ TABLE 5.2

Relevance of Existential Therapy to Current Practice

Type of service delivery setting	Private practice Clinic University setting Psychiatric hospital Health care/psycho-oncology setting
Population	Teen Adult Chronic illness Terminal illness
Type of presenting problems	Wide range of presenting problems (e.g., illness, end of life, vocational concerns, adjustment problems)
Severity of presenting problems	Wide range of severity
Adapted for short-term approach	Yes
Length of treatment	Traditionally long term
Ability to receive reimbursement	Insurance companies may reimburse with appropriate *DSM* diagnosis
Certification in approach	Certificate in the foundations of existential-humanistic practice from the Existential-Humanistic Institute Boulder Psychotherapy Institute Advanced Certification Program
Training in educational programs	College of Arts and Sciences of Seattle University offers existential-phenomenological therapeutic psychology terminal master's program
Location	Urban Rural Suburban
Type of delivery system	HMO PPO Fee for service
Credential	None
Practitioners	Professionals
Fit with *DSM* diagnoses	Certain disorders fit, e.g., mood, anxiety, and adjustment disorders

CRITICAL THINKING QUESTIONS ▶▶

1. How do you think your own cultural background has affected your understanding and acceptance of existential theory?

2. Think of an example of suffering that you have experienced that could be explained by two or three existential constructs.

3. What are the similarities and differences between European and American existentialists?

4. From the therapies you have studied so far, give examples of therapy techniques and assessment that could be

integrated into existential therapy and those that would be in conflict with existential therapy?

5. What challenges or barriers do you foresee in using existential theory to work with a client of a diverse cultural background?

SUGGESTED READINGS: IMPORTANT PRIMARY SOURCES

Books

Frankl, V. E. (2006). *Man's search for meaning* (I. Lasch, Trans.). Boston, MA: Beacon Press. (Original work published 1959)

May, R. (1969). *Love and will.* New York, NY: Norton.

Sartre, J. (1969). *Being and nothingness.* New York, NY: Washington Square Press. (Original work published 1943) [translated by Hazel Barnes]

Journals and Newsletter

International Journal of Existential Positive Psychology: http://journal.existentialpsychology.org

International Journal of Existential Psychology and Psychotherapy: http://meaning.ca/ijepp.htm

Journal of Humanistic Psychology: http://jhp.sagepub.com

Søren Kierkegaard Newsletter: https://wp.stolaf.edu/kierkegaard/publications-and-lectures/publications/newsletter-2/

Websites

All About Philosophy: http://www.allaboutphilosophy.org/existentialism.htm (Provides an introduction to existential philosophy, i.e., its basic concepts and impact)

CHAPTER 6

PERSON-CENTERED THEORY

With Jeffrey Cornelius White and Matthew E. Lemberger

Introduction

Carl Rogers's person-centered theory unquestioningly made notable contributions to the practice of therapy. His emphasis on the importance of the therapeutic relationship is now taken for granted by many present-day therapists, some of whom believe that this special type of relationship, if correctly established, is sufficient in and of itself to bring about client change. Rogers created a comprehensive theory that offered an alternative to Freudian and behaviorist-derived therapies of his time. A revolutionary thinker, Rogers was firmly opposed to any type of therapy that relied on a deterministic view that invariably led to the objectification of humans—an object called "patient." Rogers's influence can be seen clearly today in counselor training programs where Rogerian concepts such as active listening and responding empathically to the client while maintaining a nonjudgmental attitude (even if others see the person as morally repugnant or a pariah of society) are taught.

The goal of this chapter is for the reader to gain a deeper understanding and appreciation of how Rogers's theory and its applications have contributed to therapy and beyond. A theory that also has been applied to a number of additional areas, for example, unstructured psychotherapy groups, organizations, education, and even large national groups experiencing serious conflict.

▼ FIGURE 6.1

Drawing Depicting Carl Rogers

Source: The original uploader was Didius at Dutch Wikipedia (Transferred from nl.wikipedia to Commons.) [CC BY 2.5 (http://creativecommons.org/licenses/by/2.5)], via Wikimedia Commons

Historical Context

Carl Rogers (1902–1987) first published writings about person-centered theory in 1922. He ventured to China and other East Asian countries on a cross-cultural Christian social justice mission (Cornelius-White, 2012). From his early 20s, Rogers (Figure 6.1) displayed a strong interest in relationships that fostered growth and enabled a person to live authentically—an interest that would become the centerpiece for his person-centered theory. In the 1930s and 1940s, Rogers developed a therapeutic approach that he initially referred to as nondirective therapy. With the publication of Rogers's *Client-Centered Therapy* in 1951, client-centered therapy became the new term for Rogers's approach, eventually replaced by the term *person-centered therapy*. A major factor involved in the last shift in terminology was largely the result of Rogers's theory being applied to settings (e.g., schools) and situations (e.g., global conflicts) that went beyond what was implied by the qualifier "client-centered." In addition, other approaches

THE CASE OF FERNANDO: INFIDELITY AND DEPRESSION

Fernando resides in Los Angeles, California. He was born in San Salvador, the capital of El Salvador where he grew up with his aunt, uncle, mother, and older sister, Alicia. In search of better employment, more money, and better living conditions for his family, his father departed El Salvador for the United States when Fernando was only 1 year old. While his father visited San Salvador from time to time, Fernando and his family rarely saw him. However, when Fernando was six years old, to his surprise and dismay, his sister Alicia and his mother relocated to be with his father in Chicago. Five years later, Fernando reunited with his family in Chicago.

When Fernando's family members first arrived in the U.S., his father had trouble keeping a job and was only able to work part time in fast food restaurants as a short order cook. Later, he secured a full time job as a housekeeper in a local hotel. Fernando's mother stayed home with her children watching television and doing her best to learn some English and something about the U.S. culture. Fernando and his sister rarely saw their father because he worked at night, slept during the day, and when off from work gambled with his friends. Fernando and his sister also rarely spoke with their relatives in El Salvador. Fernando and his sister were quite close, but his sister ran away from home and moved to New Jersey when Fernando was 15.

Fernando is now 23 and a student in the law school at the University of Southern California. Fernando dated many women while in college and then became engaged to Elisa. His interest in women though did not subside after becoming engaged and he often hooked up with different women at local bars. Eventually, Elisa discovered that Fernando was sleeping with other women and she ended their three-year on and off romance.

Fernando described himself as "handsome," muscular, and a lady's man. He said he wished he were taller and even smarter. Fernando often talked about some common experiences he shared with others including adultery, abuse, absentee father, deceit, and moving to the U.S. to live "the Dream." As an example, he reported that one of his close friends thought he had fathered a child in one of his many adulterous affairs, but it was not the case. Fernando had a somewhat similar situation with a woman who claimed he was the father of her child when, in fact, this eventually was shown to be not true. The woman confronted him in his apartment and convinced Fernando to let her move in during her pregnancy. Though the woman refused to sleep with Fernando in his apartment, he still felt obligated to take care of her and her needs during the pregnancy. A month after the baby girl arrived, Fernando's girlfriend told him at dinner one night that he was not the baby's father and that his friend was the real father. Fernando was devastated by this news. He stopped going to the gym, could not concentrate on his studies, lost his appetite, and was quite sad, agitated and angry. Though he felt ashamed, he sought psychological help from a community clinic. During the intake, Fernando admitted to his problems with women, his repeated transgressions, and the sexual transgressions of his father and uncle. He also stated he understood why his ex-fiancée left him and that he deserved it because he was a devil.

A cultural norm for an El Salvadoran man is to be a sexual conquistador. Fernando felt guilty, however, whenever he cheated on his girlfriends, and he was especially distraught about his transgression on his fiancée. Although he felt guilt, Fernando also believed that he was so clever that he would never get caught and that eventually he would be able to stop having affairs. Interestingly, Fernando always avoided calling his ex-fiancée and other girlfriends by their name in therapy. Fernando also disclosed in therapy that he is "afraid of being left by people especially people he is close to like girlfriends." He also stated that he "did not deserve to be loved." It was revealing that his disclosures about loved ones was shared in the same therapy session where he reported that his parents planned to spend their retirement back in San Salvador.

Note: This case study will be returned to later in this chapter.

grew out of Rogers's theory during the 1950s, 1960s, and 1970s. For example, Eugene Gendlin, a colleague and junior cofounder of person-centered theory, began what became known as experiential therapy and focusing, two related but distinct approaches, which are discussed later in this chapter.

Although Rogers continued one-on-one demonstrations and interviews until his death in 1987, during the 1960s, 1970s, and 1980s it was apparent that Rogers had increasingly become involved in applying his theory to helping others in ways that transcended an individual therapy frame of reference. During his career, Rogers also inspired interdisciplinary research and applications that have continued to this day and have even expanded in their scope. Examples of such outcomes are encounter groups, family studies, educational approaches, cross-cultural interactions, and peace studies; even areas of practice such as medicine and neuroscience have felt the effects of Rogerian thought (Cornelius-White, Motschnig-Pitrik, & Lux, 2013).

research and expanding our domain

Person-centered theory, along with other related theories of Rogers's time (e.g., Adler's individual psychology and existentialism), are often credited with launching what has been called the "humanistic approach" or "third force" in psychology and therapy, contrasting it with psychoanalysis and behaviorism. This third force resulted in several prominent themes rippling throughout the psychotherapy field during the 1960s and 1970s, themes that included the importance of being optimistic about the potential for humans to grow psychologically and interpersonally. The degree of optimism present during that period allowed therapists to see and appreciate the power of facilitative relationships to foster personal change and healing (Bugental, 1964; Maslow, 1968). Rogers's 1957 article "The Necessary and Sufficient Conditions of Therapeutic Personality Change" further strengthened the new force that was building in psychology while also solidifying Rogers's reputation as the cornerstone on which humanistic psychology could be built. In addition, this article was particularly influential in the development of a line of research outside of person-centered theory that in many ways led to the principles of what comprises the basic skills required to establish a "helping relationship." These basic skills are still taught to mental health professionals at the prepracticum level and later when they receive supervised practice. The strength of this empirical research and the subjective value of a real, person-to-person relationship have been thoroughly integrated into many of the graduate programs that exist today.

Carl Rogers: The Person and Founder of Person-Centered Therapy

Carl Rogers left several explicitly autobiographical works (e.g., Cornelius-White, 2012; Rogers, 1967a), and many of his works written for professional and lay audiences have a unique autobiographical style that contributes further to understanding this remarkable person. Likewise, Rogers generated hundreds of therapy transcripts, videos, and dialogues with prominent psychologists and religious leaders, and even an Academy Award–winning documentary. In this sense, Rogers is more of an open book than most of the theorists discussed in this textbook. Rogers exhibited the transparency (i.e., genuineness) that he wrote about and presented consistently throughout his career. Likewise, several authors have written about Rogers in biographies (e.g., Thorne, 2003), and an oral history is available (Rogers & Russell, 2002), as is an interactive CD by his daughter, Natalie Rogers, a prominent theorist and author and the originator of person-centered expressive arts therapy. Furthermore, Rogers officially agreed that Howard (Howie) Kirschenbaum (1979, 2009) would write his definitive biography, and he provided Kirschenbaum with useful personal materials before his death in 1987. From all of these sources, and the numerous public appearances that Rogers made, we know more intimate details about Carl Rogers's life, thoughts, and feelings than perhaps any other major theorist.

Rogers was born in 1902 and raised in a religiously conservative home in Oak Park, Illinois (a suburb of Chicago). He was gifted intellectually, somewhat isolated, and had a keen appreciation for scientific methodology. He attended the University of Wisconsin–Madison, where he studied agriculture. After an influential 6-month trip to China and other East Asian countries in 1922—during which he was heavily influenced by the Nobel Peace Prize winner John R. Mott and such social justice theologians as Willis King and H. B. Sharman—Rogers switched his major to history on his return. He then moved to the liberal Union Theological Seminary in New York City to study religion and became a minister for a short time after graduation. He then returned to college to pursue graduate studies in psychology at the neighboring Columbia University Teachers College, where John Dewey's theories of humanistic education and philosophical pragmatism were the prevailing ideologies. In 1931, Rogers completed his doctoral requirements for his PhD.

Rogers spent about a decade in Rochester, New York, and wrote his first major book, which was influenced by the post-Freudian theories of Otto Rank (deCarvalho, 1999). While living in Rochester, Rogers worked as a child psychologist and his daughter Natalie was born. He was then offered a professorship at The Ohio State University, where he taught for 5 years and published his next book, *Counseling and Psychotherapy*, which more clearly foreshadowed the foundations of person-centered theory. Beginning in 1945, Rogers taught at the University of Chicago, where he established the Chicago Counseling Center, which would become the epicenter for person-centered research and the generator of ideas for more than 50 years. Some of the first quantitative studies of psychotherapy of any orientation and the first published transcripts of therapy sessions originated from this center. Likewise, Rogers's most influential works on individual psychotherapy were written during this time, including his 1951 book *Client-Centered Therapy*, the 1957 paper "The Necessary and Sufficient Conditions of Therapeutic Personality Change," and, most important of all, his 1959 magnum opus theory statement "A Theory of Therapy, Personality, and Interpersonal Relationships, as Developed in the Client-Centered Framework." Additionally, several influential and related theories had their origin during his Ohio State and University of Chicago periods, including play therapy (Axline, 1947), experiential therapy (Gendlin, 1962), filial therapy, a child-centered relationship enhancement family therapy (Ginsberg, 2012; Guerney, 1964), and parent effectiveness training (Gordon, 2000).

In 1957, Rogers began a joint appointment in psychology and psychiatry at the University of Wisconsin, where he would conduct a large study on psychotherapy with persons who suffered from schizophrenia. Some of his more influential students and collaborators included Charles Truax and Robert Carkhuff, who conducted hundreds of studies related to person-centered theories, and Marshall Rosenberg, who developed a model called nonviolent communication. Rogers left academia in 1963 and did not return to a full professorship or to the extensive empirical study of psychotherapy he had previously carried out, but he maintained connections to academic settings until his death. During this period. Rogers chose to focus on applications of the person-centered approach to areas beyond psychotherapy. He was a leader in the area of humanistic education and the encounter group movement of the 1960s and 1970s (Rogers, 1969, 1970).

In his later years, Rogers worked on several large-scale peace efforts in such conflict-infused areas as South Africa, Central America, Northern Ireland, and cold war Soviet bloc countries. He also continued to provide training and consulting services around the world (Kirschenbaum, 2009). It has been more than three decades since the death of Rogers; in recent years the person-centered approach in Europe, Japan, Argentina, and some other locations has seen an increase in the number of practitioners. Ironically, the increase in person-centered therapists corresponds to a decline in its appreciation as a distinct approach within the United States. Nevertheless, a renaissance of appreciation of the classic research studies in person-centered therapy and education has occurred as a result of published meta-analyses and new studies in the related area of emotion-focused therapy (which was derived from an expansion of ideas originally associated with the experiential wing of person-centered therapies; Elliott & Freire, 2008) and learner-centered instruction (Cornelius-White, 2007). Likewise, the development of common factors theory (Lambert & Barley, 2001) based on the dodo bird hypothesis (all bona fide treatments are effective), empirically supported therapy, and syntheses of component studies on specific elements of facilitative relationships (Norcross, 2001) have led to a continuing appreciation of how person-centered theory has developed the phoenix-like quality of cyclical regeneration within the research world (Cornelius-White, 2002). Table 6.1 provides a sample of comments made by Carl Rogers during his career.

Basic Concepts

Rogers believed that all humans possess an inherent capacity to grow and develop in a constructive manner. He called this capacity the actualizing tendency. For Rogers, this tendency can be aided by the experience of certain core conditions in psychotherapy, which result in a person's becoming more fully functioning. (These core conditions, such as unconditional positive regard, are explained in more detail in later sections.) Although

▼ TABLE 6.1

Quotable Carl Rogers

- The facts are always friendly; every bit of evidence one can acquire, in any area, leads one that much closer to what is true.
- The curious paradox is that when I accept myself as I am, then I can change. The good life is a process, not a state of being. It is a direction not a destination.
- The only person who is educated is the one who has learned how to learn and change.
- It is the client who knows what hurts, what directions to go, what problems are crucial, what experiences have been deeply buried.
- What is most personal is most universal.
- What I am is good enough if I would only be it openly.
- People are just as wonderful as sunsets if you let them be. When I look at a sunset, I don't find myself saying, "Soften the orange a bit on the right hand corner." I don't try to control a sunset. I watch it with awe as it unfolds.

Sources: https://www.brainyquote.com/authors/carl_rogers; and Rogers, C. R. (1961). *On becoming a person: A therapist's view of psychotherapy.* Boston, MA: Houghton Mifflin.

there are several theoretically based explanations pertaining to what person-centered therapy entails, Rogers believed his 1959 theory statement was his greatest single work on the topic, from which this section draws heavily.

Actualizing Tendency

The main foundation of the person-centered approach is a supposition that all persons are attempting to maintain and enhance themselves. This concept is called the actualizing tendency. Bozarth and Brodley (1991) described characteristics of the actualizing tendency in person-centered therapy as

- individual yet universally present for all individuals,
- holistic for the organism not just for the self-concept,
- ubiquitous and constant throughout all situations,
- directional towards realization of potentialities,
- moves towards autonomy and away from heteronomy,
- though never ending in its grit, is vulnerable to distortion and muting by environmental circumstances,
- different from self-actualizing, which represents an attachment to a self-concept away from openness to experience and therefore provides a basis for pathology,
- awareness of self and experience is a distinctively human path for internal direction,
- and finally, leads people to socially constructive behavior. (pp. 47–48)

Near the end of his life, Rogers (1977, 1980; Rogers, Lyon, & Tausch, 2013) proposed the "formative tendency" to explain motivation. The formative tendency implies interdependence in addition to autonomy as a directional focus in people's lives. Likewise, Rogers's (1951, 1969) theory of education implies a more democratic and interdependent directional tendency for people compared with independence alone. Using sociology, biology, physics, music, mathematics, and other fields, Kriz (2006, 2013) showed how humans are a self-organizing, nonlinear system, characterized by emergence (formation of order) and phase transitions (change of order) that come from within as opposed to being merely imposed from outside. According to Kriz (2007), the actualizing tendency

> is neither a belief nor an assumption in Rogers' theory, but a simple description of the consequences of seriously taking interconnectedness and relationships among processes into account . . . actualization works as an unfolding inherent order or pattern with respect to the surroundings. And the principle is not one of imposing order from outside but facilitating inherent possibilities of order. (p. 40)

Six Core Conditions

In 1957, Rogers published "The Necessary and Sufficient Conditions of Therapeutic Personality Change," which is one of the most cited and influential works found in the field of psychotherapy. In this article, Rogers presented six conditions that, if present, would lead to positive therapeutic changes. Interestingly, although identified closely with person-centered therapy, Rogers intended this work as a generic hypothesis about therapeutic change, not a statement solely restricted to client-centered practice.

It is not stated that these six conditions are the essential conditions for client-centered therapy, and that other conditions are essential for other types of psycho-therapy . . . . My aim in stating this theory is to state the conditions which apply to any situation in which constructive personality change occurs, whether we are thinking of classical psychoanalysis, or any of its modern offshoots, or Adlerian psychotherapy, or any other. (Rogers, 1957, p. 99)

The six conditions mentioned by Rogers are contact, vulnerability/incongruence, empathy, unconditional positive regard, congruence, and perception/communication. Each condition is discussed in this section.

1. *Contact.* The basis for a therapeutic relationship was that a client was in contact. Rogers was terse on what he meant by contact, but Prouty (1994) articulated elements of what it means. *Contact* refers to connecting with reality, one's self, or others through communication. Prouty developed a person-centered approach that applies when one or more of the elements of contact are not present, such as is found with people who suffer from psychosis (or severe developmental disabilities). Often these basic types of contact (with reality, with one's self, with another) are assumed to be present with clients of near-average intelligence and who do not display psychosis. Although person-centered therapists possess an appreciation of the limits of contact, these therapists also believe the approach can be facilitative and helpful regardless of whom these therapists are working with, even when the therapy process involves clients whose grip on basic points of contact are fragile.

2. *Vulnerability/Incongruence.* A state of *vulnerability* suggests that a client is suffering from some sort of internal conflict about which the client can perceive or sub-ceive and experience as anxiety or is susceptible to harm (the term *subceive* refers to having a partial or budding awareness of something). This condition provides the needed self-motivation to change (and grow) through a desire for acceptance, connection, or resolution. *Incongruence* represents a lack of self-understanding, self-awareness, and/or self-acceptance. From a person-centered position, a state of incongruence might be thought of as what another professional might call "pathology," or it can be found reflected in a client's claim that "something is wrong with my life but I'm unsure what it is." (See next section on self-concept, incongruence, and conditions of worth for more explanation.)

As with the first condition (i.e., contact), some research (e.g., McCulloch, 2001) has shown that incongruence is not a necessary condition for therapy to be applied. For example, persons with substance abuse issues who display an antisocial personality disorder, and who typically blame others for their problems while experiencing no regret or anxiety in response to their own problematic behaviors, have improved when receiving person-centered therapy. Similarly, a directive person-centered approach known as motivational interviewing has amassed a strong research base that supports the assertion that the motivational interviewing approach to therapy fosters the type of motivation required for change. When a client does not present with a vulnerable persona, the therapist utilizing motivational interviewing will specifically highlight conflict or change talk to help the client develop some awareness of his incongruence. Experiencing this awareness will activate the typical engine for change in therapy, that is, a level of motivation that enables a client to move forward in the therapeutic process (Wagner, 2013; Wagner & Ingersoll, 2012). Likewise, someone might be happy and relatively integrated but could still benefit from empathy that is displayed by the person-centered therapist in an attempt to increase the client's creative abilities. The next three conditions (i.e., empathy, unconditional positive regard, and congruence) are most commonly referred to as the core attitudes.

3. *Empathy*. Empathy was emphasized by Rogers in his writings and in many ways has become a mainstay of current therapy practice in general. *Empathy* is understanding another person from within her frame of reference. It is not a form of interpretive understanding (which is a common feature of psychodynamic approaches); rather, it is a type of understanding that is experientially grounded. Empathy occurs when the interactions between the client and therapist start to move in a steady, continuous stream or flow until a point of optimal experiencing has been achieved. It is a situation where the client's expressions and the therapist's responses converge and the client experiences an internal message that says to him, "Exactly, that's it!" Such occurrences of empathy often result in a client saying something such as "Yeah! And that makes me think about another thing . . . ."

Empathy is "hitting the target"; it is experiencing something through absorption *as if* you were the other person. The therapist has achieved an intimate understanding that is aligned with what is inside the client, aligned with the client's "head and heart." Empathy is not the same concept as sympathy (Table 6.2). Empathy has proven to be highly related to therapeutic outcome, especially with beginning (even more so than experienced) therapists. Further, positive outcomes are often experienced early in the course of treatment when empathy is present (Lambert & Barley, 2001).

4. *Unconditional Positive Regard. Unconditional positive regard* is maintaining a state of warmth, acceptance, or benign neutrality when interacting with another person. It is a way of being present: The therapist totally accepts a client's experiences, where the client is, how the client feels, what the client thinks and does. Unconditional positive regard represents a lack of judgment paired with a sense of respect for the client as an autonomous, inherently good organism. Rogers's fourth condition is not the same as being in agreement with or liking the other person's choices, nor does it represent identifying with the other person as if to say, "I am she and she is me."

Unconditional positive regard is often a challenge for beginning therapists, and it is possibly one of the most radical elements proposed by Rogers, especially when he introduced it for the first time. Despite this, it is not unusual today to find unconditional positive regard valued in other approaches, sometimes even centrally as it is in dialectical behavior therapy (a type of cognitive-behavioral therapy). It should be noted that in dialectical behavior therapy, as in other forms of therapy, the form of unconditional acceptance utilized is qualified and not accompanied by an adherence of a nondirective intent with clients.

▼ TABLE 6.2

Empathy Is Not the Same as Sympathy

In a 1956 paper, *The Essence of Psychotherapy: Moments of Movement,* presented at the first meeting of the American Academy of Psychotherapists, Rogers described what he believed to be the crucial element in psychotherapy. Rogers did not perceive psychotherapy as an independent condition or attitude, but as an *experience.* Before giving a clinical example of this crucial experience taken from a therapy session, he pointed out that this type of experience could not exist without the necessary core conditions of empathy, unconditional positive regard, and congruence acting in unison. In the example given by Rogers, the case of Mrs. Oak, the client is attempting to identify a strong emotion that she is experiencing:

Client	It's just being terribly hurt! . . . And then, of course, I've come to see and to feel that over this . . . see, I've covered it up.
	A moment later she puts it slightly differently.
Client	You know, it's almost a physical thing. It's . . . sort of as though I were looking within myself at all kinds of . . . nerve endings and—and bits of . . . things that have been sort of mashed. [Weeping]
Therapist	As though some of the most delicate aspects of you—physically almost—have been crushed or hurt.
Client	Yes. And you know, I do get the feeling, oh, you poor thing.
Therapist	You just can't help but feel very deeply sorry for the person that is you. (Rogers, 1956, p. 3)

The above exchange captures what Rogers identified as a therapeutic "moment of movement." He characterized it as an existential moment, "an experience of something at this instant, in the relationship" (Rogers, 1956, p. 3). According to Rogers, the empathic exchange (illustrated in the therapist's words above) is deeply experienced in the present moment in the relationship with the client, unlike *sympathy,* which according to Rogers is an intellectual understanding, a form of reflective compassion about another person that involves thoughts and feelings but does not involve two persons experiencing simultaneously at that deep, below-the-surface level where true empathy is found to reside.

In his presentation, Rogers emphasized that empathy is predicated on the presence of unconditional positive regard and congruence. The significance of this necessary relationship among the three core conditions was also emphasized among later person-centered advocates. For example, Jerold Bozarth, an internationally recognized expert in person-centered theory, believed it is necessary to acknowledge the intertwined relationship of all three core conditions if one hopes to fully grasp what Rogers was attempting to communicate. According to Bozarth (1988), empathy is the therapist's experience of the client's inner world (e.g., the feelings and personal meanings), "as if" the therapist were the client. It is an experiential process of being present within a shared moment with another and can be experienced only while being congruent and having unconditional positive regard. Therefore, for true empathy to occur, the therapist must be façade free, that is, authentic and in line with his internal and external experiences. In addition to this authenticity, the therapist fully accepts the client as a person of value even if the therapist cannot justify certain behaviors that the client displays.

Rogers is concerned with something that is more than a simply, readily teachable skill since Rogers's core conditions are always of a contextual nature. Specifically, empathy cannot be definition-bound; it is an experiential happening between a therapist and a client. According to Ann Glauser, a colleague of Jerold Bozarth, the type of empathy that Rogers addressed in his 1956 presentation is not easy to teach (A. S. Glauser, personal communication, January 18, 2017). This seems somewhat self-evident when one considers that unconditional positive regard and congruence must already be present for an empathic response to emerge. Furthermore, Glauser asserted that Rogers was correct to claim that it is through the immediate experiencing of empathy that the client becomes more aware, more self-accepting, and thus more integrated. (In the case of Mrs. Oak, Rogers stated, "This woman *is* the self-pity she feels—entering fully and acceptingly into it—and this is complete integration in that moment" [Rogers, 1956, p. 5].) It is empathy that better enables the client to more fully and accurately experience a personal truth. Sympathy does not offer such a result.

When empathy occurs, it is safe to assume that the therapist is sensitive enough to perceive the internal frame of the client accurately, is able to enter the existential moment with the client, and then is capable of placing herself "in the shoes" of the client. Sympathy is shallow by comparison to empathy because it does not go beyond the expression of sorrow or compassion about another person's difficulties. Although sympathy may represent some understanding of another person's problem, it essentially misses how that person feels and thinks about the problem. In addition, during sympathy-driven situations, it is not uncommon for the listener to automatically assume responsibility, at least partially, for solving another person's problem. Taking on this responsibility often leads to some form of cliché-style advice being given to the sufferer—advice that is focused on how the distressed person can or should handle what is so troublesome (Ginter & Glauser, 2012).

Sources: Bozarth, J. (1998). *Person-centered therapy: A revolutionary paradigm.* Ross-on-Wye, UK: PCCS Books; Bozarth, J. D. (n.d.). Forty years of dialogue with the Rogerian hypothesis. Retrieved January 17, 2017, from *personcentered.com/dialogue.htm;* Ginter, E. J., & Glauser, A. S. (2012). *Life-skills for college: A curriculum for life.* Dubuque, IA: Kendall Hunt; and Rogers, C. R. (1956, October). *The essence of psychotherapy: Moments of movement.* Paper presented at the meeting of the American Academy of Psychotherapists, New York.

5. *Congruence. Congruence* refers to an awareness and acceptance of one's own experiences. This condition requires the mental health professional to be integrated and self-accepting. A large part, if not all, of a congruent therapist's experience will be accepted unconditionally by the therapist. However, a therapist also may experience emotions or thoughts that are contradictory or potentially distracting to the provision of unconditional positive regard or genuine empathy. This state is often reflected in the therapist's internal monologue (e.g., "I like her," "He annoys me," or "I wonder if that book I just read would help her cope"). At its most basic level, reestablishing the condition of congruence requires only that the therapist be aware of and accepting of such lapses. This self-acceptance enables the therapist to again focus on providing unconditional understanding of the client. Therapists just need to be who they really are without hiding their experience from themselves or letting a lapse of integration distract them from being with a client in a therapeutic manner.

At a more complicated level, congruence refers to authenticity or genuineness, which denotes a willingness to share who one is and what one is experiencing with a client. Congruence refers to not hiding behind a façade and at times sharing one's own spontaneous reactions of empathically, unconditionally being with someone. This aspect of congruence often provides a challenge for many mental health professionals to understand or follow because the line between self-disclosure and genuineness is fine. Self-disclosure can be an expression of one's congruence, but it can also be an expression of one's incongruence or desire for the client to inappropriately empathize with or accept the therapist. In these cases, it is generally recommended that the therapist consult with another professional (e.g., a colleague, supervisor) about such occurrences rather than burden a client with his own unfinished business. However, there are situations, particularly in groups (less so with couples or families, and even less still with individuals), in which self-disclosures of incongruence can be the best and most genuine responses. Such self-disclosures are best articulated when a therapist is not dependent on, and does not expect, a specific response from the client and the self-disclosure can be refocused to the client's reactions and responses. For example, if the therapist repeatedly experiences annoyance toward the client, sharing this feeling may help the client better understand why she has difficulty establishing ongoing relationships with others.

6. *Perception/Communication.* The perception and communication of empathy and unconditional positive regard (and congruence in later writings by Rogers) is a condition that refers to the need for a therapist to communicate and/or for a client to perceive the core attitudes. A therapist must not only experience the attitudes internally but also convey them. Accurate empathy is communicated through word choice and voice inflection, whereas unconditional positive regard is primarily nonverbal, and congruence is often conveyed through a trustworthy, nonconflicted demeanor and an attitude of openness. Research on the three core attitudes (empathy, unconditional positive regard, and congruence) has shown that they are most predictive of positive outcomes when measured

from the client's perception as opposed to an observer or therapist's perceptions (Cornelius-White, 2002).

Development of the Person

Self-Concept, Incongruence, and Conditions of Worth. Pathology in person-centered therapy is a bit of an oxymoron because a fundamental premise of this approach is the importance of not judging clients. However, pathology from a theoretical perspective would refer to a division in the actualizing tendency due to conditions of worth. This division results in what is known as the *self*. Specifically, whenever a child begins to identify with particular parts of his experience to the exclusion of other parts, a self is formed. In other words, the self is a subset of a person's total *phenomenological field* (i.e., conscious and unconscious lived experience) and thereby the basis for incongruence. Furthermore, the self has an inherent need for consistency, which essentially means that novel experiences challenge and may require a stretching, growing, or at times shattering and rebuilding of the self as the larger actualizing tendency pushes one through the process of change.

The self is formed through conditions of worth in which a person accepts parts of her experience to the extent that her relational climate does (think of the relational climate as the real and virtual interpersonal region that surrounds a person, e.g., an infant's family). If certain experiences are not acceptable (being angry, being attracted to a particular person, disliking dresses, etc.), then this person's relational climate will discourage her from identifying with or accepting those experiences.

Therapy that provides empathy and unconditional positive regard provides a unique opportunity for a person to identify, accept, and reintegrate experiences into one's self. As more and more experiences are integrated, a person becomes more and more process-oriented and less and less attached to having to be perceived or understood by himself or others in a certain way. According to Rogers, this type of transition leads to a more fully functioning individual.

The Fully Functioning Person. Rogers was concerned with human potential and the future. Rogers believed that a person who can integrate a wide and ever-expanding set of experiences (including feelings, preferences, thoughts, facts, etc.) becomes more open to experience and lives more congruently and authentically. Such a person develops an appreciation of and valuing of concepts such as *process* and *change* and accepts that suffering is inevitable but also temporary. The person develops a sense of flow (i.e., a greater self-awareness, social awareness, meta-cognition) and an ongoing increase in skill sets that lead to additional internal integration of experiences. This person becomes increasing capable of interacting with others in a facilitative way.

Rogers (1980) identified the "person of tomorrow" or "fully functioning person" as having seven characteristics: (1) is adaptable to change, (2) is open to new experiences, (3) lives in the moment, (4) has harmonious relationships, (5) experiences internal integration that encompasses both conscious and unconscious experiences, (6) trusts human nature, and (7) enjoys the richness of life. Refer to Table 6.3 for a chronological listing of several seminal publications by Rogers.

A Chronological Sample of Rogers's Work

1951—Client-Centered Therapy   In this text, Rogers articulates the foundation of person-centered therapy, including foci on the facilitative qualities of the therapist as well as the therapeutic relationship and process. It also includes introductions to related parts of the person-centered approach, such as person-centered education.
1961—On Becoming a Person   Rogers offers a broad focus, including autobiographical disclosures in addition to psychotherapy discussions. This work also includes the role of research, creativity, communication, and other aspects of Rogers's work that articulate the power of individuals who work together and independently in advancing human potential.
1969—Freedom to Learn: A View of What Education Might Become   The first of three editions were updated in the 1980s and posthumously (with Jerome Freiberg in 1994). This work elaborated ideas on nondirective or student-centered education introduced in *Client-Centered Psychotherapy*. Its theme is that the facilitation of learning should replace teaching as the primary goal for educators. Person-centered education aims for more democratic learners and society through increased self-regulation, cooperation, and a development of people who are open to change and become experts in how to learn.
1977—Carl Rogers on Personal Power: Inner Strength and Its Revolutionary Impact   In this text, Rogers explicates how a person can translate her own actualizing tendency as a fully functioning person into systematic and cultural change. Rogers also confronted criticisms that his person-centered approach is primarily a self-centric system, including dedicating an entire chapter to illustrate the parallels between the person-centered approach and the revolutionary work of Paulo Freire. Furthermore, Rogers discussed the usefulness of his theory to diverse client groups, including ethnic and sexual minorities, economically disenfranchised groups, and others.
1980—A Way of Being   *A Way of Being* was the last major volume to be released while Rogers was still alive. It is similar in its highly personal tone to *On Becoming a Person* but chronicles developments and contributions during the 1970s across a broad array of topics.

The Therapeutic Process

Goals

For a person-centered therapist, the primary therapeutic goals are to be sincerely empathic and accepting. Another goal is to trust that the client can handle his suffering and find more adaptive ways to understand his life and act on this understanding. The therapist aims to be "right there" with the client, compassionately understanding each facet of the client's experiences.

Goals for the client are formalized in a mutually established treatment plan, a treatment that involves both therapist and client. (Rogers believed the only person who is an expert concerning the client's problem is the client, not the therapist.) In this way, the merit of the relationship becomes inductive for the client in that she can experience the types of conditions under which she is most able to actualize as a fully functioning person (e.g., unconditional positive regard, congruence). Although the therapeutic relationship can be extended to include other members of a therapy group or family members taking part in family therapy, the primary focus in person-centered therapy is on the individual's experiences in the present—the "here and now." This is to say, when the client experiences the necessary and sufficient conditions for therapeutic change, a positive outcome is expected (Rogers, 1957). According to Rogers, even in time-limited situations (e.g., therapy involving one session), the person-centered approach has the potential to provide the therapeutic ingredients needed for a genuinely felt experience to occur in the client, the type of experience that Rogers asserted led to an actual physical change within the client—the type of change that promotes positive therapeutic change (A. S. Glauser, personal communication, January 25, 2017).

Carkhuff (1969), Martin (2011), and others have discussed how a good empathic statement by a therapist often focuses on the motivational or goal-setting edge of the client's experience using words such as *want, desire,* and *change.* For example, when a therapist says something like, "You hate that about yourself and you want to find ways to improve your choices in those situations," the therapist is getting at the motivational elements of a client's experience. Such remarks will help a client realize the goals that are inherent in his conflicts and his reactions to what is being discussed in therapy. When responding, the therapist articulates the point or thrust of what the client is experiencing or expressing. A person-centered therapist is not just focusing on the manifest content of the client's remarks; rather, communication is taking place at a deeper level that matches what the client is experiencing in the moment.

Therapist's Role

I (first author) was nervous one day before going into a session, and my person-centered supervisor gave me just one word to focus on to help me with my fretting. The word was *understand.* At the most basic level, the "doing" part of the empathic therapist's role is to understand the client; that is, the therapist's role is to listen to and follow the trail of words spoken by the client. Even during those times when understanding becomes a challenge, focused listening will enable the therapist, at a minimum, to "sense the edges" of what the client is communicating about her experience. Basically, the role of the therapist is to empathize in the best way possible.

Although seemingly contradictory, it would be correct to state that a person-centered therapist has no role per se. Any attempt to "do" something to the client for any particular aim, from a Rogerian perspective, represents an attachment to a specific view toward what the client is supposed to accomplish or become. In this sense, the therapist has no role. Instead, the purpose of the person-centered therapist is to simply be with the client. The aim is to radically discard attachments to how a client is supposed to process or where the client is supposed to go. The person-centered therapist is intent on staying engaged while providing nonpossessive compassion during the client's struggle to change and grow.

At another level, the therapist's role is to be authentic, that is, to understand and be with the client but with as much presence and integration as possible. Feeling, thinking, imagining, moving, allowing one's self a complete absorption in the client's experience and reactions to those experiences and responding sincerely are part of the therapist's being genuine. In these ways—understanding, not forcing a preordained outcome, and being authentic—the overarching role of the person-centered therapist is to experience empathy, warmth, and congruence with each client.

At a more structural level, the person-centered therapist makes every effort to ensure that the client's perspective is the most essential aspect of the therapy process. Sessions are held at mutually agreed-on times, and the therapist strives to accommodate the client's therapeutic needs insofar as the therapist is comfortable with them and believes that each need reifies the conditions of worth for the client. However, the client does not completely dictate all aspects of therapy; rather, the client's position is valued and included in all therapeutic decisions made by the therapist.

Client's Role

In a sense, a danger exists in the attempt to describe the client's role from the perspective of person-centered therapy. Some person-centered supervisors, for example, suggest to their beginning supervisees not to ask questions, not to do an intake, not to review a case file, or do other such preparatory steps to honor this danger and prevent their supervisees from forming prejudgments about a person. Instead, such a supervisor would encourage the supervisee to let himself experience the person just as she is without believing or persuading the client to "do" or "be" a certain way. Although we do not subscribe to this view, believing that there are many reasons to be informed about the client and to be prepared, this sentiment is important to consider. If the therapist's goal is to avoid judgment, then the therapist must also avoid expecting something, predicting what will occur, and encouraging a specific type of role for the client because such actions would inhibit the true role of the client as conceptualized from a person-centered point of view.

However, it is possible to describe the client's role in broad terms. The client's role is to engage. Clients are to bravely confront in a radically accepting, accurately understanding, and authentic client–therapist relationship the experiences of their lives that they cannot hold, feel, or integrate into their typically conditional relationships outside the therapy room. Paradoxically, this engagement occurs best when a therapist does not force the occurrence of such an engagement but instead gets as close to or even intuitively ahead of, but poignantly connected to, wherever the client is going and whatever the client is experiencing. Clients learn to "trust the therapy process," that is, to comprehend how they learn information and trust the feelings within this unique type of engagement. Clients can be expected to also learn to internalize the accepting, understanding process from the therapist and to begin to provide more empathy and warmth to those within their lives, which further enriches their own lives and potential to learn more and grow. This type of learning is reflected in the lyrics of the song "True Colors," written by Billy Steinberg and Tom Kelly and performed by social activist and singer-songwriter Cyndi Lauper:

> If this world makes you crazy
>
> And you've taken all you can bear
>
> You call me up
>
> Because you know I'll be there
>
> And I'll see your true colors

Shining through

I see your true colors

And that's why I love you

So don't be afraid to let them show

Assessment

Assessment, like diagnosis, in person-centered therapy is a bit of a misnomer. Assessment implies judgment from an expert, but the goal for a person-centered therapist is to be non-judgmental and regard the client as the expert when it comes to his own life. However, although the person-centered approach does not view traditional forms of assessment as necessary or relevant it could be argued that a subtle form of assessment occurs as the mutual interactions unfold between the therapist and the client. It is the type of ongoing, moment-to-moment "assessment" that makes it possible for a person-centered therapist to understand and respond empathically to the client.

Strict adherence to the person-centered theory means that a therapist would avoid the types of traditional assessments used in therapy that result in a formal, medical diagnosis (e.g., a disorder listed in the *DSM*). In fact, Rogers (1951) believed that diagnostic practices are forms of a therapist evaluation of the client that create a condition of worth in the therapeutic relationship and can prove deleterious to the curative bond between the therapist and client. As a contraposition, Rogers believed that the client should be self-evaluative, as exemplified by the following statement, "In a very meaningful and accurate sense, therapy is diagnosis, and this diagnosis is a process which goes on in the experience of the client, rather than in the intellect of the clinician" (Rogers, 1951, p. 223). In this way, only the client can diagnose, because "the client is the only one who has the potentiality of knowing fully the dynamics of his perceptions and his behavior" (p. 221). For the therapist, assessment, and therefore the diagnostic process, is only valuable insofar as it facilitates the capacity of the therapist to experience empathy, unconditional positive regard, and congruence with the client.

Techniques and Strategies

The types of therapeutic techniques and strategies that are typical of the person-centered approach can best be summarized by using the words of Rogers (1951), who wrote there is a belief "that the individual has a sufficient capacity to deal constructively with all those aspects of his life which can potentially come into conscious awareness" (p. 24). This awareness emerges when the therapist facilitates the therapeutic process in such a manner that the client experiences her full sense of humanness, including the expression of feelings within a nonjudgmental therapeutic climate. In this way, formal techniques fade away in the therapeutic relationship and are replaced by genuine and authentic dialogue and action that show the client that she is understood and valued. Although the type of dialogue between the therapist and client are not proscriptive in nature, one can expect the therapist to reflect on or paraphrase what the client expresses—its content, tone, and meaning.

Additionally, a therapist might provide genuine and spontaneous feedback to the client insofar as it does not impress a sense of evaluation and worth for that client. Considered together, the dialectic and action efforts of the therapist provide the client the opportunity to be self-directive and self-reflective in therapy, which invites change and growth on the client's terms in a way that is personally relevant and meaningful.

Nondirectivity: Being Versus Doing. Early in Rogers's career, he called his approach *non-directive* (Rogers, 1942). He used this term to emphasize the acceptance of the client in a positive and nonjudgmental way, so the client could experience himself without the contamination of an evaluative outsider. In this manner, the therapist did not compel the client to do anything different with his life; instead, the focus of therapy represented a radical acceptance of the client. Therefore, both the client and the therapist could coexist in a significant relationship as congruent, authentic, and nonjudgmental beings. The focus then is on *being with* the other and not *doing to* the other.

From the nondirective perspective, the client is the authority when it comes to her own existence, and she is the primary recipient of any therapeutic change or growth that results from the therapeutic process. Therefore, according to person-centered theory, the principal focus of the therapeutic process should emanate from the client. The therapist ensures the client's safety, autonomy, and self-determination and strives to protect the client from "the inherent structural power as an authority within the therapeutic context" (Brodley, 2005, p. 2).

It should be noted that Rogers revised the name of his theory to client-centered and finally person-centered, because it was more important to focus on the human and human encounter elements over description of the therapist's attitude and behavior. Nevertheless, he denied that he ever really qualified the notion that person-centered practice was nondirective when asked directly.

> No. I think I perhaps enriched it but not really qualified it. I still feel that the person who should guide the client's life is the client. My whole philosophy and whole approach is to try to strengthen him in that way of being, that he's in charge of his own life and nothing that I say is intended to take that capacity or that opportunity away from him. (Quoted in Evans, 1975, p. 26)

Rogers and others have acknowledged that much of person-centered thinking is related to Taoism and the writings of Lao-tse, particularly with regard to the concept of *wu wei*, which has been translated in various ways, including the following: "the action of nonaction," "nondoing," "without controlling," and "spontaneous action." These variations suggest paradoxically that the most effective action is being with and being in tune with the client and effortlessly exerting effort. Rogers (1967b) wrote, "The more I am open to the realities in me and in the other person, the less do I find myself wishing to rush in to 'fix things'" (p. 21). To describe the nondirective concept of *wu wei* in relation to person-centered practice, Freire (2009) quoted a poem of Lao-tse:

> The softest water breaks the hardest stone
>
> carves the block with no effort

that which lacks substance

can enter where there is no space

thus there is strength in non-action

Teaching without words

power of *wu wei*

beyond the understanding

by the majority. (p. 329)

Reflections and Empathic Following. The technique that is perhaps most associated with person-centered therapy is active listening. *Active listening* is a process in which the therapist attends to the myriad verbal and nonverbal expressions of the client. Furthermore, a therapist who is engaged in active listening can effectively demonstrate to the client that she is accurately attending to the content and meaning of the client's expression, generally without disrupting the natural therapeutic process. As an example, a therapist might offer a head nod to demonstrate a sense of understanding concerning a significant client disclosure.

A particular form of active listening is the employment of paraphrasing and the reflection of feelings. When a therapist paraphrases a client, she tries to demonstrate immediate empathy with the client by repeating the most essential aspects of the client's prompting statement or action. Generally speaking, from a person-centered perspective, the meaning-feeling content is the most essential ingredient for an effective paraphrased statement. In this manner, paraphrasing is neither parroting the exact words of the client nor is it an interpretative reaction based on some conjectural assumptions about what has been said; instead, paraphrasing from this theoretical perspective is framed in a way to demonstrate empathy and unconditional positive regard for the client, regardless of the content of the client's prompting statement. Additionally, a paraphrase that highlights the affective content of the client's prompting statement compels the client to consider how his emotional state affects his experience of the self and the world.

It should be noted that Rogers objected to critics of the person-centered approach who might have mistakenly reduced this theory to simply reflective techniques. Rogers (1975) wrote,

> "Reflect" becoming in time a word which made me cringe. . . . The whole approach came, in a few years, to be known as a technique. "Nondirective therapy," it was said, "is the technique of reflecting the client's feelings." Or an even worse caricature was simply that, "in nondirective therapy you repeat the last words the client has said." I was so shocked by these complete distortions of our approach. (pp. 2–3)

In other words, a person-center therapist does not paraphrase to advance the therapeutic process; rather, she paraphrases because it is an appropriate and accurate experience of the therapist in relationship to a client who is disclosing important personal cognitive and affective material.

Variants and Extensions of Person-Centered Therapy

The Experiential Wing of Person-Centered Therapy

A student of Rogers, Eugene Gendlin, developed a variant of person-centered therapy first calling it "experiencing" (Gendlin, 1962) and later renaming it "focusing-oriented psychotherapy" (Gendlin, 1996). The hallmark of Gendlin's approach was to support the client in experiencing a deep connectedness, that is, connecting an affective response to an idea or phenomenon. In this process, Gendlin would encourage the client to identify where in the body this felt experience was located and associate this physical area with the experience of the mental trauma. This associative relationship was further explored in a shared manner between the therapist and client until the meaning of the felt trauma became apparent; oftentimes this occurred as the client felt a sense of relief both physically and mentally.

These qualities of a good therapeutic response are captured somewhat by the term *evocative*. Laura North Rice described the function of the empathic, unconditional therapist as one of evoking a client's experience so that the experiential part of the feeling, meaning, or goal intent is highlighted in addition to obtaining the cognitive details of the client's story or communication. Rice (1974) wrote, "The first principle of evocative responding is that the therapist should listen for and respond to reactions, either explicit or implicit" (p. 303). In other words, the story is good to hear, but the client's reactions to her own story are even better. This processing proposal model provides another avenue to assist a therapist in focusing on the client's personal meanings rather than just on the story.

Emotion-Focused Therapy

Over time, other theorists have extended Rogers's and Gendlin's ideas in a model that has been subjected to particularly rigorous and repeated evaluation, especially as a potentially superior treatment for depression compared with other approaches. This approach is known as emotion-focused therapy (also known as emotionally focused therapy and process-experiential therapy). Leslie Greenberg, Susan Johnson, and others have developed and researched this approach with individuals, couples, and, more recently, with families. In emotion-focused therapy, emotions are viewed as having an inherently actualizing potential. The problem is not the suffering and the difficult emotions but rather the client's inability to manage and use them adaptively. Emotions can help inform people of their needs and guide them toward meeting those needs.

Emotion-focused work relies primarily on evocative empathy but also engages specific proposals for tasks that may support the resolving of the problems, such as incorporating an empty chair technique to deal with unfinished business. A therapist engages a client empathically and follows him through poignant moments. If a client appears to fail to resolve a problem that represents long-standing, unfinished business, perhaps with a loved one he has lost, the emotion-focused therapist might invite the client to express himself directly to the lost loved one (using an empty chair). The therapist then follows the client empathically as the client engages with more successful resolutions, involving intense expressions of feeling, expression of needs, shifts in representations of the other, and self-validation or understanding of the other (Elliott, Watson, Goldman, & Greenberg, 2003).

Multiculturalism and Social Justice

Multicultural Perspective

Rogers's person-centered therapy has been considered a culturally appropriate approach to working with persons from diverse cultural groups (Cornelius-White, 2003; Glauser & Bozarth, 2001; MacDougall, 2002). MacDougall (2002) highlighted the importance of a culturally competent "person-centered therapy-influenced practitioner's" possessing self-awareness, awareness about the client's cultural and personal frame, and how each of these factors should be considered in the process of therapy.

This approach prioritizes the person-in-the-relationship such that culture becomes the primary mechanism for the relationship to be shared and contribute to client growth.

The client's cultural frame is an intrinsic element of the person-centered perspective, as Rogers (1951) said:

> We fail to see that we are evaluating the person from our own, or from some fairly general, frame of reference, but that the only way to understand his behavior meaningfully is to understand it as he perceives it himself, just as the only way to understand another culture is to assume the frame of reference of that culture. When that is done, the various meaninglessness and strange behaviors are seen to be part of a meaningful and goal directed behavior. (p. 494)

Although Rogers clearly valued the cultural constructions experienced by a given client, mental health professionals who adopt this perspective should remain culturally cautious. For example, some groups of people might not be as culturally receptive to the nondirective approach that is implicit to person-centered therapy, which may require the therapist to provide an explanation and some background information on the person-centered approach or display a willingness to follow implicit or explicit requests from the client for the therapist to be more directive. Members from these groups might value or request direct advice or be hesitant to self-disclose, particularly without some self-disclosure from the therapist to show mutuality and trustworthiness. In such circumstances, the person-centered therapist must remain congruent within her own self but empathize with the therapeutic needs of the client and adjust accordingly to a client's requests to the extent the therapist can also generally maintain the core conditions. Brodley (2005), one of nondirectivity's staunchest advocates, has argued that it is more directive not to direct the client when he is clearly asking for advice or interpretation or other directive activities on the part of the therapist than to paternalistically deny the client such human actions based on a misguided assumption that a person-centered therapist cannot perform such actions.

The person-centered approach has been shown to be effective in working with a variety of cultural groups (Elliott & Freire, 2008). For example, Stiles, Barkham, Mellor-Clark, and Connell (2008) found success with person-centered therapy in a diverse sample of over 5,000 clients being seen through state-funded treatments. Freire, Koller, Silva, and Piason (2005) found that person-centered therapy improved levels of resilience in approximately 100 impoverished, maltreated, and neglected children and adolescents in Brazil. One interesting finding in this study was that many of the youth who were involved in the study were initially perplexed by the nondirective approach that was utilized by the therapist, but they quickly adapted and even thrived in this type of therapeutic relationship.

Child-centered play therapy (Bratton, Ray, Edwards, & Landreth, 2009) is based on person-centered theory combined with what has been learned about children's development and the contribution that the spontaneous activity of children, commonly referred to as "play," makes to their holistic development. Child-centered play therapy allows self-healing to take place, and available evidence suggests that it is especially effective with non-Caucasian children (Lin & Bratton, 2015). Bratton, Ray, Rhine, and Jones (2005) found in a meta-analysis of 93 controlled outcome studies that the overall efficacy of play therapy was 0.80 standard deviations. Additional analysis showed that the effects were more positive for humanistic than nonhumanistic forms of play therapy.

A child-centered play therapist strives to facilitate healing and growth in a child by creating a warm environment that provides unconditional positive regard and by calling empathic attention to certain aspects of a child's activity (e.g., a child is engaged in drawing a picture). For example, a child-centered play therapist might respond to a child's conflicted feelings by calling attention to certain parts of a child's drawing. Although the therapist would not interpret the meaning of a drawing, the therapist might respond to the drawings found in Figure 6.2 by saying something such as "It looks like the hand is closed—like a fist ready to fight" and "The small face in the middle is crying—the face looks sad." (The child who drew both pictures was experiencing a stressful environment that sparked frequent arguments among family members.)

Social Justice

Rogers likely did not use the term *social justice* specifically, but he certainly exemplified what social justice encompasses today, decades before it became *en vogue* in the literature found across today's various fields of therapeutic practice. In his written work, Rogers discussed how person-centered therapy could be used to transform inequitable injustices, both for the individual and for an entire culture (see, e.g., Rogers, 1977). During his final years, Rogers spent much of his time working directly with oppressed and marginalized individuals. The culmination of these socially focused efforts resulted in a nomination for the Nobel Peace Prize for his work with oppressed groups in South Africa and Northern Ireland (see Rogers, 1987).

Rogers was admittedly slow to acknowledge the political inferences found embedded in person-centered theory and its applications, but after years of philosophical reflection and discourse with students, laypersons, and scholars, in 1977 he offered the following sentiment:

It has taken me years to recognize that the violent opposition to a client-centered therapy sprang not only from its newness, and the fact that it came from a

▼ FIGURE 6.2
Examples of a Child's Art Work

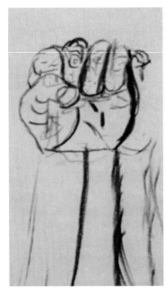

Source: Reproduced with permission from M. D. G.

psychologist rather than a psychiatrist, but primarily because it struck such an outrageous blow to the therapist's power. It was in its politics that it was most threatening. (pp. 16–17)

For Rogers, the most socially just mechanism in therapy is to disarm the overt power of the therapist and reinsert it into its proper place by virtue of the therapeutic relationship—with the client.

This idea, to reconfigure the power dynamic in therapy such that the client is trusted to be the operator of her own growth and healing, was a radical thought when it was first introduced by Rogers. In addition, person-centered therapy can be understood to be consistent with the suggestions of today's social justice scholars, who assert that advocacy behaviors should be both on behalf of and with the client (e.g., Lewis & Bradley, 2000). Therefore, it appears that person-centered therapy is perfectly consistent with these suggestions given that the therapist is charged with working within the client's worldview (the "with" advocacy posture) and in the form of social action (the "on behalf of" advocacy posture) as exemplified by Rogers's life and work.

Special Ethical Considerations

Professional ethics for mental health professionals are generally aspirational in nature, whereby the therapist is expected to practice in a manner that promotes the highest standards of conduct (Remley & Herlihy, 2015). From a person-centered therapy perspective, no specific aspirations exist that the practitioner imposes on the client, except for the necessary core conditions that the therapist maintains to promote client growth. In this manner, person-centered therapy is an appropriate and ethical approach to therapy, especially given that ethical codes in various fields of mental health are founded on the assumption that treatment must be enacted in a way that will be nonmaleficent (i.e., do no harm), promote beneficence (i.e., benefit), and support autonomy (i.e., self-determination) in the client's life. Person-centered practitioners have sometimes put a nondirective attitude forward, not as a technique or research-supported construct, but as an ethical mandate for those who accept the salience of nonmaleficence and autonomy in particular (Moon, Witty, Grant, & Rice, 2013).

In addition to general principles of ethics, a person-centered therapist should consider specific ethical circumstances that might be unique to this approach. For example, as with other therapists, during intake, a person-centered therapist is ethically responsible for informing a client of the strengths and potential limitations of his therapeutic approach. Also, if the therapist expects to be reimbursed by a third-party payer (i.e., the client's insurance company), the therapist is obligated to explain to the client the insurance company's requirement to render a *DSM* diagnosis. In addition, the client is expected to be informed about the possibility that under certain circumstances a therapist may be required to break the confidential nature of the therapeutic relationship. Even though a person-centered therapist must maintain a nonjudgmental attitude about the client in situations where a client might harm another individual, the therapist is often ethically and legally bound to work with the appropriate authorities and related individuals to ensure the safety of the client and/or others. (This is further complicated by differences that exist among various legal jurisdictions concerning the duty to warn.) Therefore, a therapist who adheres strictly to the theoretical tenets of the person-centered approach is adopting a position that might be somewhat tenuous at best and at worst a position that may be viewed as ethically and/or legally unsound.

Research Support

Rogers recorded therapy sessions on the clumsy glass disks available at the time, so he could study the therapeutic process in detail. Rogers also called for comparative research to be conducted (e.g., comparing two therapeutic approaches on their outcome). In relation to carrying out such research, Rogers persistently tried to solicit the cooperation of psycho-analysts to record their therapy sessions and test their level of success. As a result, he was accused by them of violating the sanctity of the analytic relationship. Even though they eventually agreed to have such research carried out, they restricted its extent by allowing only residents (in other words, the trainees) to be recorded, leaving the question of whose "sanctity" was actually being protected. Rogers eventually won the war over testing the effectiveness of therapy and identifying the therapeutic components that contribute to that effectiveness.

Because of Rogers's early efforts, today a large body of research exists on person-centered therapy. Rogers was the first to record and transcribe hundreds of therapy sessions verbatim so every sentence that was uttered by the client and therapist could be reviewed and studied. Such procedures were to eventually become an important part of therapy research and were also used to train future therapists. Rogers and his colleagues were the first (by 20 years) to analyze transcripts and to measure outcomes on psychometric tests (and other newly devised measures) given to clients before and after therapy, assessment measures that were also administered to control groups. Indeed, person-centered therapy was in many respects the first therapy orientation to undergo extensive empirical study that resembles today's state of the art of therapy research.

The necessary and sufficient conditions were the subject of decades of research and hundreds of studies that show the powerful impact that qualities such as empathy, warmth, and genuineness had on therapy. Rogerian research findings indicated this was true regardless of the orientation of the practitioner (Patterson, 1984). Recently, meta-analyses by Elliott and Freire (2008) pulled from the following categories of data: 203 research samples ($n = 14,235$ clients) to assess pre/post findings; 63 research samples ($n = 2,144$ clients; $n = 1,958$ controls) to assess controlled studies; and 105 research samples ($n = 6,097$ clients) to assess comparative studies (91% of these studies utilized the randomized control trial method, which is considered the "gold standard" for a clinical study). The overall aim was to determine if person-centered/experiential (PC/E) therapies have empirical support for their use. Elliott and Freire (2008) found the following: PC/E therapies were found to have a large effect size (i.e., a large amount of client change had occurred), and these gains were still being maintained at the point of early and late follow-up (greater than 12 months); clients in the controlled studies achieved large gains compared with those who received no treatment; outcomes for PC/E therapies appeared to be essentially equivalent to outcomes for non-PC/E therapies; when outcomes for different types of PC/E therapy were compared with cognitive-behavioral therapy (CBT), it was found that CBT results clearly exceeded those of nondirective-supportive therapies, but CBT outcomes were equivalent to what was called bona fide person-centered therapy, whereas emotion-focused therapy produced superior results to CBT and other experiential therapies were found to be equally effective to CBT. These findings held when Elliott and Freire (2008) limited their analyses to the sample of randomized control trial studies.

In another meta-analytic study, Lin and Bratton (2015) found support for using child-centered play therapy, a person-centered form of play therapy. These researchers synthesized the results from 52 controlled outcome studies that were conducted from 1995 to 2010. Although a good number of the studies under consideration contained relatively small sample sizes (22 had total sample sizes of fewer than 30 participants), Lin and Bratton (2015) were able to statistically account for this drawback. Out of their synthesis came a moderate effect size ($d = .47$) in favor of child-centered play therapy. Also important is that Lin and Bratton (2015) discovered that the mean effect size for studies with predominantly non-Caucasian participants ($d = .76$) was greater than that for studies with predominantly Caucasian participants ($d = .33$). The latter finding supports the conclusion that child-centered play therapy is relevant for working with diverse populations of children.

Two additional streams of research also provide broad support for the tenets of person-centered therapy: studies focused on the therapy relationship and studies focused on common factors. Bell, Marcus, and Goodlad (2013), Wampold (2001), Duncan and Miller (2000), Lambert and Barley (2001), and others have shown that certain components and common factors are present across all successful therapies, regardless of their theoretical orientation. This assertion can be made clear by referring to Lambert's 40-30-15-15 model, a model that asserts four principal elements account for positive therapeutic change. In this statistically supported model, 40% of the success is due to extratherapeutic factors (e.g., naturally occurring facilitative relationships in the client's life outside of therapy and other types of supports) and 30% is due to the therapeutic relationship (e.g., when the client receives unconditional positive regard in therapy). Only 15% of the success achieved can be traced to specific therapeutic techniques that are employed in therapy. The final 15% is due to a positive placebo effect that is due to the client's belief that she will get better. Finally, research evidence suggests that people prefer therapy founded on common factors; for example, the therapist appeared to be empathic driven and nonjudgmental in nature. Swan and Heesacker (2013) surveyed 329 individuals and found that people (with and without prior therapy experience) were more inclined to seek out therapies that were advertised as being "open and safe" rather than therapies described as "clinical and prescriptive," that is, therapies that relied on exact rules and instructions. Furthermore, Norcross (2001) compiled various research findings and found evidence for the effectiveness of the working alliance (and cohesion in group therapy), empathy, and goal consensus/collaboration. When Bachelor (2013) examined how clients and therapists conceptualized and rated the working alliance, it was found to be predictive of therapy's outcome. Specifically, Bachelor discovered that for clients, collaboration and nondisagreement concerning goals contributed to how clients conceptualized the working alliance. Additionally, examination of subsamples of research on warmth and genuineness, as measured only from the client's perceptions, was found to play an important role in therapy's success. In fact, Cornelius-White (2002) reported that clients' perception of positive regard and genuineness crossed the statistical support threshold to be considered "demonstrably effective." This author also reported that the American Psychological Association's Task Force on Empirically Supported Therapy Relationships misrepresented and undervalued the importance of general relationship elements and elevated the importance of customizing the therapy relationship.

Limitations and Criticism

The philosophic basis of person-centered therapy can appear incredibly sophisticated and even contradictory. On the one hand, Rogers believed that a congruent, empathetic, and positive relationship shared between the therapist and client is sufficient unto itself for the purposes of client growth. In this way, person-centered therapy is a relational theory. On the other hand, Rogers's theory is primarily focused on the growth and development of the particular client, as mostly independent of social circumstance (Rogers, 1977). In this manner, even in the throes of personal or social turbulence (e.g., racism, economic oppression), Rogers believed that the individual could actualize his potential.

Rogers's optimism about the potential of an individual to transcend negative social circumstance is encouraging and deserves praise. In addition, Rogers's belief in the individual's capacity to exceed her past experiences and current social inequalities can be seen as empowering for the individual client. Furthermore, Rogers asserted that his system could be socially transformative, as the actualized client will inevitably affect her world (Rogers, 1977). Interpreted differently, Rogers's system can be regarded as a philosophy that has the potential to further reinforce oppression and even place the responsibility of one's lot in life on the oppressed individual. Thus, a client who has been deeply affected by transgenerational racism, who also is working with an effective person-centered therapist—experiencing empathy, congruence, and positive regard from the therapist— is predicated to eventually apply aspects of the transformative relationship toward others outside the person-therapist context, applying these positive relational aspects even to those who have racially oppressed the client. In other words, the oppressed unconditionally accept the oppressor. Some critics have questioned the value of such an outcome and have suggested it represents an inherent weakness of the approach.

Another criticism often leveled against person-centered therapy pertains to Rogers's term *nondirective therapy*. Many critics believe that it is improbable for a therapist to be completely nondirective, and others have gone so far as to suggest that it would be imprudent to be nondirective in therapy. As stated earlier, Rogers conceded that there was some inevitable directionality implicit to any therapy relationship, but he further offered that a fully functioning therapist would do this in a way that empathetically reflects the perspective and needs of the client. Brodley (1994) asserted that nondirectivity should be perceived as an attitude rather than a description of technique or behavior.

Another criticism of person-centered therapy pertains to Rogers's perspective on client diagnosis. Rogers believed that any diagnosis that results in a condition of worth between practitioner and client should be avoided. This said, Rogers was amenable to diagnosis that was a part of treatment that moved the client toward full functioning and if the diagnosis was supported by the client. Some critics contend that it is illogical and even potentially harmful to go against the grain of contemporary psychopathological diagnoses. Other critics point to the paradox of ignoring formal assessment and diagnosis and yet assuming that every client has the innate capacity to self-actualize—a position that still calls on the therapist to informally "assess and diagnosis" throughout the therapeutic process whether the client is making progress.

We began this chapter by explaining that the necessity (if not sufficiency) of a relational foundation, as proposed by person-centered theory, has become seamlessly integrated into what represents the generic or generally accepted view of what constitutes therapy in the eyes of many people. A number of critics throughout the years have contested that the core conditions proposed by Rogers are important and even necessary for effective therapy but not necessarily sufficient for the change process to occur. One of person-centered therapy's most vocal and purist advocates, Jerold Bozarth, reexamined this specific criticism of Rogers's position. Deftly using passion and logic, Bozarth weaved both person-centered theory and decades of research findings together to create a convincing argument that persons can and do improve without experiencing therapy and can even improve in therapy sometimes despite infrequent occurrences of or low levels of empathy, unconditional positive regard, or congruence being experienced. However, Bozarth also provided compelling evidence to conclude that when therapy is imbued with such conditions as empathy, unconditional positive regard, and congruence, the conditions become sufficient enough for growth to occur; this seems especially true if the client is attuned to perceiving the presence of such conditions. Therefore, in contrast to the popular belief held by a number of professionals that a facilitative relationship might be necessary but not sufficient, Bozarth (1998) summarized his position by stating, "The actualizing tendency suggests that it is more than accurate to conclude that the conditions are not necessarily necessary but always sufficient" (p. 42).

Experiential (i.e., emotion-focused) person-centered therapists have recently provided support for another variant on the necessary and sufficient hypothesis, namely, that a facilitative relationship is necessary and sufficient but that certain extra elements (e.g., focusing, empty chair technique, etc.) can optimize the situation, that is, make it beyond sufficient. We think there is merit in all of these viewpoints, but we tend to lean toward an unconventional mix in which a facilitative relationship is not necessary, is usually sufficient, but is not necessarily optimal depending on the circumstance. Nevertheless, we acknowledge that therapy in general is less likely to do harm if Rogers's conditions are present, especially with beginning therapists in whom the quality of empathy has been shown in several research studies to predict outcome better than it predicts outcome with experienced therapists (see Bozarth, 2000).

Relevance to Current Practice

Regardless of criticisms, Rogers's ideas have proven to be some of the most significant contributions to the therapy and its body of literature. Rogers's ideas concerning the therapeutic relationship are almost ubiquitous, including other theoretical approaches that were once at philosophical odds with Rogers's person-centered approach (e.g., a type of behavioral approach know as dialectical behavior therapy). Rogers revolutionized how scholars research the therapeutic relationship, process, and outcome and what the supervision of new therapists should be focused on. Most important, Rogers embodied the theory that he created. In this way, Rogers provided a template that enables therapists to grow as a person and as a professional. Rogers was a unique person who fostered growth in others by making himself available to the people he experienced and by virtue of his unwavering belief that humans possessed the capacity to develop their lives more fully through genuine communication.

Application: Person-Centered Theory

RETURNING TO THE CASE OF FERNANDO

Recall that Fernando is a 23-year-old male who was born in El Salvador and now resides in Los Angeles, where he is attending law school at the University of Southern California. Additionally, recall that Fernando recently started seeing a psychologist in the community because he felt sad, agitated, and angry, and this was affected his appetite and schoolwork. He also reported feeling very guilty about his series of sexual transgressions, particularly his infidelity with his ex-fiancée.

After the intake session with Fernando that was conducted by a graduate student in counseling psychology, the chief psychologist decided that Aicha Yasamin would be assigned Fernando's case. Yasamin, a 34-year-old female psychologist originally from Morocco, earned her PhD in the United States and later received extensive training at Carl Rogers's Center for Studies of the Person in La Jolla, California (http://www.centerfortheperson.org). Yasamin has been practicing for 10 years, specializing in depression, relationship issues, and concerns of immigrants.

Initial Sessions. When Fernando first met Yasamin in the waiting room, he immediately looked down and barely said hello. His clothing was very wrinkled, and his shirt was not tucked into his pants. He seemed to have just awakened and perhaps had slept in the clothing he was wearing. Yasamin smelled cigarette smoke on Fernando as she walked down the hallway with him. Once in Yasamin's office, Fernando sat with his legs and arms crossed as he gazed out the window and drooped in his chair. Yasamin began

talking to Fernando and explained her credentials, approach to therapy, the parameters of confidentiality (everything she discussed was confidential except if he were a danger to himself or others, which would have to be reported to the appropriate authorities), and the fact that the clinic only permitted individuals to receive 15 sessions per year. Fernando nodded his head as Yasamin spoke, continued to avoid eye contact, and then said, "I understand." Yasamin then responded, "I'm glad to hear this from you." [*The session continued.*]

Therapist (Yasamin)	Fernando, I read the notes that were taken by my colleague after he met with you for an intake session, so I have an idea from his perspective about what led you to seek help. If you are willing, I would like you to tell me in your own words what led you to ask for counseling. This will help me to hear your concerns directly and not secondhand.
Client (Fernando)	OK. I've been real angry, agitated, and depressed lately. Can't concentrate, eat, or get out of bed. The last three weeks I just don't know who I am anymore.
Therapist	Your life seems to be unraveling in front of you, and all of these changes and the depression make you question if you even know yourself.
Client	When I look in the mirror, my past seems like a blur or a collage of unexplainable paint blots.

Therapist	You're baffled and deeply concerned about lacking clarity about your life.
Client	Sometimes I wonder if I created this collage or I was programmed by my family to cause all kinds of trouble for myself and others.
Therapist	You're uncertain as to how you got to feeling so down, but you're upset because you believe you have caused others to suffer—others and yourself.
Client	So many women, so many breakups, so many disappointments, so many fights, and still I did it again.
Therapist	Looking back, you're amazed by how many times situations repeated themselves with women, and you're upset because you did not learn from these experiences.
Client	Yeah, I did it again. Cheated on my fiancée and she gave me the boot. I deserved it as usual. I can't stand myself anymore. I'm a chicken shit!
Therapist	You're disappointed in yourself for cheating again and know your behavior is just not right. Even though you know this, you feel powerless to do anything about it, just like a scared chicken!

In this initial session, Yasamin listened attentively to Fernando and tried to display empathy, unconditional positive regard, and respect when responding to his comments. What seems obvious from the few transactions above is that Fernando and Yasamin are not quite in sync when responding to each other. As Yasamin was clearly mirroring Fernando's disclosures, it might seem odd that Fernando appeared to take the conversation in a different direction after each of Yasamin's statements except for her next to last remark. This process is not uncommon in early sessions with clients when a practitioner embraces a person-centered style of interacting. Clients, and in this case certainly Fernando, in the early stages of therapy often do not acknowledge (or maybe even "hear") their experiences in response to the practitioner's immediate reflections of their feelings.

Middle Sessions. Since his first session, Fernando has had five additional meetings with Yasamin although he missed two sessions without notifying Yasamin. In these five sessions, Fernando more fully and deeply discussed the history of his infidelities, his difficulty with anger and depression, and his recent unsatisfying dates with many different women. Fernando also verbally and nonverbally expressed not trusting Yasamin, and he even questioned her commitment and investment with regard to helping him. During these five follow-up sessions, Yasamin continued to display empathy, respect, warmth, and unconditional positive regard toward Fernando and listened attentively to his concerns about himself and his assumptions about their therapeutic relationship. We resume with some of their conversation from Session 7.

Client	I have thought more about our session 2 weeks ago and now realize you do care about me and you are trying to help me. Sitting here in your office feels weird to me though. Let's do dinner sometime. This will be more relaxing and we can get to know each other better.
Therapist	I'm glad you discovered I'm invested in helping you better understand yourself so that you can resolve your different concerns. You want to get to know me better and think meeting for dinner will help.
Client	Yeah, I know a great Ethiopian restaurant we can go to not far from the Getty Museum. How about Saturday night?
Therapist	I cannot do this, Fernando. As a professional, I have a code of ethics that I follow and greatly value, and my going with you to dinner would violate this code. Also, I can be of much more help to you in your effort to gain a better understanding about your unsatisfying and problematic relationships with women by meeting with you in my office.
Client	[Crying] I don't know what is wrong with me. I know you can't date me. Are you now going to kick me out of therapy?
Therapist	It's confusing and painful for you when you say and do things knowing better that you should act differently. You're also scared that I will say goodbye.

(Continued)

(Continued)

Client	Everyone leaves me. I'm poison!
Therapist	Such a deep painful feeling to think that everyone leaves you. I'm still here for you to help you fully understand your pain and to grow from what you learn.
Client	Thanks, you have really helped me a lot to figure out that collage and the blur in my life that I mentioned in our first session. I'm glad that you still want to help me and you are not leaving me like other people who were in my life.

In this session, Fernando was much more revealing about his deep internal feelings. He expressed a good deal of emotion, and at the same time, he responded more directly to Yasamin's statements and demonstrated that he comprehended and was able to delve further into his emotional experiences. This is a critical step in person-center counseling as it represents the client's progress in the self-acceptance process.

During this session, Yasamin continued to attentively listen to Fernando and display empathy, respect, understanding, warmth, and unconditional positive regard. A marked difference, however, with the initial session was Yasamin's willingness to genuinely self-disclose and exhibit a response other than a reflection. Yasamin's openness about her professional boundaries and her commitment to continue working with Fernando seemed to deepen their relationship and increase Fernando's trust in Yasamin and his willingness to share some of his innermost emotions.

Final Sessions. Since Session 7, Fernando has regularly attended; he has not missed a session or arrived late. He also appeared well groomed and able to maintain appropriate eye contact with Yasamin. Five sessions that had been scheduled biweekly had occurred prior to the session reported next. From Session 7 to 12, Fernando explored his relationship with his parents, the move of his sister, his bicultural identity and infidelities, and his desire to be more honest with himself and others. He also began dating a highly intelligent woman (Maria) who was attending medical school at another university in Los Angeles. At the time of this session, Fernando had been involved with Maria for 2 months in a monogamous relationship.

The following is a portion of the dialogue between Fernando and Yasamin from Session 13.

Client	I had some of those old feelings again last week.
Therapist	Which ones?
Client	I met this woman at school and had an urge to ask her for a date.
Therapist	You had an urge.
Client	Yeah, but it was cool cause I immediately started to think where is this coming from and what is it about.
Therapist	You're really pleased that you were able to have this conversation with yourself about what triggered that surprising urge.
Client	Yes, it did surprise me to have the urge, but I was also surprised that I was able to think about my feelings and not immediately act on them!
Therapist	You're real happy to realize you can control your own behavior.
Client	I guess I'm not a chicken shit anymore!

In this session, Fernando appears much more insightful about himself, far more self-accepting, appreciative and trusting of himself, and autonomous. These characteristics are all indicative of the actualizing tendency in person-centered therapy. Fernando also seemed to be listening carefully to Yasamin and reflecting back to her what he had heard. As in the earlier sessions, Yasamin displayed empathy, warmth, respect, and unconditional positive regard.

Fernando continued to see Yasamin for two more sessions. Further, he maintained a faithful relationship with Maria reporting no other times in which he considered asking another woman out for a date. By the end of therapy, Fernando's self-concept had improved greatly; he no longer doubted himself, and he was much more aware and accepting of his feelings and actions. Moreover, he understood what led to his infidelities and had confidence in his ability to effectively process any future urges to cheat on his girlfriend. Additionally, Fernando no longer felt angry and depressed; instead, he reported that he felt very happy and had gained a zest for life.

The Case of Miguel Sanchez

Miguel Sanchez is a 14-year-old Mexican American male who emigrated from Mexico City to South Central Los Angeles with his family 6 years ago. His school counselor, Mrs. Torres, referred Miguel to receive psychological services and assessment. Mrs. Torres cited a decrease in Miguel's attendance, a shift in gravitation toward a negative peer group, and potential substance abuse as reasons for her referral. Mrs. Torres reported her being particularly concerned about Miguel's recent negative behavior because he has a history of being a bright student and involved with various student organizations. Mrs. Torres called a local community mental health agency and requested that Miguel be matched with a male therapist, preferably Hispanic. Mrs. Sanchez agreed that it might be in her son's best interest to engage in psychological services and left a message at the agency that she would like for her son to begin treatment.

Ramirez is assigned to the case and contacted Mrs. Sanchez to schedule an initial assessment. Ramirez reviewed on the phone how he initially works with a new client and their family by discussing his theoretical orientation, the client's right to confidentiality, cancellation policy, a sliding scale to receive reduced fee services, and how he may work collaboratively with the school and other providers. Mrs. Sanchez confirmed that she had recently noticed a negative change in her son, and she agreed to bring him in to see Ramirez the following week.

After the initial session, Ramirez could not help but wonder if the Sanchez family situation was more complicated than they originally presented. The Sanchez family spent the first session focusing on behaviors and expectations; however, Ramirez left the session feeling as if there might be underlying unresolved issues. He made a mental note to further explore how acculturation may be affecting the Sanchez family. In the following session, Ramirez helped to initiate a conversation between mother and son as to how their experience of moving to the United States might be different as well as how it might be similar. During this session, Mrs. Sanchez tearfully explained how she felt that her son was losing his heritage by wearing baggy clothes, listening to rap music, and refusing to participate in familial and cultural activities that he once enjoyed. In defense, Miguel loudly told his mother that she embarrassed him because of the traditional clothing that she wore and by refusing to learn to read or write in the English language.

Miguel was noticeably agitated when the conversation moved to his decreased connection to his Mexican heritage. Miguel attempted to explain to his mother, in Spanish, that the only people that he can truly relate to are his new friends. A heated discussion then ensued about Mrs. Sanchez's view of Miguel's new friends' lack of morals and criminal mentality. Miguel shouted, "at least they give me respect" and stormed out of the room. Ramirez was left with Mrs. Sanchez who was sobbing with her hands held over her face.

Therapeutic Environment. Miguel returns to therapy with Ramirez, this time without his mother. Ramirez's primary agenda for the session is to hear Miguel's story from his perspective and genuinely convey his empathy and unconditional positive regard.

Therapist (Ramirez)	I hear the frustration in your voice when you describe your relationship with your mother.
Client (Miguel)	Yeah, she wants me to be just like her family back in Mexico, but I feel like she brought me here and now she doesn't want me to act like it.
Therapist	It's confusing, trying to figure out what your mother wants you to be, what you think you're supposed to be here in California, and who you really are for yourself?
Client	Yeah, it's kind of like that, you know. [*pause*] It's like I have to be a lot of different things to different people and I tried that, but I feel most comfortable being this way [*pointing down at his clothes*]. [*pause*] My mother just doesn't understand. No one does but my friends.
Therapist	You have a way in which you have found yourself, like in your clothes or with your friends, but you wish your mother would understand and appreciate these new things about you.
Client	Yeah, before we moved here, we didn't really talk much about why we would move here [*pause*] but she kept saying that it would be better for us. [*pause*] I felt like it would be better for her. At first [*pause*] but now it feels like she's blaming me for it being better only for me, and not for her.
Therapist	It's like she dragged you along telling you it was for both of you, and you didn't buy it. But after a while, you did feel like you fit in and it was better for you. But you are upset because your mother seems to not get that and at the same time she doesn't seem to fit in.
Client	Yeah, she just doesn't get me.

In this interchange, Ramirez is trying to demonstrate his empathy for Miguel. Miguel begins to experience emotion and make personalized assessments that help him to integrate his immigration experience and the conflicts between his view and his mother's on that process and his identity.

The Experience of Unconditional Positive Regard. Miguel and Ramirez developed a deep mutual bond and respect for each other, and they are able to discuss some more difficult issues that have affected Miguel's life, including his relationship with his mother.

Client (Miguel)	You know, I do want my mom to be proud of me. I also want my friends to respect me.
Therapist (Ramirez)	Miguel, you say that like those two things have to be different, your mother's being proud of you and your friends' respect for you.

Client	I feel like they are different. My mom is only proud when I do good in school and act like I did when I was a little boy in Mexico. My friends won't respect that. [*long pause*] They want me to do the things that they do.
Therapist	Like not care about school and traditional clothing?
Client	Yeah [*long pause*] and other things.
Therapist	Other things?
Client	Hanging out. Basically doing stuff that's the opposite of what my mother wants.
Therapist	Uh huh.
Client	Sometimes I want to do both. I mean, I don't want to start wearing the clothes my mom wants me to wear [*pause*] but I do like learning, but I also like hanging out with my friends and doing different things.
Therapist	So you believe that you have to do certain things for your mom to be proud of you, like being in school. And you feel that you have to do certain things for your friends to respect you.
Client	Yeah, it's kind of hard. I don't know.
Therapist	It's hard to be so many different things to so many different people in your life.
Client	Yeah.
Therapist	And that hurts and feels impossible to do sometimes.
Client	Yeah. [*long pause*] Thank you for that, man. You really get me.

Planning and Effective Implementation. For Miguel, therapy was not easy. He was experiencing a collection of real cultural and personal dilemmas. Through a relationship that was built on mutual trust and positive regard, Miguel was able to experience these dilemmas in a different light. He surmised that while he valued all of the relationships in his life and many of the behaviors expected in these often competing relationships, he would have to decide for himself how to act on his own values while respecting and responding to the values of people he loved.

Miguel developed insight into his complicity to act without really considering what he wanted or how that might affect his relationships, particularly with his mother and in school. With Ramirez, Miguel began to accept his dilemmas and conflicting feelings and learned to match his internal values with his choices and relationships.

CHAPTER REVIEW

SUMMARY AND COMMENTARY ▶▶

The person-centered approach relies on freeing the client's own potential through a facilitative relationship. A therapist's qualities of empathy, unconditional positive regard, and genuineness constitute the basis of such a relationship and have been found to be demonstrably effective in creating positive outcomes when measured from the client's perceptions. Person-centered therapy has a variety of offshoots that are more or less directive and more or less connected to other approaches. Likewise, person-centered therapy has often been regarded as a necessary foundation to most successful therapies and foreshadowed the current zeitgeist for common factors and empirically supported therapy approaches. Person-centered therapy seems to work through helping clients to accept difficult experiences, integrate them, and find more successful perceptions and actions through which to live their lives.

Table 6.4 provides additional information on the relevance of person-centered therapy. As can be seen in this table, person-centered therapy is used in a variety of settings with different populations presenting with a host of concerns. Therapy grounded in this theoretical approach can be brief or long term (one to multiple sessions) and offered in rural or urban settings. Qualified professionals who practice person-centered therapy have the potential to be reimbursed by insurance companies for their services.

▼ TABLE 6.4

Brief Overview of Current Therapy Practice

Variable	Current Application
Type of service delivery setting	Private practice Community mental health centers Clinics Psychiatric hospitals Health care settings Substance abuse clinics Military Social service agencies

Variable	Current Application
Population	Children Youth Adults Couples Families Groups Organizations
Type of presenting problems	Wide range of presenting problems
Severity of presenting problems	Wide range of severity of presenting problems
Adapted for short-term approach	Yes
Length of treatment	One to multiple sessions
Ability to receive reimbursement	Yes
Certification in approach	No additional required certification
Training in educational programs	A master's degree or a doctoral degree
Location	Urban Rural Suburban
Type of delivery system	HMO PPO Fee for service
Fits with DSM diagnoses	No

CRITICAL THINKING QUESTIONS

1. Consider an occasion in your life when you were judged and conditions of worth were placed on you. How did this affect your feelings about yourself and those people who established these conditions? How might you have experienced the occasion differently had these conditional feelings not been present?

2. Do you believe that Rogers's core conditions are both necessary and sufficient for client growth? What is it about these core conditions that leads you to that belief?

3. Do you think that working from the nondirective attitude is an effective way to work with clients? Consider ethical, political, and scientific reasons for and against this approach.

4. Have you ever experienced someone who seems to be a brilliant practitioner of *wu wei?* Can you imagine how that person might interact with a person who comes from a cultural group that sees the mental health professional as an authority?

5. What would prevent you from practicing person-centered therapy in a relatively pure fashion? Consider obstacles at a personal, work setting, political, or other level.

6. Where do you see your limitations in being able to provide empathy, warmth, and genuineness with clients? Consider skills, attitudes, and knowledge.

7. In what ways have you observed therapists, your supervisor, or yourself practice or integrate person-centered therapy?

SUGGESTED READINGS: IMPORTANT PRIMARY SOURCES ▶▶

Books

Axline, V. (1947). *Play therapy.* Boston, MA: Houghton Mifflin.

Bozarth, J. (2000). *Person-centered therapy: A revolutionary paradigm.* Bath, UK: Bath Press.

Bozarth, J. D., & Brodley, B. T. (1991). Actualization: A functional concept in client-centered psychotherapy: A statement. *Journal of Social Behavior and Personality, 6*(5), 45–59.

Cornelius-White, J. H. D. (Ed.). (2012). *Carl Rogers: The China diary.* Ross-on-Wye, UK: PCCS Books.

Glauser, A. S., & Bozarth, J.D. (2001). Person-centered counseling: The culture within. *Journal of Counseling and Development, 79*(2), 142–147.

Rogers, C. R. (1957). The necessary and sufficient conditions of therapeutic personality change. *Journal of Consulting Psychology, 21,* 95–103.

Rogers, C. R. (1963). The concept of the fully functioning person. *Psychotherapy: Theory, Research & Practice, 1,* 17–26.

Rogers, C. R. (1975). Empathic: An unappreciated way of being. *Counseling Psychologist, 5,* 2–9.

Rogers, C. R., Lyon, H., & Tausch, R. (2013). *On becoming an effective teacher: Person-centered teaching, psychology, philosophy, and dialogues with Carl R. Rogers.* New York, NY: Routledge.

Journals

The Humanistic Psychologist: http://www.tandf.co.uk/journals/titles/08873267.asp

Journal of Humanistic Counseling: http://onlinelibrary.wiley.com/journal/10.1002/(ISSN)2161-1939

Journal of Humanistic Psychology: http://jhp.sagepub.com

Person-Centered and Experiential Psychotherapies: www.pce-world.org

The Person-Centered Journal: http://adpca.org/journal

Self & Society: http://ahpb.org/index.php/self-society-journal

Websites

Association for the Development of the Person-Centered Approach: adpca.org/node/24

British Association for the Person-Centered Approach: http://www.bapca.org.uk

Carl R. Rogers Collection, 1902–1990: digital.library.ucsb.edu/collections/show/17

PCCS Books: http://www.pccs-books.co.uk (Publisher dedicated to person-centered and critical contemporary psychological theory and practice)

The Person-Centered Website: http://www.pca-online.net

World Association for Person-Centered and Experiential Psychotherapy and Counseling: http://www.pce-world.org

GESTALT THEORY

CHAPTER 7

Introduction

Although gestalt therapy predates the 1960s (e.g., *Gestalt Therapy: Excitement and Growth in Human Personality,* written by Perls, Hefferline, and Goodman, appeared in 1951), both professional and public awareness of gestalt therapy underwent dramatic growth during the 1960s, and during that decade it contributed substantially to what was called the third wave in psychology (Sinay, 1997; Smith, 1992). The phrase "third wave" was used to refer to a number of different but related approaches that opposed various features of psychoanalysis and behaviorism and sometimes opposed nearly everything that those approaches had achieved and promised to accomplish. The surge of innovative thinkers and therapists (e.g., James Bugental, Eleanor Criswell, Viktor Frankl, Abraham Maslow, Rollo May, Virginia Satir, Carl Rogers, Irvin Yalom) did not stop at opposition; they also offered viable and well-thought-out replacements for approaches many saw devoid of qualities pertaining to human values, dignity, welfare, and personal growth. This chapter covers one such approach that was in opposition to therapy's old guard. Gestalt therapy's explicit position is that the client–therapist relationship should be free of contact inhibitors, for example, interacting with the client as a person and not as an object for "mechanical processing," pursuing a type of mutual relationship that dramatically raises the possibility for clients to enact their human potential through greater self-awareness.

LEARNING OBJECTIVES

After reading this chapter, each student should be able to:

1. Articulate the contributions of the key figures in the development of gestalt theory and therapy.

2. Summarize the philosophical, artistic, historical, and psychological approaches that influenced the development of gestalt therapy.

3. Compare and contrast gestalt psychology and gestalt therapy.

4. Discuss the basic concepts underlying gestalt therapy, including views on human nature, organism and environment, figure and ground, personality, development, topdog and underdog, and character.

5. Describe the therapeutic process of gestalt therapy, including resistance, assessment and diagnosis, the therapeutic goal, the therapist's role, the client's role, and the process of change.

6. Assess the circumstances under which the various therapeutic "experiments" would be appropriate.

7. Evaluate gestalt therapy's multicultural, social justice, and ethical implications, determining where challenges may arise in the course of therapy.

8. Discuss research findings relating to the effectiveness of gestalt therapy and its various techniques.

Specifically, gestalt's key to dislodge clients from faulty perception, mental confusion, and failure to get the better of defeat rests with what is called "present-moment awareness."

THE HYPOTHETICAL CASE OF A DREAM WITHIN A DREAM

Dr. Frederick "Fritz" Perls concludes his demonstration of gestalt principles at the Esalen Institute. As participants slowly drift out of the room, the only other person remaining in the room approaches Perls. Hearing footsteps approaching from behind him, Perls turns and

(Continued)

(Continued)

experiences an uncanny sense of familiarity when he first glances up at the person who has already started to introduce himself. "Dr. Perls, my name is Dr. Manitou, but you can call me 'M' like most of my patients." Perls notices M is wearing a colorful baseball cap with an unusual design stitched into the fabric (the design appears at the end of this section).

M I'm a psychiatrist just like you are, and I have traveled for a long time to get here and watch you perform. I enjoyed your talk about "topdog"—the shoulds and oughts we carry around in our head—and "underdog." They're like two bull terriers fighting it out because they're fighting over the same bone. [*Pauses*] I've spent considerable time and effort to get here to hear you and see you perform. I'm very, very impressed. I do have a couple of questions, questions I've been unable to find an answer to and would like to hear your opinion. My questions have to do with a book I wrote and how members of my professional affiliation reacted so critically—I think my career is at a turning point. Is this a good time to ask you a couple of questions?

Perls [*Smiles and gestures for M to sit in a chair across from him.*] Funny thing about questions is that it always seems that the questioner already knows the answers.

M What? I don't understand.

Perls Let's not get trapped by a bunch of questions. If I answer your questions, we'll just spend our time exercising our intellectualizing muscle rather than attempting a much more meaningful exchange.

M Okay—what should I do? I mean—where should we start?

Perls Let's pretend you're seated directly across from one of your critics. Imagine the critic is seated in the empty chair next to mine. What do you say to your critic?

M I would tell . . . [*Perls interrupts.*]

Perls Don't look at me; talk to the critic in the chair. The person is right in front of you in the chair at this moment.

M You said the book was confusing. Maybe you're just too stupid to realize it contributes to our profession. I'm building on what I learned and experienced. You said that I am no longer a believer in the form of therapy I was trained in, that I'm a heretic and should be thrown out because my theory differs so greatly from others who practice this therapy.

Perls Too wordy. Are you aware your breathing is now out of sync with your body?

M No.

Perls You reacted excitedly, anxiously when you directed criticism toward your critic. Sometimes when we're excited, we don't breathe and the heart is stressed—like you were doing, like a fish out of water.

M What is a person to do? [*Perls interrupts.*]

Perls Person? You and I are here; is there someone else in this room? [*Pauses*] To cope with anxiety, we need to breathe. Take a moment to breathe in fully. Hold your breath. Now relax. Breathe out. Imagine exhaling all the carbon dioxide out. You're getting rid of all the bad air before you take in another deep breath of fresh air. [*Perls spends a brief period concentrating on M's breathing before he introduces an activity for M to experiment with.*] Okay M, that's good. Now imagine your critic is seated across from you. What is the critic saying to you?

M As psychiatrists go, you really are crappy—a crappy thinker who doesn't want to hear the truth.

Perls Crappy?

M Not crappy—more like shitty.

Perls   Say, "Fritz, you're treating me shitty."

M   Hmm, Fritz you're treating me shitty. [*Long pause*] No—that's not right. I'm the one who has been treating me shitty!

Perls   Go back to the critic in the chair.

M   Who are you to judge my work? Is it shitty because you don't have the guts to question the therapy's creator—THE all-knowing father figure! I have a thriving practice back home. A lot of my clients are better because I'm not afraid to try something different. [*Long pause*] Why did I let you and others get to me? I'm feeling, acting like everyone else's problems pale next to what I feel and think. I'm being a crybaby.

Perls   Say the last part again: "I'm a crybaby."

M   I'm a crybaby. After all these years, I need to grow up.

Perls   Louder. Say this much louder.

M   I'm a crybaby! After all these years, I need to grow up!

Perls   AGAIN!

M   I'M A CRY BABY. AFTER ALL THESE YEARS, I NEED TO GROW UP!

Perls   Are you aware that you closed your eyes and pulled into your body when you were saying these things?

M   My eyes, but not my body.

Perls   Okay. I want you to shut your eyes. Squeeze them shut—tighter—now tighter. Relax your eyes but keep them shut. Now, while keeping your eyelids shut, pull in your body, your arms, now your legs. Ball up. Hold this position. Hold this position. Relax now, but keep your eyelids shut. [*Before speaking, Perls takes two long puffs on his cigarette.*] What are you feeling right now?

M   I remember. [M's voice drifts off and becomes inaudible.]

Perls   Pay attention to how you are feeling at the moment. What are you feeling right now?

M   I feel empty and alone—like a little child.

Perls   How old are you?

M   Six? No, I'm eight.

Perls   Keep your eyes shut. As an 8-year-old child, what do you hear?

M   I hear and see my father across from me at the dinner table, and he is criticizing me, calling me what he always calls me—a good-for-nothing shit!

Perls   Open your eyes. Look at the chair next to me. Who is seated there?

M   My father. I can tell from his eyes he's the one who is frightened and uncertain this time.

Perls   Remember your earlier remarks about topdog and underdog? [*M nods yes.*] Okay, imagine your dad is seated in this empty chair next to me and he is dressed up as topdog and you're the 8-year-old dressed up as underdog. Talk to your father who is now seated in the empty chair across from you. What do you say?

M   Father, the joke is on you. When I'm underdog, I'm more powerful than you. I have the power to screw up all your demands, things you wanted me to do but I don't want to . . . [*Perls interrupts.*]

Perls   You're being phony.

M   Phony?

Perls   Yes "phony." I'm sure you sometimes mess things up or screw them up, as you are saying to your father in the chair—we all do this—but you don't believe it. While you were saying this to your father, your body and face were saying you don't like being given the role of underdog to play.

M   I'm topdog, too. I use underdog to get back, but I allow topdog to beat me up because I let others tell me if I have value. My dad,

(Continued)

(Continued)

still, even though he's dead. [*M pauses and starts to smile.*] I spent much of my life, even here with you, out of sync. I've been running back and forth between extremes. Just like today when I felt a bout of self-doubt and dejection coming on which caused me to stay and speak with you. I've been letting others—starting with my father—define what I want from life.

Perls Any last words for either underdog or topdog?

M I'm not perfect and I'm not a worthless shit. It's been awhile since I felt as I do at this moment.

Perls And that feels like?

M I can definitely say it's like a bag of cement has been taken off my back. Do you understand what I mean?

Perls Yah, I do.

As M walks toward the exit, he suddenly turns and bows toward Perls while removing the baseball cap he was wearing. Perls sees that the same logo stitched on the baseball cap has also been written in the center of a shaved bald spot near the top of M's head. M looks directly at Perls who realizes that M now has the appearance of someone he knows well even though he cannot recall the person's name. M, who also looks very professorial, throws a book at Perls's feet. When Perls looks up from watching the book hit the dusty floor, he notices M possesses a grin like a Cheshire cat. In one of M's hands is the end of a very long rope, which meanders about the room's floor. Perls's eyes follow the rope from its start in M's hand to its end. The end has been fashioned into a hangman's knot that has been placed around the neck of a woman in the far distance. Perls notices M's disturbingly large grin has been replaced with a gaping hole with two large fangs. Pieces of flesh begin to slump away from M's body until the now emaciated M suddenly disappears from view completely.

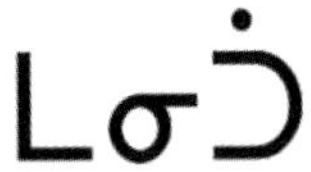

Additional background information: On awakening from this dream, Perls immediately recalls the documentary film about Algonquian Indians he watched the previous evening, and he recalls that an image very much like the one on M's baseball cap was said to symbolize a supernatural spirit called the *Gitchi Manitou,* a spirit that served to connect all parts of the world together (Figure 7.1). This supernatural entity had control over various elements of the world, such as animals, plants, trees, mountains, and rivers. Near the end of this chapter (section titled "Critical Thinking Problems/Questions"), you will be asked to reconsider Perls's dream. Specifically, you will be asked to differentiate how three different types of therapists (i.e., gestalt, psychoanalytic, and Adlerian) might utilize the reported dream in therapy.

▼ FIGURE 7.1

Symbol for Manitou

Historical Context

Although Fritz Perls is widely recognized as the person primarily responsible for the creation of and popularization of gestalt therapy, his spouse, Laura Perls, also shares credit with Fritz for the approach's initial developments as well as subsequent contributions and applications that bear her own unique style and perspective to gestalt therapy (Figure 7.2). (It should also be mentioned that although much is known about Fritz's life, much less is known about Laura's life, a person who was not driven, like Fritz, to be in the spotlight.) When Fritz and Laura settled in the United States and opened a clinic in New York City, others individuals such as Sylvester Eastman, Isadore From,

Paul Goodman, Ralph Hefferline, Elliot Shapiro, and Paul Weiss joined the couple and expanded on the work started by Fritz and Laura. Paul Weiss is especially notable for introducing Fritz to Zen Buddhism, which he infused into his conceptualization and application of gestalt therapy.

Fritz and Laura Perls

In 1893, the third child of a Jewish couple, Amelia and Nathan Perls, was born in one of Germany's ghettos. The problematic nature of this third child seemed to be sealed from birth—both for the child and the parents. Fritz's delivery was lengthy and difficult, with the physician relying on forceps to seize, hold, and then pull Fritz into a world already occupied by two sisters. Else, the oldest, was blind, and the other, Grete, was remembered by Fritz as being a "tomboy" who preferred boy's clothes and activities.

Fritz's earliest memories suggest he was born into a family environment that can be described as conflict saturated, and as Fritz's strong personality surfaced, he soon made his own unique contribution to the conflicted dynamics of an already troubled family. As a youth, he was reported to have peered under women's dresses (a behavior that went well beyond what was viewed as childhood curiosity); he was caught forging his parents' signatures; while at school, his behaviors became so disruptive he was expelled from school; he was discovered masturbating, which led to a doctor's visit and medicine being prescribed; and, when he was older, he failed to learn the basic skills associated with working at a store. Fritz's relationship with his father became so lopsided and diametric in nature that his father stopped speaking to him. Although everyone involved with Fritz hoped that something would alter Fritz's path, it was Fritz himself who assumed responsibility for his future.

▼ FIGURE 7.2

Frederick ("Fritz") Salomon Perls and Laura Perls

Fritz applied and was accepted to another school. Not only was Fritz surprised about the acceptance, he was astonished to find himself in an environment that fit his personal interest. The school was awash with philosophy, poetry, and, his greatest love at the time, the theater. Fritz finally felt connected to a world in which he flourished and grew. This was especially true when it came to the theater. He was intrigued by how actors could assume the roles they played, taking on characteristics they did not personally possess. This experience foreshadowed various therapeutic strategies later used by Fritz, such as having clients emote to an empty chair—acting as if a person was actually present in the empty chair. It was during these years that Fritz became fascinated by Max Reinhardt, manager of the German Theater, whose application of expressionistic techniques stressed the emotional dimension of life. An expressionistic approach to theater meant a director was not confined to preconceived ideas of how an actor should appear or speak on stage; rather, actors were free to display subjective reactions to various features of a play's story. In addition, expressionistic applications often resulted in everyday realities being expressed in abstract or symbolic ways that could be experienced but were difficult to describe in everyday words. The 1920 film *The Cabinet of Dr. Caligari* beautifully illustrates what fascinated Fritz about expressionism. Acting in the movie is characterized by jerks or sudden starts and stylized patterns of movements that create dancelike scenes. Painted sets for the movie depict images in abstract forms that often relied on jagged depictions of everyday objects. One of the frames from the motion picture is shown in Figure 7.3. In a short autobiography, Fritz wrote the following: "Oh, I wished Max Reinhardt, the founder of modern theater, had been there to listen to me! I wanted to make the stage real, turn the world into a stage.

▼ FIGURE 7.3

Scene From a German Expressionistic Film

Sources: Robert Wiene, director, died 1938; Rudolf Meinert, producer, died 1943; Erich Pommer, producer, died 1966; Hans Janowitz, writer, died 1954; Carl Mayer, writer, died 1944; Willy Hameister, Cinematographer, died 1938; - the movie Das Cabinet des Dr. Caligari, PD-US, https://en.wikipedia.org/w/index.php?curid=26998065.

Three dimensions, canvas, painted props" (F. Perls, 2012, pp. 1–2). It is not difficult to see the impact that theater had on the way Fritz was to eventually conceptualize and structure the process of therapy. For example, without a doubt, dreams often possess expressionistic qualities, and it was such qualities that Fritz hoped to transform so clients could absorb these qualities as they acted out their dreams.

Fritz decided to pursue a degree in medicine, a pursuit that was interrupted by his desire to serve in World War I. Due to a heart condition, Fritz was rejected for service. He sought another route to experience the war: He volunteered for the Red Cross. The war left a deep impression on Fritz. In addition to the oppressive treatment he received for being Jewish, Fritz witnessed shockingly cruel and brutal acts perpetrated on others. Before the war's end, Fritz was wounded and experienced the chaos created by Germany's introduction of chemical warfare into the war. The primary purpose was to incapacitate soldiers by inflicting blistered skin, lung damage, and blindness (death occurred with sufficient exposure).

After the war, Fritz fell into a period of extreme apathy that lingered until he discovered he could reduce his apathetic feelings by frequenting Berlin's cafés. Spending his time among intellectuals, expressionists, Dadaist artists, and others who insisted on living each day to its fullest. These associations served to revitalize Fritz enough for him to return to the university and complete his doctor of medicine studies. Believing he could thrive in New York City, Fritz left Berlin for America. He hoped to obtain the right to practice medicine, but his plans were thwarted by his inability to speak English proficiently. He returned to Berlin and moved in with his mother, all of which exacerbated the negative feelings and the self-doubt that always seemed to lay dormant throughout his life until external situations fostered their resurrection. It was only after establishing an ongoing sexual relationship that Fritz felt revived enough to improve the quality of his social life. Even more important was his decision to seek a career as a psychoanalytic therapist.

Among the therapists he encountered and learned from was Karen Horney, who encouraged Fritz to seek out Wilhelm Reich, a difficult but brilliant innovator in the psychoanalytic movement (a radical thinker who was eventually rejected by traditional analysts). Reich's influence on Perls was significant. Reich taught Perls the importance of taking an active role in therapy (i.e., going beyond just talk so that psychological tensions trapped in a client's body could be located and released) and methods to increase therapy's impact by having clients focus on the *how* of their behavior rather than understanding the *why* of their behavior.

Fritz met Laura (originally Lore) Posner while she was working with Kurt Goldstein, who was utilizing gestalt theory to better understand patients with brain lesions (Table 7.1). Laura was a gifted dancer and musician whose love of the arts became a part of her later therapeutic worldview. Fritz and Laura were drawn together and soon married. With Adolf Hitler's ascent to power, the couple decided to move their young family to South Africa where both Fritz and Laura became highly successful and well-known therapists. At this time Fritz and Laura viewed themselves as Freudian therapists interested in making a contribution to their practiced approach. But three events (which seemed to affect Fritz on a deep personal level) altered their alliance to Freudian therapy and eventually led to their co-creation of an alternative approach. First, Fritz was invited to present at a psychoanalytic conference, but his expressed views were considered by others at the conference as a deviation from well-established procedures and principles set to guide therapists. Second, a brief (less than 5 minutes) audience with Freud turned out to be a severe disappointment. Fritz's perception of the encounter was that of "being dismissed by the master." Third, Fritz's book *Ego, Hunger and Aggression* (1947) represented a greater departure from Freud's position than either Fritz or Laura realized. (In the book's first edition, Fritz acknowledged the important role and contributions made by Laura to this work.)

Ego, Hunger and Aggression was a precursor to what Fritz was to later term *gestalt therapy*. The publication set the stage for maintaining a holistic perspective of clients,

Laura Posner Perls (1905–1990): Cofounder of Gestalt Therapy

Similar to Fritz Perls, Laura Perls was initially attracted to Sigmund Freud's work, which started in her youth when the young intellectual obtained a copy of Freud's *The Interpretation of Dreams.* Early in Laura's life, she displayed a strong inclination toward academics and the art of dance and playing classical piano. (Both music and dance are excellent examples of nonverbal communication—such early artistic interests seem to mesh nicely with Laura's later focus on a client's nonverbal messages during therapy sessions.) During her pursuit of a doctorate at Frankfurt University, she encountered several intellectual luminaries of her time, including Paul Tillich and Martin Buber, both of whom pursued the meaning of human existence, and Max Wertheimer, who was associated with the founding of academic gestalt psychology. (As discussed elsewhere in this chapter, gestalt psychology should not to be confused with gestalt therapy.) During a seminar that Kurt Goldstein presented on the topic of gestalt psychology research, Laura recalls seeing Fritz Perls (who was attending the seminar) for the first time. (Fritz was 33 and Laura was 21 years old.) Laura remembers thinking at the time, "I was very young, naïve and inexperienced . . . yah, he was very impressive" (Gaines, 1979, p. 7). They were married in 1930 in Berlin, Germany. After obtaining her PhD, Laura sought training in psychoanalysis during which time she encountered and was influenced by several well-known analysts. During the early years of the Perls's marriage, Germany was increasingly falling under the influence of Adolph Hitler; as a result, significant violence and oppression were directed at Jewish inhabitants, so the couple escaped Germany and eventually settled from 1934 to 1946 in Johannesburg, South Africa. About that time, Laura Perls said, "We were terribly in love with each other" (Gaines, 1979, p. 19). In South Africa the seeds of their new form of therapy were planted, glimpses of which were expressed in a work on which Laura collaborated with Fritz to write and publish in 1942 titled *Ego, Hunger and Aggression.* This work expressed a break from the position of psychoanalysis by conceptualizing human understanding in terms of a holistic philosophical approach. According to Laura Perls,

[In] *Ego, Hunger and Aggression*, we changed from the historical-archaeological Freudian viewpoint to the existential-experiential, from piecemeal association psychology to a holistic approach, from the purely verbal to the organismic, from interpretation to direct awareness in the Here and Now, from transference to actual contact, from the concept of the Ego as a substance having boundaries to a concept of it as the very boundary phenomenon itself, being the actual contact function of identification and alienation. (Litt, 2000, p. 1)

The couple eventually left South Africa and arrived in Manhattan, New York, in 1946. At their new location they continued to refine their approach to therapy, an approach that Laura Perls stated "didn't have a name" until the 1951 publication of *Gestalt Therapy: Excitement and Growth in Human Personality* (Gaines, 1979, p. 29). According to Laura, of the three authors responsible for *Gestalt Therapy,* Paul Goodman deserved to share substantive credit for gestalt therapy's eventual shape and structure. Although *Gestalt Therapy* received sparse notice initially, attention continued to grow, and eventually gestalt therapy acquired a noticeable impact in the United States and elsewhere. Soon after the 1951 publication, Laura and Fritz established the New York Gestalt Institute, which was managed by Laura even after the estranged relationship between her and Fritz reached its conclusion.

Fritz became increasingly restless and eventually settled at the Esalen Institute on the Pacific Coast, where, according to Litt (2000), Fritz "developed a more flamboyant, theatrical 'California' style [of gestalt therapy] and became somewhat of a hippie, with a flowing white beard and flower-power clothes. Laura continued the more traditional East Coast style of gestalt therapy" (p. 1). The group therapy approaches that were practiced by Laura and Fritz also moved in different directions; Fritz's demonstrative style was individually focused and aimed to shine a light on the person in the "hot seat," and Laura's equalitarian style reached out to all the members of a group and provided ample opportunities for all to participate. In addition, while Laura continued to work as an individual and group therapist who believed strongly in the value of both therapy formats, Fritz's interest shifted away from conducting individual therapy sessions. In hindsight, it is not surprising that Laura Perls did not receive the recognition she deserved as the cofounder of gestalt therapy. In large measure Fritz Perls's innate showmanship personality led him to take center stage; for example, during demonstrations of gestalt techniques, he often displayed an amazing ability to provoke rapt attention among those observing him. Even though wide recognition for Laura's role as joint creator of gestalt therapy was not immediate, such recognition grew over time, as did recognition for her devotion to honing gestalt therapy's methods and to make known the degree to which respect and support played a critical role in this form of therapy. It required a number of years before just recognition reached all the various pockets of interested parties that had formed pertaining to gestalt therapy. For several decades Fritz Perls's long shadow continued to linger and concealed the contributions made by others, especially those that Laura had made to therapy practice, training of therapists, and theory. For example, in 1982, when Laura publically demonstrated the use of gestalt therapy before a large gathering of professionals in Germany, many of the attendees made their disappointment known because she had failed to illustrate what they had simplistically equated *to be* gestalt therapy, that is, Fritz's "hot seat" technique (Litt, 2000, p. 1). In the end, when all is weighed and measured, it is truly correct to state that gestalt therapy would not be gestalt therapy as we know it today if either Fritz's or Laura's contributions to its development were absent from the mix.

incomplete emotional expression affecting clients, the importance of being present-oriented throughout therapy, and processing what is obtained from maintaining a body-centered focus. Worse than the experience of having relatively few copies sold, this publication was viewed as a heretical work by Freudians, who relegated its content as far outside the scope of meaningful psychoanalytic practice.

The early 1940s was a turbulent period for the family. Fritz moved to New York City and was later joined by Laura and their two children, but by the late 1940s life began to settle into a pattern. In his autobiography Fritz wrote,

> In 1950, the awareness theory crystallized itself, and I coined the term "Gestalt Therapy." Designed experiments relating to the topology of awareness, to the mix-up of self and world awareness. *Gestalt Therapy*, with R. Hefferline and P. Goodman as co-authors, appeared as a book. It was jeered at by the academic gestalt psychologists, but Gestalt Therapy turned out to be no-fly-by-night: sales were increasing year by year. (F. Perls, 2012, p. 6)

The ever restless Fritz spent increasing amounts of time away from New York traveling to different training sites to spread word of this new form of treatment. In the early 1960s, Fritz experienced another period of pessimism and despondency and became convinced his age had caught up with him—he felt debilitated and inadequate. Believing the better part of his life was behind him Fritz relocated to Miami, Florida, and isolated himself in a small, dark, and dingy apartment. It was during this period that Fritz reported experimenting with LSD, a period in his life when he stated he finally grasped fully that "the experienced phenomenon was the ultimate Gestalt! It was not religion-oriented like Buber, Tillich and Marcel; nor language-oriented like Heidegger; nor communist-oriented like Sartre; nor psychoanalytically oriented like Binswinger" (F. Perls, 2012, p. 7).

While in Miami, Fritz was approached by Jim Simkin and Wilson Van Dusen. Although at first Fritz was reluctant, they convinced him to join the Esalen Institute in Big Sur, California. The decision turned out to be the right one for him and for gestalt therapy. The move supplied the impetus and conditions for Fritz to overcome his personal slump and start a new phase in his life, and Esalen served as the springboard for gaining wider attention for his form of gestalt therapy. From 1966 through 1968, Fritz's impact achieved full tilt. Taking up residence at Esalen allowed him to lecture and demonstrate various aspects of gestalt therapy while making it clear the demonstrations, what he referred to as "my circus," were not to be equated with actual gestalt therapy. However, he also asserted that what he demonstrated and spoke about had implications for achieving personal growth since gestalt therapy's theoretical foundation had wide applicability and was not limited solely to carrying out therapy. Esalen became a Mecca in the 1960s, drawing many key figures and contributors to new movements taking shape during the decade, and Fritz was correct to refer to Esalen as the "center for the third wave of humanistic psychology" (F. Perls, 2012, p. 9). The time was right for both Fritz the person and his form of gestalt therapy to take center stage.

A large segment of America's youth in the 1960s perceived the established American life as essentially phony. Societal roles once sought after suddenly took on an aura of having been manufactured without concern for individual differences. One only has to consider the confluence of numerous and troublesome events that were flowing together to understand why the word *plastic* acquired a new meaning during the decade—it was used to refer to those who were living an inauthentic existence, who were busy trying to psychologically protect themselves from what was taking place in America.

The counterculture movement that took shape in the late 1960s attracted members who were actively searching for more choices than what mainstream America had to offer. Fritz Perls's message—that many in American society were living a phony existence that seriously curtailed opportunities for actualizing their unique potentials—was a message that resonated throughout the counterculture. Table 7.2 is a brief snapshot of some of the events occurring from 1966 to 1969 that point to a social and political fabric that had become frayed and was in need of a new direction.

Fritz Perls (who was accused of being a hippie by some gestalt therapists) captured the spirit and much of the mood displayed by members of the counterculture when he wrote the gestalt prayer. The prayer took on an infamous quality for those who mistook Fritz's ode as a message that exalted a narcissistic, self-centered lifestyle. A fuller understanding of Fritz's worldview and the role that gestalt therapy could serve to promote positive human advancement (both inside therapy and on a societal level) contradicts such an interpretation. Fritz's well-known and widely circulated ode was intended to celebrate living the life of a mature individual who is free of neurotic attachments.

I do my thing, and you do your thing.

I am not in this world to live up to your expectations.

And you are not in this world to live up to mine.

You are you and I am I,

And if by chance we find each other, it's beautiful.

If not, it can't be helped. (F. Perls, 1969, p. 4)

Fritz Perls died on March 14, 1970. His last words to the nurse in his hospital room were "Don't tell me what to do." It is difficult to believe a more fitting epitaph could be found for such a fiercely independent individual. Laura Perls, who remained at the New York Institute for Gestalt Therapy rather than follow Fritz Perls, continued to reside there until her death in 1990. While Fritz's interests had increasingly focused on developing the therapeutic action and confrontation aspects of gestalt therapy, Laura's interests focused more on issues of contact and the supports involved in assisting clients to change and grow during gestalt therapy (Fagan & Shepherd, 1970; Houston, 2003; Shepard, 1975; Sinay, 1997; Stoehr, 1994; Wheeler, 2013). Even during long periods of separation, both found common ground on many issues, and both spoke out against the

A Sample of Events 1966–1970

1966
<ul><li>John Lennon makes the controversial remark about the Beatles: "We are more popular than Jesus now."</li><li>Protests against the Vietnam War escalate after the Selective Service is instructed to induct 100,000.</li><li>Black Panther Party for Self-Defense is organized.</li><li>National Organization for Women (NOW) is founded after plans are written on a napkin by Betty Friedan.</li><li>LSD becomes illegal in California.</li></ul>

1967
<ul><li>The Great Human Be-In is held at Golden Gate Park in San Francisco, where former Harvard professor Timothy Leary encourages the 30,000 attendees to "turn on, tune in, and drop out."</li><li>The U.S. Supreme Court rules that laws prohibiting mixed-race marriages are unconstitutional.</li><li>Criminal charges are lodged against Muhammad Ali for refusing to be drafted into the U.S. Army. Ali's heavyweight boxing title is taken from him.</li><li>The Beatles' album *Sergeant Pepper's Lonely Hearts Club Band*, with its counterculture message, tops various charts around the world.</li><li>For the third year, race riots flare up in major U.S. urban areas. President Johnson creates a commission to assess the reasons for reoccurring riots.</li></ul>

1968
<ul><li>Dr. Martin Luther King, Jr., is assassinated in Memphis, Tennessee.</li><li>Democratic presidential front runner Robert F. Kennedy is shot at the Ambassador Hotel in Los Angeles and dies 26 hours later.</li><li>Violent protest occurs outside the Democratic National Convention held in Chicago while it is televised in real time.</li><li>Republican Richard M. Nixon of California promises to get tough with what is taking place in the nation and is elected the 37th president of the United States.</li></ul>

1969
<ul><li>Harvard's administration building is occupied by more than 300 students, many of whom are members of the Students for a Democratic Society.</li><li>Approximately 100 American Indians occupy Alcatraz Island to protest treatment of Native Americans.</li><li>The "Smothers Brothers Comedy Hour" increasingly aligns itself with key ideas of the counterculture, which eventually leads to CBS canceling the popular show.</li><li>Charles Manson's "Helter Skelter" is initiated with the slaughter of several people, including the pregnant Sharon Tate.</li><li>Woodstock is held on Max Yasgur's farm and attracts 400,000 attendees.</li><li>"Woodstock West" takes place at the Altamont Speedway in northern California. While the Rolling Stones play their music, members of the Hells Angels Motorcycle Club, who were recruited to maintain crowd control, kill a concert attendee named Meredith Hunter.</li></ul>

1970
<ul><li>Frederick (Fritz) Salomon Perls dies and, in accordance with his wishes, a ceremony is held at the San Francisco Auditorium, where 1,500 participants gather to celebrate his life. Many of the participants dance to express their gratitude and desire to say goodbye.</li></ul>

growing body of misconceptions about what constituted the proper practice of gestalt therapy. Self-ordained gestalt therapists who had not received any formal gestalt therapy training began to appear, especially on the West Coast and then elsewhere, a trend that led some gestalt therapists to blame Fritz for the publicity he generated (both negative and positive). In truth, the fairness of such criticism is questionable since incorrect applications have occurred throughout the history of therapy. In 1910, for instance, Freud wrote on this topic in an article titled "Observations on 'Wild' Psycho-Analysis." A contemporary example is when a public schoolteacher fails to understand the proper way to apply a technique developed to eliminate the stimulus effects of disruptive behaviors through isolating a child. In this example, the elementary schoolteacher confines an unruly student for long periods of time by placing the child in a large cardboard box that is duct-taped shut and justifies the action by calling it "time out."

Finally, within days of Fritz Perls's death, a wrangling argument began to take shape when followers of Fritz pitted themselves against those associated with the New York Institute of Gestalt Therapy. Details of this passionate dispute can be found in various publications. One such source is Rosanes-Berrett's published response to articles written by Laura Perls and Ilene Serlin that appeared in an earlier edition of the same journal (i.e., *Journal of Humanistic Psychology*). Rosanes-Berrett (1993) wrote, "This article is in response to two articles in this journal. . . . It is also a description of the troubled relationship between Laura and Fritz, which seems to have polarized their respective followers. The author, who knew both Fritz and Laura Perls very well, was deeply touched by Fritz and his work and believes that Laura and her followers have misrepresented and devalued his contributions" (p. 106).

In the last analysis, if it were possible to completely abstract either Fritz Perls's or Laura Perls's influence from gestalt therapy, it is safe to assert that whatever form of therapy remained, it would significantly differ from what currently represents gestalt therapy. To go one step further, by removing their combined influences, a plausible argument could be made that gestalt therapy would not have come into existence.

Legacy

Fritz Perls was no stranger to the perils of death, having seen it up close, along with the atrocities that shaped the face of the first global war. Fritz also was no stranger to working with clients who had failed to fulfill their unique potential, choosing instead to become mired in the inertia brought about by an uncritical acceptance of overlapping familial and societal expectations.

Beginning with what Fritz believed were small but important deviations from Freudian therapy, the end result of more than 50 years of effort resulted in a therapeutic approach that significantly differed from Fritz's starting point (F. S. Perls, 1970). In the end, Fritz had developed what he viewed as a means to foster human growth and potential—a means that rested firmly on two basic, supporting foci. First, Fritz believed it was necessary to intertwine the locational and temporal nature of therapy into a singularity that he chose to succinctly express in the phrase "here and now." In other words, gestalt therapy emphasized the therapeutic process as it was simultaneously experienced moment to moment by both the client and the therapist (Gaines, 1979). Second, Fritz believed therapists must appreciate the multidimensionality of each individual client, placing a high value on the entire person—clients' thoughts, feelings, and actions and how these elements come together to form the uniqueness present in each client. Everything else associated with the approach can be seen as representing a logical outcome derived from these two foci. A few of the contributions made to therapy in general by gestalt therapy are listed next and serve as examples:

- Seeking the integration of clients' personalities is more important than analyzing their personalities to uncover repressed incidents of psychological injury.
- Drawing attention to and then strengthening clients' present state of awareness is necessary and is best achieved by a deft focus of therapeutic attention directed toward all the avenues through which clients sense the world and express themselves.
- Confronting any blocks that interfere with clients' becoming fully cognizant of what they need to develop is a necessary ingredient for therapeutic success.
- Fostering clients' acceptance of denied or alienated parts of themselves and helping them complete significant relationship tasks that linger are necessary therapeutic actions.
- Helping clients accept that reaching their full potential requires facing the inevitable fear resulting from never knowing what emotions or what reactions may erupt as a result of growing and becoming different is also a task of the therapist.
- Recognizing that mental health implies clients have moved to a stage where they are ready to take full responsibility for their thoughts, feelings, and actions is also necessary.

Fritz's views represent a category of therapy referred to as *existential-humanistic*. This term is applied to those forms of therapy that pay careful attention to the entire person rather than highlighting a single human aspect such as behavior, cognition, motivation, or some memory tied to an underlying cause for the client's problem. The term is also applied to those explanations or approaches that espouse a belief in free will, which typically finds expression in the conviction that all people are the architect (knowingly or not) of their personal destiny.

Finally, special importance is attached to a person's subjective experiences. It is this last aspect of existential-humanistic theory that is not fully appreciated when it comes to Fritz's form of therapy. It refers to how various experiences in the real world can only exist within the mind. Furthermore, the mental shape of these experiences are unique to the particular person and are always inaccessible to others even when these others are living through the same actual events (which accounts for why eyewitness testimony is such a rich pursuit in forensic psychology). Thus, it is unnecessary to attempt the impossible by trying to uncover what "objectively" has taken place in a client's life; what is of utmost importance for the gestalt therapist is to work with the client to uncover how the client currently feels and thinks about what took place. According to Frew (2008), the chief foundation on which gestalt therapy was built is composed of phenomenology, the dialogue carried on, and field therapy. These areas lay critical importance on the pattern of interrelationship established by the dynamic contributions made by both the therapist and the client. Table 7.3 provides a glimpse into Fritz and Laura's worldview.

▼ TABLE 7.3

Quotable Fritz Perls and Laura Perls

- The only state in which you can be absolutely sure is the catatonic state, where you are dead. –Fritz Perls
- I feel suspicious about all the instant things: instant contact, instant intimacy, instant sex, instant something or other, instant joy. –Laura Perls
- If you need encouragement, praise, pats on the back from everybody, then you make everybody your judge. –Fritz Perls
- It is desirable that the therapist have more awareness and experience than the [client] and more knowledge. If you have a very well educated, erudite [client] and you know nothing or almost nothing, beyond your professional stuff, you can't cope. –Laura Perls
- Lose your mind and come to your senses. –Fritz Perls
- A myth is always truer than facts: it's an integration of experiences. –Laura Perls
- You cannot achieve happiness. Happiness happens and is a transitory stage. Imagine how happy I felt when I got relief from bladder pressure. How long did that happiness last? –Fritz Perls
- Suffering is also a part of creative living and working; it's not only a curse. –Laura Perls
- Truth can be tolerated only if you discover it yourself because then the pride of discovery makes the truth palatable. –Fritz Perls
- The pursuit of happiness, per se, even if it's written in the constitution, it's a very illegitimate pursuit, it's incidental. –Laura Perls
- Guilt is nothing but reversed resentment. –Fritz Perls
- What happened mostly in schools is a lot of stuff is presented in a way in which it is expected to be repeated on the exam. People swallow it whole and spew it out on the exam and are rid of it forever after. I've never seen people who after having learned so much and stayed in school for so many years, know so very little as they do in their country [America] it's ghastly. –Laura Perls

Sources: Perls, L. (1970, 1992); Perls, F. S. (1969). *Gestalt therapy verbatim.* Lafayette, CO: Real People Press; Rosenfeld, E. (1977). *An oral history of gestalt therapy—An interview with Laura Perls.* Retrieved from http://www.fritzperls.com/publications/an-oral-history-of-gestalt-therapy/

Basic Concepts

Human Nature

Before one can accurately understand what gestalt therapy claims as its territory, one must understand that gestalt psychology and gestalt therapy overlap but are not one and the same (Table 7.4). Historically, gestalt psychologists believed that when humans encounter, observe, or undergo something over time, such experiences are taken in as a whole and not as a broken jigsaw pattern of parts. For gestalt psychologists, it is these inner processes of dynamic organization that constitute the study of psychology.

The overall definition of psychology that gestalt psychologists championed is captured in the principle of *Pragnanz*. In essence, *Pragnanz* means that human experiences are always structured in ways to perceive a meaningful totality. For example, when you recognize a friend you "perceive a friend"; you are not experiencing parts individually: voice-friend, eyes-friend, noise-friend, lips-friend, hair-friend, body-friend, movement-friend, and so forth. In fact, when some aspect of the whole differs noticeably in a friend, such as when a friend approaches you with a slight limp due to an accident, it is as if the small change ripples throughout the whole of how you perceive the person.

Gestalt psychologists are best remembered for various concepts, principles, and laws that resulted from their study of human perception. One such concept is proximity (situations where things, persons, or objects close together in space and time are seen as related to one another, i.e., creating a whole). Proximity and other concepts

Gestalt Therapy and Gestalt Psychology—"Irreconcilable" Differences

A common misconception prevails that *gestalt therapy* and *gestalt psychology* are co-equal, and if not equal, then gestalt therapy must be an extension of gestalt psychology. Fritz Perls stated "that he had never read any of the gestalt psychologists' books and that he was not a pure Gestaltist" (Schultz, 1981, p. 273). Although gestalt therapy and gestalt psychology are in fact very dissimilar in nature and purpose, they share some terminology. The most likely explanation for this can be traced to Laura Perls's academic experiences. According to Fadiman and Frager (2002), Laura Perls obtained her doctorate in gestalt psychology before becoming a psychoanalyst, and it is safe to assume that her experiences as a student led Fritz and Laura Perls to adopt some of gestalt psychology's terminology and philosophy (Barlow, 1981). Therefore, even though the precise degree to which gestalt psychology influenced gestalt therapy's creation can be debated, these two areas are not one and the same.

Sources: Barlow, A. R. (1981). Gestalt therapy and gestalt psychology: Gestalt-antecedent influence or historical accident. Retrieved from http://www.gestalt.org/barlow.htm; Fadiman, J., & Frager, R. (2002). *Personality theory and personal adjustment.* Upper Saddle River, NJ: Prentice Hall; and Schultz, D. (1981). *A history of modern psychology* (3rd ed.). New York, NY: Academic Press.

influenced psychologists' understanding of topics such as memory, insight, learning, social interactions, and aesthetic appreciation.

Gestalt Psychology and Gestalt Therapy

Of the research findings reported by gestalt psychologists, one that held great importance for Fritz was the concept of closure (i.e., persons perceiving an incomplete form, image, or sound are driven to complete the form, image, or sound). As a reader of this chapter, you can literally experience an instance of closure by looking at the blue dots that appear below. The dots, which have obvious gaps between them, are perceived as more than just seven individual dots. Our nature is to "connect the dots" and see something greater—in this case, a line.

Fritz believed that physiological and psychological incompleteness demanded closure. Furthermore, for Fritz, the failure to achieve closure was at the heart of humanity's day-to-day problems and could even serve to explain neurotic and psychotic conditions. In addition, Fritz argued that biological functioning operates according to a pervasive principle operating throughout the material universe—where Freud saw the death drive running rampant in our everyday existence, Fritz saw health as the prevailing element of existence from the earliest period of time leading up to today.

Fritz espoused the position that humans operate—think, emote, and act—as a whole functioning entity. Furthermore, as a whole all humans are much more than a simple summation of the complex systems (nervous, musculoskeletal, respiratory, circulatory, digestive) that make up the human body. It is not the parts that make each of us special; rather, it is the result of everything wrapped up and packaged within our physical skin. Each of us operates according to coordinated actions and reactions that make us who we are.

Perls also believed that not just our wholeness needed to be considered, but also that our wholeness is embedded in the outer environment or outside world. Furthermore, a basic guiding assumption of gestalt therapy is that people have the ability to self-regulate. This principle is referred to as *organismic self-regulation,* which means "the organism is striving for maintenance of an equilibrium which is continuously disturbed by its needs and regained through their gratification and elimination" (F. Perls, 1947, p. 7). This process repeats itself all the way down to the cellular level. Fritz also believed self-regulation is best described in nonmechanistic terms, for it is a natural process occurring throughout the entire organism; in fact, according to Fritz, this natural process is taking place at this moment throughout the universe.

Self-regulation also implies there is awareness in some manner or form. Organisms must be aware of themselves in order to sense an imbalance and to seek and obtain what is needed, but it should be pointed out that Fritz's form of awareness was not to be equated with what is termed *consciousness.* The two are not one and the same. Thus, while being conscious means a person is aware, awareness in Fritz's world does not guarantee the person is also completely or even partially conscious of the situation (e.g., we are not aware of imbalances in our bodies on the cellular level that require intervention of some sort, nor is it needed, nor would it add to the efficiency of this natural form of self-regulation). Finally, organism self-regulation does not guarantee health—it only means the organism does all it can with what it has at its disposal to reestablish and maintain a healthy state of existence.

Organism and Environment

Unity results from the organism and its environment, and all humans require an environment to be whole—an "environment to exchange essential substances—air, love" (F. Perls, 1969, p. 5). Without air, a person dies. If there is insufficient early nurturing, the person will wither developmentally.

The organism interacts with the environment along two avenues: either through the senses or by reacting. Both systems of interacting allow for establishing a truly amazing degree of interdependence. Whereas we have always depended on the intimate relationship we have with our environment for our health, in recent decades we have come to realize the truth in Fritz Perls's assertion that our relationship with the environment represents a true interrelationship of dependence, for now our global environment (the planet) is dependent on us humans for its health. Although the earth's environment has always posed a threat to human existence, we have entered a period of time when the sum total of humanity (increasing in number as you read this) now poses a crisis of death for what the noted futurist and inventor Buckminster Fuller called "spaceship earth."

Finally, it is important to keep in mind that when concepts such as "organism" or "environment" are discussed, other words used in conjunction with these two concepts can taint and thus distort what these two concepts are meant to convey. For example, when commonly used words such as *individual, client, person,* or *names* such as Fritz Perls are used to discuss gestalt therapy this communication implies by its very nature that these things should be considered as independent or totally self-contained entities.

Although boundaries exist and are discussed in gestalt therapy, it might be better to think of these boundaries as permeable to varying degrees since nothing or no one is totally free from or separate from what surrounds them. According to Fritz Perls, in the end everything shares a connection.

Gestalt Formation: Figure and Ground

Interestingly self-regulation's processes of awareness are tied to recognizing needs that emerge and the focused attention aimed toward fulfilling those needs to quiet the imbalance that jump-started the whole circle of events. This is where the key concept termed *gestalt* enters the picture. Fritz Perls, Laura Perls, and their colleagues concluded there was no exact word in English that corresponded to the German word *gestalt*, but its essence was referred to indirectly by a number of English words or phrases, including *unified one, something undivided, characteristic arrangement, configuration, design, set, grouping, combination of qualities, cluster, form, whole,* and *figure.* The word frequently utilized to discuss the concept in the literature is simply *figure.* Specifically, it is preferable to use the term *figure* over the other terms when discussing the concept in general, but if Fritz's form of therapy is being discussed, then the preference is to use *gestalt.*

The most prominent feature of a gestalt is revealed after we destroy the gestalt by breaking it up. The result of such an action is that the prototypical gestalt that existed once is gone; the resulting parts do not equal the original dynamic gestalt (Latner, 1973). In fact, cleaving a gestalt can extinguish it forever, as illustrated in Lewis Carroll's *Alice's Adventures in Wonderland* when all of the king's horses and all the king's men could not reassemble the pieces together to "de-extinct" the egg-shaped gestalt named Humpty Dumpty. Finally, the notion of gestalt is dependent on another concept, which is termed *ground* or *background.*

In gestalt therapy, what is undifferentiated is termed *background.* Background can be thought of as an undifferentiated soupy mixture from which reality is constructed via gestalt formation. Gestalt formation is the result of a creative process that pulls from the available background ingredients, and whatever remains outside the scope of attention comprises the undifferentiated soupy mixture or background.

Fritz Perls saw the value in destructive processes since life cannot be sustained without destruction; for humans, sustenance is inseparable from the destruction of plant and animal life for food. Fritz contended that satisfaction is tied up with destruction of the gestalt because gestalt destruction is the prelude to need fulfillment. Our lives represent a seemingly endless line of gestalt formations and destructions, all of which are tied to our needs. A final distinction should be made; a gestalt formation never causes the background to disappear since one cannot experience a gestalt without background. Gestalt and background always coexist. According to Latner (1973),

> We have seen . . . that our worlds are made of what is important to us. What is figure for us is what we know or want. The rest, phenomenological, does not exist. We create a world for ourselves according to our needs, organizing it as we live out the interplay of figure and ground. When we are interested, we are aware of what

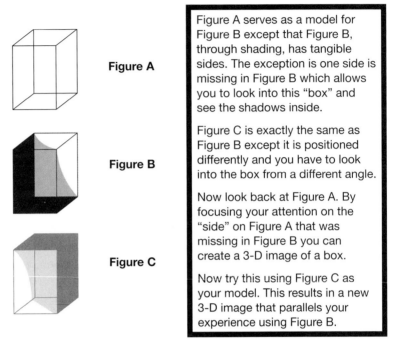

▼ FIGURE 7.4

Experiencing a Shift in Figures Using the Same Background

Figure A

Figure A serves as a model for Figure B except that Figure B, through shading, has tangible sides. The exception is one side is missing in Figure B which allows you to look into this "box" and see the shadows inside.

Figure B

Figure C is exactly the same as Figure B except it is positioned differently and you have to look into the box from a different angle.

Now look back at Figure A. By focusing your attention on the "side" on Figure A that was missing in Figure B you can create a 3-D image of a box.

Figure C

Now try this using Figure C as your model. This results in a new 3-D image that parallels your experience using Figure B.

Note: Another example of "shifting images" is provided at the start of the historical section picturing Fritz and Laura Perls. Look at the box that separates Fritz and Laura. What image do you see inside this box? Is it a flower vase or is it two faces looking at one another?

is present, as it is part of the process of discovery and invention that is the creative adjustment of the organism and the environment. Reality in this sense is flexible and changing. We make it anew continually as we live. (p. 32)

Fritz (1969) added,

Meaning is the relationship of foreground figure to its background. If you use the word "king," you have to have a background to understand the meaning of the word "king," whether it's the King of England, the king of a chess game, the chicken à la king—without its context, meaning doesn't exist. It is always created ad hoc. (p. 60)

To better understand the intimate relationship that figure and ground share, refer to Figure 7.4, which displays a Necker cube, a two-dimensional figure that allows a person to experience the moment a gestalt takes form from the background through using focused attention.

Personality and Development

Healthy Personality. Fritz Perls believed that actualizing one's innate abilities reflects healthy, mature development. Even though he aligned himself with humanism, he tended to view concepts such as Abraham Maslow's self-actualization, the highest level of human achievement and psychological health, to reflect an expression of distorted optimism concerning human existence. Such optimistic viewpoints as Maslow's simply do not give actual day-to-day existence its due. For Fritz unhappiness was as much a part of life as experiences of happiness and fulfillment.

Fragmented Personality. The opposite of achieving a mature way of moving through life occurs when we are not in touch with what we need to grow, which essentially means the person has developed an irresponsible approach to life that denotes a one-sided dependence on others. In addition, poor mental health implies the presence of a fragmented personality. Such individuals suffer holes or gaps in their personality. The fragmented personality can result from numerous factors; furthermore, such factors may become internalized at some point and operate independently of the original environmental circumstances that led to the fragmentation. For example, a society or cultural group within that society might impose its expectations on the developing child, which can result in the natural progression of early development to be sidetracked though a sort of de-actualizing blockage of growth, causing the person impacted to fail actualizing her full potential. Environments of this sort include the caste of untouchables in India or women living in regions of the world where they are viewed as "less than" the opposite sex. The latter view is often codified in such regions of the world.

Mental Processes Involved in Personality Development

The prospect of becoming a mother led Laura Perls to carefully consider the significance of infant/child experiences associated with taking in nourishment. This led to her assertion that too many parents were prematurely weaning their children from their mother's milk and moving their children to pulverized foods. Laura gave the example of the overworked parent who is consistently frustrated and impatient, who pays little attention to the actual experience of spoon feeding the child. In such situations, children will experience hurried meals that have a deleterious outcome for them because they are essentially made to "drink" their solid food rather than learn the proper way to take in food, that is, by chewing. Laura Perls was convinced the origin of the mental process termed *introjection* could be traced back to the time when a child failed to learn how to properly crush and grind his food. *Introjection* is defined as taking in ideas and information (i.e., mental food) without digesting it first, that is, without studying, pondering, or understanding. The child introjector is likely to go through life blindly accepting the beliefs and moral attitudes of others. Such a child is in danger of becoming a narrow-minded adult who can only follow an impoverished path in life that matches the "oughts, shoulds, and musts" of others.

In contrast to improper eating, chewing food correctly signifies the child is allowed the time to develop awareness of what is being chewed. Providing time for children to eat in this manner is a critical contributor for healthy child development, and Laura Perls was convinced that proper chewing, learned early in life, fostered the attainment of an ability to incorporate what is taken in later in life. (As an adult, Fritz was known to consume his food by mindfully chewing before he swallowed.) The ability to incorporate environmental elements to make them part of the person is known as *assimilation*. Assimilation is a necessary ingredient for mature and healthy living because the assimilation process enables a person to connect to the world in a variety of ways associated with full capacity learning.

Topdog and Underdog

In addition to the external forces operating on a person during development, there are also internal factors that can hinder the full expression of a healthy actualizing of one's potential. Fritz Perls reconceptualized Freud's superego, resulting in a pair of conflicting personality components. One aspect of this paired polarity is termed *topdog* and the other *underdog*, and the two compete for control.

According to Fritz Perls (1969), *topdog* (also referred to as *Super Mouse* by Fritz) is authoritarian and righteous and is the consummate bully who demands and threatens (e.g., "If you do not do such-and-such, your life will be terrible—no one will care for you or love you" or "If you do what you are thinking about, when you die you won't join your departed loved ones in heaven"). The inner voice of topdog uses words such as *ought, should,* and *must. Ought* is the weakest of the three and implies something is desirable. *Should* expresses an obligation, such as when we believe something is expected of us. Lastly, *must* (the strongest of the three) indicates a necessary condition is being imposed on us.

Using the first line only for each sentence stem below, write what comes to your mind. After completing each sentence, write the feeling you experienced responding to the particular sentence stem.

- **"I ought** _____"**

  Feeling: _____

- **"I should** _____"**

  Feeling: _____

- **"I must** _____"**

  Feeling: _____

Reflect on the sentence completions and feelings you expressed. Your responses may be very different from one another or they may all be essentially the same. The feelings you wrote may differ from one another, all may represent the same feeling or shades of the same feeling, they may strike you as being weaker or stronger than you expected, or possibly they were difficult to identify because you were somewhat emotionally numb when you completed the exercise. Considering what you have read in this chapter, write a brief comment about what you are currently experiencing as a result of this exercise. Aim to be authentic in your comment.

Comment: _____

_____

Underdog (also referred to as *Mickey Mouse*) is topdog's counterpoint. It represents that inner roadblock to taking action or doing what we believe we ought, should, and must do in life. Underdog's basic philosophy is to enjoy the day and put off worrying about what needs to be done until tomorrow. Often hiding behind a curtain constructed of excuses, apologies, defensive remarks, and crybaby tactics, the underdog's aim is always to sabotage or con topdog out of carrying through on some action (F. Perls, 1969). Often underdog is represented by a softer, lower inner voice than topdog, but nonetheless underdog can be very compelling. In fact, the inner voice of underdog at times seems to have a hypnotic quality that lulls us to sleep when we need to be awake to complete a task on time. Underdog can take a very direct form in the shape of obvious procrastination, such as when a person experiences writer's block, but this shape shifter has many forms. As a wheedler, it endeavors to influence the person by smooth flattery or by using beguiling words to get the person to consent to its goal of doing nothing. Finally, Fritz indicated that underdog usually wins out over topdog as a result of its cunning nature and because it is not as primitive as its archenemy topdog.

Figuratively speaking, topdog and underdog represent the cliché image of a miniature devil standing on one shoulder and a miniature angel standing on the other, each whispering its own version of a siren's song into the ear that is available.

Character and Individual Nature

Although Fritz Perls's concept of character refers to an aggregate of traits that form the individual nature of a person, it does not have the same connotation that most people commonly attribute to the word *character*. Perls is not using the term to suggest the individual has qualities such as honesty, courage, or the like. Instead, Fritz is applying the term to indicate a disconnect between the needs of the person coming front and center and the person successfully knowing how to fully satisfy those materialized needs in a manner that is balancing, health promoting, and conducive to actualizing the person's unique potential.

Fritz defines *character* as the development of a rigid approach to living, in which the person avoids certain aspects of life and closely adheres to a set of rules. Whether self-imposed or adopted from the outside, these rules are less about protecting the person from the many traps or dangers encountered in life and have more to do with keeping the person on the straight and narrow path of diminished living. The false envelope of perceived safety the person associates with living the straight and narrow life is what Fritz associates with the Indian word *Maya,* meaning illusion. It is not that there is a total absence of truth in what we perceive but that the truth we are able to see is just a small part of a much larger stage production called the universe. That is why a "play it safe" attitude provides no genuine protection for the person brimming with character. Furthermore, the person with great character, who relies on an unbending definition of who he is ("I'm this—I'm not that"), has difficulty dealing with changes in his world. In fact, the greater the amount of change (e.g., a natural disaster of great magnitude) is imposed on a person of great character, the greater the person's level of incapacitation or dysfunction will be. Such unexpected dramatic changes are implied in the following lyrics of American singer Everlast's song "What It's Like":

I've seen a rich man beg

I've seen a good man sin

I've seen a loser win

And a sad man grin

I heard an honest man lie

I've seen the good side of bad

And the downside of up

And everything between . . .

You know where it ends

Yo, it usually depends on where you start

The Therapeutic Process

Clients have to become firmly embedded in the *now* before they can actualize their potential. Fritz Perls's formula for the process of therapy is relatively simple, but it could produce powerful results. Basically, what is required to achieve mental health is increased awareness of present sensations, feelings, imagination, and actions. This begs a question: If achieving developmental maturity is basically the straightforward result of achieving a state of present oriented awareness, then what might account for so much ill health and interpersonal strife in the world? For many people who wind up ill-equipped to satisfy their needs, who are far from achieving their full potential, the answer can be found in what Fritz called *stage fright*. As Fritz (1969) explained,

> Anxiety is the excitement, the élan vital which we carry with us, and which becomes stagnated if we are unsure about the role we have to play. If we don't know if we will get applause or tomatoes, we hesitate, so the heart begins to race and all the excitement can't flow into activity, and we have stage fright. [But if] you are in the now, you are creative . . . if you have your senses ready, if you have your eyes and ears open, like every small child, you find a solution. (pp. 2–3)

Role of Resistance

The term *resistance* refers to those attempts during therapy when clients seek to manipulate the therapeutic environment to maintain their dependence on others. Laura Perls said resistance is a "fixed gestalt" that stays lodged in the client to block development and interrupt contact between the client and therapist (Rosenfeld, 1977). Furthermore, it would be very counterproductive, especially when such blockage reasserts its presence, for the therapist to provide unnecessary support for the client because the provision of unnecessary support at such a time will contribute further to a client's effort to maintain the status quo and avoid therapeutic change (Korb, Gorrell, & Van De Reit, 1989). For these reasons, gestalt therapists must acquire a set of background assumptions that can be called forth as needed during the therapy process to identify and confront a client's immature-based tactics intended to prevent reinstatement of growth.

Fritz spoke at length about four ways clients can manipulate others, especially therapists, in order to remain immature and irresponsible for their self-care (Clarkson & Mackewn, 1993). These forms of resistance are not one-time events in or outside therapy, and with each manifestation there is a disruption of the organism–environment cycle of satisfying needs.

1. **Introjection**: Occurs when clients take in life's experiences without devoting time to savor, relish, and appreciate these experiences in ways that allow them to literally add substance to who they are in the process of becoming. Although we might be driven to perceive the world in wholes, we are not meant to swallow our experiences whole and "choke" on them. To fully incorporate what an experience has to offer, to nourish us in ways to develop further toward our potential, requires us to chew our experiences over in the mind.

When our experiences are both ingested and digested, they become a part of us. Occurrences of introjection imply the opposite, because what has been taken in fails to contribute much if any substance to whom we are becoming. Furthermore, if things encountered are not absorbed properly, these undigested additions start to accumulate. Over time, such an accumulation lays heavily on the mind, causing a sort of mental indigestion that further interferes with an ability to judge the merits of something (e.g., societal "shoulds") for one's self. When such individuals encounter highly stressful situations and their undigested "rules to live by" offer no fitting solution, they are likely to respond in a scattered and haphazard manner. In contrast, during periods of calm they are more likely to leave an impression of being detached, incomplete, and unfinished, or they may get stuck on an idea because they have "always known it to be true."

2. **Projection**: Occurs when sensations, feelings, or thoughts experienced are rejected and attributed to other people ("Bob is such an idiot!"), objects ("Stupid computer!"), or concepts ("Socialism tricks people and turns them into stupefied parasites!"). Clients who consistently project what resides in their internal pit of unawareness (e.g., fear of being seen as stupid) to an outside target will become hypersensitive to both actual and imagined occurrences of what they repeatedly disowned through projection. Such repeat users of projection often become extremely vigilant about looking for the enemy ("stupid people") everywhere in the environment, but fail to see that the real enemy is a neurotic fear and that the enemy lies within them. They are irked by the thought they could be anything like the disowned part of themselves, and when life sours, it is always because of the "stupid boss/teacher/Democratic or Republican president," etc.

3. **Confluence**: A healthy form of confluence occurs when the newborn melds with the mother during breast feeding (Latner, 1973), but confluence can also represent an unhealthy relationship with one's world—the equivalent of an adult nursling. In addition to a strong desire to be looked after by others, this person seeks to meld with others by denying interpersonal differences (Polster & Polster, 1973). Seeking to merge trumps satisfying one's uniqueness; as a result, the person may eventually become confused or uncertain about what she feels or wants. The stronger the push is to blend with the world, the greater the pathology will become. High use of confluence is associated with a concerted effort to create a nonchanging outlook of bland but comfortable sameness. Clients who rely on

confluence block out the faces of others by holding a hand mirror turned toward their own face, not to reassure themselves they are better than everyone else but rather to assure themselves that everyone looks like them.

4. **Retroflection:** These clients are more inner-oriented than outer-oriented, and they behave in a manner marked by a tendency to do to themselves what they desire to do to others.

According to Fritz, the retroflective client has established a distinct boundary between self and what is perceived to be the environment, but retroflection makes for a terrible surveyor of boundaries. When assessing the lay of the land, this type of surveyor establishes a distinct boundary but has wrongly drawn the boundary line right through the middle of the property called "self." One outcome of the psychological act of dividing the self is a person who sometimes talks about himself as if he is talking about someone other than himself. Thus, the split client can clearly see both sides of an issue, but has to "remain on the fence" since his inner resources are not working as a coordinated whole to allow for a satisfying decision to be made. Fritz believed that when retroflection becomes chronic in nature, it can take on a physical form, such as migraine headaches, frequent upset stomach, and other types of common aches or complaints. In the end this person becomes a doppelganger who is neither fully alive nor fully dead.

Other gestalt theorists added to the list of resistances (Clarkson & Mackewn, 1993): *Proflection* denotes instances where projection and retroflection are combined to enable clients to do to another person what they desire for the other person to do to them (e.g., the cult of personality created by the media but maintained by the enthusiastic fans); *desensitization* refers to clients who deprive themselves of physical sensations through numbing (e.g., drinking several glasses of wine every evening, taking pain medications, swallowing sleeping pills); *egotism* occurs when clients try to keep in check or under control what cannot or should not be restrained; and *deflection* refers to clients who use tactics to avoid or bend attention away from themselves by joking, answering a question with a question, or changing the topic.

Assessment and Diagnosis

Preconceived ideas reached through traditional assessments or reliance on diagnostic criteria such as the *DSM* result in reducing a person to one or more abstract concepts. When a therapist makes such a judgment, the "expert opinion" forms the background from which the therapist makes decisions about what techniques are to be utilized since the actual client has been consumed by the imposed label. Fritz believed that standardized evaluations and systems of categorization superimpose artificial expectations and create illusionary boundaries between the therapist and client that filter and distort the relationship. What is required instead is for the therapist to maintain an ongoing, moment-to-moment alertness to the therapeutic process, free of preconceived labels and ideas about what to expect (Hardy, 1991; Rosenblatt, 1975).

The form of assessment and diagnosis, if it can be called that, which appears to be the most compatible with Fritz's form of therapy is what can be described as a free-floating evaluation. Thus, the key to knowing what to do in gestalt therapy is not found in the *DSM* or from the therapist handing the client a questionnaire to complete but rather through a careful attending to what is occurring between the therapist and client in the context of the here-and-now therapeutic environment that cradles them both. Specifically, the therapist goes with the flow of therapy, realizing that to unlock the unique possibility in a client requires nonjudgmental streaming. Finally, it is important to note that not all gestalt therapists are as opposed to assessment or diagnosis as Fritz Perls was, especially when conducting brief gestalt therapy (see, e.g., Houston, 2003).

Therapeutic Goal

Some critics have perceived certain aspects of gestalt therapy as being overly ambiguous, but when discussing the merits and faults of gestalt therapy, it seems more difficult to assert such a claim about its therapeutic goal, which is shared among gestalt therapists who show considerable differences in other ways. The goal of therapy is to achieve maturity.

The mature client has moved from other support to self-support. In addition, the mature client lives a life defined by creativeness, engagement, courage, and a genuine sense of purpose. Self-support is not to be confused with being fascinated with oneself or vainglory. Self-support represents a middle and balanced approach to life, as it falls between the extremes of no contact and seeking continuous contact with others. This is the type of self-support that represents personality integration, which implies the person is sensing the world accurately and, at the organism level, interacting with the environment effectively to satisfy needs. A healthy balance is obtained when the scales of self-support and experienced frustration can be made horizontal to one another or what Fritz called "zero balance" (Clarkson & Mackewn, 1993).

Therapist's Role

Effective gestalt therapy is not tied to any proscribed set of therapist-generated activities because each client is perceived to be unique. Instead, the therapist is likely to apply a combination of uniquely crafted and well-known forms of experimentation. (*Experiments* can be thought of as the actions taken by a therapist to provide learning through experience, thus enhancing awareness through a focusing of the client's attention.) The ultimate aim of all experiments is to benefit the client. The primacy given to increasing a client's awareness is evident in Fritz Perls's willingness to interrupt meaningless verbiage that hindered the expression of feelings and their associative experiences (Yontef, 1971). Finally, the therapist is walking a razor's edge that requires balanced support and fostering frustration in the client as needed through experimentation. Providing too much support will not help the client to move beyond the impasse point, where the client's fear of vulnerability and desire for self-protection merge and shut down client movement. Furthermore, an infusion of too much frustration experienced too early can cause the client to withdraw altogether from the therapist–client relationship (Yontef, 1971).

Fritz incorporated Martin Buber's notion of the "I-Thou" relationship as a cornerstone for gestalt therapy (F. Perls, 1969). This type of special relationship is defined as entering into full involvement with another, whose gifts or one-of-a-kind qualities are genuinely appreciated. Even with the inclusion of this essential relational aspect into gestalt therapy, it is better to think of the therapist as still remaining independent of assuming a single type of role. The therapist, as everyone, is a unique personality capable of acting spontaneously inside and outside a therapy session. For Fritz, gestalt therapy is not gestalt therapy unless sessions are marked by an atmosphere of genuineness that is free of the artificial exchanges we often encounter in our daily lives. (Fritz preferred offensive, harsh, or blunt language over euphemisms.)

Although therapists are free to be themselves, the paradox of the client–therapist relationship is that freedom in this case is not without obligation. For example, when a therapist self-discloses information or gives a personal opinion, the intrinsic aim of such shared spontaneity is seen as appropriate only if the underlying intention is to help the client grow and move the client closer to self-actualizing.

Client's Role

Gestalt therapy is practiced to help clients differentiate between true pains and imaginary hurts and to learn how to seek what is genuinely needed rather than going through life collecting acquisitions that seem fulfilling at the time but fail to quiet clients' real inner hunger. Thus, the client must be willing to enter into an "I and Thou" relationship. Furthermore, rather than being seen as helpless or misunderstood, the client can expect to have her dormant self-sufficient nature addressed by the therapist. It can also be expected that the therapist will avoid catering to the client's well-formulated manipulation tactics or "social games." In the end the client can expect to be confronted with the same paradox all clients involved in gestalt therapy eventually face. In other words, before a client can become strong, the client must embrace fully her perceived weakness. Fritz firmly believed that awareness and acknowledgment of what one fears energizes the client to start taking risks and to move toward fulfilling her true life path.

Techniques and Strategies

Fritz Perls said he was not the creator of gestalt therapy but rather that he rediscovered the practice of gestalt therapy since its principles and tactics are ancient. This can be illustrated by the concept of the "here and now." The *Hagakure* or *The Book of the Samurai* dates to the early 1700s and in its original form had over 1,300 excerpts that resulted from a 7-year conversation between a young samurai and an older samurai turned Buddhist monk. The following excerpt captures the essence of Fritz Perls's thinking about the importance of the here and now.

> There is surely nothing other than the single purpose of the present moment. A man's whole life is a succession of moment after moment to moment. If one fully understands the present moment, there will be nothing else to do, and nothing else to pursue. Live being true to the single purpose of the moment.
>
> Everyone lets the present moment slip by, then looks for it as though he thought it were somewhere else. No one seems to have noticed this fact. But grasping this firmly, one must pile experience on experience. And once one has come to this

understanding he will be a different person from that point on, though he may not always bear it in mind. (Tsunetomo, 1716/1979, p. 74)

In gestalt therapy, techniques are referred to as experiments for good reason. As the word implies, an experiment represents the therapist's attempt to test what the therapist believes will bring forth spontaneous feelings and promote greater self-awareness, but just like the typical lab experiment the result cannot be predicted 100%. In the case of gestalt experiments this is true because each client is unique and will respond uniquely.

Questions, Not Explanations. Rather than interpretation or explanations of what is occurring, the therapist will rely on questions to facilitate client change.

- What are you doing with your arm?
- What are you trying to avoid at this very moment?
- What are you feeling now?
- What do I (as the therapist) want from you?

Questions increase specific awareness and the client's overall ability to remain aware. Furthermore, achieving and staying in a state of awareness is not limited to the client; the therapist must also maintain a state of awareness, attuned to his own continuum of ongoing sensations, fantasies, images, prejudices, intentions, and thoughts generated by the client–therapist encounter.

Empty Chair. This experiment requires the client to speak to a chair as if it were occupied by a person related to some incomplete exchange or interaction from the past. Fritz believed that unfinished business represents incomplete, lingering gestalts that often relate to the client's previous relationship with a parent. Such incomplete gestalts also represent conflicting polarities of positives and negatives. The positives and negatives expressed toward one's parent during the empty chair experiment allows for closure. The empty chair experiment can also be used with situations (poverty), concepts (courage), and states of mind (depression) where the client speaks to these types of occupants placed in the chair. The conversation is not one-sided, as the imaginary occupant of the chair is often called on to "speak to" the client. This can be accomplished by having the client sit in the empty chair and take on the role of the other, which includes speaking for the other. As a result, the technique is also referred to as the two-chair technique.

Monodrama. The client is instructed to play a different person related to an unfinished situation. The experiment provides the client an opportunity to feel and perceive another's experience. By feeling an alternative set of emotions and thoughts, a greater depth of awareness becomes available. Again, the experiment can be done with objects, emotions, or aspects of situations that prevent client maturity. Lingering gestalts are closed as a result of greater awareness of the dimensionality of the existing polarities. Monodrama allows the client to accept a polarity as a whole rather than cling neurotically to one side or neurotically jump back and forth between the extremes.

Amplification (i.e., exaggeration). The therapist incites the client to overstate the obvious. In this case, the therapist has the client exaggerate movements and gestures, inflate what is felt at the moment, and magnify beyond the possible what a problem could create. This technique grounds the client and provides him a means to see and hear what has fostered a conflict.

Talk TO Others. The therapist discourages general, nondirected remarks. Clients are required to speak directly to others rather than interact in a manner that avoids emotional contact. This is useful in cases where client growth is prevented by an overreliance on projecting feelings, wishes, and fantasies onto others. This experiment allows for direct person-to-person contact—to say what you want and feel without justifying or explaining, without offering an excuse or arguing for your position. The price for such open communication is to accept what you hear in response while keeping your natural tendency to defend yourself contained so you can fully take in what is being said.

First Person Expression. Somewhat similar to the experiment known as "Talk TO Others," in this case a passive voice is replaced with an active voice that depends on "I" instead of "it" when talking about feelings and thoughts ("I feel," "I think," "I believe," versus "It feels a little like" "It will require some thinking" "It is just a belief"). Preferring to speak in terms of "it" implies the presence of dissociation. This is illustrated by the person who experiences anxiety and then repackages the anxiety through using vague language to refer to "it." This allows the speaker to delay doing anything because a clear target ("anxiety" versus "it") for action has not been identified. In contrast, saying "I'm experiencing anxiety" prevents dissociation from the anxiety and brings to the forefront one's own responsibility. This in turn serves to push the person to do something about the anxiety because the person cannot hide behind generalities.

Body Focus. Voluntary and unconscious corporeal manifestations represent a direct link to the inner world of the client. The manifestations can include physical movement, single gestures, repeated gestures, mirroring another's gestures, the pitch or strength of one's voice, stressing a syllable of a word, style or manner of moving (e.g., slow, rigid, relaxed, jerky) or speaking (e.g., lively, depressed, halting, threatening, macabre), posture while seated or standing (e.g., up straight or slouching), manner of walking (e.g., head held up or head held down), breathing rate and depth, changes in skin (e.g., blushing, blanching), and overall appearance. Calling attention to obvious bodily expressions will focus clients' attention on their bodies, which Fritz believed is highly conducive to fostering greater self-awareness.

Dreams. Rather than being a royal road to the unconscious as Sigmund Freud thought, dreams, for Fritz Perls, were the avenue to achieve greater awareness and significant growth by defragging the personality. This occurs in gestalt dream work by reowning disowned parts of the personality since dreams are essentially a process of disowning aspects of the personality the dreamer views as undesirable. According to Perls, acting out a dream brings to the forefront those aspects of personal reality denied by the dreamer—aspects disowned but nonetheless required to make the person whole and genuine. The following represents a brief example of Fritz Perls working with a client's dream. Earlier in the session, Muriel, the subject of the dream experiment, reports an amorphous sensation she tries to avoid. She describes this unpleasant sensation as a "swirling motion" and later as a "swirl."

Muriel   My head wants to be held. [Rests head on hand] . . . The more I rest it . . . Oh, yes! This is good . . . If I leave it free, the swirl pushes it somewhere and as I rest it on my hand, my hand is holding it and I don't feel the swirl.

Perls   So come back . . .

Muriel   Jane looks like a cat woman, peering from her hair.

Perls   Close your eyes . . . Your experience?

Muriel   Trembling, hoarseness, clearing my throat, trembling, behind my eyelids.

Perls   Open your eyes.

Muriel   I don't want to look at people.

Perls   Close your eyes.

Muriel   Stronger swirl.

Perls   Open your eyes.

Muriel   I really don't want to look at people.

Perls   Close your eyes.

Muriel   My eyes are really trembling now, I'm holding my hands, holding my head.

Perls   Can you try to integrate this? Look at us (the group) and at the same time, pay attention to the swirl, bring your swirl with you. It might be difficult, but try . . .

Muriel   Uh, oh!

Perls   Yah?

Muriel   I just, saw like, like a light of a halo behind, um, Sally's head, and as I look at Teddy's face, I see contours under your flesh, the bone structure. [*Softly*] Wow, uh–

Perls   A little discovery, a little step forward, a new way of looking. Close your eyes again.

Muriel   I want to keep them open. [Closes eyes] Now I see the sort of the phosphorescent shapes of—it's Teddy, and, I don't know—oh it's Frank.

Perls   Yah, you take them back with you. Okay, this is as far as I want to go . . . . (F. Perls, 1969, pp. 236–237)

Fritz Perls indicated that this dream, through an integration of the "swirl," first resisted then accepted and integrated, has altered slightly Muriel's perception of her world—both inner and outer aspects. It is important to note that whatever the swirl symbolized was not analyzed by Fritz; no interpretation was necessary. The "swirl" sensation was assimilated, and Muriel has moved in the direction of being more open to her experiences, even experiences she may have once avoided. Table 7.5 goes through the steps involved in starting a dream journal based on a gestalt approach to utilizing dreams for personal growth.

Gestalt Dream Journal

The "Dream Within a Dream" section appearing at the beginning of this chapter leads to an interesting question: How might a gestalt therapist use his/her own personal dream to increase awareness? Based on the dream work conducted by Fritz Perls and suggestions made by Sinay (1997) and the author of this chapter, several steps are presented here. In addition, to prevent limiting yourself to a single avenue of expression, try drawing the various elements of the dream on a single sheet of paper.

STEPS

1. Use the first person and present tense when writing out the dream. The dream should sound as if it is occurring now. Read aloud what is written to determine if the dream is expressed in present terms.
2. Now review the written content and identify what element is difficult to accept as coming from you. Are there any parts that seem unlike you? Terrible? Disgusting? Keep in mind any part you feel alienated from.
3. Take the part that seems most alien to you and imagine it is speaking to you. Record what this part says to you.
4. Has a message emerged? What is now in the foreground of your attention? Write this down—avoid evaluating or filtering what you write.
5. Take the message of the dream and imagine it is occupying an empty chair in front of you. Write what you would say to this "message." Does the message have anything else to say? Write this down.
6. At the end draw all the parts of your dream on a single sheet of paper to create a sketched out gestalt, a visual integration of the dream's parts.
7. Consider with an open mind the whole of what you have written and sketched. What comes to mind? What have you assimilated from working with your dream through writing and drawing?

Making the Rounds. A type of experiment that is well suited for gestalt group work that requires having a group member *speak to or do something with* other group members. For example, a group member making the rounds might try out some new behavior or way of interacting with others, confront an issue or group member, or make a personal disclosure about something the group member has been reluctant to reveal. This technique provides opportunities for clients to make meaningful changes in the way they live and to become people who are willing to take risks and grow.

Termination: Therapy's Closure

Fritz Perls (1969) wrote, "The crazy person says, 'I am Abraham Lincoln,' and the neurotic says, 'I wish I were Abraham Lincoln,' and the healthy person says, 'I am I, and you are you'" (p. 40). Indicators that the termination stage of therapy has been reached are a heightened ability to confront maladaptive ways of interacting, complete unfinished business, and pay attention to what one must be aware of to satisfy necessitous demands so as to sustain self-support. The client is now capable of differentiating between real-life problems and the type of nonproblems that previously imposed illusionary limits that stalled the client and drained energy. But before clients reach the point of termination, they frequently must face and work through various layers leading to maturity.

Fritz discussed five layers or categories of living with the last one associated with authentic being. First, there is the everyday *cliché layer*, which is superficial and cluttered with everyday expressions repeated with little or no investment of one's self ("Good morning," "How's it going?" "Nice coat," etc.) or worn-out gestures such as a handshake or a pat on the back. At the second layer are the common *social, as-if layers of living*, each with a set of basic rules to follow, such as the "good girl," "whiner," "geek," "grouch," "bum," "fault finder," "beauty queen," "jock," and "bully." These as-if roles seem endless in number. According to Fritz roles such as these represent a "synthetic form of existence" populated by people allowing themselves to be molded and shaped by the mere fancy of societal or cultural forces. At its worst, this stage of living can foster great distractors that interfere with healthy awareness. A prime example is the "cult of personality" mentioned earlier, where the famous or well-known person pulls our attention away from what it is critical for us to be aware of in our world. When the client self confronts, that is, moves beyond this stage of existence, the outcome is an unpleasant form of nonexistence accompanied by a terrible sense of emptiness and being adrift in the world. The client understands that to move backward is to become phony again, which is no longer acceptable because of gained awareness. The client is at an impasse where she has reached a mental cul-de-sac with no clear exit. From this impasse state of mind emerges the fourth layer, which Fritz termed the *implosive layer*. The implosive layer is in full swing when inner pressures become great enough to compress the person inward until the person experiences the equivalent of a psychological implosion that is "death-like." This inner collapse is followed by the fifth layer—the *explosive layer*. Whereas the fourth, implosive layer is analogous to the medical treatment known as maggot débridement, in which maggots devour the dead part of the person, leaving untouched what is alive, healthy, and, in the case of gestalt therapy, authentic, the fifth and final layer marks the start of a new person who is now capable of rich, full experiences that the person can fully ingest and express. Finally, Fritz mentioned four types of health-promoting explosions: The sexually blocked person explodes into orgasm, and the person dealing with a true loss explodes into genuine grief. The two remaining explosions include exploding into anger and exploding into joy and laughter (Perls, 1969, pp. 55–56).

Process of Change

Through gestalt therapy, clients realize that they do not need to depend on others to define how to live and that what has caused them to cling to an immature, inauthentic way of living largely resulted from unfinished business—incomplete gestalts—that linger and hinder self-awareness. Meaningful change is fostered through therapist-initiated experiential learning that leads clients to realize that abstract explanations and intellectualizing about why they have a problem only served to generate psychological blocks to their personal growth. Breaking through such psychological blocks is what allows clients to sense, think, emote, and act in ways that are authentic.

Limitations and Criticisms of Gestalt Therapy

Gestalt therapy has been described by Wagner-Moore (2004) as a complex, creative, yet poorly outlined and disjointed approach. For example, there is a lack of consensus on the recommended or typical length of treatment based on this approach. In addition, the technical language (e.g., gestalt, figure–ground, closure, organism–environment) remains outside mainstream thinking and can be difficult for clients to understand, which suggests that clients would profit from more time spent during intake learning some background on gestalt therapy. Other common weaknesses include the approach's emphasis in the here and now, while excluding the possible therapeutic benefits associated with examining transference reactions in terms of past relationships, and the powerful motivational factor that looking toward the future can have for some clients. Critics have argued that exalting the present over the past or future overlooks—what the author of this chapter refers to as "client time-zones"—much of what has proven to be therapeutically useful over the years.

Finally, despite the existence of numerous gestalt training institutes and universities and colleges associated with its training, there are no national or international standards for gestalt training. Academic programs related to gestalt training have been offered at Pepperdine University, Kent State University, Cleveland State University, New York University, Loma Linda University, University of Innsbruck (Austria), Gestalt Therapy and Training Centre (Australia), Sungshin Women's University (South Korea), York University (Canada), Istituto di Gestalt-HCC (Italy), and the Gestalt Institute in Mexico City. Still, there remains no national or international standards for gestalt training. In an age of empirically validated treatments and *DSM* diagnoses, the lack of agreed on standards to train gestalt therapists poses a problem for establishing the empirical validation of interventions viewed as typically falling under the umbrella of "gestalt therapy."

Application of Gestalt Therapy to Multicultural Populations

Therapists must be aware of both the inherent strengths and the limitations of using gestalt experiments when helping clients from diverse backgrounds. For example, working to integrate a client's two potentially opposing identities (e.g., being gay and religious), may be beneficial. Further, given the experiential, here-and-now approach of gestalt therapy, it may be very relevant for individuals from cultures that emphasize nonverbal as compared to verbal communication because the approach focuses on facial and other nonverbal expressions and within-body experiences.

There are possible limitations, however, of employing gestalt therapy with all multicultural populations. Gestalt therapy has been criticized as a strategy that represents the norms of the White culture of the West (Ivey, Ivey, & Simek-Morgan, 1980; Katz, 1985). For instance, the therapy's focus on self-independence may not be relevant for people from interdependent cultures. As Mocan-Aydin (2000) noted in an example of working with Turkish clients, a gestalt therapist unfamiliar with the culture would likely view a person as "phony" if he exhibited and valued characteristics of conforming, obeying authority, and keeping the peace with others. In this case, the gestalt therapist may challenge the client to achieve a more authentic sense of self that would not be congruent with a Turkish worldview and is very likely to result in the client's rejection by members of his social group. Lastly, a gestalt approach often aims to produce intense feelings and the enhanced awareness of these feelings. Such strategies, therefore, might be incongruent with those Asian clients who value emotional repression or regulation over expression (Eid & Diener, 2001; Matsumoto et al., 2008).

Social Justice

The encounter group movement, which relied on confrontation, reenactment of past hurts, and activities to achieve greater awareness and personality growth, thrived during the latter years of Fritz Perls's life (Gazda, Ginter, & Horne, 2001). This occurred around the same time Fritz proclaimed that individual therapy was essentially on the fast track to becoming defunct—a proclamation that Laura Perls said had more to do with Fritz's *Weltanschauung* (or worldview) than the general state of individual therapy (Rosenfeld, 1977). Laura was correct to assert that group therapy never usurped the throne of individual therapy and, more importantly, that Fritz's comment had more to do with his personally held image of the greater environment and its interrelationship with humanity, in other words, Fritz's views concerning how his approach can be utilized to bring about basic social changes that would engender greater self-awareness in the world, and thus greater mental health and achievement of multiple potentialities.

According to the European Association of Gestalt Therapy (EAGT), "A consequence of our field theory, the ongoing exchanging organism-environment, is that we also have a job to do on the social, ecological, cultural and political level" (Human Rights and Social Responsibility Committee, 2006, p. 1). EAGT has committed a portion of its resources to the organization's Human Rights and Social Responsibility (HRSR) Committee, a committee that takes the position that individual suffering often reflects the greater suffering and pathology taking place on a worldwide level (see http://www.eagt.org/hrscommottee.htm). Through the efforts of this committee and its parent organization, a number of social justice endeavors have already been accomplished. For example, members of EAGT have joined with members of another organization, Peace Brigades International, to promote peace and oppose threats to human rights in countries such as Colombia, Guatemala, Mexico, and Nepal. In addition, two recent endeavors of EAGT's HRSR Committee have been aimed at resolving the Israeli–Palestinian conflict and to amass a collection of writings to demonstrate how the application of gestalt theory can positively impact social, political, and cultural matters. Although examples other than EAGT's efforts can be cited, it is certain that Fritz's theoretical conceptualization of gestalt therapy has an implicit social justice element that in recent years has increasingly taken explicit form.

Research Support

Gestalt therapy has not been widely researched, and therefore it remains largely untested. Smith and Glass (1977) reported on effect sizes of multiple psychotherapies, including gestalt therapy. (An *effect size* is also referred to as a *treatment effect;* in 2009 Sawilowsky proposed the following scale for interpreting the strength of a reported treatment effect: .01 = very small, .20 = small, .50 = medium, .80 = large, .20 = very large, and 2.00 = huge.) Using meta-analysis, the researchers evaluated eight studies of the effectiveness of gestalt therapy. Their results yielded 16 effect sizes that averaged .25. Although clinically significant, this effect size was lower than that found for Adlerian (.71), psychodynamic (.59), rational-emotive (.77), client-centered (.63), and behavior modification therapy (.76). Given these results, it would appear that gestalt therapy's treatment impact was less than these other approaches.

In contrast to Smith and Glass (1977), Strümpfel (2006), who also utilized meta-analysis, found that there were no significant differences in client outcomes between gestalt therapy and cognitive-behavioral therapy, except in one study. In this one study, process-experiential/gestalt therapy, as compared to cognitive-behavioral therapy, led to larger improvements in the mastery of interpersonal issues. On the other hand, Greenberg, Elliot, and Lietaer (1994) also conducted a meta-analysis of experiential therapies, including gestalt therapy, and found that cognitive and behavioral treatments were slightly more effective than experiential therapies.

In addition to the meta-analyses involving gestalt therapy, other researchers have investigated the effects of specific gestalt strategies (e.g., the two-chair [also called empty chair] technique) on client outcomes. Results of a study by Greenberg (1980) suggested that the two-chair technique was effective in helping clients resolve unfinished emotional concerns with significant people in their lives. Additionally, the two-chair technique led to clients' greater depth of experience in comparison to empathic reflection alone. Greenberg and Rice (1981) conducted a study involving the two-chair technique as well. They also found that this strategy produced a more in-depth experience for college student clients. Further, this technique has been shown to be effective in resolving conflict splits, indecision, marital conflict, and interpersonal difficulties (see Wagner-Moore, 2004).

In a different line of research, Ellison, Greenberg, Goldman, and Angus (2009) demonstrated that experiential therapies, including gestalt therapy, were effective in treating depression and also in clients maintaining gains and improvements. Others have discovered that the gestalt approach was effective when treating individuals who had been emotionally injured by their partners (Greenberg, Warwar, & Malcom, 2008). Similarly, the two-chair technique, coupled with empathy focused interventions, has been found to be effective when helping couples resolve marital conflict (Johnson & Greenberg, 1985). Wagner-Moore (2004) cautioned, however, against using specific gestalt techniques, such as the two-chair technique, with survivors of trauma because of the potential for emotional eruptions to occur. The heightened and intense affect that often arises when using these interventions may actually harm clients with a history of trauma, rather than help them access their emotions.

Regardless of the reported results, it must be noted that gestalt therapy has not been subjected to a randomized control trial, which is considered to be the most appropriate methodology to establish an empirically validated treatment. Gestalt therapy is complex and based on a dialogue between the client and therapist and their joint creation of "experiments" useful for that client. Randomized control trials are viewed as not suitable to investigate gestalt therapy and therefore have not been performed (Yontef & Jacobs, 2011).

Relevance of Theory

Gestalt therapy has been used widely in individual therapy (see Strümpfel, 2004, for a review). However, it is also currently being employed in a group context. According to Melnick (as cited in Harman, 1984), the primary model of gestalt group therapy was created by the Gestalt Institute of Cleveland. According to this model, the gestalt therapist is the primary conductor of increasing awareness on an intrapersonal, interpersonal, and group level. According to Zinker (see Harman, 1989), gestalt group therapy is similar to Yalom's model of group therapy in that it follows specific developmental patterns grouped into four stages: (1) surface-level contact and exploration, (2) conflict and identity, (3) isolation and confluence, and (4) high cohesiveness.

Fritz Perls focused on separateness and self-reliance and sometimes seemed rather harsh in his own style. The modern version of gestalt therapy has changed a great deal in the past few decades. Aleksandrov (1997), for instance, described the approach as being less harsh than it had been earlier. Although the approach has retained its phenomenological and creative components, it also has begun to focus more on the therapeutic alliance (Wagner-Moore, 2004), and there is wide agreement that genuine client–therapist interactions are critical to successful client change.

In addition to contemporary gestalt practitioners embracing a creative approach to therapy, they also place a great deal of focus on the client–therapist relationship, which, according to Yontef and Simkin (1989), is a shift from Perls's original conception of the approach. It can be argued that this new emphasis makes it easier to integrate gestalt therapy with person-centered, interpersonal, and feminist approaches. Further, this form of gestalt therapy is congruent with the extensive research on common factors that point to the therapeutic relationship as a primary facilitator of client improvement in therapy (Norcross & Lambert, 2005).

Questioning the relevance of gestalt therapy in today's world, Wagner-Moore (2004) discussed how the flaws in Fritz Perls's early gestalt writings have left the theory as failing to "present either a coherent theoretical model or data supporting it as an empirically validated treatment" (p. 188). In contrast, others have argued that because gestalt therapy is a process theory (Melnick, 1980), it is applicable to any client population (Yontef & Jacobs, 2011). As support for this, some (e.g., Joyce & Sills, 2009) have posited that gestalt therapy is also integrative, as it includes affective, sensory, cognitive, interpersonal, and behavioral components. As a result, it has been asserted that gestalt therapy can be easily adapted to address various mental health issues presented by clients.

Yontef (1993) claimed gestalt therapy can be used as well to assist clients with more specific difficulties, such as borderline personality disorder and narcissistic personality disorder. In fact, it has been argued that there are no prescribed gestalt techniques for specialized groups of people (Yontef & Jacobs, 2011). This suggests that the approach can be practiced in different treatment contexts (e.g., individual therapy, group therapy, and crisis intervention), settings (e.g., schools, organizations), and with a host of multicultural populations (Melnick, 1980; Yontef & Jacobs, 2011).

Special Ethical Considerations

Those who practice and teach gestalt therapy are well aware of the potential ethical pitfalls of the approach and have taken steps to prevent ethical dilemmas from arising. The preamble to the EAGT code of ethics states the following:

Gestalt therapy recognizes . . . the subjectivity of the wellbeing of the individual as a phenomenological entity within their field. Since the realization of this specific goal is implemented through a dialogical approach grounded in the recognition of the autonomy and self-regulation of the individual, these codes of practice offer a meeting place for the resolution of difficulties between two or more parties. The resolution of difficulties for gestalt therapists is attained through dialogue and exchange as opposed to a hierarchical system of judgment and consequences. The code is divided into two sections. The first section states those values and principles that are inalienable rights of the individual. The second section demonstrates guidelines that honour and protect these rights. (p. 4; see EAGT Code of Ethics: Introduction www.eagt.org/joomla/index.php/2016-02-25-13-29-31/code-of-ethics)

When EAGT's ethical code is considered in its entirety, one finds there is much agreement between it and other ethical codes adopted by professional organizations in relation to areas of concern such as professional practice, client–therapist relationship, confidentiality, contracting with the client, advertising, safety issues, relationship with former clients, and other issues.

As to be expected, wording found in EAGT's ethical code is tied directly to certain features common to gestalt therapy. For example, B.1.6 of the section "Code of Professional Practice in Gestalt Therapy" states, "The gestalt therapist is aware that any acting-out, especially expressive and cathartic acting-out, requires de-dramatization achieved through detail and careful working through." As exemplified by EAGT's ethical code and other codes adhered to by gestalt therapists, it has become clear that many of the earlier criticisms and ethical concerns directed at gestalt therapy are no longer relevant.

Application: Gestalt Theory

RETURNING TO THE HYPOTHETICAL CASE OF A DREAM WITHIN A DREAM

It is necessary to address two issues before returning to the vivid dream found near the beginning of this chapter. First, the dream scenario reported earlier was created by this chapter's author and is not an actual dream reported by Fritz Perls. Second, the dream was manufactured in a manner to provide an abundance of content material, an amount that easily exceeds what is typical of a dream recalled. This was done to provide those new to the area of

dream work enough information to build support for their answer to the following question:

Question: After considering what you have read in this and previous chapters, explain how a psychoanalytic, Adlerian, and gestalt therapist would differ from one another in the way each would utilize the dream described in the "Dream Within a Dream" section of this chapter.

The Case of Miguel Sanchez

When cultural factors are cursorily weighted against various techniques within gestalt therapy, apparently but not necessarily, certain gestalt techniques could interfere with rather than facilitate the achievement of important therapeutic goals for clients from certain cultures (Niedenthal, Krauth-Gruber, & Ric, 2006). Such failed outcomes have much less to do with the implemented techniques and are much more likely connected to situations in which a practitioner's personal idiosyncrasies or biases overshadow the client's interests, such as when a therapist relies on techniques that are aimed to dazzle or outwit a client rather than paying close attention to the critical aspects of the client's difficulties. Such instances should not be mistaken for gestalt therapy. In gestalt therapy the context relevancy of a technique will determine its appropriateness, and, yes, cultural factors can play a clinically significant role in context relevancy. For example, during the first session it would clearly be counterproductive for a therapist to use a technique aimed to elicit a strong emotional reaction (to prevent intellectualizing about a problem) if the client's thinking and behavior are shaped by, for example, a Japanese cultural perspective. Such a technique would likely violate the mores of a Japanese individual because, in Japan, a therapist is culturally expected to be more subtle and willing to pursue a less direct line of conversation to discover problems and to create workable solutions (Ting-Toomey et al., 2000). Although such cultural aspects of a client's world are an essential consideration, note that contemporary gestalt therapy recognizes the importance of diversity, and its techniques can be adapted for use with a variety of cultures. This contemporary perspective is found in the following passage from Frew (2013):

> With its [gestalt therapy's] attention to the relationship between self environments, it would be a good match with clients who are struggling with their sensory self and belonging because they have recently moved to the United States or are alienated by their identification as a minority. (p. 223)

Frew's statement certainly has context relevancy for Miguel, who is struggling with the conflicted relationship he has with his mother, which is a situation that can be conceptualized in terms of *dissonant acculturation* (Rong & Preissle, 2009). Miguel is perceived by his mother as having rejected the family's cultural ethos, that is, those guiding beliefs that characterize her sense of community. The following therapy segment illustrates how the therapist uses the empty chair technique, commonly associated with gestalt therapy, to help Miguel bridge the polarizing gap between him and his mother.

Session Segment

Therapist   I see you brought your sketch book today—may I look through it?

Miguel   Yes. [He hands the sketch book over.]

Therapist   [After taking time to look through the entire sketch book, the therapist stops at the last drawing, chuckles, and looks up at Miguel.] Very interesting. I hope I never see such a cave—a cave with teeth. (See Figure 7.5.)

The Cave

The Cave

Source: Reproduced with permission from E. J. G.

Miguel	[The client laughs.] Yes—I don't think anyone wants to be—ah—*masticado y tragado* (chewed up and swallowed).
Therapist	Very true—no one wants to be *masticado y tragado*. I noticed at the top of your cave drawing that you wrote yesterday's date. Is that the day you drew it?
Miguel	Yes. It was the day I argued with my mother—same old shit.
Therapist	I want to use the empty chair again. Okay?
Miguel	Okay.
Therapist	But this time instead of speaking with your father, I want you to speak to your mother as if she's in the empty chair right now. What would you say?
Miguel	[Miguel speaks to the empty chair as if his mother is seated there.] Why do you think I'm leaving you behind—forgetting patrimonio (heritage). You don't understand what it's like having to live in both worlds.
Therapist	Miguel switch places—what would your mother say in response?
Miguel	[The client hesitates.]
Therapist	Give it a try—what would your mother say back to you.
Miguel	Miguel—I do know what it's like to live in two worlds—Mexico and here. I do it every day when I go out and work. I crossed the border for you and Alberto to have a better life. I just don't want to lose my two sons. [Miguel's eyes become watery.]
Therapist	Miguel, switch places—what would you say to this?
Miguel	I know you did this for us—the family. You did something that was very hard. I'm your son, I'm not going to disappear—you're my mother, we're family.

When used by a therapist who is in sync with the client's present state, the empty chair technique can provide a powerful avenue through which a client can become attuned to various sides of a conflicted situation. As with any technique that is introduced by a seasoned gestalt therapist, the previous sequence represents an organic event, one that is neither scripted nor predetermined by the therapist in advance. As stated by Frew (2013), "gestalt therapists do not see themselves as the architects of change. Instead, change occurs naturally within clients (not by the hand of the therapist) when sufficient attention is paid to present circumstances, self, environmental support, and readiness" (p. 222).

CHAPTER REVIEW

SUMMARY AND COMMENTARY ▶▶

Fagan (1992) compiled a long list of descriptors used to describe Fritz Perls. Many share an inimical relationship making it impossible to bring together these separate parts into a neatly packaged whole, but a reasonable sample would include the following: intelligent, engaging, disdainful, lonely, creative, power-seeking, amoral, caring, demanding, vigorous, spirited, dynamic, disruptive, disrespectful, salacious, wandering, buffoonish, rabble-rouser, independent, trendy, artistic, roguish, worldly, self-responsive, direct, hedonistic, passionate about life, and destructive (e.g., Laura Perls revealed there were times Fritz smoked up to 100 cigarettes a day). Even Fritz recognized the complexity of his impact on others when he stated, "I am astonished at my extremes of meanness and compassion" (quoted in Fagan, 1992, p. 333).

The descriptors mentioned emerged over the span of a lifetime and along the way were woven into a Gordon knot called "Fritz." Turning to a theoretical comment made by Fritz himself may at least provide a partial answer to the complexity we are left with when we consider the real Fritz Perls. Fritz wrote, "Whenever there is a boundary question, there is conflict. . . . There is always a polarity going on, and inside the boundary we have the feeling of familiarity, or right; outside is strangeness, and wrong. Inside is good, outside is bad . . . So the whole idea of good and bad, right and wrong, is always a matter of boundary, of which side of the fence I am on" (F. Perls, 1969, pp. 8–9). Virginia Satir contributed additional light to the situation when she stated the following about Fritz's and Laura's relationship; "The way in which he managed Laura at times . . . awful! But I know enough that these things are transactional and not just unilateral—that is, Laura, as well as Fritz, had responsibility for the field that they co-created" (cited in Clarkson & Mackewn, 1993, pp. 139–140).

In Fritz Perls's case, it might be accurate to say that those who are wounded by life (as Fritz was) are best able to provide a clear-eyed appraisal of what it takes to heal clients. Finally, regardless of "which side of the fence" Fritz Perls fell on for those who knew him personally, to a large degree it is irrelevant because he still deserves recognition for being a groundbreaking therapist who brought to the forefront of therapy the role that an "I-Thou" relationship grounded in the present moment, rather than the nonexistent past or future, can contribute to clients achieving a state of mature self-reliance. Table 7.6 provides a brief overview of contemporary gestalt therapy.

▼ TABLE 7.6

Brief Overview of Current Therapy Practice

Variable	Current Application
Type of service delivery setting	Private practice Schools Community mental health centers Psychiatric hospitals Health care settings
Population	Individual (child, adolescent, and adult) Group Couples and families Organizations
Type of presenting problems	Wide range
Severity of presenting problems	Wide range
Adapted for short-term approach	Yes
Length of treatment	Brief to long term
Training in educational programs	Several universities/colleges are associated with gestalt training (offering "related academic programs"). Furthermore, the Gestalt Institute in Mexico City offers degrees validated by Mexico's Ministry of Education and the Istituto di Gestalt- HCC offers degrees and programs validated by the Italian Ministry of Universities.
Location	Urban Suburban Rural
Type of delivery system	HMO PPO Fee for service

(Continued)

(Continued)

Variable	Current Application
Credential	Several training institutes provide certification: Gestalt Institute of Cleveland offers gestalt coaching, training, and certification; Gestalt Institute of the Rockies in Golden, Colorado, offers gestalt therapy certification; and Pacific Gestalt Institute offers certification in "competence in gestalt therapy."

Variable	Current Application
Practitioners	Professionals Paraprofessionals
Fit with *DSM* diagnoses	No

CRITICAL THINKING QUESTIONS ▶▶

1. Explain what Fritz Perls meant by the catchphrase, "Lose your mind and come to your senses."

2. Assume you have a problem that you believe can be solved only by seeking the assistance of a therapist. There are two equally competent and equally effective therapists in your area. One is a gestalt therapist, and the other therapist uses a talking approach to therapy. Would you seek out the gestalt therapist over the other therapist for help with your problem? Explain in detail why you would or would not select the gestalt therapist.

3. As a member of a gestalt group, you can expect the therapist to use the experiment of confrontation during the course of therapy. How would you know if the therapist was using confrontation appropriately or inappropriately? Give a tangible example of both uses.

4. Do you believe a person can gain genuine insight and understanding by not talking about an interpersonal conflict and relying solely on experiential reenactments in the "here and now?" Explain your position.

5. Return to the hypothetical dream attributed to Fritz Perls at the beginning of this chapter. Explain in detail how three different types of therapists—gestalt, psychoanalytic, and Adlerian—might utilize the reported dream in a therapy session.

SUGGESTED READINGS: IMPORTANT PRIMARY SOURCES ▶▶

Books

Perls, F. S. (1992). *Gestalt therapy verbatim* (2nd revised ed.). Gouldsboro, ME: Gestalt Journal Press.

Sinay, S. (1997). *Gestalt for beginners.* New York, NY: Writers and Readers Publishing.

Journals

The Gestalt Journal https://www.abebooks.com/book-search/title/gestalt-journal/

Gestalt Review www.gisc.org/gestaltreview/

Websites

An oral history of gestalt therapy—An interview with Laura Perls: www.awaken.com/.../an-oral-history-of-gestalt-therapy-an-interview-with-laura-perls/

Fritz Perls (An Autobiography): http://www.famouspsychologists.org/fritz-perls/

CHAPTER 8

BEHAVIORAL THEORY

With Chad Luke and Frederick Redekop

Those who say that a science of behavior is over-simplified and naïve usually show an over-simplified and naïve knowledge of the science, and those who claim that what it has to say is either trivial or already known are usually unfamiliar with its actual accomplishments.

—B. F. Skinner, 1974, p. 230

Introduction

What do we mean by behavior? What is the role of behavior in the life of an individual? How does behavior influence thinking and feeling, and vice versa? How can humans change their behavior, or, more poignantly, can behavior be changed? These are the enduring questions that this chapter addresses. Our premise in discussing these and other questions is the following: *Behavior matters and is meaningful.* Although behavioral approaches have evolved, they are still characterized by this statement. Our goal will be to make sense of the evolution of the phrase "Behavior matters and is meaningful" in practical terms as it pertains to counseling and psychotherapy (Sharf, 2012).

It is important to view behavior therapy as an evolving clinical practice. One of the ongoing criticisms of behavior therapy, as reflected in the opening quote, is that it tends to be reductionist and superficial, minimizing the complexity of human motivation and experience. Whereas these criticisms may have been more deserved in the early years of behavioral approaches, they are less accurate today. Behavioral approaches have shown that they can grow and adapt in the face of their critics, especially in response to advances in therapy research. Thus, another purpose of this chapter is to describe the historical context from which behavior therapy grew and then to describe the shifts leading to evolving contemporary behavioral approaches.

LEARNING OBJECTIVES

After reading this chapter, each student should be able to:

1. Discuss how the key players contributed to the development of behavioral theory.

2. Assess the importance of the basic concepts to the practice of behavioral therapy.

3. Critique the role of assessment in behavioral therapy.

4. Propose how you would employ each behavioral technique or strategy to assist different clients with various presenting concerns.

5. Explain the significance of the key terms presented in Table 8.8 to behavioral theory.

6. Defend the relevance and validity of applying behavioral theory to Groundhog Day.

7. Propose a set of behavioral techniques or strategies to assist Herlinda that were not mentioned in the chapter.

8. Argue that behavioral therapy was an effective treatment for Mrs. Sanchez.

Historical Context

Sigmund Freud's writings evoked powerful responses: Carl Jung, Alfred Adler, and many others developed their theories in large part as a reaction to Freud. Behavior therapy was no different. You might even say that Freud was the *stimulus* and behavior therapy was the *response*, an active response to what they saw as Freud's interminable, inaccurate, and inactive method. Behavior therapy provided an alternative for those uncomfortable with concepts such as the unconscious, drives, id, ego, superego and the like. More importantly, it provided an empirical rejoinder to Freud's eloquent anecdotal explications of the human condition. In response to the affective drives in Freudian thoughts, Skinner (1938) offered a cogent response that elucidates behavior therapy's role in altering the course of

THE CASE OF HERLINDA: THE ALARMING TEENAGER

Herlinda Morales is a 15-year-old female who presents with a variety of alarming issues. When she was 14, she cut her arms with scissors, leaving three superficial wounds on her left arm and five on her right. She has not cut her arms since that time, but she does use her fingernails to scratch her arms and legs on a weekly basis, leaving welts and scratches. She is 20 pounds overweight; she does not eat many fruits or vegetables, preferring a diet of rice and potatoes and chicken fingers. She describes symptoms of depression and anxiety, saying that she feels sad a lot of the time, that it is hard for her to get up in the morning, and that when she is around people she often feels nervous and ill at ease. She is doing poorly academically, getting no grade higher than a C.

Herlinda is a middle child, with a brother who is 6 years older and a sister who is 3 years younger. Herlinda's father is an accountant; he is Latino, born in Puerto Rico and raised in New York City. Herlinda's mother is also an accountant; she is White, born and raised in rural Maryland, with German and Dutch ancestry. Herlinda's sister is quite popular and successful academically, and Herlinda alternates between being proud of her younger sister and being very jealous of her success. Herlinda's mother set up counseling for Herlinda after she cut herself at age 14, but Herlinda did not like her first counselor and claimed, "She's old and ugly and has no idea what I'm going through." Herlinda reports that her parents fought about whether to force her to continue; she said that her father "wasn't too keen on therapy" in the first place but that her mother was strongly in favor of treatment.

An important aspect of Herlinda's situation is that she would fall in the conformity stage in Sue and Sue's (2008) racial/cultural identity model—but with a twist. In accordance with this stage, which is the first of five (conformity, dissonance and appreciating, resistance and immersion, introspection, and integrative awareness), she is self- and same group-depreciating and discriminatory toward others of a different minority, but instead of being wholly appreciative of the dominant White culture, she tends to value mainstream White culture while denigrating her mother's particular White European heritage. For instance, she makes disparaging comments about popular Latina figures such as Selena Gomez and Jennifer Lopez and admiring comments about White figures such as Taylor Swift and Miley Cyrus. But she provocatively describes her mother's family as "typical white bread Americans—they're boring and don't say anything. I think they were Nazis or something." She reports that she hates visiting her father's extended family in San Juan; "They're noisy and chaotic and dirty," she says. She describes her father by saying, "He's a typical macho guy. When he discovered that I was interested in a boy, he wanted to lock me in a closet until I'm 21." Her rejection of both cultures leaves her without potential powerful environmental supports and reinforcers, and this is a key aspect to remember in doing multiculturally competent work with Herlinda.

Note: The case of Herlinda is used later in the chapter to provide an example of behavioral therapy's application.

---

psychology and psychotherapy. Skinner wrote, "We do not cry *because* we are sad or feel sad *because* we cry; we cry *and* feel sad because something has happened" (Skinner, 1989, p. 4; italics in original).

Theorists of early behavioral approaches were not interested in asking questions about human motivation, intention, and other mentalistic concepts. They also downplayed human feelings and emotions, making them contingent on environmental cues rather than as possible generators of behavior. Finally, and perhaps most importantly, they insisted on a rigorous empirical approach. They were interested in observable evidence, preferably produced in controlled settings. Pavlov (1927) exemplified this approach, in which he famously investigated, in a laboratory setting, animal responses to stimuli that were generalized to humans. Pavlov perceived animals as machines and man, in turn, as a complex animal. Pavlov asserted that scientists can make inferences from the behavior patterns of lower animals to those of higher ones (humans): "It is obvious that the different kinds of habits based on training, education and discipline of any sort are nothing but a long chain of conditioned reflexes" (Pavlov 1927, p. 395). These conditioned reflexes were the results of the cerebral cortex responding to environmental stimuli—whether via an electrode implanted directly onto the surface of the brain or via the ear processing the sound of a bell ringing. Thus, from the Pavlovian experiments in which it was demonstrated that animal reactions were determined by environmental cues, psychology had the emergence of a science of stimulus–response in explaining human behavior.

Building on a generation of animal research, behavior therapy began to emerge as a distinct field of psychology in 1920 with Watson and "Little Albert" (Wolpe, 1973), demonstrating the emergent classical conditioning principles—in essence, a theory of learning. Wolpe (1958) concluded, "Learning may be said to have occurred if a response has been evoked in temporal contiguity with a given sensory stimulus and it is subsequently found that the stimulus can evoke the response although it could not have done so before" (p. 5).

Little Albert is the classic case of a child who was taught to fear a small white bunny through classical conditioning. Albert was not afraid of bunnies prior to the experiment, but by pairing the sight of the bunny with something that was frightening (banging of a steel rod), Albert "learned" to be afraid, not only of bunnies but of all soft, furry animals. Watson and colleagues hypothesized at least four ways through which Albert might then "unlearn" his fear, but unfortunately (although perhaps understandably) Albert's mother removed Albert from the study. Later, Jones (1924) tested one of the four suggestions for reversing this type of learning, which came to be known as counterconditioning, wherein "Peter," in another classic experiment, unlearned a fear response.

So the die was cast: Behavior therapy established itself as a distinct field of psychology. But as we shall see, the theory faced many criticisms and, in responding to those criticisms, became something new. Bandura (1977) and Lazarus (1971) offered key transitional bridges to what we now know to be behavioral approaches. For example, contemporary behavioral approaches include cognitions, function of affect, and personal historical factors. Several of these approaches merit attention as we seek to understand and apply behavioral approaches to the counseling and psychotherapy enterprise. We briefly discuss two: dialectical behavior therapy (Linehan, 1993; Neacsiu, Ward-Ciesielski, & Linehan, 2012) and acceptance and commitment therapy (Hayes, Strosahl, & Wilson, 1999; Wetherell et al., 2011).

Key Players

There are five key players that made substantial contributions to behaviorism. Their names are Pavlov, Wolpe, Skinner, Bandura, and Lazarus. Pavlov (Figure 8.1) and Skinner (Figure 8.2) are especially noteworthy since they largely established the "stimulus(S) - response (R) language" that is typically associated with behaviorism.

Ivan Petrovich Pavlov (1849–1939) had a significant impact on the field of psychology (when it became defined as the experimental study of behavior) through

▼ FIGURE 8.1
Ivan Petrovich Pavlov

▼ FIGURE 8.2
Burrhus Frederic (B. F.) Skinner

Source: Ivan P. Pavlov. U.S. National Library of Medicine.

Source: Silly rabbit [GFDL (http://www.gnu.org/copyleft/fdl.html) or CC BY 3.0 (http://creativecommons.org/licenses/by/3.0)], via Wikimedia Commons.

his work in what came to be known as *classical conditioning*. He was the first to identify that dogs would salivate at the sound of a bell ringing alone once that sound had been paired with food (Babkin, 1971). This was the beginning of animal behavior studies that would eventually be generalized to human behavior and the field of behaviorism itself.

Joseph Wolpe (1915–1997) was a South African psychiatrist who later became a U.S. citizen and who brought the field of behavior therapy to the United States. Wolpe built on the work of academic psychologists and psychiatrists of his time to develop a practice-based approach. Chief among the aspects of this approach is systematic desensitization. Wolpe believed that in most cases, anxiety was primary in what were then called neuroses. However, anxiety was not a result of some deep-seated sexual or aggressive impulse; rather, it was a response to the environment.

Burrhus Frederic (B. F.) Skinner (1904–1990) was an American psychologist who self-identified as a "radical behaviorist." He is perhaps best known for what came to be called operant conditioning, which transformed Pavlov's stimulus–response effort into behavior reinforcement. Skinner worked with pigeons and rats in the development of his theory of the role of reinforcers in the environment in shaping behavior. As radical as he was concerning behaviorism, his works in the 1970s and 1980s seemed aimed at clarifying his views to his critics: "Radical behaviorism does not thus 'behead the organism'; it does not 'sweep the problem of subjectivity under

250 ■ THEORIES AND APPLICATIONS OF COUNSELING AND PSYCHOTHERAPY

the rug'; it does not 'maintain a strictly behavioristic methodology by treating reports of introspection as merely verbal behavior'; and it was not designed to 'permit consciousness to atrophy'" (Skinner, 1974, p. 219). Table 8.1 provides a sample of assertions made by Skinner.

Albert Bandura (1925–) was Canadian-born but later became a naturalized U.S. citizen. His social cognitive theory extended radical behaviorism, transforming it into a learning theory that included cognition more explicitly than others had previously, as well as biological influences in behavioral responses. Bandura is known for the Bobo doll experiments that led to his theory of observational learning (i.e., children who observed an adult physically and verbally assaulted an inflated Bobo doll were more likely to act in a physically aggressive manner afterward). He also developed self-efficacy theory and a theory of personal agency (i.e., self-efficacy refers to the belief in one's own ability to accomplish a task). As such, he is the first among behaviorists to demonstrate the mediating role of cognitions.

Arnold Allan Lazarus (1932–2013) was a South African psychiatrist who developed multimodal therapy, a technically eclectic (vs. theoretically eclectic) theory of social learning, cognitive processes, and behavioral principles that are experimentally verifiable. It is more comprehensive and systematic compared with "broad-spectrum" behavior therapy (Lazarus, 1976, p. 6).

▼ TABLE 8.1

The Radical Behaviorist: Quotable B. F. Skinner

- No one can give an adequate account of much of human thinking. It is, after all, probably the most complex subject ever submitted to analysis . . . [but] no matter how defective a behavioral account may be, we must remember that mentalistic explanations explain nothing. (pp. 223–224)
- All selves are the products of genetic and environmental histories. . . . There is no place in the scientific position for a self as a true originator or initiator of action. (p. 224)
- Those who argue that laboratory results cannot account for human behavior in the world at large presumably believe that they know what is happening in that world, or at least that it can be known. (p. 229)
- Traditional theories of knowledge run into trouble because they assume that one must think before behaving (not to mention thinking before existing, as in cogito, ergo sum). No one thinks before he acts except in the sense of acting covertly before acting overtly. (p. 235)
- Operant theory moved the purpose which seemed to be displayed by human action from antecedent intention or plan to subsequent selection by contingencies of reinforcement. A person disposed to act because he has been reinforced for acting may feel the condition of his body at such a time and call it "felt purpose," but what behaviorism rejects is the causal efficacy of that feeling. (p. 224)
- In an operant analysis of the stimulus control of verbal behavior, we can identify the referent of abstract terms, but terms like "morality' and "justice" raise an additional problem. It can be solved by recognizing that the behavior we call moral or just is a product of special kinds of social contingencies arranged by governments, religions, economic systems, and ethical groups. (p. 244)

Source: Skinner, B. F. (1974). *About behaviorism.* New York, NY: Knopf.

Basic Concepts

One of the challenges for students and practitioners in understanding behavioral approaches is grasping the concepts themselves. In this section, we attempt to make sense of the nomenclature in preparation for translating these concepts into practice.

Empiricism Over Mentalism

The fundamental starting point for behavioral approaches is *scientific empiricism,* the view that only phenomena that can be rigorously studied are appropriate for science. In the case of therapy, for example, "mentalistic" phenomena cannot be directly observed, whereas behavior can. Therefore, behaviorism has historically focused on these observable features of humans, rather than thoughts and emotions. Thoughts and feelings of clients are impossible to observe directly, much less measure and test. *Mentalism,* a term used to describe thoughts and feelings of an individual (world of the mind), which Watson and Skinner vigorously challenged as valid and useful constructs, is the opposite of behaviorism. To the extent that mental constructs do exist, they are subsumed under behavior in behavioral approaches. This means that thoughts are merely behaviors, arising, if at all, from biological processes, rather than from some force known as the mind. Feelings are physiological responses to behavior—no more, no less.

John Watson (1924), following in the footsteps of Pavlov, not only decried the fallacy of the unconscious but also was opposed to the idea of human consciousness at all. He stated, "Behaviorism claims that consciousness is neither definite nor a usable concept. The behaviorist, who has been trained always as an experimentalist, holds, further, that belief in the existence of consciousness goes back to the ancient days of superstition and magic" (Watson, 1924, p. 2).

Present Over Past

As mentioned earlier, Freud's (1949/1989) theory and recommendations for clinical practice stimulated a powerful response. His case studies in particular, which laid out the details of patients' lives and Freud's subsequent interpretations and interventions, furnished much ammunition for behaviorally oriented theorists and therapists. Hayes (2004) described how Freud's interpretations contained in the case of Little Hans (a boy who developed a number of fears, including a fear of going outside and a fear of being bitten by a horse) were stringently criticized by behaviorists; the basic critique was that Freud's complex interpretations (involving, in this case, his standard Oedipus complex of a hostile wish toward father and an erotic wish toward mother) were simply wrong. Instead, much simpler, behaviorally oriented explanations sufficed; for Little Hans, the best explanation of his fear of horses was not the complex psychosexual one that Freud (1909/1955) advanced, but the simplest one possible: Little Hans developed his fears because of the intensely frightening experience of seeing a horse fall down and kick about with its feet (Wolpe & Rachman, 1960).

Power of Environment

Behaviorism focuses on how immediate environments shape learning and subsequent behavior. The best example of this is Skinner's operant conditioning. Think of *operant*

Schedules of Reinforcement

Schedules of reinforcement: The rate and amount that reinforcement occurs.

Fixed interval reinforcement: Happens at specific time periods, such as with set pay periods or eating schedules.

Variable interval reinforcement: Occurs at random, less predictable periods of time as with the frequency of checking a mobile phone for text messages. Eventually one will show up, but unpredictably, leading one to check repeatedly.

Fixed ratio reinforcement: Happens following a given average number of responses whereby the next response can be predicted or reinforced (Skinner, 1974) (e.g., salary increase based on pre-established level of productivity).

Variable ratio reinforcement: "Occurs after a given average number of responses but in which the next response to be reinforced cannot be predicted" (Skinner, 1974, p. 60). This last reinforcement schedule is by far the most addictive, as in the case of slot machines.

Differential reinforcement: Is a combination of positive reinforcement and extinction and is context dependent. As such, target behaviors are reinforced in particular contexts when appropriate but not reinforced when not appropriate. For example, clapping hands and cheering at a sporting event is socially appropriate and reinforced by nonverbal cues. However, clapping and cheering at the opposing team is discouraged, so such behavior may be ignored (extinction).

conditioning as examining the factors that occur immediately following a behavior (in the environment) and increase or decrease the likelihood that it will be repeated (reinforcement). Operant conditioning is the probability of something occurring in the environment following a given behavior (Skinner, 1974). *Contingencies of reinforcement* is a Skinnerian term for the consequences or outcomes of a given behavior that either increase or decrease the likelihood that the behavior will be repeated or reinforce the behavior. In other words, the probability that a behavior will be reinforced is contingent on the consequences of that action. (See Table 8.2 for additional details concerning reinforcement.)

Behavior Matters

Essentially, behavior is action—anything directly observable and measurable. Behavior is the core of behavioral approaches, as it is the only part of a person that can be directly observed and studied empirically. Behavior is the result of who we are, or, more accurately, who we are is our behavior; little else matters in terms of psychological processes. In fact, Watson (1924) was emphatic that psychology is (only) the study of behavior. The life of the mind, were it to exist at all, matters not.

Classical conditioning is a Pavlovian concept and is an excellent example of behavior. It involves the pairing of a *stimulus* with a *response*. "A stimulus is the antecedent of a response"; a response is a behavioral event" (Wolpe, 1973, p. 14). Consider a simple, common example: You eat a certain food and afterward become ill. The next time you see or smell that food you feel repulsed or maybe nauseated. This is a classically conditioned response. An *unconditioned stimulus* is an unlearned antecedent (event) that results in a response, as with the Moro reflex wherein a baby spreads her arms and then folds them back in, in response to a loud clap. A *conditioned stimulus* is a learned antecedent (event) that is paired with an unconditioned stimulus to elicit a given response (think of a bell ringing when food is presented—it previously was a neutral or unconditioned stimulus). An *unconditioned response* is an untrained (naturally occurring) behavioral event resulting

from a stimulus (salivating over food). A *conditioned response* is a trained (or learned) behavioral event resulting from an unconditioned stimulus (salivating when a bell rings). So, returning to our food example, the sickness is the unconditioned response, whereas the new food is the unconditioned stimulus. The new food becomes the conditioned stimulus while your nausea seeing or smelling the food becomes the conditioned response.

Classical conditioning was dramatically portrayed in a 1971 movie titled *A Clockwork Orange*. In this movie, the main character, Alex (played by the actor Malcolm McDowell), is a highly violent antisocial delinquent. To "cure" and "civilize" Alex, he is sent to a medical facility and subjected to aversion therapy (extinguishing an undesirable behavior by linking it with an unpleasant consequence). He is injected with medications that induce nausea, paralysis, and fear while at the same time he watches graphically violent films (Figure 8.3). After repeated exposure to this fabricated "Ludovico technique," Alex becomes extremely physically sick when experiencing or thinking about violence; that is, he has developed an aversion to violence. From a Pavlovian perspective, we see that a stimulus (viewing violent movies) was paired with a negative (nausea) rather than a positive reinforcement, resulting in "curing" Alex of his violent thoughts and behaviors.

Learning Is the Key

Social learning/cognitive theory is Bandura's (1977, 1986) theory of learning that demonstrates that most learning is mediated through cognition and occurs through observation in a social context. According to Bandura (1977), learning (as in "learned behavior") includes three main types of learning, all related to behavioral approaches. *Associative learning* (classical and operant conditioning) is the process of making an association between two stimuli or a stimulus and a response. *Nonassociative learning* (habituation and sensitization), in contrast, is a decrease or increase in response to a stimulus based on exposure. *Observational learning* (or vicarious learning) involves learning by observing someone else. Bandura also discussed what he termed *capabilities* (see Table 8.3).

Mindfulness

As evidenced by the inclusion of cognitions described earlier, behaviorism has continued to evolve and now includes a focus on mindfulness. Mindfulness is composed of different elements—a kind of amalgam of thoughts, behaviors, and emotion. One excellent example of such an amalgam is acceptance and commitment therapy (ACT; Hayes & Pierson, 2005; Hayes et al., 1999). This approach begins with a philosophical position called functional contextualism, wherein behavior is understood only within its context. Practitioners of ACT recognize the limits of language to accurately represent internal phenomena and the ways in which language can arbitrarily ascribe meaning to those

▼ TABLE 8.3

Bandura's Five Distinguishing Capabilities

Capabilities refers to metacognition in which humans have the capacity to think not only about their behavior and environment, but also about their own thinking. This allows for modifications in subsequent thinking, acting, and environment influence, particularly as each pairing of these constructs is mutually reinforcing (reciprocity).

1. **Symbolizing capabilities** mean that, rather than being consigned to trial-and-error learning as presumed in early behaviorism, humans have the capacity to use language to symbolically represent behavior and environment.
2. **Forethought capabilities** are the mediating effect that cognition can have between behavior and environment, meaning we are also not completely subject to indiscriminate reactions to the environment.
3. **Vicarious capabilities** mean that, rather than learning in a vacuum, resulting in learning by trial and error alone, humans are capable of learning from others—so-called observational or vicarious learning (Bandura, 1977, 1986).
4. **Self-regulatory capabilities** allow humans to observe their performance behavior in context. This moves them not only to shape their environment based on this but also to modify their expectations of their own performance.
5. **Self-reflective capabilities** refer to metacognition (i.e., thinking about thinking), in which humans have the capacity to think not only about their behavior and environment but also about their own thinking. This allows for modifications in subsequent thinking, acting, and environment influence, particularly as each pairing of these constructs is mutually reinforcing (reciprocity).

▼ TABLE 8.4

Mindfulness and Acceptance and Commitment Therapy

Mindfulness represents an openness toward moment-to-moment experiences without a need to mentally hold on to any particular experience in a sequence of unfolding experiences—a sort of free-flowing awareness without any mental anchors.

The Wave Analogy: Imagine that you are standing in the surf on the shore of the ocean, about chest deep. As you look out toward the horizon, you notice a large wave rolling in toward you. At this point you have a few seconds to make one of several choices: (1) You can turn and run for land, which will likely result in the wave plowing you into the ocean floor; (2) you can attempt to leap over the wave, resulting in loss of balance (unless you are a preternaturally powerful leaper) and again getting plowed under by the wave; (3) you can stand your ground, determined to fight the force of this wave (we know what happens in this scenario—same as the previous scenarios); or (4) you may choose a counterintuitive course, in which, as the wave bears down, you simply submerge yourself completely, allowing yourself to be, for a time, completely overwhelmed by the wave, only to emerge again, largely unscathed.

Tactic 4 is parallel to ACT, which builds on the mindfulness construct. In ACT, we recognize that waves of thoughts, feelings, and sensations bear down on us throughout our day. We could panic and try to run away, jump over, or fight through these waves, with predictably poor results. Or we could accept that the wave is natural, inevitable, and powerful, and prepare for calm, effective action—to briefly submerge, experience the wave, and then to regain our footing and reemerge as soon as the wave has passed. It is this approach that frees us to commit to important actions that match our genuine self—actions that are not hampered by life's ongoing distractions.

phenomena. Whereas therapists using cognitive approaches might attempt to identify and confront negative or disabling thinking, ACT therapists would direct a client to recognize that a thought is only as powerful as the attention it receives.

Therefore, rather than giving undue attention to unwanted thoughts by trying to silence them, a person would accept those thoughts as being "nothing more than thoughts." This acceptance allows a person to revoke the power that any thoughts may have over him. (See Table 8.4 for an analogy that highlights the essence of mindfulness and ACT.)

The Therapeutic Process

The contemporary behaviorally oriented therapist is concerned with quickly forming an alliance with the client around her experience of her problem, assessing the problem and how it is being maintained, formulating overall treatment goals and specifying target behaviors and how they will be maintained, and implementing a coherent and effective treatment plan.

Assessment

Assessment is one of the cornerstones of the behavioral approaches. It informs all aspects of treatment and is based on a thorough identification and understanding of the unique individual and environmental factors that cause, maintain, and affect a particular client's behavior. Behavioral therapists employ a functional assessment to acquire this information. Cone (1997) defined this type of assessment as "the activities involved in describing and formulating hypotheses about potentially controlling variables" (p. 261), and it includes three phases: information gathering, hypothesis generation, and hypothesis testing (Cone, 1997). In short, performing a functional assessment can contribute to ascertaining the targets for intervention and hypothesizing causal connections (Ivanoff & Schmidt, 2010).

Spiegler and Guevremont (2010) suggested that assessment should be multimodal as well as multimethod. Multimodal means that therapists should look for evidence from a variety of modes of human behavior—overt behavior, cognition, emotions, and physiological responses. Multimethod means that therapists should use a variety of assessment methods. Therapists typically use interviews, in which they question clients about what they would like to change and how they envision changing it. They also may ask clients to fill out self-report inventories. As Spiegler and Guevremont (2010) outlined, "There are hundreds of direct self-report inventories that are used to assess the gamut of problem behaviors clients present" (p. 87), such as anxiety, depression, eating disorders, sexual and marital problems, and so on. In addition, therapists may ask clients to keep track of certain behaviors in a diary or journal, which can help clients to become mindful of when, where, and how often these behaviors occur. Therapists may ask other people in the clients' lives to fill out instruments as well. Parents may be asked to keep track of a child's behavior; teachers and school counselors may also fill out instruments that track a student's behavior. Table 8.5 is an example of Lazarus's (1976) multimodal behavior assessment.

▼ TABLE 8.5

Multimodal Behavior Assessment

One of the best examples of a comprehensive, systematic approach to assessment that is utilized in therapy is based on Lazarus's (1976) approach. This open and full assessment can mitigate client concerns about a therapist jumping to ethnocentric conclusions regarding presenting problems. It is readily apparent that although some cultural limits persist, the assessment demonstrates a client-directed approach. For example, Lazarus (1976, pp. 30–31) utilizes the following questions in his assessment procedure, which is a neatly prescribed approach to clinical interviewing and assessment.

1. Which particular behaviors do you wish to increase, and which ones do you want to decrease?
2. What negative feelings would you like to reduce or eliminate, and what positive feelings would you like to increase or amplify?
3. Among your five senses, what particular reactions would you care to get rid of, and what kinds of sensations would you like to magnify?
4. What mental pictures or images are so bothersome that you would like to erase them, and what pleasant images would you care to bring into clearer focus?
5. Which thoughts, values, attitudes, or beliefs get in the way of your happiness?
6. In your dealings with other people, what gets in the way of close, personal, loving, and mutually satisfying interactions?
7. Under what conditions do you use drugs (including alcohol, coffee, and tobacco)?

Goals

Initially, the therapist is faced with operationally defining the client's presenting problem. What this means is that the therapist must take the client's words and use them to specifically define what exactly is happening that is problematic, when it is happening, how often, and under what circumstances. A baseline must be established, which means that an accurate picture of the situation must be established before treatment. This is done so that the effectiveness of interventions can be measured.

A hallmark of behavior therapy is to define target behaviors clearly so that they can be measured. For example, a mother may say that Jordan, her 7-year-old son, is "out of control—he bounces off the wall and never listens to a word that I say." Helping the mother to define what she means by "out of control" and "bounces off the wall" and "never listens to a word I say" is a crucial collaborative task. Goals might include teaching Jordan to recognize antecedent situations that increase his activity level, working with his mother to stop Jordan when he is ignoring her directives, asking him to direct his attention to her, having her speak slowly and clearly and directly to him, and asking him to repeat the directions that she has given. In addition, it is critical to work with Jordan's mother to help her identify situations in which she sees Jordan focusing his attention and then praising him for his self-control.

Therapist's Role

The behaviorally oriented therapist must first build a therapeutic alliance, a specific role that has increased in prominence over the years. Skinner (1989) argued that rapport building had always played an important role, and later behaviorists have paid increasing attention to the clear and significant findings in the literature pertaining to the therapeutic relationship (Iacoboni, Molnar-Szakacs, Gallese, Buccino, & Mazziotta, 2005; Rizzolatti & Craighero, 2004). For example, according to Lambert and Ogles (2004), "Reviewers are virtually unanimous in their opinion that the therapist-patient relationship is critical to positive outcome" (p. 174). In recent years it has become increasingly acknowledged that establishing a working alliance is foundational to therapeutic endeavors. Lejuez and Hopko (2006) went so far to say that "ignoring the TA [therapeutic alliance] in behavior therapy may not only be problematic on a practical level, but also may be inconsistent with basic principles that underlie behavior therapy" (p. 456).

As the relationship is established and as it strengthens, behaviorally oriented therapists actively collaborate with their clients in addressing operationally defined problems. In other approaches, the reported problem may be seen as a symptom of an underlying issue that is the "real" problem. But for the behaviorally oriented therapist, the reported problem is the problem. The straightforward, no-nonsense approach of behaviorally oriented therapists masks a successful interpersonal strategy of immediate agreement and engagement that can, in the hands of a competent therapist, begin treatment off on the right foot.

Client's Role

As in all treatments, clients are expected to provide, to the greatest extent within their power, accurate information about their situations. The client collaborates with the therapist in painting an accurate picture of how the problem developed and how it is sustained in its own particular ecosystem. In the case of Herlinda (presented at the beginning of this chapter), it is very important to establish a very specific description of the frequency of the scratches that she inflicts on her arms and the severity of the scratches in order to establish a baseline of their occurrence. The relationship that the behaviorally oriented therapist establishes with Herlinda will help her to feel safe enough to provide more accurate information, which will help in assessment, goal setting, and intervention. The therapist must also work with Herlinda to establish open and clear communication with her parents, so that accurate information can flow back and forth, with the therapist assisting them as needed.

Techniques and Strategies

Behaviorism and behavioral approaches are nothing if not replete with therapeutic techniques and interventions. This in no way implies superficiality of method. Instead, it is a testament to the long history of empiricism exploring factors leading to behavior change—behavioral interventions grew out of the clinical study of human behavior. After all, whereas depressed persons may complain that they "feel" poorly, it is the behavior that follows that must be addressed (e.g., suicidal behavior, eating habits, too much sleep, withdrawal, and other self-defeating behaviors), and interventions must decrease these negative behaviors and increase other, more functional ones.

Positive Reinforcement. The classic, core concept of operant conditioning and behavior therapy is positive reinforcement. It also happens to be a key intervention strategy in behavioral approaches. Anything that follows a behavior and increases the likelihood that it will occur again is a reinforcer (Skinner, 1974). Positive reinforcement increases the likelihood that the behavior that caused it will be repeated. In treatment, this is a powerful tool for helping clients understand and change behavioral patterns. We often direct new therapists in training to eschew "why" questions with clients, largely because clients cannot really tell a therapist why. Behavioral approaches direct attention to "what," rather than why, as in "What directly followed that action that you took when you stayed in bed all morning feeling too depressed to get up and go to work?" instead of "Why did you feel so depressed you could not get out of bed and go to work"? People continue to engage in behaviors that are reinforcers, meaning there is some "payoff" for engaging in those behaviors. In functional behavior analysis, behavior-oriented therapists analyze behaviors and their antecedents and consequents. Environmental contingencies play a large part in reinforcing behavior, even maladaptive behavior. Through positive reinforcement, therapists seek to understand those factors in the clients' environment that increase the likelihood of those behaviors being repeated, in spite of what clients may say they think or feel about those behaviors.

Negative Reinforcement. In contrast to positive reinforcement, negative reinforcement involves the removal of a negative outcome that increases the likelihood that a behavior will be repeated. Skinner (1974) used the example of taking off a shoe that is pinching your foot. Taking off the hurting shoe relieves the pain, thereby increasing the probability that you will do this again the next time it hurts. Seatbelt chimes in modern cars also illustrate the point: Click it or hear a ringing for the entire drive. In therapy practice, this means walking clients through the process of identifying negative consequences of behaviors that would best be eliminated.

Punishment. There are two types of punishment. *Negative punishment* is the withdrawal of a reinforcing stimulus, whereas *positive punishment* is the presentation of any aversive stimulus. The role of the behavioral therapist is to examine how punishment behaviors may be operating in the client's life. Punishment, although the most likely to be utilized by clients, is the least effective in long-term modification of behavior. Beginning therapists should be aware of the tendency to overuse punishment in various systems. For example, in education, bad behavior tends to be overpunished and good behavior tends to be underreinforced. Clients will have a lot of experience with these two types of behavioral interventions, but these are interventions that most likely were poorly applied and poorly followed up on.

Shaping. Also referred to as successive approximation, shaping links beginning behaviors with target behaviors. This is accomplished by reinforcing behaviors that move away from the original behavior and toward the goal, on an increasing basis. Essentially, it involves small steps in modifying behaviors. The idea here is that large-scale changes are daunting and difficult, whereas, simple, small changes seem—and are—more attainable. For example, the socially awkward client wants to feel comfortable attending an upcoming high school reunion. The behavioral therapist will assign the client homework that gradually increases his exposure to anxiety-provoking stimuli (often this will begin with *imaginal* work in session). The client will report back on his homework experience (perhaps making small talk with the cashier at a grocery store) and discuss the process with the therapist. The therapist offers feedback about the interaction and assigns increasingly intense homework followed by these debrief sessions. Shaping is an effective tool in assisting clients in making small goals and achieving small successes in changing behavior.

Thought-Stopping. Wolpe (1973) described thought-stopping as the reinforcement of an inhibitory habit. Clients often are amazed when they tell a thought to stop, and it does. The challenge, however, is to convince clients to persist in this activity in the presence of the natural recurrence of these thoughts. Clients may be able to temporarily stop a self-defeating thought through thought-stopping, but as it reoccurs almost immediately, they may convince themselves that the technique was ineffective. On the contrary, it did in fact work, but the power of the technique is in the persistence of its use over time. The key to a thought-stopping technique is encouragement by the therapist for the client to keep going.

Extinction. Wolpe (1973) described extinction as "the progressive weakening or diminishing frequency of a response when it is repeatedly evoked without being followed by a reinforcer" (Wolpe, 1973, p. 214). Extinction is what happens when you cease to reinforce a behavior. In a common parenting example, when a young child has a tantrum, yelling back or confronting the behavior can actually be reinforcing in that the child receives the parental attention the child desires. In contrast, when the caregiver ignores the behavior, the attention is not given; therefore, the behavior is not reinforced, resulting in extinction. (One caveat to this particular example is that caregivers must ensure a safe environment prior to using such an intervention.) Clients are presented with this dynamic as a goal in treatment.

ACT (Hayes, Pistorello, & Levin, 2012) has folded the extinction principle into practice. When uncomfortable thoughts and feelings enter a person's experience, often the instinctual thing to do is to confront it, numb it, or avoid it. These behaviors, however, can end up reinforcing those thoughts, as in when someone says, "Don't think of a purple elephant!" (Hearing these words, a person cannot prevent herself from imaging a purple elephant.) In contrast, ACT endorses the notion that, to the extent that thoughts and feelings are behaviors, they have limited power and influence when unattended to. Essentially, letting these thoughts and feelings move through our consciousness without challenge or confrontation extinguishes them.

Flooding. Flooding is a technique that evokes strong feelings "by exposure to either real situations or contrived imaginal situations" (Wolpe, 1973, p. 192). Similar to paradoxical intention as used by existential therapists for anxiety, flooding prescribes the problem stimulus in an intense fashion. The technique is built on the premise that dysfunctional responses to anxiety-evoking stimuli serve only to reinforce the anxiety-evoking stimuli. In addition, it confounds the original problem by adding unhelpful coping behavior to it. In flooding, clients experience the anxiety-provoking stimulus in an intense way, without engaging in their previously exercised behaviors. When the anxiety abates without client efforts, clients learn that anxiety-evoking stimuli are actually innocuous, if not reinforced through inappropriate behaviors. Flooding can be used in real-life situations, such as riding an actual elevator numerous times until the anxiety about elevators dissipates. This approach is referred to as *in vivo flooding*, or "in life" flooding. It is easy to conceive of some of the limitations to this highly effective approach (e.g., logistical considerations, safety considerations, environmental control, ethical concerns, etc.). Another approach to flooding is referred to as *imaginal*, and takes place in the mind of the client. Although physically and emotionally safer, as well as more convenient, this technique tends to be less effective than *in vivo* flooding. Imaginal flooding does have the added benefit of allowing clients to imagine anxiety-evoking stimuli that could not be implanted in the real world (e.g., debilitating fear of being a victim of a violent crime).

As with most of these techniques, flooding in particular requires additional informed consent in order that clients understand their treatment. It is not difficult to imagine the commitment needed by a client to put this much effort into an intervention and trust into a therapist.

Systematic Desensitization. Developed by Wolpe (1958, 1969), systematic desensitization is pairing a relaxed state (through progressive relaxation, e.g.) with increasingly intense anxiety-provoking stimuli until the anxiety response is replaced with a relaxed response. In one sense, systematic desensitization is a path to extinction. In discussing systematic desensitization, it is important to recall that Wolpe viewed anxiety as the source of most neuroses. Clients are gradually exposed, a little at a time, to an anxiety-provoking stimulus, after being guided into a relaxed state (Table 8.6).

Assertiveness Training. Assertiveness is the space between passivity and aggression. When individuals are unable to express their feelings appropriately to others, stand up for their rights without infringing on the rights of others, or present a point of view without "stepping on toes," they tend toward passivity wherein their needs go unmet, or toward

▼ TABLE 8.6

Systematic Desensitization: Four Steps to Consider

1. **Relaxation training.** Wolpe (1973) described a six-session deep muscle relaxation procedure that can be used. Although the types of relaxation techniques vary, Wolpe emphasized order and routine in implementing a relation technique.
2. **Creating an anxiety scale.** Clients are asked to rank-order anxiety-provoking stimuli centered on a common theme. The stimuli may begin as extrinsic (outside the person, such as fear of thunderstorms) but may trigger intrinsic fears (internal, such as a fear of dying). In determining the sources of anxiety, therapists utilize psychosocial history information, formal assessment tools, and client subjective report.
3. **Constructing the anxiety hierarchy.** In this step, the client and the therapist construct a scale, usually from 0 to 100, with 0 being the least anxiety provoking and 100 being the most anxiety provoking. Clients will identify which events or situations result in the greatest amount of anxiety and place this at the top of the scale. Working backward, the client and therapist identify, in descending order, anxiety-provoking situations in increments of one or five, depending on the list generated in Step 2.
4. **Desensitization procedure.** In this last, most crucial step, the therapist guides the client through progressive relaxation to a sufficient point that desensitization can work. Wolpe recommended below 25 out of 100 on "subjective units of disturbance." Once the client has reached the target relaxation point, the therapist will ask the client to imagine a scene set according to the lowest point of her anxiety hierarchy. Over the course of several sessions, the scenes imagined increase in intensity according, once again, to the anxiety hierarchy until the client begins to imagine previously anxiety-provoking scenes while in a state of relaxation. This process gradually decreases her sensitivity to these stimuli. In contrast to the "ripping off the Band-Aid" approach that is flooding, systematic desensitization is a gradual, and often more humane, approach to reducing anxiety.

▼ TABLE 8.7

Assertiveness Assessment and Training

Wolpe (1973, p. 84) suggested asking a series of questions such as those listed here to assess a person's typical response to various situations.

1. What do you do if after having bought an article in a shop you walk out and find that your change is several dollars short?
2. Suppose that, arriving home after buying an article on the way, you find it slightly damaged. What will you do?
3. What do you do if somebody pushes in front of you in line (e.g., at the theater)?
4. At a shop, while you wait for the clerk to finish with the customer ahead of you, another customer arrives and also waits. What do you do if the clerk subsequently directs his attention to that customer ahead of you?
5. You order a steak rare and it arrives well done. How do you handle the situation?

Once this assessment is complete, the therapist directs the client to instigate assertive behavior. It is important that only those situations wherein the client will be successful be used for practice. Examples of categories of assertive behaviors include speaking with feeling rather than using generic statements, showing emotion on your face, using contradiction when you disagree with someone, using "I statements," accepting praise by verbally agreeing with it, and being spontaneous in responding (Salter, 1946, cited in Wolpe, 1973).

   Next, it is important to use a list of assertive statements as examples to assist clients in building their repertoire. Wolpe bifurcated such statements into "hostile" and "commendatory." Hostile statements are more direct in nature, whereas commendatory statements refer to offering positive feedback to another as it is genuinely experienced. Once this list is compiled, the therapist and client can begin to role-play, or use behavioral rehearsal to practice these statements in the sessions, building confidence through positive feedback and experience.

aggression, wherein only their needs matter, thereby stepping on the rights and freedoms of others. Assertiveness training, as developed and described by Wolpe (1973), seeks to assist individuals in finding the balance between these two extremes (Table 8.7). Wolpe (1973) defined assertive behavior as "the proper expression of any emotion other than anxiety towards another person" (p. 81).

Process of Change. In behavioral therapy, clients are expected to be very active in and outside of their therapy sessions. They are responsible for making changes by increasing or decreasing their current behavioral repertoires and learning, trying, and displaying new behaviors. In-session activities and homework assignments are designed to monitor and facilitate changes in the scope, frequency, and quality of clients' adaptive behaviors. These activities and assignments also may focus on the reduction or extinction of clients' maladaptive behaviors. Through the therapeutic relationship, the behavioral therapist helps the client to accept that it is his responsibility for changing the mutually agreed upon targeted behaviors.

Terminology

Table 8.8 is an alphabetical listing of key terms introduced in this chapter.

Multiculturalism and Social Justice

One of the strengths of behavioral approaches from a multicultural and social justice perspective is the almost sole focus of current behaviors in their immediate context. Many clients

▼ TABLE 8.8

Clarification of Key Terms

1. **Associative learning (classical and operant conditioning):** process of making an association between two stimuli or a stimulus and a response
2. **Capabilities:** refers to metacognition—or thinking about thinking—in which humans have the capacity to think not only about their behavior and environment but also about their own thinking
3. **Classical conditioning:** Pavlovian concept and excellent example of behavior; involves the pairing of a stimulus with a response
4. **Conditioned response:** trained (or learned) behavioral event resulting from an unconditioned stimulus (e.g., salivating when a bell rings)
5. **Conditioned stimulus:** learned antecedent (event) that is paired with an unconditioned stimulus to elicit a given response
6. **Contingencies of reinforcement:** Skinnerian term for the consequences or outcomes of a given behavior that either increase the likelihood that the behavior will be repeated, or decrease the likelihood, or reinforces it
7. **Differential reinforcement:** combination of positive reinforcement and extinction that is context dependent
8. **Extinction:** "progressive weakening or diminishing frequency of a response when it is repeatedly evoked without being followed by a reinforcer" (Wolpe, 1973, p. 214)
9. **Fixed interval reinforcement:** reinforcement that occurs at specific time periods, such as with set pay periods or eating schedules
10. **Fixed ratio reinforcement:** reinforcement that occurs after a given average number of responses in which the next response to be reinforced that can be predicted
11. **Flooding:** technique that evokes strong feelings "by exposure to either real situations or contrived imaginal situations" (Wolpe, 1973, p. 192)
12. **Forethought capabilities:** mediating effect that cognition can have between behavior and environment, meaning we are also not completely subject to indiscriminate reactions to the environment
13. **Mentalism:** describes thoughts and feelings of an individual (world of the mind)
14. **Negative punishment:** withdrawal of a positively reinforcing stimulus
15. **Negative reinforcement:** removal of a negative outcome that increases the likelihood that that behavior will be repeated
16. **Nonassociative learning (habituation and sensitization):** decrease or increase in response to a stimulus based on exposure
17. **Observational learning (or vicarious learning):** learning by observing someone else

18. **Operant conditioning:** probability of something occurring in the environment following a given behavior
19. **Positive punishment:** presentation of any aversive stimulus
20. **Positive reinforcement:** reinforcement that increases the likelihood that the behavior that caused it will be repeated
21. **Schedules of reinforcement:** the rate and amount that reinforcement occurs
22. **Scientific empiricism:** the view that only phenomena that can be rigorously studied are appropriate for science
23. **Self-reflective capabilities:** refers to metacognition—or thinking about thinking—in which humans have the capacity to think not only about their behavior and environment but also about their own thinking. This allows for modifications in subsequent thinking, acting, and environment influence, particularly as each pairing of these constructs is mutually reinforcing (reciprocity).
24. **Self-regulatory capabilities:** allows humans to observe their performance behavior in context, which moves them to not only shape their environment based on this but also modify their expectations of their own performance
25. **Shaping:** also referred to as successive approximation; links beginning behaviors with target behaviors
26. **Social learning/cognitive theory:** Bandura's (1977, 1986) theory of learning that demonstrates that most learning is mediated through cognition and occurs through observation in a social context
27. **Symbolizing capabilities:** capacity to use language to symbolically represent behavior and environment
28. **Systematic desensitization:** developed by Wolpe (1958, 1969), pairing a relaxed state (through progressive relaxation, e.g.) with increasingly intense anxiety-provoking stimuli until the anxiety response is replaced with a relaxed response
29. **Thought-stopping:** the reinforcement of an inhibitory habit
30. **Unconditioned response:** an untrained (naturally occurring) behavioral event resulting from a stimulus (salivating over food)
31. **Unconditioned stimulus:** an unlearned antecedent (event) that results in a response
32. **Variable interval reinforcement:** reinforcement that occurs at random, less predictable periods of time as with the frequency of checking a mobile phone for text messages
33. **Variable ratio reinforcement:** reinforcement that "occurs after a given average number of responses but in which the next response to be reinforced cannot be predicted" (Skinner, 1974, p. 60)
34. **Vicarious capabilities:** capability of learning from others—so-called observational or vicarious learning (Bandura, 1977, 1986)

from non-Western cultures resist or are skeptical of insight-oriented and affect-centered therapy approaches. The straightforward nature of behavioral approaches and emphasis on what the client is doing now can ease concerns of hidden agendas and motives related to oppression. As such, behavioral approaches operate in a reassuring way to clients who may have felt uncomfortable with other approaches that focus beneath the surface of behavior.

Cultural diversity also has been fruitfully examined in behavioral assessment. Iwamasa (1997) suggested that if a therapist is ignorant of the impact of culture on a client's life, "a functional analysis of behavior may be more a function of *who* is doing the analysis, rather than *what* is being analyzed" (p. 348). It is inappropriate to approach assessment as something done from a culturally independent position; too often, therapeutic practice operates from a White European perspective that masquerades as objectivity. In the United States, the dominant White viewpoint can pretend to be "morally neutral, average, and ideal" (Sue, 2004, p. 764). Tanaka-Matsumi, Seiden, and Lam (1996) presented a culturally informed functional assessment (CIFA) interview that integrates culture into functional assessment of behavior. This assessment includes cultural identity and acculturation to assist the therapist in understanding clients' attitudes toward their culture and shows how to integrate culture into one's clinical judgment. In doing so, the therapist encourages a kind of assessment practice that does not reinforce the status quo but instead challenges its (often invisible) preeminence. Hays (2009) outlined how therapists can work with clients to help them examine their experience of oppression by dominant cultures and, from a perspective of cultural strength, empower them to change. Behavioral approaches highlight the role of the immediate environment on behavior, and contemporary iterations recognize the culpability of social systems in reinforcing antisocial behaviors. Behaviorists will always return to personal accountability, but the indictment against systemic oppression can be seen in dialectical behavior therapy, acceptance and commitment therapy, and mindfulness-based cognitive therapy (Barraca, 2012; Segal, Williams, & Teasdale, 2012; Sipe & Eisendrath, 2012). These approaches emphasize a wider perspective on behavior, including ever-widening contexts for reinforcing maladaptive behavior. Many clients are limited in their responses because of their environments. As much as they may desire to change their environments in order to change reinforcers, it is simply not a realistic possibility for them. For example, for an adolescent living in a low-income neighborhood wherein crime is a way of life, defensiveness and guarded behavior are to be expected. When this behavior is brought to school and she presents with resistance to directives out of mistrust, that behavior, in that context is labeled maladaptive. The solution? Move to a "better" neighborhood? This is likely simply not an option. Behavior therapists must be attuned to the constraints placed on clients by their environments and explore, in the type of nuanced approach advocated by Hays (2009), the cultural strengths the client possesses that tend to ameliorate social and economic injustice. Asnaani and Hofmann (2012) discuss how mindfulness activities, which incorporate a client's personal history of trauma or racism, can be used to strengthen resilience. Another possibility is the use of ACT, which teaches, for example, mindfulness, commitment to action, and awareness of thoughts without reifying them. In addition, ACT's element of radical acceptance moves clients toward meaningful changes that liberate underused personal strengths that can be applied to counter negative environmental factors such as social and economic injustice.

A Cinematic Illustration of the Concept of Radical Acceptance

A discussion of a classic movie comedy will help to illustrate the critical construct, radical acceptance, found in ACT. *Groundhog Day* is the story of Phil, a weatherman for a Pittsburgh television station. As the story opens, he is traveling to Punxsutawney, Pennsylvania, with his producer, Rita, and his cameraman, Larry, to cover the annual Groundhog Day celebration (Figure 8.4). After covering this event, they attempt to go back to Pittsburgh but are forced to turn back and spend the night in Punxsutawney. Phil wakes in the morning to find that nothing has changed. It is still February 2, Groundhog Day. Until the very end of the movie, no matter what Phil does, he wakes up to the same day.

At the beginning of the film, Phil is a deeply self-centered and unhappy man. He is very witty, but his wit is biting. He makes fun of people and pushes them away with his sarcastic behavior. He treats Larry with condescension and makes crude remarks to Rita. He has a small view of the world and what happiness is. It takes him a while to come to grips with the fact that he is reliving the same day; when he does, he acts selfishly. He discovers that he can get to know people and situations and use this acquired knowledge to manipulate them to his own ends. He steals money and seduces women.

He eventually tires of these behaviors. He realizes that what he really wants is Rita. After seeing her in action day after day, he becomes impressed with her fundamental kindness and decency. He begins to woo her. His initial attempts fail, and he becomes depressed and tries to kill himself. But he cannot kill himself because he continues to wake up in the same day. Phil is trapped in his own behaviors. He cannot seem to change things and get what he most wants in life: to have a real relationship with Rita.

At this point, Phil undergoes a transformation. How? He radically accepts that he may never win Rita's hand. He accepts that he may live the same day, over and over, into eternity. He accepts that he may never be able to change the behaviors that have caused him and others such pain. He accepts where he is and who he is.

Practicing radical acceptance of thoughts and feelings—a concept central to ACT—creates a space for new behaviors and a new life. What happens is that Phil realizes what he loves about Rita—she is

▼ FIGURE 8.4

The Movie *Groundhog Day*

the kindest person he has ever met. He says to her that he does not deserve someone like her. And he is right. It is not right that such a kind person like Rita should be with a self-centered man like Phil. Phil comes to accept his negative thoughts and feelings about himself and, in so doing, realizes the most basic of behavioral principles. He needs to change his behavior.

So he does change his behavior. He begins to act differently, regardless of his thoughts and feelings. He helps a homeless man. He catches a child who falls out of a tree. He changes the tire for some elderly women. He brings coffee for Larry, who previously was the butt of Phil's biting wit. He saves someone from choking. He treats everyone he meets with kindness. He engages in self-improvement by learning how to play the piano (because Rita has said that her ideal man knows how to play an instrument). He learns how to sculpt ice so that he can carve Rita's face. He does this over and over and over until these behaviors define him. Rather than fighting his thoughts and feelings about himself, he changes.

This is the power of radical acceptance from the ACT point of view: It allows us, perhaps for the first time, to fully and calmly accept who we are. With that step taken, we are then able to fully and calmly begin to behave in the way that will lead us toward, rather than away from, the person we want to be and the kind of relationships we want to have. We do not have to be caught up in a Groundhog Day like Phil, continually living the same day over and over and acting in the same fashion time and again. Radical acceptance involves accepting who you are; only then will you change. This is the type of change that enables a person to more effectively confront an array of personal and environmental issues, including societal factors such as the unjust exercise of governmental authority or power.

Research: Evaluating Behavioral Approaches

Behavioral and cognitive-behavioral approaches enjoy a long tradition of basing their work in empiricism—that is, only using what can be tested in controlled ways and then testing what is implemented (Hubble, Duncan, Miller, & Wampold, 2010; Miller, Hubble, Duncan, & Wampold, 2010). It is commonly recognized that behavioral approaches have generated more empirical research than any other psychotherapeutic approach. Therefore, it would be completely overwhelming to attempt a comprehensive overview of the research literature. Furthermore, as Wilson (2008) has observed, the evolution of behaviorism has resulted in a multitude of behavioral approaches, such that "it is difficult to evaluate some global entity called 'behavior therapy'" (p. 251). Therefore, we offer a practitioner-friendly approach to the extant literature on behavioral approaches.

One indicator of the voluminous research into cognitive-behavioral treatments is the work of Butler, Chapman, Forman, and Beck (2006). Meta-analytic studies, which summarize the overall status of a topic of interest, are nothing new, but so many have been generated that Butler and colleagues provided a review of 16 meta-analytic studies that cover everything from insomnia to marital problems. Butler et al. (2006) identified significant positive effects for behavioral approaches on issues ranging from generalized anxiety disorder and posttraumatic stress disorder (PTSD) to depression and eating disorders. Emmelkamp (2004) also provided a helpful overview of the status of behavioral approaches with adults, addressing their effectiveness in treating a wide range of disorders, including depressive disorders, anxiety disorders, and paraphilias, as well as relational conflict.

Behavioral approaches tend to fall nicely into what are currently referred to as evidence-based treatments (EBTs), or empirically supported therapies (ESTs). These approaches have been validated for effectiveness through rigorous research designs for the clinical conditions studied. The American Psychological Association has provided a very informative and useful resource on ESTs and EBPs (http://www.psychological treatments.org/). On this website, one may search by treatment or by disorder. For example, in searching by treatment, one encounters "Acceptance and Commitment Therapy for Chronic Pain," which has been deemed to have strong research support. A description of the treatment for this disorder is given, along with a list of references of the key research studies that support the approach. In searching by disorder, one can choose "Depression." A description of the disorder follows, along with a list of behavioral treatments with the empirical status of each. Students are encouraged to visit this website for information on the empirical status of behavioral approaches.

Limitations and Criticisms of Behavioral Approaches

It is most useful to approach a discussion of the limits of behavioral approaches from a historical perspective, primarily because of the ways those criticisms have been addressed in subsequent iterations of the approaches. One of the first limits of behavioral approaches in the early days was the marginalization of the role of cognitions and emotions. For the early behaviorists, the environment was the only determinant of behavior and therefore the only factor of consequence. Although Skinner had refuted this as a misunderstanding of his approach, this can be seen clearly in Skinner's, Watson's, and Wolpe's writings, to say nothing of Pavlov's lectures on behavior.

A second limitation is that behavioral approaches have not typically been focused on depth, understanding, and growth. Instead, they have focused on environmental contingencies that reinforce behaviors. Interventions then, have limited themselves to these contingencies in order to change problematic behaviors. Yet, we now have a clearer picture from the outcome literature that highlights the resistance of certain disorders to behavioral approaches (e.g., some anxiety disorders, delusions, hallucinations, and borderline personality).

A final limitation applies to all directive, confrontational approaches to counseling and psychotherapy. Certain clients will simply not take well to such approaches, not merely because they are resistant to change but because directive approaches can be insensitive to cultural differences, whether they be at the racial level or the individual level. That said, today's behavioral practitioners understand the vital necessity of building rapport, adapting to clients' styles and needs, and, of great significance, the role of ongoing informed consent to foster autonomy in clients (Murdock, Duan, & Nilsson, 2012).

Perhaps the most outstanding criticism of behaviorism is the mechanistic and dehumanizing way it approached human suffering. Initially, and then throughout its rigorous empirical history, behaviorists approached the human condition via studies of lower animals. Critics argued it was inappropriate to make generalizations about human behavior based on the behavior of rats or pigeons, two animals that contributed extensively to Skinner's findings and conclusions. Critics believed humans were being divested of human characteristics and their individuality. This depersonalization of human suffering was related to the second major criticism, which was that behaviorism was mechanistic in nature, that it reduced the complexity of humans and their systems (e.g., society) to observable behaviors. In the big picture, humans were being reduced to just small cogs in a large mechanism. It was also thought by critics that it was inappropriate to compare laboratory conditions to real-life situations—a laboratory environment was not the same thing as the real-world environment where people lived. Thus, the third major criticism was that behaviorists were being too simplistic in their view of behavior as all-important to the exclusion of all else.

Relevance of Theory

Behavioral therapies are widely employed in various settings (see Table 8.9), including the military, private practices, community mental health centers, psychiatric hospitals, substance abuse clinics, and social service agencies (e.g., Doss et al., 2012; U.S. Department of Veterans Affairs, 2012). Behavioral therapies are employed with both men and women and various age groups (Berkowitz, Wadden, Tershakovec, & Cronquist,

2003). Moreover, the strategies are used with individuals, couples, families, and groups (Christensen, Atkins, Yi, Baucom, & George, 2006; McCrady, Epstein, Cook, Jensen, & Hildebrandt, 2009). Behavioral therapies have been found effective for clients with various problems, including severe problems such as psychosis or borderline personality disorder (Bach, Hayes, & Gallop, 2012; Kopelowicz, Liberman, & Zarate, 2006; Linehan et al., 2006). One form of behavioral therapy, applied behavior analysis, is frequently the approach of choice when assisting individuals diagnosed with autism, whereas other forms of behavioral therapy have been used to treat anxiety, depression, insomnia, and PTSD (Foa, Hembree, & Rothbaum, 2007; Forman, Herbert, Moitra, Yeomans, & Geller, 2007; Morin et al., 2006).

Since the mid-1990s, behavioral therapists have focused on issues linked with race/ethnicity, sexual orientation, rural settings, gender, older adults, and physical disabilities (Iwamasa, 1997). Matthews (1997), among others (see Weaver, 1999), suggested culture-sensitive treatment guidelines for behavioral approaches when working with minority populations. According to the guidelines, therapists are expected to acknowledge that clients' multicultural demographic features might influence clinical judgment, treatment target behaviors, case conceptualizations, and therapeutic processes. For instance, a client's behavioral change may cause a malfunction in the person's family members if the client is part of a collectivistic family structure. Matthews also stated that the within-group differences were greater than between-group differences among minority populations. Additionally, the importance of collaboration between the therapist and the client during treatment is emphasized.

Recently, the American Psychological Association (2017) has recognized the importance of "increasing the number of racial and ethnic minority mental/behavioral health professionals and creating a culturally competent workforce to meet the needs of the expanding minority population of the United States" (p. 1). There is a lack of evidence, however, supporting the effectiveness of employing behavioral therapies when assisting members of multicultural groups. In addition, most meta-analytic studies (e.g., Abramowitz, Whiteside, & Deacon, 2005; Feske & Chambless, 1995; Hayes, Luoma, Bond, Masuda, & Lillis, 2006; Kliem, Kröger, & Kosfelder, 2010; Öst, 2007) have provided insufficient information about the relevance of behavioral therapies for multicultural populations.

In general, a wide variety of mental health professionals (e.g., counselors, psychologists, social workers, marriage and family therapists) use behavioral approaches when helping their clients. Therapists who are interested in offering a specific type of behavioral therapy can pursue a certification endorsement (Table 8.9). For instance, the Behavior Analyst Certification Board (BACB) and the Dialectical Behavior Therapy National Certification offer a certification for specialized behavioral treatments. Further, there are several associations that are composed of therapists and trainees that are interested in a behavioral approach, including the Association for Behavior Analysis International, Association of Professional Behavior Analysts, Division 25 of the American Psychological Association, the European Association for Behavior Analysis, Dialectical Behavior Therapy Association, and the Association for

Contextual Behavioral Science. Many graduate training programs offer certification in behavior analysis. Typically, BACB approves graduate-level training programs for Board Certified Behavior Analyst (BCBA) and Board Certified Assistant Behavior Analyst (BCABA) certifications.

Special Ethical Considerations

As alluded to earlier, behavioral approaches tend to be short in duration; they also are active, directive, and homework intensive. Therefore, we feel strongly that informed consent be routinely reviewed with clients to ensure they understand the risks associated with such treatment. We had discussed this briefly when we described flooding techniques earlier, but this applies to practically all modalities. Our first responsibility to our clients is to protect them from our treatments. We often remind our students that this injunction for the profession is significant because the potential "to do good" is paralleled by the potential "to do harm."

Clients must be made aware of the approach of the therapist and the implications for the role of the therapist and the client. For example, in most behavioral approaches, clients are expected to be active in articulating their goals for treatment outcomes. Paradoxically, however, the therapist's role is to set the path to reach those goals. This requires a give-and-take through ongoing assessment about the appropriateness of goals and fit with the therapist's approach. Whereas some clients will embrace these expectations, others may feel uncomfortable with both the directiveness of the therapist and with the emphasis on clear articulation of goals. For certain racial/ethnic groups and client populations, this can be off-putting and must be approached with care.

Autonomy is another ethical principle pertinent to behavioral approaches. Although clients are given the responsibility for establishing their own goals, the directive stance of the therapist can cause dependence on the therapist for ongoing support. This is a concern in all approaches, but we believe behavioral therapists need to pay particular attention to this dynamic. Our role as therapists is to foster a sense of interdependence in our clients and to liberate them from dependence on a therapist as the "authority."

Critics of classical behavioral approaches have claimed that they are superficial in assisting clients, and their assertion has merit. Ethically, our responsibility it not merely symptom reduction or change in external behavior alone. So, too, our role is not to attempt to reconstruct personalities, particularly in an outpatient setting. We must recognize that clients often do not fully realize what they need but that they also cannot achieve perfection in a clinical sense (if such a thing were to exist). Therapists owe their clients the respect of addressing their presenting problems and also helping clients map out clearer paths to wholeness. Symptom reduction is certainly part of that, but what contemporary approaches to behaviorism have done is to combine symptom reduction into a growth paradigm (see dialectical behavior therapy and ACT).

Application: Behavioral Approaches

RETURNING TO THE CASE OF HERLINDA

The behaviorally oriented therapist will gather information about the present environments that surround Herlinda. Home and school are her primary environments, and it would be vitally important to explore how these environments respond to Herlinda when she behaves in particular ways, and how Herlinda responds back. In doing so, the therapist would explore the web of actions and reactions that make up Herlinda's world; these patterns will show how Herlinda came to behave in the way that she is now behaving. The therapist must assess her situation in a culturally competent manner. Hays (2009) offered suggestions for clinically assessing and intervening in a culturally competent manner. A key concept is the idea of identifying strengths and supports that are connected to the client's culture. Herlinda is consistently negative about both her father's and her mother's culture. The therapist must keep in mind the difficulty that Herlinda has in identifying positive aspects of the cultures connected with her family and should explore cultural differences that may be causing some conflict for Herlinda. Finally, it would be important to investigate how Herlinda's cultural heritage could be transformed from a source of irritation and stress to a source of strength and support.

The therapist also would be interested in the secondary environments that Herlinda inhabits. Does she go to summer camp? Does she go to church? Does the family go on vacations? It is likely that Herlinda behaves differently in these secondary environments, and her behavior in these environments may furnish the treatment team— therapist, Herlinda, Herlinda's parents, along with any other relevant person such as her school counselor—with behavioral repertoires that could be applied to her primary environments. Again, in surveying these environments, the therapist would be interested in cultural connections. Herlinda, at

15, is engaged in identity formation, and a key aspect of this identity is her cultural status. Herlinda is an expert in finding the negative aspects of her cultural legacy, so the therapist would need to be correspondingly an expert in ferreting out positive aspects. For example, are there positive behavioral interactions that she engages with her father around his heritage—such as teasing or good-natured jokes? In unguarded moments, she admits that she liked her father's Puerto Rican *cuentos*—folktales that he told her as she was growing up. The therapist would then integrate the findings from *cuento* therapy (Constantino, Malgady, & Rogler, 1986) that describe the value in these cultural practices to promote positive personality development.

The therapist would find out how Herlinda learned and is learning to avoid certain behaviors and situations and how she has become accustomed to perform other behaviors. For example, how has Herlinda learned to avoid green salads? How did she begin to associate unpleasant sensations and taste with vegetables and pleasant sensations and tastes with blander foods such as pasta and rice? How did she learn to dislike exercise? Has she begun to avoid social situations? Has she begun to mistrust other children and assume that they will betray her confidence? Herlinda has disclosed that when she was in elementary school, a peer said that her dad was a waiter in the local Mexican restaurant. Herlinda shrugs off attempts to explore whether she feels different from the predominately White children at her school. Care must be taken to not alienate her with questions that she finds annoying while staying vigilant about the cultural aspects of her learning history.

Although she resists cultural exploration, Herlinda has a lot to say about other topics. The concerned grownups in her life have a lot to say as well. This material is important, but the therapist must guard against becoming too caught up in the verbal aspects of the material. Instead, the focus remains on the behavioral implications of the verbal reports. For example, Herlinda can be quite eloquent and funny about her lousy math teacher. The importance of this material is twofold. In a positive sense, it shows that Herlinda has a kind of comic behavioral repertoire that she, other children, and adults probably do not properly credit. She may be able to employ these comedic behaviors—her good sense of timing, her dry sarcasm, her good storytelling—in other social situations. Less positively, her comic tirades (and the therapist's reinforcing chuckles) may reinforce Herlinda's attitude toward her teacher and cause a negative cascade of behavior: Herlinda being more antagonistic toward her math teacher, which will likely cause him to be less helpful to Herlinda, which will likely lead to Herlinda trying less hard, which will lead to lower grades for Herlinda, which will lead to her to feel less competent, which will lead to Herlinda being more sarcastic about her teacher's ability, and so on.

The therapist must be careful to avoid inadvertently reinforce behaviors that carry with them negative consequences. The therapist would ask himself, "How is our very conversation tending to reinforce certain behaviors on her part and my part? Are there likely to be positive consequences from reinforcing certain behaviors and certain behavioral patterns? When I listen sympathetically to Herlinda talking about her sister, what is this reinforcing? Are there other behavioral patterns in Herlinda's peer relationships that have not been explored?"

In terms of the last question, one very interesting, less-than-helpful conversational and behavioral pattern of teenagers has been termed *co-rumination* (Rose, 2002). In co-rumination, teenagers, and in particular teen girls, make their problems worse by incessantly talking about their problems with their friends. Instead of feeling better after hanging out with friends and engaging in co-rumination, they feel worse—more discouraged, more depressed. This very interesting phenomenon plays right up a behaviorist's alley: The important thing to do with problems is not to dwell on them (in friendships or in therapy) but to take action to solve them. The therapist will be very careful not to reinforce Herlinda's tendency to ruminate on her problems and to be equally careful to focus on how their discussions can lead to actions to solve her problems.

Behavior treatment with Herlinda would proceed with a keen eye toward her multiple environments, mindful of her unique learning history, which taught her to avoid certain complex behaviors and practice other equally complex behaviors, and ever-vigilant to avoid dwelling on problems at the expense of taking steps toward resolving them. Throughout therapy, the culturally competent practitioner would be mindful of Herlinda's rejecting attitude toward her Latino heritage and seek to identify situations in which Herlinda might receive positive reinforcement for identifying with that heritage.

Returning to the Multicultural Case of the Sanchez Family

Contemporary behavioral approaches all follow a similar outline in therapeutic situations: relationship building, assessment, goals, interventions, evaluation, and follow-up (Neukrug, 2011). Various iterations of behavior therapy will address these areas differently, but in essence, assessment is the hallmark of these approaches. However, modern approaches to behaviorism made explicit the value of the relationship in treatment, and so we will begin there with Miguel, and then describe assessment, goals, and interventions.

Relation Building/Relationship

Therapeutic Relationship. The first observation that Dr. Ramirez notes to himself is that Miguel presents as angry and defensive and that his mother seems very anxious. This will require careful navigation of the relationships to honor Mrs. Sanchez's role in the family system while also acknowledging Miguel's feelings without condoning his behavior. This is a key step in working with Miguel because at this point he has not acknowledged a problem with his behavior or any desire to correct or adjust it. At the same time, Mrs. Sanchez's stress about Miguel's behavior and the subsequent pressure she is generating (toward Miguel, Dr. Ramirez, and herself) must also be addressed. Dr. Ramirez must be very intentional in how he approaches becoming an ally to the family as a whole and to the individuals as well. One of the main ways he will do this is through a thorough assessment of the behaviors exhibited by each person involved in order to gauge the effectiveness of those behaviors in reaching individual and, most important for Hispanic culture, *familismo*-related goals (Sue & Sue, 2008).

Assessment. Early on, behaviorists such as Skinner primarily focused on three aspects of behavior in their assessment: behavior of focus, antecedents, and consequents. For example, Miguel's situation would have been assessed based on the environmental conditions (environmental triggers or cues) immediately preceding his behavior and then the immediate consequences of those behaviors (contingency of reinforcement). Dr. Ramirez relies on multimodal therapy (Lazarus, 1976) in his approach to assessment.

Lazarus (1971) asserted that more areas of assessment are needed to treat the whole person. His approach highlights that all domains are relevant and focuses on practitioners learning a little about all, rather than overfocusing on one area in particular. The acronym for Lazarus's assessment approach is BASIC ID, so Dr. Ramirez would use the following for assessment:

1. **B**ehavior—actual behaviors (what Miguel and his mother are *doing*), their antecedents and consequents
2. **A**ffect—feelings that Miguel and his mother are experiencing or are likely to experience even if unaware of them
3. **S**ensation—paying attention to input based on sensory organs (sight, sound, touch, smell, taste)
4. **I**magery—"mental pictures" Miguel and his mom have about their lives and experiences
5. **C**ognition—essentially thoughts; specifically "common mistakes" in thinking, in particular, *categorical imperatives* (e.g., shoulds, oughts, musts), *perfectionism* (the denial of fallibility), and being a *victim of circumstance* (wherein our behavior is determined primarily by external factors)
6. **I**nterpersonal relationships—in Miguel's case, examining his relationship with his mother, his peers, and others
7. **D**rugs—biology, physiology and substances (naturally occurring and synthetic)

These categories allow Dr. Ramirez to systematically assess the events, attitudes, and actions of Miguel and his mother. His treatment of Miguel begins with initial assessment along the following course:

1. He obtains the Sanchez's presenting complaints (both Miguel's and his mother's).
2. He gains some understanding of precipitating events (based on each person's unique perspective).
3. He delineates various antecedent factors.
4. He examines the maintaining factors related to the presenting problem(s).
5. He ascertains some idea of what Miguel in particular hopes to derive from therapy.
6. He carefully notes overt signs of psychopathology.
7. He attempts to glean indications and contraindications for the implementation of various therapeutic styles and techniques.
8. He explores some definite indications as to whether a mutually satisfying relationship can be developed between himself and the Sanchez family. (See Lazarus, 1976, pp. 30–31)

Goals. Through the assessment described in the previous paragraphs, Dr. Ramirez is able to identify several goals that he checks out with Miguel and his mother.

Miguel's goals:

1. He wants to fit in with his American peers.
2. He wants his mom to get off his back (to stop pressuring him).
3. He wants to stop experiencing the consequences of his behaviors.

Mrs. Sanchez's goals:

1. She wants Miguel to more fully embrace and faithfully represent his Mexican heritage.
2. She wants Miguel to stop getting into trouble.
3. She wants a closer relationship with her son.

Right away Dr. Ramirez recognizes the conflicting nature of Miguel's goals, compared with his mother's. This is significant in behavior therapy because the goals must be specific, measurable, achievable, and desirable in order for clients to be invested in the work of therapy. Miguel's goals are more about staying out of trouble and fitting in—both are developmentally appropriate. Dr. Ramirez will intervene at this level of goal establishment, recognizing that there is likely much more going on with Miguel but that this is where Miguel is willing to start. Mrs. Sanchez's goals are more related to culturally appropriate behavior for Miguel and roles for them both. The next step for Dr. Ramirez is to work to bring Miguel's and his mother's goals into alignment in order to get both of their investment in those goals. Dr. Ramirez works to find common ground in their values to move them toward agreement (Hayes et al., 2012). For example, both Miguel and his mother agree that Miguel staying out of trouble is a good goal. Their respective motivations (see Weiner, 1986) for achieving this goal are different, but it is a place for Dr. Ramirez to begin. Dr. Ramirez establishes, alongside Miguel and Mrs. Sanchez, that Miguel reducing the number and intensity of his acting-out behaviors is a desirable and obtainable goal. With that, they get to work.

Interventions: Behaviors, Antecedents, and Consequents. Dr. Ramirez begins his intervention with a form of applied behavior analysis, in which he takes them through the process of understanding Miguel's behaviors in the context of the antecedents (what in his environment is occurring prior to his engaging in certain behaviors) and the consequents (what in his environment is occurring immediately following his behaviors), both of which serve to reinforce those behaviors. During this process, Dr. Ramirez discerns that the antecedents for Miguel's wearing certain clothes and avoiding family cultural functions include his being alone while at school and feeling isolated and being around his peers in class who use racial epithets, not directed at Miguel himself, but at other underrepresented groups. When Miguel distances himself from his cultural heritage (changing his clothes, music, and not attending Hispanic-oriented events), he perceives that he is more accepted by his peers, feels less isolated, and feels more a part of the predominant, White culture. These contingencies reinforce his aberrant (to his mother) behavior. Dr. Ramirez recognizes these contingencies are developmentally appropriate for a 14-year-old adolescent and also recognizes the cross-cultural ramifications of this situation. He notes to himself that part of his work will include assisting Miguel's mother in understanding her son's struggles to "fit in" as she also tries to help him maintain his cultural identity—an identity that he will likely one day regret losing.

Dr. Ramirez's working hypothesis at this point is that Miguel is bending to social pressure (real and perceived) by trying to "fit in" through these behaviors that are supposed to make him acceptable to his peers but that are also distancing him from his relationship with his mother and his heritage. The unintended result has proven to generate high levels of interpersonal stress for Miguel, in response to which he is making ineffective choices, by creating a false dichotomy (social success vs. cultural identity). Next, Dr. Ramirez identifies that one of the barriers to acclimating to a new environment is the process of adolescent development itself, and so he is careful to use change language with caution with Miguel. He is also aware of the slippery slope of acclimating resulting in acculturation: Miguel needs to feel a sense of connection in his new environment without giving up this significant part of his core identity. To that end, Dr. Ramirez addresses the issue of self-efficacy with the Miguel and Mrs. Sanchez, the notion that belief in one's abilities is a significant predictor of success, especially when combined with actual ability (Bandura, 1986). For Miguel, this means working on the four modes of increasing self-efficacy. The first mode is _mastery experiences,_ which involve personal achievement directly by Miguel. Another mode is recognizing his successes and _attributing those successes appropriately_ is key to building self-efficacy. Dr. Ramirez explains how we often have short, clouded memories, particularly in the presence of the stressors that bring us to therapy in the first place, and that his role is to systematically explore examples of Miguel's successes in social, academic, and behavioral management and to help him recall and interpret them accurately.

Two other modes are also available to Dr. Ramirez but are abbreviated here due to space. One mode is _observation,_ also called vicarious learning and associative learning, which involves drawing from the success of a similar other to build self-efficacy. The last mode is _verbal persuasion._ Given the esteem and status that Dr. Ramirez possesses in the Hispanic community in which he lives and works, he can wield great influence in the life of Miguel, in terms of motivating him to maintain his cultural identity and to acclimate to his surroundings.

Dr. Ramirez is also aware of another factor that he believes is contributing to Miguel's low self-efficacy and resultant negative behavior but which Miguel has been reluctant to discuss: anxiety. Physiological arousal can serve to enhance or decrease self-efficacy. Modest physiological arousal is associated with relaxed states and can contribute to increased self-efficacy, whereas high and aversive arousal can inhibit it. The sympathetic nervous system in our bodies alerts us to danger: the fight or flight— or freeze-response. When attempting a task, if this system is overactive, it can short-circuit our efforts toward and persistence in completing tasks. Dr. Ramirez, through his experienced listening and attending skills, has noted that Miguel talks around the topic of anxiety, describing his shortness of breath, sweating palms, and racing heart as "just anger." Dr. Ramirez believes that Miguel's acting out and his anger symptoms are most likely the result of poorly managed anxiety. As a behaviorist, Dr. Ramirez often suspects anxiety as an underlying cause of many presenting problems (Wolpe, 1973). He also knows that he can utilize a vast array of relaxation-training techniques to assist Miguel in reducing his anxiety in response to approaching a task, such as meeting new friends at school, balancing cultural heritage while living in another culture, and others. With this new insight, Dr. Ramirez proceeds.

CHAPTER REVIEW

SUMMARY AND COMMENTARY ▶▶

In this chapter, we have presented behavior therapy as an approach that grew in opposition to the dominant contemporary view, Freud's psychoanalysis. To the extent that it is necessary to set one's theory apart from the dominant view in order to establish said theory, it is also necessary that the theory evolves and "softens" its stance to establish itself as more credible and less reactionary. This happened with behavioral approaches. After an initial period in which "mentalistic" phenomena such as cognitions and consciousness and intent were eliminated (the first wave of behavior therapy), these and other mental and social aspects of human behavior were reintroduced by theorists and therapists in a second wave of change.

Thus, we find ourselves in the third wave of behavioral approaches (Hayes, 2004). These approaches have emerged in recent decades, partly in response to the environmental determinism of behaviorism and the perceived dehumanization of behavioral approaches (i.e., humans are merely animals to be trained/retrained using environmental contingencies). Behavioral approaches look very different now, because of their

evolution in response to research. They are far less likely to exalt behavior above cognition or emotion; yet, the core ethos of addressing action endures.

Today, no one can claim ownership of behaviorism, behavioralism, or a defining behavioral approach. However, the legacy of behaviorism's progenitors (Pavlov, Wolpe, Watson, and Skinner) is alive and well. Behavior matters. And when all is said and done in the therapy room, our shared goal with clients is some change in "doing." As such, therapists owe a debt of gratitude to the founders' systematic, empirical response to Freudian dominance. Regardless of one's theoretical orientation—particularly the nascent orientation of therapist-in-training—behavioral approaches deserve consideration in developing a clinical repertoire.

We began this chapter with the phrase "Behavior matters and is meaningful," and we would like to end with it as well. Clients experience any numbers of events, environments, and genetic predispositions that impact their lives. Additionally, therapists have a vast array of therapeutic approaches from which to choose. Regardless of that choice, in the end, most if not all client goals will have to do with their behavior. We may approach from the unconscious, from early environment and birth order, or through narrative; or we may approach directly through the assessment of the behaviors themselves. Managed care and client attrition limit the time we can spend helping clients experience success. Behavioral approaches are unlike any others in one simple way: They go right to the source (as they understand it)—overt behavior and its reinforcers. They provide concrete goals and specific steps to reach those goals. No matter our orientation, we must assist clients in changing their behavior—the only agreed upon power that all clients have. Table 8.9 provides a brief overview of key aspects of current behavioral therapies.

▼ TABLE 8.9

Brief Overview of Current Therapy Practice

Variable	Current Application
Type of service delivery setting	Private practice Community mental health centers Clinics Psychiatric hospitals Health care settings Substance abuse clinics Military Social service agencies
Population	Children Youth Adults Couples Families Groups Organizations
Type of presenting problems	Wide range of presenting problems

Variable	Current Application
Severity of presenting problems	Wide range of severity of presenting problems
Adapted for short-term approach	Yes
Length of treatment	Short term and long term
Ability to receive reimbursement	Insurance companies reimburse based on the company policy
Certification in approach	Behavior Analyst Certification Board Dialectical Behavior Therapy National Certification and Accreditation Association
Training in educational programs	Many graduate programs offer training programs for Board Certified Behavior Analyst (BCBA) and Board Certified Assistant Behavior Analyst (BCABA) certifications Association for Contextual Behavioral Science Association for Behavior Analysis International Dialectical Behavior Therapy Association
Location	Urban Rural Suburban
Type of delivery system	HMO PPO Fee for service
Fits with DSM diagnoses	Yes

CRITICAL THINKING QUESTIONS ▶▶

1. What role does a person's behavior directly play in influencing that individual? Think of a percentage of influence (between 0% and 100%) compared with two other factors (i.e., thoughts and emotions) to which you also assign percentages. Explain why you selected the percentages you assigned.

2. We have described behavioral approaches in terms of three developmental stages: early, later, and contemporary. What might still be missing that a fourth generation of behavioral approaches would need to address?

3. In the case of Herlinda, she has a lot going on in her life now and in the past. How do you think a therapist with a behavioral orientation would address early environmental contingencies in the present, if at all?

4. In Table 8.1, Skinner is quoted as saying, "mentalistic explanations explain nothing," yet later discussed that cognitions are important as behaviors. How would you reconcile these two positions?

5. Contemporary behavioral approaches emphasize client goals as driving treatment, yet it is the therapist who establishes what drives treatment. How do you view the prospect of "giving" clients their power in the session?

6. Learning is a major component of behavioral approaches, if not the dominant one. What are your thoughts about a treatment based primarily on training clients to behave differently as you might train a pet to sit?

7. Assuming a behavioral stance, how might you approach the process of informed consent with your clients? What would you want them to know about your approach prior to beginning therapy?

SUGGESTED READINGS: IMPORTANT PRIMARY SOURCES ▶▶

Books

Linehan, M. M. (1993). *Skills training manual for treating borderline personality disorder*. New York, NY: Guilford Press.

Martell, C. R., Dimidjian, S., & Herman-Dunn, R. (2010). *Behavioral activation for depression: A clinician's guide*. New York, NY: Guilford Press.

McKay, M., Wood, J. C., & Brantley, J. (2007). *The dialectical behavior therapy skills workbook: Practical DBT exercises for learning mindfulness, interpersonal effectiveness, emotion regulation & tolerance*. Oakland, CA: New Harbinger.

Spiegler, M. D. (2003). *Contemporary behavior therapy* (5th ed.). Belmont, CA: Wadsworth.

Williams, K. E., & Chambliss, D. L. (2015). Behavioral therapies. In B. Wolman & G. Stricker (Eds.), *Anxiety & related disorders: A handbook*. Chevy Chase, MD: International Psychotherapy Institute. Retrieved from http://www.freepsychotherapybooks .org/behavior-therapy/product/315-behavioral-therapies

Wolpe, J. (2015). *The behavior therapy approach*. In S. Arietti (Ed.), *American handbook of psychiatry* (Vol. 1). Chevy Chase, MD: International Psychotherapy Institute. Retrieved from http://www.freepsychotherapybooks.org/behavior-therapy/ product/632-the-behavior-therapy-approach

Journals

Behavior Modification

Behavior Therapy

Behaviour Research and Therapy

Cognitive and Behavioral Practice

Journal of Applied Behavior Analysis

Journal of the Experimental Analysis of Behavior

Websites

American Psychological Association, Division 25: Behavior Analysis: http://www.apa.org/about/division/div25.aspx

Association for Behavioral and Cognitive Therapies (ABCT): www.abct.org

Behavior Analyst Certification Board: http://www.bacb.com/ index.php?page=1

Behaviorists for Social Responsibility: http://www.bfsr.org/ BFSR/Home.html

Cambridge Center for Behavioral Studies: http://www.behavior .org/index.php

Skinner Foundation: http://www.bfskinner.org

Society of Clinical Psychology (APA Division 12): www.psychological treatments.org

Stanford Encyclopedia of Philosophy: http://plato.stanford.edu/ entries/behaviorism

COGNITIVE-BEHAVIORAL THEORY

Introduction

Cognitive-behavioral therapy addresses maladaptive mental health by modifying patterns of thinking, emoting, and behaving. Mental health professionals that use this approach strive to direct their clients by treating them as the expert about their lives and collaborating on treatment goals. Since the creation of cognitive-behavioral therapy, an extensive amount of empirical evidence has suggested this theoretical orientation is an effective and efficacious approach for a multitude of psychological problems. The ample amount of research support has contributed to cognitive-behavioral therapy becoming a widely utilized therapeutic approach across the spectrum of mental health practitioners (Norcross, Karg, & Prochaska, 1997).

Key Players of Cognitive-Behavioral Therapy

Albert Ellis (1913–2007) was born in Pittsburgh to a Jewish couple and was the oldest of three children (Cherry, 2017). His father was an unsuccessful businessman who typically spent time away from the family and, when he was present, paid little attention to his children. Ellis's mother was also emotionally distant from him and his siblings, and Ellis described her as self-absorbed and suffering from a bipolar disorder. Ellis was a sickly child. To overcome his difficulties, he decided that he would not be miserable about his circumstances. Instead, he began to maintain positive thoughts about his abilities and competence at the forefront of his thinking, a sort of precursor to his therapeutic approach.

Ellis found his way to psychology after earning a BA in business from the City University of New York (Kaufman, 2007). Ellis tried his hand at business and then at writing but found that the Great Depression was unfriendly to both entrepreneurs and fiction writers. Despite the difficulties associated with being a writer, Ellis realized he enjoyed writing, so he decided to persevere. Soon he was researching and writing nonfiction works that pertained to human sexuality and lay counseling devoted to the same topic. These experiences led him to pursue psychology as a profession. He obtained his MA in 1943 and his PhD in 1947 from Columbia University in the area of clinical psychology. Like many therapists in the 1940s, Ellis was initially drawn to Sigmund Freud's theory and method of practice. As a result of this interest, Ellis sought out psychoanalytic training, which he then applied to working with clients.

LEARNING OBJECTIVES

After reading this chapter, each student should be able to:

1. Articulate the contributions of key players of cognitive-behavioral theory and therapies.

2. Differentiate between cognitive theories, approaches, and strategies and behavioral theories, approaches, and strategies that are integrated into the cognitive-behavioral framework and related modalities.

3. Describe the cognitive-behavioral therapeutic process, including goals, the therapist's role, the client's role, the stages of change, and the therapeutic change processes.

4. Discuss the relationship between assessment and cognitive-behavioral theory and practice and the advantages and disadvantages of incorporating this theoretical framework into assessment practices.

5. Assess the advantages and limitations of cognitive-behavioral therapy with regard to multiculturalism and social justice (e.g., working with diverse populations).

6. Assess the advantages and limitations of integrating cognitive-behavioral theory and practice into the case conceptualization and treatment planning of diverse clientele.

▼ FIGURE 9.1

Albert Ellis

Source: OnurCaliskan6 (Own work) [CC BY-SA 4.0 (https://creativecommons.org/licenses/by-sa/4.0)], via Wikimedia Commons.

THE CASE OF ANDREA: A BISEXUAL WOMAN WITH ANXIETY

BACKGROUND

Andrea is a 36-year-old White, bisexual female who has suffered from troublesome anxiety for several years, but only recently sought help because of a panic attack she experienced. As a result of the panic attack, she was referred by her family doctor to a psychological services clinic in the general hospital of the state's capital city. Andrea has her medical degree and has been working as a general practitioner for the past 3 years at a small clinic that is affiliated with a Catholic hospital. She currently lives and works in a medium-sized midwestern town (population ~32,000), approximately 3 hours' drive from the small community where she grew up and where her father, mother, and brother still reside. She views her nuclear family as close and accepting. She attended both undergraduate and medical school in this same midwestern state.

INFORMATION PROVIDED TO THE THERAPIST

Andrea has had relationships with both women and men. Her first serious relationship was a high school boyfriend whom she thought she would marry, but she broke up with him during her first year of college, stating they had nothing in common after high school. She then casually dated for a period of time and had her first lesbian sexual experience during her junior year of college. Andrea reports that she did not date while attending medical school because she was focused on her studies and had little time to pursue either close friendships or romantic relationships. She recalls being immersed in her studies and feeling isolated during this period, partially because she felt she could not discuss her attraction to women with anyone. She says that she has always been serious ("perhaps anxious") but that her anxiety was heightened during medical school. Andrea is currently in a committed lesbian relationship. She met her partner, Callie, at a local art festival in which Callie was displaying and selling her paintings. For the past 3 months, Andrea has had (in addition to anxiety) significant difficulty sleeping and concentrating. She experienced her first panic attack 4 weeks prior to beginning therapy.

Andrea was drawn to Callie's art as well as to Callie, who seemed quite the opposite of herself: calm, confident, carefree, and comfortable with her identity. They began a friendship that developed into a romantic relationship approximately 2 years ago and have been living together for the past year. Andrea states that she is in love with Callie and has never felt so fulfilled in a relationship. Recently, Callie has expressed her wish to either have a commitment ceremony or get married in another state (same-sex unions are not accepted by many in the state in which they currently live, and there has been a recent move toward amending the state constitution to make same-sex marriage difficult to achieve). Callie would also like to take steps toward having a family.

Andrea's family became aware of her bisexual orientation after she began bringing her "friend" Callie to her parents' home for visits. She states her mother finally confronted her, asking if she and Callie were romantically involved. When Andrea confessed they were, she was surprised to learn that her family had suspected this was the case. They simply wanted her to be happy and would support Andrea's choice of partner, regardless of the partner's sex. Her family's acceptance was a relief and, to some extent, eased her anxiety regarding her sexual orientation. Andrea is not currently open about her sexual orientation in the community, feeling most people in the area will not be as accepting as her family.

The only gay, lesbian, and bisexual individuals she knows are a few of Callie's "artist" friends, and Andrea says she feels it is more acceptable by society's standards for artists to live "alternative lifestyles." Most of Andrea's professional colleagues are married, and she often hears comments from her older patients such as, "You're a pretty girl. You should hurry up and get married before you are too old to have children." Some of her colleagues have even tried to set her up on dates with men.

Recently, a nurse who works with Andrea told her that there have been some rumors about Andrea and her "roommate" and that if Andrea does not want men to get the wrong idea, she should probably live on her own since she can obviously afford it. Andrea has been feeling increasingly anxious and isolated at work. Furthermore, Andrea states that if she were to marry

Callie and have a family with her, she would be forced to become more explicit concerning her sexual orientation to others whom she typically encounters on a daily basis. Andrea reveals that she fears how coming out in the workplace and community would affect her career. She also states that she has mixed feelings about marrying a woman and bringing a child into that union. Although she loves Callie and wants to continue their relationship, she has qualms about whether two women should be married and have children. This has been a source of conflict between Andrea and Callie.

Case Discussion. Near the end of this chapter, a cognitive-behavioral therapy approach will be applied to this case.

It did not take long, however, for Ellis to become disenchanted with psychoanalysis, growing frustrated by the method's slowness, perceived ineffectiveness, and lack of empirical support. By 1953 he began to refer to himself as a "rational therapist," and by 1955 Ellis presented what was to become rational emotive behavior therapy to the psychotherapy community (his approach was originally referred to by Ellis as rational therapy, then as rational emotive therapy, and finally as rational emotive behavior therapy) (Epstein, 2001). Ellis's approach was considered revolutionary at the time and was to play a major role in moving psychotherapy practice toward a new way of perceiving and treating psychological problems. Eventually Ellis's form of therapy gained worldwide attention and a large number of adherents. Basically, it can be said that rational emotive behavior therapy, in general, caused therapists to recognize the importance of both the emotional and behavioral components of human disturbance with its special emphasis on how clients were creating problems for themselves through certain types of thoughts. Thus, by altering those thoughts that fabricate a person's problems, the person is set free.

Ellis lived in an apartment in the building that housed the not-for-profit Albert Ellis Institute in New York City. He supported the mission of the institute by donating all of his income to its operation, but Ellis did this with certain stipulations concerning his salary, living arrangement, and health care. For nearly half a century, Albert Ellis, who was considered by many authorities to be one of the world's most eminent practitioners and theorists, negotiated to be allotted a salary of $12,000 a year, provided an apartment at the institute, and receive health care (Kaufman, 2007).

Ellis's work ethic and productivity were legendary. He worked 16-hour days through most of his career, even mentoring students and holding lectures from his hospital bed during the last year of life. Ellis's bibliography of works (available through the Albert Ellis Institute) includes approximately 1,000 contributions in scholarly and professional publications (The Albert Ellis Institute, 2014). Specifically, he wrote professional journal articles, books, book chapters, forewords to books, articles for newsletters and magazines, reviews and comments concerning other works, and edited books. He also created audiotapes, videotapes, and compact disks and composed a number of "rational" therapy songs. Finally, Ellis presented at innumerable conferences and training workshops; he was interviewed for various magazine and newspaper articles and was featured in a documentary film (Editors @TheFamousPeople, 2013; Epstein, 2001; GoodTherapy, 2007–2017).

Despite his many achievements during his lifetime, the board of the Albert Ellis Institute removed Ellis from his seat on the board and canceled his weekly seminars in 2005. The board contended that payments for his health care (nursing care was required) and other costs they attributed to Ellis made the institute vulnerable to losing its tax-exempt status. Several members of the board also claimed they felt "uncomfortable with his confrontational style and eccentricities and saw him as a liability" (Kaufman, 2007, p. A1). Ellis sued the board, and a court decision in 2006 reinstated Ellis to the board. Ellis died a year later.

Aaron T. Beck (born 1921) was the youngest of three children. He was born in Providence, Rhode Island, to Jewish parents who had emigrated from Russia. Prior to his birth, his sister died as a result of an influenza epidemic, after which Beck's mother became severely depressed. According to his family history, this depression did not lift until Beck was born (Cherry, 2017).

After an infection from a broken arm escalated to a near fatal illness, Beck had to repeat a grade in school because he had accrued too many absences. It was at this point in his life when he began to doubt his intellectual capabilities. His illness also left him phobic about blood, physical injury, public speaking, and suffocation. When Beck later reflected on this period in his life, he stated that he used reasoning to alleviate his childhood fears and anxieties. Beck's self-taught cognitive skills appeared successful, as he laid to rest his worries about his mental ability, went on to enroll in medical school, and subsequently made many public presentations during his career (Seligman, 2006).

In 1942 Beck graduated from Brown University magna cum laude and later earned an MD from Yale Medical School. He initially expressed an interest in neurology during his residency but switched to psychiatry. At the time of his medical training, the most common form of treatment for psychiatric patients was either Freud's approach to psychotherapy or a regime of prescribed medical treatments, including the early use of chemical interventions. (In some instances, it was a combination of both, a sort of psychodynamic-pharmacology approach.) It did not take Beck long to become convinced that neither of these approaches was adequate to enable patients to learn how to care for themselves. Nor did these standards of treatment instill in patients any self-assurance, hope about their future, or even a lasting change for the majority of them in the grips of a mental disorder. In addition to these realizations, his passion for research moved him away from psychoanalytic theory toward developing his cognitive-behavioral therapy approach for treating conditions such as depression.

Beck concluded that people with depression suffered from faulty logic. He theorized that depressed individuals listened to what amounted to being an inner critic that made predominantly negative evaluations of themselves, the world, and the future. Beck's views concerning depression spurred him to explore the utilization of cognitive-based therapy for numerous psychiatric complaints, including anxiety symptoms, eating disorders, panic disorders, phobias, and individuals who were assessed to be a suicide risk (Aaron T. Beck Psychopathology Research Center, n.d.; Center for the Prevention of Suicide, n.d.). It was during the latter half of the 20th century that cognitive therapy amassed a tremendous amount of empirical support. In fact, cognitive therapy accrued over 200 outcome studies that indicated it was an effective treatment approach for therapy.

Currently, Beck is professor emeritus in the Department of Psychiatry at the University of Pennsylvania (Taraborrelli, 2012). During his career, Beck created a number of self-report measures for depression and anxiety. These measures are frequently considered to be the gold standard when it comes to assessing such conditions for either the purpose of treatment or for use in outcome research studies. Beck's assessments include the Beck Anxiety Inventory (BAI), Beck Depression Inventory (BDI), Beck Hopelessness Scale (BHS), Beck Scale for Suicidal Ideation (BSS), and Beck Youth Inventories of Emotional and Social Impairment–Second Edition (BYI-2).

In 2006 Beck was selected for the Lasker-DeBakey Clinical Medical Research Award, a prestigious scientific honor, and in 2010 he was the recipient of the Sigmund Freud Award presented by the New York Chapter of the American Society of Psychoanalytic Physicians. In addition to several other awards and honors received by Beck, he was awarded the 2011–2012 Edward J. Sachar Award for his contributions toward the treatment of low-functioning patients with schizophrenia. See Table 9.1 for comments made by Albert Ellis and Aaron T. Beck (Cherry, 2017; Taraborrelli, 2012).

▼ TABLE 9.1

Quotable Albert Ellis and Aaron T. Beck

Albert Ellis
- The art of love is largely the art of persistence.
- The best years of your life are the ones in which you decide your problems are your own. You do not blame them on your mother, the ecology, or the president. You realize that you control your own destiny.
- Stop "shoulding" on yourself.
- There are three musts that hold us back: I must do well. You must treat me well. And the world must be easy.
- Self-esteem is the greatest sickness known to man or woman because it's conditional.
- I get people to truly accept themselves unconditionally, whether or not their therapist or anyone loves them.
- Freud had a gene for inefficiency, and I think I have a gene for efficiency. Had I not been a therapist, I would have been an efficiency expert.
- There is virtually nothing in which I delight more, than throwing myself into a good and difficult problem.

Aaron T. Beck
- You can do therapy in a barn.
- The stronger person is not the one making the most noise but the one who can quietly direct the conversation toward defining and solving problems.
- Cognitive therapy seeks to alleviate psychological stresses by correcting faulty conceptions and self-signals. By correcting erroneous beliefs we can lower excessive reactions.
- Stop it, and give yourself a chance.
- What you might have noticed is that the approach I took during the session was to devise a hypothesis, gather data by way of experiments, see if the data confirms the hypothesis, and, if necessary, form new conclusions. In a way, it's really quite scientific.
- Cognitive therapy seeks to alleviate psychological stresses by correcting faulty conceptions and self-signals. By correcting erroneous beliefs we can lower excessive reactions.
- Some authors have conceptualized depression as a "depletion syndrome" because of the prominence of fatigability; they postulate that the patient exhausts his available energy during the period prior to the onset of the depression and that the depressed state represents a kind of hibernation, during which the patient gradually builds up a new store of energy.

Sources: AZQuotes. (n.d.). Quotes by Aaron T. Beck. Retrieved from http://www.azquotes.com/author/37421-Aaron_T_Beck; Beck, A. T. (1976). *Cognitive therapy and the emotional disorders.* New York, NY: International Universities Press; Beck, A. T. (1988). Love is never enough. New York, NY: Harper & Row; Ellis, A. (1996). Better, deeper, and more enduring brief therapy: The rational emotive behavior therapy approach. New York, NY: Brunner/Mazel; Cherry, K. (2017, June 15 [updated]). Albert Ellis biography. Retrieved from https://www.verywell.com/albert-ellis-biography-2795493; Goodreads. (2017). Aaron T. Beck>quotes. Retrieved from https://www.goodreads.com/author/quotes/91432.Aaron_T_Beck; Goodreads. (2017). Albert Ellis>quotes. Retrieved from http://www.goodreads.com/author/quotes/12929.Albert_Ellis; and The Albert Ellis Institute. (2014). About Albert Ellis PhD. Retrieved from http://albertellis.org/about-albert-ellis=phd/

Historical Context

The underpinnings of cognitive theory can be traced back to an early Greek philosophy formulated by Epictetus, a form of philosophy that focused attention on the connection between the concepts "freedom" and "determinism"—believing that it was our inherent freedom that could protect us from becoming a victim of emotional turmoil. The followers of Epictetus further asserted that human excellence was obtainable through fostering and nurturing our *prohairesis*, a term that has multiple meanings (e.g., choice, intention, moral choice, will, volition). Epictetus stated that it was prohairesis (our freedom) that enabled us to decide to live a life based on rational thinking. Furthermore, it was rationality that allowed us to maintain a healthy psychological balance that is free of emotional disturbance. Epictetus also believed it was the ability to live a rational existence that made humans different from animals since animals were incapable of breaking free from their instinctive nature. Thus, according to Epictetus, it is only humans who can choose how they will react to unpleasant, threatening, or painful circumstances. Finally, it should be noted that Albert Ellis often mentioned that Epictetus's form of philosophy provided an essential building block for rational emotive behavior therapy.

Fast forward a couple of millennia to the mid-20th century, and we find behaviorism to be in full swing in the United States. Dropping back in time a few decades before mid-20th century, we find the work of Ivan Petrovich Pavlov, along with the efforts of radical behaviorists in America, shifted psychology away from psychodynamic approaches toward behavioral approaches, approaches that were very much influenced by both World Wars. The cultural zeitgeist embraced the scientific paradigm for all things medical, including mental health. As science developed, behavioral approaches (Antony & Roemer, 2011), easily studied and replicated, proliferated.

By the 1960s, however, it was becoming increasingly clear that nonmediational approaches (e.g., radical behaviorism did not account for the potential effects of cognitive processes on behavior) were not comprehensive enough to explain all of human behavior (K. S. Dobson & Block, 1988). An example of radical behaviorism's shortcoming is a client with obsessional thinking (e.g., an obsessional thinker who suffers from a persistent thought about stabbing a child in the eye with scissors), which made noncognitive models less relevant than models that considered cognitions as an intervening factor for certain behaviors. At this time, a growing number of psychologists began to integrate cognitive meditational constructs into their behavioral work and research. Prime examples of this trend include Bandura's social learning theory (renamed social cognitive theory in 1986), Ellis's rational emotive therapy, and Beck's cognitive-behavioral therapy for depression.

By the 1980s, Bandura's research incorporated a greater holistic perspective. As a result, his work provided a much more complete understanding of the connection between cognition and behavior. For example, he put forth the model of triadic reciprocality (or triadic reciprocal determinism), a model that recognizes the interconnections between the traits of a person (e.g., belief system; cognitive processes such as thinking, reasoning, or remembering; personal preferences; temperament), behaviors expressed (e.g., actions, manner of speaking, facially expressed emotions), and relevant features of the environment (e.g., cultural patterns, other people, social groups, physical surroundings). Bandura's model is one that considers all three parts of the triad to be mutual determinants, which means that all three factors (behavior, environment, and the person himself) influence one another in a multidirectional manner. For example, if a person, who believes himself to be timid, opens a door to a noisy social gathering, he might seek out a relatively quiet spot in such an environment. But if on entering the room a familiar person, someone he finds attractive, stops him before he can find a quiet spot and this person engages him in lively, enjoyable conversation, this environmentally based event has altered his behavior and thoughts (thinking changes from uncertainty to self-assuredness). Bandura also examined how self-efficacy beliefs affect behavioral outcomes, that is, to what degree confidence in one's ability to achieve something determines whether one can succeed or not. According to Bandura (1977), the "expectations of personal efficacy are derived from four principal sources of information: performance accomplishments, vicarious experience, verbal persuasion, and physiological states" (p. 191) such as the "following modes of induction . . . attribution, relaxation/biofeedback, symbolic desensitization, symbolic exposure" (p. 195).

As a result of Bandura's research, clients were given more respect and power than what had been attributed to them via classical behaviorist theory, which basically viewed people as passive learners responding to environmental reinforcements. In the late 1960s, Bandura's paradigm of social cognitive thinking quickly transformed into pure forms of cognitive therapy, as theorists George Kelly (1991), Albert Ellis (1962, 1994, 1996), and Aaron Beck (1967, 1976, 2005) established separate but similar theories. George Kelly had gained considerable attention for an approach he called personal construct psychology (Kelly, 1955).

Bandura's Social Cognitive Theory Compared With Radical Behaviorism

Bandura's theory, and his approach to studying humans, differed noticeably from the radical Skinnerian theory and its approach to conducting research (Bandura, 1965, 1977, 1986, 1997; Bandura, Ross, & Ross, 1961). The two approaches diverged from one another in six ways:

1. Social learning studies, similar to Skinnerian research, also utilized controlled laboratory conditions, but these studies differed from Skinner's approach in that humans, and not rats or other animals, were the focus of these studies.
2. Skinner's findings with animals were extrapolated to human behavior because behavior was seen as being ubiquitous and of the same quality regardless of its origin. In contrast, Bandura's research was almost entirely carried out using humans. As a result, there was no need for an empirical leap of faith to apply the findings to humans. (Furthermore, when humans were observed in real-world settings, evidence was found, post-Banduraian research, that supported his conclusions.)
3. Radical behaviorists saw humans as passive learners (built to respond to stimuli), who lived in a world of omnipresent reinforcers, whereas Bandura asserted the learning process was an active one in which humans could choose what they wanted to learn in a wide multitude of situations.
4. Bandura painted a world of indirect reinforcement, which means that a human might learn an action through vicarious reinforcement. That is, the learner has observed someone else receiving a positive reinforcement for a certain action

(an action that the observer internalizes, i.e., has learned indirectly for future use). Bandura conceptualized the concept of reinforcement in broader terms than did Skinner, who held that reinforcement was very much a direct process rather than an indirect process.

5. Radical behaviorism took the position that unless a behavior was displayed subsequent to reinforcement, no learning had occurred. Bandura asserted that if a behavior was observed but not displayed afterward, it was not proof that no learning had taken place.

6. Finally, Bandura spoke of internalized behaviors, that is, learned behaviors that were securely in position because they were imitated and steadily reinforced for being displayed, in contrast to radical behaviorism, which claimed that humans were essentially a "behavioral tabula rasa"; that is, displayed behaviors are always in flux and open to change because new external reinforcers can alter a learned behavioral response.

Nonradical behaviorists appreciated the empirical emphasis and evaluation of cognitive therapy's effectiveness, and shortly after cognitive therapy coalesced, behaviorists merged cognitive concepts with behavioral approaches. Toward the end of the 20th century, cognitive and behavioral approaches to therapy were fully integrated (Craighead, Craighead, Kazdin, & Mahoney, 1994; Freeman, Simon, Beutler, & Arkowitz, 1989). This new form of therapy basically viewed the mechanisms of change as the combination of restructuring thought patterns and modifying behavioral responses to the environment. In part, because of the expectations of managed health care (Lawless, Ginter, & Kelly, 1999), which aimed to increase the level of shorter, greater cost-effective forms of treatment, cognitive-behavioral therapy gained the attention of many psychotherapists before and at the start of the 21st century (Gazda, Ginter, & Horne, 2001).

It should be pointed out that cognitive-behavioral therapy also had developed as a reaction to the perceived shortcomings of psychoanalytic approaches to therapy, but the influence of psychodynamic theory on the evolution of cognitive-behavioral theory is undeniable, according to Reinecke and Freeman (2003). For example, both approaches use topographic models of personality and psychopathology. That is, Freud divided the psyche into the conscious, preconscious, and unconscious domains, with an individual's behavior mediated, to varying degrees, by the id, ego, and superego. In terms of cognitive-behavioral therapy, cognitive processes are partitioned into automatic thoughts, assumptions, and schemas.

Basic Concepts

Over time, cognitive-behavioral therapy has become a school of thought encompassing an array of theories and practices on a continuum from more behaviorally oriented therapies to purely cognitive approaches; however, these various therapies share a fundamental core of features and assumptions from which their distinctions and elaborations have evolved.

Cognitive-behavioral theory suggests that people's problems largely derive from distortions of reality, which are based on erroneous premises and assumptions. During therapy, clients unravel their cognitive distortions and learn alternative, more realistic ways to understand their experiences. The aim of the cognitive-behavioral therapist is to enable clients to obtain an accurate understanding and awareness of their own cognitions and how those cognitions affect their behavior. In addition to this cognitive focus, therapists utilize behavioral strategies that require clients to behave in a certain fashion.

For instance, a client might be asked, between therapy sessions, to imagine going through the steps of a specified activity, enabling her to consider the obstacles that may arise and immediately afterward carry out that activity in the real world. Other homework assignments may require the client to keep a log for a week, using it to record any automatic thoughts that initiated negative feelings or unproductive behaviors (Beck, 1976).

Cognitive Schemas

Cognitive schemas are cognitive structures made up of both abstract and general knowledge about the attributes of a stimulus or event and the relationship among these attributes. As such, cognitive schemas are cognitive-emotional structures. Both cognition and emotion are the essentiality of cognitions.

People learn from and are shaped by past perceptions and interpretations of events, which, in turn, organize and mediate their views of the world, themselves, and others (Okun, 1990). These cognitions, which may be based on faulty or maladaptive assumptions and beliefs, become organized into enduring schemas that are an individual's template for coding and understanding life. Past consequences, interactions with others, and expectations for the future all play roles in the development of the cognitive schemas. Schemas can be adaptive or dysfunctional; are activated by events, stimuli, or stressors; and govern automatic thoughts, both emotional and behavioral, about people and life events. It is cognitions, not events, situations, or people, that help people classify life events and affect how people feel and behave. Automatic thoughts in one's conscious awareness, coming out of cognitive structures and processes, tacitly rule the way people make meaning of their world (Reinecke & Freeman, 2003). Thus, thinking, feeling, and behavior are all connected.

Schemas of cognitive distortions are components of a distorted reality. Faulty schemas can create a cyclical and "stuck" effect in the way people process and experience life. For example, when a depressive schema is the meaning system through which a person perceives past experiences, this system is also superimposed over new events and experiences as the means of evaluating and interpreting them. Strong evidence supports the conclusion that people are more likely to understand new or discrepant information they receive in terms of what they already believe, instead of using the new or discrepant information to revise their existing beliefs (Reinecke & Freeman, 2003).

Cognitive Distortions

Cognitive distortions are maladaptive ways that people process information, and they can impact people's lives in negative ways. Some cognitive distortions delineated by Beck (1976) include (1) *arbitrary influence* (drawing a conclusion based on false or missing evidence), (2) *magnification or minimization* (imagining the worst or denying importance), (3) *personalization* (relating external circumstances to oneself when there is no true relationship), (4) *dichotomous thinking* (all-or-nothing thinking), (5) *mind reading* (projecting thoughts onto others), and (6) *selective abstraction* (only recognizing part of the picture, omitting other parts) (Okun, 1990). Interrupting cognitive distortions by unearthing them, revising them, and practicing the new, adaptive cognitions is an important aspect of cognitive-behavioral therapy. The therapist is considered a coinvestigator who helps the client explore his thoughts and emotions (Reinecke & Freeman, 2003). Inductive methods are used, in which thoughts are treated as hypotheses that can be questioned, tested, and revised based on new information.

Other types of cognitive distortions include *catastrophizing* and *"should" statements*. An individual with anxiety disorder may catastrophize. That is, the individual will believe that she will undoubtedly experience negative or catastrophic results if certain actions are taken (i.e., "My life will be ruined if I fail this exam"; "If I don't go to this party, all of my friends will hate me."). Individuals with obsessive-compulsive disorder use "should" statements, reflecting an individual experiencing excessive guilt in many cases (i.e., "I should always make my friends happy;" "I should be able to handle every task my boss assigns me") (Reinecke & Freeman, 2003).

Although somewhat self-evident, it should be mentioned that therapists themselves can experience varying degrees of cognitive distortions. Thus, therapists need to be aware that they might have their own distortions related to their role and effectiveness in the therapeutic relationship. Similar to their clients, they must also check their thoughts for maladaptive, negative processes (Seligman, 2006).

Behavioral Work

As a time-limited therapy, cognitive-behavioral therapy's brevity is partially due to its instructive nature and utilization of psychoeducation and homework assignments. Effective cognitive-behavioral therapy involves a trusting relationship with the therapist, but the mechanism for change is not the client–therapist relationship as in interpersonal therapies; rather, it is in learning new ways of acting based on cognitive learning. This form of therapy is a collaborative effort in which the therapist facilitates reaching goals through teaching structured techniques and specific strategies, which the client enacts for more effective coping.

The Therapeutic Process

Goals

The primary goals of cognitive-behavioral therapy are management of symptoms and symptom reduction. Therapists help clients examine their cognitions or the way in which they view themselves and others to help them to learn new and more effective ways of behaving. The cognitive-behavioral therapist identifies measurable goals and directly approaches the targeted goals. A very important objective is to improve clients' sense of mastery and control and to enhance personal competence so that they can better approach life's difficulties. Thus, cognitive-behavioral therapy focuses on clients' competence, that is, on clients learning skills to use on their own in future predicaments.

Therapist's Role

The cognitive-behavioral therapist recognizes the prominent role that the therapist–client alliance performs in relation to successful outcomes in therapy. Therapists seek to develop an optimal level of rapport to enhance client engagement and hope. Within this relationship, the cognitive-behavioral therapist is directive, investigative, active, and structured in treatment implementation. Clients' autonomy is respected, yet the therapist directs the course of treatment. Therapists use a directive approach from the start of therapy, and these therapists often use a manual for the systematic delivery of a treatment.

Client's Role

Cognitive-behavioral therapy places the role of responsibility on the client. The client is expected to be as active as the therapist. The client is responsible to contribute to his own change. For instance, the client is expected to complete self-assessment checklists in session and at home. In addition, homework is often assigned, which the client is expected to complete. The degree of a client's willingness to participate in therapy will determine the degree of directness of the cognitive-behavioral therapist. The dyadic participation is expected to be complementary. If the client volunteers a high level of participation, a therapist is most likely to diminish her level of being directive, but if the client is less engaged than necessary, the therapist would adopt a more dominant role in the therapeutic process.

Therapeutic Change in Cognitive-Behavioral Therapy

Stages of Change. The stages of change model conceptualizes the client's situation with regard to motivation for change. There are five defined stages of change in cognitive-behavioral therapy (Prochaska, DiClemente, & Norcross, 1992), and clients' motivation for seeking treatment can vary significantly depending on which stage of change they are currently in (Figure 9.3).

Alcohol abuse is used to illustrate the five stages of change.

- *Precontemplation stage:* The first stage describes a state in which individuals are unaware (or not fully aware) of the problematic nature of their behavior, such as in the case of alcohol abuse (Dimeff, Baer, Kivlahan, & Marlatt, 1999). If precontemplative clients are judicially referred for treatment, they will most likely interpret their court referral as primarily the result of "bad luck."

- *Contemplation stage:* The second phase occurs as individuals begin to recognize some of the harmful effects of their behavior and begin to think about change. At this stage, a large degree of ambivalence accompanies any motivation to change, and individuals often struggle with both the perceived positive experiences they have had with their dysfunctional behavior, such as in the case of drinking, as well as the perceived effort or difficulty required by the change process (Prochaska, DiClemente, & Norcross, 1992).

- *Preparation stage:* The third stage of change occurs when individuals have resolved some of their ambivalence and are committed to the idea of change at some point in the near future (Dimeff et al., 1999).

▼ FIGURE 9.3

Five Stages of Therapeutic Change: Clients' Motivation for Seeking Treatment and Stage of Change

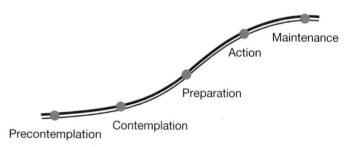

Source: Philciaccio (Own work) [CC BY 3.0 (http://creativecommons.org/licenses/by/3.0)], via Wikimedia Commons.

- *Action stage:* The fourth stage occurs as the individual makes the attempt to undergo behavioral as well as environmental changes to address the perceived problem. The individual is considered to be in the action stage for the first six months following a change in behavior.
- *Maintenance stage:* The final stage is the lifelong phase of stabilizing behavioral change and preventing relapse.

Work with clients in the early stages of change often focuses more on assisting clients to overcome their ambivalence toward change by calling attention to the discrepancy between current dysfunctional behavior and the desired goal, while simultaneously minimizing resistance (a process referred to as the therapist "rolling with the resistance," i.e., not responding in a manner that would likely elevate a client's resistance to change). During the later stages of change, when the client's self-efficacy takes center stage, the therapist serves as a resource and support for the client.

Assessment

Cognitive-behavioral therapists value outcome assessment, which is considered a vital process in treatment. They use ongoing assessment either to modify, stop, or continue interventions. Cognitive-behavioral therapists use a variety of psychological measures to examine client disorders, which include cognitive-behavioral rating scales and therapist rating scales that determine diagnosis and whether cognitive-behavioral strategies are working with a particular client. For instance, Achenbach's (1991) Child Behavior Checklist is a behavioral rating scale that elicits quantitative information and can be used by a therapists, parents, or teachers to rate and monitor the behaviors of a child client. Beck and his colleagues' Cognition Check List (CCL) is an assessment that zeros in on a client's automatic thoughts by checking their frequency of occurrence during the process of treating depression and anxiety.

The Beck Depression Inventory (BDI), the Beck Hopelessness Scale (BHS), and the Beck Anxiety Inventory (BAI) are standard assessment and outcome measures for cognitive-behavioral therapy (Beck Institute for CBT, 2016). These measures have approximately 20 items and require 5 to 10 minutes to complete. When depression is the primary concern, the BDI is helpful in assessing severity of symptoms as well as depressed mood. The BDI can be given each time the therapist and client meet for a therapy session, which allows the therapist to obtain an objective measure to gauge therapeutic progress. When a client's anxiety is of primary concern, the BAI has proven useful to ascertain what therapeutic direction should be taken to treat a client's problem. In addition to being valid for diagnosis purposes, the BAI also provides an indication about the severity of anxiety symptoms. Furthermore, the BAI has been shown to be very useful in predicting panic symptomology. The BHS also measures negative expectancies about the future and can be used in conjunction with the BDI to assess suicidal intent and behavior. The predictive validity of the BHS indicates very low false negatives, ranging between 6% and 9%. From this brief review, it can be concluded that cognitive-behavioral therapists are very interested in measuring the effectiveness of their treatments through objective analysis of data obtained with standardized tests and/or by receiving direct feedback from their clients.

The Department of Veterans Affairs National Center for PTSD (i.e., posttraumatic stress disorder) has developed two well-constructed measures for the identification of PTSD in former members of the armed forces (and current members based on special agreements). The Post-Traumatic Stress Disorder Checklist–Military Version (PCL-M) is a 17-item self-report measure that is used as a general screening tool to iden-tity veterans for whom trauma-focused treatment is appropriate. Once these veterans are identified, they are eligible for a more comprehensive assessment by the Clinician-Administered PTSD Scale (CAPS). The CAPS is a 30-item interview that is structured in a manner to determine acute stress disorder (ASD) and PTSD symptom severity, with a division between frequency and severity, as well as a determination of the degree to which current symptoms interfere with social and occupational functioning. Cut-off scores determine progressive levels of intervention from large-scale veteran psychoedu-cation to individual prolonged exposure therapy. (Note. The symptomology for ASD and PTSD overlap. ASD is assigned if symptoms have existed for less than a month; beyond that point the therapist will assess for PTSD. ASD has been found to be an accu-rate predictor of a person eventually being assigned a diagnosis of PTSD [Gibson, n.d.].)

Techniques and Strategies

To begin, the cognitive-behavioral therapist develops a treatment plan, which guides tech-niques to be employed, which typically are both cognitive and behavioral in nature. Some strategies tend to be more cognitive and some more behavioral. Some of the newer treat-ment models that have gained popularity include interpersonal and relational features.

Cognitively Oriented Strategies

Priority List. The therapist and the client might develop a cognitively and behaviorally based list that is tentative in nature so that it can be modified depending on what occurs during the course of therapy. The use of a list is especially appropriate in cases where the client initially complains of feeling overwhelmed with changes discussed. The simplest problem to solve may be addressed first in order to instill hope in the client. Overall, such lists can make the process of therapy tangible and transparent for a client. It can also serve other purposes, such as helping to categorize goals into long-term and short-term goals, provide an approx-imate time frame for accomplishing goals, break down the tasks required to meet a goal, and, obviously, list goals in order of importance. Again, such lists are best viewed as repre-senting a tentative plan that is pliable since the cognitive-behavioral therapist's hypotheses about what is contributing to the client's reported problem might require modification.

Categorizing Themes in Beliefs. Once beliefs are identified as contributing to emotional dis-tress, the cognitive-behavioral therapist can assist the client by categorizing these beliefs into particular broader themes (Parrott, 2003). Over the years, a number of broad-based themes have been identified, themes that help to explain the way clients are likely to respond to certain situations. Clients who engage in *all-or-nothing thinking* see things as perfect or horrible, and they see no shades of gray. Those who engage in *mind reading* infer what other people think or feel, and they presume the worst. Clients who *overgeneralize* view instances as happening always or never. For example, a client might state that she is "always dealt a bad hand." For beliefs categorized in the *magnification theme,* clients exaggerate the severity and/or impact of a problem. Clients who engage in *emotionally based reasoning* believe that how they feel actually reflects how they truly are; for example, they are totally worthless because they feel worthless in a particular situation. Finally, clients who *self-blame* tend to operate from a type of internal locus of control that is self-defeating because they take responsibility for negative events that are truly beyond their control. Basically, the cognitive-behavioral therapist works with the client to determine what negative, stable schema of automatic thoughts is present. (In this context, a "schema" can be thought of as a mental codification of experience that has organized the way a client will perceive and respond to a certain environmental stimuli or situations.)

A cognitive-behavioral therapist is trained to examine closely the possible meaning of words spoken by the client during sessions—especially those words that the client relies on to describe himself because such word usage often has a meaning idiosyncratic to the client. A deeper exploration into the meaning of a client's chosen words frequently provides the therapist with more information and specificity about what contributes to the client's suffering.

Cognitive techniques are employed to decrease the emotional distress experienced by clients. For instance, if a depressed client believes that no one worries or cares about her (a *generalization*) and this client is repeatedly dropped off by her mother to attend sessions, the cognitive-behavioral therapist will refer to the mother's assistance as caring behavior. The aim of this comment is to refute the client's maladaptive belief that no one worries or cares about how she is doing (the client's maladaptive belief also implies "I'm not important or lovable"). The cognitive-behavioral therapist might also offer a professional self-disclosure during a session, saying that she has enjoyed meeting with the client and strongly believes that the therapy is working (obviously this would not be said if progress was not being made). Such a self-disclosure can be expected to strengthen the working alliance.

Perspective-Taking by Client. Day, Howells, Mohr, Schall, and Gerace (2008) have suggested that therapists incorporate interventions that increase the client's *perspective-taking ability.* Specifically, Day et al. (2008) report the efficacy of *visual feedback* (i.e., clients viewing videotapes of themselves), *chair-work* (i.e., clients engaging in a dialogue between conflicting aspects of themselves), and *forgiveness therapy* (for clients who have been victimized and feel very angry). Through these interventions, clients are able to do perspective taking about their experiences and the experiences of others' and thus develop empathy for others.

Disputation by Therapist. The type of cognitive disputation used by Albert Ellis can be a directive cognitive strategy. It involves direct questioning of the client to prove or provide examples that justify a held belief. To reduce clients' defensiveness to the disputation approach, the therapist engages in searching for evidence in a sensitive manner.

Imagery. The therapist might indirectly dispute cognitions by using imagery, based on the assumption that similar neurological and emotional processes are experienced by the client when simply imagining a difficult scenario (Parrott, 2003). In this instance, a therapist could ask the client to imagine his problem and envision behaving in a different manner, with a more desired outcome. The act of imagining a difficult scene in the therapist's presence offers a safe environment in which the client learns changed emotional responses.

Motivational Interviewing. In the professional literature, *motivational interviewing* (MI) is described as "a client-centered, directive method for enhancing intrinsic motivation to change by exploring and resolving ambivalence" (Miller & Rollnick, 2002, p. 25). Motivational interviewing is not a rigid combination of therapeutic tactics so much as it is a method of being with a client that is designed to elicit the client's own change process. A key point of the motivational interviewing technique is that it respects the individual's autonomy, that is, the client's decision to change or not change, which is seen as residing with the client. In using motivational interviewing, the therapist takes the role of a collaborator trying to elicit from the client motivation, rather than adopting a role that denotes a hierarchical professional arrangement wherein the therapist imparts wisdom to the subordinate client.

In a general sense, motivational interviewing can be understood as consisting of certain principles that serve to guide the therapist's actions. With regard to the principle of expressing therapist empathy, the therapist attempts to "understand the client's feelings and perspectives without judging, criticizing, or blaming" (Miller & Rollnick, 2002, p. 37). This therapy process promotes the working relationship, client self-esteem, and client motivation to change. It should also be noted that understanding and acceptance are distinct from agreement or approval, and it is possible for a therapist to accept a client's behavior without condoning it.

One way that motivational interviewing differs from Rogerian client-centered therapy is that it is intentionally directive (Miller & Rollnick, 2002), as exemplified by another guiding principle, *developing discrepancy* in the client. The clinician helps clients to perceive and analyze a discrepancy between their current behaviors and desired life. As resistance arises in the face of change, the therapist will employ *rolling with resistance*, which means the therapist will not argue against the resistance because this is likely to cause the client to argue back and reinforce the client's reluctance to change. Rather, the therapist will acknowledge the difficulty of changing behaviors and recruit the client in problem solving. An example of rolling with the client's resistance is when the therapist acts in a manner to reactivate therapeutic movement by saying something such as "You're the person in charge. The one who really knows what she wants and you're the person who has to struggle with the ambivalence of wanting to change and wanting to avoid change because change is difficult. [Long pause] I'm here to help." The essence of rolling with the resistance is captured in a remark made by the Chinese sage Chuang Tzu who said, "To force one thing to become what it is not is to fail twice" (Xiaomin & Palmer, 2000, p. 72).

Behaviorally Oriented Interventions

Modeling Behavior. Calling on Bandura's social learning theory, which emphasizes the impact of modeling the behavior of perceived effective people, the cognitive-behavioral therapist will model behaviors that counteract a client's problematic behaviors so the client can observe and learn alternative behaviors. In general, credible models (e.g., counselors, teachers, nurses, and correctional officers) represent an excellent resource for the client to acquire other ways of responding that lead to positive client change in institutional environments (e.g., mental health clinics, public/private schools, hospitals, and prisons). In addition to the social context of people-to-people interactions that is provided by various settings, it is of utmost importance to realize that social interactions allow for ample opportunities to observe behaviors that literally can alter aspects of the observer's perception, thinking, reasoning, and remembering. Essentially, the memory of empathy (and other types of responses) can be acquired through the learning process associated with the therapeutic process. For example, before empathic behavior can appear in the behavioral repertoire of angry clients, such clients will learn compassion and understanding during the course of therapy, compassion and understanding that are soon manifested by the sight or thought of their therapist with whom they have a therapeutic relationship. Specifically, the indirect reinforcements of observation and experience (which differ from Skinner's direct reinforcements of rewards) will increase the likelihood that the client will display empathic behavior inside and outside therapy and in the future after therapy is concluded.

Behavioral Activation. The behavioral aspect of cognitive-behavioral therapy helps to modify clients' behavior caused by environmental stimuli. For instance, depressed individuals do not receive positive reinforcement from their interactions in their environment. Rather, they experience punishment, which reduces their motivation for further interactions and causes them to isolate themselves. The resulting isolation feeds into their depressive mood in a cycle of deeper depression over time. Positive reinforcement through skills training in coping with unfavorable situations and gradual introduction to interactions will help alleviate their symptoms. The underlying assumption supporting the use of behavioral activation is that "increases in overall activity related to pleasant events . . . will reduce depressive mood and other depressive symptoms" (Manos, Kanter, & Busch, 2010, p. 548).

Functional Analysis. A powerful tool used by therapists to understand the function that a client's behavior is serving is called *functional analysis*. The "ABC" of functional analysis can be used to understand the presence of depression that is promoting a painful sense of low self-esteem in a client. In this example, the ***A****ntecedent* or preceding event is two men fighting outside a bar that the client frequently visited in the past; the ***B****ehavior* is not having been successful in stopping the fight and while attempting to intervene he was knocked down in front of others; and the ***C****onsequence* is the client began to isolate himself from the two men starting the day after the fight. Soon afterward, he began to avoid other men he perceived to be similar to the two fighters. Isolation in this case functions as a means to avoid the pain of feeling like a "depressed, weak, humiliated" person. Avoidance of an aversive situation is a negative reinforcement that will increase the level of isolation from what the client is avoiding. In the short term, isolation will provide periods of freedom from the painful emotions he has been experiencing; however, in the long term, it will fuel negative emotions that simply feed a cycle of further avoidance and isolation and greater depression (Reinecke, Ryan, & DuBois, 1998). Behaviorists, therefore, favor having clients do activities that they are not motivated to do initially. Specifically, behavioral activation would involve having the isolated client perform activities that would reduce his isolation, and as a result it can be expected that the client will start experiencing pleasure in these activities. It is important, however, that these activities are based on the client's actual life and values.

Exposure Therapy. Just as behavioral activation is evidence based for treating depression, so is exposure therapy for treating anxiety disorders. There are different kinds of exposure therapy, such as imaginal exposure therapy, in vivo exposure therapy, prolonged exposure therapy, and narrative exposure therapy (i.e., NET; Neuner, Schauer, Roth, & Elbert, 2002). When NET is applied to children, it is referred to as KIDNET (Onyut et al., 2005). NET is an evidence-based therapeutic strategy for treating PTSD resulting from multiple and/or continuous traumatic stressors. It uses exposure therapy mainly through repeated narration of traumatic events until the sensory-perceptual-emotional representations of the traumatic event (i.e., hot memory or situationally accessible memory) is accepted into the autobiographical context memory (i.e., cold memory or verbally accessible memory), thereby ensuring habituation. NET is an easy therapeutic approach that lends itself to storytelling found in every culture.

Homework Methods. The cognitive-behavioral therapist might also employ behavioral means to alter irrational beliefs. The client might be asked to behave in ways that differ from her irrational beliefs and document the experiences that result, or the therapist might have the client engage in bibliotherapy (i.e., reading literature), which involves both behavior and thinking. Assigning homework is a trademark technique of cognitive-behavioral therapy. The homework assigned might be cognitive, behavioral, or both. The assignment might involve documenting activities, their frequency, potency, and duration in a checklist, and adding new activities as needed. It might also take the form of short journaling within a given number of words or self-examination of cognitions. As suggested by Reinecke and Freeman (2003), the homework assigned should flow naturally from the topics of the session and the client's life. Failed homework assignments provide information about what went wrong and how to offer a corrective experience in a future exercise.

Currently Popular Cognitive-Behavioral Therapies

Dialectical Behavioral Therapy

Dialectical behavioral therapy was developed by Marsha Linehan (1993) to treat clients who met the criteria for borderline personality disorder and who were also considered chronically suicidal (Table 9.2). Linehan postulated that a borderline personality disorder stems from more than a single cause but, at its core, can be found in the early experiences of a child who lived in an invalidating environment, whose effects linger and serve to annul any sense of personal acceptableness the child, and later the adult, may feel. As a result of such experiences, the emotional responses of these clients can fall outside the range of what is typically considered acceptable. These are emotional reactions that are poorly modulated. The person can swing between extremes (the person loves you one moment and then, what seems instantaneous, hates you for no discernable reason), a process referred to as emotional dysregulation. Furthermore, a direct attempt to change the client's faulty beliefs through traditional forms of cognitive-behavioral therapy will fail, according to Linehan, because attacking the person's faulty thinking will invariably be perceived as an attempt to invalidate the entire person and will be reacted to strongly. As an adult, such a person feels emotionally vulnerable, unable to handle conflicting elements of life, and, during stressful periods, will experience emotion dysregulation, that is, a serious reduction in emotional control. The lack of emotional control and the high degree of perceived unacceptableness (they are unacceptable to themselves and others) often finds expression in some type of self-destructive behavior.

▼ TABLE 9.2

Dialectical Behavioral Therapy: An Approach Born of Personal Experience

Marsha Linehan created dialectical behavior therapy largely as a result of her own experiences. Due to destructive behaviors that included cutting herself with any available sharp object (cutting her arms, legs, and midsection) and burning herself repeatedly with cigarettes, at age 17, Linehan was placed in a facility to treat her disorder. Her motivation to die deepened after she was confined to a seclusion room. Deprived of sharp objects and cigarettes, she started to bang her head against the room's walls and floor. Records show that she was prescribed Thorazine and Librium, given a total of 30 electroshock treatments, and subjected to a Freudian form of therapy. Misdiagnosed as suffering from schizophrenia, she was eventually discharged after 26 months with a note in her discharge record that stated she was "one of the most disturbed patients in the hospital" (Carey, 2011, p. 2). Concerning her 26 months of incarceration, Linehan said, "I was in hell and I made a vow: when I get out, I'm going to come back and get others out of here" (p. 2). After obtaining the required education and credentials, Linehan returned to help others. She took with her a new approach to treating clients, a treatment approach that evolved into what was to become dialectical behavioral therapy.

In an interview with *The New York Times*, Linehan discussed her journey from psychiatric patient to developing her own form of therapy. It is clear from her comments that certain personal experiences and the knowledge gained through professional training and practice were pulled together to create a highly effective treatment. One personal experience that convinced her of the importance of "acceptance" is highlighted here. Early in her life, while still struggling with mental health issues of her own, Linehan reported experiencing a profound experience while praying in a small Catholic chapel located in Chicago. She described this life-altering experience in the following way: "One night I was kneeling in there, looking up at the cross, and the whole place became gold—and suddenly I felt something coming toward me. It was this shimmering experience, and I just ran back to my room and said, 'I love myself.' It was the first time I remembered talking to myself in the first person. I felt transformed" (Carey, 2011, p. 2). The experience left her with a deep, lasting appreciation of how true acceptance relates positively to mental health.

Source: Carey, B. (2011, June 23). Expert on mental illness reveals her own fight [Electronic version]. The *New York Times*. Retrieved from http://www.sadag.org/images/pdf/expert%20own%20fight.pdf

Dialectical behavioral therapy requires the client to take part in both individual and group therapy, a form of treatment that can last about a year. By the end of therapy, clients will have achieved greater interpersonal effectiveness, distress tolerance, and an ability to regulate their emotions appropriately. At the core of dialectical behavioral therapy is an amalgamation of components, such as Zen mindfulness and its approach to living, a dialectics approach to conflicting elements in life, and an emphasis of validating experiences and achieving acceptance of self and others (Linehan, 1993). A brief review of each component follows.

- *Zen Buddhism component:* Clients are taught how to let go of their natural tendency to cling to thoughts and images associated with pain and suffering and develop the ability to be mindful of their surroundings while accepting the good or bad nature of events without being judgmental.
- *Validation and acceptance component:* Clients learn that the thoughts they have, feelings they experience, and behaviors they display during any particular real-life situation are the logical outcome of their past and current life and a reflection of their personal strengths and weaknesses. For a client suffering from the vicissitudes of borderline personality disorder, the power of being able to achieve a sense of acceptance cannot be overestimated.
- *Dialectical component:* This component pertains to clients developing the ability to recognize and identify opposing aspects of their life. In addition, clients obtain the realization that some things in life can be changed and some things cannot be changed, that these two attributes of change apply to them and others, and

that this is all right. Most important is the realization that if they are to change for the better, they must confront the conflict created when they chose to refute their current view of themselves for what they are capable of becoming. The level of difficulty involved in accomplishing this critical task becomes apparent when one genuinely considers what it means for these individuals to accept their unacceptableness by embracing who they really are—this process is analogous to fighting fire with fire.

Linehan's treatment approach consists of individual therapy, skills training groups, telephone consultations, and the use of a consultation team. It is a form of therapy that requires regular consultation meetings with teams of therapists who provide feedback and support to each other. The provision of support is an essential part of dialectical behavioral therapy because working with clients diagnosed with a borderline personality disorder can be very difficult and therapy sessions can be very intense.

Acceptance and Commitment Therapy or ACT

ACT is said as one word; it is not pronounced using each separate initial. Steven C. Hayes's ACT therapy is aimed at transforming the way we look at psychopathology (Rousmaniere, 2013). Hayes believes that therapists should move away from conceptualizing client problems as reflecting some form of maladaptive behavior covered in the *Diagnostic and Statistical Manual of Mental Disorders (DSM)*. Specifically, Hayes has advocated moving the concept of psychopathology away from its content (symptoms) and its form (highs, lows, course of disorder) toward viewing psychopathology in relation to its context. In an interview Hayes stated, "An honest examination of it [*DSM*] points to it being a billion dollar failure" (Rousmaniere, 2013, n.p.). Furthermore, Hayes believes that once a therapist (or client) begins to focus on *DSM* symptoms (treating problems like they are an illness), the client's innate problem-solving mechanisms become stymied. The major aim of ACT is to regain a focus on the psychology of what is normal rather than abnormal. An important assertion of ACT is that clients going into therapy should not be viewed as "broken," so there is no need for them to be "fixed" (or cured).

ACT interventions consist of utilizing mindfulness strategies and personal acceptance combined with behavior-change techniques and a strong infusion of commitment to one's values.

In ACT, rather than teach clients to cognitively master their negative emotions, troublesome memories, disruptive thoughts, or unpleasant sensations, ACT's goal is to teach clients to recognize the presence of such mental events as they occur, to accept them for what they are, and psychologically consider each of these as representing an individually unique experience, especially those that clients had previously identified as unwanted. According to ACT, this is a process that is opposite of what is often practiced in therapeutic settings where a form of "therapeutic avoidance" is taught. For example, clients are expected to overcome certain negative thoughts, that is, learn to avoid them. Hayes believes there is more to therapy than just being focused on taking time to identify, dispute, and change certain cognitions. Therapists should be providing the type of support that enables a client to do a better job with those parts of their lives that they care the most about (e.g., family members or some work-related passion they have never been able to fully pursue). ACT emphasizes assisting clients to clarify what personal values are genuinely important to them and then act on those values. According to Hayes, when clients act on values that are important to them, they experience greater vitality and psychological flexibility. Possibly of utmost importance, by taking action on values, clients establish a personal meaning for living.

ACT seeks to apply evidence-based principles related to human affect, behaviors, and cognitions (Hayes, 2004; Hayes, Follette, & Linehan, 2011; Hayes, Strosahl, & Wilson, 2016; Hayes, Villatte, Levin, & Hildebrandt, 2011). The process of therapy involves clinical behavior analysis; that is, the therapist and client actively work as a team to explore and estimate the nature of past and current patterns of interacting with others, which leads next to determining how and what is required for the client to move toward a fuller, meaningful life based on personal values (an accomplishment that takes place regardless of any counterproductive thoughts and feelings that remain present). ACT assumes that the key to accurately perceiving what feeds the problems reported by clients can be obtained via a process represented by the acronym FEAR. The four components of the process FEAR allow a therapist to obtain a detailed understanding of what is supporting a client's problem. FEAR stands for the following:

- **F***usion* with one's thoughts, joining with a problematic thought
- **E***valuation* of an experience from a judgmental stance
- **A***voidance* of an experience judged unacceptable
- **R***eason* given for subsequent behavior

The healthy alternative to FEAR is to ACT. This acronym stands for the following:

- **A**ccept reactions and be present in the here and now.
- **C**hoose a valued direction.
- **T**ake meaningful action.

Trauma-Focused Cognitive-Behavioral Therapy

A variant of cognitive-behavioral therapy, called trauma-focused cognitive-behavioral therapy (TF-CBT; O'Callaghan, McMullen, Shannon, Rafferty, & Block, 2013), emerged as a result of models that were developed to better understand information processing and emotional dysregulation. Over time, cognitive-behavioral theorists and researchers have learned a great deal about the ways in which traumatic experiences can disrupt core cognitive processes and turn them into pathological fear structures. It is these pathological fear structures that result in children (Cohen, 2005) who suffer from PTSD to incorrectly perceive normal situations as dangerous or unsafe and to see themselves as being too incompetent or too vulnerable to handle these negative situations (Reinecke & Freeman, 2003).

There are eight components to TF-CBT when used with children, which are summarized by the acronym PRACTICE (Bisson & Cohen, 2006). The eight components are listed next.

- **P**sychoeducation and parenting skills training
- **R**elaxation training
- **A**ffective expression and regulation of feelings
- **C**ognitive coping
- **T**rauma narrative development (creating relevant narratives [stories] concerning a trauma) and processing of narratives generated
- **I**n vivo gradual exposure to triggers associated with the child's PTSD
- **C**onjoint parent and child therapy sessions
- **E**nhancing the safety and future development of the child

Before any of these interventions are introduced, the therapist must build trust and rapport with the child and the child's parents. Moreover, parents are integrated into the therapeutic process because they are essential to the progress of their child; even if a parent cannot give adequate support, that parent remains an important aspect of treatment (Griffin, 2007).

TF-CBT with children usually consists of 12 to 18 sessions and is considered brief therapy. According to Griffin (2007), termination involves three steps. First, the therapist predicts setbacks and then helps the client (and parents) establish plans to handle setbacks that might occur after the therapy has been terminated. Second, a discussion takes place concerning how parents are to fulfill the role of a continued resource and support for their child through difficult times. Finally, there is a graduation ceremony to celebrate the children's accomplishments in facing their traumatic events and understanding that the traumatic events are in no way their fault.

Trauma-Focused Cognitive-Behavioral Therapy and Veterans

Serving in the military can result in trauma of various causes. During combat a soldier may witness frightening events, lose a friend, or experience bodily injury. In addition, other events, such as sexual harassment and sexual assault, can have a traumatic effect that goes unreported (Figure 9.4). The Department of Veterans Affairs and the Department of Defense (VA/DoD) have used TF-CBT with large numbers of veterans who returned from Iraq and Afghanistan suffering from psychological trauma (Fischer, 2015; Foy, Ruzek, Glynn, Riney, & Gusman, 2002; VA/DoD, 2010). The VA/DoD (2010) concluded that cognitive restructuring and exposure therapy (in vivo and imaginal forms are utilized) are two of the more effective treatment modalities for veterans with trauma. The VA/DoD also views psychoeducation, relaxation training, and coping skills management as effective and indispensable parts of their treatment protocol.

Interestingly, TF-CBT computer-based interventions have been used with veterans in the early stages of their reaction (i.e., an acute stress reaction) to a trauma for the purpose of preventing the

▼ FIGURE 9.4
Military Sexual Trauma

DanielBendjy/Vetta/Getty Image

Note: Another cause of PTSD is referred to as military sexual trauma (MST), which has been linked to incidents of sexual harassment and sexual assault. The National Center for PTSD reports 55% of women and 38% of men serving in the military have experienced sexual harassment. Of the women serving in the military, 23% have reported sexual assault.

development of PTSD. Computer-based interventions resemble individual services in that this form of intervention can be specialized to meet what each veteran requires (Draper & Ghiglieri, 2011). A genuine advantage of these computer-based interventions is that they require fewer resources than what individual therapy requires because clients complete work online and therapists get involved when necessary. Finally, clients without a personal computer may access their treatment through a VA center's computer lab.

Group therapy allows therapists to work with multiple veterans at a time, thus saving time and financial resources for the institution. Group therapy also provides social support, allows for the development of basic social skills through social learning, and provides an intervention for social isolation and alienation due to trauma reactions. Medical consultations are also provided to those clients involved in TF-CBT group work, given their prolonged, significant symptomatology. Medication is also utilized as an adjunctive treatment when therapy proves to be insufficient (VA/DoD, 2010).

Individual cognitive-behavioral therapy is an excellent form of treatment for those clients who experience significant distress following trauma (VA/DoD, 2010). Also it is not surprising that veterans who feel uncomfortable sharing in a group or who have extreme social deficits are likely to find individual TF-CBT more conducive to their treatment than group therapy (VA/DoD, 2010). The use of individual therapy provides a higher level of care because it furnishes clients with more time and resources than computer-based interventions or trauma-focused group therapy and by its very nature relies on a concentrated form of attention that many victims of trauma find helpful. In addition, those clients assigned to individual cognitive-behavioral therapy are offered medical consultations as needed. Even though differences can be found across the various forms of treatment used in VA hospitals, TF-CBT is implemented in some form in all the different treatments utilized whether computer-based intervention, group therapy, or individual therapy. By applying TF-CBT across the board, it guarantees that clients will experience consistency in their treatment, especially when they move between the different forms of treatment.

Multiculturalism and Social Justice

Cognitive-behavioral therapy encompasses many possible therapies, which have proven to be effective for an array of client issues. Although cognitive-behavioral therapy's ideographic or individualized applications of principles in assessment and treatment make it receptive to variability in client characteristics, there remain inherent problems that need to be addressed and adapted for culturally sensitive treatment of multicultural clients (Coleman, 2003).

Hays (1995) identified three limitations in cognitive-behavioral therapy with multicultural clients. First, cognitive-behavioral therapy purports to be a value-neutral approach; however, no therapeutic intervention is free of social bias. The assumption of a "value-neutral approach" itself shows an inherent bias toward a dominant social view in the United States. The result of applying such an approach universally is that it can cause the therapist to overlook the concerns of clients from marginalized groups. For example, cognitive-behavioral therapy emphasizes self-control as empowering and simultaneously blames clients' beliefs about injustice, not seeing the latter as a potential step toward self-empowerment. Therapists are expected to be cognizant of any personal prejudicial attitudes held toward the lesbian, gay, bisexual, and transgender (LGBTQ) population, as well as value-based diagnoses of transgender experiences as gender identity confusion. Therapist biases may manifest as avoidance of sexuality issues in therapy or the assumption that a client is heterosexual. At a minimum, cognitive-behavioral therapists should simply ask direct, nonjudgmental questions that convey an attitude of acceptance. In this way, they communicate that sexual orientation is suitable for the therapy hour (Safren & Rogers, 2001). Multicultural awareness of one's own heterosexism and of the profession's traditional disregard for diversity in sexual orientation and sexual identity will enable the therapist's cognitive-behavioral treatment to be culturally sensitive (American Psychological Association, 2012).

The second limitation of cognitive-behavioral therapy (Hays, 1995) is that insufficient scrutiny is paid to a client's family and personal history. Although cognitive-behavioral therapy emphasizes the uniqueness of the individual at the present time, it rarely focuses on the immigration or sociopolitical history that the individual brings to the treatment. Cognitive-behavioral therapists should be familiar with historical events and the reactions of gay and lesbian clients to these events, for example, 1993's Don't Ask, Don't Tell policy, which was rescinded on September 20, 2011; Proposition 8 in California, which overturned a state court ruling legalizing same-sex marriage; the Defense of Marriage law; and which states resisted the most and which states resisted the least to the idea of same-sex marriage. With regard to personal history, cognitive-behavioral therapists need to know a client's issues surrounding GLB identity, such as the coming out process (Purcell, Campos, & Perilla, 1996). The therapist should be aware of a client's involvement in GLB social, cultural, and political issues, as well as how the client interprets what is meant by "societal oppression" (Safren & Rogers, 2001). Understanding the sociopolitical climate that GLB persons currently endure will assist the therapist in providing culturally sensitive therapeutic treatment.

According to Hays (1995), the third drawback to using cognitive-behavioral therapy is that its heavy reliance on a rational perspective and scientific methodology reinforces a stereotypically European American worldview, which is believed to devalue other worldviews that privilege other forms of knowledge, such as intuition, mind-body-spirit-environment holism, sensory perception, or Eastern enlightenment, and social behaviors of modesty, nonassertiveness, and introversion. Understanding cognitive-behavioral therapy's limitations with diverse clients allows for clinicians to adapt cognitive-behavioral therapy's effective treatments to better fit diverse populations.

The American Psychological Association (2012) issued a number of guidelines for conducting therapy with GLB individuals that fall under five themes: psychologists' attitudes, GLB relationships and families, diversity issues, and economic and workplace issues, as well as touching on psychologists' training and education. Truncated, paraphrased versions of 17 of American Psychological Association's recommended guidelines are presented here.

Theme: Attitudes Toward Homosexuality and Bisexuality

1. Strive to understand the effects of stigma (i.e., prejudice, discrimination, and violence) and its various contextual manifestations in the lives of LGB people.
2. Understand that same-sex attractions, feelings, and behavior are normal variants of human sexuality and that efforts to change sexual orientation have not been shown to be effective or safe.
3. Strive to recognize the unique experiences of bisexual individuals.
4. Strive to distinguish issues of sexual orientation from those of gender identity.

Theme: Relationships and Families

1. Recognize that the families of LGB individuals may include people who are not legally or biologically related.
2. Strive to understand the ways in which a person's LGB orientation may have an impact on his or her family of origin and the relationship with that family of origin.
3. Recognize that families of LGB people also go through a painful coming out process.

Theme: Issues of Diversity

1. Strive to recognize the challenges related to multiple and often conflicting norms, values, and beliefs faced by LGB members of racial and ethnic minority groups.
2. Consider the influences of religion and spirituality in the lives of LGB persons.
3. Strive to recognize cohort and age differences among LGB individuals.
4. Strive to understand the unique problems and risks that exist for LGB youth (e.g., homelessness, suicide, drug abuse, trafficking).
5. Recognize the particular challenges of LGB individuals with physical, sensory, and cognitive-emotional disabilities.
6. Strive to understand the impact of HIV/AIDS on the lives of LGB individuals and communities.

Theme: Economic and Workplace Issues

1. Consider the impact of socioeconomic status on the psychological well-being of LGB clients.
2. Strive to understand the unique workplace issues that exist for LGB individuals.

Theme: Education and Training

1. Strive to include LGB issues in professional education and training.
2. Increase knowledge and understanding of homosexuality and bisexuality through continuing education, training, supervision, and consultation. (APA, 2012, pp. 12–27)

In 2013 the board of the Association for Lesbian, Gay, Bisexual and Transgender Issues in Counseling (ALGBTIC), a division of the American Counseling Association, published updated competencies pertaining to counseling lesbian, gay, bisexual, queer, questioning, intersex, and ally (LGBQQIA) individuals (ALGBTIC LGBQQIA Competencies Taskforce, 2013). The update provides an in-depth look at the concerns of diverse sexual orientations and identities and includes ally individuals, as well as those who identify as intersex, questioning, and queer.

Ally and intersex areas had not been commented on before in the professional literature and have become two sources of burgeoning study. The ally portion of the update divides competencies into subsections. The first subsection offers counselors, who identify as allies, a frame of reference and lists 23 competencies. The second subsection lists 16 competencies for counseling those who identify themselves as allies. Because many counselors are not familiar with the intersex population, the intersex section of the document covers basic information about individuals who possess characteristics of both sexes, that is, intersex characteristics that are related to chromosomes, genitals, testes or ovaries, or sex hormones (ALGBTIC LGBQQIA Competencies Taskforce, 2013, pp. 27–28). The document lists 19 competencies that pertain to intersex individuals.

Overall competencies are arranged in eight sections (A–H): A. Human Growth and Development (19 competencies), B. Social and Cultural Foundations (12 competencies), C. Helping Relationships (18 competencies), D. Group Work (21 competencies), E. Professional Orientation and Ethical Practice (13 competencies), F. Career and Lifestyle Development (12 competencies), G. Assessment (17 competencies), H. Research and Program Evaluation (9 competencies). Altogether the competencies presented are very thorough and certainly meet the counseling organization's goal of formulating competencies that offer the means "for creating safe, supportive, and caring relationships with LGBQQIA individuals, groups, and communities that foster self-acceptance and personal, social, emotional, and personal development" (ALGBTIC LGBQQIA Competencies Taskforce, p. 2).

Finally, cognitive-behavioral therapy's commitment to science and empirically supported treatments is helpful when working with LGBQQIA clients. This commitment to a scientific approach is especially important because some gay and lesbian clients may request behavioral therapy or religious counseling to change their sexual orientation (Yarhouse, 1998), but it has been empirically demonstrated that conversion treatment is both ineffective and has "potentially damaging effects" (Haldeman, 1994, p. 226). The musician, singer, and songwriter Lou Reed wrote the song "Kill Your Sons" in response to his parents having him undergo a form of conversion therapy that relied on electrically induced seizures (i.e., electroconvulsive treatments) to "cure" his attraction to other males. Figure 9.5 shows Reed as a high school student and provides the opening lyrics from "Kill Your Sons."

Lou Reed

"Kill Your Sons"

All your two-bit psychiatrists are giving you electro shock

They say, they let you live at home, with mom and dad

Instead of mental hospital

But every time you tried to read a book

You couldn't get to page 17

'Cause you forgot, where you were

So you couldn't even read . . .

Don't you know, they're gonna kill, kill your sons

They're gonna kill, kill your sons

Source: English: Freeport High School. [Public domain], via Wikimedia Commons.

Special Ethical Considerations

Both proponents and critics of cognitive-behavioral therapy have outlined several salient ethical concerns that need to be addressed when working with this form of therapy. Cognitive-behavioral therapy often takes a psychoeducational approach to therapy. In this teaching design, the therapist can become an objective expert who dictates the domain of rational and irrational thoughts. However, the powers (authority) of others are often sources of distress that some clients already carry when entering therapy. Therefore, therapists need to be mindful of how much client–therapist power differential they allow in the therapeutic relationship and how even subtle displays of power can be detrimental to successful outcomes. For example, power can be abused when a therapist uses intervention strategies that do not coincide with what the client wants.

Proctor (2008) stresses the integral role that supervision plays in diminishing the damaging effect of power in the therapeutic relationship. Supervision assures that the therapist is acting from a therapeutic position, not from a position of overriding power or personal biases. Regardless, ruptures in therapeutic alliances may occur when a client does not follow an intervention laid out by the cognitive-behavioral therapist. As the objective individual in the power position, the therapist should consider making an attempt to correct the client's resistance toward a therapeutic intended strategy, but deciding to do so can lead to a therapist overstepping a boundary that previously prevented the therapist from abusing her power. As with therapy in general, the interplay of power and neutrality is evident among cognitive-behavioral therapy practices, and therapists must remain mindful of how these characteristics of therapy practice can be distorted in ways that create a toxic atmosphere marked by the therapist seeking to be dominant in the therapist–client relationship (Proctor, 2008).

Cognitive-behavioral therapists rely on empirical measures to conduct and validate their work. The notion of integrating empirical science with the art of therapy puts an emphasis on a client's observable, overt behaviors. This emphasis can sometimes lead to deemphasizing the client's qualitative-oriented experiences in therapy (R. B. Miller, 2004). Such personal experiences, not easily or meaningfully quantifiable, are likely to be overlooked because of the importance placed on measureable, objective therapy data. Another drawback of cognitive-behavioral therapy is that it can result in a therapist emphasizing the perceived positivity or negativity of specific social roles and the explicit behaviors associated with such roles. These are roles that are generally deemed by society's majority as either appropriate or inappropriate (e.g., being sociable [judged appropriate] versus unsociable [judged inappropriate]). In addition, both the client and the therapist are expected to value order, structure, and reasoning during the process of cognitive-behavioral therapy (Miller, 2004). These aspects of cognitive-behavioral therapy can inadvertently lead to imposing values of middle-class U.S. culture on the client. Thus, it is recommended that the client and therapist build their own positive, personal relationship before strict cognitive-behavioral therapy methods are implemented.

Evaluating the Theory

Research Support

A frequently noted strength of cognitive-behavioral therapy is the extensive research base (Chambless et al., 1998; Leichsenring, Hiller, Weissberg, & Leibing, 2006; Leichsenring & Leibing, 2003), supporting its application to a wide array of client issues and *DSM-5* disorders. The approach has also proven its effectiveness across various populations (Dobson & Dobson, 2009; Hofmann, Asnaani, Vonk, Sawyer, & Fang, 2012; Kanter, Manos, Busch, & Rusch, 2008). D. J. G. Dobson and Dobson (2009) provided a review concisely summarizing the research evidence in support of the cognitive-behavioral approach for specific mental disorders. Cognitive-behavioral therapy has been found to provide greater positive results compared to individuals receiving no intervention, being placed on a wait-list for treatment, and those individuals assigned to a different but typical form of treatment, for a wide range of mood disorders (e.g., Ball et al., 2006; Cuijpers et al., 2013; Wampold, Minami, Baskin, & Tierney, 2002), substance abuse/dependence (e.g., Davis et al., 2015; Denis, Lavie, Fatseas, & Auriacombe, 2007), sleep/insomnia (e.g., Okajima, Komada, & Inoue, 2011; Wang, Wang, & Tsai, 2005), eating disorders (e.g., Rosenblum & Forman, 2002), personality disorders (e.g., Leichsenring & Leibing, 2003), anxiety/panic disorders (Kendall & Southam-Gerow, 1996; Otto, Pollack, & Maki, 2000), and psychotic disorders (e.g., Lawrence, Bradshaw, & Mairs, 2006).

It also was the recommended treatment for specific phobias (e.g., Choy, Fyer, & Lipsitz, 2007), social phobia/anxiety (e.g., Craske et al., 2014; Heimberg, 2002), PTSD (e.g., Bradley, Greene, Russ, Dutra, & Westen, 2005; Ponniah & Hollon, 2009; Van Etten & Taylor, 1998), and bulimia nervosa (e.g., Hay, Bacaltchuk, Stefano, & Kashyap, 2009). Other research results have indicated it could be an effective treatment with severe mental health disorders. For example, Morrison et al. (2006) and Morrison et al. (2003) concluded this form of therapy seems to contribute to the prevention of schizophrenia in high-risk populations, and Lam et al. (2003) focused on studying bipolar disorder and concluded cognitive-behavioral therapy might also serve as a relapse-preventer for this particular disorder. Others have uncovered evidence for its use to treat pathological hoarding (Steketee, Frost, Wincze, Greene, & Douglass, 2000; Steketee, Frost, Tolin, Rasmussen, & Brown, 2010) and gambling (Ladouceur et al., 2001; Sylvain, Ladouceur, & Boisvert, 1997).

The previously cited research demonstrates the effectiveness and possibilities of cognitive-behavioral therapy in individual therapy, but investigators also have written about cognitive-behavioral therapy's potential for positive outcomes when delivered in a group therapy format (e.g., Burlingame, MacKenzie, & Strauss, 2004; March, Amaya-Jackson, Murray, & Schulte, 1998; Wilfley et al., 1993), couple and marital therapy (e.g., Baucom, Shoham, Mueser, Daiuto, & Stickle, 1998; Gurman, 2008), and family therapy (e.g., Kendall, Hudson, Gosch, Flannery-Schroeder, & Suveg, 2008; Wood, Piacentini, Southam-Gerow, Chu, & Sigman, 2006).

Although the cognitive-behavioral approach is generally considered a short-term treatment modality (e.g., lasting 16 sessions or less; Dobson & Dobson, 2009), practitioners have demonstrated that cognitive-behavioral therapy can be useful in even fewer sessions. Brown et al. (2005) examined a suicide prevention program with a 10-session limit and discovered it decreased individuals' likelihood of attempting suicide again. These researchers also used a follow-up period of 18 months and found the rate for reattempts was roughly 50%.

Limitations and Criticisms of the Theory

This form of therapy has been criticized as representing a "manual-based therapy" where a therapist relies too heavily on treatment manuals. Attackers argue that manuals provide a narrow procedural focus that, if routinely followed, results in a cookie-cutter style of therapy in which the therapist overlooks the human in the client. In response to such criticisms, cognitive-behavioral therapists argue that this condemnation of treatment manuals is based on a misunderstanding of their use. These defenders assert that, when properly used, a manual serves as a resource for treating a client's presenting problem and that competent therapists are flexible enough to address any new concerns or permutations of a client's original presenting problem during the course of therapy. Finally, defenders point out that attention directed toward issues that emerge does not mean the therapist forgets the original therapy goals but will continue to rely on those goals to guide the therapeutic process to its end (Kendall et al., 2008).

Proponents of feminist therapy, multicultural counseling, and ecological systems of therapy have criticized cognitive restructuring techniques. Followers of these postmodern methods of therapy work with clients whose belief systems and ways of thinking are constantly challenged in mainstream contexts. Therefore, the direct disputation techniques utilized by cognitive-behavioral therapists can reasonably be viewed as an action that leads further to objectifying these clients. This is true because alternative ways of thinking and perceiving are often labeled as irrational simply because they do not conform to what has been called the European American worldview.

Despite political efforts to change the African American experience pertaining to racism (Figure 9.6), racism has persisted to this day as a major problem in the United States. In the case of African American clients, long-standing de facto and de jure racism (e.g., Jim Crow laws that enforced racial segregation) can affect their psychological health (Harrell, 2000). Race-based discrimination has been empirically connected with physical ailments as well as low self-esteem. This is particularly pertinent considering the multitude of scenarios that are felt as racist discriminations. According to Harrell (2000), there are six scenarios that contribute to racism-related stress: single discriminatory events, vicarious discrimination, chronic-contextual discrimination, collective discrimination, transgenerational transmission of traumatization by racism, and microaggressions. DeGruy

▼ FIGURE 9.6

President Lyndon Johnson Signing on July 2, 1964, the Historic Civil Rights Act

Source: Lyndon B. Johnson is sworn in as President of the United States on Air Force One following President John F. Kennedy's assassination. Nov. 22, 1963. LBJ Library photo by Cecil Stoughton, 1A-1-WH63.

(2005) proposed a syndrome, post traumatic slave syndrome, as a summation of multi-generational racism-related stress. If the previously mentioned factors are not considered in therapy, a psychotherapeutic intervention may overlook a primary source of stress. Watkins and Terrell (1988) reported that African American clients who are initially mistrustful of therapy can be expected to harbor very low expectations of treatment outcomes, particularly if the therapist is White.

Although challenging cognitive distortions is of primary importance to cognitive-behavioral therapists, if a client describes experiences of racism, the therapist must refrain from challenging the client's perceptions of an event as discriminatory because the client may perceive the therapist's response as a form of microaggression (Constantine, 2007).

Because trust is essential to a therapist's perceived credibility, it is critical that clients are given sufficient time to warm up to the therapeutic framework and for a therapist to be willing to openly discuss racial differences between the client and the therapist that are likely to impede therapeutic progress (Fuertes, Mueller, Chauhan, Walker, & Ladany, 2002). It may also be helpful to find commonalities (e.g., shared interests) on which to build a therapeutic alliance (Fuertes & Ponterotto, 2003; Roysircar, 2009; Toporek, 2003). Once the therapeutic alliance has been developed, the therapist can focus on specific techniques of cognitive-behavioral therapy and, if needed, modify any techniques in ways to better fit the cultural perspective of the client seeking assistance (Aponte, 2004; Pantalone, Iwamasa, & Martell, 2010; Rossello & Bernal, 1996).

Relevance to Current-Day Practice

Along with extensive empirical support, cognitive-behavioral therapy is an accepted approach within the managed care system in the United States. Insurance companies commonly reimburse psychological providers that use cognitive-behavioral therapy for two main reasons. First, its cognitive and behavioral interventions are designed for specific disorders (Crawley, Podell, Beidas, Braswell, & Kendall, 2010); mental health professionals who utilize cognitive-behavioral strategies typically base their treatment on a diagnosis derived from what is provided in the *DSM* (American Psychiatric Association, 2013). Second, it is a form of therapy that is short term in nature. Many of the cognitive-behavioral therapy manuals available for therapists to use are structured for a treatment length of 12 to 16 sessions (Chambless et al., 1996) or less than 20 sessions (Young, Weinberger, & Beck, 2001). Cognitive-behavioral therapy can be easily adapted to serve people from rural, urban, or suburban locations. See Table 9.3 for current cognitive-behavioral therapy practice settings.

The numerous benefits of the cognitive-behavioral therapy approach have placed great demands on training centers and facilities. Today, many graduate programs and private organizations offer cognitive-behavioral therapy training for students and professionals. These training opportunities vary from academic courses to weekend seminars. Training can also be obtained through some prominent cognitive-behavioral therapy training organizations, including Academy of Cognitive Therapy, American Institute for Cognitive Therapy, Beck Institute for Cognitive Behavior Therapy, and National Association of Cognitive-Behavioral Therapists. Because many mental health professionals employ cognitive-behavioral therapy, two organizations (National Association of Cognitive-Behavioral Therapists and Academy of Cognitive Therapy) have established credentialing requirements to distinguish professionals that have completed the proper training. The credentials awarded by these organizations are based on degree attained, total number of training hours, and past experiences (Academy of Cognitive Therapy, 2018; National Association of Cognitive-Behavioral Therapists, 2018).

Applying Theory to Therapy

RETURNING TO THE CASE OF ANDREA

Andrea was initially hesitant during the intake process to address issues other than her anxiety. However, she was forthcoming to the therapist's direct, nonjudgmental questions about her relationship history. At intake, the therapist and Andrea discussed the ways in which her sexual orientation may be connected to her anxiety, and Andrea agreed that it would be useful to address both concerns in therapy. The link between anxious behaviors and the client's sexual orientation was deemed important to revisit throughout therapy. When asked at the end of the intake session how she felt about working with the therapist, Andrea expressed that she found the clinical interview to be balanced with a personal yet objective approach.

Andrea's treatment was based on a therapeutic approach in which the therapist would utilize cognitive restructuring strategies, psychoeducation, and various behavioral oriented exercises. The therapy was designed to tackle Andrea's anxiety, develop supports within the GLB community, and assist Andrea with her ongoing coming out process (Safren & Rogers, 2001; Purcell et al., 1996). Treatment began with psychoeducation about the therapist's cognitive-behavioral approach. Andrea was quite responsive to a logical, stepwise approach as it fit well with her framework as a physician. Because of Andrea's scientific background, education, and intelligence, the therapist also brought in current articles regarding research on lesbian families.

Andrea was surprised to learn that research has shown lesbian families to be much like heterosexual families, with positive relationships occurring between the parents and their children, and no differences noted in the children's development trajectory (Bos, van Balen, & van den Boom, 2005). Andrea said that this information opened her eyes to the possibility of having a healthy nontraditional family. Psychoeducation also focused on the cycle of panic attacks, teaching relaxation techniques, and improving Andrea's sleep habits (Basco, Glickman, Weatherford, & Ryser, 2000). Medical consultation was provided by the hospital's psychiatrist for her panic attacks and insomnia.

The prejudice and discrimination found in societal norms and mainstream culture can contribute to the creation of repetitive, negative thoughts and faulty beliefs concerning same-sex sexual attractions (Safren & Rogers, 2001). As a result, many GLB individuals struggle with internalized homophobia, which can lead to or exacerbate problems (Purcell et al., 1996). Thus, identifying and challenging cognitive distortions about sexual orientation is an important aspect of conducting cognitive-behavioral therapy with this population (Purcell et al., 1996).

The therapist and Andrea began the task of cognitive restructuring. Andrea completed a thought log as homework in order to elicit and examine her automatic thoughts, identify maladaptive assumptions, and challenge these automatic thoughts and underlying biased assumptions. Andrea decided it would be useful to write down all her automatic thoughts about being in a long-term committed lesbian relationship. Her automatic thought log included the following statements: "Lesbians and bisexuals are dirty," "Professionals cannot be bisexual," and "It is selfish for two women to have children." The therapist and

Andrea discussed how some of these thoughts might be rooted in societal prejudices that Andrea had internalized and made into assumptions.

The therapist assessed the degree to which Andrea's cognitive distortions about sexual orientation had been integrated into the schema of her sexual identity. The therapist and Andrea examined Andrea's automatic thoughts, beginning with Andrea's statement that "lesbians and bisexuals are dirty." When asking Andrea what came to mind with this statement, Andrea recalled movies and pornography that displayed lesbian scenes. She remembered how men in college had talked about these images being especially gratifying for them as well as the vulgar language they used to describe these images. In response to her thought that "professionals cannot be bisexual," Andrea stated that she knew very few bisexual or lesbian women, and none of them were professionals. As an intervention, the therapist and Andrea developed alternative statements to her automatic thoughts.

Because it is not unusual for sexual minorities to worry about issues pertaining to isolation, the therapist was sensitive to the absence of social supports in Andrea's life. Isolation may result from the hostility, prejudice, and discrimination that GLB persons are subjected to. Furthermore, sexual minorities may not share their minority status with their families. For those clients who are suffering from feelings of social isolation and alienation, it is important to identify positive environments where sexual minorities can receive support and make connections (Safren & Rogers, 2001).

To challenge her first two statements (i.e., "Lesbians and bisexuals are dirty" and "Professionals cannot be bisexual") behaviorally, the therapist asked Andrea to attend a meeting for the Gay, Lesbian, and Bisexual Alliance (GLBA) at a nearby university as a homework assignment. The therapist knew that students, professors, and community members were involved with this group, and the therapist herself attended the meetings as an ally. Andrea attended the meeting with Callie. Andrea came to her next session, obviously brighter, and began to talk about the meeting. She stated that there were lots of different people there, including professors and even a lawyer who was lesbian. Andrea also explained "that none of the people seemed dirty to her" but were "just like

(Continued)

(Continued)

everyone else." She and Callie had made plans to see the lawyer and her partner socially the following week, and the two also decided to continue attending the GLBA meetings.

Treatment proceeded with Andrea continuing her thought log, utilizing her new skills in challenging her cognitive distortions, implementing relaxation techniques, practicing new sleep behaviors, and forming connections with a supportive community.

Andrea gradually developed a more positive sexual self-image, and her symptoms of anxiety lessened to a manageable level. However, Andrea still felt anxious about being "out" at work. It was not long before Andrea and Callie began to discuss moving to a nearby city, where many of their friends from the GLBA lived and they might feel more accepted. Andrea and Callie could imagine being able to begin a family in this new location.

Returning to the Multicultural Case of the Sanchez Family

When focusing specifically on Latino youth, utilizing culturally sensitive cognitive-behavioral therapy is important. According to Gonzales, Germán, and Fabrett (2012), 25% of the Latino population is under 18 years old, which accounts for approximately 11.3 million Latino youth living in the United States. Many of these children and adolescents are exposed to a variety of serious challenges of an educational, social, and psychological nature. When researchers contrasted Latino youth to the general population of the United States, they found that Latino youth had greater rates of anxiety, depression, drug abuse, excessive absenteeism and dropping out of school, problems with the law, and unexpected teenage pregnancy (Gonzales et al., 2012). Ecological circumstances place Latino youth and their families at risk for a number of potential problems (Gonzales et al., 2012). For example, family and community poverty related to low educational and social economic status contributes substantially to Latinos holding low-paying and unstable jobs. Approximately 30% of Mexican Americans live below the poverty level. When a therapist works with members of this population, the sociocultural and political contexts of their circumstances are important considerations.

The collectivistic, largely relational characteristics of Latinos are also important to consider in conducting therapy. The therapist should provide ample opportunities for the child client to connect with his heritage culture; for example, provide opportunities for the parents to inform their child of the importance and significance of ethnic identity to them and any relevant information the parents believe they should share concerning their immigration journey. A promotion of bicultural competence and adaptation should also be thoughtfully incorporated into the therapy process. Further, Gonzales et al. (2012) recommend including the family in therapy, thereby aiming to increase the bicultural competence of the family system as a whole rather than just of the Latino child.

One approach that can be incorporated into therapy is called *cognitive behavior modification,* which was developed by Donald Meichenbaum (2009). This way of dealing with situations is based on social learning principles and the differentiation and interaction among cognitive events, cognitive processes, and cognitive structures. The term *cognitive events* is used to refer to the conscious, automatic thoughts that are easily accessible and retrieved on request. Examples of cognitive events include attributions, expectancies, internal dialogues, or thoughts that occur from trial-and-error-thinking (Meichenbaum, 1995). Cognitive events for Miguel and his mother would be their attributions for disrespectful behaviors of one person toward the other.

Cognitive processes include the automatic and unconscious ways in which mental representations are shaped and transformed into schemas. These processes influence how people appraise, selectively attend to, and/or recall events, as well as what information they seek that is consistent with their own beliefs. According to Meichenbaum (1995), examples of cognitive processes include (a) *confirmatory biases,* also referred to as *myside bias* (i.e., available information [new, incoming information or information recalled] is interpreted in a manner, regardless of what the information objectively means, to confirm one's preexisting beliefs); (b) *self-fulfilling prophecies* (i.e., making a prediction based on a strongly held false belief, but the prediction itself is influential enough to evoke the occurrence of what was predicted); (c) *mental heuristics* (i.e., relying on simplistic rules that rapidly narrows one's focus to a single aspect of a complex situation, which can lead to making a poor decision because of what was ignored); and (d) *metacognition* (i.e., involves thinking about thinking; that is, it represents a higher level of mental processing that critically reviews who we are as a thinker and what we do to achieve successful learning). For Miguel and his mother, their American-acculturation orientation (for Miguel) and Mexican-enculturation orientation (for Miguel's mother) form their schematic lens for analyzing information.

Finally, *cognitive structures* are the core and basic principles that organize thoughts into patterns and schemas. They include the assumptions, beliefs, and meanings that determine the way one sees oneself and the world, further shaping and influencing one's behavior. For Miguel it is the gang peer group, and for Miguel's mother it is *marianismo,* the female gender role. These factors influence how they see themselves and the world around them. Meichenbaum (1995) cautioned that psychological dysfunction occurs from the interaction between flawed principles, which inform one's interpretations of experiences, and negative automatic thoughts, such as negative self-attributions or hopeless evaluations of the world. Changes in thinking, feelings, and behavior are sought by the therapist through the careful attention paid to the interactions among the client's cognitive events, processes, and structures.

The *element of focus* is the way in which the individual processes new information cognitively and affectively and incorporates the information into existing structures, thus continually transforming and reorganizing experiences to maintain unity and promote effective problem-solving skills. Miguel and his mother are experiencing maladjustment because of their impairments in completing the cognitive reorganization process. In Miguel's case, his inability to adapt to experiences of discrimination, feelings of marginalization, and alienation from the family has resulted in him joining a gang and using drugs. To cope with the demands of the second culture, Mrs. Sanchez has resorted to traditional Mexican ways. The final goal in therapy is for the therapist to help Miguel restructure processes of self-knowledge and knowledge of the world, so that the client may complete the cognitive reorganization process whenever the client comes to a standstill (Okun, 1990). This goal would apply to both Miguel and his mother because they have reached an impasse situation where neither can progress.

Many features of cognitive-behavioral therapy are congruent with Latino clients' culture and their interpersonal experiences (Organista, 2006). The psychoeducational aspects of the cognitive-behavioral therapy model is useful in helping Latino clients reconceptualize the therapy experience as less of a treatment for *personas locas* (crazy people) and more of a learning experience on how to better deal with a problem with the guidance of an expert. Also, the cognitive-behavioral therapist will direct his or her attention to what comprises the here and now of a problem situation; this focus on the present, combined with the approach's short-term, problem-solving nature, often makes it a better fit with the systemic and logistical difficulties faced by low-socioeconomic status clients and immigrant clients. These individuals often have to contend with limited financial resources, unreliable modes of transportation, and frequent difficulties or crises. Likewise, the situation/environment-based structure of the cognitive-behavioral therapy model permits therapists and clients to address multiple contexts, such as family relationships, school, and work.

Based on the working hypothesis that Miguel is experiencing significant depressive mood as well as significant family relationship problems, two specific goals are proposed and agreed on: (1) Diminish depressive feelings by raising Miguel's sense of possessing sufficient power to influence events in his life and (2) strengthen family relationships by working with the client and his mother on articulating and establishing a good balance between family obligations and extrafamilial relationships.

Initial sessions will focus on the essential cognitive-behavioral therapy theme of how thoughts influence mood and, thus, behavior. Later sessions will focus on how beliefs about and interactions with others (particularly family members) affect mood. These later sessions would include the participation of Miguel's mother. During the first session, the rationale of cognitive-behavioral therapy and the essential rules that govern therapy will be covered and the establishment of goals discussed, that is, diminishing depressive feelings and exercising greater control over behavior, thereby increasing positive feelings and strengthening relationships. The concept of depression is presented and connected to Miguel's feelings and experiences. At that point the focus moves to various ways of thinking (with an emphasis on distorted ways of thinking). For example, depressed thinking can be conceptualized as a person being too judgmental while maintaining a tenacious grip on negative thoughts. Thus, using Miguel's way to define various words, he will be instructed on how to recognize and differentiate between thoughts that are opposites (e.g., important vs. unimportant, optimistic vs. pessimistic, beneficial vs. unbeneficial, etc.). In addition, cognitive errors that commonly distort a person's thinking will be covered (e.g., overgeneralizing, adopting rigid rules, catastrophizing, and "black and white" thinking where something is judged either "good" or "bad" but never somewhere in the middle). At this point in the therapeutic process, the therapist will move toward explaining how Albert Ellis's A-B-C-D fits the client's situation. (**A** stands for the **a**ctivating event, the particular situation that sets off a chain reaction, **B** represents Miguel's **b**eliefs and associated thoughts about the particular situation, **C** stands for the **c**onsequences that result from distorted beliefs and thought, and **D** represents Miguel consciously and actively **d**isputing the faulty beliefs and maladaptive thoughts he experiences.)

Many of the components within the cognitive-behavioral therapy framework are complementary to the Latino culture, such as the short-term time frame of therapy, which decreases the amount of time and financial resources required to access mental health. Another example includes the acknowledgment in cognitive-behavioral therapy of an individual's multiple contexts and how one must continually work to cognitively restructure one's schemas to fit the different situational demands of each context; this also is a common process for Latino/a immigrants acculturating to multiple contexts (i.e., neighborhood, school, and church), while they attempt to sustain enculturation to the family of origin's ethnic identity. Obviously, a person may experience agitation while going through such a process due to lack of capacity for handling enculturation and acculturation simultaneously. In explanation, Gonzales et al. (2012) claimed that enculturation and acculturation processes, understood in this framework as cognitive processes, create two different schemas of environmental demands.

Complex lifestyles from ascribed (by peers) and prescribed (by family) identities may be addressed by exploring the cognitive structures that embody Miguel's assumptions about what it means to be acculturated, to fit in, and what kind of status or privilege is associated with each aspect of his life. For example, a cognitive-behavioral therapist may help Miguel examine his differing assumptions and expectancies about participating in familial and cultural traditions, doing well in school, skipping class, and hanging out with a perceived negative crowd. Examining each cognitive event and its respective structure and process may promote understanding and integration of the various identities and contexts present in his life. Additionally, ethnic identity will be addressed by assessing the degree to which pride is felt for one's heritage and the schemas of how one conceptualizes cultural identification that influence behaviors. Miguel's stress due to detachment from his Mexican heritage ultimately creates overall restlessness and insecurity in him. Addressing ethnic identity in this way may reveal possible negative cognitions in both Miguel and his mother, resulting in polar opposite behaviors, marginalization in Miguel, and the separatism experienced by his mother.

Several components of the cognitive-behavioral therapy framework exist that may be refined to be more culturally sensitive, making the therapeutic approach applicable to the Latino/a client's experience and ultimately making the approach more effective for change. One component subject to modification may be the concept of irrational beliefs because it inherently does not consider social changes, individuals within larger groups, family system influences, work-related issues, role of community organizations, and so forth. For example, Miguel's idea that only his friends respect him, implying that his mother does not, may be seen as irrational by a therapist. However, the culturally sensitive therapist takes into account the present difference in acculturation levels between Miguel and his mother. It may appear to Miguel that his mother's lack of effort to acculturate is what has caused him to feel disrespected by his mother, i.e., because she does not fully understand his perspective. At the present time, the majority of Miguel's absolutist beliefs must be seen in the context of his increasing acculturation to mainstream society relative to his mother. Therefore, when using the A-B-C-D technique, the goal would not be to completely dispel the irrational thought (lack of respect), which it is not if viewed at a deeper level, but to contextualize Miguel's view of being disrespected and understand under what cultural norms and conditions it has evolved. Taking this type of approach to handle the issue of "being disrespected" can be expected to lessen this belief's mediating impact and ultimately the strain it brings about in the mother–son relationship. By understanding how Miguel's feelings of disrespect from his mother (B) caused him to storm out of the room (C), and not his mother's expression of his new friends' lack of morals and criminal ways (A), would positively improve the relationship between Miguel and his mother, as well as alter his belief of how much *respeto* (respect) his mother holds for him and vice versa.

Another modification could be the way the therapist directly challenges the client's irrational or incorrect cognition as a mechanism for change. This type of therapeutic action is likely to provoke resistance in the Latino/a client and increase feelings of disrespect. A more culturally sensitive approach would include conveying *respeto* alongside the assertiveness required when addressing Miguel about his unhelpful thoughts or beliefs (Organista, 2006). The cognitive-behavioral therapist may incorporate the Latino value of *simpatia* (warmth, friendliness) in her approach by being less confrontational and more relaxed in addressing the client's thoughts and beliefs. To additionally avoid appearing impersonal to the Latino client, the therapist should refrain from beginning the sessions with the presenting problem, as is common in cognitive-behavioral therapy practice. Rather, the therapist may foster Latino values of *confianza* (trust) and *personalismo* (formal friendliness) in the very first session by establishing a therapeutic alliance, which emphasizes the importance of the relationship. In addition to using selective therapist self-disclosure, this could be achieved by means of *plática*, or small talk, where the therapist maintains a "balance between task-oriented formality and warm personalized attention to the client" (Organista, 2006, p. 81).

In efforts to improve familial relationships and reach a place of biculturalism, a protective factor for Latino youth (Gonzales et al., 2012), it would be culturally sensitive of the cognitive-behavioral therapist to implement some exercises and homework assignments that involve both the client and his family in addition to those activities that only require the client's participation. By doing so, the therapist promotes the Latino value of *familismo*, that is, a prime emphasis on "family centrality and loyalty" (Organista, 2006, p. 81), which, in Miguel's case, may restore participation in Mexican American cultural activities while helping his mother embrace his individual acculturation status.

The culturally sensitive cognitive-behavioral therapist will guide Miguel and his mother to closely examine how their cultures—past and present—are driving their thought processes, assumptions, interpersonal behaviors, and attitudes. This collaborative exploration and its discoveries can be liberating for Miguel and his mother, who have otherwise been isolated through the institutionalization and internalization of discrimination.

CHAPTER REVIEW

SUMMARY AND COMMENTARY ▶▶

Clearly, cognitive-behavioral therapy is employed to treat a large array of problems presented by different types of clients. Despite the extensive research supporting its use, there are several limitations of cognitive-behavioral therapy that have been mentioned in this chapter that deserve further attention. Additional research is needed to study cognitive-behavioral therapy's application with diverse clientele, its applicability with comorbid disorders, and its long-term efficacy (Epp & Dobson, 2010). Further, many cognitive-behavioral studies utilize randomized controlled trials (and other means to control extraneous factors that could affect the results), a research standard that provides the researcher the confidence to state findings are factually sound and valid. A reader of this textbook might find it curious then that a seemingly paradoxical problem enters the picture when research is conducted with tight control over external influences. Basically, the more a researcher creates an "experimental, laboratory style" of study, the more problematic it becomes for the researcher to generalize the results to real-world therapy settings. In a true sense, it can be argued that whereas one of cognitive-behavioral therapy's greatest strengths is its empirical research approach, one of cognitive-behavioral therapy's limitations is the lack of research to support its use in real-world clinical settings. Table 9.3 is a current overview of the practice of cognitive-behavioral therapy.

▼ TABLE 9.3

Brief Overview of Current Therapy Practice

Variable	Current Applications
Type of service delivery setting	Private practice Community mental health services Psychiatric hospital Health care setting Substance abuse clinic Military Social service agency
Population	Child Teen Adult Couple Family Group
Type of presenting problems	Wide range of presenting problems

Variable	Current Applications
Severity of presenting problems	Wide range of severity of presenting problems
Adapted for short-term approach	Yes
Length of treatment	Brief (approximately 20 sessions or less)
Ability to receive reimbursement	Insurance companies will reimburse pending *DSM* diagnosis.
Certification in approach	Yes
Training in educational programs	Assumption College's Master of Arts in Counseling Psychology program covers cognitive-behavioral therapy (theory and practice) and addresses common problems/mental disorders (e.g., attention deficit hyperactivity disorder [ADHD], anxiety, conduct disorder in children, depression, and substance abuse).
Location	Urban Rural Suburban
Type of delivery system	HMO PPO Fee for service
Credential	Certified Cognitive Therapist Diplomate in Cognitive-behavioral Therapy Certified Cognitive-Behavioral Therapist Certified Cognitive-Behavioral Group Therapist Certified Cognitive-Behavioral Group Facilitator
Practitioners	Professionals Paraprofessionals
Fit with *DSM* diagnoses	Yes

CRITICAL THINKING QUESTIONS ▶▶

1. Some have criticized cognitive-behavioral therapy for its manualized, routinized approach to psychotherapy. What are some pros and cons of a treatment that lends itself to a manualized approach, as cognitive-behavioral therapy does?

2. A key assertion of cognitive-behavioral therapy is that an individual's suffering is rooted in faulty thinking in the present. What are your thoughts on and reactions to this assertion?

3. Are there any psychological disorders you can think of that might not lend themselves to a cognitive-behavioral therapy–oriented treatment? Are there any particular situations in which cognitive-behavioral therapy might not be applicable? Which ones, and why?

SUGGESTED READINGS: IMPORTANT PRIMARY SOURCES ▶▶

Books

Beck, A. (1988). *Love is never enough.* New York, NY: HarperCollins.

Beck, A., Rush, J., Shaw, B., & Emery, G. (1979). *Cognitive therapy of depression.* New York, NY: Guilford Press.

Beck, J. S. (2011). *Cognitive therapy: Basics and beyond* (2nd ed.). New York, NY: Guilford Press.

Ellis, A., & Blau, S. (1998). *The Albert Ellis reader: A guide to well-being using rational emotive behavior therapy.* New York, NY: Citadel Press.

Ellis, A., & Dryden, W. (2007). *The practice of rational emotive behavior therapy* (2nd ed.). New York, NY: Springer.

Ellis, A., & Harper, R. (1997). *A guide to rational living* (3rd ed.). North Hollywood, CA: Wilshire Book Company.

Journals

Behavioral and Cognitive Psychotherapy

Cognitive and Behavioral Practice

Cognitive Therapy and Research

Websites

Albert Ellis Institute: http://albertellis.org

Beck Institute for Cognitive Behavior Therapy: http://www.beckinstitute.org

Cognitive Dynamic Therapy Associates: www.cogdyn.com

CHAPTER 10

REALITY THERAPY AND CHOICE THEORY

iStockphoto.com/BrianAJackson

Introduction

Reality therapy and choice theory represent a model of therapy that operates from a cognitive and behavioral base that is grounded in the present not the past (Wubbolding et al., 2004). The approach's originator, William Glasser, held the belief that a happy and effective life relies heavily on the personal decisions that a person makes (he believed the same about mental health, e.g., people choose to be depressed). The idea that the choices we make in the present that are of utmost importance in defining a person's current life struck a chord with a vast number of drug counselors, teachers, therapists, and individuals (especially individuals who were pursuing a self-help approach to changing their circumstances). One of Glasser's precepts is that everyone is responsible for his or her own behavior and the results that a behavior causes. In Glasser's world, no one is free of personal responsibility because people are capable of accurately evaluating situations and selecting the appropriate behavior to meet realistic, healthy expectations, such as when a person is provided an opportunity to fulfil one of the key human needs described by Glasser, such as love, friendship, or social cooperation. Human suffering is the result of individuals simply failing to use their strengths to effectively deal with problems and choosing instead to allow problems to block them psychologically from implementing those very actions that would generate a happier life. According to Woo (2013), Glasser asserted that there is a single reason for individuals to seek therapy, which is that they are unhappy.

People can fail to take control of satisfying their own needs in an assortment of ways. For example, when a person indulges in unrestrained self-pity. The British writer, actor, comedian Stephen Fry (n.d.) said the following about self-pity:

> Self-pity will destroy relationships, it'll destroy anything that's good, it will fulfill all the prophecies it makes and leave only itself. And it's so simple to imagine that one is hard done by, and that things are unfair, and that one is underappreciated, and that if only one had had a chance at this—only one had had a chance at that—things would have gone better, you would be happier.

Glasser would agree with Fry's remarks since he asserted that people identify and select everything they do or become, including the misery they experience in life (Vitello, 2013).

HYPOTHETICAL CASE STUDY: THE STREET ARTIST WHO MEETS REALITY AND IS CONFRONTED WITH CHOICE

The sound of the phone dissolved Angela's dream and she instinctively grabbed for the receiver on the nightstand while Eduardo lay in bed, quiet and motionless listening to Angela's conversation. Eduardo heard Angela's voice start off lethargic and then instantly explode into a loud frantic tone that he had come to associate with their son Felipe being in trouble. Eduardo could make out that Felipe had been arrested.

"Arrested again—it can't be?" is the question that started to repeat itself in Eduardo's thoughts even though he knew that this was nothing more than a hope that had somehow become twisted into a question. Eduardo lay there slowly calculating whether this was the third or fourth time that Felipe had been arrested for graffiti—unless he had stepped over a line and done something worse.

At 3:31 a.m. Eduardo and Angela found themselves at the local jail to post bail, but this time they were told by the person behind the protective glass that because

there had been a "serious probation violation," they could not use a property bond to obtain Felipe's release as before. The charges were parole violation and vandalism of state property, and Felipe was being held until his court date. Eduardo and Angela were then told that their son had painted an image on a drawbridge, and when the drawbridge was opened "a male sex organ—drawn the length of the bridge— would rise until it was straight up in the air—graffiti that could easily be made out for what it was even from a pretty far distance" Until the graffiti was removed, a large number of people visited the site to see the drawbridge raised for river traffic (Figure 10.1).

Much to the surprise and embarrassment of Felipe's parents, two days following the arrest an article, "Teenager Charged with Obscene Graffiti," appeared in "The Blotter" section of the local paper. The article stated the following: *Officers caught a teenager drawing obscene graffiti on the town's drawbridge*

▼ FIGURE 10.1

Street Art

iStockphoto.com/AntonioGuillem

near the high school. The officers were on patrol at the time of the incident. Both officers saw 17-year-old Felipe M. Menéndez standing next to 103 Hooper Street across from the abandoned Milledge building with the trunk of his car opened. In the trunk of the car the officers found a great number of paint cans, markers, and various graffiti stencils used to mark buildings and stop signs. A friend of Felipe's arrived at the scene and reported she had dropped off Felipe just a few minutes ago to pick up his car. The friend later confessed she had lied once she saw Felipe was in trouble and that Felipe had actually called her after he had painted the bridge "to drive over and see his newest piece of art." Felipe's friend told the officers she had left her infant at home and needed to return. An officer followed her to her residence to make sure the child was all right. The teen mother was reported to the Department of Family and Child Services because her child had been left unattended. Felipe, the alleged painter of the graffiti, was charged with vandalism of state property and arrested.

At court Felipe was found guilty, fined equal to the cost of the paint removal, and sentenced to time served plus 200 hours of public service. In addition, Felipe was required to attend a special counseling program that the city's judicial system had developed in cooperation with the local college. The presiding judge informed Felipe that he expected to receive a monthly counseling report concerning Felipe's progress in the program. Any violation of probation would result in an additional 7 months of incarceration. Because staying in school was not part of the conditions of his parole, Felipe dropped out of high school.

COUNSELING COMMENCES

Felipe was reluctant to say anything during the first session, but with about 10 minutes remaining Felipe said he had been seen by a psychiatrist before and that he had been told his problems were due to things that happened to him as a child, that he was "some kind of antisocial type of person." Felipe concluded by saying, "That's just a bunch of horseshit—I'm my own person. I do what I want to, not because I was traumatized by my older brother's death."

Raul, the therapist assigned to work with Felipe, looked at him and said, "I agree totally you are not being controlled by something in your past and you are not suffering from something like antisocial personality disorder. You're not suffering from any form of mental disease. And I agree that you are living your life as you choose. I have one question to ask—have your choices in life made you feel good about yourself and others?" Felipe was surprised by the therapist's comments—he knew how to "read people," and he was sure the therapist believed what he just said even though it seemed to contradict much of what Felipe had been told before. During the second session, Felipe entered the room with a sketch pad. When asked about the pad, Felipe reported it was "nothing, just stuff—projects I'm working on." When asked to see "the stuff," Felipe handed over the pad, which contained a number of drawings. Felipe said he drew the pictures with the intent to later draw them on a much bigger scale on buildings around the city. The last drawing in the sketch pad caught the therapist's attention because of the quality of artistry involved and because the image looked vaguely familiar. The therapist realized who was depicted in the drawing after asking Felipe the identity of the model for the drawing and Felipe said, "I saw it on a sheet of paper that was lying on the corner of your desk last week—I'm good at remembering things I see and drawing them later." The therapist smiled after realizing he had never seen William Glasser depicted in the style of street art which he knew was different from what most people simply referred to as *graffiti*. Felipe could see that the therapist was genuinely interested in the drawing (Figure 10.2).

The session was devoted to asking questions about how different images could be made with spray paint, what kind of spray paint was used, and how Felipe had developed his unique style of drawing and painting over the years. Felipe also talked about Banksy, a well-known street artist from London whose work was easily accessible through Google (see Note 1). Felipe felt good but somewhat confused by the session's end because previous encounters with either law enforcement personnel or therapists had felt like interrogations or attempts to find out the hidden meaning behind his street art. Even though he always expected the police, and later the judge, to view his work as vandalism, he was surprised by

(Continued)

(Continued)

▼ FIGURE 10.2

Client's Drawing of Glasser

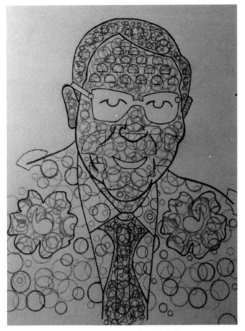

Source: Reproduced with permission from M. J. G.

Raul's reaction. The adults he previously encountered all saw his public art as nothing more than the destruction of property, and they seemed solely focused on uncovering a reason for his "striking out against society," a reason he was certain they would use against him to lock him up in jail or "cure him" of something they say he has. But this time the person assigned to work with him seemed different. Here was someone who expressed an interest in what he was interested in. When Felipe was explaining the difference between graffiti and street art, Raul even understood some of the words such as *tag*. This was a person who knew who Banksy was and who had actually seen some of his art in London, someone who could appreciate the clever way Felipe inserted

messages into his art, like Banksy, either by adding a few words or through the very image itself that he had created.

At the third session, Felipe spoke about the reason he selected the drawbridge to paint on. Felipe picked the drawbridge because it went up and down throughout the day across from the vice principal's office at his high school. Felipe had been referring to the "old vice principal" at his school as "VP" for Viagra Prick ever since the vice principal asked Felipe to step into his office before the morning class bell sounded to tell him, "I know you've been up to something at this school ever since you've arrived. You'll be graduating in a month and just because no one here ever caught you doing anything I just want you to know what I think will happen—you're destined to spend your life in jail before you're 21 years old. Soon you'll be held legally accountable. Now get out of my office." (In truth Felipe had never done anything more at school than sneak off to a backstage section of the school's theater to smoke cigarettes.) Students at Felipe's school, along with the vice principal, were aware he referred to the vice principal as "VP"—an inside joke that several of the students shared with faculty at the school after the penis drawing appeared on the drawbridge.

Further aspects of this case are presented near the end of this chapter. The brief discussion at the end illustrates a few salient features of the above hypothetical case and briefly addresses what would have most likely taken place during the remaining sessions that would enable the therapist and Felipe to reach a successful termination to therapy.

Note 1. Banksy is "arguably the most influential, provocative and inspiring artist from the street art scene" (Mathieson & Tapies, 2011, p. 15).

Note 2. Even though the case is fictitious, the photograph in Figure 10.3 is based on a real-life event similar to what is described in this chapter. A similar photograph was published in the newspaper *The Moscow Times,* accompanied by a newspaper article that reported members of the street artists group known as Voina painted a giant penis on a drawbridge prior to the scheduled 2011 St. Petersburg Economic Forum as a message about unchecked governmental powers. The humor intended behind the image rising every time the drawbridge was raised was not lost on either residents of the area or visitors to the bridge. The site became a popular tourist attraction with people posing for photographs until the painted image was removed.

The Roots of Reality Therapy and Choice Theory: William Glasser

William Glasser was born on May 11, 1925, to Ben and Betty in Cleveland, Ohio. It is probably safe to assume that neither of his parents imagined the widespread contribution that William would have on therapy's future when, in 1965, *Reality Therapy: A New Approach to Psychiatry* was published. For Glasser, the meaning of life resides with our seeking to satisfy our basic needs, a pursuit that is inevitably tied to the choices we make in life. Whenever we reach a low point in life, regardless of who we are or what is taking place at that time, we can either choose to buckle under life's pressures or decide to choose from the available alternatives to discover the best way to satisfy our needs. Positive choices lead to a real sense of self value and help to usher in and maintain a healthy interpersonal life.

Glasser asserts that too often people find themselves involved in a power struggle to wrestle from life what they need, but any such persistent misuse of power promises to keep them in a perpetual unsatisfied state of existence. For Glasser choice implies responsibility, an essential quality of existence that all too often is taken away from those treated in psychiatry. Utilizing *DSM* labels, psychotropic medications, and sometimes confinement to a psychiatric hospital are various ways one profession has deprived others of responsibility and prevented them the freedom of making many important choices. For Glasser, psychotic and nonpsychotic clients all require the same thing—more responsibility and the freedom to make choices to satisfy their needs.

For a radical thinker, Glasser's academic career started off as nondescript. Once he graduated from Cleveland Heights School, he entered the CASE School of Applied Science and completed a BSc in 1945. Afterward, he chose to work as a chemical engineer, but soon his interest shifted to psychology and he entered Western Reserve University to earn a master's degree in psychology. During this period, Glasser was inducted into military service and was assigned to test the effects of poisonous gasses developed by the Germans during World War II. After being discharged, Glasser reentered his graduate program at Western Reserve University and completed his master's degree in psychology in 1948. A year later, he returned to the same university and enrolled in its medical program. In 1953, Glasser began his internship at the Veterans Admiration Center located in Los Angeles, California. After completing his internship, Glasser began his psychiatric residency at Brentwood Veterans Neuropsychiatric Hospital in Los Angeles, where he was assigned to a ward reserved for males diagnosed with schizophrenia.

▼ FIGURE 10.3

William Glasser

Source: Dr. William Glasser, psychiatrist, at the 2009 Evolution of Psychotherapy Conference in Anaheim, California by Brother Bulldog. https://commons.wikimedia.org/wiki/File:WilliamGlasser.jpg. Licensed under CC BY-SA 3.0 https://creativecommons.org/licenses/by-sa/3.0/deed.en.

The first of several turning points in Glasser's life occurred in 1956 when he assumed positions that divided his time between the Ventura School for Delinquent Girls and UCLA's Neuropsychiatric Institute and Outpatient Clinic. It was during this time that Glasser met a fellow psychiatrist, G. L. Harrington, whom Glasser remembered saying to him "join the club," which was essentially an invitation for Glasser to reject the very foundation on which psychiatry was built—the bedrock known as mental illness. It should be mentioned that although Glasser rejected the concept of mental illness early in his career, he recognized brain pathology as a reality, exemplified by diseases such as Alzheimer disease, brain tumors, multiple sclerosis, and Parkinson disease (Glasser, 2003, pp. 14–15).

It turned out that Harrington was much more than simply a nonconformist. This professional maverick was successfully treating patients displaying schizophrenic behaviors with a much higher success rate than were professionals using either traditional psychotherapy or psychotropic medications. This notable achievement was accomplished by increasing the patient's level of freedom and treating the patient as a responsible person capable of planning his future. For Glasser, this remarkable psychiatrist was to take on the role of an older, wiser, and trusted teacher whom Glasser came to regard as his "mentor." Harrington's influence nurtured Glasser's own thoughts and led him to the realization that opposing the ingrained mantra of mental illness, clung to so strongly by conventional psychiatry, provided him with an opportunity to be creative and to develop a much more effective way to treat his patients. Glasser embraced these contradictions and used them as a teacher, even if on the surface the treatment approach he developed seemed counterintuitive to what psychiatry was advocating.

For Glasser, mental health was soon to become a public health issue that spread beyond the walls of psychiatric hospitals, clinics, and the private practitioner's office. It was to encompass other areas such as managing the affairs of a business, assisting couples and families, and educating children. Glasser viewed all of these areas as providing avenues to fostering healthy interactions that would nurture a genuine appreciation of self and others, and most important of all, prevent occurrences of what was labeled "mental illness."

After completing his residency requirements in 1957 (he became a board-certified psychiatrist in 1961), Glasser started working for the California Youth Authority as a lecturer with a clear focus on changing how mental conditions were to be viewed and treated. The publication of *Mental Health or Mental Illness? Psychiatry for Practical Action* (1960) soon followed. During this time his influence gradually snowballed and Glasser was increasingly invited to share his ideas on how public schools in California and elsewhere could change for the better. In 1962, Glasser named his approach to treatment *reality psychiatry* only to conclude that his ideas were not limited to psychiatry, thus causing him that same year to change the name of his approach to *reality therapy*. While maintaining a private practice and continuing his association with Harrington (referring to and seeking information and guidance from his mentor), Glasser began what was to become a life-long effort to methodically apply his ideas to various areas, such as addictions and corrections. A career peak (one of many to come) was achieved in 1965 with the publication of *Reality Therapy: A New Approach to Psychiatry.*

In 1967 another significant achievement occurred when the Institute for Reality Therapy was established in California. Several publications followed, eventually reaching a publication total of more than 30 books, along with numerous articles. If the early years of his professional life represent Glasser's "reality therapy period," then the middle years marked a period that might be labeled Glasser's "control theory period" of thinking (e.g., Glasser, 1984). Glasser became familiar with the work of William Powers through reading his book, *Behavior: The Control of Perception* and soon after consulted with Powers on various theoretical ideas. Subsequently, in 1985 Glasser wrote *Control Theory: A New Explanation of How We Control of Lives* and in 1994 *The Control Theory Manager*. In 1995, while in Ireland to discuss his theoretical views, attendees of a presentation shared their opinion that the prominent use of the word *control* to describe his most recent efforts was misleading to those interested in his work because he spoke and wrote strongly in favor of rejecting the external controls humans seek to place on others and that are placed externally on humans by various systems. A year later, while spending several months in Australia, Glasser replaced the term *control theory* with *choice theory* during various talks. During the 1990s and continuing into the current century, Glasser's body of work might be aptly referred to as Glasser's "choice theory period" of conceptualizing. At the same time, the name of his institute was changed to the William Glasser Institute. Currently, independent institutes and facilities associated with Glasser's approach are found throughout the United Kingdom and Europe, Central and South America, Australia, and New Zealand. In addition to the regional groups found in New England, the Sunbelt, and the West Coast of the United States, in 2010 the William Glasser Association International was established and charged with organizing international conferences and activities.

In 1990, Glasser was presented with the honorary degree of Doctor of Humane Letters, Honoris Causa, from the University of San Francisco for contributions in the field of counseling. The American Counseling Association also presented him with its Professional Development Award in 2003, and a year later again honored Glasser and his body of work with the "Legend in Counseling" award. In 2005 Glasser was presented with the Master Therapist designation by the American Psychotherapy Association, and in that same year he was recognized with the Life Achievement Award by the International Center for the Study of Psychiatry and Psychology. Finally, in 2006, Pacific Union College in Angwin, California, awarded Glasser an honorary Doctorate in Education.

In 2008, Glasser witnessed the establishment of the William Glasser Institute for Research in Public Mental Health in the Department of Psychology at Loyola Marymount University, an institute supported through foundation donors. In the same year Achievement, Inc., a Japanese based company, celebrated 20 years of utilizing Glasser's ideas in a business setting. William Glasser and his wife, Carleen Glasser, were invited to participate in a speaking tour in Japan and to see the release of Glasser's *Eight Lessons for a Happier Marriage* in Japanese. By the time that the 29th William Glasser Institute International Conference was held in Edinburgh, Scotland, reality therapy and choice theory were actively being applied in over 35 countries with more than 77,000 trained in Glasser's approach and nearly 11,000 who have become certified in reality therapy.

Newspaper Announcement for *Beehive*

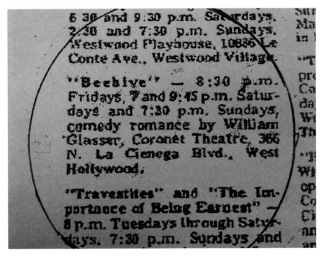

Source: 1977, February. "Beehive." *Star News.* pp. 28.

Note: This clipping is several decades old and appeared on p. 28 of the *Star News*, a newspaper published in Pasadena, California. The newspaper printed this announcement on Thursday, February 1977 and it reads as follows: "Beehive" - 8:30 p.m. Fridays, 7 and 9:45 p.m. Saturdays and 7:30 p.m. Sundays, comedy romance by William Glasser, Coronet Theatre, 366 N. La Cienega Blvd., West Hollywood.

The William Glasser Institute website provides a listing of Glasser's accomplishments, which span approximately 50 years and includes a play written by Glasser in 1975. It is not surprising to find the play listed considering Glasser's creative nature and the unique contributions he has made throughout his life. Figure 10.4 depicts the original clipping obtained from *Star News* announcing the time and location of the William Glasser's production, which was performed for several months during 1977.

Biographical Sources: Photograph and biographical information accessed via the William Glasser Institute (2012a, 2012b, 2012c, 2012d); additional information obtained via Wubbolding (2000, 2003, 2011).

Reality Therapy and Choice Theory

Glasser's thinking evolved and changed over time, and to a large extent Glasser operated from a creative and additive perspective that kept pace with various societal changes. Without a doubt he displayed an unusual willingness to be open to new ideas throughout his career. In addition to his comfort with going directly to a source to seek counsel and advice, he made sure to pay tribute to others for the role they played in his conceptualization of reality therapy and choice theory. G. J. Harrington and William Powers greatly influenced Glasser's own approach to therapy and theory. G. J. Harrington was an early and very significant influence in Glasser's professional life, an influence that eventually led to a number of the basic concepts comprising reality therapy and, eventually, choice theory.

Glasser also sought out William Powers later in his career, and it was this relationship that influenced Glasser's conceptualization of what was termed *control theory*. Powers described the brain as a dynamic process system for the acquisition, storage, and use of input. Furthermore, the brain functions to automatically maintain a desired state of need satisfaction, utilizing various behaviors until a needed balance is achieved.

According to Glasser, once he isolated what constituted the basics of human motivation, he was able to subsequently focus on emphasizing the importance of avoiding those aspects of a client's problem that defy change. Springboarding from the notion of behavior, Glasser came to believe that the totality of a person's internal and external activity provided a comprehensive picture of each person, but consistent with his earlier conceptualizations, Glasser also concluded that of this behavioral totality, only certain aspects could be changed relatively easy: essentially what we call observable behavior and conscious thought (European Association for Reality Therapy, 2012a; William Glasser Institute, 2012b, 2012c).

It is important to recognize that although Glasser adopted, modified, and reassembled what he learned from others, Glasser was an independent thinker who did not approach the work of others in a wholesale manner. For example, Glasser abandoned an idea central to Powers's theory, the notion of perceptual levels, and replaced it with perceptual filters. Another concept introduced by Glasser, the qualitative world, referred to how humans place a value on all that they perceptually process. During this period of reconceptualization, two of Glasser's previously used terms, *perceptual error* and *reorganization*, were respectively replaced by the terms *frustration* and *creativity*. For Glasser, the term *frustration* was a much closer approximation of what the earlier term was intended to reference in day-to-day life, and the term *creativity* was seen by Glasser as a better descriptor for what he was trying to describe. Glasser was aiming for a transformative quality that exceeded a simple rearrangement of those elements that define a person's approach to living and interacting with others.

Glasser's final major shift in thinking occurred near the end of the 20th century and is captured in the following words: "I decided in the spring of 1996 to call what I teach, *Choice Theory* [emphasis added]. I changed the name because of my significant alterations to the original Control Theory. In my view people often misinterpreted the concept of control" (William Glasser Institute, 2012b, n.p.). Parish (2010) helps to clarify where Glasser arrived in his thinking and the application of what those thoughts meant when she wrote,

> Choice Theory seeks to help us to better understand why we do things and why we should do them better, and Reality Therapy is a specific procedure that is intended to help us to take more "efficient control" of our lives by recognizing the error of our ways, and to look for—and implement—more efficient thoughts and/ or actions so that we might more likely secure what we want and avoid getting what we don't want. (p. 10)

Table 10.1 provides a sample of quotations that provide a glimpse into William Glasser's own qualitative world and what he came to believe and value about the innate strengths of humans. Glasser believed humans are capable of assuming responsibility and taking effective action as a result of adopting a philosophy of choice—an approach to living that fuses personal freedom with personal control to enable humans to make life-changing choices even in the most extreme situations, such as when a person has been pinned with the label of "psychotic" and subsequently institutionalized by a well-meaning expert, as a result of psychiatry's protocol. Prone to harm rather than help, too many psychiatrists today mistakenly assign diagnoses of no value—they have essentially become the duped dispensers of the newest psychotropic drug whose effectiveness is measured not in mental health increments but rather the dollars the newest magic bullet generates for the pharmaceutical companies.

Major Concepts

The remainder of the chapter is devoted to providing an overview of Glasser's approach to therapy, specifically, those qualities and techniques viewed by Glasser as important for therapists and other professionals to possess if they hope to facilitate the type of changes

▼ TABLE 10.1

Quotable William Glasser

- What is important is what is happening now . . . recounting of the past serves to insulate the patient from the important details of the present where his defective ego is now functioning. (1960, p. 168)
- When I asked him [Dr. Harrington] when he believes a patient is ready to have therapy terminated, [he said] "When, after a long period of treatment, he begins to talk about how much he needs a new car and how much less he needs you." (1965, p. 153)
- Conventional psychiatry wastes too much time arguing over how many diagnoses can dance at the end of a case history, time [is] better spent treating the ever-present problem of irresponsibility. (1965, p. 49)
- In Reality Therapy . . . we rarely ask why. Our usual question is What? What are you doing—not, why are you doing it? (1965, p. 33)
- In Reality Therapy we are much more concerned with behavior than with attitudes . . . waiting for attitudes to change stalls therapy whereas changing behavior leads quickly to a change in attitude. (1965, pp. 27–28)
- Talking in one's sleep, slips of the tongue, phobias, and compulsions are examples of behaviors obviously based on unconscious mental processes. But we are doing therapy, not research into the cause of human behavior, and we have found that knowledge of cause has nothing to do with therapy. (1965, p. 53)
- Very few of us realize how much we choose the misery in our lives. (1976, p. 1)
- Total objectivity is a myth. (1998, p. 47)
- Drugs provide pleasure; they cannot provide happiness. For happiness you need people. (1998, p. 88)
- It may be easier to go from unhappiness to mental health than from out of shape to physically fit. (2003, p. 21)
- External control is very simple. In a relationship is a belief that what we choose to do is right and what the other person does is wrong. Husbands know what's right for wives and wives for their husbands. The external control attitude . . . will eventually destroy that relationship. As I said, we are social creatures. We need each other. Teaching everyone the dangers of external control and how it can be replaced with choice theory, is the heart and soul of a successful public health program. (2005, pp. 20–21)

Sources: Glasser, W. (1960). *Mental health or mental illness? Psychiatry for practical action.* New York, NY: Harper & Brothers; Glasser, W. (1965). *Reality therapy: A new approach to psychiatry.* New York, NY: Harper & Row; Glasser, W. (1976). *Positive addiction.* New York, NY: Harper & Row; Glasser, W. (1998). *Choice theory: A new psychology of personal freedom.* New York, NY: Harper & Row; Glasser, W. (2003). *Warning: Psychiatry can be hazardous to your mental health.* New York, NY: HarperCollins; and Glasser, W. (2005). *Treating mental health as a public health problem.* Chatsworth, CA: Author.

Glasser advocated for teenagers, adults, couples, families, groups, organizations, and larger systems. For Glasser, people enslave themselves to unhealthy culs-de-sac of their own making and it is by becoming fettered to these dead-end relationships and social structures that they guarantee themselves lives of distress. Glasser's overarching goal in all cases is to break with destructive life patterns so that people can reach their full level of happiness through a process that directly confronts what holds all of humanity back.

Human Nature

Once human nature is reduced to its essential characteristic, we find that humans are motivated to seek fulfillment of needs. Specifically, there are five needs (also referred to as genetic instructions by Glasser) that drive human action (Wubbolding, 2000, 2003). These needs are inborn, tend to be general in their aim, and represent a universality that transcends any specific culture (Wubbolding, 2000, 2003).

Although water, food, and warmth are necessities for all living things, it is the special conglomeration of needs identified by Glasser that differentiate humans from other living things on earth. The necessities of human existence are (1) *survival,* or the preservation of oneself from harm or destruction; (2) *freedom,* which implies the person is free from outside restraints but also encompasses the ability to stand alone and think for oneself; (3) *fun*, especially social fun, to take part in enjoyable playful activities; (4) *power*, the capability of doing or achieving something toward which effort is directed; and (5) *belonging*, the critical social aspect necessary to sustain healthy life. The need to survive is the only one listed that Glasser considers physiologically based; the four remaining needs he considered to be psychological. Although there is a tendency to see similarities to Abraham H. Maslow's conceptualization of needs, differences between Maslow's and Glasser's views outweigh any similarities. For example, Glasser does not arrange the five needs in any sort of ascending hierarchy; all five are significant when it comes to need fulfillment. In addition, Glasser champions the self-determining quality of all humans rather than the self-actualizing quality that Maslow believed pertained to relatively few individuals.

Commonly used words such as *crazy, lunatic,* and *deranged*, along with a number of technically derived words found in everyday use, such as *neurotic* and *psychotic,* all point to one type of situation where the person is not satisfactorily fulfilling one or more of Glasser's listed essential needs. It is this failure to achieve need satisfaction that has led to a breakdown of functioning in the person's motivational world, especially the interpersonal aspect. Although this explanation, or variations of it, has served as a jumping off point for other theorists to explain the turmoil clients may experience, the difference between other theorists and Glasser is relatively broad. The magnitude of the difference can be appreciated when one considers that Glasser refused to include any of the predominant theoretical approaches adopted by his own profession. In the foreword to Glasser's *Reality Therapy,* Mower (1965) identified six assumed truths of traditional therapy (popular at the time Glasser trained to become a therapist) that he opposed: "the reality of mental illness, reconstructive exploration of the patient's past, transference, an 'unconscious' which must be plumbed, interpretation rather than evaluation of behavior, and change through insight and permissiveness" (p. viii).

Human Development

According to Glasser (1985), images enter our awareness through two filters (low and high). The low-level filter labels things—that object or event is a car, baby, party, wedding, and so forth. The high-level filter assigns value to the image we take in (positive or negative, and even neutral). Those things that satisfy needs are viewed as positive and those that work against need fulfillment are negative; other things are unimportant and thus neutral. Wubbolding (2000) added a third filter, which is an understanding filter that represents the perceived connections between the various images formed. Furthermore, as Wubbolding pointed out, the use of metaphors in therapy allows one image to be more fully understood in relation to another image. In addition, metaphors can helps a client see the special meaning behind various images, which helps to foster a sense of teleological purpose and can give new direction to the client's life. Also, as suggested by Wubbolding, utilizing metaphors during the course of therapy often helps a client make the connection between certain ineffective thoughts and specific ineffective actions. Finally, in relation to human development, Wubbolding (2003) discussed the importance of quality time interactions. These are relationships that require effort and are characterized especially by each person's wants and interpersonal needs being satisfied, the absence of criticism and complaints directed toward each other, and their repetitive nature (they are not a one-time encounter). Everyone experiencing such interactions, regardless of the ages of those involved, benefit positively and achieve greater mental health. It is assumed that, compared with fully developed adults, children need longer periods of quality time interactions to thrive and maintain good mental health.

Glasser asserted that all humans have the same basic needs and only differ from one another in the manner (i.e., effectiveness) in which they seek to satisfy those needs. From birth onward, we encounter a series of different relationships that play a formative role in our lives, and even though these relationships can mold our manner of seeking need satisfaction, the outside world does not dictate our behavior. Glasser firmly believed we are the primary source of our behaviors and not the accumulation of outside encounters we have with others (i.e., mother, father, family, teachers, spiritual leaders, friends, conjugal relationships, employers, etc.). In addition, even when our observable behaviors are the result of making a poor choice, from a Glasseresque perspective, the poor choice-maker should not be blamed or criticized for those "bad choices" because at the time the choice was made, it was likely the best possible choice the person could have made at that specific point in her life, regardless of whether or not we understand why that is the case. For Glasser, criticizing bad choices is useless, for time is better spent getting the person to make better choices starting now and as the person contemplates moving forward with her life.

Quality World. Glasser's concept of the "quality world" explains how our wants are tied to the five needs described earlier. Specifically, the quality world represents how each person would like to have needs fulfilled. Due to its dynamic nature, each person's quality world changes over time (the wants of a child morph into the wants of an adolescent whose wants morph into those of an adult). In each person's mind we can find a unique arrangement of wants, for example, images of enjoyable places, people the person is drawn to, hobbies or interests, strong beliefs, enjoyable types of interactions scripted out, and so forth. This heterogeneous pictorialized combination of wants is what Glasser (1985) referred to as our "mental picture album," which is inseparably tied to the five human needs.

In her song "Mercedes-Benz," Janis Joplin beautifully illustrated how a person might seek to fulfill a need for belonging through an expressed *want* of some status-imbued object. "Lord, won't you by me a Mercedes-Benz / My friends all drive Porsches/ I must make amends" (cited in Kaplan, 2002, p. 838). In light of these lyrics, understanding Glasser's full message about wants and needs allows us to appreciate the truth embedded in the cliché "Money can't buy you happiness."

Two Personalities—Two Pathways. According to Glasser, a person's approach to the world reveals one of the two general personality pathways that can be taken (Glasser, 1972; Wubbolding, 2000). Wubbolding (2003) stated that the personality representing a less effective pathway is referred to as *regressive* in nature and is marked by three stages: giving up, subsequent choices, and negative addictions.

The following is an actual case the author of this chapter is familiar with, one that perfectly illustrates how this type of personality unfolds. Carl started the first grade in the early 1950s, and it was during this time that he developed a "giving up" attitude. Finding it difficult to read, he recalls the teacher ridiculing him in front of the other students, even on some occasions adding sarcastic criticisms the other childrens' negative remarks about Carl. Things came to a head when near the end of the school year Carl asked to read a passage during "reading time." The teacher allowed it, but after stumbling over each word with a growing amount of frustration, and after several other students began snickering, Carl stopped reading. When Carl's mother met with Carl's first-grade teacher to find an explanation for Carl failing the first grade, she was told: "Your son will amount to nothing. He's the son of a musician and my son is a musician and I can tell you he has amounted to nothing!"

At school, Carl's needs for fun, belonging, power, and independence were rarely met which created the prerequisite for Stage 2 developing, that is, the subsequent choices Carl was to make. Carl's choices reflected one or more aspects of what Glasser has termed *total behavior*—actions, thinking, feeling, and physiology, that is, the four elements of behaviors intended to fulfill quality world wants. Subsequent years for Carl were marked by actions that are associated with being a class bully; his thinking revolved around "how boring school was," a place that conjured up feelings of anxiousness, fear, resentment, and full-blown anger, and physiologically Carl became more susceptible to illnesses, becoming "sicker" more easily and for longer periods of time than many of his classmates.

The final stage, addictions, comes into play when a person such as Carl adopts harmful or injurious behaviors while misperceiving them as need fulfilling when in fact they are pseudo-need-fulfilling. Consumption of alcohol and other drugs can provide a temporary sense of fun along with a fleeting belief that one is free, powerful, and connected to others, even if it is little more than seeing one's self belonging to a group of "societal rebels without a cause." Earlier in his conceptualizations of what caused people to suffer, Glasser might have spoken of this type of personality as developing a failure identity, but the term lost its significance for Glasser over time since everyone (even seemingly lost causes) can move toward developing a "winning personality," where the person is effectively meeting needs (Wubbolding, 2000). Considering this as the ultimate outcome hoped for, and according to Glasser available to essentially everyone via his approach, the term *failure identity* fell by the wayside. (We can apply the same type of scenario to Glasser himself. Glasser initially chose psychiatry as a career but soon afterward chose to reject what his profession practiced and subsequently decided to create a new form of therapy. All the evidence available indicates Glasser's new choice offered him much more satisfaction than if he had decided to stay with his first choice.)

It should not be a surprise the second type of personality described is positive in nature and represents an effective life direction where the three stages can be described as seeking change and growth, utilizing effective behaviors, and developing positive addictions (Wubbolding, 2000). The person is displaying effective healthy actions, feelings, physiology, and thinking—the opposite of what is occurring with the first personality outlined earlier. It is especially noteworthy to consider the role that thinking plays in differentiating both types of personalities. Whereas the kind of thoughts found to dominate in the first personality type tend to enslave these individuals because they chose to become attached to such thoughts, in the second type of personality the thinking style actually facilitates acquisition of what is needed to experience a healthy, fulfilling life. In addition, Glasser repackaged the everyday notion of addiction by differentiating between negative and positive forms. The latter type, positive addiction, is intended to refer to behaviors that allow one to increase self-esteem and personal strength. Developing qualities that help sustain us through difficult times can help to inoculate us against adopting a "giving up" attitude. Negative addictions are activities related to drugs, alcohol, smoking, overeating, and excessive use of caffeine, whereas positive addictions are activities such as running, meditating, and other types of activities that promote health and are performed at a set time each day. In his 1976 book *Positive Addiction,* Glasser wrote, "We drink, smoke, and eat too much because it's easier than disciplining ourselves to say no. I am not recommending that we should be more rigid or contentious, for that too is weakness. It takes strength, however, to be warm, firm, humorous, and caring and still do what we know we ought to do" (p. 5).

Therapy

Although reality therapy shares commonalities with several well-known forms of therapy, reality therapy should not be confused with those approaches (Wubbolding, 2011). The existentialist Jean-Paul Sartre said, "Man is fully responsible for his nature and choices." Certainly both Glasser and existential therapists see "choice" as central to defining and achieving human growth. Sartre also wrote the line "Hell is other people" in his play *No Exit.* The meaning of this phrase is more complicated than a cursory glance would provide. According to Sartre,

> "Hell is other people" has always been misunderstood. It has been thought that what I meant by that was that our relations with other people are always poisoned, that they are invariably hellish relations. But what I really mean is something totally different. I mean that if relations with someone else are twisted, vitiated, then that other person can only be hell. . . . But that does not at all mean that one cannot have relations with other people. It simply brings out the capital importance of all other people for each one of us. (Quoted in Morgareidge, 2005, n.p.)

Although Sartre's explanation is in line with Glasser's views concerning unhealthy relationships, beyond such similarities to existential informed therapies, existentialism's views pertaining to the human condition tend to be rather bleak compared with what is found in Glasser's writings.

Keeping in mind there are definite limits to comparing Glasser's work with other therapeutic approaches, it is safe to say that his views are similar to the client- or person-centered approach in terms of here-and-now optimistic quality and reality therapy's elevation of the therapeutic relationship to a critical status, although reality therapy's emphasis on changing behavior rather than focusing on feelings or allowing the client to take the lead are important differences. Furthermore, although Glasser seems to share a clear affinity with behavioral therapists, who also adopt a straightforward pragmatic approach to clients that is dependent upon behavioral change as a key to successful therapy, the two are fundamentally different in that behavioral therapists view behavior as often outwardly caused whereas reality therapists view behavior as inwardly caused. Overall, the therapy that shares the greatest degree of similarity to reality therapy is Adlerian therapy, a fact recognized by Glasser himself (Wubbolding, 2000). But even in this linkage there are differences. For instance, although both approaches place importance on family relationships, reality therapy emphasizes the present and not the past.

Beyond points of overlapping similarity, for the most part reality therapy appears to be an approach developed largely by Glasser independent of other well-known approaches to therapy and counseling. The exception obviously is Glasser's early rejection of psychodynamic approaches, which he was familiar with due to his psychiatric training, and it was the psychodynamic explanations and techniques that Glasser referred to when he explicitly rejected traditional psychiatry when he wrote *Reality Therapy: A New Approach to Psychiatry.*

Goal of Therapy

The overall goal of therapy is to assist the client in developing a new approach to life by abandoning the use of control to wrestle from others what the client wants or needs. In the short run, the controller may "satisfy" one-sided desires or expectations believed to make him happy, but there always comes a time of reckoning. Sometimes the eventual accounting that takes place has strong, tangible unpleasant results such as jail time, but even if such harsh outcomes do not materialize Glasser believed a reliance on trying to control the outside world creates a path that dead-ends at unhappiness and dissatisfaction. This is why few people have difficulty understanding the implications of the well-known lyrics sung by the Rolling Stones:

No, you can't always get what you want

No you can't always get what you want

But if you try sometimes

You just might find

You get what you need. (M. Jagger/K. Richards, on *Let it Bleed* album, 1969)

But to get just enough of a need satisfied to stay afloat in today's world is not really living, is it? Life has much more to offer us and we have much to offer life, according to Glasser.

Interestingly, even those who do not force their way through life by choosing a deliberate self-serving approach often cannot report they are experiencing a blissful existence. Life takes effort and planning. It seems fair to assert that the majority of life's travelers are stuck somewhere in the middle of the continuum between the two extremes of destination—misery and bliss—with much room left for change. Glasser's point is that the majority of people inhabiting the world can improve on how they satisfy their needs and interact with others. The goal of therapy is essentially the same for all clients even though the exact circumstances and story of each client are unique. The reality therapist aims to help those relying on a psychology of external control to understand why life is not matching their wants. An initial step is to have the client real-ize self-control is a genuine possibility whereas other-control is doomed to fail.

In conjunction with this aim is the importance of the client assuming responsibility for her life, which means using choice in a manner that leads to genuine need satisfac-tion and enjoying a life of healthy, nurturing relationships. Taking responsibility for ourselves eliminates one of the greatest impediments to a satisfying life, for it is the veil of irresponsibility that hides true reality and allows us to justify our blaming of others for being dissatisfied in life. Assuming responsibility removes this veil, and our finger of blame can only point toward us for the life we experience. Of equal impor-tance is the complementer—the realization that if I cannot control others, then they cannot control me—and the subsequent realization that everyone is confronted with the responsibility of finding happiness. In Glasser's view, there is no question that I am completely responsible for my own happiness (which does not mean I cannot support others achieving happiness). It turns out that life really is a mutual give-and-take prop-osition that requires good compromising skills.

Therapist's Role

Even more important than what the therapist does not do (e.g., the therapist *does not* diag-nose or label) is what the therapist does. In fact, Glasser viewed the role of the therapist as critical to therapy's outcome since it is the therapist who must create the special envi-ronment in which the client learns to genuinely trust the therapist and the process of real-ity therapy. One way to achieve this is to ask the client if there are any topics he does not want to discuss during the course of therapy and then respecting the wishes of the client. Wubbolding (2000) discussed the relationship in terms of "always be"—always be cour-teous, determined, and enthusiastic. This translates to the client experiencing a sense of being respected, that the therapist is hopeful, and that the therapist is seeking to understand what strengths the client brings into therapy.

The therapist works hard to create this special environment in various ways. In addi-tion to displaying appropriate disclosure, the therapist can be expected to display warmth, authenticity, and an accepting attitude. The therapist is also skilled at adopting a non-critical stance even though there are times the therapist will use confrontation. Listening for themes is important because themes will reveal something about wants or aspects of a "giving up" personality that can be used to help the client better understand her con-tribution to current problems. Similarly, metaphors used by the client can reveal aspects of the client's ineffective thinking and/or behaviors that can be used by the therapist to facilitate change (e.g., Client: "I feel like an abandoned dog that has been kicked around." Therapist: "So what are you doing about getting up, brushing yourself off, and seeking out others?"). In reality therapy, the therapist is expected to take the lead, which explains why this form of therapy is seen as being directive in nature. The therapist must also have achieved a level of healthiness congruent with Glasser's theoretical views; that is, the ther-apist must have achieved need fulfillment in an effective and prosocial manner.

The therapist operates under various assumptions: (a) All clients share the same genetic-based needs for independence, fun, love, power, and survival; (b) all clients are basically good by nature and desire to grow and become better people; (c) dysfunction or turbulence in the client's life is due to one or more needs not being met; (d) the essence of therapeutic work is to identify specific sources of frustration; and (e) ultimately, it is the client's responsibility for accurately determining how to satisfy what is wanting, so needs are met.

How important is establishing the right environment before commencing the work of reality therapy? It is critical if the therapist hopes to effectively help the client to establish healthy, prosocial goals; establish the requisite details of how to reach those goals; determine which therapeutic techniques will help the client the most; correct for any hindrances to progress during the process of therapy; and effectively serve as the client's preceptor who is expected to encourage the client throughout the process until success is met and termination can begin.

Client's Role

Once the client accepts the idea he is responsible for his life, the client is expected to maintain a current time focus throughout the therapeutic process and, with the assistance of the therapist, decide what choices are necessary to make his life better (Wubbolding, 2011). During the course of therapy the client is expected to avoid the all too common tendency to look to how others—either from the past or the present—have caused the client to be miserable and unsatisfied. Even if the client were to find a childhood event that fully explained why he does what he does today, it will would be viewed as totally irrelevant to conducting effective therapy. The past itself simply constitutes a historical record—nothing more nothing less.

When a client looks to the past for an explanation, the client is allowing herself a potential way to avoid effective treatment. Allowing such memory-travel provides the client a means to make excuses for who she is, which further allows the client to avoid accepting responsibility for her own current life. It is this avoidance of responsibility that hinders the client from making effective, health-promoting decisions.

Of course, making effective, health-promoting decisions in the time frame of now can be frightening for some clients because it requires new skills and ways of thinking. Also, therapeutic decision making implies there are important alternatives that must be considered, and where there are alternatives, there are mistakes to be made. (It is not surprising that some clients display a strong desire to cling to old patterns of thinking and acting—at least they know what to expect compared to the unknown territory they are likely to find themselves in if they begin making different types of choices.) But choosing to not choose one's life direction or allowing someone else (e.g., a therapist) to choose for us is not a good solution for clients experiencing an unsatisfactory state of existence.

The following nonsequenced listing summarizes some of the lessons that a client can expect to learn during the course of therapy. The client will learn to do the following things:

1. Differentiate between those things in life that he can control and those things he cannot control.
2. Take on responsibility that promotes true freedom and self-control.

3. Appreciate that the past is gone and since it cannot be resurrected it should remain undisturbed and buried.
4. Recognize that occurrences of frustration point directly to the use of ineffective ways to fulfill needs, which are also linked to current unfulfilling relationships (or the absence of relationships).
5. Avoid doing more of what he has been doing since it is the client's present thoughts and actions that have failed to bring the much needed satisfaction.
6. Avoid focusing on feelings and instead narrow one's efforts to changing current actions and thoughts, which are believed to be easier to change than feelings.
7. Accept the idea that effective change requires maintaining an exclusively present time orientation because problems are experienced in the present, not the past or the future.
8. Accept that happiness in life is tied directly to one's acceptance that everyone possesses personal strengths that can be identified and called on to make effective, health-promoting choices.

Therapeutic Techniques and Strategies

The Therapeutic Relationship. The therapeutic relationship is marked by an atmosphere of trust in which the client believes the therapist is genuinely interested in her and is willing to assist her in developing the means to live a satisfying life. The therapist values the client and is genuinely interested in seeing her life change for the better; as a result, the therapist becomes a part of the client's quality world. Glasser saw the client and therapist as cocreators of what has been termed a *professional friendship* (William Glasser Institute Ireland, 2009). This is not to be confused with what is typically meant solely by the word *friendship*, which denotes a type of intimacy that would be counterproductive to the type of successful therapeutic outcome Glasser advocated. It is important that the client not be too dependent on the therapist, and even less so as therapy progresses. It is the client's responsible, independent actions that will net the full benefits of what is offered by this form of therapy.

As a "professional friend" to the client, the therapist remains realistic throughout the course of therapy as to what will occur during the process. It is important to remember that on entering therapy, the client is being led to adopt a life perspective that counters how he currently perceives the world as operating. The client can be expected to make excuses, try manipulation, and display reluctance to adopt full responsibility for his total behavior. He may even display uncertainty about making choices that do not provide any of the illusionary safety nets he relied on prior to entering therapy.

Overall, Glasser's position is that therapy is very fluid and organic in nature. Reality therapy represents a process that can accommodate many different therapists' styles to engender client growth. Furthermore, various techniques associated with other therapeutic approaches have been incorporated into reality therapy. The remainder of this section sketches what can be expected to typically occur as the process of reality therapy unfolds and leads to achieving therapeutic goals.

By the time the therapist and client start to move in the direction of addressing unfulfilled needs, the client sees therapy as a safe environment to work out concerns and views the therapist as a kind, beneficent, and worthy helper who will assist the client in developing needed relationships that are mutually satisfying.

Often Used Strategies. Therapeutic strategies are more than just a skilled way of interacting with a client and should be seen as extensions of the theoretical underpinnings that constitute Glasser's approach (i.e., techniques that will keep the client focused on her present life, identify unsatisfactory elements of the interpersonal world, recognize what is modifiable, acknowledge displaced responsibility, and learn new ways of thinking and interacting to satisfy wants/needs).

In addition to the creation and careful maintenance of a supportive environment throughout the course of therapy, it is important for the therapist to maintain a determined attitude, enthusiasm, courteousness, genuineness, and empathy. The therapist can also be expected to use techniques such as paradoxical intention (refer to Viktor Frankl's logotherapy), which essentially has the client do more of what the client fears or desires to avoid. Other techniques used are attending skills, applying and appreciating humor, incorporating role-playing tactics, listening for and using metaphors and themes expressed, providing feedback to the client, confronting contradictions and excuses, utilizing reasonable amounts of self-disclosure, providing teaching/instruction, formulating action plans, creating client contracts that specify doing and/or not doing something, allowing the client to experience consequences for his behavior (as in other forms of therapy, consequences that may prove harmful are not ethically permissible), and discussing problems revealed using the past tense and using either the present or future tense when discussing positive solutions (Wubbolding, 2000, p. 239). Finally, when a client uses certain nouns to describe a state of mind or feeling the therapist changes those nouns to verbs by adding an *-ing* suffix. For example, depression becomes *depressing,* anxiety becomes *anxiety-ing,* and anger becomes *angering.* This change calls attention to a situation that is not fixed in time but rather a situation that the client has chosen to enact now. When words like *depression* are used by the client, the attempted payoff is freedom from responsibility, as a person with depression is generally seen in our society as less capable and in need of care by others.

Techniques That Play a Central Role in Reality Therapy. Wubbolding formulated two overarching techniques, **WDEP** and **SAMI^2 C^3,** which are central to the success of reality therapy (European Association for Reality Therapy, 2012b). They serve to anchor all reality therapists to Glasser's special form of therapy, but neither should be viewed as representing a rigid step-by-step procedure. At what point the therapist enters the process is a judgment call based on what is best for the client. It is for this reason that Wubbolding (2003) refers to **WDEP** and **SAMI^2 C^3** as the "cycle of counseling."

The **WDEP** technique involves the following foci:

W = Wants: It is critical to explore the wants, needs, and perceptions of the client (the therapist will also share her wants and perceptions concerning the client). It is important to obtain a commitment from the client early in the process because a positive outcome will dependent on the client's commitment to change. Wubbolding measures the level of commitment by assigning a value 1 (lowest) to 5 (highest). The five values correspond to the following descriptions of commitment: 1 = I don't want to be here [in therapy], 2 = I want the outcome, but not the effort, 3 = I'll try, I might, 4 = I will do my best, and 5 = I will do whatever it takes (Wubbolding, 2003, p. 272). The therapist always accepts the level reported, but if it is too low for planning to take place then the therapist works with the client to move him to a higher level.

Asking questions that are intended to discover what the client wishes, craves, or desires plays an essential role in reality therapy. Here are a few examples.

- How do the wants you express fulfill your need for belonging?
- If you had a genie you could summon to carry out your wishes and you decided that you wished you could be someone else, who would that person be?
- What prevents you from obtaining what you desire in life?

D = Direction and Doing: This component requires a careful examination of the client's total behavior. The client's actions and typical self-talk (negative and positive) provides a real sense of the client's direction in life. As in the previous process component, the therapist will devote time to continuing to build a strong therapist–client relationship solidly tied to trust. Looking for and encouraging the client's strengths are important aspects of the "direction and doing" process component (and throughout the entire process when an opportunity is provided). Questions at this point are intended to provide details, keep the focus on present time and on the client rather than others, and reveal something about the client's actions, thoughts, feelings, and physiological dimension (i.e., the client's total behavior). The classic question that is both short and capable of getting at all of what was just mentioned is this:

- What are you doing?

E = Evaluation: Having clients evaluate their own actions and thoughts by weighing the consequences of their actions helps clients develop the much needed skill of self-evaluation, which in turn leads to developing the ability to self-regulate appropriately. In addition to confronting clients with ineffective outcomes that result from certain actions, the therapist will also have clients evaluate components of their actions through questioning. It is essential that clients develop good self-evaluation skills if they are to succeed in the real world outside of therapy. Again, questions play a very important part of getting the client to self-evaluate.

- Are you moving in a direction that matches the goals you want to achieve?
- Did sleeping until noon today get you closer to enrolling in the community college you want to go to?
- Is that "want" realistic, or does it fall into an area beyond what you can obtain at this time?
- How will enrolling in college meet your current needs?
- Is your present behavior getting you what you want the most now?

P = Plan: The therapist will collaborate with the client to develop effective plans to achieve goals by determining what new behaviors are required to satisfy the client's needs. At this stage, client commitment is an essential ingredient. Beyond having the client commit to the decided plan, the therapist can expect to go through the planning process a number of times until the client reaches a point of being able to genuinely take control of her life as well as developing plans independent of the therapist. The time and effort devoted to working toward developing effective plans to achieve established therapeutic goals contribute to successful therapy since even the partial success of developed and implemented plans, with the therapist's encouragement, reinforces client movement as well as strengthens the client's ability to commit to later plans that may be even more difficult to achieve.

Planning is critical to the therapy process (Wubbolding, 2003, 2007). Effective planning ultimately depends on the client's ability to successfully construct doable plans. Wubbolding lists eight qualities to consider during planning and refers to these qualities via the acronym **SAMI^2 C^3** (Wubbolding, 2003, p. 275).

S = Simple: The plan is uncomplicated.

A = Attainable: If the plan is too difficult or too long range, the client is likely to become discouraged and not follow through.

M = Measurable: The plain is precise and exact. The client is encouraged to define a clear answer to the question, "When will you do it?"

I = Immediate: The plan is carried out as soon as possible.

I = Involved: The therapist is involved if such involvement is appropriate. The involvement is, of course, within the bounds of ethical standards and facilitates client independence rather than dependence.

C = Controlled by the client: An effective plan is not contingent on the actions of another person but is, as much as possible, within the control of the client.

C = Committed: The therapist helps the client to pledge firmly to put the plan into action.

C = Continuously carried out by the client: When a plan does not work exactly as anticipated (which is the norm rather than the exception during the early phase of this stage), the therapist works to help the client develop a new plan with consideration of why the earlier plan failed. The idea is come up with plans that are characterized by repetition because these are considered the most productive type to construct. A single plan, where the outcome might happen once, can be a starting point, but the most effective type of plan is one that can serve as a prototype to confront many future situations.

Even though the various aspects of therapy described can be considered as building on one another, it is certain that the client and therapist will return to some aspect of the treatment process used earlier before termination is reached. Finally, Wubbolding (2000) stressed the therapist should avoid actions that are counterproductive to a successful outcome. Actions such as arguing, criticizing, dominating, allowing the client to give up too easily, and overlooking client excuses all fall into this category.

Process of Change

The change agent in Glasser's approach hinges on clients accepting that they have the ability to meaningfully *choose* in life. The process of change means that clients no longer place themselves at the mercy of others or society, adopt a victim mentality to explain their problems, or develop a psychological disorder such as depression to free themselves from personal responsibility. Chronic complaining about one's life and psychological symptoms are indicators that clients have chosen to live an unfulfilling, dissatisfying lives. Change comes when clients understand, incorporate, and act on the basic assumption that they have an inherent ability to choose how to interact with the world—that they are capable of quieting that sense of hopelessness and despair that prevented them from taking appropriate action.

Moving Beyond the Reality Therapy of the 1960s

To more completely appreciate Glasser's later contributions to what actions contribute to healthy relationships (compared to actions that are destructive) and what exactly he meant by choice theory, read Glasser's 1998 book, *Choice Theory: A New Psychology of Personal Freedom,* in which Glasser listed what he considered to be 10 self-evident truths pertaining to choice theory (Table 10.2) and seven healthy interpersonal habits along with their unhealthy counterparts (Table 10.3).

Choice theory can be viewed as an important shift in how Glasser conceptualized various aspects of his overall approach. This is not to say the importance of choice was

▼ TABLE 10.2

The Ten Axioms of Choice Theory

1. A person can only control his/her behavior not the behavior of others.
2. All a person can provide to others is information.
3. Every long-lasting problem is connected to one or more interpersonal problems.
4. Interpersonal problems are manifested in our current life.
5. While the past may have affected who we are today the past cannot be changed and we are left to seek the fulfillment of our needs this day or plan how we might satisfy our needs beyond this day.
6. We can only satisfy needs by matching them with the *pictures* comprising our *quality world.*
7. The essence of being human is found in our manner of *acting* in the world.
8. All behavior is to be considered *total behavior* which is made up of four constituent parts: *acting, thinking, feeling,* and *physiology* including all physical and chemical processes.
9. All *total behavior is chosen,* but we only have direct control over two aspects of total behavior which are *acting* and *thinking.*
10. All total behavior is represented by verbs and designated by the behavioral aspect that is the most distinguishable.

Source: William Glasser Institute (2012c, n.p.).

▼ TABLE 10.3

The Seven Caring Habits/Seven Deadly Habits

Caring Habits	Deadly Habits
1. Accepting	1. Nagging
2. Encouraging	2. Blaming
3. Listening	3. Complaining
4. Negotiating differences	4. Bribing, rewarding the person in an attempt to control
5. Respecting	5. Punishing
6. Trusting	6. Threatening
7. Supporting	7. Criticizing

Sources: Glasser (2003); William Glasser Institute (2012c, n.p.).

overlooked earlier, but after adding to, taking away from, and reconsidering differing aspects of his approach for several decades, it is as if all the major theoretical pieces fell into place to form a coherent image. Considering that Glasser spent the bulk of his professional career changing and refining earlier views, it is difficult to understand his work if only two or three of his books are read at random. A better way to accurately grasp some of the changes that took place leading up to choice theory is to chronologically review a sample of Glasser's works. Such a sample is provided in Table 10.4.

Reviewing the chronologically arranged sample of books found in Table 10.4 reveals consistencies and changes that occurred in Glasser's thinking over time. For example, a noticeable characteristic found throughout his body of work, one that has become more noticeable over time, is his interests in going beyond just helping clients to helping large groups of people and entire systems—an interest that has taken on a more global focus in recent years. One also finds Glasser to be a strong advocate for large-scale proactive steps aimed at enhancing mental health throughout society, rather than continuing to rely on systems that intervene after problems have become firmly rooted in individuals and groups. As a reader of this textbook, what can you conclude about Glasser from the sample of books appearing in Table 10.4?

Research Support

During the past three decades, there have only been a few studies published in the *International Journal of Reality Therapy* that examine the efficacy or effectiveness of reality therapy. Perhaps this is because unlike other approaches, reality therapy supports a treatment plan that appears to be flexible when based on the client's wants and needs. This plan also should be initiated by the client (Wubbolding, 2000). Considering that empirical studies on therapeutic outcome require standardized procedures, it is not surprising that conducting a study on the efficacy or effectiveness of reality therapy has been a challenge for decades.

A Chronological Sample of Glasser's Work

1960—*Mental Health or Mental Illness? Psychiatry for Practical Action*
Discusses how normal functioning deserves greater attention because it is associated with happiness and worthwhile achievement. Glasser list three criteria to consider: the person and his or her needs, the world or reality in which each person lives, and the ego as a negotiator between the world and the person. Glasser advocated for proactive approaches to increase mental health in society.
1965—*Reality Therapy: A New Approach to Psychiatry*
Form of therapy developed by Glasser that opposed key components of psychiatry's approach to treatment. Specifically, Glasser advocated against psychodynamic therapy, *DSM* diagnosis, and the use of medicine to treat what was wrongly called mental illness.
1969—*Schools Without Failure*
Discusses the deficiency in school environments and contemporary education's approach. Glasser offers an alternative that leads to students seeing the relevance of involvement that leads to greater participation and fosters greater thinking ability.
1972—*The Identity Society*
Reviews Glasser's position that, because survival is not the concern it once was for humans, humans have turned their attention to self-development and identity, which has shifted the goal of motivation in ways that allow for the discussion of what can be termed *identity motivation*.
1976—*Positive Addiction*
An exploration of how people can purposely seek what is termed positive forms of addiction such as meditating or long distance running. It is hypothesized that positive addictions can help people overcome negative addictions such as eating, gambling, or drug-related problems.
1981—*Stations of the Mind: New Directions for Reality Therapy*
Reviews how the human brain functions in conjunction with needs, allowing Glasser to provide an explanation for why humans think and act as they do. Everyone perceives the world from needs-tainted lenses. Discusses a therapeutic approach that is more humanistic than the forms of behavioral therapies that dominated this period of time.
1984—*Take Effective Control of Your Life*
Thoughtful suggestions that allow one to increase happiness. This practical guide is based on Glasser's years of counseling experience. The work expands on Glasser's *Reality Therapy: A New Approach to Psychiatry*, covering topics such as creativity and reorganization, psychosomatic illness as a creative process, chemical control of our lives, conflict, criticism, and how the use of control theory can lead to greater self-control.
1984—*Control Theory (revised and retitled Take Charge of Your Life)*
Presents the science of choice theory, which provides an explanation for human behavior and how establishing genuine internal control in one's life generates freedom and taking charge of one's behavior, which allows for healthy choices being made to achieve a more satisfying and enjoyable life. The potential impact of such changes affects the individual and spreads out to others making the world a better place. Topics covered include psychosomatic disorders, diseases, being parents, relationships, and marital discord. The views presented are illustrated with examples.
1986—*Control Therapy in the Classroom*
Provides reasons for why large numbers of students, who are capable of learning, have been turned off of education and as a result make minimum or no effort to learn. Glasser illustrates how control theory can be used to create the type of team-building experiences that dramatically increase the level of satisfaction and fun students encounter.
1994—*The Control (Choice) Theory Manager*
Covers the importance of achieving quality work produced by happy, satisfied workers, which emerges when the too typical style of boss-management is replaced by lead-management.
1998—*The Quality School*
The bossy managerial style of schools automatically places teachers and students in a relationship destined to generate hostility. Glasser seeks greater collaboration between these two former adversaries and discusses how this can generate an atmosphere in which students come to believe there is a health-promoting quality in the tasks they are given as well as a positive quality inherent in this type of teacher–student relationship.

1998—*The Quality School Teacher*

Further elaborates on what is covered in *The Quality School*. The book offers practical, detailed advice that enables teachers to create what has been termed the *quality classroom*.

1998—*Choice Theory: A New Psychology of Personal Freedom (see Note)*

Attempts at controlling others have dominated much of human history right down to the present. Glasser argues strongly for a rejection of the external control psychology that has dominated human interactions and replaces it with a noncontrolling type of psychology that leads to freedom and health-sustaining relationships.

1998—*Choice Theory in the Classroom*

Discusses the use of learning-teams intended to harness the type of team spirit seen in sports but in this case directed toward classroom activities where learning generates excitement and genuine engagement.

1999—***The Language of Choice Theory*** *(coauthored with his wife, Carleen Glasser)*

Provides examples for four categories of relationships in which the recipient of a message (employee, lover, student, and child) is more likely to respond favorably by changing a controlling type of comment into a comment that allows the recipient choice.

2000—*Getting Together and Staying Together*

Represents an update of Glasser's earlier work, *Staying Together*. The update explores the issue of compatibility and how choice theory can be applied to improve intimate relationships.

2000—***Reality Therapy in Action*** *(in 2001, this work was printed in paperback and retitled Counseling With Choice Theory: The New Reality Therapy)*

Represents an updated and expanded version of Glasser's seminal 1965 book, *Reality Therapy*. The update incorporates choice theory and discusses how choice theory and reality therapy, when applied and practiced, are inseparable components contributing to the final outcome.

2001—*Fibromyalgia: Hope From a Completely New Perspective*

With the medical field failing to find a pathological component to those suffering from the condition, Glasser explains how symptom improvement can be achieved through the application of choice theory.

2001—*Every Student Can Succeed*

Provides a means for teachers to reach a new level of teaching that promises to create a student environment in which students feel included in their education. This results in a genuine interest in learning and generates a sense of being competent learners who are guiding their own destiny.

2003—*For Parents and Teenagers: Dissolving the Barrier Between You and Your Teen*

Covers the tremendous drawback to using external control in relating to teenagers. Glasser argues the advantage to allowing choices to be made by teenagers. Applying choice theory to parent–teenager and teacher–teenager relationships can foster positive and loving relationships.

2004—*Warning: Psychiatry Can Be Hazardous to Your Mental Health*

Reviews how mental health was sidetracked by mental illness because of the inherent money-earning potential of medical-based treatment. The primary force behind the embracing of mental illness over mental health lies with the billions of dollars generated by the drug industry. Glasser argues it is not an illness that plagues humanity but rather the condition of unhappiness. It is this unhappiness that should be taken care of through ways that promote mental health rather than mental illness.

2007—*A-Ha Performance: Building and Managing a Self-Motivated Workforce*

Explains how motivation for change must come from the inside. Externally created motivation is faulty because it does not lead to people achieving their true potential.

2007—***Eight Lessons for a Happier Marriage*** *(coauthored with his wife, Carleen Glasser)*

Provides examples of couples experiencing difficulties and offers examples of how such difficulties could be altered so that lasting, loving relationships can flourish.

Note: The books appearing in ***bold font*** are recommended for those interested in obtaining a detailed update of Glasser's concerns and views pertaining to therapeutic applications.

More recently, however, Loyd (2005) examined the effectiveness of reality therapy for adolescents in a school setting. In this study, students ($N = 68$) were assigned to either a treatment or control group. Outcome assessments were made at pretherapy, posttherapy, and follow-up. Students in the treatment group received five sessions of reality therapy. Participants in the control group, in contrast, also received five sessions of reality therapy principles but after the posttherapy assessment. Results showed that at posttreatment, students in the treatment group significantly improved in three psychological needs (power, freedom, and fun). The control group also improved at the follow-up test after exposure to the principles of reality therapy. In addition, the positive effects for the treatment group were maintained at the follow-up testing. Neither group, however, demonstrated significant improvement in the psychological need for belonging.

Despite the paucity of outcome studies involving reality therapy, a meta-analysis project was conducted by Radtke, Sapp, and Farrell (1997). Radtke et al. examined 21 studies that included therapeutic outcomes of reality therapy. A moderate overall effect size was discovered (an *effect size* is also referred to as a *treatment effect*). This meta-analysis has been criticized because the studies included were ineffective in controlling the outcome variables. It has also been criticized for assessing the outcomes of the treatment and control groups with nonequivalent measures.

In contrast, other studies have supported the effectiveness of reality therapy for clients with substance abuse issues (Wesley, 1988), domestic violence concerns (Rachor, 1995), depression (Ingram & Hinkle, 1990), rheumatoid arthritis or osteoarthritis (Maisiak, Austin, & Heck, 1995), and disruptive behaviors (Edens & Smyrl, 1994). Studies conducted outside of the United States have also reported on the effectiveness of reality therapy. Peterson, Chang, and Collins (1998) examined the effect of reality therapy on undergraduates in Taiwan. Results revealed that four of the undergraduates' psychological needs improved after treatment.

The results of a study in South Korea further supported the effectiveness of reality therapy. In this study (Kim, 2008), college students ($N = 276$) participated in either a treatment group for Internet addiction or a control group. Students exposed to reality therapy reported significant improvement in the reduction of symptoms of Internet addiction. In yet another study, Prenzlau (2006) examined the effectiveness of reality therapy for clients with symptoms of posttraumatic stress disorder in Israel. The results revealed reductions in clients' somatization rumination behaviors.

Relevance of Theory

The applicability of reality therapy for diverse settings and populations is quite promising because of its emphasis on the client's perspective in the treatment process. Individuals may encounter reality therapy in a school setting, private practice, psychiatric hospital, substance abuse clinic, social service agency, or military setting (e.g., Carbo, 2006; Edens, 1995; Posada, 1991). Clients with a disability and from various racial, ethnic and socioeconomic backgrounds, as well as adolescents, adults, couples, families, and inmates (e.g., Carbo, 2006; Owens, 2002; Wicker, 1999; Wubbolding, 2000) may benefit from reality therapy. This approach is frequently employed with adolescents in a school setting.

Culturally sensitive treatment is highly emphasized among therapists who embrace choice theory and reality therapy. For instance, Wubbolding (2000) addressed the need for reality therapists to be aware of individual differences in religious backgrounds by focusing on the characteristics of each religion. Brinson and Kottler (1995) also stressed the importance for reality therapists to recognize that the needs of minority clients are diverse. Reality therapists are required to be aware of the potential barriers experienced by such clients seeking and receiving psychological services. More specifically, Wilson and Stith (1991) claimed that when working with African American clients, reality therapists must be aware of social oppression, the clients' social support system and values, barriers to communication, and the importance of being genuine throughout the treatment process.

Reality therapy can be found in urban, rural, and suburban settings. Depending on the service provider's affiliation, clients receiving reality therapy may be covered through their Health Maintenance Organization and/or Preferred Provider Organization. Insurance companies will reimburse clients for the cost of receiving reality therapy based on the particular company's policy.

The William Glasser Institute has provided training programs for several decades. Approximately 77,000 individuals have completed the institute's basic course (William Glasser Institute, 2012b). To obtain certification in choice theory or reality therapy, trainees are required to complete courses offered by the institute. The institute also provides continuing education credits for the American Association of Marriage and Family Therapy, the National Board for Certified Counselors, and licensed clinical social workers. Additionally, various centers for reality therapy in the United States provide training programs and continuing education credits for the National Board for Certified Counselors, National Association of Alcohol and Drug Abuse Counselors, Ohio Counselor Licensing Board, Ohio Social Worker Board, Alcohol and Drug Abuse Counselors, Ohio Psychological Association–Mandatory Continuing Education, and Kentucky Department of Education Bulletin Board.

Social Justice and Multiculturalism

Social Justice. Choice theory asserts that humans are self-determining entities whose choices create the matrix for our behaviors, thoughts, emotional states, and physiological experiences. Embedded in choice theory is an explanation of how control can go wrong and be used to attempt domination or command of others. The purpose of control can inevitably be reduced to an effort to regulate and guide others in ways to fulfill our unmet needs. During the 1990s and the beginning of the current century, Glasser increasingly promoted choice psychology to replace the type of control psychology that plagues people worldwide.

If enough inhabitants of the world stopped faulting others or things for their disappointing lives, embraced the responsibility and freedom that lies dormant in so many, and began to make healthy choices, perhaps the world could be changed for the better. To a large extent choice theory relies on the very language we speak, and finding new ways to positively craft our use of language on a daily basis is one of the goals of Glasser's theory. What makes this goal impossible (or for the optimists among us at least highly improbable)? The answer is people. It is interesting to think that we have the power to act responsibly but for the most part simply choose not to do so, and instead make the choice to wallow through life by staying in a dead-end job, maintaining poor-quality relationships while we inhabit a place on earth that promises only a paltry level of happiness. The examples in Table 10.5 illustrate how making simple adjustments to typical patterns of speaking can easily bring about a choice theory–driven form of communication. The examples provided in Table 10.5 are modeled after the 52 examples published by William Glasser and Carleen Glasser in their book *The Language of Choice Theory,* in which they discuss external control psychology and assert that external control represents "a plague on all of humanity" and that choice theory offers all of us a direct opposite (Glasser & Glasser, 1999, p. viii). The Glassers emphasized that the relations we require to provide optimum need satisfaction are typically not short term in nature, and even though the use of external control may place us in a position of the winning competitor who comes in first by dominating the other, no relationship can endure such an interpersonal battlefield for long. Eventually the winner in such contests loses, for example, through divorce, loss of a friend, turned-off student, or departure of the family's black sheep never to return. By comparison, choice theory provides an uncomplicated restructuring of everyday language that fosters collaborative efforts to find creative solutions to life's problems. The message found in this coauthored book echoes an earlier theme often repeated by William Glasser throughout his body of work: The only behavior we can control is our own.

Multicultural Perspective. Glasser's approach is effective for dealing directly with controversial or sensitive issues. Any topic that has polarizing potential and easily produces tension and strife are good topics for reality therapy, including sexually transmitted diseases, racial issues, clashing cultural differences, and so forth. The reason for this therapeutic suitability lies with the approach's emphasis on equality throughout the treatment process and the expectation for therapists to help clients build meaningful and fulfilling relationships.

Therapists applying reality therapy have been trained to understand the importance of the client–therapist relationship and to foster relational ingredients that contribute to establishing a strong client–therapist bond. Specifically, the therapist is expected to pay close attention to even slight details or impressions while maintaining an acute mental and emotional sensibility, and to be especially aware of and responsive to the feelings and expressed concerns of the client. Nor is the therapist to criticize a client's action that represents the type of ineffective approach that reality therapy was designed to counteract. It is clear from the focus placed on the importance of the client–therapist relationship, especially in terms of establishing and maintaining trust throughout the approach, that this method seems especially suited to handle sensitive issues.

Reality therapy is commonly practiced in several Asian countries. When discussing this practice, Jusoh and Ahmad (2009) emphasized the importance of therapists awareness of multicultural issues such as family relationships for Koreans, nondirective communication for Japanese individuals, and the therapists' role in the treatment of Taiwanese college students.

Choice Theory: Changing Communication Patterns

Communication That Fosters Control	Communication That Fosters Choice
Teacher to Student "If you drop further behind in your schoolwork, you will fail."	**Teacher to Student** "You feel way behind. Rather than focus on what you have not done, let's focus on what it will take to graduate from high school this spring. Just do the work I assign, show me you know what to do, and this class won't hold you back. There are 4 months left in the school year. I'm on your side, so come to me when you need help. You have enough time to pull this off."
Supervisor to Supervisee "It's that time of the year—time for annual evaluations. Here is what I wrote down—there are a few things you need to consider and need to improve on by our next annual evaluation meeting."	**Supervisor to Supervisee** "Instead of just handing you an annual evaluation, I decided to take time and ask you several questions. First, tell me what part of your daily work assignment you're best at—that enables you to display your talents. Second, what would you like to improve on by next year at this time? Third, would you be willing to help someone else in the company who plans to strive for improving in the area you think reflects your best work? Fourth, would you be willing to speak with an employee who selected the area you want to improve in as the area she excels in to get some suggestions as to how you might improve?"
Adult to Child "Go to bed, Billy. Nine o'clock is way too late for a child your age to stay up on a school night. For the last time, go to bed or you can forget about going over to Tommy's this weekend!"	**Adult to Child** "Billy, you can stay up if you remain quiet and don't disturb me or your dad. When you get sleepy, you can go to bed, but before I get too tired and can't keep my own eyes open, do you want me to read a story out of your favorite book?"
Lovers "I'm frustrated because all we do is work, go to bed exhausted—we don't even take time for sex any longer and every spare minute is devoted to one of us taking care of our 6-year-old and baby."	**Lovers** "Honey, we seem to rarely have time for one another and this includes sex. We seem more busy blaming one another for things, and lately I seem to be blaming you even more. I love you and I want to enjoy life with you rather than fighting because both of us feel unsatisfied. What do you think we can do to get out of this cycle of blaming each other and find new ways to strengthen our relationship?"

Criticisms of Reality Therapy and Choice Theory

When reality therapy was first introduced, it was criticized for its simplicity and lack of technical language. However, Glasser purposely strove from the beginning to present his ideas in a straightforward, jargon-free style of writing. Glasser was interested in reaching the largest possible audience in order to have the greatest possible impact on those who were having a difficult time satisfying their needs. Glasser was determined to demystify the process of mental health from the start.

Another criticism is that Glasser's approach is a watered-down version of one of the other major approaches. This has proven to be false, even in the case of Adlerian therapy, which Glasser recognized as having several points of convergence with his own theory. Even a fleeting examination shows the two approaches (reality therapy/choice theory and Adlerian therapy) to be significantly different from one another in key areas and philosophy.

It is appropriate to criticize Glasser's body of work in terms of his views pertaining to mental health and pharmaceutical treatments. It seems somewhat strange to think that Glasser viewed people as basically good, but that he would unequivocally accuse people involved in creating pharmaceutical treatments as being basically bad. It is reasonable to argue that Glasser's views in this case are both premature and needlessly extreme in light of recent developments in newer treatments for various disorders. In addition, the wholehearted rejection of transference events, unconscious motivation, occurrence of dream symbols, as well as the value for some clients to ferret out repressed memories and familial conflicts is the type of position that is somewhat surprising when the available evidence for their existence is objectively considered.

Overall, the one criticism that cannot be refuted is that after approximately five decades, Glasser's approach still lacks a sufficient body of strong research to support various theoretical and practice assumptions, including reality therapy's/choice theory's application to populations outside the United States. This is a criticism to which Glasser called attention. In an issue of the *International Journal of Choice Theory and Reality Therapy*, Glasser outlined his future vision for the journal:

> I am . . . looking forward to seeing more juried articles with an international flavor reflecting the use of Reality Therapy and the teaching of Choice Theory in diverse cultures around the world. I am very impressed with the research initiatives already being pursued by Loyola Marymount University and their efforts to coordinate national and international studies, occurring simultaneously via the internet. I eagerly anticipate seeing some excellent articles being submitted by CT/RTC [Choice Theory/Reality Choice Therapy] Scholars from different universities in the United States and from the country of Australia. All these universities have great potential to fulfill the mission of the Institute. (Glasser, 2010, p. 12)

Application: Reality Therapy and Choice Theory

From a multicultural perspective, reality therapy possesses some potential shortcomings that merit consideration when working with clients. The emphasis that is placed on the ability of individuals to make choices to fulfill essential needs might place a client at odds with the standards of the client's group, community, or culture. Although some instances exist in which a divergence of needs may be desirable (e.g., a gang member who seeks to act in ways counter to the gang's needs), the ramifications of fulfilling individual needs over collective needs deserves to be weighed during the course of therapy, and although this is a genuine concern, the issue of individualism versus collectivism that surrounds reality therapy is somewhat offset by Glasser's belief that clients must assume responsibility for their actions and his belief that fulfillment of one's needs should not conflict with the needs of other people.

REVISITING THE HYPOTHETICAL CASE STUDY: THE STREET ARTIST WHO MEETS REALITY AND IS CONFRONTED WITH CHOICE

THERAPEUTIC ENVIRONMENT

Raul established a genuine relationship of healthy client–therapist interactions through the skillful use of empathic listening and by focusing on Felipe's frustrations tied to high school, the vice principal's treatment of him, and his street art as a way to communicate his frustrations. Whenever Felipe injected feelings into the session, Raul used those times to discuss how feelings were natural but how expressing negative emotions was not the same thing as taking positive action—action that would not add to the storehouse of frustrations Felipe had already acquired.

WANTS, DOING, DIRECTION, AND EVALUATION

As a client Felipe is naturally verbal, and in agreement with his artistic slant he often uses metaphors to describe situations, especially as a means to describe what he wants out of life. As therapy progressed, Raul used Felipe's metaphors as a means to decipher Felipe's wants and the needs tied to those wants.

The brief passage that follows took place after a number of sessions. Despite the brief nature of this exchange, it points to what Felipe defines as what he wants out of life and an instance of where Felipe evaluated the likely consequence of enacting a thought he was having.

Felipe School is boring—a waste of time and the vice principal sucks big time. Someday I'll paint the entire outside of the school—with my SiG-RAF-FiO [a group of graffiti artists of which Felipe was a member] friends—we could do it in one hour. [Felipe starts to smile and laughs briefly.]

Raul It's an enjoyable thought you're having, but if you carried this thought out, who would be surrounded by bars?

Felipe I should just paint the bars around me. That's why I was smiling—I saw myself painting my own jail.

Raul [Raul laughs.] You ever hear the expression the best revenge is success?

Felipe Yeah—but how do I do that with what I want to do? [Long pause] To be an artist?

Raul That's why we are here—to figure it out.

Subsequent sessions helped Felipe to clearly see that being a member of SiG-RAF-FiO allowed him to satisfy several needs he was not able to satisfy at school. Specifically, membership allowed him to create more of a balance in his life, providing a means to better fulfill several needs. His street art allowed him to accomplish a sense of power through achieving the art he had planned out in his sketch pad. Producing street art increased his sense of self-worth, recognition, and fame. It also offered him an escape from a school environment that tried to "squeeze enjoyment out of life."

PLANNING AND EFFECTIVE IMPLEMENTATION

Planning was difficult at first, not because of Felipe's level of commitment (that was high), but rather because he sought to accomplish too much. Instead of keeping it simple and attainable at first, he was trying to take giant steps to achieve his goal of being an artist.

Within a couple of sessions and with Raul's assistance, Felipe was able to implement a series of plans that effectively allowed him to complete a GED and enroll in a community college to earn a 2-year art degree. A 6-month follow-up by the therapist found that Felipe was doing well at school and that he had acquired a part-time job at a local art store. The proprietor of the store allowed Felipe to paint the entire front of the store with a beautiful mural incorporating contemporary street art themes and several images from Renaissance painters. After the follow-up Raul drove past the art store, as suggested by Felipe, to see his art. Raul noticed that in one corner of the work of art Felipe had painted the face of William Glasser as it had appeared in Felipe's sketch book.

Coming out of Glasser's mouth were the spraypainted words: *Raul—Lo hiciste bien* (i.e., *Raul—you did good*).

The Case of Miguel Sanchez

An additional complexity involved in applying Glasser's approach is the existence of environmental or cultural factors (e.g., oppression or discrimination) that can hinder a client's attempts to fulfill needs and wants. Wubbolding (2008) has recognized that there are times when existing factors can significantly narrow the range of choices available for clients, but he also believes that even though such a case is true, there still remain choices to be made and among those remaining are some choices that can lead to life-affirming changes. Let's not forget that in his early career, William Glasser successfully worked with clients who were diagnosed as schizophrenic and experienced a variety of systemic forces that obstructed their recovery.

Seemingly, as Glasser (1998) asserted, key principles of the approach do apply universally, so a therapist is likely to encounter cultural differences that can be utilized in ways to adapt the approach to a new cultural perspective. Wubbolding (2000) reported aspects of Japanese culture that require changes be made to Glasser's approach when it is used in Japan. For example, the use of a direct question technique to elicit a direct answer is not effective with Japanese clients. Wubbolding discovered that directly confronting a client's personal issue goes against the grain of Japanese culture, and he advocated a much more subtle and indirect line of discussion to uncover problems and find solutions.

The following segment is taken from a session that occurred at a point in the therapeutic process in which Miguel struggles to make productive choices that will allow him to assume ownership of his destiny.

Session Segment

Miguel   *Hola.*

Therapist   *Hola.* [Pauses before speaking again.] You look different somehow. I sense that you have chosen to work on what we had talked about last time—not "depressing" yourself.

Miguel   Yeah, I'm thinking about and doing things that make me feel better about myself.

Therapist   Like what?

Miguel   Art—drawing. I had stopped doing drawings for a long time. I was looking through one of my old sketch books on Saturday and found a drawing that meant something to me. So I used some kind of special copy paper my art teacher has, and after copying the drawing, I used my mother's iron to transfer the copy to a T-shirt, the T-shirt I have on today. [Dr. Ramirez has Miguel stretch his T-shirt, so he can obtain a clear image of the drawing. See Figure 10.5.]

Therapist   *Muy impresionante* (very impressive). We've talked about your interest in art before and your finding a way to apply what I believe to be a wonderful talent. Am I correct?

Miguel   Yes. We talked about it a couple of weeks ago.

Therapist	The colors in your drawing remind me of *Día de los Muertos* (Day of the Dead) masks and the celebration itself. Your drawing has also caused me to remember a Nahautl poem that I learned a long time ago. I think I can still recall the words. [Dr. Ramirez recites the poem. See note at the end of this section.]

▼ FIGURE 10.5

Miguel's Drawing

Let us consider things as only lent to us, oh, friends;

Only in passing are we here on earth;

Tomorrow or the day after,

As your heart desires, oh, Giver of Life,

We shall go, my friend, to His home.

[The therapist briefly laughs as Miguel smiles.]

Therapist	Your drawing reminded me of things I haven't thought of for quite a while. Let me ask you, why were you attracted to this image out of all the images in your sketch book?
Miguel	Well, it reminded me of why my brother once told me that we celebrate *Día de los Muertos*, so we can be reminded that nothing stays the same. He said it's to remind us to make the most out of life because we won't always be here.
Therapist	Yes, he's right. It's what we are doing here—what we are working on when you come here. Correct?
Miguel	Yeah.
Therapist	You're beginning to make choices that feel right for you. You are starting to act in ways that tell me you recognize what we've talked about a lot—you know, that you are capable of choosing how to live your life.
Miguel	Yeah. When I first came here, I only wanted to talk about things—like my father's leaving.
Therapist	Yeah—you were stuck in the past, which neither you, nor your brother, nor your mother could change, but you can choose not to live in the past. [Pauses for a few moments.] You know what part of the drawing reminds me of you.
Miguel	*Cráneo* (skull).
Therapist	*Serpiente* (snake).
Miguel	*Qué* (what)? [Miguel smiles before speaking again.] Because I bite?
Therapist	No. What happens with a snake as it grows and gets larger?
Miguel	Hmm. It sheds its old skin. I'm changing—I'm shedding the old me.
Therapist	You're a smart guy—don't let anyone ever tell you that you're not.

Even though this section represents a snippet of a session, abstracted from a series of sessions, it illustrates a therapist who applies several guiding principles of reality therapy, principles that the therapist found easy to incorporate into his personal style of interacting with clients. Specifically, the session brings up important considerations, such as how feeling depressed (i.e., *depressing*) is a condition we choose to create (Glasser, 2003) and that dwelling in the past does little or nothing to help a client discover how to fulfill reality therapy's five genetically grounded basic needs, which are survival, love and belonging, power, freedom, and fun. The therapist keeps the focus on Miguel's art, which is an area of achievement for Miguel; this focus resulted in Miguel's feeling worthwhile. In addition, his artistic ability has enabled Miguel to nourish his need to belong and connect with others (e.g., Dr. Ramirez and his art teacher at school), so this talent created a renewed sense of pleasure and provided Miguel with a possible career direction to pursue that is more connected with the person he sees himself becoming.

Note. The Nahautl poem is available via UNC Institute for the Study of the Americas (http://isa.unc.edu).

CHAPTER REVIEW

SUMMARY AND COMMENTARY ▶▶

If someone unfamiliar with Glasser was asked to describe Glasser's personality based solely on the photograph appearing at the beginning of this chapter—the dapper grandfatherly individual with glasses—it is unlikely that the first word to come to mind would be *radical*, but that characteristic lies at the heart of this unique professional.

Glasser adopted a direct and often uncompromising approach to mental health treatment and issues while also advocating for significant reform to professional and social structures. Although there are other psychiatrists who have tackled the sticky problem of what exactly is meant by "mental illness," few if any started off their professional career by claiming all of the disorders appearing in the *DSM* (except for what could probably be described on a single page) were nothing more than part of a great mythos created by psychiatry, a profession whose freedom of inquiry had largely evaporated under the shackles of powerful pharmaceutical companies.

Glasser serves as a steadfast reminder that it is important for all of us to periodically examine carefully the underlying system of beliefs that guide our own endeavors. As Glasser would point out, it is our choice. Of course the ever present fear when such an examination is contemplated is that we will uncover a number of unproved or false collective beliefs that we have used in the past to justify what we do. It is interesting that when William Glasser concluded psychiatry's own system of beliefs lacking, to say the least, the professional apocalypse that we might have expected to occur for Glasser never really materialized. In fact, his rejection of psychiatry's dogma was the start of a very productive and professionally rewarding journey for Glasser. Without question, William Glasser qualifies as a genuine professional gadfly whose form of therapy and theory has benefited many lay people, professionals, and clients. It seems fitting to say: *Bill—Lo hiciste bien.*

This chapter's review of William Glasser's contribution to therapy and theory concludes with Table 10.6, which summarizes various salient points about his approach.

▼ TABLE 10.6

Brief Overview of Current Therapy Practice

Variable	Current Application
Type of service delivery setting	Private practice Clinic Psychiatric hospital Health care setting Substance abuse clinic Social service agency Schools
Client Population/ Treatment Arena	Child Teen Adult Couple Family Group Organization
Type of presenting problems	Wide range of presenting problems
Severity of presenting problems	Wide range of severity of presenting problems
Adapted for short-term approach	Yes
Length of treatment	Short term (brief)
Ability to receive reimbursement	Insurance companies will reimburse based on the company policy.
Certification in approach	The William Glasser Institute provides Choice Theory/ Reality Therapy Certification.
Training in educational programs	Many graduate programs offer courses that cover reality therapy.

Variable	Current Application
	The William Glasser Institute provides reality therapy training programs (http://www.wglasser.com). The Centre for Reality Therapy provides training in reality therapy (http://www.realitytherapywub.com). There are institutions that offer a master's degree in conjunction with choice theory/reality therapy training. If specific requirements are met. Whitworth College and Graceland University grant graduate credit to students enrolled in their programs, and the Institute for Reality Therapy SA, Inc. (affiliated with the William Glasser Institute–Australia) offers a graduate diploma in reality therapy.
Location	Urban Rural Suburban
Type of delivery system	HMO PPO Fee for service
Credential	Certification in reality therapy/choice theory are offered via William Glasser Institutes located world wide.
Practitioners	Professionals Paraprofessionals
Fit with *DSM* diagnoses	No

CRITICAL THINKING QUESTIONS ▶▶

1. Consider the meaning of the Zen koan, "The way we do one thing is the way we do everything," and explain how this koan applies to William Glasser's life.

2. Present two carefully thought-out reasons for concluding that mental illness is a myth.

SUGGESTED READINGS: IMPORTANT PRIMARY SOURCES ▶▶

Books

Glasser, W. (1965). *Reality therapy: A new approach to psychiatry.* New York, NY: Harper & Row.

Glasser, W. (1998). *Choice theory: A new psychology of personal freedom.* New York, NY: Harper & Row.

Wubbolding, R. E. (2000). *Reality therapy for the 21st century.* Philadelphia, PA: Brunner-Routledge.

Wubbolding, R. E. (2011). *Reality therapy.* Washington, DC: American Psychological Association.

Journals

International Journal of Reality Therapy

International Journal of Choice Theory and Reality Therapy

Websites

European Association for Reality Therapy: https://wgii.ie/wgii/european-association-for-reality-therapy/

Institute for Reality Therapy UK: http://www.reality_therapy.orguk

William Glasser Institute: http://www.wglasser.com

William Glasser Institute Ireland: https://wgi-uk.co.uk/

CHAPTER 11

FEMINIST THERAPY APPROACHES

iStockphoto.com/Dean Mitchell

Introduction

Oxford University opened in 1196 as a *studium generale,* that is, a place to seek knowledge and was officially granted a charter to serve as a university in 1248. The year 1196 provides just one of many ways to measure when certain rights were obtained by women. In the late 1800s, the first women's colleges were established at Oxford University. By 1920, women were allowed the status of full membership at Oxford University (University of Oxford, 2017). It would take 724 years before women were accepted as full members in one of the oldest, continuously operating institution of higher learning in the world.

As evident by Oxford's history, it was the late 1800s and early 1900s that marked a shift in women's rights in England, the United States, and elsewhere. Figure 11.1 shows a photograph taken in the late 1800s of New Zealand's first female doctor, and it was during the 1800s that Charles Fourier, a French philosopher, created the commonly used term *feminisme* (feminism).

In the United States the late 1800s and early 1900s represented a time that is now referred to as feminism's first wave, a period during which women were granted the right to vote. The second wave of feminism started during the 1960s, a period in American history that saw escalating social chaos and turmoil. It was a time when a large number of women began to openly challenge what constituted a type of gender apartheid that was widespread, systemically created, and focused on creating what seemed for many women to be a hermetically sealed existence. In the early 1960s, Betty Friedan wrote the now widely read *Feminine Mystique,* which pushed for role change in women's lives. By the decade's end, Kate Millet published her doctoral dissertation as a book, titled *Sexual Politics.* This book essentially became the bible for a second wave of feminism. It captured the essence of what women were confronted with on a daily basis (Sehgal & Genzlinger, 2017).

It is interesting that many women do not recognize themselves as discriminated against; no better proof could be found of the totality of their conditioning. Patriarchy's chief institution is the family. It is both mirror of and a connection with the larger society, a patriarchal unit within a patriarchal whole. As the fundamental instrument and the foundation unit of patriarchal society, the family and its roles are prototypical. Serving as an agent of the larger society, the family not only encourages its own members to adjust and conform, but acts as a unit

LEARNING OBJECTIVES

After reading this chapter, each student should be able to:

1. Articulate the contributions of key players of feminist theory.

2. Place the development of feminist theory and therapies into a historical context.

3. Summarize the basic concepts underlying all feminist therapies (e.g., gender, marginalization, personal experience, etc.).

4. Recognize the importance of addressing politics and dominant culture values when using feminist therapy techniques.

5. Describe the therapeutic process of feminist therapy, including goals, the therapist's role, the client's role, and the therapeutic change processes.

6. Recall feminist therapy strategies, including empowerment, therapist self-disclosure, gender role analysis, and power role analysis.

7. Examine the integration of feminist therapy and the concept of intersectional identities.

8. Discuss both the theoretical and practical advantages and disadvantages of using this kind of therapy, taking both the therapist and client into account.

▼ FIGURE 11.1

Margaret Cruickshank

Source: Photographer unidentified [Public domain], via Wikimedia Commons.

THE CASE OF TIM, A TRANSGENDER CLIENT

Dr. Smith was a therapist in private practice who used cognitive-behavioral therapy (CBT) with many of his clients. Although Dr. Smith had been trained in relationally treatments, he felt most comfortable with using CBT and thus chose it whenever possible. Tim, a new client, sought therapy because of his growing fear of being in public places. Because Tim was transgender, he had experienced a great deal of discrimination and abuse in both his previous workplace and in his recreational activities. Tim was biologically a woman. However, he dressed in male clothing, preferred to be referred to as he/him, and was saving money to have sex reassignment surgery.

Dr. Smith had no previous experience with transgender clients and felt uncomfortable with some of the emotions that Tim shared. Dr. Smith was secretly disgusted by Tim and communicated microaggressions (e.g., subtle verbal exchanges that communicate a critical or disrespectful attitude) on a regular basis without awareness that he was acting out implicit biases against his client. Because Tim often spoke of his attraction to women, Dr. Smith believed that Tim was a lesbian. Furthermore, on several occasions, Dr. Smith called Tim by his original female name, Teresa, which appeared on his insurance card, and would use female pronouns periodically. It never occurred to Dr. Smith to reflect on his biases about transgender individuals, and he never corrected himself or admitted his mistakes to Tim. Tim felt that Dr. Smith was not empathic and that he kept therapy on a superficial level.

Dr. Smith diagnosed Tim with gender identity disorder even though Tim was presenting with social anxiety or social phobia. Dr. Smith chose to use CBT for Tim's treatment because he could not imagine fostering an authentic relationship with someone so confused about personal identity. Tim decided to terminate the therapy after 6 weeks. His anxiety about being in public places had worsened, and he felt fairly certain that Dr. Smith made inaccurate assumptions about his transgender identity and did not see him for who he was (Figure 11.2). Additionally, it did not feel worth the time, money, or effort to attend therapy that was superficial in nature. Dr. Smith was surprised by this early termination and felt that Tim was being noncompliant to the 12-week contract they had agreed on during the first session. Dr. Smith did not explore the ways in which he might have been responsible for Tim's early termination.

▼ FIGURE 11.2

A Therapist's Hurtful Assumptions Can Cause a Client to Self-Terminate

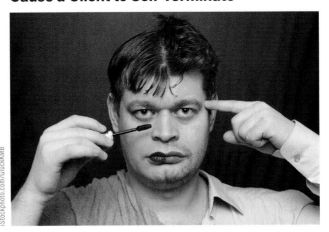

iStockphoto.com/GluckKMB

Case Discussion. Near the end of this chapter the case of Tim is discussed in greater detail to illustrate how a feminist therapeutic approach can be applied to his situation.

in government of the patriarchal state, which rules its citizens through its family heads. (Millett, quoted in Sehgal & Genzlinger, 2017, p. B13)

Finally, the 1990s third wave feminism has in many ways broadened the term *feminism* to include issues of diversity, recognizing that it was not just White, well-educated women who were confronted with challenges, but all women were involved in the struggle for equality.

This chapter covers the history and main premises of feminist theory and its impact on therapy as it is practiced today. Feminism has had a profound effect on a number of areas, including biology, movies and televised programs, businesses, literature, music, art, politics, civil rights, theology, jurisprudence, and language, and also what is of main interest to us—counseling and psychotherapy.

Key Players in Feminist Therapy

Jean Baker Miller

Jean Miller (1927–2006) was born in and reared in the Bronx, New York City. Noticed by teachers at an early age as a gifted student, she received scholarships to attend Hunter College High School and Sarah Lawrence College. She pursued her education in medicine at the Columbia University College of Physicians and Surgeons, earning her MD in 1952. Miller completed her postgraduate work at Montefiore Hospital and continued with a psychiatric residency at Bellevue Medical Center, Albert Einstein College of Medicine, and the Upstate Medical Center. She then received psychoanalytic training at New York Medical College. Miller also received a research fellowship at Albert Einstein College of Medicine.

▼ FIGURE 11.3

Jean Baker Miller

Source: US National Library of Medicine via Creative Commons.

In 1973, Miller moved to Boston to teach at Boston University. Her book *Toward a New Psychology of Women,* published in 1976, was considered a breakthrough. Her description of "the relational model" was a revolution in understanding human development and society. Her theory argued that psychological problems found their source in the disconnections of fulfilling relationships that are a human necessity. Internationally distributed and translated in many languages, Miller's *Toward a New Psychology of Women* became a launching pad for women's psychology. She demonstrated that her theory could be applied to all aspects of her professional life. In 1981, Miller served in the role as the first director of the Stone Center for Developmental Services and Studies at Wellesley College in Boston. There, she placed emphasis on the prevention of psychological problems in women. Subsequently, Miller became the director of education at the Stone Center. Still applying her relational model, she created a group that encouraged discussion and collaboration among women. The result was a collection of ideas and exchanges, published under the title *Women's Growth in Connection.* Later, in 1995, she headed the Jean Baker Miller Training Institute at Wellesley College.

Among her many accomplishments, Miller was a clinical professor of psychiatry at Boston University. She lectured at Harvard Medical School and was the recipient of the Distinguished Career Award from the Association for Women in Psychology. Although

Miller belonged to the second wave of feminists, her integration of cultural factors in therapy was a bridge to today's third wave of feminism.

Relational–Cultural Theory (RCT). RCT was created at the Stone Center by Jean Baker Miller, Janet Surrey, Judith Jordan, and Irene Stiver to address the concern that traditional psychology reflected the thinking of White, middle-class, heterosexual males. A basic assumption of RCT is that humans experience the same reality (Jordan & Hartling, 2002). In addition, RCT proposes that authentic mutual connectedness and empathic relationships are essential to the development of healthy human beings. Growth-fostering relationships are typified by the "five good things": (1) zest or well-being, (2) ability to take action in a relationship and other situations, (3) knowledge of oneself and the other individual, (4) an increased sense of worth, and (5) a wish for more connections (Jordan & Hartling, 2002; Miller, 2003). RCT recognizes that each person in a relationship has multiple social identities, such as gender, race, sexual orientation, and class, which act as the defining framework for a relationship (Miller, 2003).

Lenore Walker

▼ FIGURE 11.4
Lenore Walker

Denver Post/Getty Images

Lenore Walker became a well-known specialist in the field of psychological treatment of victims of domestic abuse. She was a pioneer in speaking up against domestic violence and advocating for battered women's rights. Walker's academic work began with an ABPP degree (i.e., specialty in professional psychology) from Hunter College of the City of New York, and she earned a master's degree from the same school. Walker worked in the New York City school system as a staff psychologist, where she made important contributions to the efforts to improve reading levels and decrease mental health issues. After she received her doctorate in education from Rutgers University in New Jersey, Walker worked with troubled children from abusive homes. The patterns she noticed in their behaviors led her to investigate the phenomenon further, and she discovered that the mothers of her abused child clients displayed similar behaviors as their children, a finding that added to our understanding of abuse. Walker taught at Rutgers Medical School from 1972 to 1975. She worked as a faculty member at Colorado Women's College (1976–1981) prior to founding her own practice, centered on family violence and violence against women. During this period, she served as a supervisor of doctoral students at the University of Denver's School of Professional Psychology. Walker also became involved in forensic psychology, specializing in domestic violence and associated cases.

A member of the American Psychological Association (APA), Walker has been involved in many APA divisions and has served as president of Divisions 35 (Society for the Psychology of Women), 12 (Society of Clinical Psychology), and 46 (Society for Media Psychology and Technology). Walker has written several books about feminist psychology and domestic violence. Recipient of many awards, Walker earned the APA and National Women's Health Award, an APA Presidential Citation for her work in feminist and forensic psychology, and the APA Division 43's Family Psychologist of the Year award. Walker's publications include "*The Battered Woman; Terrifying Love: Why Battered Women Kill and How Society Responds*" and "*Abused Women and Survivor Therapy: A Practical Guide for the Psychotherapist.*"

Although her early career as a woman working with children was argued to place a ceiling to her career, Walker found her child clinical work a powerful asset because it opened her eyes to the effects of domestic violence on mothers. Her most important study was on battered woman syndrome. *Battered woman syndrome* generally occurs when a woman is repeatedly submitted to physical and mental abuse by a partner or authority figure. Over an extended period of abuse, a symptom pattern appears, such as fear or a perceived inability to escape. Walker spent her career advocating for victims' rights and finding the source and treatment of domestic violence in families. Walker has argued that societal changes were necessary to decrease domestic violence. Walker's operationalization of the feminist construct of empowerment as the treatment of the battered woman syndrome and the prevention of domestic violence and violence against women shows the transition between second wave and third wave feminists.

Laura Brown

Laura Brown grew up in Cleveland Heights, Ohio. Her involvement in social justice led her to major in psychology and in 1972, she earned a BA cum laude from Case Western Reserve University, and in 1977, a PhD in clinical psychology from Southern Illinois University, Carbondale. She did her predoctoral internship at the Seattle Veterans Administration Medical Center. Brown has lectured in the United States, Canada, Europe, Taiwan, and Israel and has taught in several universities, including the University of Washington and Washington School of Professional Psychology. Brown is a Diplomate in Clinical Psychology from the American Board of Professional Psychology.

Through publication of more than 100 articles and book chapters, Brown has enriched and advanced the fields of feminist theory and therapy. Considered part of the second wave of feminist therapy, she has focused her work on feminist therapy, lesbian and gay issues, assessment and diagnosis, trauma treatment, ethics, standards of care in psychotherapy, and multicultural competence. Brown is considered to be one of the pioneers in developing feminist theory and therapy.

A distinguished member of the APA, Brown is a fellow in 10 of its divisions. Brown served as president of APA divisions 35 (Society for the Psychology of Women), 44 (Society for the Psychological Study of Lesbian, Gay, Bisexual and Transgender Issues), and 56 (Trauma Psychology). She also is the founder and director of the Fremont Community Therapy Project, a low-fee feminist therapy training clinic.

Brown's numerous awards and recognitions include the APA's Distinguished Professional Contributions to Public Service award, the Sarah Haley Award for Clinical Excellence from the International Society for Traumatic Stress Studies, the Carolyn Wood Sherif Memorial Award from the Society for the Psychology of Women, and the Society of Clinical Psychology Lifetime Contributions to Diversity award. Brown's works include "Subversive Dialogue: Theory in Feminist Therapy"; "Feminist Therapy"; and "Cultural Competence in the Treatment of Complex Trauma."

Brown revealed on her website that for many years she worked with a cotherapist, a Staffordshire bull terrier (Figure 11.5) named Schmulik

▼ FIGURE 11.5

Brown's Cotherapist, a Staffordshire Bull Terrier Named Schmulik ("Schmu")

Source: Spcenter (Own work) [GFDL (http://www.gnu.org/copyleft/fdl.html) or CC BY-SA 3.0 (https://creativecommons.org/licenses/by-sa/3.0)], via Wikimedia Commons.

inappropriate

▼ TABLE 11.1

Quotable Jean Miller, Lenore Walker, and Laura Brown

Jean Miller

- My biggest obstacle was the attitude of many classmates and many faculties at medical school. They acted as if they believed women should not be there, and some were even more crudely sexist in their jokes and comments. They created a generally chilling atmosphere. However, a few classmates, and later, interns and residents, were not this way. (Quoted in U.S. National Library of Medicine, 2015)
- I wanted to find work that would help people, that would be interesting, and that also would enable me to make a living. At the time of graduating college in 1948, my friends could find only clerical jobs. There were not many fields open to women, at least that I was aware of. (Quoted in U.S. National Library of Medicine, 2015)

Lenore Walker

- For some women, going through the legal system may be frustrating and frightening due to their lack of knowledge of the system. Services for battered women may seem unattainable to her if she lives in a rural area; however, this is not the case. She feels she is in a no-win situation. If she leaves, she didn't try; if she stays, she must like it. This is how people view the situation. (Walker, n.d.)
- There's no question I'm an advocate for battered women. But I'm also a scientist. Because I will advocate for battered women doesn't mean I will not tell the truth about science. . . . I am not saying O. J. Simpson is not a batterer. What I am saying is because you are a batterer that does not make you a murderer. I believe that all of the work I have done in trying to measure battered woman syndrome and trying to present it in legal cases cannot tell us alone whether O. J. Simpson could have killed these people. You need other information. . . . I hope to be able to publicize the tragic consequences of domestic violence with the caution of looking at individual people's behavior. I really believe the Achilles' heel of the battered women's movement is the quick and harsh rush to judgment without enough information. (n.p., as cited in Boxall, 1995)

Laura Brown

- I have often told people I'm training that one of my goals is to put myself out of business. As a specialist in trauma, I work with survivors of the worst that humans can do to one another. And thus in my optimistic heart I try to imagine a day when the supply of work for trauma specialists will dry up and disappear. (Brown, n.d.)
- I see the people with whom I work, survivors of appalling childhood trauma, who are gentle, loving, decent human beings, good partners, good parents, good and contributing members of society. I see people seeking and finding non-violent, non-traumatizing paths to change the world around them. I join with others in working to stop the epidemic of gun violence in the United States. And then I go back to work. As the Talmud famously says, the one who heals one life heals the entire world. Today, let's each of us heal one life–your own, someone else's life. Heal the world. (Brown, n.d.)

Sources: Brown, L. (n.d.). About psychological trauma. Retrieved from *http://www.drlaurabrown.com/*; Boxall, B. (1995). Abuse expert stirs uproar with Simpson defense role: Trial: Psychologist Lenore Walker says she is testifying to bar either side from distorting data on battered women. *Los Angeles Times.* Retrieved from http://articles.latimes .com/1995-01-29/news/mn-25821_1_battered-women; Miller, J. B., & Stiver, I. S. (1997). Relationships revisited. *The New York Times.* Retrieved from http://www.nytimes.com/ books/first/m/miller-connection.html U.S. National Library of Medicine. (2015). *Biography: Dr. Jean Baker Miller. Bethesda,* MD: Author. Retrieved from https://cfmedicine.nlm.nih .gov/physicians/biography_225.html; and Walker, L. (n.d.). *The cycle theory of battering.* Retrieved from http://www.transitionhouse.ca/THEORY.html

("Schmu"). Starting in 1995 and for many years, Schmu worked alongside Brown, bringing healing, love, and kisses to many hurt clients. Although Schmu is no longer present, his spirit has been kept alive through Brown's encouragement to trainees to bring therapy dog "interns" with them to the Fremont Clinic, which holds clinical training. Currently, Brown has a full-time practice in psychotherapy, consultation, and forensic psychology in Seattle. In Brown, one sees the intersectionality of the identities of the 1970s and 1980s second wave feminists and the third wave feminists of the late 1990s and the new millennium. See Table 11.1 for comments made by Jean Miller, Lenore Walker, and Laura Brown.

Historical Context

Feminist psychotherapy, as indicated by its name, is a theoretical orientation whose principles are centered on the experiences of women. The movement began in the late 1960s with meetings of what were known as *consciousness raising groups,* where women came together to contemplate the ways in which their lives were impacted by their gender's subordinate status.

Pioneers of the movement, such as Hannah Lerman, Carol Gilligan, Jean Baker Miller, and Judith Lewis Herman, were also inspired by the civil rights movement. Considered a grassroots phenomenon with no official founder, feminist psychotherapy took flight on the wings of the feminist movement of the 1960s and 1970s. Proponents of feminist psychotherapy framed mental health problems as stemming from restrictive gender roles, stereotyped cultural expectations, and societal inequalities, rather than dysfunction within the individual (Worell & Remer, 2002). Prior therapy approaches seemed to have had an emphasis in helping women adjust to their gender-assigned roles. As women struggled and fought to be recognized as equal members of American society, feminist psychotherapy aimed to give women the freedom to express themselves against societal oppression.

There are various theories of feminist psychotherapy. Four enduring feminist theories, liberal, cultural, radical, and socialist, comprise what is labeled as the second wave of feminism (Enns, Sinacore, Ancis, & Phillips, 2004; Evans, Kincade, & Seem, 2011). *Liberal feminism* focuses on helping individual women overcome maladaptive socialization patterns, such as pleasing others and conforming to gender role expectations. *Cultural feminism* maintains that oppression stems from societal devaluation of women's strengths. *Radical feminism* focuses on the belief that oppression comes from patriarchy. Those in the radical feminism group, along with *socialist feminists*, seek to change societal patterns through activism (Evans et al., 2011).

Feminist psychotherapy is not just for women anymore. Other feminist therapies—postmodern, women of color, and transnational feminism—forming the third wave offshoots of the original theory of the empowerment of women, integrate current multicultural concerns with the traditional feminist perspective (Enns et al., 2004). *Postmodern feminist* theory focuses on self-reflection and flexibility within networks of relationships, and the *women of color* approach defines feminism as a commitment to abolishing any and all forms of oppression, including racism, sexism, and classism. According to women of color feminist theory, no woman is only a woman (Enns et al., 2004), but rather, every woman plays many different roles within many different social contexts and groupings. *Transnational feminism* examines the interconnections between religion, nationalism, and gender and calls for the building of linkages among feminists around the world (Enns et al., 2004).

Although there are now many forms of feminist therapy, at its core, feminist theory focuses on the effects that social, political, and other systemic influences have on women's levels of satisfaction, distress, and pathology. Thus, clients' problems must be understood in the context of a sociocultural perspective (Worell & Remer, 2002). In other words, the theory looks at how the experience of being a member of a certain culture, for example, the female culture, affects clients' mental health and well-being. Certainly, when the word *culture* is presented, the demographic that comes to many people's minds is race, ethnicity, or immigrant origins rather than gender. It is easy to overlook that any and all subgroups have their own cultures, and women are no exception.

Feminist therapy examines the interactions between a minority culture and the larger society, and how these interactions affect the members of the smaller subculture. In fact, feminist therapy is easily adaptable for use with members of any minority culture because it focuses on clients' subjective experiences of sexism, racism, classism, and other types of social, cultural, and political discrimination and oppression (Worell & Remer, 2002). Given that the theory can easily be viewed as culturally oriented, rather than strictly

▼ FIGURE 11.6

Gender Is Not a Given

Source: Assistant on assignment for F.U.S.I.A. [Public domain], via Wikimedia Commons.

gender oriented, it is plain to see that feminist therapy need not be applied only to women. Viewed from this angle, it seems that the principles of feminist therapy can, and should, be applied to both females and males of any cultural, racial, or ethnic background. However, the question that is raised is what is prioritized first in feminist therapy—gender, race, ethnicity, or cultural heritage?

Basic Concepts

The principles of feminist therapy are structured around acknowledging the oppressed status of women, or any minority group, and empowering members to make positive changes at individual and societal levels (Brown, 2010). First and foremost, a particular value of the feminist perspective is emphasized. After all, who has a better handle on the subjective experience of the female condition than the very people living it? Feminist therapists communicate genuine respect for women's viewpoints and opinions.

Gender

It is important to understand the social construct of gender. According to Lev (2004), *gender* is a social construct that sorts individuals into natural categories of women and men that are thought to derive from their physiological female and male bodies. Gender, as defined by society, is a binary dichotomy, male or female, and is not presented as a continuum or as fluid. According to Lev (2004), *gender identity,* in contrast, refers to a self-identified or subjective understanding about one's gender, regardless of one's biological sex (Figure 11.6). *Transgender* is an overarching term for persons whose gender identity and gender expression are not aligned with the socially prescribed gender norms linked to their biological sex, a binary female or male at the time of their birth (American Psychological Association, 2015; Singh, Meng, & Hansen, 2014). Within this umbrella term are included transsexuals (cf., Livingston, 1991), who find their physiological bodies do not capture their true sex and who struggle to find alignment between sex and gender (Lev, 2004).

To provide support for people of all gender identities, it is important to understand the expectations that society has in place regarding gender. Even among highly educated professionals, ignorance prevails. The most recent (fifth) edition of the *Diagnostic and Statistical Manual of Mental Disorders* (*DSM-5;* American Psychiatric Association, 2013) has categorized "gender dysphoria" as a diagnosable problem for individuals (Pfäfflin, 2011). This diagnosis emphasizes that transgender individuals may be diagnosed because of the severe distress and dysphoria that they may experience regarding their gender identity, rather than meeting diagnostic criteria due to identifying outside of the gender binary. This diagnosis of "gender dysphoria" is a linguistic improvement from the previous *DSM* edition (*DSM-IV-TR*; American Psychiatric Association,

▼ TABLE 11.2

Continuums of Gender Identity, Gender Expression, Sexual Orientation, and Biological Sex

Gender Identity (psychological sense of self)	Man	Transgender	Woman
Gender Expression	Masculine	Androgynous	Feminine
Sexual Orientation (romantic/erotic response)	Attracted to women	Bisexual	Attracted to men
Biological/Physical Sex (anatomy, chromosomes, hormones)	Male	Intersex*	Female

*Intersex refers to having both male and female sex characteristics such as chromosomes, gonads, sex hormones, or genitals.

2001), in which "gender identity disorder" suggested that the diagnosis related to the existence of the individual's gender identity itself (Pfäfflin, 2011). Societal support must derive from a place of understanding and compassion, but it cannot exist while transgender individuals are still considered to be mentally ill by the psychiatric profession and, consequently, by the majority of the population.

Despite the significance of transgender identity, the literature does not thoroughly examine the wide and diverse range of gender identities. *Cisgender* (umbrella term for individuals "whose gender identity and biological sex at birth match") issues and individuals have been more thoroughly analyzed and studied throughout history than transgender issues will likely ever be (Litosseliti & Sunderland, 2002). It is difficult to accurately identify the needs of the transgender community without examining them through research, and counselors and psychologists have a responsibility to try to supplement the existing incomplete and insufficient research.

Maguen, Shipherd, and Harris (2005) argued that sex and gender should be seen as lying on a continuum and that gender is an expression of sex. Table 11.2 shows how gender identity, gender expression, sexual orientation, and physical sex each lie on a continuum. Sexual orientation is included to demonstrate its difference from gender identity and physiological sex.

Table 11.2 also shows how each phenomenon can be independent, thus allowing for intersectionality of gender identity, gender expression, sexual orientation, and physical self, resulting in the individuality of a person. For instance, a woman could be androgynous in gender expression and a man could be bisexual in his sexual orientation.

Marginalization

Societal marginalization of women and other minority groups can be understood using the example of transgender people. Transgender individuals, as true margins of society, are at the greatest risk for social discrimination and ostracism (Carroll, Gilroy, & Ryan, 2002). As Bornstein (1994) noted,

> There is most certainly a privilege to having a gender; when you have a gender, when you are perceived as having a gender, you don't get laughed at in the street, you don't get beat up, you know which public bathroom to use, and when to use it, people don't stare at you or worse, you know which form to fill out, you know what clothes to wear, you have heroes and role models, you have a past. (p. 127)

Chapter 11 • FEMINIST THERAPY APPROACHES   ■   365

Societal practices of stereotyping, categorizing, and stratifying people have a large effect on individuals' sense of connection and disconnection (Walker & Miller, 2001). Discrimination, like transphobia and gender oppression, impedes everyone's ability to participate and engage in growth-fostering relationships (Jordan & Hartling, 2002). Because of the experiences of transgender persons as margins of society, targets of daily discrimination, victims of hate crimes, and transphobia, it is clear these individuals have had to employ survival strategies to fit into the few relationships that are available, thereby becoming less and less genuine in their relationships (Jordan & Hartling, 2002).

Self-in-Relationship

In classical psychology, mental health is achieved when one separates from parents and family of origin and functions as a fully autonomous individual. Feminist theory argues that this theory does not fit for women or for culturally diverse individuals from collectivist cultures. For these women and culturally diverse individuals, the primary experience of self is relational, and the sense of self is developed in the context of significant relationships (Jordan, Kaplan, Miller, Stiver, & Surrey, 1991). The emphasis shifts from separation from relationships to being-in-relationship as the primary factor contributing to self-development.

Feminist therapy investigates disconnection in relationships. Although disconnection is understood to be a normal and inevitable aspect of relationships, the mode by which the disconnection is resolved has a major impact on one's psychological state. For instance, if a person feeling hurt responds authentically with her feelings and the other person responds empathically, the relationship and relational competence can be strengthened (Jordan & Hartling, 2002). This is known as mutual empowerment (Jordan et al., 1991). However, if a person who is hurting is not able to respond authentically or her response is received with indifference, hostility, or denial of the experience, the hurt person often begins to leave parts of herself out of the relationship in order to hold on to that relationship (Jordan & Hartling, 2002). Stratification in relationships similarly interferes with mutuality, and differences may be interpreted as opposition (Miller, 2003). Feminist therapy views relationship disconnections as the source of psychological problems.

Good Mother/Bad Mother

The early mother–daughter relationship is of crucial importance in relational–cultural feminist theory. The specific attachment between mother and daughter strongly affects a woman's sense of self and her level of interpersonal relatedness. Early in the mother–daughter relationship, a mutual reciprocal process develops in which both are "energized to care for, respond to, or attend to the well-being of the other" (Jordan et al., 1991, p. 37). Mothers teach their daughters "good mothering" practices, starting when their daughters are quite young, by subtly reinforcing gentleness and concern for others. Daughters simultaneously pick up on their mother's anxious feelings when enacting "bad mother" qualities that the mother typically devalues in herself. Thus, a little girl is "deeply affected by her mother's unconscious identification with her as 'good' or 'bad' mother and takes on the characteristics of her own mother in an unconscious process of identification" (p. 41). This identification can lead to problems in adulthood, such as caring for others at the expense of oneself and intense difficulty separating from destructive relationships. Thus, being overly nurturing and dependent in relationships must not be blamed on the traits of a woman but rather located in her socialization.

Personal Experience

A major principle of feminist theory is the acknowledgment of the worth of female contributions, both to the therapeutic situation and to the world in general (Worell & Remer, 2002). Traditionally silenced and devalued by patriarchy, women find their voices within the context of therapy and identify their experiences with the experiences of other women. It is in therapy that women reflect for the first time on their experiences as a woman, both challenges and oppression, as well as the successful and joyful experiences they have had.

Personal Is Political

Another very important principle of feminist theory is the truism, "The personal is political." This phrase is intended to highlight the idea that intrapersonal conflicts (i.e., conflicts within oneself) are not purely personal, but are embedded in the legal, political, economic, and social structures of society that disadvantage and disempower women (Crenshaw, 1989; Fine, 2010). These systemic structures are viewed as the creators of mental health problems, as evidenced by another feminist theoretical principle—the rejection of the disease model. In feminist theory, "pathology" is seen as a woman's best approach at coping with the constant oppression and restrictive social norms under which she lives (Brown, 2010). This system-based conceptualization of psychological distress suggests that the dominant culture (i.e., men and society as a whole) must also change if the minority is to ever achieve equal status (Worell & Remer, 2002).

Integrated Analysis of Oppression and Egalitarianism

Two final principles of feminist therapy are the integrated analysis of oppression and the construction of an egalitarian relationship between therapist and client. *Integrated analysis of oppression* involves the understanding that men and women are victims to institutional oppression, traditional beliefs, and stereotypes, which furthermore influence individual beliefs and perceptions, including those held by the victim.

Egalitarianism empowers women clients and demonstrates respect for them, in that they are ensured equal footing and an equal voice in the therapy process with the therapist. Following the development of this cooperative and collaborative relationship, the therapist–client dyad can then work effectively together to analyze how a client has been pigeonholed into certain female roles by societal expectations and how fulfilling these prescribed roles may influence a client's levels of satisfaction and distress (Worell & Remer, 2002).

Important Concepts in Relational–Cultural Therapy

The Therapeutic Relationship. Relational–cultural therapy emphasizes connection in relationships, making the therapeutic relationship particularly important (Frey, 2013). A client *must* feel safe in the therapeutic relationship in order to move toward authenticity and toward more adaptive relationships. Once a client and a therapist have developed a strong relationship, the therapeutic work can begin to provide corrective relational experiences, in which negative relational images are challenged and reshaped (Jordan, 2009).

Growth-Fostering Relationships. Growth-fostering relationships are characterized by several improvements in functioning. These types of relationships typically result in an increase in energy, as well as an increase in creativity and productivity. They also result in a better comprehension of one's own experience and a greater sense of self-worth. Because these relationships result in improvements in functioning, they are also characterized by a desire for more connection (Jordan, 2009). Two critical components of growth-fostering relationships are that they are *authentic* and *mutual*.

Authenticity. Authenticity refers to feeling comfortable in expressing one's feelings, experiences, and thoughts with an awareness of how this affects the other person in the relationship (Hartling, Rosen, Walker, & Jordan, 2004).

Mutuality. Mutual empathy is when there exists a willingness to impact and to be impacted by another person. Mutual empathy involves being able to empathize with another person not only in one's ability to connect but also to disconnect (Hartling et al., 2004). Mutual empowerment refers to the sense of personal strength that evolves from a relationship (Frey, 2013). In a mutual relationship, there is involvement, commitment, and sensitivity between two people (Frey, 2013).

Relational Confidence. Relational confidence involves tolerating the fear of establishing new relationships and finding support to cope with a new situation rather than facing it alone. According to Jordan (2004), "As misunderstandings are renegotiated and empathic failures are reworked, the client slowly develops a sense of relational confidence" (p. 41).

Relational Resilience. The concept of relational resilience has to do with the capacity to reestablish connection following a disconnection (Frey, 2013; Jordan, 2004). It also refers to the capacity to reach out for help. This is critical for healing because without relational resilience, the strategies of disconnection may never be challenged and the individual will remain isolated.

Relational Images. Relational images "develop early in life and are carried from one relationship to another, sometimes subject to modification (growth), and sometimes limiting our expectations in ways that anchor us in the relational past. Our expectations of relationships are held in these relational images" (Jordan, 2009, p. 26). These images can be either positive or negative.

Controlling Images. Controlling images are beliefs given to us by the dominant cultural values. They hold people in their societal "place" and involve the notion that societal change cannot happen, leading clients to feel disempowered. Controlling images are problematic because they can produce a sense of shame and humiliation in an individual. According to Jordan (2009), "Shame is a powerful way to silence and isolate individuals, but it also plays a large role in silencing and disempowering marginalized groups whose members are strategically, if often invisibly, shamed in order to reinforce their isolation and thus their subordination" (p. 29).

Disconnections. An instance of disconnection occurs when a person feels misunderstood or invalidated in some way. During the life of a woman an instance of a disconnection or acute disconnection happens often. Chronic disconnections or continued acute disconnections may result in some form of diagnosed psychopathology (Jordan, 2009).

Therapeutic Process

Feminist therapy, primarily theory driven, has at its core an epistemology of empowerment set against the backdrop of each client's larger sociopolitical context. Feminist therapy has a strong emphasis on egalitarianism and empowerment of clients, as well as a close attention to power, gender, and social location as determinants of resilience and distress in human existence (Brown, 2010).

Goals

Empowerment of the client is the core goal of feminist therapy. *Empowerment* is the means through which clients take charge of their lives. The therapist seeks to help all clients find their voice by facilitating the discovery and strengthening of their intrinsic abilities, and, furthermore, by advocating changes in society so that individuals' voices might be heard and respected. Empowerment of clients requires self-acceptance, self-confidence, and authenticity. Authenticity is desirable on both sides of the therapeutic relationship—authenticity to self from the client and transparency toward the client from the therapist.

Another major goal of feminist therapy is the "deepening capacity for relationship and relational competence" (Jordan et al., 1991, p. 53). Relational competence is the personal understanding of one's ability to impact change in relationships and the sense that one is valued in relationships. Within such a relationship, other aspects of the self, such as autonomy and creativity, can develop (Jordan et al., 1991).

Therapist's Role

Feminist therapists must question and reevaluate their own beliefs and perhaps stereotypical views that they might have been carrying since childhood. Authenticity and transparency are not only owed to the client but also to oneself. Self-awareness of personal biases can be heightened through further education and additional training that specifically examines how acting or feeling in a particular way could create unwanted barriers for oppressed clients. Thus, therapists must be aware of their own biases if they are to effectively confront them during therapy sessions.

Through gender and power analyses, therapists empathically understand clients and are able to monitor their own biases concerning cultural and societal beliefs. Gender analysis supports clients through identifying and reevaluating beliefs that have been internalized since childhood. These socialized beliefs reflect the stereotypical gender differences reinforced by a patriarchal society that have deeply affected individuals during their development. A power analysis helps clients recognize the differential power between genders and the ways in which this influences their lives.

The therapist's goal is not to "rescue" the client, as this would maintain oppression and would not empower. The client is not expected to remain passive and dependent. The therapist assists the client to define her own view of power and to identify what beliefs have been internalized about power since childhood (Greene, 2010). Through an egalitarian relationship, both therapist and client search for the causes of the client's symptoms (instead of assigning a diagnostic label). The client is given an expert position, which gives her access to her own voice and an active role in her treatment. The therapist helps the client de-pathologize her experiences. In training future therapists, a relationship of caring is the most important element between supervisees and their supervisors in the clinical training area, which is analogous to the connection that the therapist and client make when taking perspective of each other's gender cultures.

Client's Role

The client has an active role and participates in her therapy. She must find empowerment in order to find her own voice. The client is invited to practice self-acceptance by identifying that her distressed states are not caused by inner deficits but rather by an imbalance of power in society.

The client is considered an expert in determining what she needs and wants from the therapeutic process, keeping in mind that there is an egalitarian partnership between the client and the therapist. Once trust is established, the client, within the therapeutic alliance, is encouraged to face feelings (including anger) that she may have denied to herself or prevented from expressing while trapped within the expectations created for the genders by patriarchy (e.g., a "good" woman should not express anger loudly).

Assessment

Although the majority of feminist therapists do not give diagnostic labels to their patients, it is required by most forms of health insurance. Labels tend to pathologize clients and do not take into account the causal components of social injustice and oppression in clients' lives. Many feminist therapists prefer to use gender role analysis (i.e., analysis of prescribed roles for men and women) as an alternative to assessment. Gender role analysis has five steps, which help clients to recognize how their behaviors might be affected and shaped by traditional gender role beliefs and expectations. The five steps are (1) identify early beliefs, held since childhood, of traditional gender roles; (2) identify and discuss both positive and negative beliefs about gender role; (3) analyze what expectations have been internalized; (4) decide which beliefs should be processed; and (5) develop a therapeutic plan.

During assessment, transgender clients, for example, should be asked which pronoun they prefer others to use when referring to them (he/his/him; she/hers/her), and the therapist must adhere to the client's wishes (Vanderburgh, 2007). A therapist should keep in mind the importance of assessing the full client, including all dimensions of personality and sociocultural characteristics, such as minority race or ethnicity, class, and religion, in addition to the client's self-assigned gender and sexual identity.

Many individuals who identify as transgender may use the phrase "M to F" (MTF) or "F to M" (FTM) to indicate that they have transitioned from male to female or vice versa. Tim, the client presented in this chapter, uses the term FTM to describe his transition. On the other hand, other transgender individuals may consider their gender identity apart from the socially constructed gender binary of female and male (Korell & Lorah, 2006). Transgender individuals can have any sexual orientation and should not be confused with same-sex sexual orientation as in homosexuality (Lombardi, 2001). For instance, Tim, an FTM heterosexual, wants to have sexual relationships with women. On the other hand, an MTF individual may choose to remain with her wife of many years even though she is now openly a woman.

Having a transgender identity does not mean having a mental disorder, but there are occasions when transgender persons may experience distress because of indecision or confusion about gender expression (Korell & Lorah, 2006). This experience of distress has been defined by the *DSM-5* (American Psychiatric Association, 2013) as gender identity disorder. It is important that this diagnosis be used appropriately and not automatically assigned to any client who identifies as transgender. To accurately diagnose gender identity disorder, there should be persistent discomfort regarding one's assigned sex and clinically significant impairment or distress in occupational, social, or other realms of functioning (American Psychiatric Association, 2013).

Therapeutic Change

Therapist empathic attunement is the primary agent of change, while intellectual insight is secondary (Jordan et al., 1991). Therapists must represent themselves authentically and decrease boundaries in order to experience what the client is feeling. This attunement is more than what would be utilized by traditional approaches. Time is spent helping the client appreciate the integrity of the interplay between cognition and affect and honor the unique female conflict of "self-other boundary oscillation" (Jordan et al., 1991, p. 284). Through the therapist–client connection, relational memory is reorganized and the individual feels empowered to form healthy relationships outside of therapy.

Change occurs when clients are able to identify and accept that their problems are not intrinsic as personality traits within themselves but rather are consequences of the power imbalance between genders that is maintained by inner and outer reinforcements (e.g., one's enjoyment of making sexist jokes; sexist jokes being applauded and encouraged by listeners). Changes happen within clients when they take conscious stock of their inner abilities and rights, which are not to be measured or compared to others (such as with a normative sample) through the use of limited instruments and measures developed in a patriarchal society.

Techniques and Strategies

The overarching goals of feminist therapy provide a base that supports practical variation across therapists and clients, making feminist therapy easily integrated with other theoretical approaches. Rather than prescribing particular interventions, feminist therapy supports an emphasis on tailoring interventions to meet each client where she is with her own skills, abilities, strengths, and capacities. This results in fluidity within the practice of feminist therapy, allowing for a client-focused model in which outcome and effectiveness are determined by the therapist and client in a collaborative and flexible fashion.

Empowerment. Empowerment cannot be given to a client. The client must realize for herself her inner abilities and strengths and develop these with the support of a feminist therapist. Given the lead in this area of self-empowerment within the therapy process, the client has already seized the construct of being personally powerful and can further enhance her skills toward building a stronger self.

Therapist Self-Disclosure. Therapist self-disclosure includes sharing personal information or experiences with the client. One example of therapist self-disclosure is feeling comfortable acknowledging to transgender clients an inability to understand all aspects of their transgender experience. The therapist exhibits humility and expresses a desire to learn from the client's experiences. The therapist is also much attuned to where the client is at the present moment and the ways in which the sharing of herself or himself—as the therapist experiences the client (e.g., positive countertransference)—will empower or help the client.

Gender Role Analysis and Intervention. Gender role analysis is an original intervention of feminist therapists. By considering the impact of the social construction of gender, both therapist and client can evaluate how their experiences are informed by gender differences. Within a patriarchal society, traditional psychotherapy treats women's symptoms as pathological rather than the consequences of society's neglect and distortion of women's true intellectual, sexual, and social needs.

Power Analysis and Power Intervention. Power analysis and power interventions help clients to have active consciousness of the power differential between genders in society. It aims to empower clients to assess what powers they have access to. Clients take control of their lives through actively participating in their own therapy treatment, for example, through bibliotherapy, assertiveness training, reframing and labeling, and group work. Clients also gain control of their lives through advocacy, not only for themselves but for others as well, the latter involving social action and going beyond personal interest.

Multiculturalism and Social Justice

Sussman (2004) explains the role of culture in definitions, management, and interpretations of illness. It is through the process of socialization that individuals learn how to experience, view, and deal with illness. The medical belief system and social organizations that function within a culture shape the meaning of illness, interpretation, and management. These contexts provide the lens through which individuals perceive and interpret symptoms and illness. These contexts influence whether individuals decide to seek care and how they choose sources of care, develop treatment goals and expectations, evaluate treatment, and decide whether to continue, cease, change, or supplement care (Sussman, 2004). Societal contexts similarly shape therapists' assumptions, values, and biases about clients, which affect their assessment and treatment practices. In fact, their very professional training is steeped in the societal belief system, also called worldview, as to what are maladjustment, mental disorder, and healing.

Therapist critical self-awareness is a key tenet of feminist therapy (Jordan & Hartling, 2002). Critical self-awareness is an especially necessary component when working with Tim, the client case presented in this chapter, who identifies as transgender. The therapist spends time getting in touch with personal feelings of being different from the client and utilizes this self-awareness when providing the client with therapy. Lack of self-awareness regarding transgender stereotypes could complicate countertransference reactions as a result of therapist prejudice and possible attributions of blame. Similarly, therapists' ignorance about their own implicit stereotypes and attitudes can lead to microaggressions. *Microaggressions* are subtle and commonplace verbal or behavioral exchanges that communicate derogatory, insulting, or demeaning messages. Often unintentional, these tiny aggressions from the therapist can create disconnection between the therapist and client. Should therapists commit unintentional microaggressions against transgender clients, feminist therapy allows the space for the therapists to acknowledge their microaggression, learn about themselves from this mishap, and move toward repairing the connection with clients. For instance, Dr. Smith, Tim's former therapist, needed to apologize to Tim for making the mistake of calling him by his previous female name, Teresa. He could have been transparent about needing current knowledge on transgender people, which would make him better understand Tim's gender identity, and about his mistaken assessment of Tim as a lesbian. Dr. Smith's acknowledgment of his limitation would increase his authenticity as a person, and his perceived credibility with Tim would increase because he would show himself to be continuously educating himself about his client's needs.

Feminist therapists are aware that different types of unearned power and advantage accrue because of various categories of social identity (Jordan & Hartling, 2002). Transgender individuals may be accustomed to having their reality ignored or denied, as well as experiencing an isolated existence most of the time. Feminists are aware that those at the center of the distribution of privilege and advantage hold the power of naming reality for others less privileged than they, defining deviance and norms, and eliminating the potential of open conflict with individuals who are forced to the margins (hooks, 1984). Women who have experienced marginalization may have suppressed mutuality and authenticity in relationships, thus reducing or interfering with the formation of growth-fostering relationships and inflicting on themselves disconnection, silence, shame, and isolation (Jordan & Hartling, 2002). These issues are at the forefront for feminist therapists when working with clients (Jordan & Hartling, 2002).

Feminist therapy focuses not only on the therapist's awareness of different forms of unearned advantage and privilege, but also on assisting the client to better understand the importance of difference in social privilege, as the latter is the result of imbalances in power and privilege (Jordan & Hartling, 2002). This is an especially significant issue when addressing transgender individuals because of their unique experience of marginalization and low privilege. Sexism, racism, heterosexism, ableism, and other types of oppression will affect a transgender client differently throughout life, especially with regard to the time before, during, and after transitioning (Carroll et al., 2002). For example, an individual who is FTM and passes within society as a male might experience male privilege for the first time, whereas an individual who is MTF might be experiencing sexism as a woman for the first time (Carroll et al., 2002). Privilege should be assessed with regard to a client's status because assessing privilege can be used to deal with oppression.

Additionally, intersectionality of identities, such as race, class, and gender, might be salient for the individual and are important to acknowledge within the therapeutic process. Feminist therapy is the foundation for an increasing array of research on psychological problems in conjunction with issues of racism, sexism, heterosexism, classism, and gender oppression (Carroll et al., 2002).

Although feminist therapy was initially created to comprehend women's psychological experience of oppression, it is increasingly being utilized to obtain a better understanding of all human experience (Jordan & Hartling, 2002). Feminist therapy would be a good fit for a transgender individual because it examines gender issues as a central tenet, promoting an integration of a person's strengths through his or her gender identity. In addition, because gender tends to be more fluid among individuals who identify as transgender, aspects that are historically attributed to women may exist within a transgender individual regardless of sex differences (Fee, Brown, & Laylor, 2003).

Ethical Considerations

Although feminist therapy allows for necessary revisions in the psychological understanding of women, the paradigm has some limitations. First, therapists are required to have an even higher level of self-awareness than is typically necessary. Second, many therapists may be uncomfortable with deeply experiencing others' difficult emotions, which could lead to compassion fatigue or vicarious traumatization. Third, therapist self-disclosure could lead to blurring of boundaries between the therapist role and the client role. Fourth, feminist therapy may be less useful as a brief intervention. Time is needed to build a strong therapeutic relationship that will reorganize relational memory of the client. Due to some health care restrictions, many clients do not have the economic means to participate in long-term therapy.

American Psychological Association Guidelines for Practice With Transgender and Gender Nonconforming People

The following APA (2015) ethical guidelines, rationale, and applications encourage psychologists to have knowledge, skills, and awareness when serving transgender individuals, an underserved population. Transgender and gender nonconforming (TGNC) persons have a gender identity that does not fully align with their assigned sex. Population estimates range from 0.17 to 1,333 per 100,000, or a surveyed 0.5% of the population. High rates of stigma and discrimination are experienced by this population, which are related to a high propensity of depression and suicidality in TGNC individuals. Barriers to mental and medical health care are common, including denial of care. Less than 30% of mental health professionals and graduate students report familiarity with TGNC issues (APA Task Force on Gender Identity and Gender Variance, 2009). As such, the APA guidelines intend to maximize the effectiveness of mental health–related services.

Foundational Knowledge and Awareness

Guideline 1. Psychologists understand that gender is a nonbinary construct that allows for a range of gender identities and that a person's gender identity may not align with sex assigned at birth. (p. 834)

Gender identity is defined as a person's inherent sense of being in relation to feminine, masculine, or alternative gender characteristics, or a blend or absence of such. This is as opposed to a binary construct, particularly one in which gender identification is always aligned with the sex assigned at birth. Identification as TGNC is not inherently pathological; however, such individuals may experience distress linked with gender discordance as well as with stigma and discrimination. Health care treatment in the 1960s and 1970s focused on reinforcing binary gender, with the ideal outcome being that individuals feel comfortable with their assigned sex, or if not, the opposite, with a heavy emphasis on passing.

Embracing a nonbinary understanding of gender is essential to the affirmative provision of care for the TGNC population (Bess & Stabb, 2009; Langer, 2011; Shipherd, Green, & Abramovitz, 2010). By understanding gender as a spectrum, therapists have increased capacity to assist in care. Supporting TGNC individuals in genuinely articulating gender identity and lived experience is, therefore, central. Many such individuals are isolated. Therapists supporting exploration of identity and acceptance of ambiguity by displaying nonjudgmental behavior can help to counteract pervasive stigma.

Guideline 2. Psychologists understand that gender identity and sexual orientation are distinct but interrelated constructs.

Sexual orientation and gender identity are theoretically and clinically distinct (APA Task Force on Gender Identity and Gender Variance, 2009). The latter is defined in terms of the individual's sexual attraction to other people, as opposed to the former, which is the felt, inherent sense of gender, often nascent in early childhood. Unfamiliarity with gender identity may obscure TGNC awareness as sexual discordance, which is incorrect. Sexual orientation and gender identity are interrelated (Munoz-Plaza, Quinn, & Rounds, 2002) in the sense that in adolescence, children go through similar overlapping developmental phases of sexual orientation identity and gender identity, such as initial self-realization, other- and self-stigma, discomfort, transition, and resolution. Therapists may assist in the differentiation between sexuality and gender identity through the provision of acceptance, support, and understanding without imposing outcomes. Information on TGNC identity may need to be provided, including the language with which individuals describe their experiences.

Guideline 3. Psychologists seek to understand how gender identity intersects with the other cultural identities of TGNC people.

Gender identity and expression may have significant intersections with other identities of individuals, such as racial, educational, religious, or cultural identities. Some intersecting identities may hinder empowerment, such as being a White transgender female, for those individuals in a state of transition into a less privileged identity (i.e., giving up White male privileged identity). The complexity of identities may obstruct access to community or family support, especially in the case of traditional religious beliefs. Therapists who help clients to find supportive resources in these other roles may facilitate affirmative expression. Therapists may assist in informing and supporting

TGNC people to navigate systems of power and privilege, as well as help manage stigmatized identities (e.g., being an African American transgender male).

Guideline 4. Psychologists are aware of how their attitudes about and knowledge of gender identity and gender expression may affect the quality of care they provide to TGNC people and their families.

Therapists should be aware of the biases they may hold about TGNC individuals. Lacking knowledge or training in offering affirmative care can restrict the effectiveness of delivering service and perpetuate barriers (APA Task Force on Gender Identity and Gender Variance, 2009; Carroll et al., 2002; Shipherd et al., 2010). Therapists experienced with lesbian, gay, and bisexual clientele may not be familiar with TGNC needs or possess relevant skills. The ethics codes of the American Psychological Association and the American Counseling Association specify that psychologists and counselors must practice within the boundaries of their competence, which, in the case of TGNC services, may be improved through education, supervised experience, or consultation.

Therapists should possess basic understanding of the TGNC population and their needs, and therapists are encouraged to utilize evidenced-based practices. TGNC individuals may benefit from active and collaborative engagement in decision making with their therapists, given their historical disenfranchisement. Therapists are encouraged to explore their personal beliefs on gender and sexuality (Carroll et al., 2002; Whitehead, Thomas, Forkner, & LaMonica, 2012), as well as identify and fill gaps in personal knowledge or understanding. It is recommended that TGNC clients are referred to knowledgeable providers in the absence of such competency.

Stigma, Discrimination, and Barriers to Care

Guideline 5. Psychologists recognize how stigma, prejudice, discrimination, and violence affect the health and well-being of TGNC people.

Guideline 6. Psychologists strive to recognize the influence of institutional barriers on the lives of TGNC people and to assist in developing TGNC-affirmative environments.

Discrimination is a common experience for TGNC people, from a misunderstanding of their identity to the assumption of psychopathology to blatant marginalization. Experiencing physical violence, including police violence, is significantly common for TGNC individuals. This discrimination extends to harassment in educational settings and lack of adequate educational policies. These kinds of inequities contribute to significant economic disparities; for instance, 90% of TGNC respondents have reported workplace discrimination (APA Task Force on Gender Identity and Gender Variance, 2009). These issues are particularly salient in the military, including services provided by Veterans Affairs, where "transsexualism" is cited as a medical exclusion. When coming out, TGNC individuals in the workplace are faced with very difficult career, physical (e.g., restroom usage), and mental health care choices.

Given such economic and workplace challenges, TGNC individuals may engage in "survival sex" or sex work or sell drugs for income (APA Task Force on Gender Identity and Gender Variance, 2009; Bucholtz, Liang, & Sutton, 1999). These illegal activities place them at risk for police harassment, along with the probability of mental health symptoms and health risks (Haas, Rodgers, & Herman, 2014). TGNC individuals who are incarcerated report isolation, rape, and assault both by inmates and prison personnel (Baldwin, 2013), as well as involuntary solitary confinement, a further mental health risk. Health care access is another major area of discrimination. TGNC people may not feel comfortable seeking medical services or primary health care. This is particularly salient for transgender men, who still need regular gynecological care. This discrimination extends to poor insurance coverage.

The awareness of the impact of anti-trans prejudice can assist in mental health care. Therapists may facilitate emotional processing of negative experiences and help transgender individuals identify resources. Specific needs may vary from navigating public spaces, seeking legal recourse for discrimination, and treating trauma symptomology. Therapists may assist in accessing social service systems such as housing resources. Social justice may extend to locating affirmative spiritual communities. Therapists may also furnish documentation that affirms gender identity to seek and secure appropriate accommodations. They may also assist in strategizing sharing gender history with employers or helping employers to develop appropriate policies.

Gendered restrooms are a major public discomfort, frequently demanding a careful concern of others' negative reactions to transgender individuals' presence in a female or male restroom. Therapists can advocate for gender-neutral restrooms. Many TGNC people may be concerned with being pathologized or have previously been so, and frequently are asked to secure a letter of endorsement from a mental health professional, confirming the stability of their gender identity, in order to access a legal institution, a surgeon, or an endocrinologist (APA Task Force on Gender Identity and Gender Variance, 2009; Bucholtz et al., 1999). Therapists may also ask TGNC clients for feedback on their therapeutic treatment and advocacy. They must be aware of how cues in the workplace environment may affect the comfort or safety of TGNC clients. In addition, it is advised that therapists be aware of language cues, such as gender-specific pronouns, including in paperwork or outreach materials.

Guideline 7: Psychologists understand the need to promote social change that reduces the negative effects of stigma on the health and well-being of TGNC people.

The lack of appropriate TGNC public policy results in the lack of legal protections for TGNC people, including in housing and employment. Such systems are particularly marginalizing of individuals who do not undergo medical transition. Therapists are encouraged to inform trans-affirmative public policy, as well as identify and improve systems that permit violence, discrimination, lack of health care access, and other systemic inequities. Given the frequent occurrence of barriers, especially in the obtaining of legal documents (e.g., a driver's license), therapists may assist in attending to experiences of fatigue and trauma, offering advice about alternate avenues of recourse, appeal, or self-advocacy (Singh et al., 2014; Shipherd et al., 2010). Therapists may consult the National Center of Transgender Equality for additional information, and they may participate at the different levels (i.e., local, state, national) to support TGNC-affirmative policy changes (APA, 2015).

Evaluating Theory

Research Support Overall

The increased research on gender and women in the past 50 years is tied to the work of feminists, who have brought these topics to the forefront of the U.S. sociopolitical scene. The feminist movement for egalitarianism has served as the catalyst for numerous other theories, such as on rape, domestic violence, and sexual abuse, as well as exploring gender as a new avenue of research.

Eagly, Eaton, Rose, Riger, and McHugh (2012) describe two definitions of feminism in psychology; one is belief-based and the other behaviorally based: (1) belief in the political, social, and economic equality of the sexes, and (2) the advocacy movement organized around this belief. Accordingly, research fits into two categories: furthering knowledge about gender equality and using research as a catalyst for societal and cultural change. Eagly et al. also note that not all researchers who examine topics like sexism, gender roles, or gender stereotypes declare their work as "feminist," even though it fits into the two feminist research categories.

The first wave of feminism in the United States resulted in women obtaining the right to vote. The research that occurred during this time was marked by studies challenging the belief that women were intellectually inferior to men. After this point, research on women dropped off significantly and did not pick up again until the second wave of feminism began in the 1960s (Eagly et al., 2012).

The dearth of research on women in the first half of the 20th century drove feminist researchers to do research on gender differences so as to alleviate the pervasive theoretical bias against women. This turning point is known as the second wave. From 1975 to 1983, there was a massive outpouring of literature on sex role attitudes and gender stereotypes. Social psychology was quick to incorporate gender stereotypes and sex role attitudes into its already attitude- and stereotype-heavy theoretical base. The greatest upward trend occurred at the tail end of the second wave, with approximately 1 in 10 articles covering sex differences, gender, and women. Subsequently, when the Equal Rights Amendment was defeated in 1982, the number of publications dropped (Eagly et al., 2012).

The third wave of feminism brought about a second peak in the late 1990s, again with 1 in 10 journal publications involving feminist topics (Eagley et al., 2012). The late 1990s saw a second upward trend in articles, as increasing research on the interaction between gender with race and ethnicity continued its upward trend. In addition, research examining the effects of intimate partner violence increased sharply in the 1990s, following the Violence Against Women Act enacted in 1994 (H.R. 4970—112th Congress; Eagly et al., 2012).

But the new millennium saw a drop in published articles. Recent decreases in the number of articles on sex differences, gender, and women (Eagly et al., 2012) seem to parallel the rise of social and economic conservatism in the United States. The prevalence of women and gender in articles is greatly predicted by the prevalent sociopolitical status of women.

However, despite these up and down trends, a substantial portion of articles published every year involve women and gender in some capacity (Eagly et al., 2012). Psychology is no longer dominated by men; in fact, the majority of faculty members in psychology departments are now women. Examining the spread of feminist research across journals shows that understanding women and gender is embedded in the basic areas of psychology. A breakdown by discipline shows that women and gender topics are in almost 25% of all articles published in social processes and social issues, as well as in developmental psychology (16%), personality (12%), and social psychology (12%; Eagly et al., 2012). From 2000 to 2009, the psychology of women and gender ranked third in production among all classification codes, producing 52,824 articles. The next closest topic was developmental psychology, producing 31,147 articles. The only two classifications that ranked higher were psychological and physical disorders (147,870 articles) and health and mental health treatment (128,027 articles), which have both seen significant increases as emphasis has shifted toward empirically based treatment and diagnostics.

The nine topics that Eagly et al. (2012) used to understand how feminist topics have gotten into the literature are race and ethnicity, sexual orientation, gender stereotypes and role attitudes, gender and depression, social class, work–family issues, intimate partner violence, abortion, and sexual harassment. These nine topics contribute to three dimensions of feminist research: diversity of gender (race and ethnicity, sexual orientation, transgender issues, social class), mainstream research (gender role attitudes and stereotypes, gender and depression, and work–family issues), and advocacy and activism (abortion, intimate partner violence, and sexual harassment).

Research on the diversity of gender serves two functions: to further explore the feminist emphasis on social context and to continue the struggle to overcome the overwhelming bias in psychology to represent the educated, industrialized, and European American members of U.S. society. Race and ethnicity and social class have been "hot button topics" within the psychology of gender, women, and sex differences. Over the past several decades, race and ethnicity and social class have seen a steady representation within a subset of psychology. As gay and lesbian issues move to the forefront of the sociopolitical stage, sexual orientation is showing an upward trend as well (Eagly et al., 2012).

The three topics that represent the more traditional research areas—gender stereotypes, gender and depression, and work–family issues—are those that fit easily into preexisting fields of psychological research. Gender and depression has seen an increase in publications in the past decade, as the many disciplines of psychology have sought to explore why research has revealed that women are more susceptible to depression than men. In traditional psychology, broad theories were developed to show that vulnerabilities to depression were caused by biology, with cognitive and affective personal traits compounding negative life events. Feminist therapy has refuted this theory of depression.

The activist areas, such as intimate partner violence, abortion, and sexual harassment, express another function of feminist psychology: to effect social change through research. This function does not easily mesh with traditional psychology and, in varying ways, is controversial in the sociopolitical theater (Eagly et al., 2012). Intimate partner violence, also known as domestic violence, is one of the single largest threats to the safety of women today. For instance, in the state of New Hampshire, almost half of all homicides are related to domestic violence, and in all of the partner homicides, the victim is female and the perpetrator is the woman's current or ex significant male other (State of New Hampshire, 2012). The significant increase in awareness about women's safety coincided with the passing of the Violence Against Women Act of 1994 (H.R. 4970—112th Congress), which was renewed in 2013 by Congress, although it should be noted that a steady flow of research on intimate partner violence preceded this landmark bill. This controversial topic that 30 years ago had never received any attention has almost doubled in article production in the past decade and is advancing the literature's knowledge about women's vulnerabilities with regard to physical and emotional safety and depression.

It would appear that the more attention controversial topics on women receive, the more research is done on them, followed by a decline in interest. However, some of the archetypal topics of feminist psychology, gender role attitudes and stereotypes, gender and depression, and work–family issues, have found their own ground to stand on. The issues of gender and race and intimate partner violence have established themselves as sustainable topics for research and should continue to be covered in publications. The popular introductory texts in psychology show that a significant emphasis is placed on teaching gender and women's concepts to the broadest of audiences. Feminist psychology has managed to advance the field of psychology significantly in the past 50 years, and "gender differences" and "women" have become a vital part of social and individual psychology.

Research Support for Feminist Therapy. Although controlled studies involving feminist therapy have been conducted, researchers mostly have examined various tenets important to this approach. For example, Chandler, Worell, Johnson, Blount, and Lusk (1999) investigated client experiences with feminist therapy using a scale that measured empowerment. With either very brief (four or fewer sessions) or longer (seven or more sessions) treatment, individuals in feminist, as compared to other therapy approaches, improved significantly more on the empowerment variables; these changes were sustained at a long-term follow-up (Chandler et al., 1999). Other positive changes have been found that may be linked to therapists' use of feminist therapy. For instance, Prochaska and Norcross (2002), in a review of feminist therapy, determined clients receiving feminist therapy had shown significant changes in political/social awareness, career interests, self-perceptions, perceptions of sex roles, and changes in their attitudes.

Extrapolating from the literature on the factors important to positive outcomes in the therapeutic relationship, in general, it is apparent that clients receiving feminist therapy can benefit from this approach. Factors that have been found to contribute to positive outcomes in therapy include, for instance, an egalitarian approach, empowering clients during the therapy process, and increasing the clients' voices in therapy. All of these factors are basic to the feminist approach to therapy. Further, each of these factors is now considered to be an essential component of empirically supported treatments (Bohart, 2005). Specifically, various aspects of an egalitarian therapeutic relationship, such as collaborating on treatment goals, creating a strong therapeutic alliance, and tailoring treatment to the client, have been found to improve outcomes in therapy (Norcross, 2002). It is possible, therefore, to consider feminist therapy to be evidence based in and of itself because of its reliance and amplification of these factors shown to be important in client outcomes (Brown, 2006).

Limitations and Criticisms

Because of their cultural understanding of the family, kin, neighborhood, and collective "we," many traditional racial and ethnic minorities may consider the early feminist models selfish and self-centered. The one-on-one dyadic relationship present in therapy is not the same as network relationships that promote social support, resilience, and survival of the group. Such social relationships are societally prescribed and observe ascribed roles (Roysircar, 2012) and are thus counter to basic assumptions of feminist therapy.

There exist many threats to the use of feminist therapy, particularly for those therapists reliant on third-party payment (Ballou & Hill, 2008). There is also a movement toward exclusive use of evidence-based practice (although there is little consensus on what can be considered good evidence; Norcross, Beutler, & Levant, 2005). Brown (2010) perhaps best articulated this contradiction by stating, "It can be extremely difficult for a therapist to hold fast to an ethic of client empowerment and the creation of feminist consciousness when sitting in the room with her or him and the client is the managed care staff person who is counting symptoms and symptom reduction, not empowerment" (p. 94).

Relevance of Theory to Current-Day Practice

In January 2009, at the National Multicultural Conference and Summit, a group of feminist psychologists participated in a rousing session that provided the standing room only audience a great appreciation for the importance of feminist psychology. According to Martha Banks (2013), "The progress [of feminist therapy] has been amazing and the future holds much promise." According to Amazon.com, since 2008, 246 books were published on feminist therapy. One compelling article (Baumgold-Land, 2010) reported the growth of the use of feminist therapy in Israel in the past 22 years and discusses the creation of the Counseling Center for Women in Jerusalem. Currently the center has 28 therapists, 6 administrative staff, and 12 student trainees.

California seems to have a large concentration of practices focusing on the use of feminist therapy. Practitioners help clients with social phobia, trauma, eating disorders, family relationships, depression, anxiety, stress, anger management, assertiveness coaching, managing the stress of bicultural relationships and acculturation, body image, self-worth, love and work, and grieving and loss. Men, women, adolescents, and children also benefit from this therapeutic approach. In fact, it is used for family relationships (e.g., relationship problems, building better communication, intimacy, and parenting skills, adolescent behavior, couples, and children). Feminist therapy is successfully used for women and men from different ethnic, racial, and sexual backgrounds. It has been successfully used in very difficult contextual situations, such as therapy with incarcerated populations (Marcus-Mendoza, 2004). Feminist therapy is used in group work as well. For example, anger and assertiveness groups are held for women who are primed to develop and enhance conflict resolution skills or who have experienced abuse, trauma, or bullying either as a child, a teen, or an adult (Brown, 2008, 2010).

As such, the overarching goals of feminist therapy provide a base that supports practical variation across therapists and clients, making feminist therapy easily integrated with other theoretical approaches. Feminist therapy supports an emphasis on tailoring interventions to meet each client's skills, abilities, strengths, and capacities. This results in fluidity within its practice, allowing for a client-focused model in which outcome and effectiveness are determined by the therapist and client in a collaborative and flexible fashion. The subjective nature of the actual practice of feminist therapy allows for its delivery across multiple settings, clients, and client needs (Brown, 2010). Adding to the integrative and variable nature of feminist therapy is the consideration of clients' subjective cultural and social locations (Brown, 2008).

Examination of a client's current definitions of reality and her congruence with emotional, cognitive, relational, and behavioral experiences allows for affirmation and validation of individual experiences (Smith & Douglas, 1990). Because feminist therapy is integrative, it also supports the utilization of somatic interventions (Brown, 2010). For example, the subfield of feminist psychopharmacology (Jensvold, Halbreich, & Hamilton, 1996) incorporates the encouragement of clients to exercise judgment and regard of personal values in consideration of psychotropic medications and seeks to influence those prescribing such medications to do so in a nonoppressive and empowering manner (Brown, 2010).

Research findings suggest that therapists improve their effectiveness with all clients when they are culturally competent (Coleman, 1998), and the broad field of psychotherapy is consistently moving toward improved attention to multicultural factors. Modern feminist therapy offers a framework for addressing each client's individual, cultural, and sociopolitical needs and goals (Brown, 2010). This entails consideration of a client's multiple roles and identities that help define his reality. Further, feminist therapy has an inherently biopsychosocial approach that leads to a holistic means of understanding client distress and development (Brown, 2008), which is easily integrated with other theoretical and technical approaches to therapy. Due to its flexibility, ability to be integrated with other therapeutic approaches, and influence on other fields, feminist therapy has increased in use within the fields of psychology and counseling (Brown, 2010).

Applying Theory to Practice

Relational–cultural therapy (RCT) is a feminist intervention model that is of particular value when working with marginalized clients. Although RCT is rooted in feminism and stems from examining the complexities of women's development (Jordan & Hartling, 2002), aspects of this therapy can be applied affirmatively to work with other clients who have been oppressed and are low-privileged. According to RCT, the impact of disconnection caused by empathic failures, relational violations, and interpersonal injuries can cause individuals to keep certain aspects of themselves hidden in order to maintain a relationship (Jordan & Hartling, 2002). The denial, anger, or depression family members, friends, partners, and other loved ones may experience in response to relatives who are different and do not follow conventions can result in disconnection and the *central relational paradox*, that is, being loved as well as rejected (Miller & Stiver, 1997). The central relational paradox is likely to occur in situations when criticized or less powerful persons are unable to represent themselves or their feelings in a relationship, or when they are faced with a response of additional injury, indifference, or denial of their paradoxical relationship experience (Jordan & Hartling, 2002).

RETURNING TO THE CASE OF TIM, A TRANSGENDER CLIENT

The relational–cultural therapy (RCT) model would apply well to the transgender experience of feeling disempowered, ignored, and ostracized by combating those nontherapeutic (i.e., personal) relationships with a positive therapeutic alliance that creates mutual empathy. Miller's (2003) "five good things"—zest or well-being, ability to take action in a relationship and other situations, knowledge of oneself and the other individual, an enhanced sense of worth, and a wish for more connections—would greatly assist a transgender individual in enjoying life, becoming empowered, having a better sense of self and being in relationships, increasing self-esteem, and increasing a wish to connect with others apart from the therapeutic relationship. By working toward creating a more authentic self, the transgender individual can work through gender identity issues with the therapist, as well as other issues that arise, related and unrelated to the transgender identity. For instance, cognition and affect may be disorganized. If the client is also undergoing hormone therapy, she may be dealing with significant emotional change often referred to as a "second puberty" (Carroll et al., 2002). Therapist empathic attunement would be an affirmative way of helping a client notice the interplay and nuances between adolescent emotional turmoil and her otherwise mature cognitions.

Tim's second therapist is Dr. A. Ware, a feminist therapist. Because Dr. Ware had no experience treating transgender clients, she decided to explore her possible biases and assumptions through writing self-reflective journal notes. Dr. Ware was committed to her own self-work with regard to *transphobia* (inherent fear of transgender individuals) and explored the defensiveness, projections, anxieties, intellectualization, fears, and guilt that might block a positive therapeutic relationship (Roysircar, 2003a). Prejudicial attitudes may have a significant impact on transference and countertransference reactions (Comas-Diaz & Jacobsen, 1991). Dr. Ware's self-reflective journaling made it clear to her that she was experiencing prejudicial thoughts toward Tim and relying on her understanding of lesbian, gay, and bisexual (LGB) people to conceptualize Tim's problem.

Dr. Ware decided to address her self-awareness of her GLB bias and reliance on stereotypes about sexual orientation by contacting a colleague who was actively involved in the transgender community and was educating therapists about gender identity. Dr. Ware believed that to foster a real relationship with Tim, she needed to integrate a greater understanding of transgender individuals into her work. She asked her colleague to serve as her supervisor with regard to Tim's case to help her become more sensitive toward Tim's transgender identity. These consultations

(Continued)

increased Dr. Ware's understanding of how sexual orientation and gender identity are two separate aspects of a person's makeup that may have intersecting impacts on the individual person. Dr. Ware also attended an experiential 2-day feminist therapy workshop that focused on countertransference, therapist bias, the use of self-disclosure, and empowerment training. Outside of this workshop, Dr. Ware read journal articles, viewed media presentations, and read an autobiography about transgender identity to increase her understanding.

Dr. Ware understood what transgender identity means to Tim, a specific client, the language and pronouns to use with Tim, and the impact of being transgender on Tim's peer group, family, community, and society. There is very little language that describes the transgender experience in inclusive and affirmative ways (Korell & Lorah, 2006). Therefore, it was important for Dr. Ware to assess on an individual level how Tim identified and which gendered or nongendered language Tim would prefer in therapy.

Dr. Ware argued that to define transgender individuals as mentally ill was to stigmatize them (Vanderburgh, 2007). She further contended that the *DSM*'s gender identity disorder as a diagnosis, coupled with a history of repeated exposure to hate crimes and experiences

of oppression, may predispose Tim to a posttraumatic stress disorder (PTSD) diagnosis. This dual diagnosis would complicate therapy. Keeping in mind these potential diagnoses, Dr. Ware used the feminist approach to intervene with Tim's gender identity concerns and the hurts and pains of exclusion.

Dr. Ware felt it was important that she disclose to Tim how she was educating herself about transgender identity because authenticity can help deepen the therapeutic alliance. She communicated that their work would be done collaboratively and that sharing the therapeutic experience would help to remove some of the client–therapist power differential. Dr. Ware also explained how therapy progresses and why she believed it is helpful with transgender clients. Tim appreciated Dr. Ware's efforts and respectfulness and agreed to continue treatment with her. After asking Tim about preferred pronoun usage, Dr. Ware learned that, instead of the pronouns *he/his*, Tim now felt most comfortable with the use of *ze/hir*. Both Dr. Ware and Tim experienced growth through their relationship with each other. Tim was able to address interpersonal issues that ze had been experiencing, which were directly impacting hir struggles with transition, thus decreasing symptoms and strengthening the therapeutic alliance.

Returning to the Multicultural Case of the Sanchez Family

Although the Sanchez family has been living in the United States for 6 years, it cannot be assumed that family members speak English fluently. Therefore, it is essential to assess their proficiency in English. Given that Miguel has been faring successfully in an American school system, it is likely that he is at least proficient in English as a second language. His mother, on the other hand, cannot read, write, or speak English. Hiring a professionally trained translator, then, is necessary to communicate with Mrs. Sanchez and to give her a voice in therapy. Research has shown that clients are more willing to continue treatment if a skilled and carefully trained bilingual interpreter is present to bridge the linguistic gap between the client and the therapist (Altarriba & Santiago-Rivera, 1994). It is possible that in the past, Miguel was required to assist his mother with this translation task through "language brokering." Young children learn languages much faster than adults, and, consequently, often take on the role of mediator between their parents and non-Spanish-speaking members of society. As teenagers grow older, they might come to resent this adult-like responsibility to help their parents (Altarriba & Santiago-Rivera, 1994).

During the intake with Mrs. Sanchez and her son Miguel, it is important to be sensitive about their immigration status. Because we do not know if Mrs. Sanchez is a legal immigrant, it may be prudent to hold off on paperwork at first. According to Diaz-Lazaro, Verdinelly, and Cohen (2012), "Many Latina immigrants, particularly those who are undocumented, are leery of filling out much paperwork for fear of legal consequences" (p. 85). A feminist therapist will keep in mind that the first visit may also be the last if clients are worried about immigration issues. Although immigrants usually experience acculturative stress in their second culture, research has found foreign nativity to be a protective factor against mental illnesses (Algeria, Mulvaney-Day, Woo, & Viruell-Fuentes, 2011). This information is good news for Miguel's mother.

There seems to be an obvious difference in the level of acculturation between mother and son, a fact that can trigger *acculturative family distancing*, an intergenerational family conflict caused by gaps in acculturation and communication style between parents and children (Hwang, 2006). Adolescence is a typical time period for the emergence of acculturative family distancing, as the child struggles with his developing identity (both personal and ethnic) while embedded in the European American culture. Miguel has adopted the fashion of his peers (e.g., baggy clothes) and their cultural interests (e.g., rap music). He seems to be well acculturated to the teen culture. In fact, he resents his mother's enculturation or desire to retain her traditional language and culture. The dual-opposite process of acculturation and enculturation might produce conflicts across generations in families and increase the risk of psychological issues for adolescents (Gonzales, German, & Fabrett, 2011; Roysircar-Sodowsky & Maestas, 2000). An assessment of Mrs. Sanchez using a bilinear model of acculturation might indeed reveal that she is at the separation stage of acculturation; that is, she avoids as much contact as possible with the dominant culture, while her son might vacillate between integration and assimilation (Roysircar, 2003b, 2004). A further inquiry concerning how much contact Miguel has with his own traditional culture might reveal, if he has none at all, that he is indeed in the assimilation stage, a stage characterized by a rejection of one's own culture (Roysircar, 2003b, 2004).

Acculturative family distancing may be aggravated for Miguel because he is able to discern the level of discrimination he experiences as a result of his Mexican ethnicity. Gonzales et al. (2011) suggest that perceptions of discrimination increase as children grow older. In fact, as adolescents have more interaction with mainstream society, they also experience more instances of discrimination. Miguel might be a victim of insidious trauma, resulting from microaggressions, a form of discrimination that affects minority individuals on a daily basis through apparently banal ways, for example, media portrayal of one's group in a stereotypical manner. Miguel has expressed to his mother that his friends give him respect; perhaps his peer circle is the only place that he feels respected within the dominant society.

It is important for a feminist therapist to have some background knowledge about Latino traditional values and to seek out this knowledge. A common misconception is to see Latinos as a homogeneous group when, in fact, a great heterogeneity exists among them. However, there are some common values, such as *familismo, machismo, marianismo,* and *respeto* that tie together all Latino cultures. *Familismo* refers to the strong bond of loyalty, solidarity, and reciprocity that individuals share within the family group. *Familismo* has been found to be a great protective factor for psychological health, and presenting its positive aspects to Miguel could help him to find common ground with his mother. *Machismo* is a value that posits that because of their gender, males are in a privileged position in society and are to be viewed and treated as authority figures (Comas-Diaz, 1987).

Marianismo gives some power back to women. It puts forth the belief that women are superior to men morally and are able to withstand much suffering (Comas-Diaz, 1987). The idea is that a mother sacrifices herself for her children and the family, and it is in her right to expect a form of "worship" from her children. Keeping this in mind might help us to understand how deeply Miguel's attitude hurts Mrs. Sanchez. She may feel shame around the mother–son conflictual relationship, specifically around Miguel's rebellious behavior. She expects her son's behavior to reflect *respeto* (respect), a traditional value that she may feel that she has earned as his mother, as a woman, and possibly for all the sacrifices that she has made to bring him to the United States.

In a multicultural case involving a woman, feminist therapy is a fitting approach. Essentially, the conflict between mother and son has to do with how each interacts with the European American society, and how these interactions influence their relationships both with each other and with their own selves, the very reciprocal influences and sociocultural factors that feminist theory is designed to examine. Miguel affects and is affected by the host culture in a very different way than is his mother. This difference in reaction to the cultural, social, and political systems has recently begun to strain their relationship. Feminist therapy has framed mental health problems as being rooted in restrictive gender roles, stereotyped cultural expectations, and societal inequalities, rather than stemming from dysfunction within the individual.

The therapist treating Miguel and his mother should focus on understanding and exploring the perspective of a male Mexican American teen growing in his *machismo*. Miguel has communicated that his new friends give him respect, a fact that he likes. Therefore, the therapist should also be sure to communicate genuine appreciation for Miguel's unique contributions to the therapy process and to his peer relationships. The same principle applies to Mrs. Sanchez. Feminist theory dictates communicating to clients that their voices can and will be heard and acknowledged.

Mrs. Sanchez values the traditional Mexican behaviors of *marianismo* and *machismo*. The therapist can empower her by allowing her to choose to keep these values, while also pointing to Miguel's *machismo* expression. Research has shown that Latinas perpetuate these traditions to help them cope with the socioeconomic stresses that they experience within the dominant culture (Comas-Diaz, 1987, 2006). Rather than imposing the traditional American feminist value of empowerment on Mrs. Sanchez, it is important to recognize that she can choose her own mode of empowerment, which may be *marianismo*.

Because Mrs. Sanchez is Mexican-oriented, helping her to feel comfortable with the therapy process may involve alternating therapy questions with the use of *pláticas* (informal conversation, small talk; Diaz-Lazaro et al., 2012). The use of *pláticas* aims to establish a rapport with Mrs. Sanchez in a culturally congruent manner. The therapist understands Mrs. Sanchez's possible mistrust of him, an acculturated Mexican American professional, and of the therapeutic situation as a whole.

The egalitarian relationship between the client and the therapist offers the experience that each participant is an expert and brings his or her own particular knowledge to the session. Within this relationship, all participants, like Mrs. Sanchez and her son Miguel, are valued equally. It is important for the therapist to reflect on his position of privilege and implied power, as it might be perceived by the client during therapy (Brown, 2010). The therapist's goal is not to "rescue" his client, as this would maintain oppression and not empower. Empowering Mrs. Sanchez would consist of helping her to see what independence and strength she may gain by learning some English. However, this might be at odds with her values of *familismo, marianismo,* and *respeto,* as she might consider relying heavily on her son for language and culture brokering as normal family functioning.

Miguel shows behaviors common among immigrant children, and the therapist might want to let Mrs. Sanchez know that many immigrant teenagers distance themselves from their native culture so that they may adapt to their new environment (Roysircar-Sodowsky & Frey, 2003). The therapist does not justify criminal activities, but instead introduces to Mrs. Sanchez the idea that her son is not completely at fault. The therapist may also present to Mrs. Sanchez the social, bicultural, and familial pressures that Miguel is under. This can lead to reframing symptoms of distress as signs of strength and as possible forms of adaptive communication on the client's part (Evans et al., 2011).

The therapist might reframe Miguel's symptomatic behavior and rejection of his cultural practices as manifestations of coping mechanisms. He may ask Miguel what he likes about his second culture and his Mexican heritage and what he does not like, which is a method of empowering him to clarify his cultural identification. The therapist might ask Miguel about the value of *familismo.* If Miguel can consider some part of *familismo* as a strength that enables him to face microaggressions coming from European Americans, this recognition might encourage him to spend more time with his family, perhaps attending Mexican cultural celebrations with them.

Another possible intervention is to introduce Mrs. Sanchez to Mexican American bicultural women who value both their second and original cultures and are able to balance the retention of relationships and cultural identity found in the dominant society (Roysircar, 2003b, 2004). These individuals can live in both majority and minority groups without compromising their many contextual identities (Roysircar, 2004). Through exposure to these bicultural Mexican Americans and their ideals, Mrs. Sanchez may feel less threatened by the idea of adopting some practices of European Americans and interacting with them. However, it is crucial to go about this acculturation intervention carefully. It is very important to keep in mind feminist therapy constructs of empowerment, choice, and the egalitarian therapeutic relationship. Mrs. Sanchez must be an equal partner in the decision to exercise the intervention of meeting bicultural Mexican Americans in the community. She must not be pushed to abandon her cultural values or to engage in these meetings because of a perceived power differential between herself and the therapist and/or between herself and bicultural Mexican American women.

Because feminist therapy is no longer uniquely restricted for use with female clients, its sociocultural roots make it ideal for treating psychological disorders in minorities. The Sanchez family belongs to an oppressed group that could benefit greatly from the empowerment provided by feminist therapy. A few modifications might be necessary to make feminist principles applicable, and with the care of a culturally sensitive and aware therapist, feminist therapy could become a powerful healing tool for the Sanchez family.

CHAPTER REVIEW

SUMMARY AND COMMENTARY ▶▶

In her 1963 book *The Feminine Mystique,* Betty Friedan, a second waver, examined the status of women through the eyes of European American, middle-class U.S. women of the 1940s and 1950s. She highlighted how these women were brought up into the socially defined role of a woman being restrained, homemaking, child-bearing, husband-serving, and unthinking. That image, she said, was a transformation from the feisty women of the late 19th and early 20th century United States, who demonstrated on the streets for improved working conditions and the right to vote (Figure 11.7). In light of the sexualization of girls and women in current U.S. media and clothing fashion, the increasing trafficking of girls and women worldwide (including the United States), the utilization of rape as a weapon of war worldwide, and the increase of rape in India, one may wonder whether there is a downward swing in the feminist movement. There seems to be a bipolar nature in the current status of women. More women than men are attending college, including medical and law schools; women are in the workplace in large numbers, and they are increasingly elected into the U.S. Congress and Senate. Some women are top bankers, CEOs of companies, presidents and deans of universities, newscasters, astronauts, war journalists and political commentators, and award-winning film producers, directors, screenwriters, and comedians. At the same time, women are gang-raped by members of school athletic teams. Recently, women in the United States have been allowed to participate on the battlefront, even as sexual harassment and rape of women in the U.S. armed forces have captured the national news. On the homefront, numerous young women are choosing to be stay-at-home mothers, divorce rates have not appreciably declined, and birth rates for Whites have declined, even as political conservatives rally around pro-life and anti-LGBT+ morality and the traditional definition of marriage.

An explanation for unevenness and paradoxes in the status of women through history is that feminism, like all social movements, evolves and responds to the zeitgeist of the times. Feminism is not obsolete; it is just different from what it was during the first and second waves. The objectification of women, which Friedan called "the problem that has no name," is now out in the open and is reported and debated more than ever before.

▼ FIGURE 11.7

Women Protestors

Source: Paul Thompson [Public domain], via Wikimedia Commons.

Gail Sheehy (2013), a second wave feminist, who comprehends today's young feminists, says that they do not beat on themselves for failing to "have it all" as did some of their "superwomen" predecessors, ambitious women in their professional careers but who came home to begin the second shift. Today's women are seeking, at their own pace and sense of time, a happy balance among work, love, and family. Sheehy believes they do not see themselves as trying to navigate between work and home. According to Sheehy, some women today may even perceive that feminism garners privileges but comes up short when it comes to their love lives.

Sheehy's (2013) catchy article title "The New Feminists: Young, Multicultural, Strategic, and Looking Out for Each Other" captures the notion that today's feminists come in a variety of colors, may stall their personal and professional lives, know how to utilize their mentors, and know how to mentor other women. Many of these feminists work for nonprofit organizations that advocate for social justice, prevention of violence, education of girls, GLBT+ issues, prison reform, and patient medical education, and they work hard for funding their causes. In other words, today's feminists and the feminist movement itself are not defined by others, and they have many choices. Currently, feminism has to go beyond just taking into account gender; it also must consider immigrant status, language capacity, and economic capacity and must extend to other intersections of identity such as class, race, ethnicity, immigrant or refugee status, ability, sexuality, sexual orientation, gender identity and expression, geography, and internationalism. Without question, at this point in time, feminism is more inclusive and broader than Friedan's feminism. Table 11.3 is an overview of current feminist therapy practice.

▼ TABLE 11.3

Relevance of Feminist Therapy to Current Practice

Variable	Current Applications
Type of service delivery setting	Private practice Clinic Psychiatric hospital Health care setting Substance abuse clinic Military Social service agency Crisis line/hotline Support group (e.g., survivors of incest) Women's shelter (also called women's refuge or battered women's center)
Population	Child Teen Adult
Type of presenting problems	Wide range of presenting problems (e.g., anxiety, depression, stress, and posttraumatic stress) Issues frequently dealt with: gender bias, empowerment, assertiveness, rape, domestic violence, career issues and career trajectory, body image, incest, eating disorders, sexual abuse, self-blame, discrimination, oppression, sexual harassment, leadership style and gender.
Severity of presenting problems	Wide range of severity

Variable	Current Applications
Adapted for short-term approach	Yes
Length of treatment	Highly variable
Ability to receive reimbursement	Insurance companies will reimburse pending *DSM* diagnosis.
Certification in approach	Lewis and Clark College, Portland, Oregon, offers certificate programs through its Education and Counseling Department. For example, a certificate is available in the area of eating disorders. ProChoices Community Therapy Clinic, Vancouver, Canada, offers a certificate program in feminist narrative therapy for graduate students and practicing professionals.
Training in educational programs	Feminist theory/therapy is covered to varying extents in graduate training programs. Some universities and colleges provide additional programs or supplemental training, including the Jean Baker Miller Training Institute at Wellesley College, Massachusetts.
Location	Urban Rural Suburban
Type of delivery system	HMO PPO Fee for service
Credential	Northwestern University, Evanston, Illinois, offers programs to add credentials to a professional's degree in areas such as advanced feminist theory, queer theory, and sociology of sexuality.
Practitioners	Professionals Paraprofessionals
Fit with *DSM* diagnoses	No. The *DSM* system is built on a form of biological reductionism that supports the medicalization of treatment. The connection between sociopolitical forces and women's mental health issues is not a primary focus.

CRITICAL THINKING QUESTIONS ▶▶

1. Discuss the main tenets of feminism. How can these be applied to work with clients from differing cultural backgrounds (e.g., race, ethnicity, gender, sexual orientation, religion)?

2. How do societal forces disempower women, men, and transgender individuals?

3. Compare the goals of feminist therapy with the goals of other types of therapy.

4. What are some ways in which a therapist's biases can affect work with clients who have been marginalized because of their gender?

5. What are some similarities and differences between feminist therapy with Tim and that with the Sanchez family?

6. How do societal forces affect the feminist movement and the research conducted on feminism?

SUGGESTED READINGS: IMPORTANT PRIMARY SOURCES ▶▶

Books

Ballou, M., & Brown, L. S. (Eds.). (2008). *Rethinking mental health and disorders: Feminist perspectives.* New York, NY: Guilford Press.

Friedan, B. (1997). *The feminine mystique.* New York, NY: Norton.

Henley, N., Meng, K., O'Brien, D., McCarthy, W., & Sockloskie, R. (1998). Developing a scale to measure the diversity of feminist attitudes. *Psychology of Women Quarterly, 22*(2), 317–348.

hooks, b. (1984). *Feminist theory: From margin to center.* Boston, MA: South End Press.

Jordan, J. V. (2009). *Relational–cultural therapy.* Washington, DC: American Psychological Association.

Miller, J. B., & Stiver, I. P. (1997). *The healing connection: How women form relationships in therapy and in life.* Boston, MA: Beacon Press.

Walker, M., & Miller, J. B. (2001). *Racial images and relational possibilities* (Talking Paper No. 2). Wellesley, MA: Wellesley College, Stone Center.

Journals

Affilia: Journal of Women and Social Work

Feminist Studies

Feminist Theory

Gender & Society

Hypatia: A Journal of Feminist Philosophy

Journal of Lesbian Studies

Journal of Women, Politics & Policy: A Quarterly Journal of Research & Policy Studies

Journal of Women's History

Meridians: Feminism, Race, Transnationalism

Nashim: A Journal of Jewish Women's Studies and Gender Issues

off our backs: A Women's News Journal

Psychology of Women Quarterly

Signs: Journal of Women in Culture and Society

Women and Health: A Multidisciplinary Journal of Women's Health Issues

Women and Therapy

Women's Studies Quarterly

Websites

American Psychological Association Division 35: Society for the Psychology of Women: http://www.apadivisions.org/division-35

Association for Women in Psychology: http://www.awpsych.org

Documents From the Women's Liberation Movement (National History Education Clearinghouse): http://teachinghistory.org/history-content/website-reviews/22796

Emancipation of Women 1890–1930 (video): https://www.british pathe.com/video/emancipation-of-women-1

Feminism (BBC radio): Melvyn Bragg and others discuss 20th-century feminism and its empowerment of women: http://www.bbc.co.uk/programmes/p00545b0

Psychology's Feminist Voices: http://www.feministvoices.com

CHAPTER 12

POSTMODERNISM

Constructivism and Social Constructionism

Introduction

The term *postmodernism* has various connotations, but it is typically applied to ideas and events that collectively represent a dramatic shift in the way we interact with and perceive the world around us. Even though this game changer initially affected areas mostly comprising the arts, postmodernism's spreading, pervasive effect eventually spread to psychotherapy, most notably, in the form of narrative therapy. If we refer to one of the areas initially affected, architecture, the reader is provided a visual interpretation of this particular movement (Figure 12.1). The postmodern design of the Dancing House captures the essence of what postmodernism represents, that is, an overthrow of the rules that had governed how an architectural structure should be built. In general, postmodernism represented a tearing down of the explicit and sometimes unspoken, but understood, values of what was known as modernism, a contemporary movement that rested on a belief that human life could be improved by discovering universal truths through the expert use of rationality and the empirical scientific method. Postmodernism took the opposing position that discovering universal truths was a myth. In addition, the formal and technical languages used by experts were not to be trusted because such languages were used to maintain a power differential between the experts and all others, a difference in power that

enabled the experts (e.g., academics, historians, religious honorifics, scientists, politicos, intellectuals, and traditional therapists) to control or oppress others. There are many phrases and sections found in George Orwell's classic novel *1984* (Orwell, 1949) that intelligently capture key points made by postmodernists. One such section appears below.

> We know that no one ever seizes power with the intention of relinquishing it. Power is not a means, it is an end. One does not establish a dictatorship in order to safeguard a revolution; one makes the revolution in order to establish the dictatorship. The object of persecution is persecution. The object of torture is torture. *The object of power is power.* (Italics added; Orwell, 1992)

The remainder of this chapter reviews the main premises of the postmodern movements of *constructivism* and *social constructionism* and considers how the major constructs derived from these movements have been applied to psychotherapy. Even though these two postmodern movements overlap in many ways, major and subtle differences between the two movements exist and these differences are explored in this chapter.

[handwritten note:] ★ Important — what does this mean?

The Dancing House Located in Prague, Czech Republic

We want to remind readers, as discussed in the first chapter of this textbook, terms such as *therapist, client,* and *therapy* or *psychotherapy* are used throughout this textbook. The reason for this reminder is that some notable contributors to the areas covered in this chapter strongly advocate the use of other terminology. This is illustrated by the stance taken by narrative therapists who believe terms such as *counseling, psychotherapy, treatment, patient,* and *therapy* should not be used; similarly, Michael White preferred the term *conversationalist host* rather than *therapist* when referring to his role (Murdock, 2009). The terms rejected are seen as a means to assert power over those who seek assistance for their problems.

Key Players of Constructivism and Social Constructionism

Michael J. Mahoney

Michael J. Mahoney (1946–2006), a behaviorist, made important contributions to cognitive psychology and constructivism (Marquis, Warren, & Arnkoff, 2009). He was allowed to enroll in Joliet Community College, Illinois, with a probationary status, since he had not completed high school. His interests were somewhat broad in scope, and he acquired more course credits in philosophy than in his eventual major, psychology. Mahoney was intrigued by what philosophy taught him in the areas of beliefs and thoughts. Before finishing college in Illinois, he moved to Arizona for health reasons, a decision made in part by an allergist who emphasized that the dry climate there would help with his respiratory problems. Mahoney did not realize at the time that he would have to reapply to get into a different college. When he tried to register at Arizona State University, which he supposedly chose by flipping a coin, personnel at the university informed Mahoney he had to choose a major before starting. Mahoney panicked and sought career advice from a therapist he had randomly selected from the telephone directory. Mahoney told the receptionist he could only see the therapist once, but that this meeting was very important to his future. The therapist gave him 2 hours of his time, and Mahoney expressed deep appreciation toward the therapist at the end. The therapist was Milton H. Erickson, the famous psychiatrist and psychotherapist who specialized in hypnosis. Mahoney reported that the appreciation he felt was because the therapist endorsed his decision to declare a major, which turned out to be psychology. Unknown to Mahoney he enrolled in a psychology department that was thoroughly Skinnerian in its focus—a radical form of behaviorism (Mahoney, 2008a).

As an undergraduate "psych tech," Mahoney resorted to what amounted to a constructivist tactic (he essentially entered into the "story" of several individuals receiving his assistance) to change behavior when other attempts did not work. For example, in a Catholic hospital, one patient diagnosed with catatonic schizophrenia thought he

THE CASE OF JUSTINE

Justine's heritage is French. Justine's parents emigrated from Paris in 1969 to settle permanently in the United States. Her father chose to resettle in Lafourche Parish in the state of Louisiana (where many of the inhabitants spoke Cajun French). The reason for moving was that Justine's father wanted to obtain a PhD in chemistry at a university in the United States. Justine, who is 40 years old, and her younger brother were both born in America. Soon after acquiring his doctorate, Justine's father was employed by one of America's top chemical firms, located in New Orleans. Justine's mother did not work outside the home and focused on taking care of the children and home. Justine's parents managed to merge much of French culture into their current life in the United States; at home they predominately spoke French (and occasionally used common Cajun French phrases), ate customary French food, and periodically traveled to Paris to spend time with family there. One of Justine's earliest memories pertained to when her father returned from work each day and on seeing Justine he would look down at her and say in Cajun French, *"Un 'tit chien lafourchais"* (child from Lafourche) and she was expected to reply *"Père"* (father). This was always followed by her father and her laughing. However, the parents also embraced the lifestyle of their adopted country. They lived in a middle-class neighborhood and provided their children a strong education intended to prepare them for professional careers. Justine attended Nicholls State College in Thibodaux and then earned her law degree, JD, at Tulane University.

Justine had a strong emotional bond with her French heritage and history and continued to maintain several French customs. Justine's mother died approximately 4 years ago due to a postsurgery pulmonary embolism. Justine currently resides in New York City with Tomás, who is originally from Spain, and their 3-year-old daughter. Justine is pregnant with a second child. Currently, Justine is a nonpracticing lawyer, choosing to be a full-time mother. Tomás's job requires that he travel frequently, and he is often away for weeks at a time.

Justine decided to meet with a private practitioner in Manhattan because, in her words, she "feels confused about several choices she has to make." Justine reported that she feels cut off from others and ambivalent when she considers her current life. These concerns arose recently when she discovered that her father was in a new relationship with a "young Cajun woman living in Lafourche Parish," which he had kept secret from Justine. This discovery left Justine feeling angry and confused. Justine also finds her father judging and pushing her, while he currently finds that Justine (which he revealed in a recent phone conversation) has become distant and seems to want to circumvent any kind of confrontation. Justine tells the therapist she feels very close to her first-born child but worries about what will happen to her child if she "can't remain strong."

Case Discussion. Near the end of this chapter, the case of Justine will be returned to illustrate the application of a postmodern therapeutic approach.

was Jesus. This person stayed in his bed stretched out as if he had been crucified, but when the patient adopted a different pattern of behaving, it was very unsettling for staff members and other patients. One night the patient started to yell and moan as loudly as possible. Despite medication he was given, the yelling continued and the psychiatric ward became increasingly chaotic and the typical patterns of behavior displayed by other patients deteriorated. Because little progress was made to quiet the patient, Mahoney took action by going to the nurses switchboard and connected himself to the room of the once catatonic patient. Assuming what Mahoney thought was a "god-like tone" he said, "This is God the father—Go to sleep!" in an authoritative manner. The patient, who thought he was Jesus, suddenly stopped yelling and moaning. When the nurse on duty went to the patient's room, she found him to be comfortably asleep (Mahoney, 1974).

Mahoney graduated and went on to graduate school. While Mahoney was a graduate student, he had an onsite job in a treatment program designed to help predelinquents. He found that the children there responded differently from what he had expected when he applied standard behavioral techniques. For example, whenever a certain child at the facility was instructed to go to bed, his reaction to this instruction was to display uncontrollable anger. The well-known techniques Mahoney was familiar with (e.g., a token economy where tokens are earned and exchanged for a valued reinforcing event, time out for unacceptable behaviors, and verbal praise utilized for behaviors that increasingly matched a target goal) failed to make a difference with this child. The child continued to display the behaviors associated with a tantrum until Mahoney noticed that one evening the boy went to bed without displaying any inappropriate behavior. Mahoney concluded that because he had given the child a choice among the bathrooms to take his shower that this action was what mediated the change in the child's behavior. Mahoney tested his suspicion by allowing the child to choose what color towels he wanted to use when showering. Mahoney found this further contributed to a positive change. In another case a girl who liked to receive candy from Mahoney refused to do so one evening. Mahoney decided to ask her why she had responded in this manner, and she told Mahoney that it was because he was using candy in an attempt to control her. As a result of these types of reactions, Mahoney moved toward interventions that required him to work jointly, collaboratively with these children to achieve desired goals.

While at Arizona State University, as an undergraduate student, Mahoney had become interested in the social cognitive learning theory of Albert Bandura. Later, while studying for his doctorate at Stanford University, Mahoney got the opportunity to study with both Bandura and with Bandura's former advisee, Jerry Davidson. These experiences and contacts led Mahoney to question B. F. Skinner's assertion that adults interact with children in ways to enable them to learn a language—specifically, by reinforcing correctly spoken words (a process that starts with reinforcing close approximations) and then by reinforcing correctly arranged words that create sentences. Mahoney wrote to Skinner expressing his doubt concerning language acquisition (i.e., thoughts). Skinner wrote a short response back. Later, at a meeting arranged by his Stanford professor Carl Thoresen, Mahoney received a stern warning from Skinner concerning Mahoney's interest in probing thoughts and processes related to thoughts that Skinner indicated was a form of mentalism that would cause Mahoney to travel down a mistaken and a fruitless line of research (Mahoney, 2000).

Later in his career, Mahoney became the founding editor of *Cognitive Therapy and Research* and the executive editor for the internationally read *Journal of Constructivism in the Human Sciences*. Such professional involvements positioned Mahoney to converse and debate with cognitive psychology icons such as Aaron Beck, Albert Ellis, and Donald Meichenbaum. He met and maintained communications with Viktor Frankl and Sophie Freud and was influenced by both. Concerning Sophie Freud, Mahoney stated, "She has helped me to discover and appreciate the constructivist developments in psychodynamic theory" (Mahoney, 2000, n.p.). Mahoney had Buddhist friends, was drawn to feminist therapy, and was attuned to the positive psychology movement. Mahoney traveled nationally and internationally on conference and colloquium circuits, visited universities, and dialoged with well-known professionals, always learning from them. He taught at different universities in the United States and abroad. Because Mahoney drew from influences in cognitive therapies, humanistic theories, existentialism, and other areas, his style of writing was imbued with an expansive quality (Mahoney, 2003, 2004, 2008b).

As a constructivist, Mahoney was known to be extremely self-reflective and introspective. Although he was a pioneer of constructivism, he also recognized its limitations (Mahoney, 1995). First, he wondered how a constructivist therapist is able to know what is wrong or what is best for the client. Second, the experiences of a therapist represent inherent biases that may alienate or ignore the subjectivity of the client. He openly wondered how any therapist could conceptualize a client's problems without prejudice toward any part of the client's story. Third, there is no solid bedrock of leaders within the constructivist field because a leadership structure would reflect objective, hierarchical powers and paradigms that postmodern theories opposed. Mahoney (1995) believed that these limitations were not confined to the constructivist approach but were present within all psychotherapy theories and their applications. Mahoney believed that an important tool to remedy some of these limitations was to build an awareness of the biases and inherent elements of objective power that a therapist inevitably brings into a therapeutic relationship (Mahoney, 1995). Furthermore, he also believed that there is no one true appraisal of reality, which makes assessment and diagnosis a less essential part of the therapeutic process (Mahoney, 1995).

Mahoney (2000) stated that radical/extreme behaviorism had several theoretical weaknesses, which included the following:

1. The attempt to press associationism beyond its warrant
2. The tendency to either deny cognitive processes or to redefine them as relatively simply connections between presumably isolated events (whether defined as stimuli, responses, or something else)
3. The claim that a pattern (habit) can be totally eliminated from a person's repertoire
4. An authoritarian and dogmatic tendency that denies the meaningfulness or warrant for knowledge claims that fall outside of the positivist (or logical positivist) approach to epistemology [acquisition of knowledge] (n.p.)

Fervent advocates of a Skinnerian form of behaviorism delivered harsh attacks toward Mahoney for expressing such criticisms. They were especially intolerant of Mahoney's position when he proposed that findings in cognitive studies may have relevancy for psychotherapy practice. In response to an article by Mahoney that appeared in the *American Psychologist,* titled "Scientific Psychology and Radical Behaviorism: Important Distinctions Based in Scientism and Objectivism," those who took an opposing view wrote a scathing letter in 1991, endorsed by scores of radical behaviorists, which was published in *Behavior Analyst.*

When not engrossed in psychological theory and practice, Mahoney was a writer of fiction and poetry. He was also a successful weightlifter, receiving national awards and recognition for his accomplishments; in fact, Mahoney served in 1980 as the psychologist for the American Olympic Weightlifting Team competing in Moscow.

Mahoney suffered from periodic depression throughout his life and committed suicide in 2006 at his home in Newport, Rhode Island. When he was younger, Mahoney had anxieties associated with his academic performance, and he suffered from persistent uncertainty about decision making. When he became a professional, he applied relaxation techniques on himself to silence such inner pressures. One wonders whether he accepted his diagnosis for treatment or if he accepted the inevitability of depression, per his tenet, "I view development as a lifelong process of complex self-organization in which core processes change less, change more slowly, and change more fitfully (non-linearly) than other life processes" (Mahoney, 2000, n.p.). With regard to his constructivist theory and clinical practice, one can also wonder what possible directions Mahoney might have taken, given this statement:

> I speak from the heart and to the heart as often as I can, and I encourage my clients to do the same. I feel very grateful for the privilege of participating in their lives, and I enjoy my work now even more than ever. If my life patterns continue as they have over the past 30 years, I will continue to explore and expand in ways that I cannot now anticipate. I look forward to that adventure. (Mahoney, 2000, n.p.)

See Table 12.1 for assertions made by Michael Mahoney during his career.

Kenneth J. Gergen

Kenneth J. Gergen (born 1934) grew up in Durham, North Carolina. His father, John J. Gergen, was a professor at Duke University and was chair of the mathematics department. Kenneth Gergen was a professor at Swarthmore College for 10 years and served

▼ TABLE 12.1

Quotable Michael Mahoney

- Of central importance to psychotherapy practitioners is the realization that the processes underlying human psychological change are nonlinear and complex, thereby preventing perfect predictions of what will happen to the particulars of any given individual's life. (pp. 260–261)
- The single most distinctive feature of constructivism is the assertion that all cognitive phenomena—from perception and memory to problem solving and consciousness—entail active and proactive processes. In less technical terms, the organism is an active participant in its own experiences as well as in learning. (p. 100)
- Psychoanalysts, behaviorists, cognitivists, existentialists, and humanists can all find many threads of their respective traditions in the conceptual tapestry woven by psychological constructivism. (p. 113)
- The experience of change is relative to each individual and cannot be separated from the predominantly tacit and personalized experience of stasis. (p. 323)
- The separation between knowledge and existential phenomena, itself a forced distinction with centuries of inertia, is no longer tenable. (p. 176)

Source: Mahoney, M. J. (1991). Human change processes. New York, NY: Basic Books.

as chair of its psychology department. He also assumed the position of Senior Research Professor at the same institution. His contributions to academia are such that he has served as a visiting professor at several other institutions of higher learning, including Adolfo Ibanez University, Kyoto University, Sorbonne, University of Heidelberg, University of Marburg, and University of Rome. Some of his most noteworthy publications, i.e., "*An Invitation to Social Construction*," "*Realities and Relationships*," "*The Saturated Self*," and "*Toward Transformation in Social Knowledge*" have had a significant effect on constructivism's arena of scholars and practitioners. Gergen has displayed an array of interests that span areas such as hostility, dissension, and social harmony; language related to communication; cultural appraisal; moral duty and obligation; reality and virtuality; stories about the self and identity; and assessment and research methodology. Mary McCanney Gergen, a social psychologist, collaborated with her husband Kenneth Gergen on various projects. For example, she coedited the book *Social Constructionism: A Reader* with him and cowrote *Social Constructionism: Entering the Dialogue*, which was published by the Taos Institute, an institute focused on issues related to constructionism. Because of her numerous achievements, especially those in the area of feminist thought, Penn State University bestowed the title of Professor Emerita on Mary Gergen, a title that allowed her, after retiring in 2006, to retain her status as a professor. Mary Gergen has made important and insightful contributions to constructivism and was cocreator of and responsible for, along with Kenneth, publishing the electronically distributed *Positive Aging Newsletter* dedicated to deconstructing/reconstructing views about aging while emphasizing its positive potentials. The newsletter is read by approximately 12,000 subscribers. (As a side note, another famous family member is Kenneth's brother David Gergen, who has served as a political advisor to several American presidents starting with Ronald Reagan. David Gergen has been a frequent commentator on current politics on the Cable News Network [CNN].)

In 1957, Kenneth Gergen received a BA from Yale University and in 1962 a PhD from Duke University in experimental social psychology. Gergen is a founder and a current administrator for the Taos Institute, an institute devoted to providing learning experiences for both students and professionals. Taos's specific goal is to discuss and research social constructionism as it exists in literature and in everyday application.

In general, Gergen's numerous publications have served as a catalytic spark that influenced the thinking and efforts of many other professionals. From the standpoint of an experimental social psychologist, early publications by Gergen questioned notions taken to represent crucial foundational presumptions that had been relied on to develop other ideas and explanations. For example, he questioned whether an entity referred to as a "coherent self" actually existed. Furthermore, in his 1973 article, "Social Psychology as History," appearing in The *Journal of Personality and Social Psychology*, he took the stance that those behavioral patterns examined and discussed by social psychologists were "historically perishable," which implied that once research findings and related conclusions were published, and widely accepted, those findings and conclusions became susceptible to an "illness" that one of the authors of this textbook refers to as "truth decay" (whose dominant symptom is a loss of validity over time). What was being proposed by Gergen had profound implications for the dispersal of what seemed to constitute acquired knowledge—that is, instead of contributing to an increased amount of solid, enduring knowledge, social psychologists were unintentionally involved in documenting findings that had the power to alter, in the future, what had been discovered in the first place. This can be illustrated by referring to a series of social psychology experiments carried out by Stanley Milgram, who reported in his 1963 study that participants were willing to respond as instructed by an authority figure even if it meant another person could suffer pain and injury. Milgram (1963) reported that 26 of the 40 participants in his study agreed to give another person a maximum electric shock equal to 450 volts, which, according to Milgram, was "two steps beyond the designation: Danger: Severe Shock" (p. 376). Based on Kenneth Gergen's assertion, once Milgram's findings about obedience to an authority were published and dispersed (it was discussed in psychology textbooks and in articles appearing in magazines and newspapers), the wide availability of his findings would eventually alter how the general population would respond to a perceived authority. Therefore, it is not possible for social psychology (and other fields in psychology) to create a lasting foundation of accurate knowledge; rather, psychology's predominant effectiveness resides in its ability to document events that serve to change how people respond to situations in the future. Interestingly, Gergen's seminal and controversial article later resulted in him being presented an award based on the article's high rate of citation in other publications.

Gergen also was credited with helping to create a crisis in social psychology because of a 1978 article he wrote on the topic of "generative theory" that appeared in *the Journal of Personality and Social Psychology*. In this article, Gergen suggested the possibility that theoretical suppositions do not actually lead to studying social interactions. He concluded that a theory should not be evaluated for accuracy but rather its likelihood to open up new areas of interests to act on. Gergen argued that an empirical approach to knowledge acquisition was not foolproof; in fact, such an approach should be considered seriously flawed. For Gergen, knowledge is never independent of its social context. It is social relationships that determine what is valuable, reasonable, and congruent with life. Empirical studies are incapable of such outcomes. Gergen expressed this notion by reworking René Descartes's famous dictum "I think therefore I am" to read "I am linked therefore I am." This rewording was intended to reroute psychology's focus by proposing that what we call "mental processes" are not exclusively "in the head" but rather emerge from the relationships we have with others (Gergen, 2006; Gergen, Schrader, & Gergen, 2008). Gergen believed that scientific theories were inescapably tainted by many factors such as moral beliefs, political implications, and the historical period during which they evolved and as a result should never be weighed in terms of their accuracy or truth-rendering potential. Instead their value should be determined by asking a question: Does the theory produce results that have pragmatic implications for humans?

Gergen served as president of two divisions of the American Psychological Association: Theoretical and Philosophical Psychology and Psychology and the Arts. In

Quotable Kenneth J. Gergen

- If we view our emotional expressions as culturally constructed and performed, we not only avoid the problems of stasis and imperialism, we also open new vistas of possibility. (p. 104)
- As we construct local realities and invest them with value, so do we also plant seeds of conflict. We come to see those who don't share in our way of life as lacking in some way—taste, sophistication, know-how, conscience, ability, intelligence, and the like. When we become committed to these realities and values, the potentials for conflicts are intensified. (p. 114)
- As elsewhere, we in the West typically presume the universality of our truths, reasons, and morals. Our scientific truths are not "ours" in particular, we hold, but candidates for universal truth. That the world is made up of atoms and individuals who possess emotions is not for us a matter of cultural belief. Any reasonable person would reach the same conclusion. Yet, as we presume reality and truth of our own beliefs, so do we trample on the realities of others. We unwittingly become cultural imperialists, suppressing and antagonizing. (p. 27)
- The idea of social construction may seem simple enough. But consider the consequences: if everything we consider real is socially constructed, then nothing is real unless people agree that it is. (p. 4)
- Our predictions should not be colored by what we hope to see; science focuses on what is the case, not what ought to occur from the researcher's standpoint. (p. 59)

Source: Gergen, K. J. (2009). *An invitation to social construction* (2nd ed.). London, UK: Sage.

addition to his many scholarly publications, he served as a reviewer for a large number of professional journals and he fulfilled the duties of an associate editor for two professional journals, *American Psychologist* and *Theory and Psychology*. Table 12.2 contains quotes from Kenneth J. Gergen.

Robert A. Neimeyer

Robert A. Neimeyer (born 1954), in addition to maintaining a private practice, is a professor in the Department of Psychology at the University of Memphis. He also serves as the editor in chief of the journal *Death Studies* (formerly known as *Death Education*) and the *Journal of Constructivist Psychology* (formerly known as *International Journal of Personal Construct Psychology*). Among the hundreds of scholarly works Neimeyer has published, books of high significance include *Advances in Personal Construct Psychology*, *Constructivist Psychotherapy*, and *Development of Personal Construct Psychology*. Neimeyer is a Fellow of the Division of Clinical Psychology in the American Psychological Association, and in 2006, he was awarded the George A. Kelly Award for Outstanding Contributions to Constructivist Psychology by the Constructivist Psychology Network.

Robert Neimeyer is widely known as a psychologist who chose to specialize in the field of *thanatology,* a specialty area that studies human reactions toward death that includes cognitions, emotions, and behavioral responses (thanatology also includes the study of factors associated with suicide). According to VandenBos (2007) prior to the 1960s, thanatology was almost exclusively confined to those who were religious-based practitioners and theologians. Even though existentialists' interest in death, as a central philosophical concern, predates the time period mentioned by VandenBos, after the 1960s there was a steady growth of interest by other groups of professionals. This increase of interest led to a better understanding of how the death of a loved one can negatively impact those left in a state of grief. Neimeyer has devoted his private practice to helping individuals and families, confronted with transitions and losses, to create ways to overcome their apprehension toward the future, states of disruptive mental confusion, intense and painful longing for the deceased, and the separation anxiety experienced by children. In addition, Neimeyer conducts grief workshops throughout the United States and in other countries.

Neimeyer has applied his constructivism approach to research, practice, and teaching; all three of these areas have been guided by his interest in grief, loss, and suicide intervention (Neimeyer, 2000, 2004, 2012; Neimeyer & Mahoney, 1995; Neimeyer, Winokuer, Harris, & Thornton, 2011). One of the most prominent concepts espoused by Neimeyer is that symptoms of a bereaved person are significant in terms of *meaning-making*. He believes that *meaning reconstruction* is a natural reaction to personal loss that resides at the center of the grieving process. Books by Neimeyer that deal with meaning reconstruction include *Death, Loss and Personal Reconstruction*, *Lessons of Loss*, and *Meaning Reconstruction and the Experience of Loss*. Neimeyer also provided a scientific oriented perspective that examined the association of grief with the response to trauma-related loss in his 2006 article "Complicated Grief and the Reconstruction of Meaning: Conceptual and Empirical Contributions to a Cognitive-Constructivist Model." In addition, Currier, Neimeyer, and Berman (2008) provided an overview of findings pertaining to the therapeutic effectiveness of working with those suffering the death of a loved one. It is important to note that Neimeyer's applied writings offer practitioners models and case descriptions that connect concepts to real-life situations related to losses. Finally, his 2009 book titled *Art of Longing: Selected Poems* was the result of Neimeyer joining with painters, photographers, and sculptors from various countries to produce a book that pictorially combines their creations with his poetry. Neimeyer's intention was to create a book that allows readers to meditate on their loss and grief.

Neimeyer's body of work provides an excellent description of how life stories can become fragmented as the result of a personal loss, and how processes pertaining to meaning-making can facilitate adaptation. He has suggested several principles to help facilitate the process of meaning-making during work with a client in grief therapy, such as assisting the client to discover a meaning in the loss, maintain a connection to the personal loss, and become reoriented to a new world as a result of the loss. He discusses how issues can be reintegrated into one's life. His approach to grief work, termed *meaning reconstruction*, advocates for healing that involves the processes of telling and retelling of stories (narratives) in which the departed person is part of these stories, and advocates for helping the client to establish new meanings that reaffirm and serve to reconstruct a life without the person who is gone. Table 12.3 contains comments made by Neimeyer.

Historical Context

▼ TABLE 12.3

Quotable Robert A. Neimeyer

- I have tried to use . . . theory in a generative way, to envision new constructivist practices—biographical, interview-based, reflective, metaphoric, poetic, and narrative—that help bereaved people take perspective on their losses and weave them into the fabric of their lives. (pp. 15–16)
- Some people narrate their losses in an "external" voice, focusing on objective events in a way that might be reported by an outside observer ("My mother died of emphysema in the fall. All of her children were there at her bedside, sitting in vigil. Nurses came and went, sometimes gesturing one or more family members into the hall for a medical update."). Others engage in a more "internal" and emotional narrative process ("When my mother lay dying, I felt a cascade of emotions, from hope, to despair and loneliness, to deep sadness. But above all, I had a sense of awe and privilege to be there."). Still others present a more "reflexive," significance-seeking account ("My mother's death made me aware of the fragile order of life, and the critical importance of sharing these life transitions as a family."). (p. 15)
- The emergence of extremely high risk behaviors, such as actual acts of self-injury sufficient to mandate one-on-one observation, was predicted not only by hopelessness, not only by self-negativity and impaired problem-solving, but also by the unique impending disorganization of patients' construct systems regarding the social world. (p. 13)

Source: Neimeyer. R. A. (2004). Constructions of death and loss: Evolution of a research program. *Personal Construct Theory & Practice, 1,* 8–20.

After the World Wars, psychologists were focused on the development and use of empirical, scientific methodology to support conclusions, a focus aimed at uncovering evidence-based findings that could be verified by others. Thus, the aim of psychological research was generally perceived to be discovering effects that always occurred if certain conditions were present, that is, laws that governed human behavior. At the center of psychology, represented by behaviorism (e.g., B. F. Skinner) and cognitive psychology (e.g., Albert Ellis), was found an unshakable assumption that psychologists were on a path to find out exactly "what makes people tick." The world seemed to be knowable, a knowability that was within reach.

Constructivism

Postmodernists arrived with their theory of constructivism and turned the assumptions of science on their head (Neimeyer, 1995). Rather than an objectively knowable world that can be captured by science, constructivists argued that the divergent realities held by people made the reductionist approach to understanding humans a literal impossibility. Thus, systems built on scientific verifiable results that can be generalized to all humans are destined to fail. Compared to the assertion of universal truths, divergent realities are assumed to be socially constituted, historically situated, and in which "language constitutes the structures of social reality" (p. 13).

Before constructivism existed, as we know it today, there was personal construct theory, a theory developed in the 1950s by the psychologist George Kelly. George Kelly began to confront the psychological needs of farming communities in the Midwest affected by the Dust Bowl and Great Depression. He helped farmers construct fictional identities to be utilized for short periods of time. Although this was an intervention aimed at alleviating the stress of the circumstances, Kelly also encouraged the individuals in these depressed farming communities to adapt their fictional identities to different ways of living that could then be assessed to determine if such constructed identities were viable. This practice foreshadowed narrative therapy strategies that would be popularized decades later (Neimeyer & Bridges, 2003).

Constructivism focuses on the creative, meaning-making aspect of an individual's thoughts. There is also an emphasis on the subjective construction of reality and how past perceptions affect the way people define and perceive their generated reality. No two realities are alike as each individual constructs personal meanings. Constructed realities represent a multitude of possible ways that individuals can categorize people, places, and environments in their experiential world.

According to Neimeyer (1995), an individual possesses an innate propensity to perceive patterns (schemes or configuration) in the world around him. Furthermore, the individual is subsequently affected by the way he cognitively organizes the perceived patterns that pertain to himself, others, contexts, and by the way these unique perspectives—ways of thinking about something—are arranged (Brabender & Fallon, 2009). This process of methodically organizing patterns supports a person's individualized realities and associated constructs. A specific understanding of the realities that a person harbors can be obtained when they are shared by this person through interactions carried out within his immediate community.

Even though constructivism strongly endorses creative cognitive activity, it claims not to endorse solipsism, that is, mind over matter. (According to philosophers, *solipsism* means an individual can only be certain of her own mind existing, and because this is the only certainty, then the individual can assume that everything else, including other people, in the universe are just constructs of her mind.) Constructivism takes a pragmatic position that people must adopt a position that corresponds with their physical and social environments (i.e., the material world). The criterion for such a corresponding relationship includes the degree to which a person's constructed knowledge anticipates events, promotes an awareness of one's freedom to exert desired change, and it corresponds to what constitutes the person's material world, or as Neimeyer (1995) stated, this involves "pragmatically useful organizing schemes for guiding human action" (p. 15).

Social Constructionism

A related line of thinking is *social constructionism*. This form of constructionism was advocated by Gergen and Gergen (1991). According to them, this form of constructivism's epistemology (i.e., nature of knowledge) represented a socially based acquisition or knowledge. Specifically, the Gergens drew attention to the important role that language and other forms of communication (e.g., body language) plays in creating socially embedded meanings. For example, there are a number of social processes tied to communicating one's power, such as wearing tailored suits or expensive jewelry, climbing the corporate ladder, or driving an expensive car. These avenues allow for socially embedded meanings to be communicated, and as a result they have an impact on how one's experiences are accounted for and explained. Thus, attention needs to be on both the obvious and the subtle meanings that language conveys, as people collectively (in their local communities) generate descriptions and explanations for the world they inhabit. In contrast to the "applicable universal knowledge" offered by science or other sources of authority, it is the local-based knowledge created by an individual's language of self-reflexivity that requires our attention. Self-reflexivity represents interpretive articulations that pertain to the generation of knowledge, which typically includes a consideration of whether a power differential has contaminated the value of the knowledge generated (D'Cruz, Gillingham, & Melendez, 2007).

Because human experience rarely seems to unfold according to one's plan, to make sense of any unanticipated or off-kilter situation encountered, a person constructs a "story" to explain why things went askew, but these stories can easily change in subtle (and sometimes dramatic) ways when repeated over time. For example, the meaning and memories a client has of her fight with her husband the previous week is likely to change several times when she is asked about it (e.g., her story will differ depending on who is asking or the context in which the story is repeated). Even if a reality show had contracted with the couple to record the couple's marital life, what would a therapist do if the couple remembered an argument that cannot be found in any of the recorded episodes? Even if the therapist came across a visual or auditory recording of the argument, it would not furnish a complete picture of what had taken place; for example, it would not include the context leading up to the argument or what took place after the argument (Peterson & Peterson, 1997). This would force the therapist to admit that visual or auditory records of life do not show all that is taking place, and if a fight is found, it only represents one portion of what was involved in the couple's argument and it would fail to provide a holistic understanding (Peterson & Peterson, 1997). The point is that knowledge is relative, a type of relativeness that helps to create different interpretations or even contradictory interpretations in different contexts (societal, family, and personal). It is through reflexive knowledge-construction, facilitated by a "narrative" therapist, that a client discovers her inconsistent roles in various contexts of an interpersonal nature.

Social constructionism's aim is to displace "grand narratives" that are based on research-derived knowledge that claims objectivity and replace them with *local narratives* that reflect a specific context, culture, and community. These are narratives that include other persons, local institutions, and what is culturally shared—these are aspects of existence that are also immersed in a historical time frame that determines an individual's perspective moment to moment. Furthermore, it is assumed that a client is continually constructing reality and is producing new knowledge via a socially infused process. Thus, to better understand social constructionism, one must accept that theoretical assertions have a pluralistic quality not found to be present in what traditionally have been considered to represent infallible guiding information (Peterson & Peterson, 1997).

Social constructionism has sociological roots that began with the *sociology of knowledge* (i.e., the examination of the link between thinking and the social context within which that thinking manifest) proposed by Max Scheler in the 1920s and further developed by Karl Mannheim in the early 1990s (Barber, 1993; Karácsony, 2008). These were German philosophers who questioned basic principles or beliefs held by institutions such as religion. It was not long after Max Scheler that sociocultural forces replaced "purely" historical forces (e.g., Hitler's Germany or World War II) as the central factor in directing people's behavior, course of events, and the relevance of knowledge in various situations (Hruby, 2001).

Although postmodernism did not find strong expression in American psychology until the 1990s, its roots can be seen in the works of Immanuel Kant (1724–1804), Giambattista Vico (1668–1774), and Hans Vaihinger (1852–1933) (see Urmson & Rée, 1989). These philosophers claimed that knowledge was "an active structuring of experience, rather than a passive assimilation of 'things in themselves,' uncontaminated by human knowing" (Neimeyer & Bridges, 2003, p. 273). Influenced by these ideas, psychologist George Kelly began the psychology of personal constructs in the 1930s and 1940s. Kelly believed that humans form construct systems that create order and meaning in their lives and help them determine their reactions to events they encounter. In addition, before the postmodernists formulated and put forth their explanations, William James, John Dewey, and George Herbert Mead proposed a somewhat similar philosophical position in America, a position that William James christened *pragmatism* (Haggbloom et al., 2002). All three criticized what was called foundationalism (i.e., whose tenets were considered true and self-dependent on scrutiny), essentialism (i.e., it is possible to discover universal human truths or transhistorically valid principles), reductionist science (i.e., belief that complex phenomena can be reduced to their complex ingredients), and mechanical determinism (i.e., the universe, including humans, are essentially machines whose operations are knowable through science). These philosophers highlighted the priority of the intersubjective, social, and communal dimensions of experience, language, and inquiry. The word *inquiry* (or disciplined inquiry) is used by social constructionists in opposition to deductive, positivistic empirical research.

The term *pragmatism* has often been applied to social constructionism and has even been referred to as *neopragmatism* by Polkinghorne (1992). Polkinghorne (1992) stated that the litmus test to determine whether knowledge is of a pragmatic nature is to ask "whether it functions successfully to fulfill intended purposes. . . . The more open we are to increasing and revising our patterns, and the greater the variety of organizing schemes we have at our command, the more likely we are to capture the diversity . . . that exists in the world" (pp. 151–152). The neopragmatic scientist is one that expects science to be part of clinical inquiries (via "curious" questions), and the neopragmatic scientist is one whose practical applications lead to successful outcomes.

Postmodernism is a reaction to modernist beliefs that grew out of the Age of Enlightenment of the 18th century. Modernism placed full faith in the rational human mind. From a modernist perspective, cognitive processes can be objectively studied (e.g., checking off daily negative thoughts in a checklist), and language has the ability to accurately convey the content of one's mind (such as an individual's responses to cognitive, intelligence, and objective and projective personality tests). However, modernists also agree that a person's presentations are usually subjective and, therefore, inaccurate. In therapy, a client's distorted thinking must be corrected by a therapist with a rational perspective because the therapist, educated in research, recognizes the underlying cognitive causes of and cures for psychopathology. Constructivists, on the other hand, would consider client presentations as narratives of his own local realities and not as truths or distortions.

From the postmodern perspective, the modernist tendency is to elevate knowledge gained through scientific research, an approach that places hierarchical value on rationalness and devalues individuals' stories or narratives about their world. According to postmodernism, there is no such thing as unchanging truths obtained via studying natural phenomena (this includes humans) and isolating their properties, determining the relationships among those properties isolated and how outside factors might affect those properties. The described procedure is dependent on using empirical, scientific methods (i.e., logical positivism). Constructivists believe that all "human 'realities' are necessarily personal, cultural, and linguistic constructs—although they are no less substantial or important for this reason" (Neimeyer & Bridges. 2003, p. 275). If there is an objective reality, it is considered to be outside of human consciousness and language (Gergen, 2001).

Gergen (2011) cites three tenets that have shaped the development of theoretical social constructionism.

1. Social philosophies that challenged the realities taken for granted by the general population arose in an effort to reveal the political goals that institutional realities seek to achieve (e.g., Hitler's anti-Semitic propaganda that initially hid the desire to exterminate all Jews).

2. Inherent linguistic and rhetorical routes in academic science highlight the various forms that language can take for scientists and other experts to use so they can stake a claim as to what equates as important knowledge. It turns out that this inherent power of language does not always lead to consequential findings; rather, it is mostly used to create abstract structures so that scientific findings and conclusions can be pinned to those creations. We are then told by the same people who reported the findings and related conclusions that we are to trust them when they say what has been reported is to be considered as "evidence" for the existence of an objective reality that applies to everyone.

3. The final tenet, according to Gergen (2011), was stimulated by Thomas Kuhn's *The Structure of Scientific Revolutions*. In this work, Kuhn claimed that the thinking carried out by scientists is governed by a specific paradigm. Furthermore, in Kuhn's opinion, the findings of science do not come about because of some worldly consensus concerning the importance of scientific findings; rather, they come about because of a type of communal negotiation that takes place among scientists who determine how available resources (e.g., government grants) are to be used. An example of such an occurrence is the development of NASA and the burst of space science in the 1960s, 1970s, and 1980s.

Narrative Theory

Narrative theory is grounded in postmodern social constructionism theory and proposes that meaning is created through storytelling, a process in which language is crucial (Bruner, 2004). Even though narratives are considered unique to each individual (Polkinghorne, 2004), they are considered to be socially constructed for two reasons: (1) The language in which a story is told is itself manufactured and given meaning through social processes (Bruner, 2004), and (2) narratives are "guided by unspoken implicit cultural models of what self-hood should be, might be—and, of course, shouldn't be" (p. 4). Ultimately, "self-making" is viewed as the process of both forming and sharing narratives (Bruner, 2004).

Within narrative theory, voice is considered to be "the way in which a story is told . . . [and] represents a weaving together of multiple voices" (McLeod, 2004, p. 22). Personal authorial voice occurs when individuals are active tellers of their stories. This form of voice allows individuals to feel that they have agency, that is, the capacity to exert personal power in their lives (Ahearn, 2001). Narrative strategies include the use of metaphors. The therapy process includes locating metaphors within clients' narratives and using them as tools to enable clients to externalize problems that they need not feel guilty for creating (Legowski & Brownlee, 2001). Also, since because a basic aim of narrative therapy is to change problematic stories, metaphors may be used in ways to help clients reconstruct the stories they carry with them into therapy. Specifically, metaphors can provide clients with a sense of personal, authorial voice to paint a picture of how they see their situation. Such a personal, authorial voice can be fostered through a careful selection of metaphors that offer clients a language that is congruent with their experience and "enhance the client's perception of being heard" (Wickman, Daniels, White, & Fesmire, 1999, p. 393).

Conclusion About Constructivism and Social Constructionism

Whereas social constructionism pays close attention to the client's social environment, pure constructivism remains focused on the meaning-making constructs produced by a client. The two positions are neither identical nor mutually exclusive; rather, they depend on one another. Postmodern therapists choose the theory they will call to the forefront when working with a client, while simultaneously keeping aspects of other theory in mind to be called on if needed. Table 12.4 provides a comparison of constructivism and social constructionism.

▼ TABLE 12.4

Comparison of Constructivism and Social Constructionism

Constructivism*	Social Constructionism
1. Origins are tied to philosophy, experimental psychology, and developmental psychology. 2. Reality is constructed individually. 3. Emphasis is on the processes of individual cognition. 4. Focus is on the meaning-making process of the individual. • Reality is subjectively constructed. • No two persons' realities are alike. • Perceived patterns/schemes of the world support people's constructions and individual realities. • People must achieve an adequate fit with their physical and social realities; thus, an emphasis on pragmatism is a critical element of constructivism.	1. Historical roots are tied to sociology. 2. Reality is constructed linguistically and socially. • Social constructionism highlights how language and various social conventions influence the accounts of people (what they claim). • Descriptions and explanations are collectively developed by people in their local communities. • People's language of self-reflection interprets the social world. • Knowledge is relative, subjective, and pluralistic, leading to diverse and even contradictory personal realities. • Clients present local narratives that reflect a specific culture, context, and community. • A heavy emphasis is placed on the social aspect comprising knowledge, the "situatedness," or social context that impinges on a person's observations. • People are challenged by inconsistent social roles imposed by interpersonal and cultural contexts.

*The terms *constructivism* and *constructionism* are generally considered interchangeable (VandenBos, 2007). The term *constructivist* is used in this chapter in a generic manner to refer to an adherent to any one of the three positions (i.e., constructionism, social constructionism, and narrative therapy), unless greater specificity is seen as required.

Basic Concepts

Contemporary constructivist thought from the 1990s has ties to philosophy that called attention to an active mind that organizes information and produces meaning (reality is created, not discovered as claimed by science). As Gergen (2001) puts it, "To tell the truth . . . is not to furnish an accurate picture of what actually happened but to participate in a set of social conventions, a way of putting things sanctioned within a given form of life" (p. 806). Language does not have inherent meaning but is given value and meaning within a specific context. The concepts provided in this section are endorsed by adherents to both constructivism and social constructionism.

Self

The self is relative. The self "represents the distillation of our shifting efforts to engage the social world" (Neimeyer & Bridges, 2003, p. 276). When we detect what is called "self," we are detecting a narrative derived from our interaction with other persons. William Lax (1992), a social constructionist therapist, describes it as our discourse with others. Thus, the self, who we are, is displayed each time a person repeats her story with others. Although people's narratives about their selves seem to have a one-to-one correspondence with what is called "real," they are actually constructs (nothing more, nothing less) that arise out of people's experiences and various environmental, cultural, and genetic factors. From this perspective, *people are their constructs*. What we can glean from this is that the behaviors people engage in throughout the day are much more likely to be situationally driven than internally driven. If this is correct, then behavior may be more in flux and open to change than we typically assume.

According to Gergen (1991), there was a quixotic view concerning the self that was held during the 19th and 20th centuries that essentially figuratively portrayed the self as a window to understand the complexities that make a person a person or, as Gergen stated, the "world of the deep interior" (p. 20). Congruent with intrapsychic therapy and appearing in the 18th-century Age of Enlightenment, this view emphasized an individual's beliefs, opinions, and intentions and elevated discovered knowledge and industrial progress. It was believed that human beings were knowable in a material sense and that human problems had a remedy. Conversely, in the postmodern view, people are a "plurality of voices vying for the right to reality," and their beliefs about reality are a "product of perspective" (Gergen, 1991, p. 7). Humans are tied to context (historical and present) and as such are "in a state of continuous construction and reconstruction," designated by the presence of "reflexive questioning" (i.e., where previously gathered information is incorporated into a question) and "irony" (i.e., incongruity between what is expected and what actually occurs; words spoken/written might convey one meaning, but they have an opposite outcome than what is conveyed, e.g., voting laws written to protect voting from fraudulent voters, but whose language is used to prevent members of a minority from voting in an election; Gergen, 1991, p. 7). From the previous discussion it is reasonable to conclude that the self of constructivism is relative, is more than one in number, is local and contextual, and falls within the limits of possible experience, meaning that the self is immanent.

Meaning-Making

Whereas postmodern therapists acknowledge that there are biological and genetic factors that influence psychopathology, and some believe that diagnosis can be useful at times, they recognize that such perspectives are culturally and historically constructed and must be used cautiously. Pathology and distress usually arise when there are "challenges to the client's meaning-making process" (Neimeyer & Bridges, 2003, p. 279). This occurs when a person has not revised his meaning-making systems to adjust to changes in relationships and environments. Meaning-making systems are often formed around early experiences and relationships and are maintained despite life changes. Because there is no ultimate truth and tangible self to be discovered, the focus becomes one's constructs and processes of meaning- making, which determine how one interacts with the world and views oneself.

Local Knowledge

The dictionary meaning of *local* refers to the space and parameters of a particular place or locality. In social constructionism, local knowledge refers to the common language spoken and the process that is embedded in one's local community that is used to understand life events, relationships, and the self. Thus, the exchange between the therapist and client will have a specific local nature. What transpires between the therapist and client is to be considered *open* rather than *closed;* that is, it lacks the type of control typical of psychology which seeks to apply generalizable research findings to therapy settings (Peterson & Peterson, 1997, p. 215). Local cultures serve as a manifold means for people to connect; these cultures are responsible for fashioning numerous narratives that characterize individuality. People are pragmatic in nature and repeat what works which includes identities that they rely on and the social roles that accompany those identities. Repeating various social roles is likely seen by the client as required to protect local imaginings, cultures, opinions, and people. Everyone participates in various local communities that embrace established stories and manner of imagining and thinking that allow for everyone to perceive themselves as comprehended and of significance to others in a particular community (Peterson & Peterson, 1997).

The Therapeutic Process

The client's story serves as the organizing principle, and narratives supply the characteristics and contexts for a client's constructions and the client's account of experience. Knowledge and awareness, and every other quality related to human experience, are viewed from the perspective of a storytelling client. How a client experiences therapy is influenced by the self-knowledge summoned through the collaborative interactions that take place between the client and the therapist. The therapist is better thought of as fulfilling the role of a coauthor since both individuals are involved in the process of rescripting the client's narrative-based problem (Guidano, 1995).

Narrative Therapy

Narrative therapy goes hand in hand with constructivism and social constructionism. In response to the rigidity of the modern scientific era, Michael White and David Epston of

New Zealand developed narrative therapy, a process-focused paradigm that rejects the scientific approach. This philosophy identifies the power imbalance in the dominant therapist-receiving-client relationship and empowers the client as a competent individual with the power to heal herself (Carr, 1998). To establish the client as "healer," narrative therapists apply constructivist ideas, removing pathology from within the individual and instead viewing pathology as a product of how that individual has come to understand herself through current and past social narratives. The theory of narrative therapy proposes that people interpret their reality through conversations with others and that cultural structures and values, established through interpersonal interactions, create each person's identity (Polkinghorne, 2000). These conversations become the stories that define each individual's interpretation of her personal timeline that starts in the past and ends in the future, placing the client currently somewhere between the two extremes. The client's stories become problematic by the way people impose meaning on them. Narrative therapy provides the opportunity for change conversations, resulting in the replacing of earlier stories of perceived reality with preferred personal constructs. Narrative therapy was established to help people remove themselves from the cultural stories people find themselves in by creating a new self-generated story more representative of one's individuality (Polkinghorne, 2000). Narrative therapy, thus, might tend more toward individualism, whereas culturally sensitive practices, by comparison, might tend recognize collectivism. The bicultural integration of both individualism and collectivism may not be simple, particularly because these two orientations or belief systems arise in contrasting cultures, Western and Eastern (Roysircar, 2009; Roysircar & Pignatiello, 2011). Next, the respective therapy processes of constructivism and social constructionism are discussed.

Constructivism

Goals. Goals are almost solely identified by the client; in fact, the goals are often known to the client long before entering therapy (Neimeyer & Bridges, 2003). What becomes apparent is the client is often in a state of suffering, and his way of being in the world is distressing. The goals of therapy are revealed to the therapist over time and often altered throughout the process of therapy as the client's stories unfold (Neimeyer & Bridges, 2003).

Goals that arise are often determined through moment-to-moment interactions between the client and therapist. Careful attention is paid to the client's use of language and nonverbal communication in attempts to identify areas where the client wishes to gain more self-knowledge. The therapist's manner of paying attention to the tier that comprises a client's communication "ensures that the therapist is attending at the appropriate level of the epigenetic [i.e., organically evolving] model, with due attention to personal, interpersonal, and cultural factors of relevance to their immediate work" (Neimeyer & Bridges, 2003, p. 290). In addition, the constructivist therapist emphasizes overarching goals that relate to therapeutic outcomes, such as client empowerment, relational openness, self-awareness, and ability to enact her preferred self-narrative (Neimeyer & Bridges, 2003).

Therapist's Role. From a distance it might seem that the constructivist therapist is less active than most. In actuality, the constructivist therapist is active internally and externally

(Neimeyer & Bridges, 2003). The therapist is attentive and continually makes a concerted effort to ascertain the client's current state of being. The constructivist therapist is always ready to intervene, posing open-ended questions that are aimed at finding deeper meaning. The therapist is process-oriented while he enacts an empathic, respectful, and fully engaged approach to the revealed narrative and to the self that is unfolding (Neimeyer & Bridges, 2003). The constructivist therapist does not decide which meanings to attach to the client's narrative, but instead guides the client in identifying meanings of personal relevance. The therapist is a representation of the social world of the client, who then is able to try out preferred selves with the therapist (Neimeyer & Bridges, 2003).

Client's Role. The client is expected to be active and engaged. It is essentially the client's self-knowledge and activity level that produces long-standing change (Neimeyer & Bridges, 2003). Although each client–therapist relationship is perceived to be unique, there are two common expectations: One is that the client relies on self-reflection throughout, and the second is that the client fulfills the role of an active contributor to what occurs during therapy sessions. The client is expected to engage in the process of therapy by attributing meaning to patterns of being in the world. The meanings identified by the client can then be explored by both client and therapist to trigger insight, which can lead to changes in behavior.

Assessment. The type of exploratory assessment process utilized examines the client's ways of being, that is, his relationship with the environment, significant others, and himself. Thus, the assessment procedure utilized is a multisystemic approach (Neimeyer & Bridges, 2003). Assessment involves understanding the client's world of meaning. Because constructivism is a process-oriented intervention, the assessment process becomes one of therapeutic value in and of itself and is not solely for diagnostic purposes (Neimeyer & Bridges, 2003). The client and therapist collaboratively explore a variety of salient themes in the client's narrative, related areas of struggle, and his available internal and social resources. The therapist and client also determine together what the client's ideal self or preferred self looks like (Neimeyer & Bridges, 2003).

- **_Laddering in Assessment:_** A constructivist assessment technique, laddering, involves the "unpacking" of a client's symptoms and how they are tied with her sense of self (Neimeyer & Bridges, 2003). Laddering can assist the client and therapist in identifying personal constructs that involve ambiguity. For instance, if a client both loves her father and fears him, the process of laddering can help the client explore which feeling is more dominant and what the implications are for feeling both (Neimeyer & Bridges, 2003). The process of laddering is composed of a series of straightforward questions aimed at identifying "both ends" to any construct that the client identifies. Next, the therapist would seek to determine which end the client tends to associate herself (Neimeyer & Bridges, 2003). In this example (i.e., loving and fearing one's father), the therapist might ask the client if she prefers to love or fear and might wonder if the client wishes to be more of one or the other. The client and therapist together can develop a hierarchy of meaning through the laddering process. This assessment tool allows for the client to acquire a strong sense of agency, with the therapist's questions prompting the client to understand the meaning behind her own personal constructs.

Therapeutic Change. Narrative therapy creates an opportunity for the reauthoring of the client's narrative (i.e., story of self) by focusing on elements of experience that have been trivialized by others or by the dominant culture. Thus, through reauthoring of one's narrative, a client's identity, lives, and problems can be changed. Clients internalize unreasonable societal standards and believe that societal goals therein are attainable. Therapists help clients examine the dominant narratives of their lives in light of power and oppression that have subjugated the individual into continual isolation, evaluation, and comparison. The therapist helps the client to develop an alternative narrative of the marginalized self to replace the dominant narrative of pain, thus releasing the client's suppressed narrative, which brings about change.

Techniques and Strategies

Narrative therapy is a popular practice of constructivists. In narrative therapy, the client's story emerges in the context of the interactions between the therapist and client. The therapist acts as a joint author (coauthor) of the client's new narrative. In a sense, it would be impossible not to fulfill this action because, according to this theory, even the presence of the therapist alone has an influence on the narrative that develops (Lax, 1992). Often, clients have established fixed narratives that can hinder them from seeing their lives from new perspectives and from addressing problems that have arisen. Therefore, the therapist's role is to co-construct with the client new stories, which are somewhat different from previously held stories. Together, they expose and deconstruct the client's dominant discourse—the person's mode of organizing knowledge, ideas, or experience that is rooted in language— and replace it with an alternative narrative. Instead of coercing the client into adopting new narratives, the therapist merely facilitates the conversation (Lax, 1992).

For the narrative therapist, culture is a "supportive framework within which people can construct a viable sense of identity, but, on the other hand, limiting the repertoire of possibilities that they can endorse or even perceive" (Neimeyer & Bridges, 2003, p. 280). The therapist is careful not to impose her own culture onto the client, but rather to examine the supportive and oppressive qualities of a client's culture.

A client's personal history is not remembered like it is in a psychodynamic theory, but instead is re-created and constructed as stories. According to Lax (1992), "Insight can be considered merely a new understanding which makes sense to the person at the moment in time: it is not the discovery of some truth about one's existence" (p. 74). The therapist offers a certain perspective to the client's situation, and the client either rejects this view or finds that it fits. This view is not considered the "correct" perspective but is one of many ways of perceiving a client's life, which can aid in the development of new narratives that allow the client to see and address life situations differently. Clients develop "ever more comprehensive and adequate theories of life, as authoritative 'authors' of their own life stories who selectively draw on the storehouse of available cultural forms to craft satisfying ways of 'moving forward' at individual and social levels" (Neimeyer & Bridges, 2003, p. 280). Therefore, narrative therapy represents an ongoing, collaborative process between the therapist and client in which old narratives give way to new narratives for addressing difficulties and living more fully. The specific interventions (Carr, 1998) used by therapists to achieve such a goal are described next.

Externalizing the Problem. An important step in reauthoring a problematic narrative is externalizing the problem, which is done by asking questions and using language that refers to the problem as external to the client, including possibly giving the problem a name. The problem is thus reframed. Rather than being helpless, as a result of such an interaction, the client has gained power over his problem.

Excavating Unique Outcomes. The act of "digging out" unique outcomes is important because these are past experiences that defy the themes of the dominant narrative creating problems for the client. For example, a client who describes herself as depressed and ineffective has surely experienced agency at some point. Such outcomes did not have to be dramatic in nature; they can be as simple as a period of time when she succeeded in bringing her children to school every morning. Eliciting those shining moments in a client's life helps to accelerate a change process because it reminds the client that she has the ability to author her own life.

Thickening New Plots. After unique outcomes are excavated, it is useful for the therapist to ask questions that place those positive moments of agency in a context. The linking of successful experiences create a larger story that marks the beginning of change in the client's self-narrative.

Linking the New Story to the Past and Extending It to the Future. This step in the therapeutic process involves asking the client questions that result in the client finding stories from his past, when he felt isolated or marginalized, and then having the client picture different ways of experiencing the future that are congruent with his newly developed story.

Outsider Witness Groups. Social resources such as members of the client's family and individuals that comprise the client's outside social structure can be called on to assist in the narrative change process. When the client has begun to link situations with the new story, it is important that she share what has been archived with people outside of therapy or bring people into therapy to share the new narrative and also work to further solidify the newly created story outside of the therapeutic encounter.

Therapeutic Documents. A powerful technique is to utilize documentation in narrative therapy, such as providing the client with letters or process notes written by the therapist and using letters composed by the client that are provided to one or more of the client's communities of associates. The utilization of documentation in this manner involves a collaborative effort.

Re-membering Practices and Incorporation. In grief work, rather than encouraging a client to deal with grief by putting the deceased behind him, *re-membering* facilitates the presence and incorporation of a loved one. This form of therapeutic reconnection encourages a client to hold the loved one close rather than forget the countless ways the deceased connected to his life story.

Taking-It-Back Practices. Here the client is invited by the therapist to share her therapeutic experience with others. This type of sharing has the positive effect of strengthening the client's story, making it a more powerful guide for the person's future social interactions.

Social Constructionism

Goals. The goals of the social constructionist and positive/virtues-based therapy include becoming what one truly wants, much like an ideal self (Wong, 2006). Often in psychotherapy, goals surround a negativistic perspective, such as lessening depression or reducing self-harm behavior. In therapy's virtues-based view, the client's language is of utmost importance; in contrast, using the expert-based language of pathology only fosters more pathology (Wong, 2006). White and Epston (1989) believed that symptoms can have an oppressive quality tied to one's society. Instead, a depressed person might choose the goal to have a more meaningful existence or to obtain a higher level of fulfillment from his job or relationships. Similarly, a goal for a client engaging in self-harm behavior might be to care for herself more frequently in different ways of living and knowing and to seek enjoyment and love or any variety of strength-focused goals.

Therapist's Role. A key characteristic of the social constructionist's role is to help decipher the meaning behind clients' subjective experiences. Wong (2006) asserts that because clients typically are unaware of the strengths they possess, part of a therapist's responsibility is to help clients identify what inherent assets they already have in an attempt to expand on their strengths. The therapist's role is also to recognize and identify how cultural and systemic forces influence both the therapist and client and which strengths they denote as important to have and access (Wong, 2006). The therapist, additionally, is responsible for being continually aware of her own morals because the therapist's perception of what is and is not acceptable can negatively influence the therapeutic encounter (Wong, 2006).

Client's Role. The client's role within a social constructionist, virtues-based therapy that rests on the therapist's integrity is one of high activity. The client is expected to share her subjective experience along with the ways in which she makes meaning out of experiences. The client and the therapist are equally active. Wong (2006) describes this situation as one where the therapist and client are inseparable. With the therapist's guidance, the client is expected to develop positive goals and actively pursue the desired state of being (Wong, 2006).

Assessment. Integrating social constructionism and positive psychology (which focuses on psychological states such as joy and felicity and the characteristics of strengths) allows for a more balanced view of the individual (Roysircar, 2012; Seligman, 2002). Both positions' center of attention is on virtues and strengths of the person instead of limitations and psychopathology, although both positions recognize how diagnoses can be used as a way in which clients can make meaning of their suffering. Social constructionism provides avenues for clients to understand how their pain can be the result of a greater societal influence (Wong, 2006). As noted by Wong (2006), integrating the two perspectives allows for a more holistic view of suffering—internal traits (positive psychology) and external causes (social constructionism)—which would be appealing to managed care systems and allow for clients to rely on their own internal resources (e.g., resilience [positive psychology]) to face everyday social challenges. Much like in constructivism, social constructionists assess together with their clients what and who they would like to become and how to promote their inner strengths to achieve this ideal way of being (Wong, 2006).

Therapeutic Change. Contrary to the rationalist's point of view via Albert Ellis, the client does not have incorrect beliefs that a therapist must challenge in order for the client to adopt what the therapist sees as a more accurate view of the world. Instead, the therapist and client function as a team that coordinates its efforts to co-construct fresh, adaptive narratives (Lax, 1992).

Techniques and Strategies

Together, the client and the strength-focused social constructionist seek to make new meanings out of a client's personal experiences. How clients live and interpret their pain and suffering will transform such subjective experiences, allowing for greater life fulfillment and purpose. Wong (2006) states that combining a strength-promoting approach with social constructionism involves four phases in treatment: explicitizing, envisioning, empowering, and evolving.

- ***Explicitizing Phase***. In this first phase, the client and therapist decipher inner strengths possessed by the client, strengths that are believed to be inherent within the client's presenting problems. Often, the therapist will validate any painful experiences the client brings into a session, while pointing out the strengths that are implicit within the narrative about client pain. For instance, if a client were describing a severe trauma that occurred during childhood, the therapist might point out to the client how far he has come since then and is more so thriving than merely surviving.
- ***Envisioning Phase***. During the envisioning phase, the client and therapist together determine what strengths the client wishes to expand on and develop further. The therapist might ask a client about a particular goal, such as the desire to be fulfilled in life, and then ask what strengths are needed for the client to achieve this goal. The therapist would want to know the idiosyncratic meaning that the client applies to any given character strengths so that these hold personal significance for the client.
- ***Empowering Phase***. The empowering phase occurs when the client is given opportunity to develop the character strengths that are desired and needed to accomplish the goals she developed. One technique that is used (Wong, 2006) is to allow the client to write to herself as someone who is admired, while all the while describing how it would be beneficial to possess such strengths. Another aspect of this phase is acknowledging how situational variables or external resources play into character strengths.
- ***Evolving Phase***. The final phase is the termination, or evolving phase. This phase is heavily focused on the client's growth over the course of therapy and how building on strengths is a life-long endeavor.

Multiculturalism and Social Justice

Therapist Cultural Self-Awareness

There is limited reference in the postmodern literature concerning a therapist's own cultural biases and the possible effects of such biases on the therapist's ability to facilitate and co-construct narratives with a client. According to Lakes, López, and Garro (2006), handling the problem constructed by a client requires, from the start of therapy, a cultural based process that incorporates both the client's and the therapist's worldviews. As Lakes et al. (2006) explain, "[When] clinical encounters are successful it is because the practitioner and client are able to read each other well or create a shared narrative" (p. 383). Because the therapist and client are to co-construct a new narrative, the therapist has to be particularly cautious of imposing his own worldview onto the client, especially in situations that involve a cultural or ethnic experience different from the therapist's.

Therefore, as the literature on multicultural counseling competence emphasizes, the therapist must become aware of her biases, values, and assumptions because, left unexamined, these will often manifest in the therapeutic process and hinder effective treatment (Roysircar & Gill, 2009). As an example, a White American female therapist might become aware of her own subtle disapproval of Justine's (case vignette at the beginning of this chapter) choice to be a stay-at-home mother, rooted in her own belief that women should not depend on men for financial security. Or the therapist's countertransference might be that Justine has the privilege to be a stay-at-home mother, while the therapist has no such entitlement as a single parent. If the therapist is not aware of such potential personal judgments, she might subtly encourage Justine to explore her story of dissatisfaction with her choice to stay at home and deemphasize its positive aspects, thus prompting Justine to develop a new negative story, which, otherwise, might not have occurred.

Understanding the Client's Worldview

Understanding the worldview, religion, and cultural background of a client aids in helping therapists gain an awareness of their own stereotypes about those different from themselves. The deeper the understanding is, the more a therapist benefits. In addition, the possibility of pathologizing the client is decreased if the therapist becomes aware of what is considered "normal" in the client's culture and community (Roysircar, 2005, 2013), but it is also important for a therapist to realize that having a little knowledge does not guarantee a fuller understanding of a client's actual situation. For example, if a therapist only knows that it is normal for Asian Indian families to be closely knit, the therapist might assume that an emotional divide between two members of an Asian Indian family is not normal. However, research findings indicate that gaps in acculturation pertaining to situations that include first-generation immigrant parents and those parents' children reared in the United States is associated with more conflict among the generations (Hwang, 2006; Roysircar, Carey, & Koroma, 2010). Hwang (2006) states that in such situations, "When parents are less physically affectionate, use more interpersonal space, and have more reserved or controlled facial and physical expressions, children may misinterpret this as their parents being emotionally cold or distant" (p. 401). Thus, because of an existing intergenerational acculturation gap, "the active and passive choices that children make in retaining, changing or surrendering cultural values can place children at risk for developing relationship difficulties with their parents" (p. 402). Having a deeper understanding of the value conflicts between first- and second-generation clients (Roysircar et al., 2010) will help the therapist develop insight into the cultural contexts influencing clients. Such a therapist will be much more likely to offer assistance that is in line with a client's unique cultural circumstances.

In conducting narrative therapy, it is important for a therapist to identify the presence of any oppressive aspects of the client's culture and how these can play out in a client's stories. Assisting the client to formulate a narrative free from external oppression is the primary goal of this therapeutic approach. However, this can create a risk, that is, the possibility of the therapist devaluing the client's culture. If a therapist is cognizant, for example, of the ways in which the client has adopted the American ideals of independence and autonomy, then there is a greater potential for the therapist to devalue collectivism and family influences (Roysircar & Pignatiello, 2011). Jaipal (2004) reported a study in which an Indian sample was found to place significantly more emphasis on a social identity component of the self-concept compared to an American sample. Suppose, for example, that a depressed client from such a culture, one who is living in the United States and is currently having a difficult time juggling responsibilities, revealed to her therapist that she feels an obligation to "invite a parent to stay with me for a while" (the client's mother lost her husband in a car accident). A therapist who does not know that her remark reflects an obligatory duty that a family member is expected to fulfill might mistakenly believe her remark is tied to what had been discussed in previous sessions about "feeling guilty for leaving her family behind"; as a result, the therapist remains focused on pushing the client to let go of the guilt of living away from her family. Along similar lines, studies have shown, according to Nagayama-Hall (2001), that "separation from a group could create a loss of identity and additional risk for maladaptive behavior for an interpersonally oriented person" (p. 506). Therefore, one aspect of narrative therapy might require a therapist to help a client define her "group" and help the client seek out community and interpersonal connections, as well as reconnecting with her loved ones. Finally, Fuertes and Ponterotto (2003) encourage therapists to explore with clients any applicable concerns that they may have about social and cultural differences related to being male or female. Other examples include the way one group of people might be identified as being recognizably different from other groups (e.g., Muslim head covering); what it means for membership to a certain group to be based on commonalities, such as shared national or cultural tradition; what the shared attitudes, goals, practices, and values are that are typically linked to certain societal characteristics or socioeconomic backgrounds; and any other diversity-related factors that might play a role in the client's current life.

A therapist should also be sensitive to a client's feelings about being in therapy. It is wise for the therapist to remember that "the whole social enterprise of psychotherapy, which involves self-reflection, self-analysis, and verbalizations of private feelings to a stranger/therapist on a hired contractual basis is a fairly recent social construction arising in a Western individualistic context" (Rastogi & Wampler, 1997, cited in Jaipal, 2004, p. 296). There may be unknown factors that need to be addressed. For example, in Indian culture, to admit psychological problems to outsiders brings shame on the family. Finally, a therapist should let a client who is unfamiliar with the therapy process explore his thoughts and emotions at a pace that allows the client to feel comfortable.

Making Cultural Generalizations

A therapist should also avoid making generalizations about her clients; ideally a therapist should remain focused on recognizing the ways in which the client is an individual who is influenced by his culture, community, and personal factors. Lakes et al. (2006) wrote, "A one-size-fits-all within the group approach is an essentializing view that may inadvertently promote group stereotypes in the guise of cultural sensitivity while failing to address individual needs" (p. 381). Therefore, even when a therapist is familiar with the culturally related influences on a client, the therapist should also recognize that the client is a unique individual regardless of how closely that person feels connected to his cultural group.

Ethical Considerations

In narrative therapy, a therapist frequently encourages a deep level of self-description on the part of the client, which can resurrect vivid imagery of painful memories. Before attempting this level of exposure, a bond of care and trust must be achieved with the client, even though constructivism does not address essential therapeutic conditions and therapist attributes (other than the therapist is to fulfill the roles of collaborator, coauthor of narratives, and facilitator). Another consideration is that the process of therapy is known to cause clients to emotionally gravitate toward their therapist. Because of the possibility of such a reaction occurring, it is very important for a therapist to be careful about imposing his own stories and viewpoints on a client who is experiencing a transference reaction; to do so would negate the philosophy behind the constructivist theory of dual and multiple realities.

Although a pioneer of constructivism, Michael Mahoney (1995) was reflective about its ethical implications. First, he wondered how the constructivist therapist is able to know what is wrong or what is best for the client. Second, the experiences of the therapist represent inherent biases that may alienate or ignore the subjectivity of the client. This leads to the question: How does the therapist conceptualize the client's issues without bias? Third, there is no solid bedrock of leaders (sources of authority to call on) within the constructivist field. This is because such leadership structures are viewed as an objectified, hierarchical framework that is used to collect power directed toward oppressing others, and such archetypal structures are opposed by postmodern theories. According to Mahoney (1995), an important tool to remedy some of these limitations is to build an awareness of the elements of "objective power" that a therapist unfailingly brings into a therapeutic relationship. Mahoney (1995) also stated that there is no one true appraisal of reality, which he believed made assessment and diagnosis less essential to therapy. But Mahoney's stance simultaneously raises ethical questions concerning what should be considered as essential components of the therapy process. Some professionals would argue that assessment and diagnosis are of critical importance. Furthermore, to receive third-party payments from an insurance company, the expectation is that a competent therapist is capable of assessing and diagnosing a client's condition.

Evaluating Theory

Research Support: Ways of Discovery

In the 1990s, practitioners provided transcripts of client sessions that allowed for a description of what the therapy process entailed and to reveal the types of unique, positive outcomes that emerged from constructivist forms of therapy (see Hoffman, 1992, for an example from family therapy; see Neimeyer, 1993; White & Epston, 1990, for an example from individual therapy). Overall, constructivist researchers studying narrative therapy have remained focused on clients' stories and related factors such as the collaborative efforts of therapists; this focused interest has relied on a number of qualitative applications. Constructivist researchers tend to approach research from an angle that is largely different from the way research has been conceptualized and carried out to study aspects of the various theoretical approaches covered in earlier chapters of this textbook. Although such procedures are congruent with the constructivist theory itself, according to Neimeyer and Bridges (2003), it has proven to be a barrier to conducting what would constitute experimental investigation. Thus, because of what comprises a constructivist research perspective, in general, research on therapy's effectiveness is not seen as an attempt to map objective reality. The only true reality of importance is the subjectively created reality formulated by individuals.

Currently, there are several methods that a constructivist researcher can use to carry out a study, a viable set of procedures, rules, and assertions that are employed to better understand various aspects of the theory, such as how language usage can either oppress or free an individual to live fully, and so forth (Raskin & Bridges, 2002). According to Neimeyer (1993), the *mutual orientation method* refers to an approach to research where both the person collecting data and the contributor of data provide something to the effort and both obtain something back. Such an approach is very much in line with the collaborative spirit of the theory. Sarbin (1986) and Viney (1987) referred to other methods such as narrative analysis and discourse analysis. There are different forms of *narrative analysis* where, for example, the narrative therapy process is scrutinized to uncover aspects of what takes place. For example, the process might be analyzed primarily in terms of the content of stories told throughout the course of therapy or analyzed by focusing on incidents that provide an understanding of how a client's social world might be shaping the realities she creates. Sarbin (1986) and Viney (1987) also mention *discourse analysis,* which utilizes sources such as transcripts of sessions, films or videos, and vocal recordings to analyze. The aim of this approach can be thought of as finding the "story within the story," which goes beyond just the words that can be found within a transcription or some other document. Specifically, it is a detailed examination of the structure of a conversation or a story whose scope lies beyond single words or sentences—beyond what the surface reveals. This can be illustrated by Raffee's (2016) effort to find the connection between discourse and power. Raffee examined the rhetoric of the Australian national government, specifically that of the Australian Prime Minister and the Minister for Indigenous Affairs, to ascertain whether the government's form of intervention to combat incidents of child sexual abuse was a genuine attempt to help Aborigines with their concerns. By going beyond the surface discourse, Raffee concluded the real intent of the national government had less to do with helping and more to do with controlling the Aboriginal population. Another method was advocated by Feixas and Villegas (1991), who discussed the use of *textual analysis,* which is used for analyzing material dealing with the person's life. This is done by extracting and analyzing information from autobiographical texts (e.g., autobiographical novels, such as Lydia Davis's *The End of The Story* and Hunter S. Thompson's *Fear and Loathing in Las Vegas*; diaries written by individuals such as Anne Frank and Harry S. Truman; and other written sources dealing with the writer's personal story). Taking another approach, Mahoney (1991) suggested using "process-sensitive measures of human change" (p. 451), and Neimeyer developed and used the Death Index (Neimeyer & Epting, 1992) to study areas pertaining to thanatology. Howard (1986) provided a succinct summary statement concerning types of research: "By broadening the range of acceptable explanations in psychological research and modifying slightly the evidence-collecting procedures in the practice of counseling, the gap between the two might be lessened to the benefit of both undertakings" (p. 61).

Grounded Theory. The term *grounded theory* provides a rationale intended to support the collection of qualitative data and how those data can be examined. Grounded theory's ontological position is that there is no single objective reality that can be agreed on. Thus, grounded theory accepts the possibility for multiple interpretations and different phenomenological realities to emerge via qualitative approaches. Views concerning grounded theory and how it is to be defined vary. One expert in the area defined it as follows:

> Grounded theory is a systematic method of analyzing and collecting data to develop . . . theories. This method begins but does not end with inductive inquiry. It is a comparative, iterative, and interactive method. The emphasis in grounded theory is on analysis of data; however, early data analysis informs data collection. (Charmaz, 2012, p. 2)

Epistemologically speaking, grounded theorists embrace the phenomenal nature and grounds of knowledge and those procedural approaches that agree with the subjective quality that marks knowledge acquisition. One of grounded theory's applications in counseling and psychotherapy has relied on a semi-structured type of questioning protocol that utilizes face-to-face interviews that can take several hours to complete. These face-to-face interviews are guided by the open-ended responses of an interviewee, which can sometimes result in an intense interaction between the interviewee and interviewer. The discourse that occurs allows for the hermeneutic examination (i.e., a method interpretation focused on the personal experiences captured through the face-to-face interview). In collecting qualitative data, grounded theory researchers must acknowledge the biases and the expectations they had for a research study. Schreiber (2001) stated, "What is needed is for the researcher to recognize her or his own assumptions and beliefs, make them explicit, and use GT [grounded theory] techniques to work beyond them throughout the analysis" (p. 60).

It can be concluded that constructivist grounded theory research operates on the belief that the results are co-constructed creations, for example, involving the researcher (e.g., therapist) and the participant(s) (client[s]). This is a type of co-constructed creation influenced by background experiences and unique characteristics that participants and researchers bring with them to the study (Charmaz, 2009; Thornberg &

Charmaz, 2012). Constructivist theory and research have influenced faculty in training programs, as well as practicing therapists, enabling them to become more aware of certain components of therapist–client communications and research endeavors, such as self-reflexivity, i.e., the capacity to examine, consider, and analyze one's own behaviors and thoughts in relation to what is currently taking place, whether it is part of the therapeutic process or part of conducting research (Hoshmond, 1989; Roysircar, 2004; VandenBos, 2007).

Limitations and Criticisms of Theory

There is no one voice of constructivism. Differences include the (a) extent to which reality is constructed individually (constructivism) or linguistically and socially (social constructionism), (b) nature and existence of the self, (c) degree that cognitive terms are used (some in the area exclude such terminology entirely), (d) how much the therapist pushes for and is involved in moving the client toward change, (e) degree that constructivists advocate for or against realism (i.e., that some universals exist on their own), (f) endorsement of pragmatism (i.e., attributing value to practicality), and (g) use of a narrative model of psychotherapy (Neimeyer, 1995). Neimeyer (1995) concluded that the acknowledgment and tacit endorsement of pluralism in the theory has led to a polyphony of voices.

Narrative therapy arouses criticisms also. Is the use of narrative therapy appropriate and ethical in all cases, for instance, with people with limited language skills or who do not proficiently speak the language that the therapist uses? Narrative therapy is unlikely to meet the needs of families who are worried about tangibles such as meals, medical costs, clothing, sufficient money for rent and utilities, and steady employment.

Narrative therapy involves considerable self-monitoring, self-reflexivity, and a lot of talking. Constructivist therapists should consider if a client is capable of and will be comfortable with such a process rather than assuming this form of therapy is generally a good fit for everyone. Research is needed to provide acceptable evidence that this approach is not harmful to clients. If it is found to have a potential for harm, then it is crucial to clarify the degree of harm and the context in which this is likely to occur. However, one problem with finding an answer to such questions is that the frequently used methods that pertain to quantitative outcome studies are deemed inappropriate by constructivists' researchers and theorists.

The constructivist viewpoint has raised other questions that have yet to be answered. Can a narrative therapist collaborate with therapists of other theoretical orientations? How is traditional family therapy (which leans toward objective research and belief in realism) to be incorporated into such an approach? How is the relative influence of clients and therapists in the coauthoring process conceptualized? In what situations does the therapist become overly dominant in guiding the plot of a narrative? And considering its theoretical foundation, if narrative therapy were to become a dominant narrative itself, would it lose its usefulness or applicability?

There is a plethora of professional literature that focuses on what are considered essential "common factors" in therapy. These include a therapist's empathy and warmth, capacity to establish a working alliance, and the ability to conceptualize cases and implement interventions along relationship-building lines. Related concerns addressed in the literature include a therapist's cross-cultural empathy composed of the therapist's felt and expressed affect, perspective-taking on cultural and immigrant communities, and relational engagements that enable a therapist to bridge the therapist–client cultural divide (Roysircar, 2009; Roysircar & Gill, 2009). Postmodern theories do not address such components of the therapeutic relationship, and many professionals consider this to be a major drawback to accepting this approach as truly viable.

Crossley (2003) reported that constructivism and social constructionism are unable to address psychological questions about self and identity. Postmodern theorists have argued that it is impossible to make universal claims about what is called the "self" because definitions of the self cannot be given a commonplace characterization or application. This position acts in clear opposition to decades of work by some of the greatest thinkers in psychology, who critically investigated areas such as personality, psychotherapy, and human developmental theories, which produced elaborate constructs about self and identity. This also holds true of multicultural psychology that espouses a number of self-related concepts, for example, *collective self,* which is that part of the self-concept that develops out of relationships linked to others, groups, or categories such as race; *interdependent self-construal,* which is often associated with non-Western cultures and emphasizes the connectedness and the development of a self-image that emerges from being embedded in the interactions comprising social networks that are capable of influencing one's social behavior, emotional reactions, and values; *spiritual self,* which is a multifaceted internal image that is shaped by cultural experiences that provide meaning for existing, values to live by, a bond among groups, and confidence that there is something greater than self; *independent self-construal,* which emphasizes the uniqueness, separateness, and independent nature of the person that is often associated with what is called "Western cultures"; and *racial and ethnic identity,* which is that part of one's self-image derived from being associated with a certain race or ethnic group (VandenBos, 2007). Because there is no essential nature of self that is either recognized or agreed on by constructivists, the term often used as a replacement for *self-concept* is a person's *constructed reality* or some related term or notion. Crossley (2003) believes that it is a severe theoretical limitation that the construct of self has been abandoned by postmodernism because there is both subjectivity and objectivity within social contexts, as well as in uniting individual, social, and cultural forces that help to define the self.

Current Mental Health Delivery System

Neimeyer and Bridges (2003) and Genovese and Atwood (2014) believe that the constructivist approach, which currently extends well beyond the United States, has much to offer to therapy. A variety of training centers have developed throughout Central and South America, Australia, and Europe in attempts to explore the meta-theoretical implications and utility of postmodernism (Neimeyer & Bridges, 2003). Applications of constructivism in education and business have proven fruitful as well, helping teachers and managers gain insight into how children and consumers perceive the world and make meaning out of their experiences.

Social constructionism is predominantly practiced in individual therapy by private practitioners and in university counseling centers. However, trends have indicated a movement toward integrating this perspective into already formulated treatment modalities, such as couples and family therapy (Wong, 2006) and Adlerian therapy (Watts, 2003). Social constructionism has also been useful for group therapy, in which group members can decipher meaning-making and how reality is constructed within society's social settings. Social constructionism and constructivism practices have also found residence within social work (Parton, 2003).

Applying Theory to Practice

RETURNING TO THE CASE OF JUSTINE

In narrative therapy, the first step for the therapist is to identify the client's dominant discourse by using "curious" questions. Justine's presenting complaints are a continuous minor depression, fatigue, and a nagging sense of discontentment. By permitting her to quit her job, splurging on a beautiful apartment in New York City, and agreeing with her on having a second child, her husband, Tomás, was doing everything in his power to make Justine happy. But nothing was making her happy. A narrative therapist might first guide Justine toward externalization of this depression by asking questions such as "When did this depression set in?" and "When depression shows up, what does it say to you?" "What name would you give this depression?" These questions would help Justine begin to take a step outside of herself and examine at a metacognitive level how her stories about herself and her relationships with others contribute to her depression and discontentment. This process might reveal that Justine holds multiple, conflicting narratives that pull her in different directions. Choosing to be a stay-at-home mom, she feels that she somehow is not fulfilling her full potential as a lawyer, and she often feels socially isolated. On the other hand, she wants to be the "best mother" she can be and feels that the only way to do this is to stay at home.

Furthermore, Justine and the therapist could examine the ways in which these two narratives (i.e., being a professional woman and being a good mother) are informed by her French culture, mother and father, and professional life in the United States. For instance, the therapist might guide Justine to explore the narrative, "I can only be a good mother by staying at home." This process might reveal that this particular narrative is largely informed by her mother's values. Justine's mother was, in many ways, the foundation of the family, upholding traditions and maintaining family cohesion. Justine has some guilt around not fulfilling her mother's expectations. For instance, after learning of Justine's engagement to "a Spaniard," her mother would often say, "You are ashamed of yourself, of being French." Following her grandmother's death Justine kept only one of her grandmother's possessions. When Justine took only one item to remember her grandmother by, Justine's mother commented that there would be "no one to whom I can pass on my things." Therefore, Justine's decision to leave work may have been an attempt to embrace her mother's values and relieve some of the guilt she feels.

An alternative scenario might be that Justine, as a U.S.-born, second-generation French woman, may uphold the parenting values of many American women who recognize that their job pressures interfere with the quality of their home life with young children. Therefore, they leave their jobs to raise their children, while their husbands are the primary wage-earners. However, a seemingly conflicting narrative might be that by not working, Justine is failing to contribute to the family's financial security and to her own security, and that she is not taking advantage of her intelligence and training as a lawyer. This view is partly influenced by "American" values of success, gender equality, and individuality, which Justine has internalized through her upbringing in the United States.

In addition, when her father recently visited, he had encouraged Justine to go back to work, saying, "Now is the time for you to be working, building your career." Like many foreign-born first-generation immigrants, Justine's father, a relatively successful professional himself, now retired, never feels completely secure about his children's future. All her life, Justine heard her parents emphasize saving for the future. Justine feels somewhat disconnected from her father's value of productivity and yet seeks his approval. For instance, as she showed her father her large apartment in New York City, she felt self-conscious of her affluent life with Tomás, and at the same time she felt "a quiet slap of rejection" when she realized from her father's silence that none of it impressed him. Her academic and career choices previously had often been an attempt to receive her father's approval. Therefore, her own voice that disapproved of her staying at home may partly be an embodiment of her father's criticisms of this choice.

Justine feels constantly pulled between these two narratives and others (such as about her husband and father) and senses disapproval no matter what lifestyle choice she makes. Narrative therapy could begin to help Justine externalize her conflicting voices, facilitating progression to the next stage, which is deconstruction. Deconstruction might occur, first of all, by exploring Justine's marginalized narratives. For instance, she might realize that a part of her also feels a strong confidence in her choice, her quiet and peaceful life at home, and her play activities with her son. This alternative narrative could be emphasized and strengthened.

The therapist would also draw on Justine's desire to connect to her departed mother, her increasingly self-sufficient and individuating father, and her French heritage. As Justine explores her narratives about her parents, she might begin to see them as people with admirable qualities as well as flaws. She could then begin to relinquish her guilt around not fulfilling all of their stories about who she is, allowing her to make active choices about what values, both American and French, she wishes to embrace or reject. Justine's new narrative could be a fusion of previously disconnected and seemingly conflicted stories about her identity. She could see herself as a French American woman, rather than a French and an American woman. Last, by recognizing her conflicting emotions toward her parents and her husband, she could begin to explore her narratives about their lives and their relationships with her. This would allow her to further mourn the loss of her mother and attempt to bridge the emotional gaps between herself, her father, and her husband.

Returning to the Multicultural Case of the Sanchez Family

The case vignette of Miguel and his mother is presented in Chapter 1. Social constructionist therapy may be particularly applicable to families. By allowing for multiple interpretations of a situation, social constructionist therapists are uniquely poised to help family members in conflict arrive at more functional ways of understanding themselves, each other, and the whole family system because no one individual in the system can be said to be correct. Particularly when one member is going through adolescence, family conflict may persist around themes of autonomy and authority. Social constructionists can help the family "restory" rebellious adolescent behavior in a more affirming way.

It is critical for therapists to understand that immigrants face many challenges: financial stress, prejudice, stress of acculturation, family conflicts due to acculturation and communication differences between parents and their children, the use of English as a second language, and so on. (Roysircar & Pimpinella, 2008). Conceptualizing some of these hardships as they relate to distributions of power and privilege is necessary (Roysircar & Pimpinella, 2008). As discussed by Gonzales, German, and Fabrett (2011), when juxtaposed with data for the U.S. population in general, "Latino youth are exposed to a number of challenging conditions that place them at increased risk for social, educational, and psychological difficulties" and higher "rates of anxiety, depression, juvenile arrest, substance use, school dropout, and teenage pregnancy" (p. 259). Latino adults are confronted with many challenges, including a lack of English proficiency and strong ties to home communities. Such ties can hinder acculturation just as when individuals often speak their native language rather than English and continue to be primarily involved in the culture and traditions of their heritage culture.

Developing a Narrative. Narratives involve individual family members creating or co-creating their personal stories in order to explore each person's multiple identities in different contexts, including social, cultural, and familial arenas. Narrative therapy directly acknowledges issues of power, privilege, and oppression by recognizing that certain social practices may grant or prevent an individual from having certain privileges and powers. Such issues can be assessed and addressed through the creation of a viable story, which also works to distance treatment from pathologizing the "problem" by "depersonalizing" it and seeking to focus on the individual's or family's strengths. Dr. Ramirez may begin this process by explaining the task of creating a narrative. He may initially instruct both Miguel and Mrs. Sanchez to share their story independently of each other in order to be more able to understand their individual perspectives; that is, how they understand themselves and each other. They may speak, write, or act out their stories.

After this storytelling, Dr. Ramirez may help them to deconstruct their stories to define common themes, which may include culture, immigration, peer involvement, and prospective substance use. It is often the case that individuals perceive their stories through the lens of the problems at hand rather than positive life stories. Deconstruction can aid each of them by analyzing the emotions and representations in their respective stories as well as by shifting the focus from problem-oriented to solution-oriented. The family members may be encouraged to rewrite their stories based on the deconstruction process. This is meant to empower the individual and to bring about yet another meta-perspective.

Developing a Family Metaphor. Eventually, Dr. Ramirez may work with the clients on the abstract task of building a family metaphor (Neimeyer & Neimeyer, 1994). Metaphors can help to express complex, deeply hidden emotions and constructions. Dr. Ramirez could present this task by asking them to compare their family to another, unrelated construction. He may start by asking, "People have different images of what families are. If I were to say to you, 'Families are like _____,' how would you fill in that blank?" (Neimeyer & Neimeyer, 1994, p. 90). After responding privately to themselves, Miguel and his mother may share their answers to these probes aloud.

Dr. Ramirez will highlight dissonance and agreement among these metaphors through discussion. Through the narrative processes of loosening, tightening, shrinking, and stretching metaphors, the therapist explores and deepens the family's connection to shared metaphors. These processes encourage collaboration in the family and deepen the imagery by increasing visual, auditory, and emotional tones embedded in the metaphors (Neimeyer & Neimeyer, 1994). Because metaphors may speak to underlying issues that family members are not otherwise able to convey, this activity may improve their understanding of one another (Neimeyer & Neimeyer, 1994).

The Family as a Meaning-Making System. Although Mrs. Sanchez has suggested that Miguel enter therapy, individuals are seen as intrinsically embedded in the family system, which becomes the medium of problems as well as the arena for their resolution. Even though Miguel has been identified as the source of the problem, social constructionists would not define any single individual as problematic. Seeing a teenager as "troubled" is only one way among many others to view the adolescent's behavior, and social constructionists would consider the family context as an important source of meaning that shapes the behavior of all members.

An approach that situates the presenting complaint amid a complex family-based meaning-making system is most consistent with social constructionism. For instance, the absence of a father figure suggests the stories of Miguel's father may be an important opportunity for exploration.

The therapeutic endeavor with the Sanchez family will benefit from a family genogram activity. Although the task of creating the physical chart of family relationships is structured enough to provide Mrs. Sanchez and Miguel directives to work collaboratively on a task, the process is likely to elicit stories and memory sharing between Miguel, his mother, and Dr. Ramirez. This task will function as an assessment as well as an intervention to the extent that Dr. Ramirez is allowed into some of the more intimate narratives about family dynamics and values. If problematic narratives are revealed in the process of creating the genogram, Dr. Ramirez can begin reconstructing these stories into preferred narratives.

The notion of *respeto* can be expected to contribute to the style of the communication and system of familial meaning-making between Miguel and his mother. *Respeto* implies compliance and a sense of duty that results in describing and preserving boundaries associated with particular types of relationships for the purpose of avoiding interpersonal conflict. Although *respeto* may be an important concept around which Mrs. Sanchez and her son have different narratives, its tenets may impede the therapeutic usefulness of the concept by virtue of the top-down communication patterns it imposes on the family system. It will be important for Dr. Ramirez to have a sense of both Miguel and Mrs. Sanchez's conceptualizations of *respeto* in their family life. Social constructionist therapy assumes an equal distribution of power across all individuals in the therapy room, but families may have particular value systems that preclude certain kinds of communication or ways of understanding the power of individuals in relation to others in the system.

Immigration and Acculturation as Transformative Meanings. Miguel's assertions of independence mark a transition that brings instability to the family system. As migration is often a source of unexpressed pain in immigrant families, loss and grief are possible themes around which the Sanchez family has organized narratives. The manner in which a family system deals with immigration-based losses often has profound implications for how its members establish identities in the second culture.

From a narrative perspective, Miguel and his mother have deeply held stories around the context of their culture of origin and the way they identify themselves vis-à-vis their cultural transition. Processing the loss of their culture of origin context may require them to reauthor those stories and how they define themselves in relation to each other and their lives in the United States. Miguel and his mother hold the power to decide whether immigration and acculturation narratives operate dominantly and destructively in their family system. Assuming that Miguel and Mrs. Sanchez support Dr. Ramirez's suggestions about the role of divergent immigration narratives in their lives, the goals for therapy are conceptualized as the following: (a) Miguel and Mrs. Sanchez understand themselves more fully through an exploration of lived stories; (b) through witnessing the unfolding of the other's stories in therapy, they come to understand and more fully appreciate one another; (c) as a unit, they develop a preferred narrative of family resilience, strength, or bravery in place of long-standing immigration narratives of grief and loss; and (d) they enter into a period of satisfaction with their own level of acculturation and allow the other to be more fully situated in whichever level of acculturation is self-defined.

Miguel's Construction of Self. It is important that Dr. Ramirez understands how Miguel has made sense of his context and his behaviors within that context. Whereas it is unsurprising that an American teenager of Miguel's age would increasingly define himself in relation to his peer groups, it is also possible that he is distancing himself from his parental attachments earlier than his same-age Mexican peers. Childhood has been shown to extend further into teenage years for Latinos than for other cultures. This early distancing may be a fruitful avenue of meaning to explore. Dr. Ramirez will need to understand how Miguel understands his own emerging independence in relation to his peers.

Miguel's Stories of Immigration and Acculturation. The status of the Sanchez family as immigrants likely feeds into a set of stories around cultural identity that are entrenched in the family conflict. In addition to having acculturated to differing degrees, Miguel and his mother seem to share dissatisfaction with the extent of each other's acculturation. This is evidenced by Mrs. Sanchez's concerns that Miguel is abandoning his roots in favor of reckless behavior and by Miguel's embarrassment at his mother's traditional Mexican clothing and inability to speak English. Dr. Ramirez will need to understand how Miguel conceptualizes his identity vis-à-vis his cultural history and acculturation. Miguel's autobiographical account of his immigrant transitions will likely become the substance of therapeutic explorations. Through a process of revealing any destructive immigrant narratives operating in Miguel's life, Dr. Ramirez can help Miguel see ways to change his realities by restorying them.

Once the destructive content in Miguel's immigrant narratives is revealed, Dr. Ramirez will listen for inconsistent threads in his stories. One narrative in Miguel's life may be that because he is Mexican, he won't have any friends unless he engages in certain activities. When Miguel naturally recounts an occasion when an individual was friendly to him outside the context of these activities, Dr. Ramirez will explore the meaning of these friendly interactions with Miguel. These therapeutic opportunities are called "innovative moments" or "sparkling moments." By noting alternatives to dominant narratives operating in a system, these innovative moments provide the therapist an opportunity to help the client reconceptualize the family issue and create a new narrative. This reauthoring process would include Mrs. Sanchez as an indelible member of the family meaning-making system.

Mrs. Sanchez's Stories of Immigration and Acculturation. Regardless of the circumstances around their immigration from Mexico, the event has likely impacted Mrs. Sanchez's life in profound ways. As she seems less acculturated than her son, perhaps her approach to the mainstream culture in the United States has been one of reluctance. Both Dr. Ramirez and Miguel can act as witnesses to Mrs. Sanchez's stories of immigration and acculturation. Perhaps through this process of telling and renegotiating these stories, the Sanchez family will become more invested in developing a shared narrative around the psychosociopolitical upheaval of immigrating.

The Co-constructed Story of Immigration and Acculturation. Dr. Ramirez will help Mrs. Sanchez and Miguel transform their own stories, such that newly compatible narratives operate in each of their realities. Hopefully, they will have developed a greater desire to have a shared narrative that is broad enough to account for the ways in which they have adapted similarly and ways they have adapted differently. As Dr. Ramirez is working with them to understand their own narratives, he may also facilitate conversations in which they take on each other's perspectives. This is especially relevant as Miguel and Mrs. Sanchez have such opposing definitions of the problem.

Dr. Ramirez may ask Miguel, "How do you think your mother feels about your recent changes?" He may also consider how his old and new friends view his new behaviors. Mrs. Sanchez may be invited to consider why Miguel wishes that she adapt her behaviors to match those of the dominant culture. She may also consider how those with whom she comes into contact in the community view her traditional dress. It is hoped that if they are able to begin to consider how the other is thinking, Miguel and his mother will be able to modify their own personal beliefs and assumptions about one another and begin to understand their own roles in the family system.

Language as the Medium of Reality. From a social constructionist perspective, language is the medium of reality and change. Dr. Ramirez must assess the degree to which Mrs. Sanchez communicates in Spanish and English and the degree to which Miguel engages in language switching. This initial language assessment will not only provide critical information about whether social constructionist therapy with this family is viable, but it may also reveal important stories about the role of language in the Sanchez household. The success of therapy with Mrs. Sanchez and Miguel is dependent in large part on the degree to which the therapist is able to operate with both of them in their language of choice or in switching languages. Because so much of social constructionism is built on the metaphor of storytelling, language fluency for the therapist is imperative. As such, the demands on the clinician to understand the subtleties of clients' stories in this paradigm are immense, given that clients may hold dominant narratives that are organized by more than one language.

CHAPTER REVIEW

SUMMARY AND COMMENTARY ▶▶

This chapter focused on constructivism, social constructionism, and the narrative approach to therapy. These three areas hold views that are attuned to the importance of situations, meaning derived from situational context, the plural and local aspects of life, pragmatism, social constructions, self-reflexivity, interactions based on collaboration rather than being structured by an authority, and the value of narrated stories that are subjective in nature but not spurious accounts of life. This chapter also examined the ways in which constructivism and social constructionism may contain implicit cultural biases and illustrated how a constructivist perspective can be culturally adapted to the Sanchez family, an adaptation that demonstrated how postmodern theories can be utilized with diverse populations. For decades, mental health professionals have been developing and fine-tuning innovative treatments to attempt to mitigate human suffering. While it would be imprudent to throw away all of their hard work simply because their accomplishments lacked certain postmodern ingredients, we need to consider how postmodern-dependent theories and the therapeutic tools that surfaced because of those theories can be utilized to fit our current times, concerns, and settings.

Finally, postmodern extremists seem to create more questions than they can answer. This is especially true when it comes to their complete lack of faith in humans being able to ascertain exactly what is implied by the phrase "objective reality." When a radical postmodernist chooses to reject the idea that there is a knowable reality that encompasses all humans, this rejecter of realism has allowed for ontological fuzziness to fill the void that remains. This ontological fuzziness comes dangerously close to what philosophers have referred to as *solipsism*, a term that literally means the only thing a person can assume to exist is himself or herself. If solipsism is correct, then "others" are nothing more than what we are likely to call simulations today—these are simulations created by the one, existing mind in the "universe." This scenario might strike a reader of this textbook as absurd, but Greek philosophers who originally raised the possibility, and even current-day philosophers, have failed to find a satisfactory means to dismiss the likelihood that actuality is the result of an extreme egocentrism associated with a single person. In fact, a version of this belief led to creating the storyline for the movie *The Matrix* (Figure 12.2). Interestingly, the possibility that humans are constructed simulations was seriously considered and debated in a recent *Scientific American* article

▼ FIGURE 12.2

Are We Mindfully Created Simulations?

Source: © 1999 Warner Bros. Entertainment Inc. (US, Canada, Bahamas and Bermuda); © 1999 Village Roadshow Films Limited. (All Other Territories).

(Moskowitz, 2016). While such a reality is an intriguing by-product of extreme constructivist thinking, if one adopts the type of pragmatism endorsed by constructivism, one can conclude that solipsism is a nonissue because the outcome (whether solipsism is true or not true) would not change your life as you experience it now. This chapter concludes, as other chapters have, with a table (Table 12.5) that provides an overview of current practice of the approach discussed in this chapter.

▼ TABLE 12.5

Brief Overview of Current Therapy Practice

Variable	Current Application
Type of service delivery setting	Private practice
	Clinic
	Psychiatric hospital
	Health care settings

Variable	Current Application
Client population	Child Teen Adult Couple Family
Type of presenting problems	Wide range; also utilized with various therapeutic formats, i.e., play therapy, individual therapy, couples and family therapy, and group therapy. The narrative approach has been applied to a wide array of client problems, e.g., interpersonal conflict, anxiety, depression, trauma, grief and loss, substance abuse and addiction, aggressive behavior, specific phobias, lack of confidence, sexual identity issues, low coping skills in children and adolescents, eating disorders, chronic illness, and psychosis.
Severity of presenting problems	Wide range, including schizophrenia
Adapted for short-term approach	Yes
Length of treatment	Brief to extended
Ability to receive reimbursement	Insurance companies will reimburse with appropriate *DSM* diagnosis.

Variable	Current Application
Certification in approach	Interested parties may obtain training via various avenues. For example, the Dulwich Centre (created by Michael White and David Epston) offers online training, intensive workshops, and continuous training, and will consider requested training events. Also, New York City's Columbia University, School of Professional Studies offers a Narrative Medicine Certification of Professional Achievement.
Training in educational programs	Many graduate programs have incorporated this approach into their existing curriculums. Columbia University, School of Professional Studies offers an MS in narrative medicine.
Location	Urban Rural Suburban
Type of delivery system	HMO PPO Fee for service
Practitioners	Professionals and paraprofessionals
Fit with *DSM* diagnoses	No

CRITICAL THINKING QUESTIONS ▶▶

1. How is the world viewed by constructivists and by social constructionists? Which view do you agree with more, and why?

2. How is the acquisition of knowledge explained by constructivists and by social constructionists? Which position do you agree with more, and why?

3. What are four differences that distinguish objectivism from constructivism?

4. Explain in what ways co-construction is utilized in therapy.

5. What type of clients do you believe would benefit the most from working with a narrative therapist? Explain why.

SUGGESTED READINGS: IMPORTANT PRIMARY SOURCES ▶▶

Books

Bruner, J. S. (1990). *Acts of meaning.* Cambridge, MA: Harvard University Press.

Neimeyer, R. A., & Mahoney, M. J. (Eds.). (1995). *Constructivism in psychotherapy.* Washington, DC: American Psychological Association.

White, M., & Epston, D. (1990). *Narrative means to therapeutic ends.* New York, NY: Norton.

Journals

Constructivism in Psychotherapy

Narrative Inquiry

Websites

Dulwich Centre: www.dulwichcentre.com.au (Michael White & Cheryl White are codirectors of the narrative therapy Dulwich Centre, Adelaide, Australia.)

Narrative Approaches: www.narrativeapproaches.com (David Epston and Michael White are internationally recognized for the contributions they have made to narrative therapy. They coauthored the classic resource, *Narrative Means to Therapeutic Ends.*)

CHAPTER 13

FAMILY THERAPY APPROACHES

iStockphoto.com/Ridofranz

Introduction

The word *family* often conjures up an image of the first group of people who dominated our lives. We may join a family through birth, which is often referred to as our *family of origin* or through a circuitous route, such as a *blended family*, which includes offspring from another relationship. In most families a child is wrapped in a protective environment that nurtures, but a family can also do the opposite, such as wrapping a child in a cloak of secrecy to conceal abuse. Fortunately, most individuals' early family experiences fall somewhere "betwixt and between," that is, somewhere toward the middle rather than the extremes of smothering parental love that creates a sense of engulfment or forfeited parental love that leaves a sense of desertion. These and other severe family situations have been identified as the causes of later attachment problems for the individuals. Although few, if any, children completely traverse early family experiences free of any negative residue, the typical familial environment provided for the majority of children generally seems to be good enough to meet critical developmental needs and wants.

Interestingly, after we leave our childhood family behind and become emancipated, of-age adults, we realize that no one fully breaks away from their family. Even when the turmoil associated with one's early family would justify a complete break, a strongly dysfunctional family can linger in the shadows throughout a person's life. It seems that some family members, even when physically absent, can invade thoughts unexpectedly or even trespass at night into the private territory of one's dreams. Many psychological ligaments, both negative and positive, have the power to cause us to revert to the psychological dynamics of our earliest family.

Clearly the word *family* is more than a simple descriptor that specifies who is related to whom; familial relationships can extend well beyond blood ties, as adopted children can affirm. In addition to the indelible influence our early family experiences have on our lives, it is equally important to realize that our presence in the family also impacted other family members in ways that cannot be erased from their lives. Take a moment and consider how you would define the word *family* and then write your definition in the space provided in the box at the top of the next page.

LEARNING OBJECTIVES

After reading this chapter, each student should be able to:

1 Compare individual and family approaches to therapy.

2 Identify the key figures and theories that laid the foundation for family therapy approaches.

3 Discuss assumptions about family dynamics, the therapist's role, the family's role, assessment, goals, the change process, and termination for five commonly used family therapy theoretical orientations.

4 Conceptualize working with a family, paying particular attention to the techniques that would be used from the perspective of each of the five family therapy orientations.

5 Appraise the ways in which family therapies account for and address multicultural and social justice factors.

6 Critically examine ethical issues that may arise in family therapy.

7 Discuss research findings relating to the effectiveness of family therapy and its various techniques.

8 Identify the limitations of family therapy approaches, and propose ways a family therapist could address these limitations.

```
Family =
```

I encourage you to share your definition with others: a friend, a family member, or a student in class. If you are sharing with a friend or family member, I recommend first ask the other person to define *family* and then compare the two definitions. Look for similarities and differences in the descriptions shared. Is either definition comprehensive enough to be considered definitive? You most likely realized from this activity that finding a comprehensive and decisive definition for the word *family* is not easy and that there may be no single definition that everyone can agree on.

Returning to the Issue of Defining the Word *Family*

Traditional definitions of what a family represents, for example, any group of persons closely related by blood, as parents, children, grandparents, uncles, aunts, and cousins, are destined to fall short, especially considering that family therapists apply the word *family* even to two-person couples with no children. Also, a couple does not have to be married to be regarded as comprising a family. Such a couple can certainly share commitments in ways equivalent to those of married couples. The term *cohabitation* is applied to couples who decide to live together for financial or other reasons. Contemporary therapists recognize family configurations well beyond the age-old marital categories of married, separated, and divorced. One finds a number of descriptors used in current literature to describe families, including *single-parent families*, *grandparent-headed families*, *gay* and *lesbian families*, *binuclear families* (in which both parents are involved in raising their children), *stepfamilies* that are formed through remarriage, *latchkey families* in which school-aged children of working parents spend part of their day unsupervised, *serial relationships* that entail several long-term relationships or marriages, and so forth. When we consider linguistic traditions or cultural aspects, the demarcation of the word *family* grows even more complex. It is even possible among the constellation of possible family types to find families where the living and the dead share equal footing in this world. Each fall in the Mexican state of Puebla, graves are cleaned, painted, and decorated with yellow marigold flowers during the *Días de los Muertos* (Days of the Dead), a week-long event that culminates with a night vigil at family graves that ends with living family members sharing sugar skulls, bread of the dead, *mole poblano*, and other indigenous foods with dead ancestors who revisit the world of the living on the night of November 1 (see Thompson, 1999).

Freedom From Want, by Norman Rockwell (Figure 13.1), depicts several generations of a family gathered for a special dinner. Few would mistake the image as something other than a family gathering, but there

▼ FIGURE 13.1

Freedom From Want by Norman Rockwell

Source: Goku iroshima [Public domain], via Wikimedia Commons.

HYPOTHETICAL CASE: A FAMOUS FAMILY ENTERS THERAPY

Seven members of a family enter therapy and during the initial session, various remarks and answers to questions were noted by the family therapist. One of the big challenges for a family therapist is to find a way to organize the relevant information in such a way that it aids in assessing a family's situation, so it can be used later to discuss how generational and intergenerational factors relate to the family's problem. The abundance of valuable, complex, and entangled information that is sometimes gathered at the start of therapy can be a little overwhelming, even for a competent therapist.

Family therapy is predicated on the belief that it differs from individual therapy in various ways beyond the wealth of information that a therapist can obtain and later sift through to find answers. One important difference is that family therapy allows a therapist to personally observe the *family dynamics* (i.e., patterns of relating to one another) that permeate a family's interactions. Although some common patterns can be identified across families, dynamics that are unique in nature exist for every family. The question becomes how to mesh the information gathered with what occurs during family therapy sessions. It should be mentioned that the therapist's notes (Table 13.1) will be revisited near the end of this chapter to further discuss how a therapist can organize family information to best determine a family's problem(s) and to provide a useful visual tool that can be referred to during the course of therapy.

▼ TABLE 13.1

Therapist's Handwritten Notes (page 1 of 5 pages)

Same-Sex Marriage

would be much less agreement concerning how accurately the image depicts contemporary times. *Freedom From Want* portrays just one of the many possibilities of what might be considered a family today.

Even the once widely held notion that marriage is a legal or religious ceremony that formalizes a man's and a woman's decision to live as husband and wife, has undergone considerable change. For many present-day Americans, an excludable definition that requires a mixed-gender coupling as central to what constitutes marriage has become an unsupportable position with divisive undertones. The difference of opinion about what constitutes a marriage was cleverly depicted by a well-known satirical magazine. *MAD* magazine's drawing represented a take-off on another well-known painting by Norman Rockwell, titled *The Marriage License* (To view MAD's image go to https://www.madmagazine.com/blog/2012/10/18/norman-rockwells-marriage-license-reimagined). *MAD*'s revisionist version of Rockwell's painting squarely points to the issue of the role of state governments in authorizing marriages (or not) through the granting of a license. Increasingly, the issue of same-sex marriage was framed as a civil rights issue by proponents who consider the problem to be similar to what occurred when racially mixed marriages were considered illegal in the United States. In *Loving v. Virginia* (1967), Chief Justice Earl Warren of the U.S. Supreme Court commented on the unconstitutionality of state laws that prohibited interracial marriage:

> To deny this fundamental freedom on so unsupportable a basis as the racial classifications embodied in these statutes, classifications so directly subversive of the principle of equality at the heart of the Fourteenth Amendment, is surely to deprive all the State's citizens of liberty without due process of law. (Section II, para. 2)

▼ FIGURE 13.3

The White House Celebrates the Court's Decision

Source: White House Photographer (White House Press Office) [Public domain], via Wikimedia Commons.

Forty-eight years later, the Supreme Court in *Obergefell v. Hodges* decided in favor of same-sex marriage (see Figure 13.2). In 2015, Associate Justice Anthony Kennedy, the author of the majority's opinion, wrote the following:

> No union is more profound than marriage, for it embodies the highest ideals of love, fidelity, devotion, sacrifice, and family. In forming a marital union, two people become something greater than once they were. As some of the petitioners in these cases demonstrate, marriage embodies a love that may

endure even past death. It would misunderstand these men and women to say they disrespect the idea of marriage. Their plea is that they do respect it, respect it so deeply that they seek to find its fulfillment for themselves. Their hope is not to be condemned to live in loneliness, excluded from one of civilization's oldest institutions. They ask for equal dignity in the eyes of the law. The Constitution grants them that right. . . . It is so ordered. (Section V, para. 4)

Figure 13.3 shows the White House illuminated in rainbow colors after the Supreme Court ruled on same-sex marriage.

Family Therapy

A reader may ask, beyond providing a deeper appreciation of the complexity implied by words such as *family* and *marriage*, what has family therapy done to advance our understanding of and ways to treat problems that are brought into therapy? The brief answer is that such an appreciation has enriched the practice of therapy overall through a unique perspective of what creates and sustains problems in families and through what can be done to solve those problems. The remainder of this chapter is devoted to examining this branch of therapy.

Between Family and Individual Therapy: Differences

Even though certain features of family and individual therapy overlap, in general, family therapy differs from individual therapy in what it uncovers. Family therapists have discovered the following:

1. For a wide variety of problems, participation by the entire family in therapy rather than just one member of the family is a more efficient and effective approach than the use of individual forms of therapy.
2. It is beneficial for therapists to expand their attention beyond the affliction (disorder) of the individual to include the affliction (dysfunction) of the family.
3. Professional responsibility can no longer be confined simply to the individual who is identified as "having the problem"; the responsibility extends to significant others in the identified client's life.
4. Although attention still needs to be paid to what is initially described as problematic, therapists must direct their attention to also finding exceptions to the problem's occurrence. Call attention to, and building positively on, such exceptions will significantly reduce the number of required sessions.
5. Consideration of the role that interpersonal dynamics contribute to maintaining problems, beyond intrapsychic dynamics, is an important contributor to successful treatment.
6. Therapeutic change requires much less, or even no, attention to processing client-to-therapist projections (e.g., transference reactions).
7. A focus on clients' strengths contributes more to achieving rapid gains in therapy than does maintaining a focus on clients' "weaknesses"; in fact, a focus on "weaknesses" prolongs the time spent in therapy and in some cases even intensifies the level of dysfunctional behaviors already present.

8. Initiating change begets change, which essentially means that as therapists initiate a change in the family system, the family is likely to benefit from the therapy. (These improvements reflect even counterintuitive changes being suggested.) For example, before the first session ends, a therapist outlines a homework assignment that requires an arguing couple to argue even more than they have been before they return for the next session. In this case when the couple returns, they say they failed to argue more; in fact, they report fewer arguments. A deft exploration of this outcome by the therapist will help the couple identify what occurred in their interactions to decrease the amount of arguing that occurred.

9. Because problems are seen as residing at the family level, not at the individual level, family therapists develop holistic ways to assess the nature of system-wide problems. One such assessment tool is known as the *genogram*, which is basically a drawing that helps to isolate a family's history of important events (e.g., abortion, divorce, or suicide) and behavior patterns that span several generations. (Later in this chapter an example of a genogram, based on the hypothetical case of a famous family, is provided.)

Family Therapy: Historical Context and Points of Origin

Whereas some early therapies eventually moved from an individual format to a family format (e.g., Nathan Ackerman and psychoanalytic-based family therapy), some practitioners showed interest in family dynamics in the early 1900s. Alfred Adler was one such practitioner, one who made important contributions in the early 20th century that are still used by family therapists. Whereas many earlier practitioners found it difficult to move beyond an individual form of assisting others, Adler was an exception in that much of his theory had direct implications on helping families. Prime examples of Adlerian concepts that pertain directly to family functioning are *family constellation*, which was used to denote the entire set of relationships that characterizes a family and was theorized by Adler to be affected by factors such as the number, ages, gender, and birth order of the family's members; and *guiding fictions*, a term used to denote principles that guide goal-directed behavior and contribute to the formation of each member's particular *lifestyle*, or characteristic way of interacting with others and reacting to hindrances that block one from achieving a life-defining goal (Bitter, 2009; VandenBos, 2007). Adlerian theory also offers suggestions and techniques for fostering healthy family interactions, such as the use of *family councils* in which family meetings are convened to discuss matters that will affect the entire family. Thus, before the family makes a decision, all members of the family, including young children, are provided a respectful and genuine opportunity to express their thoughts and feelings. In addition, Adlerian therapists have used what is known as *logical consequences* to address undesirable family behaviors. If a father reports, "I delay family meals when my son is late coming home, which is often and usually without any kind of excuse provided. When the family finally sits down to eat, the conversation soon erupts into a fight about getting home on time for dinner." An Adlerian is likely to instruct the family to eat dinner on time with the understanding that the consequence for being late, regardless of which family member is late, is to eat leftovers that have been put away (Carlson, Watts, & Maniacci, 2006; Dreikurs, 1968). Adler proved to be a systems-oriented thinker even though he did not use the systemic language that is common to family therapy today.

General Systems Theory: The Bedrock for Family Therapy

The family systems perspective that is prevalent today in family therapy can generally be traced to concepts that were proposed by a Viennese professor of biology, Ludwig von Bertalanffy, who wondered why a sponge pushed through fine mesh material resulted in an organic mush but pulled itself back together from the mush to form a completely functioning sponge. This and other intriguing observations eventually led Bertalanffy to write his widely influential book *Problems of Life: An Evaluation of Modern Biological Thought*, which announced his plan to establish a universally applicable theory that was based on the common attributes of systems. One of Bertalanffy's generalizable concepts was *equifinality*, which was used to describe situations in which organisms that encountered a roadblock to their growth responded by finding a new pathway to reach an endpoint. This concept foreshadowed later findings in other areas, such as medicine, in which a brain injury activates the neurological plasticity that is inherent in the human brain and results in some sort of compensatory solution for the losses that were sustained. Interestingly, equifinality can even be used to explain why divergent family therapies can all produce desirable changes. This situation is analogous to when a child at the local playground jumps onto a moving merry-go-round, grabbing the handrails that section off its many points of entry. From a systemic perspective, each approach to family therapy offers a different point of entry to assist families with the same problem.

Bertalanffy also asserted that each stage in an organism's (an organism is a system) development is a qualitative change that has distinct properties. The extent of these qualitative changes can easily be demonstrated by referring to the types of changes that water (H_2O) undergoes. If the temperature falls to freezing, water becomes an icy solid. Raising the temperature of that ice to above freezing causes the solid to once again take the form of water, and if the temperature continues to rise to the boiling point, the liquid water will evaporate. Although H_2O represents the constant throughout, at each stage of change it shows stark qualitative differences. Growth, according to Bertalanffy, also displays such stark qualitative differences. Another important systemic implication Bertalanffy abstracted from the observation of live systems is that isolating the chemical elements that support growth tells us nothing significant about life itself. Thus, if we want to understand any system (e.g., a family), we have to work with the whole system, not with an isolated part of that system (e.g., a family member). He also concluded that biological systems are open, not closed, to environmental influences and that such systems often do not wait to be acted on since they are capable of acting before being acted on—as is the case with bored adults who are unwilling to passively accept their state of boredom and act to overcome the ennui. Rather than wait for something exciting to come along, they take action to dispel their languor. In sum, Bertalanffy realized that a biological system represents a dynamic whole rather than a fixed whole.

So what is the significance of Bertalanffy's body of work? It altered our general perception of how the world functions, which led to new questions, and answers to these new questions led to new applications and discoveries, such as game theory, cybernetics, and communication theory. In the case of Bertalanffy, it is certainly appropriate to apply the frequently misappropriated phrase "paradigm shift" to the widespread influence of his work, including the creative momentum that emerged from systems theory to produce various family therapies.

Gregory Bateson

A major contributor to systems-based therapies, post-Bertalanffy, was Gregory Bateson, even though Bateson was never a practicing therapist. Bateson proposed a cybernetic explanation for how the mind operates in which the mind acts as a self-correcting system that seeks a *dynamic homeostatic balance*. Even when the mind has achieved such a balance, it remains vigilant to identifying and processing vital information in its environment. Bateson also believed that the body and the surrounding environment are to be viewed as extending into one another rather than existing independently of each other. Hampden-Turner (1981) illustrated this symbiotic relationship by referring to the image of a person who suffers from blindness walking along a sidewalk and tapping a walking stick. By tapping the walking stick, the person receives critically important information about the sidewalk. Tapping reveals what is safe (a level sidewalk) and what is dangerous (the edge where the sidewalk drops off and can cause one to stumble and fall). Hampden-Turner uses the described situation to ask, "As the person uses the walking stick to tap the sidewalk where is Bateson's cybernetic mind located?" If your answer is "in the person's head," you are incorrect because the key attribute of the cybernetic mind is information gathering. Thus, the correct answer is that the cybernetic mind is located at the tip of the walking stick.

Bateson's interest in information processing also led him to examine the communication patterns among families, which led to his seminal finding that some patterns of conflicted communication combined with other factors had the power to "split the soul" of a child (i.e., widely known as the *double bind*). In such situations a parent might say to a child, "I love you more than anything in the world," but the tone of the parent's claim along with the parent's facial expression simultaneously communicates, "I resent you for being in my life." Bateson discovered that children exposed to an unending string of contradictory messages are more likely to be diagnosed later as suffering from a mental disorder.

Contemporary Family Therapy

The new means to conceptualize the role of systems—started by Bertalanffy and further added to by Bateson and others—led to a cogent, new language for organizing the problems that are reported by families. This new language had sufficient explanatory power to demystify the array of dysfunctional interaction patterns that have been found to hinder a family's functioning. This language also provided family therapists with a new means to conceptualize and create therapy techniques and to apply a systemic standard to guide the therapy process to its completion.

The term *feedback loops* is one example of the new language that emerged. This particular term is used to refer to a self-sustaining chain reaction that frequently occurs among family members. A *positive feedback loop* refers to situations such as when an adolescent violates a family rule and is grounded for 2 weeks, but the punishment serves only to amplify familial conflict and the likelihood of violating the family rule again. A *negative feedback loop* means the parental action taken serves to effectively constrict the probability that the rule will be violated again.

▼ FIGURE 13.4

Analogous to Linear Causality

▼ FIGURE 13.5

Analogous to Circular Causality

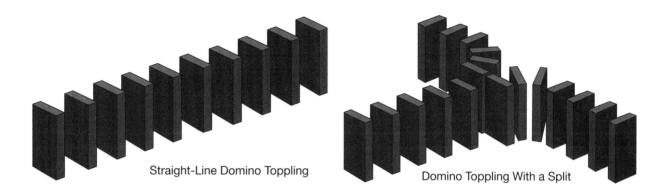

Straight-Line Domino Toppling

Domino Toppling With a Split

One of the most far-reaching outcomes of systemic thinking is that it counters the belief that problems brought to therapy developed through a straightforward, linear cause-and-effect manner. Linear cause-and-effect explanations force the therapist to vigilantly search for that one traumatic event that set into motion a chain of events that led straight to the client's presenting problem (Watzlawick, Beavin, & Jackson, 1967). This type of explanation is like having a row of standing dominoes (Figure 13.4). Pushing the first domino over (i.e., the traumatic event) starts a sequence of toppling dominoes (i.e., a sequence that leads directly to the reported problem). In truth, family-embedded problems rarely, if ever, follow such a straightforward pattern. The causal complexity that is generally found in families is much more similar to the pattern of domino toppling as illustrated in Figure 13.5, where *circular causality* occurs. Circular causal events often have multiplying causes and a reciprocal quality that is not found in linear cause-and-effect sequences (Hoffman, 1981). When a circular causal problem takes hold and goes unabated, it can assume the dimensions of an emotional maelstrom by the time a family has decided to enter therapy.

Five Approaches to Family Therapy

Many individuals have contributed substantially to the field of family therapy, and a list of contributors (and their respective theoretical positions) is likely to include Nathan Ackerman (psychoanalytic family therapy), Murray Bowen (Bowen family systems theory), Steve de Shazer (solution-focused therapy), Albert Ellis (rational emotive behavior family therapy), Carl Whitaker (emotionally focused therapy), Salvador Minuchin (structural therapy), Virginia Satir (experiential approaches), and Michael White (narrative therapy). Other theoretical perspectives that are associated with family therapy include attachment theory; collaborative language; contextual therapy; couple, marital, and family enrichment models; Milton Erickson–based family therapy; feminist family therapy;

medical family therapy (e.g., physiological reactions to stress, biofeedback, neurofeed-back, neuropsychology); Milan systemic family therapy; MRI brief therapy; object relations therapy; and second order cybernetics.

A single chapter cannot possibly capture the wealth of knowledge and experiences that have accumulated over several decades. The solution is to discuss a representative sample, but which approaches should make up this representative sample? The answer lies in a large-scale survey study of family therapists in the United States and Canada reported by Bradley, Bergen, Ginter, Williams, and Scalise (2010). In this study, participants rank-ordered those theoretical perspectives that were "most valuable to their work" in family therapy. Five family approaches emerged as the top choices from among 23 contenders, and these are listed with the percentage of family therapists selecting each one in parentheses: Albert Ellis's rational emotive behavior family therapy (60%), Steve de Shazer's solution-focused therapy (55%), Murray Bowen family systems theory (51%), Salvador Minuchin's structural therapy (45%), and Virginia Satir's experiential approaches (37%).

Cognitive-Behavioral Family Therapy: Rational Emotive Behavior Family Therapy

Although several individuals, such as Aaron Beck and David D. Burns, recognized that mental activity itself could serve as a powerful conditioner of human behavior, Albert Ellis

▼ FIGURE 13.6
Albert Ellis (1913–2007)

Ellis was a psychoanalytically trained therapist who practiced as a marriage and family therapist in the 1940s. Growing increasingly dissatisfied with the outcomes of his approach, which provided his clients with insights about how early childhood experiences were linked to current difficulties but which failed to provide lasting relief, Ellis concluded it was not the experiences encountered in life but rather how these experiences are evaluated and what we tell ourselves about these experiences that can be problematic. This approach led Ellis to formulate a therapy approach he originally termed rational emotive therapy and later rational emotive behavior therapy (REBT). Ellis wrote about his new approach well before the emergence of what was termed cognitive therapy, and he produced what seems to be an endless line of publications, including *A Guide to Successful Marriage*, *The Art and Science of Love*, and *Sex and the Liberated Man*. Ellis's interest in sexual behavior even predates that of the famed sexologists William H. Masters and Virginia E. Johnson.

Source: OnurCaliskan6 (Own work) [CC BY-SA 4.0 (https://creativecommons.org/licenses/by-sa/4.0)], via Wikimedia Commons.

had the greatest impact on the field of family therapy, according to L. P. Bergen, executive director of the Association of Marital and Family Therapy Regulatory Boards (personal communication, January 23, 2014). Ellis's theory is discussed in more detail elsewhere in the textbook. The purpose of this section is to review how his approach relates to family therapy.

Family Dynamics

The term *family dynamics* refers to key factors that affect how family members interact not only within the family but also outside the family, in other interpersonal systems (i.e., neighborhoods, employment and educational situations, social media, professional associations, etc.). Ellis's position informs us that families are not "born" to interact either irrationally or rationally; such styles of interacting are learned. For example, thinking is malleable during childhood and can be forged by significant others in the family system to take either a rational or irrational form. When irrational beliefs are accepted as truths by a child, such beliefs have the power to compress a child's perception of the world and reduce certain events to one-dimensional encounters. Over time, an irrational belief can result in a deep rut in the way a person thinks, which can make it difficult for a person to veer away from the established path of an irrational belief. According to Ellis, it is an accumulation of rigidly held irrational beliefs that lie at the center of a family's reported problem.

Therapist's Role and Family's Role

According to Ellis (2001), the role of the family therapist is active and directive, although the therapist remains an empathic professional throughout the therapeutic process, from beginning to end. The therapist is expected to function as a knowledgeable expert who teaches, directs, urges, and maintains an approach that is seasoned with a dose of egalitarianism and tempered by unconditional acceptance of the family. Although Ellis asserted the importance of the therapist–family relationship, he cautioned therapists not to be too personable and warm—being too amiable was likely to result in family members seeking approval from the therapist during the course of therapy for each success the family achieves. According to Ellis, the seeking of such praise was counterproductive since a central aim of his approach was to prevent a family from relying on outside acceptance as a measure of its value (e.g., "Everyone must like us; otherwise, we have a terrible family!"). When the family can recognize its very nature, which includes its failings and imperfections, the family has taken a significant step toward achieving a happier and more satisfying style of family living. Ellis succinctly captures the essence of what he believes to be the quintessential family therapist's role when he wrote that the therapist is to be "authoritative without being authoritarian" (Ellis, 2001, p. 161). Interestingly, when some first-time viewers watch a video recording of Ellis as he demonstrates his approach, they are left with the impression that Ellis's form of therapy is too confrontational for him to claim it to be "tempered by unconditional acceptance of the family," but as pointed out by Wolfe (2007), such a reaction is mistaken since rational emotive behavior family therapy embraces a wide range of confrontational styles.

The family's role in therapy basically requires a commitment to learning new ways of thinking and reacting. To fulfill its role, the family is expected to participate in learning activities during and between sessions. Family members are also expected to stay focused in the present because understanding early family history and other past influences are unessential to bringing about change. Ellis also asserted that the therapist is to assume that family members possess the necessary level of freedom to decide their collective fate. In sum, the family is expected to work actively to address irrational forms of thinking that prevent the family from functioning at a healthier, more realistic level.

Assessment and Goals

For Ellis, family assessment was ongoing and relied on a systems perspective that he reduced to four points: (1) Assessment is ongoing and focused on how family members communicate among themselves. This type of assessment will also provide windows of opportunity to intervene. (2) In studying families, it is essential to devote attention beyond what each family member's behaviors, expressed emotions, and revealed thoughts might mean, for it is the contextual meaning of what comprises the entire organization of a family system that is important for the therapist to consider. (3) It is necessary for a therapist to turn diligent attention to emerging patterns in family interactions and not just to the apparent linear exchanges that might misdirect both the therapist's thoughts and actions. It is the environmental unfolding of events that leads to the family's therapeutic progress. (4) System-generated principles that help the therapist understand the typical complexities found in families that are undergoing therapy must be considered when those explanations provide sufficient explanatory power (Ellis, 2001, p. 159).

Any specific goals that are developed represent a collaborative endeavor and can be expected to dovetail with the three overarching goals common to this form of family therapy. First, the therapist aims to help family members learn how to self-monitor thinking patterns. Second, the therapist equips family members to generalize what was learned in therapy in an effort to enable the family to confront any future troublesome family interactions that emerge after therapy. Third, the therapist aims to help family members learn ways to positively reinforce those family patterns that sustain a healthy family environment.

Techniques and Termination

Although cognitive-behavioral-oriented family therapists are likely to use traditional behavioral techniques, such as modeling, positive reinforcement, extinction, and thought stopping, such therapists will obviously be focused on uncovering the irrational beliefs that lie at the heart of what has spurred dysfunctional patterns to take hold in the family, and although the problem reported by the family (e.g., "father is argumentative and doesn't support our interests") must be acknowledged, a therapist's actions will be focused on specifically identifying those irrational beliefs that connect to the reported problem. The therapist will use well-reasoned logic to dispute the irrational thoughts that are provoking the current problem when those thoughts are identified and exposed.

For Ellis, family interactions typically represent a mixture of rationally embedded desires, preferences, wants, wishes, and mistaken beliefs. Problems can develop when mistaken beliefs collide with natural desires, preferences, wants, and wishes. Using the earlier example of the father who is reported as being very argumentative and not supportive of other family members' interests, the therapist discovers the following scenario is not unusual.

A father promises his teenage daughter that he will attend her afternoon softball game but fails to make the game. Working late, the father suddenly realizes he has missed his daughter's game at which point he adopts an irrational point of view. The father says to himself, "It's terrible I wasn't able to leave work in time to make my daughter's game. I'm a shitty parent just like my dad." Furthermore, the father's initial irrational reaction of excessive self-blame gets tagged with additional irrational thoughts that blossom into anger toward the family (e.g., "I work long and hard to give this family what it needs. I can't do it all—it pisses me off that when I get home my wife will say I don't support her or my daughter's needs!").

Ellis's central contention is that that the father is capable of preventing himself from overweening such extreme self-blame by letting rational thinking rule the day because the father possesses the ability to replace his crooked thinking with a more realistic evaluation of situations that can go astray. In the previous situation, the father could have self-spoken: "I regret I was not able to leave work in time for the start of my daughter's game—I'll plan better next time. If I leave now, I can still probably get there in time to see her pitch for two or three innings." In addition to the therapist's confronting the father's excessive catastrophizing of certain events that are followed by an argumentative response, the therapist will explore solutions that will enable the father to be present at important family events and explore whether the wife and daughter also harbor any irrational expectations that have contributed to the negative family dynamics.

Two primary techniques relied on by Ellis are summarized below. (The first one lies at the heart of what defines this approach as used in family therapy.)

- *ABCDE Technique:* Family members learn that problems and therapeutic changes fit a sequence that Ellis associated with the letters A, B, C, D, and E. In this technique, the **A**ctivating event is the father's missing his daughter's game. Irrational **B**eliefs tied to how terrible it is to have missed the game result in inappropriate **C**onsequences of excessive self-blame. The solution for the father is to **D**ispute his irrational beliefs with the guidance of the therapist. The therapeutic **E**ffects that follow basically comprise a new philosophy for living through which the person lives a life that is dominated by rational thinking and beliefs, and family members' feelings and interactions are essentially in alignment during shared events.
- *Homework Assignments:* Ellis was a strong advocate of giving homework assignments tailored to the specifics of the family's current problems. When such assignments were given, the family was instructed to provide a report of the

results, which were then used to further assist the family in finding ways to effectively dispute irrational, family-defeating interactions. Family therapists will also use such assignments to track the family's progress from session to session.

Finally, the therapist knows that the termination phase of therapy has been reached when the family is capable of realistically addressing faulty expectations held by family members, confronting demeaning self-statements that hinder healthy interactions among family members, and challenging entrenched attributions that contribute to family members automatically misreading other family members' words and actions.

Process of Change

Family members become aware of faulty thinking and its link to dysfunctional reactions (affective and behavioral) in the family. New knowledge and thinking skills lead to a rational approach to living inside and outside of the family. It should be kept in mind that Ellis was not advocating a rational approach to living that diminishes other important human qualities. Even the writer Eugene "Gene" Roddenberry, who created the extreme logical positivist Mr. Spock, understood that a logical way of life leaves ample room for positive feelings and the ability to connect "humanly" with others, that is, Captain Kirk and others stationed on the starship Enterprise.

Solution-Focused Therapy

Steve De Shazer was trained as a classical musician, played the saxophone as a jazz musician, became a therapist after earning a master's degree in social work, authored several books that contributed significantly to the development of family therapy, and is recognized as the creator of solution-focused therapy, which is known for its short duration. This form of therapy utilizes a strategic orientation to intervention; that is, interventions are developed to fit the problem. Rather than thinking of the "briefness" associated with this form of therapy as an externally imposed requirement, it is much more accurate to think of the short duration as an *outcome* of the inherent nature of the approach developed by de Shazer. De Shazer was a close friend of John Weakland, who served as Insoo Berg's supervisor while she trained at the Mental Health Research Institute in Palo Alto, California. De Shazer met Berg at the institute, and they later married and opened the Brief Family Therapy Center in Milwaukee, Wisconsin, in 1978. It was while de Shazer was traveling in Europe to demonstrate and discuss his approach to therapy that he died in Vienna in 2005. Insoo Kim Berg, who had contributed substantially to the approach, died approximately two years after de Shazer.

Family Dynamics

De Shazer believed family behavior is largely driven by a healthy perspective on life that relies on the combined resources and competencies of its members, yet there are times when the family system falters, and in some situations, the family may succumb to what is perceived to be an insurmountable problem. These problems possess a systemic quality both in their origin and how they prevent the family from finding a solution. According to de Shazer, the real problem is not so much what the family has identified as the problem, but rather the way in which the family has dwelled on the problem, such as inflating it until it overshadows all that is positive in the family's life. Problem preoccupation has become "problem occupancy," which only serves to evict family strengths and competencies while leaving enough room for dysfunctional interactions to progress.

Therapist's Role and Family's Role

The therapist fulfills the role of a change expert, who is responsible for creating the means for positive change to occur in the family. This process starts with moving the family from its initial *problem-oriented mindset* (i.e., which supports problem-promoting interactions) toward a *solution-oriented mindset*. This shift in orientation is largely accomplished through a display of future-directed optimism and hope and by calling attention to the family's competencies and strengths. It is the family's role to call on its inherent expertise pertaining to understanding what constitutes healthy functioning, and when such functioning has been reestablished, neither the therapist nor anyone else other than the family has this unique type of expertise.

Assessment and Goals

A traditional approach to assessment, aimed at identifying the exact ingredients and causes for a problem, is excluded from this approach's range of tools. Metaphorically speaking, the form of assessment used can be called "doughnut assessment." Just as the "hole" helps to define the simple glazed doughnut, what the family members have "left out" of their story during the initial session helps to define the shape of therapy to come. For example, after listening to the family's reason for seeking help, the therapist will shift attention to gathering information about what the family is overlooking. Specifically, the therapist will move the family from its problem-oriented focus toward a solution-oriented focus through a series of probes aimed at revealing exceptions to the reported problem, that is, times when the problem is absent from the family's day-to-day life. Filling in the "hole" allows the therapist to discover potential solutions that the family has failed to recognize. The positive interactions that are identified represent those instances when innate family strengths and resources, or changes in family patterns, were in play and prevented emergence of the family's reported problem; this information provides the means for the therapist to design therapeutic strategies uniquely tailored to fit a particular family's character.

Using a collaborative platform to operate from, the therapist will assist family members in establishing meaningful goals that are concrete in nature, positively stated, future directed, and attainable in the here and now. In setting goals, the therapist purposely avoids the use of technical jargon and instead relies on the family's vernacular to discuss and finalize the goals of therapy, which is an approach to goal setting that helps to demonstrate to family members that the therapist has heard and grasped what they have expressed.

Interestingly, de Shazer claimed that a competent solution-focused therapist should be able to render successful therapy even if the therapist is kept in the dark about the family's presenting problem. However, this claim was never intended to imply that a therapist should refuse to hear about the problem because this approach would likely be perceived by the family as lack of interest that, according to de Shazer, would greatly diminish the chance for a successful therapeutic outcome.

Techniques and Termination

This form of family therapy is driven from the start to concentrate on solution finding. Devoting a lot of time to probing for details about the problem will do little more than create a fogbound situation that hinders the therapist from discerning and moving toward a viable solution. Furthermore, because de Shazer believed that any change to the family system has the potential to produce a succession of positive changes (if monitored for results and appropriately built on), he advocated that the therapist's time is best spent implementing techniques that are solution driven as soon as possible.

The therapist will amplify all positive changes that are reported by the family throughout the course of therapy. The emphasis from session to session on what has changed for the family is central to this approach and often leads the therapist to inquire about positive changes that have occurred between sessions. In fact, the importance that is given to acknowledging and amplifying positive changes that are reported by the family is illustrated by the therapist on meeting the family for the first time: "Since scheduling this appointment and arriving for your first session, what has changed for the better in the family?" De Shazer and others (e.g., de Shazer & Molnar, 1984; Sharry, 2007) have provided general guidelines for implementing solution-focused interventions. For example, the basic formula for the first session is to (1) pay attention to how the family overcomes urges to give into the problem cycle; (2) look for resources, strengths, and coping skills that are possessed by the family; (3) consider therapeutic alternatives to the family's repetitive recycling of the problem; and (4) jump-start system changes as soon as possible. Thus, as the first session concludes, the family is very likely to be provided a task to complete prior to the next session. Often the task lacks definitive instructions, for example, "Before the next session, I want the family to do something different—where you sit at the table to eat, see a movie, take a long walk around the neighborhood—do something that breaks with routine." The task is presented in a way that the therapist communicates that the family will know what constitutes something different and is capable of carrying out the task. Even if a suggested task takes an unexpected direction, at a minimum, the outcome will provide the therapist with information about family homeostasis, that is, how its members interact in order to maintain stability within the family and how such interactions might relate to the persistence of problems in the family.

An important aim of the approach is to disrupt the recursive nature of the reported problem in ways that fit the family's basic nature that can take different forms, such as energetic, serious-minded, humorous, or demonstrative. For example, a couple seeks help to end periodic arguing that recently resulted in one spouse pushing the other spouse. An attempt to identify why the couple argues would likely only serve to reinforce negative aspects of the situation and delay effective treatment of what could evolve into a serious pattern of domestic violence. On the other hand, on learning that both spouses share a humorous outlook and even connect positively through the jokes that they play on one another, the therapist might prescribe the following:

> When the husband has experienced the kind of work day he knows "is likely to contribute to a heated argument at home," he is to ring the doorbell when he arrives home, wait 30 seconds, and enter the house walking backward. The ringing of the doorbell and delayed entry allows the wife to walk to the door to greet him and the husband's walking backward provides a signal he has had a difficult work day.

Although the actual problem is not being directly attacked by the therapist, a change has been introduced into a well-choreographed pattern of dysfunctional interaction. This example is similar to a case that de Shazer reported in *Patterns of Brief Family Therapy* (1982), in which the couple reported at the next session that they had started to laugh as the husband entered their home walking backward, which is a response that de Shazer identified as marking the starting point for finding a lasting solution.

As the therapist communicates during the first session that positive change is possible for the family, despite what seems like an unchangeable problem, the therapist instills hope in the family, which can be strengthened by introducing a positively oriented assignment. This process is illustrated by the therapist who assigns a couple to do something that will "pleasantly surprise" the other spouse before they return and concludes by saying neither spouse is to reveal what they have done prior to the next session. At the next session it is not unusual for the couple to discover that each reports an event that was not the actual event meant to "pleasantly surprise" the spouse. This assignment demonstrates to the couple that even a relatively slight change made in their lives had the power to shift them away from negative expectations toward more positive expectations.

Techniques associated with this approach are not intended to be applied in any sort of prescribed or mechanical manner, for a key feature of this approach is its interest in working with a family's unique qualities in order to facilitate positive change. In other words, regardless of how much families may appear to be similar, no two families are ever exactly alike, and all families require that the therapist craft tasks and use techniques in ways that fit the unique and subjective world of the family. The following elements comprise a sample of techniques that are common to solution-focused therapy (de Shazer, 1982; de Shazer & Molnar, 1984; Sharry, 2007).

- *Compliment:* An essential element of the technique is for the therapist, using the communication style of the family, to make a positive statement on which the family can agree. This action helps to build a *yes-set* for the family by relabeling the therapy situation in a manner in which the family is more likely to accept (i.e., say "yes" to) a subsequent task or intervention implemented by the therapist. For example, the therapist might say, "Based on what both of you have done so far, it's obvious to me that you are parents who love your child a lot! I have found that caring parents are the ones willing to work especially hard in therapy to set things right." After both parents nod in agreement, the therapist turns the focus of both parents to their teenage daughter's strengths and abilities by saying, "Let's now talk about what your teenager can do for herself while she's at school."

- *Normalizing:* In addition to drawing attention away from the family pathologizing the problem, this technique creates optimism in family members since they learn that similar concerns thought by other families to be insurmountable have been overcome. For example, the therapist might normalize a situation by saying, "Listening to your problem reminds me of other families I've worked with, and to answer your question about whether you guys are crazy, the answer is no—not at all. We'll work together to find a solution that fits."

- *Miracle Question:* This is a useful technique for situations in which the family has difficulty recalling exceptions to their presenting problem. Switching from a failed attempt to find exceptions to the reported problem, the therapist might say, "If you were to wake up tomorrow and the problem you reported no longer existed, tell me how family life would be different from what it is now?" The responses gathered can then be used to create what would constitute exceptions to the problem.

During the course of therapy, the therapist will obtain the degree of positive changes that have accrued in family functioning by asking the family to respond to *scaling questions* (de Shazer & Berg, 1988), such as "Using a scale of 0 (zero) to 10 with 10 being the absence of your troubles and zero no change in how you were functioning when you started therapy, how would you rate yourselves now as a family?" Scaling questions allow for an ongoing evaluation of the therapy process, a means to gauge the outcome of tasks successfully completed, and notification when the point of termination has been reached.

Process of Change

Desirable changes in the family are brought about by directing attention to and utilizing the dormant strengths and abilities that are already possessed by the family. In fact, embedded family strengths and abilities emerge via what the therapist orchestrates toward bringing about successful termination.

Bowen Family Systems Therapy

Bowen was born January 31, 1913, in Tennessee where his family had resided since the American Revolution. After earning an MD from the University of Tennessee, he moved to New York in 1938 to intern, but his plan to become a surgeon was placed on hiatus due to his serving in World War II. After the war he decided to specialize in psychiatry, and he relocated to the Menninger Foundation in Topeka, Kansas, which was known for its psychoanalytic approach. Bowen later joined the staff at Menninger and worked there until 1954 when he left to serve as the chief investigator on a project funded by the National Institute of Mental Health. Bowen's research led him to oppose the view that schizophrenia and alcoholism were individual "illnesses" since their genesis was tied to dysfunctional family interactions. This view meant to Bowen that psychiatric treatment focused on the individual was misguided—a conclusion with radical implications for psychiatry.

Family Dynamics

Every family is an inheritor of a multigenerational past, which is often capable of motivating the actions of family members in the present. This dynamic can become problematic when a family allows these echoes from the past to rigidly influence the family's interactions. This is the type of family that exhibits lower levels of differentiation (i.e., family personalities display a higher degree of unhealthy homogeneity than healthy heterogeneity) and higher levels of disruptive anxiety. As is to be expected, such families often lack the resilience to effectively counter challenges to the family (e.g., a serious illness, a child who goes away to college, the loss of a job) and as a result are likely to seek help when such "overwhelming" challenges take place.

Therapist's Role and Family's Role

Bowen was the consummate scientist–practitioner who advocated reliance on hypothesis testing to guide, instruct, and work with families. His research led him to believe that a key element of the therapist's role was to help a family understand how lingering aspects of their extended family were able to comingle with their present lives to create problems. The family's role is to collaborate in identifying, examining, and countering troublesome interactions of a multigenerational pedigree—those types of interactions that blocked the expression of mature, healthy interactions among family members. Finally, to effectively apply this approach, Bowen believed therapists had to become knowledgeable about their own family-related issues, including but not limited to family-of-origin matters; otherwise, their therapeutic work would be compromised because a therapist's own family issues would certainly contaminate the process and hinder satisfactory therapeutic closure.

Assessment and Goals

Bowen (1985) asserted that it was useful to assess the level of differentiation that is present in a family (pp. 472–486). The term *differentiation* referred to those families in which the members had developed a clear sense of self that allowed for mature, independent decision making and action. The term *fused* referred to families in which the members were so emotionally and cognitively intertwined that their sense of self had dwindled, or to the situations of children who had been left undeveloped and in a shadowy state. This latter type of family suffered from a poverty of unique ideas and opinions since its members had opted to unquestionably accept the values and beliefs of another person, so they represent a perfect gathering of yes-men and yes-women. Bowen's research supported the conclusion that as the level of differentiation that is present in the family increases, a family is more likely to benefit from family therapy. Finally, goal attainment can be thought of as two-tiered in nature. Successful achievement in moving a family away from its reliance on dysfunctional interaction patterns, a primary goal, invariably means that the family has essentially overcome the original conflict or problem that it struggled against.

Techniques and Termination

Bowen identified several common interaction patterns that are used in response to anxiety. For example, *coercive interactions* between spouses take place when one spouse seeks to cause the other to think and act as desired; *conflicted interactions* are situations where blame is directed toward the other spouse; and interactions that target a child serve to relieve the tension that is felt by other family members. Another reaction to anxiety that often accompanies the previously described interactions is *emotional cutoff,* which occurs when a person minimizes the interpersonally generated anxiety by emotionally separating from its source (e.g., a scapegoated child who "emotionally hides" when the family is troubled). Furthermore, dysfunctional reactions are often played out interpersonally in what Bowen termed a *triangle,* which is the basic building block of all interpersonal environments. "A two person relationship is unstable in that it automatically becomes a three person system under stress" (Bowen, 1985, pp. 424–425).

Bowenian therapists utilize a number of techniques, such as the *genograms* (see the fundamental example provided later in this chapter), *coaching,* and *de-triangulation.*

- *Coaching:* The therapist actively provides support and encouragement. This is especially helpful when a family member who has gained greater differentiation is learning a new skill. For example, while the therapist is helping a family member practice what to communicate to another family member, the therapist might say, "You've made great progress dealing with responsibility issues pertaining to your parents' alcoholism. This is difficult for you, but I'm confident you're ready and you can do it. I'm here to help you sort out what needs to be said."
- *De-triangulation:* Two members of a family (e.g., mother and daughter) can interact effectively until tension rises (e.g., daughter's choice of a boyfriend comes up), and it is at this point that one can predict that the twosome becomes a threesome (someone else is drawn in: father, older sister, aunt, etc.). The primary purpose of triangle formation is to dilute the anxiety that is felt—not to solve a perceived problem ("Carl, I want you to explain to your daughter why this guy is wrong for her!"). De-triangulation requires that the therapist remain objective and not "take sides" when conflict erupts and use knowledge gained about specific triangle formations within the family to work toward preventing their reappearance. For example, a therapist might say, "Carl, I've noticed that when Sally expresses concern about Julie's boyfriend, the outcome is a pretty intense argument, the kind of argument where you are soon pulled into the conflict. I want to try something if all three of you agree—for each of you to say what you feel and think about the situation the family's struggling to overcome. The rule we'll follow is that no one is

punished or criticized later for what is said. [All three agree to participate]. Okay, let's start with Julie, while keeping in mind that neither of you will interrupt her. When she's finished, Sally will go next and then Carl. Julie, what would you like to say?"

De-triangulation moves from a technique to a family skill once the family is able to interrupt such triangles in the future and chooses instead to listen respectfully and nondefensively to what other family members have to say about a concern.

Termination takes place once a family has acquired the skills to block repetition of counterproductive and destructive interaction patterns. Its members have successfully dealt with their family-of-origin issues, issues that had blocked differentiation and prevented family members from developing the unique personal qualities that would enable them to critically assess situations, form opinions, make decisions, and interact on a person-to-person level inside and outside of the family.

Process of Change

Through instruction, guidance, and posing questions that are grounded in Bowen's theory, the therapist facilitates the cognitive processing of mutigenerational influences uncovered during family therapy. Thus, change results from the family's comprehending the presence of multigenerational influences, gaining specific knowledge about how these influences affect family interactions, and applying what was learned in therapy in order to alter dysfunctional patterns and foster greater differentiation.

Structural Therapy

Salvador Minuchin was born in San Salvador, Argentina, where he practiced pediatric medicine until 1947, when he chose to serve in Israel's military to defend the state's right to exist. After obtaining psychiatric training in the United States, he returned to Israel to treat refugee children; he later returned to the United States and studied at the William Alanson White Institute founded by Erich Fromm and Clara Thompson to provide psychoanalytic training that emphasized social activism. Concurrent with his training, Minuchin worked at the Wiltwyck School for Boys, where he moved from relying on what he had been trained to use to a family-focused approach detailed in the book *Families of the Slums: An Exploration of Their Structure and Treatment*. In 1965 Minuchin accepted a position that divided his time between serving as a professor of pediatrics and child psychology and director of the Philadelphia Child Guidance Center. His approach to therapy was contested, and an official complaint was lodged with the American Psychiatric Association (APA). Possessing both investigative and sanctioning authority, the APA judged Minuchin's therapeutic approach to be sound. Subsequently, in 1974 Minuchin published *Families and Family Therapy*, which is widely considered to be a seminal work in family therapy. Moving to New York City in 1981 he established his own therapy center that was later renamed the Minuchin Center for the Family. In 1995 Salvador Minuchin retired from the center he founded, and in 2017, at age 96, he died from heart disease.

Family Dynamics

The manner in which family members respond and interact relates directly to a family's structure, which is based on rules that control the family's operation; boundaries that provide seclusion and privacy; roles that are typically played out; and various alliances, coalitions, and hierarchies that exist within the family system. *Enmeshed* and *disengaged* were two family structures that Minuchin regarded as problematic. The former structure entangles its members in an intense family involvement in which conformity is valued and individualism is tantamount to betrayal, whereas the latter structure creates an anemic style of family involvement in which disjointed interactions are typical.

Therapist's Role and Family's Role

The therapist juggles connecting to the family and managing the therapy process, which involves remaining active, considering the past while staying oriented in the present, and monitoring family communication patterns—a role that is aimed at fully grasping the family system's operation. This course of action allows identification of, and targeting for change, those organizational aspects of the family that represent functional incompetence. The family's role is to shift its attention from interpersonal myopia (e.g., "Our teenager is wrecking our family by staying out past midnight") to a structure-directed focus (e.g., "Our rule about her curfew may have caused more problems than her sometimes coming home later than we expected") that can lead to appropriate solutions.

Assessment and Goals

The therapist creates a working alliance with family members called *joining,* which is the kind of relationship that allows the collection of pertinent information while the therapist interacts with family members; such interactions can spotlight those structural elements that power the family system and subsystems (Minuchin, 1974). Structural elements to look for are hidden alliances, the quality of system-wide and subsystem boundaries, family roles, and whether the family has undergone any event of a transitional or transformative nature that has impacted its operation (e.g., worsening of parental alcoholism has forced a child to become the decision maker). The therapist will also consider distancing tactics used by family members to disengage from one another (e.g., revealed in the seating arrangement of family members on their entering the therapy room).

Techniques and Termination

The following techniques provide a sense of what can be expected during the course of family therapy.

- *Setting Boundaries:* When privacy is a scarce commodity and "being your own person" challenges the structural system, a system in which boundaries can easily disintegrate or bleed into one another, the therapist will focus on boundary construction. To pique the curiosity of family members, the therapist might start this process by saying something like, "Has anyone heard the saying, 'No man is an island'"? After receiving confirmation that family members have heard this before, the therapist continues by saying, "I think it is equally true to state, 'Every man is an island.' I bring it up because it doesn't sound like anyone has very much private time, which is important. Let's take a few minutes to discuss this and see how we might provide some breathing room for everybody."

- *Enactment:* Discussing a problem, such as spouses arguing, can make the problem more abstract than real. This technique would require the couple to re-create a typical argument during the session. This provides the therapist with an opportunity to change critical aspects of the enacted argument and explore with the couple the effect that these changes have on their thoughts and feelings.

- *Rule Challenge:* It is not unusual for family rules, especially a rule that contributes to the family's problem, to be vocalized in the form of a saying. For example, a father may reveal a family-based belief about staying strong and not giving in to adversity by repeatedly espousing, "Rocks don't have to worry about damage from the rain!" Such instances open up an opportunity for the therapist to explore how a family has misapplied a family rule. Any rule that is rigidly applied across situations will likely hinder the family's ability to function effectively. Furthermore, families' adopted sayings often have a counter saying that can be introduced to prompt discussion (e.g., "Over time even the hardest stone can be worn away by drops of water").

- *Reframing:* Offering an alternative explanation by relabeling something said, an alternative that gives hope, can cause positive change to occur. A mother nods her head in agreement to the father's remark, "We don't know what to do about our son; no one else in our family's needs to see a therapist for help." To this statement the therapist responds, "It took a lot of strength to come here—to take positive action rather than hide from a problem; let's see how we can best channel that strength." (*Reframing* has become a ubiquitous technique that is used by therapists today who represent a wide array of theoretical persuasions. Hanna and Brown [1995] ascribe the technique's origin to Watzlawick and his colleagues in the 1970s with other terms, such as *relabeling, positive connotations*, and "ascribing noble intentions" being used to describe the same process.)

- *Unbalancing:* The therapist "objectively sides" with a member or subsystem to counter a problem-provoking aspect of family life. For example, the therapist states, "You know, I've heard the same thing from other families over the years, and your daughters have a point that we should pay attention to during the remaining time."

Termination is reached when organizational changes needed have been accomplished. At this point, boundaries no longer disintegrate and bleed into one another. The boundaries that are established through therapy are maintained, and the operative rules that are established create the desired effect on how the family and subsystems communicate, interact, and function in the general sense.

Process of Change

The change process is facilitated by the therapist's joining with the family, guiding and directing the therapeutic effort to help the family make necessary structural changes, as well as ensuring that boundaries are reset to match any structural changes that are established.

Experiential Approach

Starting as a family practitioner by 1955, Virginia Satir was teaching a family dynamics course to psychiatric residents at the Illinois State Psychiatric Institute. Later she held the position of training director for the Mental Research Institute in Palo Alto, California, and then for the Esalen Institute, in Big Sur, California. Satir's career path led to her developing intimate professional associations with other early contributors to the field of family therapy, such as Gregory Bateson, Jay Haley, John Weakland, and Don Jackson, who used the term *conjoint* to refer to treating the whole family. In 1964 Satir published one of the field's classic works, *Conjoint Family Therapy*, a work whose style is clear and exacting and provides a detailed outline of Satir's position on three topics: family theory, communication theory, and theory and practice of therapy. In the preface of the 1964 edition Satir states, "I was one of many who experimented with observing the person labeled 'schizophrenic' in the presence of his family, rather than by individual treatment alone." This and other experiences led Satir to conclude, "Any individual's behavior is a response to the complex set of regular and predictable 'rules' governing his family group, though these rules may not be consciously known to him or family."

Family Dynamics

Satir paid close attention to how family communication and self-esteem intermingled to drive behavior within and outside of the family sphere of family activity. In addition to disrupting the expression and development of autonomy and individuality, Satir linked low self-esteem to elevated anxiety and interpersonal uncertainty. A family that is built on a foundation of low self-esteem will have major fault lines running through it, and attempts at communication during periods of high stress will eventually rupture the precarious family bedrock and create a dysfunctional upheaval. Satir found that problems (e.g., marital discord) often beget problems (e.g., a child's behavior becomes problematic—the proverbial "identified patient" of the dysfunctional family).

Therapist's Role and Family's Role

The therapist's job is to strengthen self-esteem through comments (e.g., "You're of value" and "It's not wrong to want things for yourself") and by voicing recognized strengths (e.g., "You've carried through on doing what you never thought you could—that's great!"). Note, however, that Satir was not saying that we should elevate others' self-esteem without regard for their actual capabilities (e.g., every player on the middle school soccer team is given a special award so that no child feels rejected). Falsely elevating self-esteem has its own pitfalls.

The therapist will also establish rules that promote discussion of what is painful (e.g., "Since it's important for everyone to be heard, all family members will be allowed to speak without interference"), show how family-based defenses are a means to avoid what is painful (e.g., anger is used to mask the pain felt), delineate faulty roles and their function, model clear communication, and call attention to faulty verbal and nonverbal communication patterns. The role of the family members is to stay attuned to the here-and-now context of the therapy process while they devote special attention to communicating clearly and listening to others without becoming defensive.

Assessment and Goals

Satir devoted an entire chapter in *Conjoint Family Therapy* to describing her use of *family-life chronology* (see Satir, 1964, pp. 112–135). Satir typically started a family-life chronology by asking questions about the problem, then shifting her attention to the parents by asking questions about each parent's family of origin, when they met, and the expectations each had about living together (e.g., marriage). This process is followed by the therapist's asking both parents about living together prior to having children and their expectations about parenting. Each child is also given an opportunity to discuss his parents in general and in specific situations (e.g., when they seem to be having fun, when they disagree). A family-life chronology serves several purposes. It allows a therapist to gather information to better structure the therapeutic process, and it provides opportunities to make comments about specific family-of-origin influences that have impacted each parent. Near the end of this process, Satir would reassure family members that therapy would provide a safe environment in which to express themselves, emphasizing the important role that clear communication will play during the sessions. She brought the chronological process to closure by summarizing what she had learned and by making remarks that would instill a sense of hope in the family. For example, Satir might say, "It appears that everyone in the family works very hard to make everyone else satisfied and happy, but in the end no one appears to be very happy or satisfied. This is something we'll work on, and I have the impression that by therapy's end the pain everyone is experiencing can be laid to rest."

Techniques and Termination

Satir's form of family therapy was oriented in the here and now and often was experientially based. A variety of techniques were used to bring about system changes that would enable a family's members to thrive and grow (Satir, 1964; Schwab, 1990). Several of these techniques are described next.

- *"I" Messages:* Having clients use the pronoun *I* when communicating forces the speaker to assume responsibility for expressed thoughts and feelings.
- *Challenging Hurtful Stress Responses:* Satir identified four habitual reactions to stress that hamper communication and self-esteem. *Blamers* confront stress through aggressive action that diminishes other family members. *Placaters* handle stressful situations by diminishing the self and agreeing with others. Family members may use words, such as *wilting, child-like, worn-out, vulnerable,* and *clingy* to describe the *placater. Computers* approach stressful events by diminishing both the self and others and are identified as being rigidly objective, unfeeling, distant, and

obsessively concerned about being appropriate and correct. *Distractors* respond to stress by diminishing the self, others, and the context of the stressful situation, often portraying the situation as irrelevant to the family. After a stressful situation subsides, others in the family are likely to recall the distractor's reaction as being off-kilter, spacey, out-of-touch, confused, and directionless. The aim of challenging these ways of responding to stress is to instill a new habituated response that Satir termed *being real*. This type of approach to stress comes about through developing new competencies that are aligned with the self, others, and the actual context of situations. According to Satir, family members who change in this manner are often described as congruent, integrated, unique, alive, and creative.

- *Sculpting:* Family members are physically molded or positioned during therapy in ways that symbolize how a speaker perceives that her message is being received (or not received in many cases). The images created through sculpting often linger as powerful reminders. For example, if a family member complains that "no one pays attention when I'm trying to talk about something that concerns me," the therapist could sculpt the situation by positioning each member of the family in a corner of the therapy room, instructing them to stare into the corner while each member of the family takes a turn speaking about something that they consider to be important.

Treatment is completed when each family member regards himself as others in the family perceive him; they are free from allowing past family models (families of origin) to influence current family interactions; their behavior matches their messages; they use the first person pronoun *I* when speaking; they are capable of acknowledging healthy separateness; and parents are able to deliver clear questions, statements, directions, and intentions when they speak to each other and to their children.

Table 13.2 provides a compilation of quotations that are arranged by the five major proponents who are highlighted in this chapter, the creators of therapies that have continued to inspire and remain influential forces in the practice of family therapy.

Process of Change

Satir's approach enables the family to understand that the symptoms that they report are not confined to one person (the "identified patient") but reflect a system-wide problem. Change is largely due to helping the family move away from incongruent functioning toward congruent functioning through teaching and allowing family members to experience and learn to communicate in ways that nurture self-esteem.

Appropriate Client Populations: Family Therapy

Bergen, Bigham, Ginter, and Scalise (2013) found that even with larger numbers of college students who are graduating from marriage and family programs (with master's degrees in marriage and family therapy programs that are accredited by the Commission on Accreditation for Marriage and Family Therapy Education [COAMFTE]), family therapy remains largely a multidisciplinary profession whose members train in a wide variety

Quotable Virginia Satir, Salvador Minuchin, Murray Bowen, Steve de Shazer, and Albert Ellis

Virginia Satir

- Problems are not the problem; coping is the problem.
- We must not allow other people's limited perceptions [to] define us.
- Adolescents are not monsters. They are just people trying to learn how to make it amongst the adults in the world, who are probably not sure themselves.
- Parental validation does not imply uncritical approval of everything a child wishes to do. Parents are the socializers; they must teach the child that he [or she] is not the center of their world or the world at large.
- The most psychologically influential roles people play are sex-linked roles.
- Defenses, as I see them, are simply ways of enhancing self-esteem and defending against attacks on self-esteem. So the therapist does not have to "destroy" defenses in order to produce change. He [or she] exerts as [his or her] efforts [reduce] terror, reducing the necessity for defenses.

Salvador Minuchin

- We may label as deviant what is actually the creative attempt of a family organism to develop a new shape—the shedding and becoming that precede a butterfly.
- The touchstone for family life is still the legendary "and so they were married and lived happily ever after." It is no wonder that any family falls short of this ideal.

Murray Bowen

- The problem in the patient is a product of imperfections in the parents, and the parents a product of imperfections in the grandparents—continuing back for multiple generations.
- Emotional illness is a multigenerational process.
- Systems thinking . . . is [aimed] directly at getting beyond cause-and-effect thinking and into a systems view of the human phenomenon.
- Labeling with a diagnosis invokes the ills of the societal projection process, it helps to find the problem in the patient, and it absolves the family and society of their contributions.

Steve de Shazer

- Find out what works [with the family], and do more of that.
- Problem talk creates problems; solution talk creates solutions.
- In a multicausal open system it is difficult to label "cause-effect" as "event 1 caused event 2."

Albert Ellis

- People don't just get upset. They contribute to their upsetness.
- The art of love is largely the art of persistence.
- There's no evidence whatsoever that men are more rational than women. Both sexes seem to be equally irrational.

Sources: Bowen, M. (1978). *Family therapy in clinical practice.* New York, NY: Jason Aronson; De Shazer, S. (1982). *Patterns of brief family therapy: An ecosystemic approach.* New York, NY: Guilford Press; Ellis, A. (2001). *Overcoming destructive beliefs, feelings, and behaviors: New directions for rational emotive behavior therapy.* New York, NY: Prometheus Books; Minuchin, S. (1974). *Families and family therapy.* Cambridge, MA: Harvard University Press; Minuchin, S., Nichols, M. P., & Lee, W.-Y. (2007). *Assessing families and couples: From symptom to system.* Boston, MA: Pearson; Satir, V. (1964). *Conjoint family therapy* (Rev. Ed.). Palo Alto, CA: Science and Behavior Books; and Schwab, J. (1990). *A resource handbook for Satir concepts.* Palo Alto, CA: Science and Behavior Books.

of professional programs that are associated with various professional groups, such as psychiatry, pastoral counseling, psychology, psychiatric nursing, mental health counseling, and social work—professional groups that are frequently listed by these therapists as their primary affiliation. As might be expected, the range of disciplines represented in the field of family therapy matches both the breadth of problems and types of clients whom family therapists encounter. In general, family therapists work with couples and families with problems such as drug abuse, drug addiction, alcoholism; parent skills training; anxiety disorders; bipolar and depression-related concerns that affect the family; bereavement and complicated grief reactions; problems related to separation or divorce; relationship conflict between couples or among family members; attention-related disorders in children; sexual dysfunction in adults; trauma-related events, such as rape or sexual abuse of a child; and posttraumatic stress disorder in a family member who is returning from combat. A common misconception is that family therapists primarily work with families as the unit of treatment. In fact, researchers (Bergen et al., 2013; Bradley et al., 2010) reported that 48% to 52% of family therapists' clinical work time is devoted to seeing individual clients, but it is important to realize that even when working with an individual rather than a family, family therapists can be expected to utilize a systems theory perspective to assess, plan, and implement therapy.

Multiculturalism

Multicultural family therapy literature encompasses a variety of factors, such as age, ethnic group, gender, nation of origin, race, religion, sexual orientation, and socioeconomic class. These are factors that are known to affect a "sense of self, help-seeking patterns, openness to therapeutic interventions, definitions of family, and varied and complex functioning in the couple and family relationship" (Poulsen & Thomas, 2007, p. 144). Therefore, a family therapist should consider the presence of such factors—not limiting attention solely to the contribution that one or more of these elements may have made to a family's problem but also looking at how such factors can help a family therapist understand how they inform a theoretically based approach to family therapy. This can be illustrated by the case of an Asian Indian couple who entered family therapy. Although the marriage had been arranged and the husband was afforded greater influence and power than the wife by the extended family, the husband and wife desired a relationship that was more equitable than tradition dictated; the couple reported a high level of marital satisfaction but complained that they lack privacy; the husband reported his mother frequently complains about how the recently married couple interact with her and others (family members and neighbors). The husband stated that his mother recently said, "You're more loyal to her [the wife] than me."

According to Dupree, Bhakta, Patel, and Dupree (2013), this situation represents a traditional cultural perspective, and understanding that such couples regard themselves "holistically as part of a larger family" (Dupree et al., 2013, p. 324) better enables the therapist to formulate a therapeutic plan to help the couple discover a viable means to establish harmony within the larger family while meeting their need for intimacy. According to Dupree et al. (2013), family theories that can inform the therapy process include Bowen's family systems therapy (i.e., special attention being applied to problems of triangulation, emotional cutoff and gridlock, and how multigenerational transmission has played a role in what the couple has reported), Minuchin's structural therapy (specifically tackling roles and boundary issues), and de Shazer's solution-focused therapy (i.e., focusing on the positives of a traditional family structure while creating solutions that will facilitate short-term therapy for the couple).

Social Justice

Kosutic and McDowell (2008) reviewed the content of diversity and social justice articles published in family therapy journals during a recent 10-year period. One outcome of this study was that Kosutic and McDowell were able to abstract from these articles practical ways for family therapists to address significant social justice concerns in the lives of family members. Ten examples of how a family therapist, during the course of treatment, might ferret out and work with important social justice issues contributing to a family's problem are listed.

1. Use and promote the use of inclusive language that affirms differences while showing acceptance and support. (A family therapist's use of inclusive language helps to convey a genuine interest in working with the family to solve a problem.)
2. Construct a genogram that incorporates pertinent cultural information.
3. Call the family's attention to cultural myths, stereotypes, and cultural narratives for the purpose of exposing their hidden assumptions and contradictions.
4. Ask questions about a family's social context and sources of oppression.
5. Discuss openly any oppressive social messages that have become internalized by family members and others.
6. Help family members develop narratives about the ways they have coped, overcome hardships, and used their strengths as a means to resist oppressive internal messages.
7. Foster personal and family identities that affirm the strengths that family members possess.
8. Identify and utilize larger system interventions that meet a family's needs, such as health clinics, support groups, and advocacy groups in their immediate community.
9. Discuss the invisibility of various groups (e.g., ethnic groups, uninsured workers, females, first-generation college students, gays, minimum-wage workers) when important issues are publically debated and policies are being considered.
10. Acknowledge the reality of oppressive systems in the family's environment while modeling the importance of taking steps to foster change (e.g., the therapist becomes visibly involved in the government that controls and makes decisions for a town or city).

Too often, family problems (parent–adolescent conflict, marital dissatisfaction, partner abuse, etc.) represent manifestations of larger system forces (lack of teen supervision in society, overworked and underpaid parents, male privilege, etc.) that are being played out at a societal level. Systems theory is not limited to the therapy room, nor is it like a light switch that can be flipped off as a family therapist exits the therapy room. Systems theory extends to the entire world in which we live.

Special Ethical Considerations

Working with a family can pose unique ethical challenges for a family therapist. The concept of family secrets and the use of paradoxical or deceptive techniques are used to illustrate such challenges.

Family secrets can take several forms. An *intergenerational family secret* is a secret shared among members of different generations (e.g., "Before your great-grandmother married, she worked as a prostitute in Storyville, the red-light district of New Orleans").

Generational family secrets are confined to members of just one generation and are known to all, some, or to just one member of the family (e.g., the spouse who was involved in an extramarital affair). During the intake phase of family therapy, the family therapist is expected to provide information about confidentiality, especially as it pertains to situations in which confidentiality does not apply, such as when a family secret is revealed. Failure to address how a revealed secret will be handled by the family therapist can be problematic, especially if one member of the family reveals a personal secret to the family therapist but desires that the shared information remain hidden from the other family members. For example, prior to her husband's arrival from work to attend the session, a wife tells the therapist that the couple's recent sexual difficulties date back to her one-time sexual encounter with a coworker, which her husband is unaware of. Just moments before her husband arrives, she then asks the family therapist not to share this information with her husband.

Revealing such a secret during individual therapy does not have the same implications as it does when it is selectively revealed during couples therapy because failing to openly address the revealed secret has compromised the family therapist's ability to work effectively with the couple. By agreeing with the wife's request to preserve the secret, the family therapist has effectively allowed what had been a therapeutic relationship to undergo triangulation. This triangulation event prevents the wife from assuming responsibility for her actions.

It is not unusual for family therapists to utilize *paradoxical or deceptive techniques*, which have been shown to produce meaningful therapeutic gains for a family. Even though the use of such techniques might seem opposed to therapy's general aim of encouraging open communication during therapy, from an ethical standpoint the question of whether or not a paradoxical or deceptive technique is appropriate to use will depend on whether the family therapist makes a carefully weighed decision. Specifically, the therapist should ask whether using a straightforward technique, in place of a paradoxical or deceptive technique, would result in a useful outcome. If the answer is "it would," then the use of the straightforward technique is preferable to a technique that employs concealment or ambiguity.

Research Findings

Fine and Fincham (2013) succinctly capture the challenge of confronting anyone who is interested in finding support for family therapy's theoretical foundation when they wrote, "The lack of a single, unifying perspective [due to multiple theoretical positions] makes it more difficult to integrate findings across studies" (p. 6). Keeping this caveat in mind, this section provides a review of various studies that support theoretical concepts covered in this chapter.

Evidence provided by Cowan and Cowan (2002) supports the conclusion that systemic-based interventions, both those focused on parental dynamics and those focused on parent–child dynamics, lead to greater psychosocial and psychological functioning (i.e., lower likelihood of psychopathology) among the children in a family. A different set of studies found that certain factors led to a deeper, systemic understanding of family dynamics that helps to explain why children in the same family can act differently to identical displays of parental conflict. A number of researchers (Davies, Forman, Rasi, & Stevens, 2002; Gerard, Buehler, Frank, & Anderson, 2005; Grych, Raynor, & Focco, 2004; Skopp, McDonald, Manke, & Jouriles, 2005) reported that various factors can play a significant role in mediating the effects of parental conflict on children; these factors include children's style of regulating emotions, unique configuration of children's personality attributes, general sense of children's security, and personal temperament (e.g., a child with an active nature will respond differently from one whose natural predisposition is to be quiet). Such factors help to explain why some children withdraw from ongoing parental conflict, whereas others may intervene through triangulation by joining with one of the parents.

Consistent with Bowen's conceptualization of how various family subsystems can influence other family subsystems, as well as the entire family, researchers have found that after divorce, the boundaries between children and the custodial parent often weaken in ways that result in the children becoming a support system for the custodial parent. In the case of remarriage, researchers have found that triangulation is a common occurrence for newly created blended families, commonly known as stepfamilies, in which one or both parents have children from a previous relationship (Alexander, 2003; Baxter, Braithwaite, & Bryant, 2006; Biblarz & Gottainer, 2000; Coleman, Fine, Ganong, Downs, & Pauk, 2001; Jurkovic, Thirkeild, & Morrell, 2001). Empirical support has also been found for one of the basic assumptions of cognitive-behavioral family therapy, which holds that certain types of mental images or thoughts contribute directly to occurrences of inappropriate and elevated anxiety or depression (e.g., Beck, 1979).

Limitations and Criticisms

Beyond the many strengths that family therapy brings to therapy in general, certain aspects of family therapy require closer scrutiny. In real-world settings, in which a single therapist is available for family therapy, one finds that as the number of family members who participate increases, a corresponding increase in the likelihood for a family member to be "lost among the many" follows, such as a when a young child's expression of concern goes underaddressed because the child lacks the interpersonal sophistication and skills of the older participants. Because a family therapist's attention is always selection-based, the therapist will focus on some members more than others. As a result, the chance always exists that the interests of the one, whether intentional or not, may be sacrificed to some degree for the greater good of the whole.

As alluded to earlier, family therapy is also susceptible to criticism as a result of some family therapists' reliance on the use of deceptive techniques to initiate change in the family system. In general, the use of deception goes against the grain of general therapy practice, especially for those therapists who regard therapy as an open and collaborative process. A final criticism that should be mentioned is the failure of many family therapists to fully apply systems thinking outside the therapy room. Although it is certainly logical to expect family therapists to make an effort to confront societal forces that are known to negatively impact families, in truth many family therapists do not make a concerted effort to tackle such societal forces. Interestingly this is often due to the constraints of various systems that make up a large part of their lives, leaving them with little time or energy to devote to such an effort (e.g., a social worker with a very large case load who provides family counseling for the Department of Family and Children's Services). Such systemic situations do not justify a family therapist (or anyone else) not taking any action against negative societal forces since even a series of small efforts can have an accumulative effect.

Application: Family Therapy

RETURNING TO THE CASE OF A FAMOUS FAMILY SEEKING FAMILY THERAPY

Table 13.3 presents the basic information collected on all 13 family members discussed in the initial session. A review of the information in the table reveals that converting the handwritten information in this manner provides a much clearer sense of each family member as well as that person's relationship to others in the family. Still, the table falls short of revealing the interplay of different generations in an easily digestible format. This is where the *genogram* (diagram portraying a family's history) comes into play. The genogram depicted in Figure 13.7 serves as an example of how the family therapist converted the family's story into a readily understandable configuration made up of compact information, but it is important to emphasize that the genogram contains more than a simple holistic and visual arrangement of salient family features.

The genogram provides a backdrop for the family therapist to refer to, a sort of *mise-en-scène,* which can be used to illuminate intergenerational relationships and those key interconnections among family members that lie at the heart of the family's current problem(s). The genogram presented is intended to introduce the reader to some of the components that are used to construct a basic genogram. In addition, a few examples of graphic notations that the family therapist typically relies on to construct a genogram appear at the bottom of Figure 13.7. Instead of listing names and ages, which is typically done when constructing a genogram, numbers and generic descriptors (e.g., second daughter) were used. These numbers and descriptors correspond to what is found in the therapist's summarized notes appears in Table 13.3. (Finally, readers should remember that genograms can be much more elaborate than the one presented here.)

What Famous Family Was Used to Construct the Genogram?

The family referred to for constructing the genogram (see Figure 13.7) is a virtual family well known to millions of TV viewers—the Simpsons. Members attending the hypothetical session were Grampa Simpson, Mother Simpson, Homer, Marge, Bart, Lisa, and Maggie. This particular virtual family provides an abundance of familial information, both generational and intergenerational information, which spans close to 30 years. (The TV

TABLE 13.3

Family Therapist's Notes

No.	Relationship	Description
1	Grandmother: half-brother's mother	Worked as a circus performer.
2	Grandfather: father's side (attended session)	Retired watchman who guarded a building to "protect it from fire, wrongful taking, and vandalism." Currently resides in a retirement home. Emphasized he had dressed up for the session (he was wearing his "favorite bolo tie and bedroom slippers"). During the session he reported he was "forced to come—I don't like spending time with this family." When asked what he felt good about, he said, "I'm proud of fighting in the army during WWII." Note: During the family therapy session, he fell asleep.
3	Grandmother: father's side (attended session)	Introduced herself by saying, "I'm the reason we came in for family therapy." Self-described as a "die-hard social activist and old hippy" who had been assumed dead. Her reappearance was reported to have created problems for her son (second-generation father) who reported he is having a difficult time adjusting to knowing his mother "is alive—not dead—and that she abandoned him."
4	Grandfather: mother's side	Mother (second generation) reported they were just a typical, caring couple with three daughters, herself being one of the three.
5	Grandmother: mother's side	See description 4.
6	Brother: father's side	"Half-brother" to father. Graduated from an Ivy League college. Described by the family as being "very driven" to succeed. Former CEO in the car industry. Grandfather reported this son resulted from "sex with a carnival floozy when I was young—he was put up for adoption after he was born." Affectionately referred to as "Uncky" by third-generation son and first daughter.
7	First twin sister: mother's side	Both twins are older than the remaining sister. First twin works for the Department of Motor Vehicles. Has always parted hair in the middle to distinguish herself from the other twin. Father stated, "She hates me."
8	Second twin sister: mother's side	Also works for the Department of Motor Vehicles. Smokes "lots of cigarettes," according to her family. The two oldest children simultaneously added that she "always has us massage her feet."
9	Father (attended session)	Works as a safety inspector at a power plant. He has held the same entry-level position for years (liked by fellow workers but referred to as a "dunderhead"). Obese due to poor diet and abuse of alcohol (weighs between 239 and 260 lbs.). During the session, he laughingly referred to his drinking of beer as "me killing my brain." Has undergone coronary bypass. Age 36.
10	Mother (attended session)	Has worked as a realtor, substitute elementary school teacher, among other jobs. Mandated to complete a class for "road rage." Also reported having a gambling addiction at one point in her life. Launched a community program called "Families Come First." Reported that her "real job has been to hold the family together." Expressed concern for her husband since he discovered that his mother was alive and not dead. Age 36.
11	Son (attended session)	When something negative occurs (e.g., some object is broken or taken), he is the one first suspected. Said to shift blame to others even when he is not sure of what he is being accused of doing. Described as "devious, underachieving, and a school-hater that likes to make prank phone calls to the local bar that his father goes to after work." Age 10.
12	First daughter (attended session)	She is the second-born and middle child. Tends to see things as either "right or wrong" and strives to do the right thing. Expressed an interest in environmental issues, animal rights, and Buddhism during the session. Appears to be a precocious child who possesses considerable musical talent. Age 8.
13	Second daughter (attended session)	Described as the "baby of the family." Age 1.

Example of a Basic Genogram: A Famous Family

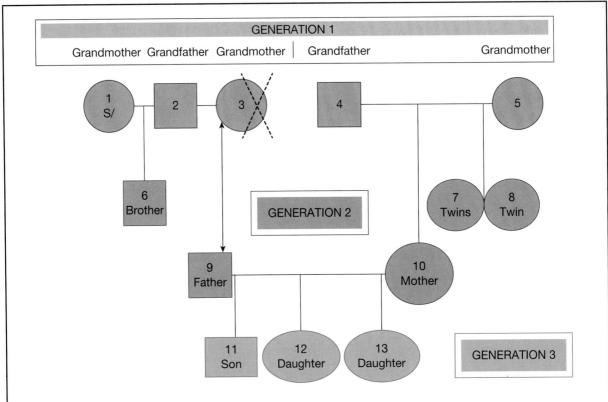

Genogram Symbols Frequently Used by the Therapist

(Both Standard and Unique Symbols Are Represented)

Square = male; **Circle** = female; **Triangle =** unborn child (in utero); **Horizontal Line** = marital or equivalent relationship; **Vertical Line** = offspring; **Double Arrow Line** = primary relationship conflict; **X-ed Out** = died, suicide, or murdered; **Triangle** (with "**A**" inserted) = abortion; **Triangle** (with "**S**" inserted) = stillborn; **D/** = divorced; **S/** = separated; **EN/** = empty nest; **Broken Line** = incorrect belief (e.g., told a person died, but person is still alive).

show debuted December 1989 and has over 600 episodes.) The easily obtained information facilitated the creation of the basic genogram depicted in Figure 13.7 (see Richmond, Gimple, McCann, Seghers, & Bates, 2010). How a genogram might be used in family therapy is further explored in the ongoing case presented in each of the 12 theoretical chapters (i.e., the case of Miguel Sanchez).

The Case of Miguel Sanchez

One advantage of maintaining a systems perspective during therapy is that this approach lowers the chance for a therapist to overlook important information, such as a factor that contributes significantly to a family's problem. The broader, systemic view embraced by various forms of family therapy is positively correlated with the level of complexity that is present when therapists work with families. In light of these remarks, one interesting criticism that has been directed toward Bowen's style of family therapy (the form of family therapy illustrated in this case example) is that this approach is too complex and difficult to follow at times (Kaplan, 2000). Admittedly, Bowen's published works can challenge a reader, but in truth this challenge is more likely due to the complicated nature of family dynamics and the influence of various systems beyond the immediate family rather than Bowen's style of presentation. In such a situation of analyzing and writing about family dynamics, complexity begets complexity.

While individual therapy carries with it its own form of complexity, the difference between conducting individual therapy and family therapy is analogous to how clients might allow a therapist to view a personally meaningful mosaic (mosaic pieces that come together to reveal the person). A close look at the mosaic depicted in Figure 13.8 will soon reveal that the overall image is formed by using a number of smaller images (representing family relationships and other influences). In situations that involve individual therapy, only a small portion of the mosaic is made available to the therapist for understanding a family-related problem. Conversely, family therapy that involves the entire family comes close to presenting the entire mosaic for the therapist to analyze and understand a problem's causes. A complete mosaic offers the whole picture and offers a rich source of information, which helps the therapist to decide how to best approach a family's difficulties.

Family therapy for Miguel and his mother commenced when Dr. Ramirez constructed a genogram. Because of the nature of the presenting problem, a family that was obviously experiencing the tension of existing between two cultures, Dr. Ramirez carefully constructed a genogram that included pertinent cultural information. A culturally grounded genogram often provides a clearer snapshot of what is occurring within the family than what could be obtained otherwise. This type of genogram will help to shorten the duration of family therapy because this approach will allow Dr. Ramirez to more quickly separate critical from noncritical cultural factors that are contributing to the mother–son conflict. Furthermore, the genogram creates a reference point for discussing the family's concerns and allows Dr. Ramirez to hypothesize that part of the family's difficulties are of a multigenerational nature. Bowen believed that sometimes interaction patterns can exist in a family and transfer to subsequent generations. Bowen also believed these multigenerational patterns are tied to how each generation is likely to respond to anxiety-provoking events (McGoldrick & Hardy, 2008). This case illustrates the power of familial events that led to a pattern of handling stressful events through what Bowen (1985) termed *emotional cutoff*, which is a withdrawal from and avoidance of emotionally provoking encounters across generations.

▼ FIGURE 13.8

Faces Become Mosaics of Family Influences

Source: w:User:William Meyer (User-made photograph) [Public domain], via Wikimedia Commons.

The following segment of one session illustrates how this hypothesis was addressed by the family therapist. The therapist's exploration of a multigenerational factor leads to Mrs. Sanchez and Miguel's obtaining greater insight into one critical aspect of their shared problem.

Session Segment

Therapist   So if I understand correctly, Miguel, you remember when your father left your family to start a new family?

Miguel   Yes, he left us and I used to blame my mother, but my older brother sat me down and explained it was not my mother's fault, that she even left Mexico—the country she loved—on her own—to come to the U.S. to make a better life for us. *Mi padre nos abandonó* [My father abandoned us].

Therapist   Rosa, when we were working on the genogram, you mentioned that your husband's father, Miguel's grandfather, also left his wife to start a new family. Sometimes patterns repeat themselves in families, from one generation to the next. Does that sound true—in this situation?

Mrs. Sanchez   Yes, I think so—but Miguel's grandmother couldn't leave Mexico. Her father expected her to return to his house, and she did so. I saw how difficult this had been for her—for her to go back and live in her father's house. At her age, it was hard for her. I did not want to do the same—return to my family in Mexico. I decided to come here, to the U.S.

Therapist   Rosa, in what other ways were these two events—the husbands' leaving—similar?

Mrs. Sanchez   I don't know.

Therapist   After leaving, how did your husband respond to you and to your two sons?

Mrs. Sanchez   After a while he stopped checking on his two sons. It didn't take him too long to act as if he didn't have any sons, any wife. Miguel said it—*él nos abandonó* [he abandoned us].

Therapist   What about your husband's father?

Mrs. Sanchez   I remember Miguel's grandmother saying pretty much the same—he left her and his son behind. Like he never had a family.

Therapist   I don't know if you two remember this, but when we started I mentioned that I would be looking for patterns that repeat from generation to generation. Patterns that carry over to the next generation—descendants. Patterns that are tied to how the next generation responds to anxiety—how

	a family may react during difficult times, stressful times, like trying to adjust to a new country. [The therapist pauses to give both Rosa and Miguel a chance to respond.]
Miguel	Yes, but how does this—a pattern of acting explain what's happening now?
Mrs. Sanchez	I think I remember what you said before. Can you say more?
Therapist	Both of you have struggled to make a new life in the United States. And sometimes this effort has resulted in anxiety—worry or feeling uneasy. Especially during times one or both of you were uncertain about the future, those times you didn't know what was going to happen.
Miguel	So you're saying my grandfather and my father handled their difficulties by withdrawing from others. When I had a problem at school, I also pulled back—I wanted to drop out, and that led to me and my mother fighting. Is this what you're getting at?
Therapist	Yes, and do you remember the first time you came in with your mother to see me? You got up and left the room and went to the waiting room. That reaction may have been your way of dealing with an unpleasant situation, something you were unsure about.
Miguel	Hmm.
Mrs. Sanchez	Are you saying we are trapped by what happened? That we are—*los prisioneros de nuestro pasado* [prisoners of our past].
Therapist	Yes and no. Yes, previous generations can affect us negatively—also positively. No, neither you nor Miguel is trapped by the past. We can always choose to act differently. Especially once we understand what's been going on. [Pauses for a moment.] I see our time is up. We'll discuss this more next time we meet. Will both of you think about what we uncovered. Think about it before the next session?
Miguel	Hmm. Yes.
Mrs. Sanchez	*Sí* [Yes].
Therapist	*Buena* [Good].

Murray Bowen achieved significant breakthroughs in terms of understanding family dynamics, both healthy and unhealthy, and his ability to conceptualize and apply what he learned about families significantly advanced systemic thinking. Bowenian concepts are invaluable tools for rendering effective treatment, but a full application of these tools requires a type of understanding that occurs in conjunction with an understanding of how Bowen's concepts, such as *fusion* and *differentiation* (Bowen, 1985), can differ from culture to culture. Without achieving this combined understanding, a therapist might easily mistake certain behaviors between family members as proof of the existence of unhealthy fusion (i.e., a loss of self in which the lack of separation from other family members is accompanied by a dysfunctional blending of feelings and thoughts). But what may constitute unhealthy fusion in one culture may actually represent a healthy norm in another. Santisteban, Mena, and Abalo (2013) nicely summarize what is at hand here. They acknowledge that despite the considerable diversity that exists between and within some ethnic groups, which can noticeably complicate the application of therapy, neither type of diversity will invariably create difficulties for a therapist if the therapist genuinely understands and appreciates each type of diversity. Santisteban et al. (2013) stated, "Fortunately, family systems therapists embrace rather than shy away from complexity" (p. 247).

CHAPTER REVIEW

SUMMARY AND COMMENTARY ▶▶

▼ FIGURE 13.9

A Mobile Representation of a Family

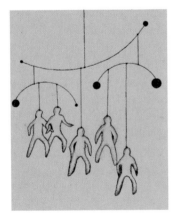

Source: Reproduced with Permission by E. J. G.

Family interactions are analogous to the mobile depicted in Figure 13.9, which uses pieces of string to keep the family figures suspended and in balance. As with all mobiles, however, this balance can be easily upset by the touch of a finger. Sherry Turkle, Director of the MIT Initiative on Technology and Self, has closely examined how advances in technologies are altering relationships.

In addition to technology-related factors that were already known to upset the balance of important family relationships (e.g., Internet pornography, cyber bullying, Internet cheating), Turkle's (2011) recent findings suggest that family therapists will be increasingly confronted with challenges that pertain to how developments in gaming, sociable robotics, mobile technology, and social networking negatively affect the ways in which people choose to interact and the process of forming a personal identity. According to Turkle, these technologies are enabling people to create and share with other online users, a virtual identity or avatar (in some cases, multiple avatars). Whereas an avatar can maintain a sense of interpersonal safety for its creator by removing the emotional risks that are often associated with rejection by another, an avatar-to-avatar relationship cannot guard against loneliness or the sense of incompleteness that can result from failing to connect intimately with an authentic person. The drawback of technologically fabricating a false self to use online is reflected in the song "Do You Want to Date My Avatar" (lyrics by Felicia Day, music by Jed Whedon):

Grab your mouse and stroke the keys

Here in cyberspace there's no disease

Pick a time, send a tell to me

Just pay, just pay a small subscription fee

Do you wanna date my avatar?

She's a star

And she's hotter than reality by far

Wanna date my avatar?

One could argue that the new forms of system-related problems referred to by Turkle can only be fully resolved by relying on a systems theory perspective, which is an inherent strength found in the various family therapies reviewed in this chapter. This chapter concludes with Table 13.4, which offers a brief overview of the current practice of marriage and family therapy and is not intended to represent an exhaustive summary of the areas listed.

▼ TABLE 13.4

Brief Overview of Current Therapy Practice

Variable	Current Application
Type of service delivery setting	Private practice Clinic Psychiatric hospital Health care setting Military Social service agency
Client population	Child Teen Adult Couple Family
Type of presenting problems	Wide range. Those specifically associated with couples and families and the types of problems associated with the various individually oriented therapies covered in previous chapters.
Severity of presenting problems	Wide range
Adapted for short-term approach	Yes
Length of treatment	Brief to long term
Ability to receive reimbursement	Insurance companies will reimburse with appropriate *DSM* diagnosis.

Variable	Current Application
Certification in approach	Marriage and family therapists who obtain the Marriage and Family Therapy license or certificate have met high educational and clinical experience criteria. All states require a master's or doctoral degree and supervised clinical experience.
Training in educational programs	Many graduate programs offer courses in marriage and family therapy. In addition, the Commission on Accreditation for Marriage and Family Therapy Education's (COAMFTE) scope of accreditation includes three types of programs: master's degree programs, doctoral degree programs, and postgraduate degree clinical training programs, which provide clinical education in marriage and family therapy to trainees with a master's or doctoral degree in MFT or in a closely related field. A COAMFTE program may allow for specialized training in a particular modality or treatment population.
Location	Urban Rural Suburban
Type of delivery system	HMO PPO Fee for service
Credential	The National Credentialing Academy (NCA) was established to provide a national certification system. It recognizes those who have met their standards in training and experience and adhere to their ethical standards. NCA credentialing provides a measure of professionalism for interested parties, but NCA asserts that it is not a substitute for state licensure and strongly encourages professionals to obtain state licensure. Contact information: ncacademy@stx.rr.com
Practitioners	Professionals
Fit with *DSM* diagnoses	No

CRITICAL THINKING QUESTIONS ▶▶

1. Explain how individual therapists and family therapists might differ in the meaning they assign to the comment, "We all have baggage."

2. Identify one advantage and one disadvantage for a couple contemplating marriage to visit a family therapist.

3. Bill Clinton acknowledged attending family therapy while he was governor of Arkansas. Select one of the following—Benazir Bhutto, Theodore Roosevelt, Frida Kahlo, John F. Kennedy, Helen Keller, Oprah Winfrey, Eleanor Roosevelt, George W. Bush—and discuss how her/his family of origin might have impacted her/his life in either a positive or negative manner.

SUGGESTED READINGS: IMPORTANT PRIMARY SOURCES ▶▶

Books

Ellis, A. (2001). *Overcoming destructive beliefs, feelings, and behaviors: New directions for rational emotive behavior therapy*. New York, NY: Prometheus Books.

Turkle, S. (2011). *Alone together: Why we expect more from technology and less from each other*. New York, NY: Basic Books.

Journals

Couple and Family Psychology: Research and Practice

Journal of Family Psychology

Journal of Marriage and Family Therapy

Journal of Systemic Therapies

Websites

American Association for Marriage and Family Therapy: www.aamft.org

Lois Paff Bergen, PhD, Executive Director, Association of Marriage and Family Therapy Regulatory Boards, i.e., AMFTRB: lois@amftrb.org (https://amftrb.org/)

CHAPTER 14

MULTICULTURAL AND INTERNATIONAL APPROACHES

Introduction

This chapter covers the main premises of multicultural and international approaches to therapy and applies concepts of oppression, empowerment, and subjective meaning of self-identity to the case of Tyrone and concepts of immigrant acculturation to the case of Miguel and his mother, Mrs. Sanchez. The historical context of multicultural psychology is analyzed. Select models of multicultural and international therapy competencies are presented. The roles of the client and the therapist, the nature of their relationship, use of assessment, intervention examples, therapeutic goals, and client change processes are explicated. The discussion includes professional ethics for practice with ethnic, racial, and cultural minority clients; research on the effectiveness of multicultural competencies and culturally adapted therapy interventions; relevance to current mental health delivery systems; and an overall evaluation of the multicultural approach.

Note: The acronyms *APA* and *ApA* are used in this chapter when citing works listed in the reference list; unless otherwise indicated, these acronyms stand for the American Psychological Association and the American Psychiatric Association, respectively.

Key Players

Derald Wing Sue

Following World War II, Derald Wing Sue, PhD, was reared in Portland, Oregon. He was one of six children. His father was an immigrant from China and married his mother in the United States. Both parents had a third-grade education. Sue and his family experienced prejudice because of their Chinese heritage, and because of these early experiences Sue gravitated toward the research issues of racism and multiculturalism. D. W. Sue received his doctorate in 1969 and began working at the University of California, Berkeley, Therapy Center. In 1972, D. W. Sue and his brother, Stanley Sue, as recent graduates and young psychologists, founded the Asian American Psychological Association (AAPA). D. W. Sue was AAPA's first president, and over the years, he and his brother led AAPA to develop into one of the most successful ethnic minority professional associations in psychology.

Although Sue enjoyed working as a therapist, he found that sociopolitical and other oppressive, external forces contributed to the problems of his diverse client base. He realized that through academic training and research, he could influence

LEARNING OBJECTIVES

After reading this chapter, each student should be able to:

1 Compare and contrast the main aspects of the inferiority model, the culturally deprived model, and the culturally different model.

2 List at least 10 cross-cultural and multicultural counseling competencies.

3 Give the definitions of race and ethnicity.

4 Describe a person with four intersecting identities other than race, ethnicity, sex (male/female), and age.

5 Defend Helms's (1990) Black racial identity model from Cokley's (2002) arguments against racial identity models.

6 List the goals of multicultural counseling.

7 Describe a situation where self-disclosure is useful in a multicultural interaction.

8 Discuss important considerations of cultural bias when doing multicultural assessment, including the clinical interview and clinical judgment.

9 List potential ethical considerations when counseling ethnic and racial minorities.

10 Discuss Berry's (2001) bilinear model of immigrant acculturation adaptation as it relates to the case of Miguel and his mother, Mrs. Sanchez.

THE CASE OF TYRONE

Tyrone is a Black man who perceives himself as invisible because others fail to see his true self. He expresses that his true self is obscured by the different roles he plays that are tied to societal stereotypes and racial prejudices. He is an intelligent man, reflective, and a gifted orator, but throughout his youth he proved to be naive about people's intentions. His youthful optimism was gradually destroyed by a chain of traumatic events.

Tyrone sought a good education and attended college on a scholarship. The predominately White committee that eventually decided to award Tyrone the scholarship had undergone a contentious debate during their review of Tyrone's application. Tyrone was grateful for the scholarship but blind to the racial attitudes of his benefactors. Once in college, he took on the role of a disciple of Booker T. Washington while accommodating discrimination and slights. Tyrone agreed to take a White board member on a tour of a Black community. It was during the tour that Tyrone repeatedly stated his contempt for Black people's poverty and their ignorance as well as his belief that he was not like them. His remarks were viewed by the White board member as extreme and contrary to the school's desired public image.

Tyrone believed that his expulsion was a betrayal of his trust in his White benefactors.

Since childhood, Tyrone has been conflicted about race relations. According to his interpretation, when his Black community and family praised his conduct, it was because he was doing something against White people's wishes. Tyrone moved to a major city, where he hoped to find employment to pay for college. The city did not meet this expectation, and Tyrone began work in a paint factory. His employment ended shortly after an explosion in which he was injured. Tyrone became involved in a Black Brotherhood, an organization in which his linguistic skills were admired. He became the Brotherhood's spokesperson but found

▼ FIGURE 14.1

The Journalist Touré

Source: Joshua Simpson [CC BY-SA 3.0 (https://creativecommons.org/licenses/by-sa/3.0/deed.en)].

that he was forced to embrace many inauthentic selves as a means of meeting others' expectations.

In his youthful journey, Tyrone encountered Touré, a journalist and author of the book *Who's Afraid of Post-Blackness: What it Means to be Black Now* (see Figure 14.1). He also encountered White men who were blatantly racist, Black men who succumbed to the roles of White men, and White men who fought for a Black cause.

He encountered Black people who fought for civil rights but had varied ideas about how a Black man should fight for and achieve a better life for the Black community. Some people found Tyrone to be too Black, whereas others saw him as not Black enough. Each time Tyrone succumbed to the expectations of others, he was not himself. His life appeared to be a struggle to define himself against the expectations of society.

Case Discussion. Near the end of this chapter, the case of Tyrone is discussed in greater detail to illustrate how the approaches covered in this chapter can be applied to his situation.

the course of change in professional psychology. So he moved into academia and occupied positions at various universities. He is the former president of the American Psychological Association's Society of Counseling Psychology (Division 17) and the Society for the Psychological Study of Culture, Ethnicity and Race (Division 45). He is a member of the American Counseling Association and a Fellow of the American Psychological Association.

Sue is most known for his conceptualization of multicultural competencies and racial microaggressions. He and his research team at Columbia University's Teachers College took on a 10-year study of the causes, manifestations, and impact of racial microaggressions. Their groundbreaking efforts led to a taxonomy of racial microaggressions that empowers people of color by making the invisible visible. He performed extensive writing and multicultural research in education and psychology years before the academic community perceived it favorably. His concepts and theories have established a pathway for a generation of younger scholars interested in issues of multicultural psychology and mental health (Zalaquett, n.d.a).

▼ FIGURE 14.2
Derald Wing Sue

Photo courtesy of Derald Wing Sue

Melba J. T. Vasquez

Melba Vasquez, PhD, ABPP (diplomate of the American Board of Professional Psychology), was the first Mexican American/Latina and woman of color to be elected president of the American Psychological Association in 2007. She is known for creating inroads for minority groups that are traditionally underserved by psychology. Vasquez grew up in various small towns in Texas, where she was affected by her family's participation in grassroots civil rights activities. One of seven children, she was a first-generation college student.

Vasquez started her career as a middle school teacher of English and political science. While she was studying for her master's degree in school therapy, a faculty member encouraged her to pursue her doctorate. It was her interest in the psychology of discrimination, human behavior, and resilience that motivated her to pursue her PhD. Melba Vasquez was in the first cohort of the American Psychological Association's Minority Fellowship Program, which supported much of her doctoral education, and in 1978, Melba Vasquez earned her doctoral degree in counseling psychology from the University of Texas at Austin.

During her entire career, Vasquez has been instrumental in implementing standards linked to ethical responsibility for psychologists. As a member of the APA's Board of Social and Ethical Responsibility for Psychologists (later renamed the Board for the Advancement of Psychology in the Public Interest), she was integral to the APA, canceling its investments in South Africa during apartheid and raising awareness about HIV/AIDS. Vasquez is the cofounder of two APA divisions: the Society for the Psychological Study of Ethnic Minority Issues (Division 45) and Trauma Psychology (Division 56).

Janet E. Helms

Janet E. Helms, PhD, has described her life as "much like everyone else's" (Institute for the Study and Promotion of Race and Culture, 2011, para. 1). Yet, since graduating with her doctorate from Iowa State University in 1975, Janet Helms has been a driving force in psychology—contributing innovative empirical research and theories on racial identity and gender issues.

Helms grew up in Kansas City, Missouri. She was the second of seven children and the eldest daughter. Since the second grade, Helms knew that she wanted to work with people, practicing as a psychologist and treating children with autism. Over time, her life path veered into mathematics at the University of Missouri–Kansas City; however, Helms realized that she was not like other math students and sought the human element of psychology. She ultimately attained her bachelor's and master's degrees in psychology from the University of Missouri–Columbia. (Institute for the Study and Promotion of Race and Culture, 2012).

After completing her doctorate in 1975, Helms became an academic; she has now published over 60 articles, written 21 book chapters, and given scores of presentations. Similarly, she has garnered a dozen awards, including being the first recipient of the Teachers College Columbia University Janet E. Helms Award for Scholarship and Research Mentoring in 1991.

Paul Bodholt Pedersen

Paul Bodholt Pedersen, PhD, is considered a pioneering international researcher from the United States and had a prolific and distinguished career. Having grown up in Iowa and later traveled to Europe and Asia, Pedersen focused on understanding how different people respond in culturally unique ways. Paul Pedersen attained his associate's degree in 1956, his bachelor's degree in history and philosophy in 1958, his master's degree in American studies in 1959, another master's in theology in 1962, a third master's degree in therapy and student personnel psychology in 1966, and a doctorate in Asian studies in 1968 (APA, 2010).

Pedersen became an academic and published over 40 books, 100 articles, and scores of book chapters. His work, as he stated, is intended not as competing "with or opposing psychoanalytic, humanistic and behavioral orientations but rather . . . [explores] how a culture-centered perspective complements and strengthens all approaches to therapy and communication" (Zalaquett, n.d.b, para. 8). His cultural awareness is evidenced by his extensive international endeavors, such as working in the United States, Malaysia, Taiwan, Australia, South America, and Europe. Suffering from Parkinson's disease, Paul Pedersen moved into a retirement home in Minnesota, but he continued his writing and professional commitments to the American Counseling Association (ACA) and APA. He died in January 2017.

See Table 14.1 for statements made by Derald Wing Sue, Melba J. T. Vasquez, Janet E. Helms, and Paul Bodholt Pedersen.

Historical Context

During the first half of the 20th century, mental health issues of ethnic and racial minorities were identified by developmental and clinical psychologists (Lal, 2002; Sokal, 1987), whose image of the mental health client were their White clients. This "White Man" model was challenged during the second half of the 20th century by a growing cohort of psychologists who were both European Americans (e.g., Gilbert Wrenn, Allen Ivey, Paul Pederson) and racial and ethnic minorities (e.g., D. W. Sue, Janet Helms, Thomas Parham, and Patricia Arredondo).

▼ TABLE 14.1

Quotable Derald Wing Sue, Melba J. T. Vasquez, Janet E. Helms, and Paul B. Pedersen

---

Derald Wing Sue

- Although overt expressions of racism (hate, crimes, physical assaults, use of racial epithets, and blatant discriminatory acts) may have declined . . . its expression has morphed into a more contemporary and insidious form that hides in our cultural assumptions/beliefs/values, in our institutional policies and practices, and in the deeper psychological recesses of our individual psyches. . . . Racism has become invisible, subtle, and more indirect, operating below the level of conscious awareness, and continuing to oppress in unseen ways. (Sue, 2010, p. 8)

Melba J. T. Vasquez

- I knew there would be a contingent of APA members that preferred that the association stay away from these controversial topics [i.e., topics pertaining to immigration reform]. But I did not become a psychologist to understand human behavior and then hold onto that information while I observed society at a distance. Simply put, the contributions being made by psychologists are too relevant to ongoing social concerns [to] not try to bridge the "disconnect" between research and public policy in order to: help others understand the psychological factors related to the immigrant experience; and contribute to decision-making on immigration policies. (Vasquez, 2014, n.p.)

Janet E. Helms

- Many people erroneously use a person's racial categorization (e.g., Black versus White) to mean racial identity. However, the term "racial identity" actually refers to a sense of group or collective identity based on one's *perception that he or she shares a common racial heritage with a particular racial group. Racial designation or category and ethnicity per se are confusing issues in the United States.* (Helms, 1990, p. 3)

Paul B. Pedersen

- Culturally competent counselors are accurately aware of culturally learned assumptions by themselves and their clients, comprehend the culturally relevant facts and information about a client's culture and are able to intervene skillfully to bring about positive change through counseling. (Pedersen, 2002, n.p.)
- I have spent my life studying multiculturalism. We each belong to many different cultures. I tell my students sitting in their chairs they have a thousand people sitting with them whom they've gathered over a lifetime. Those persons include friends, family, enemies, fantasies, and other imaginary personalities. Those persons in our head control our behavior, and that makes up what we call our culture. All behaviors are learned and displayed in a cultural context. Accurate assessment, meaningful understanding, and appropriate intervention require that we become familiar with our many different selves. (J. Jensen, 2012, n.p.)

Source: Helms (1990), J. Jensen (2012), Pedersen (2002), Sue (2010), and Vasquez (2014).

Deficit or Inferiority Model

Drawing from Darwin's writings (cf., Darwin, 1859) on the heritability of traits and a hierarchical perspective on race, with superiority ascribed to the Aryan race, psychology evolved in a professional and cultural context assuming that the White male was perched at the apex of the evolutionary ladder and perceived as dominant in civilized life and intelligence (Galton, 1870).

A true paradigm-shattering event took place with the 1859 publication of Darwin's *On the Origin of Species by Means of Natural Selection, or the Preservation of Favored Races in the Struggle for Life.* Darwin's model pushed aside other evolutional models of the 1800s, such as the Lamarckian model of acquired characteristics (e.g., giraffes that stretched their necks to eat leaves from high tree branches passed on the characteristic of longer necks to their offspring). Darwin provided a brilliantly argued position asserting that the process of natural selection was behind the myriad life forms found on earth. The phrase "natural selection" refers to when an organism is better adapted to meet the conditions of its environment and as a result is more likely to survive, which Darwin associated with producing more offspring. After the publication of *Origin of Species*, a number of eminent individuals started to publicly support Darwin's position, including statistician Sir Francis Galton and biologist Thomas H. Huxley, who coined the term "Darwinism."

In the early 19th century, insanity was thought to result from the demands that civilization put on an individual, while "primitive societies," with no civilization, were viewed as placing no demands on their people. European civilization, in contrast, demanded intellectual involvement and organized production from its people. The general belief at the time was that the demands of civilization overwhelmed individuals with "mental weakness" and they became "insane" (Gauchet & Swain, 1999). As colonization spread, it was discovered that rates of mental illness, along with infectious diseases, tended to increase among the "primitive people."

In his 1871 book *The Descent of Man*, Darwin set out to build on his earlier work by discussing, in much greater detail, three areas: (1) evidence gathered that supported the claim that humans, like all known species, had descended from an earlier version of what they are now; (2) distinct developmental features comprising the evolutionary journey specifically taken by humans, and (3) similarities and differences between existing human races. Darwin believed that animals and humans were similar in a number of ways. For example, he believed that animals also experience complex emotions, display love and a desire to receive love, show wonder and curiosity, and display reasoning and imagination. In Darwin's eyes, it was the degree to which animals and humans differed in such qualities that made humans biologically special. Darwin considered some groups of humans (such as Englishmen) to be highly intelligent and possessing the level of organizational skills necessary to start the industrial revolution. Such groups were considered by Darwin to be "civilized" and, from an evolutionary perspective, much more advanced than groups that he termed "savage." Examples of the latter were "negroes" and "Australians" (i.e., aboriginal people). In *The Descent of Man*, in the section titled "On the Affinities and Genealogy of Man," Darwin wrote the following: "At some future period, not very distant as measured by centuries, the civilised races of man will almost certainly exterminate and replace throughout the world the savage races" (Darwin, 1871, p. 201).

There was a widely accepted notion during Darwin's time that members of savage races lacked the intelligence and motivation required to function in a civilized environment. It was believed that if such inferior persons were assigned to carry out civilized forms of work, their inherent mental weaknesses, which could not handle the stress experienced, would cause them to go insane. In the 19th century, colonialism was spreading, and those coming from "civilized countries" reported back to their homelands that among the primitive people in occupied territories, there had been a noticeable rise in mental illness and communicable diseases due to the inferior inhabitants' inability to adapt to the civilized changes imposed on them (Gauchet & Swain, 1999). In conjunction with the proliferation of such false beliefs about the superiority of some groups (and the spurious evidence to support this), a new term emerged: "social Darwinians." Many advocates of 19th-century social Darwinism viewed wealth as an indication of evolutionary superiority, while living in poverty was indicative of being an "unfit" human. Social Darwinism was used to justify the full or partial political control of nonsuperior others and their country. This belief allowed settlers to occupy the country and exploit the inferior inhabitants through various economic measures. Social Darwinism allowed for the rationalization of both racism and the assertion that northern European (Anglo-Saxon and Nordic) groups were evolutionarily superior. These details may create the notion that we are supportive of social Darwinism. We may encourage young college students to adopt the ideology of social Darwinism. We need to be attuned to conservative political climate of the U.S. that is currently pervasive. Let's prevent Charlottesville, VA.

In weighing the various evolutionary factors discussed by Darwin, Sir Francis Galton (1870) concluded that when a group of people achieved civilized status, the process of natural selection was thrown out of kilter. Galton feared that if natural selection was hindered from fully functioning, as it did when a group became civilized, then this breakdown in the natural order would allow unfit traits to pool and eventually spread throughout the group, leading to a sort of evolutionary rot.

Galton and many others feared the possibility that if left unchecked, inherited weaknesses would cause a slowdown of human evolution, could even offset any further civilized advancement, and could possibly even throw things in reverse for a period of time. Galton was also convinced he had the solution to prevent this from happening. Galton termed his solution the science of "eugenics," which he believed could reinstate an orchestrated form of natural selection by controlling the mating and production of human offspring. Various versions of Galton's new science were carried out in a number of countries, including the United States when the state of Indiana passed a law that required the sterilization of individuals deemed inferior. Eventually over 30 states had eugenics-inspired laws (Kluchin, 2009; Selden, 2005). In Nazi Germany, this effort led, during the 1930s, to the sterilization of thousands of Germans deemed unfit (Black, 2003). Eventually the Nazi eugenics program selected Germans of high intelligence and superior physicality to mate for the purpose of adding to what was already perceived as a superior race. Obviously, Nazis' interest in eugenics expanded to a level aimed at eliminating entire races and groups of perceived undesirables.

At the beginning of the 20th century when neurological theories of human functioning became popular, Western science utilized its science to justify racism proposing that African Americans had smaller frontal lobes (Bean, 1906), resulting in "more developed inferior mental faculties such as smell, sight, manual ability, corporeal sense, and melody, while Whites, on the other hand, would have developed higher mental faculties such as self-control, ambition, ethical and aesthetic sense and reason" (p. 163, Raimundo Oda, Banzato, & Dalgalarrondo, 2005, p. 163)

Intelligence tests proved particularly beneficial as instruments to sort a society that was emerging as increasingly heterogeneous because of the rate of high immigration in the late 19th and early 20th centuries (Gerber, 2011). Numerous immigrants were from eastern and southern Europe and were viewed as inferior to the earlier immigrants arriving from England and northern Europe (Reed, 1987; Roysircar & Pimpinella, 2008).

Concerns about this increase of immigrants played into eugenics fears of a number of leading psychologists such as Lewis Terman (1916), who developed the Stanford-Binet intelligence test (cf., Jensen, 1969), and James Cattell (Sokal, 1987), who developed the 16PF tests. The freed slaves of African descent, many of whom that had relocated into northern states, were considered to be a threat to racial purity.

Twisting science to confirm White superiority had real life-and-death consequences, especially given what had taken in applying eugenics.

During the same period, assessments to measure intelligence emerged. The first intelligence test was developed by Alfred Binet in France to identify children who would not profit from public education due to poor mental ability. Lewis Terman imported the Binet-Simon test and from it created the Stanford-Binet test of intelligence (Jensen, 1969). It was Terman who developed the original concept of IQ and created a scale that labeled different ranges of IQ scores (e.g., the lowest was termed "definite feeble-mindedness" and the highest "near genius or genius"). Other tests, such as Rorschach's ink-blot test and various personality tests, were being developed and increasingly utilized in the United States (Sokal, 1987). At the same time that psychological testing was proliferating (often used to highlight the deficiencies possessed by certain groups), the rate of immigration was becoming a concern (Gerber, 2011; Laughin, 1920). The migration of those tagged inferior was seen as an internal threat to racial purity and White supremacy. Such concerns rested on explanations that collectively comprised what is called the "deficit model," a model that asserted that certain groups in the United States suffered from multiple deficiencies in those areas believed to characterize White racial superiority.

Fighting the Deficit Model

In the 1930's, Howard Hale Long, an African American psychologist and a Harvard PhD, was employed in the Washington, D.C., public schools. Long claimed it was not intellectual inferiority, but problems of inequality in educational resources that resulted in the lower academic achievement and inequality in test scores for African American students (Guthrie, 1998). Among other minority psychologists who made significant contributions to refuting the arguments advocating racial inferiority were Albert S. Beckham and Herman G. Canady. In the 1930's, Beckham, a recipient of a Ph.D. from New York University, addressed the influence of urban environments on intelligence scores of Black children. Similarly, Canady questioned the role played by differences in race between the examiner and examinee in obtaining accurate results on intelligence tests (Guthrie, 1998). Canady demonstrated the importance of creating rapport with minority children to acquire the most accurate assessment of intelligence. He also contributed research that pointed out the difficulty in establishing similar testing environments for White and Black participants. By the time World War II arrived, psychologists of color were successfully challenging the findings of psychometric and scientific racism.

In the mid-1920s, a different view began to emerge, one that was in direct opposition to the deficit model. Increasingly, professionals began to oppose the idea that there were immutable racial differences and that hierarchies of racial superiority existed. The unquestioned superiority of Whites on a number of important psychological characteristics (i.e., intelligence, intrinsic motivation, ability to restrain sudden and unreflective urges, and so forth) was coming to an end. A perennial question argued by philosophers and psychologists was referred to as the *nature versus nurture question.* The nature position asserted that human qualities are innate (the deficit model represents this side of the argument) while the nurture position believed it is environmental factors that determine human traits (the current position is that both make us who we are). The move toward nurture was clearly reflected in the growing opposition toward the idea that intellectual differences depend solely on one's race.

A noteworthy example of research findings that fueled the growing resistance to claims of White superiority is illustrated by the breakthrough work carried out by Otto Klineberg, who later in his career promoted psychology internationally (Klineberg, 1965). Klineberg was a social psychologist, and his comparative research focused on students' intelligence scores. Klineberg's findings led him to conclude that the discrepancy in intelligence scores was attributable to social and economic differences between African Americans and Whites. Klineberg's research into racial differences led him to make a number of other assertions, assertions that often resulted in strong pushbacks. In a *New York Times* obituary for Klineberg, Lambert (1992) wrote the following:

> [Klineberg's] views were controversial. When he was quoted in 1931 saying there was no scientific basis for racial superiority barring interracial marriage, the New York Herald-Tribune, in an editorial against him, said his assertions ran counter to most ethnologists' assertion, "any intelligent farmer's knowledge of barnyard biology" and "American experience." (n.p.)

In addition to Klineberg, psychologists of color were drawn to providing cogent arguments to counter various forms of scientific racism, especially the type of racism that permeated psychometrics (Guthrie, 1998). In the 1930s, George Sanchez, a psychologist working in New Mexico, called attention to the cultural elements comprising Chicano children's lives. According to Sanchez (who had studied group differences and the scores of Spanish-speaking children on repeated tests), when assessment tests that had been validated using only White children were administered to Chicano children, the test results were automatically invalidated. Sanchez's explanation for such invalidation was that the language, values, and cultural experiences of White children differed too much from the language, values, and cultural experiences of Chicano children (see Sanchez, 1932). Also in the 1930s, others such as Howard Hale Long, Albert S. Beckham, and Herman G. Canady decided to throw down the equivalent of a psychometrics gauntlet (Guthrie, 1998). Long, a graduate of Harvard with a doctorate in educational psychology, was employed by the Washington, D.C., public school system to work with students. Through his pioneering work, Long asserted that it was not intellectual inferiority that was the cause of poor performance and lower intelligence scores, but the problematic inequality and insufficient resources. Beckham focused on identifying characteristics of city life that negatively impacted the intelligence scores of Black children who were attending schools in New York. Canady narrowed his exploration to what took place during the testing process itself. For example, he was interested in whether a difference in race between the examiner and the child being tested could skew results. Canady's research eventually led him to report that creating an atmosphere of rapport was a necessary ingredient for properly assessing a child's abilities. Therefore, it was critical for an examiner to develop a relationship with the child to be tested, a relationship in which the examiner and the child felt they understood each other, one that was imbued with the kind of empathy that would make communication possible and the testing process easy for both participants. Finally, Canady successfully pointed out the hurdles that confronted psychologists interested in creating testing environments that were of equal quality for White and Black students. Calling attention to the types of differences that could take place between these two testing environments was of critical importance, since Canady found that such differences invariably contributed to Black students performing poorly compared to White students. By the 1940s, psychologists of color had drawn significant attention to the inappropriateness of administering tests developed using one cultural group to a different cultural group. Layer by layer, the veneer hiding the embedded scientific racism that detracted from accurate testing was being torn away.

Civil Rights Movement

After World War II, an increasing number of psychologists began to view psychology through the lens of social justice. This change in perspective matched what was taking place during and after the war. The violent struggle taking place between the United States and fascism exposed the inconsistency between the ideals of equality and America's democracy. The civil rights agenda of the National Association for the Advancement of Colored People (NAACP) came to the forefront, and the NAACP, along with other organizations, was energized to put an end to discrimination in the country's military forces and in the public arena. During 1941, hundreds of thousands of Whites were being hired and prepared for industries geared toward war. Asa Philip Randolph, a civil rights activist and labor organizer, threatened to march on Washington, D.C., unless African Americans were provided equal access to the jobs being filled. In response to Randolph's concerns, President Franklin Roosevelt issued Executive Order 8802, which created the Committee on Fair Employment Practices to address discrimination complains (Jones, 2013; Kesselman, 1946).

After the war, the effort to fight discrimination continued to gain momentum (Gardner, 2002), drawing the attention of many individuals, including a number of psychologists. Two urban-based psychologists who brought about change that advanced fair and just relations between the larger society and African Americans were Mamie Phipps Clark and Kenneth Clark. Mamie had started investigating the areas of racial preference and identity while she was at Howard University. Kenneth joined her effort, and their work unequivocally demonstrated that racial rejection was directly tied to damaging self-awareness and self-esteem early in the lives of African American children.

Their research findings motivated Mamie and Kenneth Clark to establish the Northside Center for Child Development in New York City. The Center's overall aim was to study and call attention to the misuse of psychological testing, specifically testing that was being used to incorrectly label a disproportionate number of African American as mentally deficient and place them in classes established for the "retarded." Based on the Clarks' own assessment of these children, they concluded that many of them were actually above average in intelligence. This situation was psychologically damaging and immensely limited these children's chances for future success. The Clarks took on the New York City School Board, a confrontation that led to a protracted legal battle. In the end, the Clarks prevailed. Interestingly, the strategic steps taken by the couple essentially became a template to fight other instances of inappropriate testing that had long-term negative effects on minority children. One such situation taking place in the state of California led to a class-action court case known as *Lary P. v. Riles* (Frisby & Henry, 2016). The defendant was the California Department of Education, and the plaintiffs represented a class of African American children placed in special education classes expressly designed for students classified as "educable mentally retarded." Both the NAACP Legal Defense Fund and the U.S. Department of Justice Civil Rights Division were involved in the case. During proceedings, the Bay Area Association of Black Psychologists shared research data and gave their opinions concerning the inappropriateness of using standardized intelligence measures with minority children. The court ruled in favor of the plaintiffs, severely restricted the use of psychological tests for placement purposes, and established a monitoring system to oversee testing efforts to prevent future misplacement of children.

While the Clarks in their positions at the Northside Center were focused on effecting positive social change, the Supreme Court of the United States in May 1954 ruled in its landmark decision, *Brown v. Board of Education of Topeka Kansas*. In this court case, the Clarks presented their Black and White doll studies with African American children, showing that the children preferred White dolls (Clark & Clark, 1940). The Court ruled that segregation by race in public schools was unconstitutional. This was a momentous and historic ruling and one that contributed added impetus to the growing civil rights movement (see Figure 14.3).

In line with the efforts of the Clarks, Rosenthal and Jacobson's (1968) research pointed out the influence of expectation and labeling on the performance of school children on intelligence tests. Although not fully investigated until Steele and colleagues' research on stereotype threat (Steele, 1997), there was an increasing awareness that negative labeling of ethnic minorities could cause a self-fulfilling prophecy and restrict their academic and job success.

Similar to the efforts of the Clarks, Rosenthal and Jacobson (1968) uncovered findings that supported the conclusion that the expectations one holds toward a child can be influenced by the label (e.g., below average, average, or above average) assigned to that child based on the child's IQ score. The significance of Rosenthal and Jacobson's research became more fully appreciated when Steele (1997) published research pertaining to "stereotype threat." The term refers to situations where individuals perceive

▼ FIGURE 14.3

Court Decision Ends Segregation

Source: 1954, May. "Segregation in Public Schools Ended by Court." *The Bee.* pp. 1.

themselves as being in danger of confirming some stereotypical notion associated with their social group. Thus, widely held ideas or images that provide a grossly oversimplified view of a certain type of person increase the chances that a self-fulfilling prophesy will be activated. For example, a teacher's prediction that a minority student (based on an IQ score) will perform poorly in her or his class will indirectly or directly cause the child to perform as predicted (Steele & Aronson, 1995).

In the context of the American civil rights movement, around the time the Clarks were battling "separate but equal" school segregation, research on mental health and social class gained momentum. George Albee (1986) posited that a society could prevent mental disorders on a mass scale by reapportioning its resources to respond to problems in education, drug abuse, housing, and nutrition among low-income children.

When Hollingshead and Redlich (1958) systematically removed the possible influence of other variables (e.g., age, marital status, race, religion, or sex), a procedure called partialing or regressing out a variable, they found a clear correlation between social class and mental illness. Specifically, they uncovered an association between mental illness and lower social class status. These researchers also found that individuals who fit the lower class profile were less likely to see a professional for problems or receive any therapy for their mental illness that would be considered universally valid to treat their condition. Such individuals were also much more likely to be confined to institutional facilities permanently.

By the mid-1960s, the struggle of the civil rights movement started to impinge on psychology in the United States and leaders in the American Psychological Association. One strategy was to turn to George Albee and Kenneth B. Clark for leadership as sequential presidents of the American Psychological Association. Looking back, this milestone proved to be a critical moment in changing the face of psychology in the United States.

Culturally Deprived Model

A new explanation for the differences between minority groups and the majority White race in America arose during the civil rights movement. Reissman (1962) reported that a number of children who were considered to be culturally disadvantaged actually possessed above-average potential to succeed in life. Thus, according to Reissman, some members of a disadvantaged population—those who had relatively low IQ scores—had encountered deficiencies in the types of experiences provided by their family or racial group that had adversely influenced their development. Rather than earlier explanations that depended upon innate deficiencies genetically passed on to the next generation, Reissman was advocating an explanation dependent on non-innate, socially transmitted deficiencies passed on from generation to generation primarily through the socialization process (starting at infancy) carried out by parents and other family members. From this perspective, the mental health and other characteristics (i.e., habits, beliefs, and knowledge) that a child displays in school and elsewhere are a direct outcome of the training and instruction received in the context of the child's early environment.

The prototypical model of a healthy culture was considered to be the White middle-class. Well-meaning therapists and psychologists were motivated to raise Blacks and other minorities "up" to their standards. The cultural strengths of minority communities were not given any credit, and little attention was given to the successes of ethnic minorities when rearing their children successfully in spite of the oppression present in mainstream society. A cogent response to this failure to recognize the strengths of ethnic and racial minorities was voiced by Joseph L. White, one of the founders of the Association for Black Psychologists (ABPsi) and the first to utilize the phrase "Black Psychology" in print (see http://www.aaregistry.org/historic_events/view/joseph-white-paved-way-black-psychology; https://www.youtube.com/watch?v=2bm6ek6swGg). Here is an excerpt from his article, "Toward a Black Psychology":

The assumption from the *culturally deprived model* was that the standard of a healthy nurturing environment was the White middle-class American family. Therapists and academic psychologists committed to seeing African Americans and other minorities advance to this prototypical standard of mental health were surprisingly oblivious to the implications of adopting this kind of position. It is difficult from today's perspective to understand why those who were trying to help minorities did not realize that one group's values, family strengths, resilience, ways to deal with conflict, and so forth cannot be hijacked and superimposed onto another group. Even though on the surface the culturally deprived model might have appeared to represent a step forward in the explanation of racial and ethnic differences, its wholesale disregard for cultural strengths found in each race and ethnic group resulted in a step backward.

> Most psychologists take the liberal point of view which in essence states that black people are culturally deprived and psychologically maladjusted because the environment in which they were reared as children lacks the necessary early experiences to prepare them for excellence in school, appropriate sex-role behavior, and, generally speaking, achievement within an Anglo middle-class frame of reference. Possibly, if social scientists, psychologists, and educators would stop trying to compensate for the so-called weaknesses of the black child and try to develop a theory that capitalizes on his [her] strengths, programs could be designed which from the get-go might be more productive and successful. The black family represents another arena in which the use of traditional white psychological models leads us to an essentially inappropriate and unsound analysis. Maybe people who want to make the black a case for national

action should stop talking about making the black family into a white family and instead devote their energies into removing the obvious oppression of the black community which is responsible for us catchin' so much hell. (White, 1970/1972, pp. 43–45)

Ethnic and racial minorities were to be defined on their own terms, according to ethnic and racial minority counselors and psychologists. Further, identity was created in the community of origin and not imposed on minorities by Whites, however well-meaning. By 1968, there was a younger generation of African American psychologists who viewed being Black as an indicator of positive identity. These individuals became weary of waiting for APA to take action on their concerns about pursuing social justice for minority communities. As a result, at the September 1968 APA annual convention, a small group of Black Psychologists formed ABPsi. The association immediately challenged APA's leadership to demolish the legacy of racism in testing and the failure to establish appropriate psychological services, and urged APA to pursue policies and procedures to admit minority students into graduate programs in psychology (White, 2004; Williams, 1974).

Toward the end of the 1970s, ethnic and racial minority counselors and psychologists had reached a critical mass of individuals and the pace of change to pursue "a multicultural psychology" was substantial enough to launch the next stage of the struggle: creating multicultural competencies (D. W. Sue, Arredondo, & McDavis, 1992) with concurrent education and training in the appropriate delivery of multicultural services by all counselors and psychologists.

Joseph L. White's remarks (White, 1970/1972, pp. 43–45) made it clear that the responsibility to define African Americans resided with African Americans. It is the community of origin where identities are forged to begin with, and it is up to the members of such a community to determine "who or what a person is." Those outside a community who attempt to define what constitutes a healthy "identity" for members of that community are falling prey to hubris. It could be argued that such a well-meaning action to assist minorities is simply another form of racism hidden behind a misplaced desire to help, a desire resting upon the type of exaggerated confidence that causes one group to think they know what is best for another group.

The late 1960s brought a noticeable increase in young African American counselors and psychologists who saw being Black as positive and shared among themselves the same generational views. Tired of the lack of attention that social justice issues garnered in relation to the needs of minority groups, a small group of African American psychologists at the 1968 American Psychological Association's (APA) annual convention met and created the Association of Black Psychologists (ABPsi). After its creation, ABPsi moved forward and confronted leaders of the larger organization, APA, to take action against racism, especially as it related to psychological tests and the testing of minorities. The group also strongly advocated changes in the provision of services to minorities and pushed for APA to take a course of action that would lead to new policies for recruiting minorities interested in pursuing graduate degrees in the profession (White, 2004; Williams, 1974). As a result of such concerted, forceful efforts, within approximately a decade the number of African American counselors and psychologists had achieved the necessary size to produce a sustained effort that allowed them to continue to strive for and achieve needed changes, such as working to create a viable form of multicultural psychology. A critically important subsequent accomplishment was the specification of multicultural competencies that were securely moored to requisite education and the application of what had been learned through research (D. W. Sue et al., 1992).

Culturally Different Model

The culturally different model abandons the value judgments of diversity as genetic inferiority or culturally deprived and embraces the assumption that cultural differences must be recognized and respected as naturally occurring differences among the human species. The perspective for health moved away from a European American middle class male to a contextually bound frame of reference. Further, the universalistic application of psychological methods and theories based on a European American paradigm was challenged. Population-specific psychologies emerged from assumptions that it was not possible for White counselors and psychologists to remain stuck in their cultural context to sufficiently comprehend and promote the psychologies of culturally diverse groups (Cross, 1971; Padilla & Ruiz, 1973; Sue, D. W., 1981; Sue, D. W. et al. 1982; Sue, S. 1999; Trimble, 1981; Wrenn, 1962).

The *culturally different model* operates from the premise that various ethnic and racial groups differ in how they take in information and comprehend the world. Each culture has its own culturally derived ideas that provide vital information about how to be and act in a culturally congruent manner. Advocates of the culturally different model believe it is a mistake to consider one culture superior to another. Different cultural perspectives simply represent naturally occurring developments that occur among the various cultural groups that make up the world's population. A major outcome of the culturally different model was that there was no longer a reference being made to a single standard or apex of what constituted psychological and emotional well-being (e.g., archetype of the American middle-class Aryan). Acceptance of the culturally different model also led to challenging the universal soundness of theories and therapies viewed as solely tied to a European American paradigm (e.g., early psychodynamic theories and therapies based on a monocultural view of the world).

From the ashes of the deficit and deprivation cultural models arose population-specific psychologies and explanations that prevented counselors and psychologists, regardless of their own cultural ties, from remaining fixated on their personal cultural frame of reference. The culturally different model moved these professionals toward considering how they could promote and practice therapy that embraced cultural diversity (Cross, 1971; Padilla & Ruiz, 1973; D. W. Sue, 1981; D. W. Sue et al., 1982; S. Sue, 1999; S. Sue, Fujino, Hu, Takeuchi, & Zane, 1991; Trimble, 1981; Wrenn, 1962). The argument was that

> dominant methods of psychological research, the problems selected as important to pursue, and the demographics of the data gatherers have conspired against

developing a psychology of individuals that emerges from the experiences and per-spectives of those who occupy different places in the social order. (Trickett, Watts, & Birman, 1994, pp. 20–21)

The culturally different model opened up new lines of research, since this model escaped the obvious racism of the deficit model and the subtler form of racism that permeated the cultural deficiency model, whose pseudo-accuracy still depended on the existence of a racial hierarchy. After the arrival of the culturally different model, each ethnic, racial, or cultural group could be studied on its own merit. As pointed out by Helms (1995), this meant that White racial identity could now be studied as unmistakably different from what constituted African American racial identity (Cross, 1995; Khanna & Johnson, 2010; Sellers & Shelton, 2003). This particular model also supported the conclusion that minorities within the dominant culture respond to their social environments in terms of a multiple cultural context and thus behave and think from a bicultural perspective (Sodowsky, Lai, & Plake, 1991).

One should not assume that, because the culturally different model was arguably much better than the models it succeeded, it did not pose any challenges for academics and practitioners. Take, for example, the area of psychometrics. Even though it is safe to say that psychologists have not devoted the necessary time and effort to creating the number of culture-specific intellectual assessments needed, it can also be said this is not entirely their fault, because the culturally different model brought with it a new complexity that requires careful scrutiny. This can be illustrated by referring to the psychological theory and test construction methods associated with the science of psychometrics. For example, when one sets out to create either a culture-fair intel-ligence test or a culture-free intelligence test, the challenges rapidly begin to build up. The aim of a *culture-fair intelligence test* is to develop an assessment that provides IQ scores that are unaffected by social status or cultural experiences, and the aim of a *culture-free intelligence test* is to develop an assessment that completely gets rid of any quality that would either be in favor of or against any type of cultural influences. Concerning the latter, VandenBos (2007) stated that "the creation of such a test is probably impossible" (p. 251), and when he remarked on the former, VandenBos con-cluded that whatever the creator used to construct test questions would be riddled with problems. According to VandenBos, regardless of how the test questions were constructed, they would unavoidably "reflect certain cultural norms in some degree, hence [might] tend to favor members of certain cultures over members of others" (p. 251). VandenBos illustrated his point by quoting a prominent psychologist who had developed several IQ tests that have been used extensively for decades. This psy-chologist said, "A circle in one place [i.e., culture] may be associated with the sun, in another with a copper coin, and [in] another with a wheel" (D. Wechsler, 1966, as cited by VandenBoss, 2007, p. 251).

Regardless of the specific challenges mentioned above, operating from the cultur-ally different model does require caution and taking steps to avoid cultural prejudice from seeping into situations that involve either the construction of an assessment or the administering of an assessment. The following recommendations have been made concerning both of these situations (see American Educational Research, 2014; ApA, 2013b; Cofresi & Gorman, 2004; Drasgow & Probst, 2005; Herzig, Roysircar, Kosyluk, & Corrigan, 2013; Roysircar, 2005, 2013; Roysircar, Colvin, Afolayan, Thomspson, & Robertson, 2017; Roysircar & Krishnamurthy, 2018): (1) A coordinated push should be made by professional groups to develop minority culture–specific and universal test items in conjunction with corresponding instructions for scoring; (2) all psychological assessment studies conducted should incorporate ethnic minorities; and (3) professionals who rely on testing others should utilize, as much as possible, nonverbal measures, structured intake interviews, and qualitative interviews.

Internationalization of Psychology

In the 21st century, as internationalization is intensifying its influence around the world, psychologists and counselors from the United States leave behind a sense of self-sufficiency about their European American theories when serving in international settings while simultaneously trying to increase their understanding of therapy as it is practiced in other cultures and nations. The profession of counseling psychology is addressing the many challenges of our global era, such as the mass trauma of natural and human-made disasters, by examining European American psychology's assumptions and practices as they are applied throughout the world. Special attention is given to the significance of accommodating European American psychology's purposes, roles, and functions to cultural and international differences. Instead of McDonaldizing therapy worldwide (i.e., relying on an assembly line type of mentality that seeks standardization), therapists should always display respect for local healing practices while simultaneously considering how such practices can be effectively incorporated into their approach (see Gerstein, Heppner, Stockton, Leung, & Aegisdottir, 2009).

Models of cross-cultural therapy competencies in helping persons from various locales around the world also have been deemed important in this regard. Four such models have appeared in the professional literature, including one (Heppner, Leong, & Gerstein, 2008) that focuses on employing knowledge about the cultural context and the subsystems in cross-cultural activities and another (Ægisdóttir & Gerstein, 2010) that has adapted the three-component (awareness, knowledge, and skills [AKS]) multicultural competencies model (D. W. Sue et al., 1992) to include a fourth component, motivation. The third model, called the cross-national cultural competence model (Heppner, Wang, Heppner, & Wang, 2012), integrates a systems perspective and the AKS model. The fourth and final model, the dynamic-systemic-process model of international competencies (Gerstein, Hurley, & Hutchison, 2015), is the most elaborate and detailed model, claiming that it

> is guided by the assumption that individuals' learning and development of international competencies is continuous, not sequential but recursive, constantly evolving, cumulative, and highly dynamic. Further, it is assumed that change is a constant and inevitable aspect of the human experience, and as a result, individuals' affect, cognition, and behavior (e.g., international competencies) is complex,

fluid, and in a reciprocal relationship with the environment. Stated differently, it is believed that individuals' competencies are both shaped by and shape the environment. (Gerstein et al., 2015, pp. 241–242)

When therapists have developed the ability to be empathic with the cultural experiences of clients who are not European American, they are well prepared to do work with a diverse clientele. "Cultural empathy" is described as:

the attitude and skill to effectively bridge the cultural gap between the clinician and the client; one that seeks to help clinicians integrate an attitude of openness with the necessary knowledge and skill to work successfully across cultures. It involves a deepening of the human empathic response to permit a sense of mutuality and understanding across the great differences in value and expectation that cross-cultural interexchange often involves. (Dyche & Zayas, 2001, p. 245)

Psychologists and counselors of the future will be expected to interface with individuals from a highly diverse range of cultural backgrounds. A variety of cultural concepts could be applied to a diverse range of human behaviors and contexts that are new to most counselors and psychologists (Moodley, Lengyell, Wu, & Gielen, 2015; Poyrazili & Thompson, 2013). Already, children of immigrants are attending schools in many of the major cities worldwide, such as Toronto, New York, Berlin, London, and Paris. For instance, in 2012, two thirds of the students in New York City's public school system were from minority and immigrant cultures. Consequently, the school counselor in a New York City public school must be ready to assist students whose parents have relocated to the city from 40 nations around the world (Roysircar, 2006). For such a counselor, exposure to the literature on practices in therapy across cultures is a preparation for the essential task of understanding how the world may be perceived by students (clients), their extended families, peers, and neighborhood friends (Moodley et al., 2015; Roysircar, 2006).

Basic Concepts

Culture

The American Psychological Association's Multicultural Guidelines (APA, 2017) defines the term culture as "belief systems and value orientations that influence customs, norms, practices, and social institutions, including psychological processes (language, care-taking practices, media, educational systems)" (p. 165). According to APA (2017) "culture has been described as the embodiment of a worldview through learned and transmitted beliefs, values, and practices, including religious and spiritual traditions. It also encompasses a way of living informed by the historical, economic, ecological, and political forces on a group" (p. 165).

One way that therapists can acquire more information about their client's cultural context is by utilizing the fifth edition of the American Psychiatric Association's *Diagnostic and Statistical Manual of Mental Disorders* (*DSM-5*) (ApA, 2013a). This manual includes criteria for taking into account cultural variations in displays of disorders, provides structured information about cultural concepts of distress, and features a clinical interview tool. The Cultural Formulation Interview (CFI) helps therapists evaluate cultural factors (i.e., cultural definition of the problem, stressors, causes, support, self-coping, role of cultural identity, previous help-seeking, barriers, and preferences) that affect the client's perspectives, behaviors, responses, and options for treatment (ApA, 2013b). Therapists can use this interview tool along with personality evaluations to acquire a more holistic understanding of the client.

Cultural Paranoia

The experience of many immigrants can be characterized as culture shock, which may include paranoid aspects (Whaley, 1998). Individuals who suddenly become immersed in a different culture without adequate knowledge of the cultural norms, language, and economics of the host society as well as social resources are likely to experience paranoia or the fear of doing something wrong as a natural response to this transition (Whaley, 1998). However, when psychopathology does develop in immigrants, paranoid psychosis is found more frequently than affective disorders (Whaley, 1998).

Paranoia can also be viewed as an adaptive response to the environment for individuals who experience oppression in the dominant culture (Whaley, 1998). Within the therapeutic relationship, paranoia can develop, especially when the client is from the oppressed culture and the therapist from the dominant culture. Therapists may misinterpret this type of paranoia as a symptom of psychosis. Socioeconomic status also has a critical role in the development of paranoia. Whitaker (2002) stated, "Behaviors and emotions that can lead to a diagnosis of schizophrenia—hostility, anger, emotional withdrawal, paranoia—go hand in hand with being poor" (p. 173). Therefore, in therapy, cultural factors, effects of immigration, race, and socioeconomic status should be considered when attempting to understand a client's paranoia.

Biculturalism

Multidimensional models of acculturation (Berry, 2001; Roysircar, 2004a) posit that positive mental health outcomes are correlated with bicultural adaptation, wherein individuals are competent in both their culture of origin and the host culture. *Bidimensional acculturation* has been defined as the process of adapting to the host culture while maintaining an identity with one's culture of origin. It is also the process by which persons comprehend and incorporate beliefs, values, and behaviors of the host culture in the context of their culture of origin (Roysircar, 2004b). LaFromboise, Coleman, and Gerton (1993) discussed the *alternation model*, in which a person can alternate between each of two cultures depending on the context and not give one more preference than the other. This context-based cultural flexibility has also been called the "diaspora experience" and is believed to provide an individual with the highest chances for mental well-being.

Race and Ethnicity

Race is defined as a complex construct without precise or clear scientific or theoretical meaning, though it is often used in psychological theory and research (Helms, Jernigan, & Mascher, 2005). Race is often understood as a biological-race construct, yet a racial group is not monolithic due to within-group diversity. Consider for a moment: Is there a pure, intact race in the United States?

Helms (1995) posited that race is a sociopolitical and socioeconomic construct determined by how a group ranks or positions itself in relation to other groups. For example, how does White American society understand its power status, privilege, and institutional policies when it compares itself to African Americans? People use sociopolitical hierarchy for their own convenience, and this practice sets up power differentials (power vs. oppression) regarding which group gets something and which group does not. *Ethnicity*, in contrast, has been defined as a group's acceptance of the practices of its culture of origin and the perception of belonging to a reference group (Ponterotto, Casas, Suzuki, & Alexander, 2010). Ethnicity refers to a commonality within a group, which is often based on nationality, language, traditions, and history (Roysircar, 2004b).

Intersectionality

Intersectionality takes into account the multiplicity of cultural/social contexts and roles to which individuals belong, are shaped by, and identify with (Howard & Renfrow, 2014). Therapists are encouraged to be aware of the perspectives of individuals shaped by the multiplicity of their social contexts, some marginalized, some privileged. Both privileges and discrimination are inherent to different contextual identities of an individual. Therefore, systems of inequality (e.g., racism) are transformed by the intersections of multiple identities (e.g., a Black lesbian feminist having African American communal support as well as women's support). Intersectionality is more than the sum of parts (e.g., Black + Woman + Lesbian + Class), but is a transformation of inequalities and privileges of unidimensional systems. Intersectionality captures the vast within-group variations in identity development found among members of ethnic and racial groups (Shin, 2015). Intersectionality theory argues that focusing solely on the influence of ethnicity and/or race on identity development fails to consider the multiple social identities that intersect within one's life, keeping invisible the forces of patriarchy, heteronormativity, ableism, class oppression, and other types of systemic, institutionalized discrimination (Shin, 2015).

Stereotype Threat

According to Steele and Aronson (1995), *stereotype threat* is described as the risk of confirming a negative stereotype attributed to one's group (see Figure 14.4). As a type of self-fulfilling prophecy, stereo-type threat occurs when an individual adheres to the negative evaluations of others about one's own group. For instance, Steele and Aronson (1995) explored the influence of stereotype threat upon African American intellectual test performance. The researchers described how a lifetime of being exposed to negative prejudices can eventually be internalized, causing "inferiority anxiety" (Steele & Aronson, 1995). *Inferiority anxiety* is triggered by situational cues and causes an individual to be threatened and thereby meet the negative standards held by others (Steele & Aronson, 1995). In fact, Steele and Aronson (1995) described

▼ FIGURE 14.4

Being a Person Means Being Stereotyped

how inferiority anxiety can lead members of the stereotyped group to become defensive and blame other groups for the anxiety, avoid seeking opportunities, and even facilitate the development of a victimized identity—all of which contribute to a lack of success in life.

Racial Microaggressions

Racial microaggressions are defined as subtle, everyday insults toward individuals belonging to a group of people of color about whom negative stereotypes are held (D. W. Sue et al., 2007). Individuals who commit microaggressions are typically unaware that they are doing so and may even be unaware of the implicit negative prejudices they hold against other groups (D. W. Sue et al., 2007). According to D. W. Sue et al. (2007), there are three types of racial microaggression: microassault, microinsult, and microinvalidation.

Microassaults are explicit expressions of prejudices and are typically viewed as traditional, overt racism. For example, the use of racial slurs to demean another individual is a microassault and is most likely a conscious process for the individual. *Microinsults* are subtle verbal or nonverbal snubs directed toward individuals of color. For instance, when an individual asks a light-skinned person of color, "Where are you from?" and he or she does not seem to put it to rest when the answer is the United States or Canada, there is likely a microinsult implicit in this interaction. *Microinvalidations* discount the subjective experience, feelings, or thoughts of a person of color. For instance, when an African American male expresses frustration that he is not being treated the same way White customers are being treated at a restaurant, he may be told to relax and that he is overreacting. Microinvalidation is implicit within this commentary and serves as a subtle way of belittling the experience of individuals of color.

Implicit Racism

Research on subtle racism (e.g., Dovidio, Gaertner, Kawakami, & Hodson, 2002; Dovidio, Kawakami, & Gaertner, 2002) and stereotype threat (Steele, 1997) bears on the present topic. For instance, Dovidio, Kawakami, and Gaertner (2002) investigated the effects of explicit and implicit racial attitudes on White persons' perceptions of interactions with Black individuals. According to these researchers, *explicit racial attitudes* can influence "deliberative, well-considered responses for which people have the motivation and opportunity to weigh the costs and benefits of various courses of action" (p. 62). Alternatively, *implicit attitudes*, according to Dovidio, Kawakami, and Gaertner (2002), can influence "responses that are more difficult to monitor and control [e.g., eye movements, blinking] or responses that people do not view as an indication of their attitude and thus do not try to control" (p. 62). Dovidio, Kawakami, and Gaertner (2002) revealed that the explicit prejudice of White participants was significantly associated with ratings of their verbal friendliness but not with ratings of their nonverbal behaviors. Implicit prejudice, as measured by a response-latency task, was significantly associated with ratings of their nonverbal friendliness but not with ratings of their verbal behaviors. Thus, implicit and explicit racism have a low correlation with each other.

Racial Identity

Helms (1990) described racial identity as a "sense of group or collective identity based on one's perception that he or she shares a common racial heritage with a particular racial group" (p. 3). Helms's (1990) *Black racial identity model* is considered the predominant model in the therapy literature. Racial identity development is overcoming internalized racism, internalized societal racial stereotypes, and negative conceptions of the self and one's own group (Helms, 1995).

There are certain assumptions about the development of racial identity (Wijeyesinghe & Jackson, 2012). For instance, the general identity issue for Whites is said to be the abandonment of racism, which can also be interpreted as entitlement. The general issue of development for Blacks involves overcoming internalized racism. This development occurs in successive racial identity statuses, and maturation is sequential. Healthy development is the capacity to be aware of and give up the normative strategies of one's racial group for coping with race-related information. Discomfort in unresolved situations is thought to be the catalyst that strengthens existing statuses, creates new higher-level ones, or promotes regression to an earlier, less mature status (Helms, 1995).

Kevin Cokley (2002) posited that emphasizing racial identity may become a problem when it unwittingly prescribes prejudicial beliefs or stereotypes about a person's ascribed racial group. Internalized racialism occurs when one identifies with any stereotype attributed to one's racial group, be it positive or negative, based on one's or others' (false) assumption that racial categories have immutable and innate characteristics. An African American's internalized racialism would be evidenced by such an individual's belief that Black people are members of a definable, monolithic racial group. Thus, racial identity is undergoing ongoing theory development.

"Emic" (Multicultural) and "Etic" (Cross-Cultural) Approaches

Etic, as described by Leong, Leung, and Cheung (2010), pertains to the universalist approach of cross-cultural psychology, as in the use of acculturation theory to understand diverse groups of immigrants in various contexts and countries. *Emic* is best described as the indigenous approach (Leong et al., 2010), such as understanding the effects of racism on African Americans through racial identity theories and doing healing and resilience-building by using African American religious or spiritual traditions. The *etic approach* can be characterized by general knowledge about a cultural phenomenon (Leong et al., 2010), such as the acculturation of immigrants, cultural values of independence versus interdependence, and worldview systems, whereas the *emic approach* involves culture-specific knowledge and awareness (Leong et al., 2010), such as African American racial identity, the Chinese stigma of loss of face, and the Asian Hindu work philosophy of Dharma. Although some tensions exist between the etic and emic approaches, Leong et al. (2010) argued that integrating both can yield new insights for culturally sensitive practice. Within therapy practice, it is important to grasp generalized information regarding client help-seeking attitudes, stigmas, and mental health behaviors along with how an individual client interprets his or her experience of loss of face when speaking to a therapist. Understanding both *nomothetic* and *idiographic* features of a culture is paramount in understanding idiosyncrasies of a client from a different background (Roysircar, 2013). Therefore, both the etic (cross-cultural) and emic (multicultural) approaches, when integrated, produce the soundest and most culturally sensitive therapeutic approach.

The Therapeutic Process

Practitioners are better equipped to prevent ethical violations and promote beneficence to their clients with increased attention to multicultural dynamics in therapy. They need to demonstrate multicultural competencies, which are described in the following sections.

Goals of Therapy

Multicultural therapists need to expect and attend to the mistrust their clients might have toward the therapeutic process. Creating goals for treatment is important in guiding therapy in directions that best suit the client. Nelson-Jones (2002) outlined 12 goals for multicultural therapy: (1) reconciliation, (2) support, (3) coping with posttraumatic stress, (4) helping with acculturation and assimilation, (5) avoiding additional marginalization, (6) addressing racial and cultural discrimination, (7) helping clients to manage close cross-cultural relationships, (8) helping clients to manage intergenerational conflict, (9) helping long-stay transients and expatriates, (10) helping with gender role and equality issues, (11) attaining higher levels of development, and (12) establishing the "good society."

The therapist acts as a social change agent and helps identify institutional factors that oppress and inhibit the client's cultural beliefs and practices (Nelson-Jones, 2002). An overall goal of multicultural therapy is to help the person express himself or herself within a culture. Through the process of reconciliation and support, the client can help shape what he or she views as the good society. The goals that remain in the process are not linear and can be implemented during different times in therapy, depending on the presenting issues of the client.

Lakes, López, and Garro (2006) presented the *shifting the cultural lenses* model, which requires moving between two cultural perspectives—that of the client and that of the therapist. This allows both the client and therapist to operate from the same, shared narrative. This model emphasizes the process of defining the problem from the perspective of both the client and the therapist. This approach validates the client's perspective while still utilizing the therapist's knowledge of the presenting problem. It allows for more successful treatment because of mutual understanding. People create their meanings from personal, cultural, and linguistic constructs, and it is in these contexts that the therapist and client bring forth meaning. This model also involves the externalization of negative beliefs and an examination of how those beliefs have been acted on in the client's life.

Another goal of multicultural therapy is to increase client resilience and decrease client trauma. The American Psychological Association's Task Force for Re-envisioning the Multicultural Guidelines for the 21st Century (APA, 2017) has encouraged psychologists to actively strive to take a strengths-based approach in working with individuals, families, groups, communities, and organizations that seek to build resilience and decrease trauma, while also understanding resilience and trauma within a cultural context.

The Therapist's Role

Self-Disclosure and the Multicultural Relationship. Therapist self-disclosure can strengthen the alliance as long as professional boundaries are maintained. Disclosure can confront similarities and differences between the therapist and client, which can encourage discussion about the roles of cultural factors in therapy. The goal of self-disclosure should always be to strengthen the alliance. Finding common interests and similarities can help the therapist and client create a base for more personal, even difficult aspects of psychotherapy (Roysircar, 2009a). The multicultural relationship is supportive, empathic, and an interpersonal alliance built on expressed differences and similarities. The alliance is of primary importance in multicultural therapy (Roysircar, 2009a), which can disagree with the growing trend of empirically supported treatments.

Therapist Awareness of the Client's Worldview. The therapist must approach the client's cultural beliefs in a judgment-free manner and be responsive to the client's beliefs about what is true, values about what is good or best, and other factors connected to identity (see Figure 14.5). Building a competence in the client's background and reflecting this knowledge and a desire to learn more can increase the client's comfort in therapy. To comprehend the influence a client's culture has on her or his life, the therapist must evaluate the person's own degree of cultural awareness and perspective. If this assessment is not conducted, the therapist takes the risk of misattributing cultural factors to the client's presentation (Toporek, 2003).

Culturally Appropriate Intervention Strategies. In the area of application, the therapist comes to realize that the individualistic orientation of European American psychotherapy informs the perception of what is normal and acceptable and what is pathological. The therapist realizes that multicultural and social justice concerns are not inherent to mainstream European American therapies. Multicultural competency entails adapting one's theoretical approach by both recognizing and adhering to human diversity factors that best suit the client and lead to a successful outcome. Multicultural sensitivity or indigenous therapeutic adaptation should not be an "add-on"; it should be part and parcel of competent therapeutic skills. An integral component in making sound intervention strategies includes developing the skills and knowledge to comprehend the client's personal, cultural, and universal identities. Understanding the core conditions of safety, support, and rapport is required to make successful interventions and build the alliance (Fuertes & Ponterroto, 2003).

▼ FIGURE 14.5

Factors of Identity

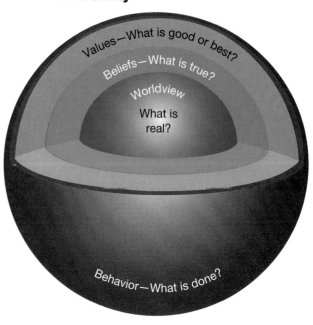

The Client's Role

Multicultural clients have a higher likelihood of remaining in therapy if the counseling strategies used are congruent with their values and beliefs (Griner & Smith, 2006). Clients may be passive and expect the professional provider to do the job rather than being actively engaged in carrying out their own treatment. Cultural minority clients need psychoeducation on what therapy is, therapy outcomes, and the type of treatment they will undergo. This direct guidance will elicit client compliance.

Multicultural Assessment

Multicultural evaluation involves engaging in a number of decisions. The first decision revolves around whether an emic (multicultural) or etic (cross-cultural) focus will be used (Draguns, 1996). At the beginning of the assessment, however, it is important to consider how a client would view the evaluation. Individuals that are representative of some minority cultures, for instance, where assessment rarely occurs or where information gathered from such an evaluation has disadvantaged them, can lack trust in the use of semi-structured and structured evaluation procedures. Consequently, individuals who are minorities may feel compelled to respond, and the therapist may not gather valid data. In such instances, the evaluation should be performed according to the "narrative structure" of what is familiar to the client (APA, 2013b; Roysircar, 2005, 2013). If at all possible, the therapist should employ both an etic and an emic lens to obtain a more complete profile of the person being evaluated (Draguns, 1996). This requires investigating how the person's perceptions, mores, and behaviors are similar to and different from those of the individual's minority culture as well as the dominant culture. Such a process can be conceptualized utilizing *multicultural ecological assessment* (Roysircar, 2013), which emphasizes the changes in environmental systems that immigrant clients may experience. It is also essential that the therapist comprehends the client as a person who cannot simply be understood in terms of majority/minority contextual variables. The therapist, therefore, utilizes dynamic sizing (S. Sue, 1998), defined as having the ability to perceive the individual's uniqueness and to generalize the person's issues in the evaluation and intervention processes (S. Sue, 1998).

Due to the observation that cultural groups vary in how they cope with external and internal stressors (Kuo, Roysircar, & Newby-Clark, 2006), it would appear inadequate to believe in the findings of a psychological evaluation based on *DSM* criteria without taking into consideration, as a mediator variable, the client's culture (Roysircar, 2005). Furthermore, the American Psychological Association's policy (APA, 2006) on evidence-based practice posits that it is critical to design and implement interventions based on the client's value preferences against a background of current research along with therapist expertise.

The Clinical Interview. Semi-structured interviews have been found to result in increased diagnostic accuracy with ethnic minorities (Aklin & Turner, (2006). Open clinical interviews were found to increase the likelihood of misdiagnosis, which resulted in poorer treatment outcomes for minority clients. African American and Latino clients are disproportionately overdiagnosed with schizophrenia and affective disorders compared to White clients. Therapists overpathologize symptoms expressed in ethnic minorities due to their lack of multicultural awareness and training. Therapists often apply rigid diagnostic criteria found in the DSM without considering additional sources that could contribute to a more accurate diagnosis (Aklin & Turner, 2006).

When creating a semi-structured interview, therapists must include culturally relevant questions that are responsive to cultural issues. Being responsive to these factors in the initial interview will lead to a more accurate diagnosis and increase trust between therapist and client. Creating structure within the interview protocol ensures that relevant information is covered with every client and that criteria are met for various diagnoses. Such questions do not assume homogeneity in clinical presentations and background but instead are flexible to the client. Aklin and Turner (2006) outlined several examples of assessment tools that can be implemented in the semi-structured interview: the Symptom-Driven Diagnostic System (SDDS), Primary Care Evaluation of Mental Disorders (PCEMD), and the Mini-International Neuropsychiatric Interview (M.I.N.I.). These tools have brief administration times (approximately 15 minutes), are sensitive to client characteristics, and are diagnostically sensitive (Aklin & Turner, 2006).

Clinical Judgment. Utilizing clinical judgment should not be equated with simply making a diagnosis. It is much more than that, since it represents a complex skill that typically involves stages such as gathering client data via an intake interview, administering a psychological evaluation/assessment to gauge a client's psychological functioning (this stage may or may not lead to making a DSM diagnosis), thoughtfully weighing treatment options (which may include making a referral), and rendering a prognosis that concerns the likelihood for improvement. In addition to possessing the expected competence that comes with administering psychological tests and the interpretation that follows, it is of critical importance for the therapist to make an informed effort throughout the clinical judgment process to prevent errors from taking place—the types of errors that can occur when the therapist allows a personal feeling, guess, or opinion to intrude into the process. The accuracy and effectiveness of any treatment recommendation made requires the therapist to sustain focused attention on the client's needs while simultaneously maintaining an appropriate level of objectivity during each stage of the process. It may be surprising to a novice, but it is not always easy for a trained professional to strictly adhere to the process as it is intended. For example, a seasoned therapist has typically acquired an intuitive ability over time that can prove invaluable when working with a client in the context of ongoing therapy, but the type of therapy shortcut that results from this intuitive wisdom should never be confused with taking a shortcut during the clinical judgment process. The two shortcuts are not the same. According to Spengler, Strohmer, Dixon, and Shivy (1995), therapists' "assessments are accurate to the extent that they are based on what is known, do not overlook important client data, and lead to efficacious interventions" (p. 508). In truth, as recognized by Spengler et al. (1995), therapists too often resort to utilizing their personal experiences, unchecked expert consensus about some matter, or a self-proclaimed approach for administering assessments that is roughly correct but not well-founded. According to Spengler et al. (1995), such incidents increase the likelihood of an erroneous clinical judgment being made.

Spengler et al. (1995) indicated that for a therapist to remain competent, she or he must stay abreast of the professional literature, particularly literature that relates to the types of clients a she or he is currently working with. However, it is also important for a therapist to maintain a practical familiarity with current multicultural issues. This is especially true for practice issues for which a therapist may not have received adequate (or any) preparation during his or her training program. Examples of issues that therapists have been increasingly confronted with in recent years are PTSD in refugees (e.g., Kleijin, Hovens, & Rodenburg, 2001), acculturation stress experienced by first-generation immigrants (e.g., Roysircar-Sodowsky & Maestas, 2000), generational gaps tied to a family's decision to immigrate to the United States (e.g., Hwang, 2016; Roysircar, Corey, & Koroma, 2010), traumatic reactions associated with the severe mental stress or physical injury resulting from an intense encounter with racism, and the other-and-self-alienation that plagues both Native Americans and African Americans (e.g., Leary, 2005; Turner & Pope, 2009). A good guiding principle concerning the professional literature is to look for publications appearing within the last ten years, but one should keep in mind that there are exceptions to this rule, since much can be gained by reading older seminal publications. These are groundbreaking publications that have remained relevant and are known to have strongly influenced later developments in the mental health field. Finally, if a therapist discovers there are insufficient resources to stay up-to-date, she or he should keep in mind that there are other ways to ways to learn about the latest developments and trends. In fact, professional organizations often encourage the use of alternatives, as per the American Psychological Association's Code of Ethics that pertains to competence (APA, 2010), which asserts that in such situations it is the therapist's responsibility to consult with knowledgeable professionals or to seek supervision for an area that requires strengthening.

Techniques and Strategies

Addressing Systemic Disparity. Health care, law enforcement, education, and the judicial system are only a few of the many systems impacted by widespread disparities. The social inequities that individuals face in these systems have tremendous negative psychological effects. Because of therapists' central role in helping individuals cope with negative experiences, it is necessary that they continually recognize and educate themselves about these disparities and how structural disparities promote oppression and affect each group and each individual differently. They must also advocate for human rights and justice and equal access to resources (APA, 2017).

A Therapist's Intersectional Perspective. Awareness of individual and cultural differences in the multitude of domains that make up identity has been recognized as essential to effective clinical care (Roysircar, Dobbins, & Malloy, 2010). Intersectionality, by its broadest definition, incorporates the vast array of cultural/social contexts and roles that individuals are shaped by or subscribe to. Intersectionality stands in contrast to linear, or "single-axis," models that privilege singular dimensions of difference and encourage the derivation of knowledge from the notion that all members of a group have essentially the same experience (Grzanka, 2014). To understand an individual in the therapy setting, it is not enough to acquire and apply a knowledge base of group difference (race, ethnicity, gender, sexual identity, religion, etc.) and view that individual through that single-axis lens. A given sense of identity will likely comprise interacting contexts of multiple identities and their associated privileges and oppressions, informed by the power, social dictates, constraint, values, strengths, and perceived deficits of those identities. To have any hope of understanding a client, therapists begin with a foundational assumption that a client's experiences are constructions of a multitude of identity aspects working in a dynamic interplay to form perspectives and responses, with a focus on how the contexts of those identities inform the biases with which a client and a therapist will formulate the world around them. A therapist's intersectional framework encourages a depth of curiosity and willingness to learn from diverse identity perspectives necessary for holistic psychological care (APA, 2017).

Using a Strengths-Based Approach. In general, therapists have made an attempt to move away from a traditional model of therapy based on a client's disorder or diagnosis, which focuses on weaknesses. In contrast, the strengths-based model emphasizes the individual and cultural strengths clients have (e.g., resilience, adaptation, coping skills) in the context of their environment (APA, 2017). According to Roysircar, Thompson, and Boudreau (2017), the strengths-based approach takes into account an individual's external strength resources in his or her culture, heritage, and community as well as various positive contextual factors (e.g., family, communalism, religion). Not only can focusing on strengths produce client empowerment, but it also allows the professional and the client to have a reciprocal relationship in their approach to care and promoting positive change. This model uses a collaborative therapeutic approach, where clients are not passive recipients of professional expertise but active participants in their own healing and growth. The strengths-based model does not ignore the present problems of individuals; however, it does focus on the coping and problem-solving skills clients already employ with the goal of improving these skills to minimize future risks. It is important for the therapist working with strengths-based interventions to capitalize on the meaning and the expression of strengths within the client's cultural experience. The client has a unique understanding of his or her personality characteristics and how these characteristics interact with his or her community. Therefore, clients are seen as experts in terms of understanding how they can impact the therapy process and also how to make the therapist aware of how to respect their clients' cultural values and needs.

Developing the Therapeutic Alliance. A strong therapeutic alliance must be built and maintained for the therapist to work effectively with the client. The alliance must reflect flexibility, honesty, respect, empathy, and openness from the therapist to the client (Fuertes & Ponterotto, 2003). Attending to the client's past and present experiences both inside and outside therapy is crucial. An integral component of therapy includes the facilitation and processing of affect, which is often a gradual experience. The therapist must abstain from including stereotypes when creating the therapeutic frame, and must attend to the diversity factors a client presents and introduces as important and meaningful.

Cognitive Match Model.[2] The cognitive match model pertains to the degree to which congruence is present between the worldviews of the client and the therapist (Roysircar, 2009a). Cognitive match can be thought of as being situated among the key ingredients necessary for effective therapeutic outcomes. It contributes significantly to the conceptualization phase of therapy, since it allows for a substantial amount of information to be obtained from a client, which contributes directly to deciding what therapeutic techniques and strategies are most appropriate and the specific goals that need to be constructed to successfully treat a client's concerns. Overall, cognitive match allows for the therapist to better foster and enhance skills known to advance the therapeutic process from start to finish (S. Sue & Zane, 1987). Martinez-Taboas (2005) discussed a client case that provides a glimpse into how various therapeutic elements, especially cognitive match, can come together to drive effective therapy. In the case described, it was critical for Martinez-Taboas to demonstrate the genuine respect he held for the spiritual beliefs that made up the client's worldview. While successfully connecting with the client along this dimension, he made the decision to rely on a combination of experiential techniques and cognitive behavioral tactics, which were introduced in such a manner as to make them a meaningful part of the therapy process for the client. The client revealed details about the psychogenic seizures she was experiencing, which she believed had a spiritual connection. The overarching goal the client hoped to accomplish was to confront the spirit of her grandmother so she could rid herself of the lingering fear and guilt that had persisted after the grandmother's suicide. The client's primary goal was accomplished through the frequent use of an empty-chair technique throughout the course of therapy. The empty-chair tactic allowed the client to speak extensively to the imagined grandmother seated before her and allowed closure to take place. Martinez-Taboas's case presentation is an excellent illustration of a cultural conceptualization that included the client's relevant spiritual beliefs, a form of spiritualism common to her culture that also provided the client with an explanation for her problems and a means to overcome those problems. The case also demonstrates how widely used, common therapeutic techniques can be effectively reframed when a client's particular worldview is kept in mind (LaFromboise & Malik, 2016).

Lakes and colleagues (2006) have pointed out that, in addition to ascertaining what the client wants to spotlight in therapy, a therapist should not overlook the elements of a client's immediate interpersonal environment that the client considers to be important. Such elements provide useful information that can be referred to by the therapist during the course of therapy as needed to facilitate therapeutic progress. But most important, by ferreting out these elements, the therapist is in a much better position to convey his or her understanding and appreciation of the depth and width of a client's experiences. Communicating in this way about the client's experiential world is very likely to result in a feeling of empowerment for the client, which will contribute to fostering a collaborative atmosphere that feeds and strengthens the developing therapeutic coalition. Therapists are much better prepared and able to traverse any cultural divides during the course of therapy when they accurately comprehend the local aspects of a client's worldview, such as the contributions made by family members, religious connections, and the various relationships he or she has established in the local community. Furthermore, it is safe to expect that a client's personal identity will be intimately tied to a familial hierarchy and the local social structures; both of these serve to promote the development of loyalties that provide a strong sense of support. These are the types of loyalties that often grow strong and endure the entire span of an individual's life (Shonfeld-Ringel, 2000; Sodowsky, 1991).

Racism Acknowledgment Model.[2] The various complexities and nuances of prejudice, discrimination, and antagonism are common events in the lives of many ethnic minorities, but the frequency and tone of such events are infrequently experienced by White Americans. This difference in experiences can make it difficult for a White therapist to fully grasp what these occurrences are like. Of particular concern are situations like the one described next, where differences in experiences interfere with the effectiveness of a therapist. In this example, a minority client reports experiencing "ongoing anxiousness" that she attributes to an argument that occurred the previous month outside her apartment building. The argument involved "someone from the neighborhood" and ended with the person using a racial slur. If the therapist assesses this situation's possible danger for the client and finds that the client is not worried about the incident repeating itself, the therapist may assume it is only the anxious feeling that needs to be dealt with in therapy. Operating from such a position, the therapist may incorrectly limit the therapy process to overcoming an "irrational emotion" that he believes resulted from exaggerating the importance of the undesirable events reported. The therapist decides to use an approach that has the client assume responsibility for her feelings. Furthermore, he encourages the client to practice behavioral and cognitive strategies to diminish her anxiousness and suggests several methods that can be used to increase personal accountability while identifying irrational emotional reactions to situations. It can easily be argued that it is not appropriate to place this client in the position of assuming responsibility for a racist event that she did not cause. It is also obvious from the example provided that the therapist missed the big picture and was too quick to decide what was needed for the client. Finally, the case illustrates that the most effective therapeutic approach to dealing with racism-based anxiety is not to limit therapy solely to intrapersonal factors (see Roysircar, 2009a).

According to Fuertes and colleagues (2002), therapists who assist clients in the areas of identity development, societal oppression, and aspects of the intersectionality that automatically comes with having multiple group identities have found that even when African American clients neglect to discuss racial issues within the context of therapy focused on the areas mentioned above, they still benefit from the therapeutic process. Other findings have also been reported. For example, pulling from what we know about Black racial ideology and an African American cultural identity to structure interventions pertaining to the utilization of role modeling, connecting with community resources, and applying consciousness-raising group tactics that call attention to some shared concern, has been shown to effectively increase a sense of empowerment in participants (Utsey, Bolden, & Brown, 2001). Finally, Thompson, Alfred, Edwards, and Garcia (2006) found that infusing an after-school prevention program called the "Heritage Project." with social justice advocacy strategies proved to be pivotal to the project's effectiveness with African American children. Specifically, including social justice advocacy strategies in the program's structure increased the impact that the program's teaching of Janet Helm's racial identity theory (i.e., Helms, 1995) and African American history (which emphasized the values, strengths, and resilience of African Americans) had on the children participating in the project.

Acculturation Model.[2] Researchers (e.g., Frey & Roysircar, 2006; Kim & Omizo, 2006) report that it has been determined that the factor of acculturation has a crucial influence on Asian ethnic groups in terms of the following: help-seeking actions related to mental health concerns, the degree that available resources are used, and their way of thinking about and feelings toward therapy. There is a consensus among those in the mental field that it is important for therapists to be cognizant of Asians' attitude toward seeking assistance, an attitude that appears to be associated with their level of acculturation. It is believed that knowing about such an attitude will prepare therapists to devote more time to exploring and addressing any concerns that a beginning Asian client may have about entering therapy (which is also likely to reduce the level of dropout among such clients). Atkinson, Thompson, and Grant (1993) pointed out that when a therapist starts to work with a less acculturated Asian client, it is critical for the therapist to fulfill a role that portrays the therapist as an adviser, advocate, and facilitator who makes taking action easier for clients who want to use indigenous support systems and healing systems that are available in the client's environment. When the therapist finds that a sufficient increase in the client's level of acculturation has taken place, the therapist should adapt his or role to meet this change. At this stage, the therapist should incorporate the roles of consultant and change agent. Finally, when judged appropriate, the therapist should take on the full-fledged role of a psychotherapist. Roland (2006) and Roysircar (2004a) both assert that therapists should recognize that working with clients who have bicultural identities can also prove to be a challenge, because it is not unusual for them to not be fully comfortable with operating within the structure that is typically associated with a traditional Western therapeutic approach. This lack of comfort is true even though biculturally oriented clients can be expected to have a stronger sense of self and a greater level of self-assurance than Asians who are less acculturated (Roland, 2006; Roysircar, 2004a). It should be concluded that a therapist is responsible for having the knowledge and skills necessary for being therapeutically responsive to the range of acculturation levels that he or she is likely to encounter as well as knowledgeable about the continuum that comprises the various combinations of external-internal racial and cultural accounts for the cause, or set of causes, or manner of causation responsible for a client's condition. In addition to possessing knowledge about possible etiologies, a therapist must also be attuned to the approach needed to assist clients in developing specific, measurable goals that will effectively yield the desired results. Finally, as much as possible, the goals developed should serve to inoculate the client against similar types of problems in the future (Atkinson et al., 1993; Roysircar, 2009a).

Unmet expectations can have a strong impact on disappointed immigrants' emotions and attitude, but unmet expectations for their new country are not the only problem experienced. For example, some therapists are called upon to mediate conflicting views among family members who clash on issues arising from a second-generation child who has been "Americanized" due to his or her school and social experiences. Without the assistance of a therapist to help such a family find a workable solution, it is likely that the family will become fractured and increasingly dysfunctional. The therapist will be careful not to readily endorse the kind of independent self-construal identity that has formed in such situations and that is sometimes supported by nonfamily members, who make comments to the effect that the individual "is in America now, and in America a person is free to be whoever or whatever the person wants to be." Generally, the therapeutic aim is to help the family better understand the nature of such conflicts and to help the family members find a solution to prevent further discord. In these cases, it is not unusual for therapists to hear and respond to double-bind messages made by the second-generation family member, who feels he or she is caught between two irreconcilable and undesirable courses of action, and comments by parents who "just want" their child to return to his or her "cultural roots." The second-generation family member might say something like, "My parents always told me they wanted me to benefit from being in America; to fit in and be successful. I don't understand what the problem is." When the therapist judges it to be the right moment, he or she will introduce various topics (in a genuinely respectful and sensitive tone) for the family members to talk through so they can better understand the elements that feed their conflict and so they are not responding to each other purely at an emotional level. The therapist may decide to introduce topic questions that could serve as a jumping-off point in helping the family find a workable solution. For example, the therapist might have all family members specifically identify and discuss the difficulties associated with separation from the culture one feels strongly connected to or the difficulties, within and outside the family, associated with growing up in a country to which one's parents chose to immigrate so there would be more opportunities for themselves and their children.

One consideration that the therapist should keep in mind is that second-generation offspring may psychologically experience less pressure to maintain or suppress one or more of the elements (e.g., language, accent, clothing, career interest) of his or her family's culture, and it is not unusual for a second-generation child to believe it is up to him or her to decide what it means to be an American, Indian, Asian, Hindu, and so forth (LaFromboise & Malik, 2016; Roysircar, Carey, & Koroma, 2010). According to Roysircar (2009a), in the end, a competent therapist is capable of identifying how such contextual factors play off one another, how contextual factors relate to mental health and illness, and the role of acculturation and enculturation in clients' problems and successes. Roysircar indicated that this is what lies at the center of successful therapy.

There are several recognized reasons for Asian Americans displaying disinterest in utilizing mental health assistance. Frey and Roysircar (2006) have reported that potential Asian American clients, those with low acculturation, shy away from therapy. Low acculturation has been tied to a number of explanations given by Asians for not seeking therapy, which can be summarized as follows: certain practices attributed to their religion or faith; little or no information about the accessibility of therapeutic services or what is provided in therapy; too few multiculturally competent Asian professionals who also possess the needed linguistic skills; shame resulting from their culture stigmatizing conventional forms of American therapy; and a general uncertainty concerning the reliability, ability, and trustworthiness of therapists. The predominant framework through which Asian Americans watch, assess, and decide how to best interact with their surroundings also contributes to their sparse use of therapy services. Specifically, one can expect Asian Americans to be aligned with a worldview that is strongly collective in nature, and as a result, they are most likely to seek assistance and guidance within a family or from a co-ethnic group member in whom they have a great deal of trust. Available research supports such a conclusion. For example, the collective nature of Japanese students' perception of their world was found to strongly account for the majority of them going to a family member when they experienced a personal concern (Roysircar, 2009a; Yeh & Inose, 2002).

▼ FIGURE 14.6

Martin Luther King Jr.

Social Justice

The racial history in the United States has conferred social protest and civic responsibility to the African American leaders of APA and the Association of Multicultural Counseling and Development (AMCD) (Roysircar, Thompson, & Boudreau, 2017). Numerous African Americans demanded to have their voices heard during the civil rights movement (see Figure 14.6) and corresponding movements in the mental health fields (White, 2004). Social justice is an important value of AMCD's presidents, displayed most frequently by their inclusion of marginalized groups—African Americans, Latinos, Asian American/Pacific Islanders, and American Indians—in AMCD's governance (*Journal of Multicultural Counseling and Development*, 2010; Roysircar, Colvin, et al., 2017). Psychology and counseling associations have also embraced inclusiveness along a host of domains (e.g., gender, language, religion and spirituality, physical ability, sexual orientation, and age). These professional associations have been active advocates of societal change by developing accessible and equitable local community involvement (Clauss-Ehlers & Weist, 2004; Espelage & Poteat, 2012; McCabe & Rubinson, 2008; Roysircar, 2006; Thakore et al., 2015; Thompson et al., 2006).

Social justice advocacy deals with oppressive systems that negatively influence individuals' development and entails informing and assisting decision makers (Lee, 2007; Toporek, Gerstein, Fouad, Roysircar, & Israel, 2002). Social justice advocacy establishes citizen therapists and psychologists who support less privileged and low-income clients as well as address issues of welfare, health care provision, public health, and access to therapy (Aldarondo, 2007). Therapists are expected to move outside the comfort and safety of their office to offer more inclusive services in communities of interest (Ratts & Hutchins, 2009). Social justice advocacy establishes a socially responsible voice for oppressed and marginalized populations (Gerstein & Ægistdóttir, 2007; Goodman et al., 2004; Ratts & Hutchins, 2009; Roysircar, 2009b; Toporek, Lewis, & Crether, 2009).

Ethical Considerations

The American Psychological Association's Multicultural Guidelines (APA, 2002, 2017) are relevant to current-day practice because they help therapists understand the rationale for focusing on multiculturalism in training, education, practice, research, and consultation. These guidelines provide therapists with basic information and current empirical research that supports the guidelines and demonstrates their significance.

Empirically supported therapies (ESTs) and culturally sensitive therapies (CSTs) represent two different orientations to treatment in the United States. While there is not adequate empirical evidence to indicate that any of the ESTs are effective with ethnic minority individuals in the United States, nor is there adequate empirical support indicating that CSTs are efficacious in reducing symptoms (Roysircar, 2009a). Unlike ESTs, however, CSTs are at the beginning stage of development. Moreover, there are within- and between-group differences that might justify altering a particular type of therapy to better meet the needs of a particular client." Some therapists may contend that there are similarities in human behavior across groups and, therefore, that tailoring specific strategies may be unnecessary, but such an approach is based on the identification of universal behaviors and not the identification of heterogeneity. Simply including ethnic minorities in therapy research is not likely to yield an understanding of the cultural relevance of theories, assessment methods, and interventions. It is also a failure of research to include ethnic minorities in broad categories such as ethnicity and race and not identify defining characteristics of a cultural group or an individual (e.g., language skills, immigrant generation status, class, religion or spirituality, sexual identity, marginalization, acculturation, and family composition).

Numerous therapists in the United States often utilize therapy strategies that were developed with White American individuals in mind. These strategies do not account for the experiences of minorities and can result in premature termination, negative mental health help–seeking attitudes, and the underutilization of therapy by minority clients. Leong and Lee (2006) urged therapists to investigate what features of their theoretical approach are universal and have application to all groups and which aspects are peculiar to White Americans and, therefore, can lead to cultural gaps. Such an investigation would enable therapists to identify "culturally specific" constructs to fill those gaps (Aguilera et al. 2016; Hwang, 2016; LaFromboise & Malik, 2016; Milburn & Lightfoot, 2016).

The presence of spirituality in ethnic minority communities often affects the social, religious, and political behaviors of its members (Cook & Wiley, 2014; Ibrahim & Dykeman, 2011; Roysircar, 2003a; Schlosser, 2006). It is proposed that psychology should not completely separate science and spirituality. As argued by Richards and Bergin (2014), mental health professionals that are spiritually competent display an attitude and approach to therapy that draws upon, respects, and utilizes the spiritual and cultural resources of diverse groups. Awareness of the religious practices and customs of a client who identifies strongly with a particular religion can help establish an effective therapeutic alliance. Spiritually and culturally competent therapists earn more trust, credibility, and respect from spiritually diverse clients, leaders, and communities. Resistance to client spirituality is antithetical to good therapy. Furthermore, researchers have discovered that religiously committed persons appear to have greater life satisfaction and subjective well-being, adjust better to loss and crisis, display less depression, and are less inclined to use illegal drugs and alcohol (Richards & Bergin, 2014).

Evaluating Theory

Research Support

Research on evidence-based practice is relatively new in multicultural therapy. Griner and Smith (2006) did a meta-analysis of 76 studies and found an overall positive effect of culturally adapted mental health interventions. These interventions led to significant client improvements across various conditions and outcome assessments. Interventions with groups of same-race individuals were found to be four times more effective ($d = 0.49$ effect size) than those offered to groups comprising mixed-race participants ($d = 0.12$ effect size). This suggests that cultural adaptations to mental health strategies may be more effective when such adaptations are specific to a particular racial or ethnic group. Interventions provided in the clients' native language were found to be twice as effective as those performed in English (Griner & Smith, 2006).

Fuertes and colleagues (2006) investigated the role of therapists' multicultural competencies (MCC) using 51 therapy dyads (client and therapist). Therapists who rated themselves higher on MCC experienced a better working alliance, and their clients viewed them as more competent, attractive, and trustworthy. For clients, "MCC [was] significantly associated with their feelings of the working alliance, perceptions of therapist empathy, combined ratings of therapist expertness, attractiveness, and trustworthiness, and their satisfaction with treatment" (Fuertes et al., 2006, p. 487). Clients' ratings of therapists' general competence (perceived expertness, attractiveness, and trustworthiness) were also positively associated with therapists' multicultural competencies.

Increasingly, it is recognized that diversity training is intrinsic to preparing persons for therapy practice (see http://www.apa.org/ed/accreditation/about/coa/). Smith, Constantine, Dunn, Dinehart, and Montoya (2006) performed a meta-analysis of 45 unpublished and published studies undertaken from 1973 through 2002 that were designed to investigate the effectiveness of diversity education in graduate training programs. The findings revealed that individuals who had received some type of multicultural education scored higher on different multicultural competence instruments than those who had not received such education. Further, it was found that multicultural education interventions that were "explicitly based on theory and research" (p.132) were nearly twice as beneficial as those that were not.

Pope-Davis et al. (2002) found that some clients of color accepted the cultural limitations of their therapists but also blamed themselves if their therapists lacked information about people of color. These clients edited their responses to their therapists and restricted their self-disclosure. Important information that these clients thought therapists should know included culture-specific knowledge about relationships and family structures as well as knowledge of racism and other forms of discrimination, gender role issues, cultural beliefs about therapy, cultural identity issues, communication styles, and cultural norms for behavior (Pope-Davis et al., 2002).

LaRoche, D'Angelo, Gualdron, and Leavell (2006) developed and assessed the Culturally Competent Relaxation Intervention (CCRI) with 25 Latino adults in a pilot study that required them to participate in 8 weekly 1-hour group sessions. During the first 30 minutes of the sessions, participants talked informally and reviewed psychoeducational material. During the last 30 minutes, participants learned and practiced a relaxation exercise (i.e., progressive muscle relaxation, diaphragmatic breathing, and guided imagery). The authors found that the level of collectivism was related to the number of times that the participants utilized the allocentric imagery exercise—which they were encouraged to use as many times as possible following the second session. Using a pre-post measurement of anxiety, LaRoche et al. (2006) found a reduction in anxiety based on the number of allocentric imagery exercises carried out.

Constantine (2007) examined the relationships between African American clients' perceptions of White therapists' racial microaggressions, the working alliance, the therapists' general and multicultural competencies, and therapy satisfaction. She found that perceived microaggressions were negatively linked with perceptions of the working alliance along with therapists' general and multicultural competencies. Since clients of color may be acutely aware of and/or sensitive to therapists' behaviors in terms of culture and race, therapists' awareness of the potential influence of their behaviors on their clients is critical. In striving to develop cultural self- and other-awareness as an aspect of multicultural competence; and commitment to investigating the effect of one's nonconscious and deliberate interactions with culturally and racially diverse clients is inherent to offering effective care (Comas-Díaz, 2000; Hays, 2016; Helms & Cook, 1999; LaRoche, 2013; Roysircar, 2004b; Tummala-Narra, 2016).

Fuertes and colleagues (2002) qualitatively investigated White American therapists' impressions of their therapy when helping African American clients. Therapists described the following facilitative factors with respect to their work with African American clients: (a) being direct yet sensitive to racial issues, (b) communicating a sense of openness, and (c) displaying acceptance of the historic effects of racism. The therapists reported favorable therapeutic outcomes, including reduced depressive and anxiety symptoms, and positive impressions of therapeutic processes, such as better rapport, increased intimacy, client self-disclosure, and overall improved client participation and involvement in therapy.

Limitations of the Multicultural Theory

Leong and Lee (2006) posited a framework, the *cultural accommodation model* (CAM), that they believe can be implemented to overcome some of the challenges confronting cross-cultural applications. The underlying assumption of CAM is that there are universal, group, and individual dimensions in understanding a culture. Evidence-based practice with specific cultures is needed to investigate the validity of CAM. That is, it is not yet known which cultural variables of the group dimension should be accommodated into the therapy process. For example, salient ethnic group–specific variables for Asian Americans would be the accommodation of interdependent self-construal, collectivism, and high context communication (i.e., *vocal inflection* [changes in the forms of words used], *paralanguage ingredients* [intonation, speed of speaking, hesitation noises, gestures, and facial expression], *kinesics* [body movements that represent a type of nonverbal communication], and proxemic interactions [degree of space between the client and the therapist that is established by the client]). As with evidence-based practice, CAM needs to be validated to determine if such accommodations would be beneficial for Asian American clientele. This validation process would need to be repeated with any and all appropriate cultural groups.

Multicultural competence is often described as preoccupied with the cultural differences of discrete racial, ethnic, and nationality groups. Such a description risks promoting group stereotypes. Thus, cultural competence should be geared toward a process-oriented approach rather than a content- or group-oriented one (Lakes et al., 2006). Thus, it is not the level of match between the client's and therapist's worldviews (i.e., multicultural competence, cognitive match) that matters, but rather that each person is operating from a shared narrative with a therapist. This model emphasizes the process of describing the problem from the perspective of both the client and therapist instead of basing assumptions on putative cultural differences (Lakes et al., 2006). Lakes et al. (2006) drew from an anthropological conceptualization of culture in terms of what is at stake for the client in the local social world and from the social constructionist idea of shared narratives between therapists and clients. Social constructionists propose that to understand the actions of others, a person must place such actions in the context of a story that is being told. The key strength of the process model is that no assumptions are being made about a group; rather, evidence is collected to ascertain what is important for each unique case (González, Biever, & Gardner, 1994; Young & Collin, 2004).

Thus, the intervention is tailored to the individual rather than based on group-specific variables. As culture is seen as different for each family or each locality, this model provides an open-ended view of the definition of culture. Lakes et al.'s (2006) suggestion that cultural competence should be geared toward a process-oriented approach is based on the observation that taking a group-oriented approach assumes rigid boundaries between the dominant culture and minority groups. Specifically, the group-oriented approach assumes that the characteristics of the group automatically apply to the individual. Lakes et al. (2006) proposed that a process-oriented approach would reduce stereotyping, as the therapist could not assume that all characteristics of a culture applied to the individual (e.g., collectivism in Latino American families). The process-oriented approach allows for individual needs to be addressed but still requires cultural sensitivity. Lakes et al. found support for the need for a co-created narrative in their observation that therapy is successful when the problem is articulated from both the therapist's and client's perspectives.

The importance of the local social world is supported by the observation that what occurs in an individual's daily life is critical in treatment. Culture affects this local social world, but therapy allows for an individual's daily needs to be addressed and does not permit the assumption that all cultural beliefs, attitudes, and practices are inherent to the individual. Thus, the definition of culture, for that individual, remains open-ended. Understanding culture from this perspective, rather than simply as a set of attitudes, beliefs, and practices, allows the therapist to address individual needs while remaining aware of the cultural differences of the individual.

Relevance to Current Practice

It is especially critical to discuss therapy in a multicultural framework because of the growing diversity of clients and their cultures that therapists encounter. As therapists continue to learn more about culture and diversity, they become more informed about how treatment should progress. At the onset of this millennium, people of color comprised roughly a third of the population, and this number is expected to rise to at least 50% by the year 2050 (Colby & Ortman, 2014). Additionally, school-aged children are the most diverse age group in the United States, with 37% of this group being non-White as opposed to 28% in the general population. Some researchers estimate that under these trends, by the year 2025, the typical public school classroom will be 50% non-White. The populations of some cities and towns in Texas, New Mexico, and California are already 50% minority.

It has become increasingly accepted within counseling and psychology that therapists must competently assist diverse groups of individuals. Indicators of a commitment to serving diverse populations are apparent in the creation of ongoing conferences (e.g., the Cross-Cultural Winter Roundtable Conference of Teachers College, Columbia University, which has been convening since 1978; the biennial National Multicultural Conference and Summit, which emerged in 1998) along with the establishment of peer-reviewed journals focusing on issues unique to diverse populations, such as the *Journal of Multicultural Counseling and Development*, the *Hispanic Journal of Behavioral Sciences*, *Cultural Diversity and Ethnic Minority Psychology*, the *Journal of Cross-Cultural Psychology*, and the *Journal of Black Psychology*. Further evidence of this commitment can be found in the variety of guidelines endorsed by the American Psychological Association, including the *Guidelines on Multicultural*

Education, Training, Research, Practice, and Organizational Change for Psychologists (APA, 2002), which were revised in 2017 and titled *Multicultural Guidelines: An Ecological Approach to Context, Identity, & Intersectionality*, and the *Guidelines for Psychological Practice With Lesbian, Gay, and Bisexual Clients* (APA, 2012). APA has acknowledged the importance of offering competent care to diverse populations of individuals by requiring that, in part, to secure APA accreditation, graduate programs must have a clear plan to provide trainees with knowledge regarding the influence of diversity on human behaviors.

The therapy profession is committed to serving multicultural populations in the United States, as demonstrated by the publication of multicultural articles in its top-tier journals—the *Journal of Counseling Psychology*, *The Counseling Psychologist*, and the *Journal of Counseling & Development*—and by the textbooks that constitute required reading for its students, such as Brown and Lent's *Handbook of Counseling Psychology*; Ponterotto, Casas, Suzuki, and Alexander's *Handbook of Multicultural Counseling*; Toporek, Gerstein, Fouad, Roysircar, and Israel's *Handbook of Social Justice in Counseling Psychology: Leadership, Vision, and Action*; and Gerstein, Heppner, Aegisdottir, Leung, and Norsworthy's *International Handbook of Cross-Cultural Counseling: Cultural Assumptions and Practices Worldwide*.

Multicultural and International Books. Below is a list of multicultural and international fiction and nonfiction books that practitioners can read as casebooks to conceptualize the experiences of children, adolescents, and adults from a multicultural or international framework.

- Alexie, S. (2007). *The absolutely true diary of a part-time Indian*. New York, NY: Little, Brown.
- Alverez, J. (1992). *How the Garcia girls lost their accents*. New York, NY: Plume.
- Bloom, A. (2008). *Away: A novel*. New York, NY: Random House.
- Chopra, D., & Mlodinow, L. (2011). *War of the worldviews: Science versus spirituality*. New York, NY: Harmony Books.
- Chua, A. (2011). *Battle hymn of the Tiger Mother*. New York, NY: Penguin.
- Cisneros, S. (1989). *The house on Mango Street*. New York, NY: Vintage Books.
- Cleave, C. (2009). *Little bee*. New York, NY: Simon and Schuster.
- Diaz, J. (2007). *The brief wondrous life of Oscar Wao*. New York, NY: Riverhead.
- Dias, J. (2012). *This is how you lose her*. New York, NY: Riverhead.
- Divakaruni, C. (2010). *One amazing thing*. New York, NY: Voice/Hyperion.
- Ellison, R. (1995). *The invisible man*. London, UK: Vintage.
- Erdrich, L. (2012). *The round house*. New York, NY: HarperCollins.
- Erdrich, L. (2010). *Shadow tag*. New York, NY: HarperCollins.
- Eugenides, J. (2002). *Middlesex*. New York, NY: Picador.
- Fadiman, A. (1997). *The spirit catches you and you fall down: A Hmong child, her American doctors, and the collision of two cultures*. New York, NY: Farrar, Straus, & Giroux.
- Kaling, M. (2011). *Is everyone hanging out without me? (and other concerns)*. New York, NY: Crown.

- Kwak, J. (2010). *Girl in translation*. New York, NY: Riverhead Books.
- Lahiri, J. (2003). *The namesake*. New York, NY: Houghton Mifflin.
- Leary, J. (2005). *Post traumatic slave syndrome: America's legacy of enduring injury and healing*. Milwaukie, OR: Uptone Press.
- Lee, C. R. (1996). *Native speaker*. New York, NY: Riverhead Trade.
- Manji, I. (2011). *Allah, liberty, and love: The courage to reconcile faith and freedom*. New York, NY: Free Press.
- Margolick, D. (2011). *Elizabeth and Hazel: Two women of Little Rock*. New Haven, CT: Yale University Press.
- McBride, J. (1996). *The color of water: A Black man's tribute to his White mother*. New York, NY: Berkeley.
- Mitter, S. S. (1991). *Dharma's daughters: Contemporary Indian women and Hindu culture*. Piscataway, NJ: Rutgers University Press.
- Nye, N. (1999). *Habibi*. New York, NY: Simon Pulse.
- Pipher, M. (2003). *The middle of everywhere: Helping refugees enter the American community*. New York, NY: Harcourt.
- Rogriguez, L. (1993). *Always running: La vida loca, gang days in L.A.* New York, NY: Simon & Schuster.
- Satyal, R. (2009). *Blue boy*. New York, NY: Kensington.
- Tatum, B. D. (1997). *Why are all the Black kids sitting together in the cafeteria? And other conversations on race*. New York, NY: Basic Books.
- Thakrar, P. V. (2010). *God=mc²: Getting spirituality down to a science*. Providence, RI: Om Enterprise Group.
- Torres, J. (2011). *We the animals*. Boston, MA: Houghton Mifflin/Harcourt.
- Touré, M. E. D. (2011). *Who's afraid of post-blackness? What it means to be black now*. New York, NY: Ward.
- Ward, J. (2011). *Salvage the bones*. New York, NY: Bloomsbury.

Applying Theory to Practice

RETURNING TO THE CASE OF TYRONE

Tyrone is living the pain of identity conflicts because he has assumed many identities according to the expectations of different groups of people he has associated with. Counteracting identity conflict involves establishing a subjectively consistent and meaningful racial identity that results in a positive self-image and embracing a value system that promotes social and personal well-being (APA, 2008; Comas-Díaz, 2012; Sellers, Smith, Shelton, Rowley, & Chavous, 1998). Thus, rather than minimize the pain of identity conflict, Tyrone has to honor the pain of finding his true self.

With increasing self-awareness, Tyrone recognizes an alternative view of his self (e.g., persistent student, bicultural, realistic, community oriented, spiritual). In coming to accept himself for who he is, Tyrone is able to appreciate the elements that make him a unique being of African American heritage. He finally finds meaning and purpose in his worldview of time: about the past, the present, and the future.

The current ideologies of both the White dominant social group and the African American reference group carry a hidden power that constrains the roles and responsibilities available to Tyrone. As a result, Tyrone's problems are based in social, political, and cultural contexts over which he has no control. The competing dominant and minority social contexts have invalidated Tyrone's individual meaning, creating psychological problems, such as depression and overcontrolled hostility (Vontress & Epp, 1997).

Racial minority status in the United States affects every aspect of life: "Dark skin places an undue burden on Black men in their struggle for self-definition and identity, education, access to networks providing employment and career information, political and economic power, and decent neighborhoods in which to rear their children" (White & Cones, 1999, p. 5). To help Tyrone, multicultural therapy will involve the unfolding of personal, cultural, and environmental characteristics that are new to Tyrone and will contribute to his resilience, his picking himself up, and his success as these prevail in the face of minority status challenges.

MULTICULTURAL INTERVENTIONS

For Tyrone, it will be important to separate out what he did and did not have control over as a young adult. For instance, he feels shame for being expelled by his college, for his loss of scholarship, and for not being able to catch up later. The therapist could interpret these events as being allowed by the system. Tyrone was failed by both an educational system and a parental subsystem that were supposed to look out for his future. The economic conditions of the country have caused African Americans to have the highest unemployment rate. Tyrone took all the blame on himself, and he coped

by taking on new socially prescribed identities or symbolic invisibility.

Making Meaning of Contexts. Culturally exclusive and racist contexts create climates that limit psychological growth and result in internalized racism for an individual. Multicultural therapy concerns itself with the individual as situated within sociopolitical, socioeconomic, and intergroup contexts and recognizes that many "pathologies" are culturally inflicted rather than internal to the individual. As noted by Roysircar (2009b), being well adjusted in an unjust world could be considered pathological in and of itself.

Tyrone is trying to negotiate his life in a culture steeped in racism that degrades him a little at a time on a daily basis. This has a cumulative effect on his internalized sense of worthlessness. Helping Tyrone to externalize the problem rather than pathologize his reaction will be a step in the direction of separating his identity from the cultural indignities he endures.

Valuing the Client's Prsonalized Racial Identity. Multicultural therapy can help Tyrone discover where the dominant and minority racial attitudes are different from his own attitudes toward himself and others. Tyrone may have developed an internalized hatred toward his own reference group as well as hostility toward the White dominant group by acquiring the cultural biases and prejudices of both groups. The consequences of such ill feeling can be depression, poor self-esteem, and a sense of worthlessness (Vontress & Epp, 1997). The work of multicultural therapy will include helping Tyrone uncover meanings about diverse societal contexts in which he is grounded (family, potential friendships, college availability, the White dominant society, and the African American minority) that do not fit the experience of despair and emptiness. He will find uniquely positive outcomes in these contexts and will be able to build on them. Therapy will also involve the externalization of negative beliefs and an examination of how those beliefs have acted on his life to his detriment.

Testimony Therapy: The "Us" of a Community Culture. The emphasis of testimony therapy is

(Continued)

(Continued)

"communitarian" and situates the person within a community culture. It emphasizes "us" rather than "I," consistent with an Afrocentric collectivistic worldview. This is an emic therapy approach that can be utilized with Tyrone. Akinyela (2005) contrasted the Eurocentric "I think, therefore I am" with the Afrocentric "I am because we are and because we are therefore I am" (p. 10). Spirituality permeates Afrocentric thought and is what unifies African Americans across classes, genders, regional backgrounds, educational statuses, ages, and religions.

For Tyrone, this could be an opportunity to deal with his parents and the confusion and pain he feels in leaving them behind. It will also be an opportunity to highlight his potentially positive relationships with his sister and her children, as well as with his high school mentor who encouraged him to go to college. He seems to be unaware of his capacity to form and hold relationships and instead is focused on the pain of his invisibility and betrayal by people with organized power. The fear that invisibility generates could be surfaced and explored as part of his interpersonal sufferings.

Returning to the Multicultural Case of the Sanchez Family

Miguel is a 14-year-old Mexican American boy who immigrated to the United States with his family at the age of 8. Miguel complains of a lack of respect from his mother, an inability to relate to her or connect with his Mexican heritage, and embarrassment over his mother's low acculturation. His mother complains of Miguel's lack of respect for his cultural heritage and his new criminal friends. Miguel's guidance counselor cites a decrease in school attendance, movement toward a negative peer group, avoidance toward participating in the Mexican Heritage Festival, and potential substance abuse. Interventions will be appropriate for Miguel's age and developmental stage, his cultural heritage, and his acculturation level. These interventions will address his problems in school, his involvement in a gang, and his cultural rift with his mother.

Given Miguel's multiple identities as an adolescent, Mexican American, male, immigrant, school student, and gang member, multicultural therapy is sensitive to his multidimensional contexts. Roysircar, Arredondo, Fuertes, Ponterotto, and Toporek (2003) suggest, "Demonstrations of cultural competence and interest in relevant aspects of a client's cultural background may increase the likelihood that a client will feel understood and helped in the therapy relationship" (p. 41). Multicultural therapy with Miguel and his mother is framed within the 3 × 3 model of multicultural competencies of awareness, knowledge, and skills, as these competency characteristics interact with therapist assumptions/values/biases, awareness of the client's worldview, and intervention strategies (Roysircar, 2003b; D. W. Sue et al., 1992). This tripartite model of multicultural competencies provides the foundation for culturally sensitive practice.

A culturally sensitive therapist first examines his or her stereotypes about young Mexican American men. According to Gonzales, Germán, and Fabrett (2012),

"Stereotypes of Latinos often include expectations of academic incompetence and, for Latino boys, assumptions about the propensity for violence and delinquency" (p. 259). Miguel's therapist closely examines his own self-awareness in terms of common Latino youth stereotypes. The therapist examines and corrects his affective, cognitive, and behavioral aspects of self-awareness (the first multicultural competency) so that Miguel does not perceive him as holding racist beliefs that can disrupt the therapeutic alliance (Roysircar et al., 2003). Furthermore, the therapist has the knowledge (the second multicultural competency) that bias is an inherent result of one's socialization in a cultural group and understands also how the therapist's own multiple identities (educated, middle class, highly acculturated, a professional, young adult, gender) impact his or her interactions with the client (Roysircar, Dobbins, & Malloy, 2010).

The therapist incorporates culture-specific knowledge (Roysircar et al., 2003) important in understanding Miguel's experiences and reactions. Knowledge of the challenges and dangers Latino youth are exposed to in the United States is paramount in Miguel's case. As a foreign-born youth, Miguel may find himself navigating multiple sets of values, norms, and expectations, which can vary a great deal across family, neighborhood, and school contexts (Gonzales et al., 2012). The dual process of retaining one's country-of-origin culture while learning English and the norms and values of the United States can lead to an increased risk for psychopathology and distress for Latino adolescents (Gonzales et al., 2012). According to John Berry's (2001) bilinear model of immigrant adaptation, individuals who choose assimilation (like Miguel) as a strategy may experience psychological stress due to weakened ties with and support from their original culture. Miguel may feel he must deny his cultural values and instead embrace the values of the mainstream culture to be successful in navigating the challenges of adolescence.

To compound this challenge, 30.1% of Mexican American families live below the poverty level (Gonzales et al., 2012). Low socioeconomic status and neighborhood conditions of poverty create barriers in development for Latino youth and create an increased risk for emotional, behavioral, and cognitive problems (Gonzales et al., 2012). Families living in low-income neighborhoods are exposed to social disorganization, which may precipitate deviant peer activity. According to Gonzales et al. (2012), associating with deviant peers leads to an increased risk for school dropout, delinquency, and depression in mid-to-late adolescence. The referral questions posed by Miguel's therapist draw attention to the importance of knowledge regarding the risk to Latino adolescents involved with a deviant peer group.

Knowledge around the conflicts that can arise due to differences in English proficiency and communication styles between immigrant youth and parents (Hwang, 2006) is an important consideration in Miguel's case. According to his case history, Miguel expresses frustration and embarrassment with his mother's lack of English language skills. Gonzales et al. (2012) described a phenomenon termed "cultural brokering" whereby children may find themselves in the position of having responsibility to negotiate important family matters on behalf of their parents. Miguel may be experiencing a disruption in normative parent/child roles and feeling an enormous burden to assist his family. Furthermore, cultural brokering can negatively impact Miguel's ability to invest in his own developmental and educational needs. Language, according to Falicov (1998), is symbolic of memory, affect, places, and family alliances. Differences in choice of language may symbolize loyalty between past and present, or between stances on the decision to stay in the new country or to return to the homeland (Falicov, 1998). An understanding of the symbolic and affective qualities of language in Miguel's family is an important aspect of understanding his case in a culturally sensitive manner.

Youths acculturating at a faster rate than their parents may discard their culture of origin, leading to parent-child conflict and the loss of social and emotional and support from their family members (Roysircar, Carey, & Koroma, 2010). Miguel expresses feeling emotional and social disconnection and a lack of respect from his mother, as evidenced by his statement that the only people he can truly relate to are his new friends. Miguel's clothing, music, and open rejection of his family's cultural activities demonstrate his different acculturation adaptation as compared to his mother's. The verbal conflict and visible agitation between Miguel and his mother during the intake interview are indicative of the conflict experienced by the Sanchez family due to acculturation differences within their family.

With an emphasis on understanding individual differences within a family, an immigrant group, and an ethnic community, multicultural therapists reduce stereotypes and promote cultural empathy for the client (Roysircar, 2009a). They also recognize the diversity of an individual and the interweaving or interfacing of the individual's particular gender, race, religion, age, socioeconomic position, sexual orientation, and life experience, which are expressed through multiple identities (Roysircar, Dobbins, & Malloy, 2010). While multicultural therapists recognize the importance of working within the particular beliefs and values of a client, they also understand that individual and family meanings grow out of interactions within the context of present sociopolitical and class junctures. Multicultural therapy, therefore, relates to themes of cultural diversity, legal justice, social justice, poverty, gender, politics, and power.

Assessment

Miguel's therapist may choose to use the Narrative Assessment Interview (NAI) (Hardtke & Angus, 2004), a brief, semi-structured interview strategy designed for administration pre- and post-therapy and at other post-treatment periods to assess client change in psychotherapy (Hardtke & Angus, 2004). For the purposes of this assessment, narrative is defined as the description of personal events or stories that occurs within the context of the therapy hour (Hardtke & Angus, 2004). This interview's findings are primarily qualitative in nature and based on case study data.

The open-ended format of the NAI will allow Miguel's therapist to create a space where Miguel can share his self-knowledge. Stories of the reasons, timing, and conditions of his immigration, the characteristics of the community in which he lives, his family structure, the importance of cultural practices to him and his family, acculturation, experiences of racism, ethnic identity, and the pressures of adapting to multiple facets of Miguel's life contexts will be considered in a culturally sensitive qualitative assessment. Thus, Miguel's assessment will be a dynamic process that is as much an intervention as it is an assessment.

Interventions

Multicultural therapy skills assume that individuals can be guided to change their understanding of past experiences, analyze biased assumptions by using varied perspectives, interpret or reinterpret traumatic events, integrate their life experiences, develop a sense of agency by taking a lead in their life development, adopt more flexible ways to process and adapt to varied contexts, and become better able to create life-empowering experiences in the future. When multicultural therapy is used with children, the idea is to allow the child to express feelings, heal from past trauma, symbolically externalize inner cultural conflicts, vicariously identify with multicultural leaders and role models, and role-play with the therapist solutions and alternative outcomes. The goal is to allow the child to learn while being guided by the therapist. In this way, the child can develop greater self-esteem and social/collectivistic/family esteem, become a master of making sense of cultural and racial experiences, and find meaning in an integrated multicultural or bicultural life.

Culturally sensitive interventions incorporate critical aspects of culture, such as spirituality or religion, individualism/collectivism, independence/interdependence self-construal, and family structure and roles, while addressing developmental and cultural adjustment concerns. The interventions address cultural history, social values, family systems/extended family, acculturation level, language and cognitive processing styles, and culture-specific stories/materials or multicultural texts. If an intervention is not relevant to an individual's culture, acculturation level, and developmental stages, then the individual might not benefit from the specific intervention. The cultural match theory posits that clients adhere to and benefit more from strategies that fit with characteristics of their own culture (LaRoche et al., 2006).

For instance, *cuento therapy* interventions (use of folktales) have been successful with Puerto Rican youth in New York City from a low socioeconomic status and single-parent homes who are at risk for joining a negative peer group (Malgady, 2010). In Malgady's study (2010), the assumption underlying cuento therapy was that Latino marginalized adolescents with behavior problems would better benefit from stimuli culturally relevant to their life as opposed to mainstream treatments. Further, these adolescents had experienced emotional distress growing up in a cultural environment from which they were alienated, which led to weakened cultural values (these values not being reinforced by the mainstream society), a lack of pride in cultural roots, and the inability of a single-parent household in poverty to serve as an agent for their socialization (Malgady, 2010). The cuento therapy approach is also deemed appropriate in Miguel's case because this modality is congruent with the Hispanic oral tradition of passing down cultural and familial values through stories.

Mrs. Sanchez's low acculturation and possibly her low socioeconomic status leave her unable to be the agent of Miguel's socialization. Miguel is at risk for joining a negative peer group and feels a lack of cultural pride. Because of the problematic similarities between Miguel and the adolescents in Malgady's study (2010), two interventions used in this study will also be useful for Miguel: hero/heroine histories/biographies and folktale/cuento therapy.

The first intervention applied, hero/heroine histories/biographies, entails the selection of appropriate nonfictional characters from Mexican or Mexican American history or biographies that can serve as role models for Miguel. These figures' life stories will feature themes such as confronting racial/ethnic prejudice and poverty, educational and athletic achievement, and maintenance of a positive self-image and cultural pride (Malgady, 2010). Miguel will listen to the life story of the chosen role model and witness the hero go through life struggles similar to his. The goal of this intervention is to have Miguel relate to the hero so as to imagine overcoming similar problems in his own life and make changes.

A second intervention will be the use of folktales. Folktales have been traditionally used as a way for families and cultures to pass down values and provide solutions for everyday problems. Cuento therapy represents a culturally sensitive form of narrative therapy designed to be used with Latino children who live in two cultures (Constantino, Malgady, & Rogler, 1986). Similar to the hero/heroine model of therapy (but using fictional characters), cuento therapy's purpose is to get individuals to focus on a culturally relevant folktale hero/heroine and to utilize the character as an idealized self as well as an achievable role model (Comas-Díaz, 2006). The idea is for the client to learn the hero's or heroine's lesson and adapt it to his or her own life.

Last, the use of *dichos* is a particularly useful intervention. Dichos are Spanish proverbs or sayings that teach life lessons in a culturally specific way. Comas-Díaz explained, "As one-liner interventions, they provide 'flash' psychotherapy. For instance, the dicho 'El que canta, sus penas espanta' (The person who sings scares his or her sorrows away) articulates the value of a positive outlook in life" (Comas-Díaz, 2006, p. 443). Falicov (1998) found that dichos could be a very powerful communication tool for therapists who have knowledge of them and use them appropriately. Dichos promote cultural resilience by offering adaptive strategies and responses to oppression and other societal ills (APA, 2008; Comas-Díaz, 2006).

Miguel can take perspective on his new life of adaptation as one that accepts his traditional and new cultures simultaneously, sees that his mother is not his enemy but instead respects him, opens the door for family therapy, and creates stronger self-esteem, social self-esteem, and cultural identity that protect him from the negative influences of his peer group.

There are language differences between the therapist, Miguel, and Mrs. Sanchez, new immigrants, whose English language abilities are limited. Miguel probably speaks nonstandard English. A translator should be considered, but because the therapist is himself a Latino, he may conduct bilingual therapy if he has the necessary skill set to do so (Roysircar, 2013). Other psychotherapy interventions may include (a) consultation with the family's minister to understand religious/spiritual healing methods, (b) psychoeducation regarding acculturation, dominant language differences, and racism, and (c) solution-focused and role-playing strategies to build communication, social skills, and responsibility taking.

SUMMARY AND COMMENTARY ▶▶

Exercising multicultural competence in therapy practice entails balancing the application of cultural knowledge, attention to clients' uniqueness, and an appreciation for within-group cultural heterogeneity in such a way that stereotypes, derived from less complex descriptions of diverse cultures, are avoided. There is a very fine distinction between being sensitive to the implications of an individual's membership in a specific group and losing sight of the same person's individuality and intersecting identities (APA, 2017; Comas-Díaz, 2000; Hays, 2016; Helms & Cook, 1999; LaRoche, 2013; Roysircar, 2004b; Tummala-Narra, 2016).

However, the translation of a large body of knowledge and understanding to culturally sensitive treatment and skills is paramount. Studies have illustrated that multiculturally competent therapy practice recognizes dynamics that may emerge in cross-racial and cross-cultural therapeutic relationships. Further, the research has suggested that multiculturally competent therapists address racial and cultural issues directly in an effort to foster therapeutic relationships where culture has value and relevance. Moreover, clients' understanding of their therapists' ability to attend to their cultural concerns and therapists' multicultural competencies is probably enhanced through therapists' openness and willingness to allow culture to enter the therapeutic relationship (APA, 2017). Last, studies have illustrated the complexities of therapists' racial-cultural self-awareness, particularly their awareness of racial microaggressions. See Table 14.2 for an overview of current practice-related issues.

▼ TABLE 14.2

Brief Overview of Current Therapy Practice

Variable	Current Application
Service delivery setting	Private-practice offices Schools and universities Clinics Psychiatric hospitals Health care settings Rural outreach centers Disaster crisis centers Other (e.g., refugee camps)

Variable	Current Application
Client population	Child Teen Adult Couple Family Specific populations (e.g., international students and workers, refugees, asylum seekers, immigrants, temporary immigrants, undocumented immigrants)
Presenting problems	In addition to mental disorders (e.g., depression), clients seek assistance with issues such as cultural identity, social class/poverty, gender, gender preference, conflicts due to religion, sexual orientation, trauma, immigration status, discrimination, oppression, marginalization, and, in the case of refugees and asylum seekers, adaptation and functioning after resettlement.
Severity of presenting problems	Wide range of severity
Adapted for short-term approach	Yes
Length of treatment	Brief to extended
Ability to receive reimbursement	Insurance companies will reimburse with appropriate *DSM* diagnosis.
Certification in approach	The University of Missouri (Mizzou Online) offers a 12-credit-hour graduate certificate in multicultural education. Also, the Department of Human Development and Psychological Counseling at

(Continued)

(Continued)

Variable	Current Application
	Appalachian State University has a certificate program (i.e., systemic multicultural counseling certificate) that prepares individuals to work with diverse and marginalized groups.
Training in educational programs	Graduate programs have incorporated the approaches covered in this chapter into their existing curriculums.
Location	Urban Rural Suburban
Delivery system	HMO PPO Fee for service
Practitioners	Professionals and paraprofessionals

Variable	Current Application
Fit with *DSM* diagnoses	The answer is "yes" and "no." The *DSM-5* includes the Cultural Formulation Interview, which is intended to help therapists evaluate cultural factors (i.e., cultural definition of the problem, stressors, causes, support, self-coping, role of cultural identity, previous help-seeking, barriers, and preferences) that affect the client's perspectives, behaviors, and options for treatment. Even with the positive changes found in the *DSM-5*, the *DSM* system continues to be aligned with Western psychology's perception of what constitutes *normal* and *abnormal* conditions.

CRITICAL THINKING QUESTIONS ▶▶

1. What influence, if any, do you believe your own cultural heritage will have on your role as a therapist?

2. Do you believe that you possess any biases that will make it difficult to provide culturally competent therapy to any multicultural groups that are different from you?

3. How would you know if the use of therapist self-disclosure is appropriate to use in strengthening the therapeutic relationship?

SUGGESTED READINGS: IMPORTANT PRIMARY SOURCES ▶▶

Books

Helms, J. (1990). *Black and White racial identity: Theory, research, and practice*. New York, NY: Greenwood.

Pedersen, P. B., Draguns, J. G., Walter J., Lonner, W. J., & Trimble, J. E. (2008). *Counseling across cultures*. Thousand Oaks, CA: Sage.

Ponterotto, J. G., Casas, J. M., Suzuki, L. A., & Alexander, C. M. (2009). *Handbook of multicultural counseling*. Thousand Oaks, CA: Sage.

Roysircar, G., Arredondo, P., Fuertes, J., Ponterotto, J., & Toporek, R. (2003). *Multicultural counseling competencies*. Alexandria, VA: Association for Multicultural *Counseling* and Development. (Reprinted 2010; Spanish translation 2007)

Sue, D. W. (2010). *Microaggressions in everyday life: Race, gender, and sexual orientation*. New York, NY: Wiley & Sons.

White, J. L., & Cones, J. H., III. (1999). *Black man emerging: Facing the past and seizing a future in America*. New York, NY: Routledge.

Journals

American Psychologist

Asian Journal of Social Psychology

Cultural Diversity & Ethnic Minority Psychology

International Journal for the Advancement of Counselling

International Journal of Psychology

International Perspectives in Psychology: Research, Practice, Consultation

International Psychologist

Journal of Counseling & Development

Journal of Multicultural Counseling and Development

Journal of Muslim Mental Health

Journal of Social Issues

Psychology International

Revista Interamericana de Psicología/Interamerican Journal of Psychology

Websites

AMCD Multicultural Counseling Competencies: http://www .counseling.org/Resources/Competencies/Multcultural_ Competencies.pdf

American Counseling Association: www.counseling.org

APA 2017 Multicultural Guidelines: http://www.apa.org/about/ policy/multicultural-guidelines.aspx

NOTES ▶▶

1. The section "Historical Context" is based on Leong, Pickren, & Tang, 2012, and Valencia & Suzuki, 2001.

2. The text under the headers "Cognitive Match Model," "Racism Acknowledgment Model," and "Acculturation Model" is based on Roysircar, 2009a.

CHAPTER 15

MOVING TOWARD A PERSONAL THEORY OF COUNSELING AND PSYCHOTHERAPY

A Wealth of Theories and Therapies

This final chapter is designed to help readers to look back and carefully reflect on what they have read. By this chapter's end, readers will be asked to use their understanding of what was covered in this textbook to construct their own personal theory of counseling. The authors of this textbook (referred to simply as "we" for the remainder of this chapter) know from personal experience that such a task is far from easy, and it requires effort, thought, and self-reflection to arrive at an acceptable answer. Also, over time, we all realized that our first answer was not our final answer to constructing our own personal theory of counseling. The task is much like starting a long journey without a clear view of the destination rather than a short, predictable journey whose destination can be seen in the distance. We have found that when we have given the same task to others, they invariably report having gained a more accurate and personally insightful understanding of the various theories, especially in terms of theoretical convergence and divergence.

From past experience, we have come to expect many readers will experience an initial sense of being at least somewhat overwhelmed on hearing they are expected to reconsider previously covered theoretical positions and then construct their own personal theory of therapy. This reaction can often be traced to the sheer number of theoretical positions they will have to reconsider, and each position provides a fairly complex and unique way to conceptualize the causes of clients' problems and the exact methods for rectifying those problems. We want to emphasize that what might first strike readers as an insurmountable challenge can easily be reframed to become a genuine advantage for the task at hand. In other words, to explain this assertion more clearly, we unequivocally maintain that the magnitude of theories available for consideration actually provides a comprehensive pool of information for readers to pull from to formulate their own approach. Finally, to facilitate completion of the task of designing your own personal theory, we will now discuss various traits, special qualities, and other aspects of the theories that this book has covered. Such an approach will help readers move from a knowledge, comprehension, and application level of thinking toward the level of thinking required to build a theoretical approach to therapy, which is a level of thinking that is dependent on analysis, evaluation, and synthesis of the various approaches (see Anderson & Krathwohl, 2001; Bloom, Engelhart, Furst, Hill, & Krathwohl, 1956; Ginter & Glauser, 2010).

Before moving on to issues that are considered critical in this final chapter, we want to point out that the current number of extant theoretical approaches raises an interesting question:

LEARNING OBJECTIVES

After reading this chapter, each student should be able to:

1 Propose a connection between witnesses providing testimony during a murder trial and the proliferation of theoretical explanations surrounding mental health issues and their treatment.

2 Plan your journey to find your own theoretical approach relying on the seven elements of formulating your personal theory of therapy.

3 Assess the strengths and limitations of the four therapeutic approaches described in Table 15.1 based on the six areas represented in this table.

4 Defend the argument that therapy is a blend of science and art.

5 Critique the benefits and limitations of the forms of integration.

6 Formulate your personal theory of counseling and psychotherapy to effectively treat Mrs. Sanchez.

What process nourished the proliferation of theories during a span of time that covered over a century in length?

One explanation can be uncovered by asking a second question.

What is the *connection* between witnesses providing testimony during a murder trial *and* the proliferation of theoretical explanations surrounding mental health issues and their treatment?

Do not read ahead before you write your answer to this second question in the box below.

> The *connection* between these two seemingly unrelated situations (i.e., witnesses testifying and the number of approaches to therapy) is . . .

We believe that the connection between the two divergent situations lies in what has been termed the *Rashômon effect*. The term was coined by Valerie Alia, who used the term in an article appearing in *Theaterwork*. It is a term that was subsequently used by her in a number of later publications (Alia, 2004). Alia derived the term from the title of Akira Kurosawa's internationally acclaimed movie *Rashômon* (Figure 15.1). The movie portrays a story that defines the exact elements for a true Rashômon effect.

Kurosawa's movie is set in 12th-century Japanese culture and features the unanticipated meeting of the three primary characters in a forest. The pivotal scene of the movie unfolds when the three characters give different versions of what might be or not be consensual intercourse between the wife and bandit and what could either be the murder of the samurai or an incident in which the samurai takes his own life. A trial is held, and the samurai's wife, bandit, and the deceased samurai (through a medium who channels his spirit) present their own versions of what had transpired between them. The film's director portrays each version of what takes place according to each person's testimony. The director's purpose was not to provide the viewer of the movie a single, accurate depiction of events, as is often typical of heinous crimes depicted in movies. Rather, Kurosawa's motivation was to provide images for each of the stories that were convincing and "true" from each presenter's perspective, which leaves the viewer of *Rashômon* completely uncertain as to what story represents the truth. Thus, the Rashômon effect can be defined as contradictory, plausible versions of an event that leave the recipient of them to decide which version(s) are in accordance with actuality. (The Rashômon effect may have even played a role in the answer you gave earlier in the box, that is, if your response and the responses of several others answering the same question were both contradictory but plausible.)

▼ FIGURE 15.1

Rashômon

Possibly, the Rashômon effect provided you not only with an insight that will help you better understand why theories proliferated over time but also with an understanding why the founders of major theoretical approaches were similarly convinced of the truth of their own positions, such as what occurred between Alfred Adler and Sigmund Freud and later between Carl Jung and Sigmund Freud. (Incidentally, Yalom [2002] made an interesting observation concerning two sharply contrasting appraisals of Freud's work—appraisals that either confirm or deny his contributions. These two categories of divergent opinions outlived Freud and continue to this day. According to Yalom , one of the outcomes of treating psychoanalysis as unworthy of serious consideration is that "a whole generation of mental health practitioners has been educated with a critical and wholly uninformed view of the man [Freud] whose ideas compose the very foundation of psychotherapy" [p. 217].)

The point being made is twofold. First, plausible but theoretically different explanations and the resulting forms of therapy that are associated with them are understandable in light of the Rashômon effect. Furthermore, in the early years of theory development, advocates for a certain approach often felt very strongly about their perspective's accuracy and suitability to treat mental disorders, so the number of positions being defended eventually led to research studies that were intended to empirically test the various approaches to find which one was best. This process resulted in considerable controversy and polarization among theorists and practitioners. Arguably the publications that created the most discussion were written by Eysenck (1952, 1965), who concluded psychotherapy, compared with no treatment, produced either no or minimal benefits or gains. Later, Glass and Smith (1978) and Smith and Glass (1977) reported

Margaret Mead and Gregory Bateson

Source: 1938 photo of Mead Archives and Gregory Bateson, Library of Congress.

Note: Photograph taken in 1938 of Margaret Mead and Gregory Bateson, her husband, during a field trip to Papua, New Guinea. Source: Mead Archives, Library of Congress.

on meta-analysis results that challenged Eysenck's earlier conclusions by showing the general effectiveness of psychotherapy. Their studies were followed by a number of studies that were implemented by others that also found psychotherapy to be effective. It appears that the various major approaches covered in this textbook, for the most part, can be considered as effective, with no clear victor emerging as the best in all cases.

Sometimes the Rashômon effect has led to life and death decisions, such as what occurred during the famous witch trials in Salem, Massachusetts. In other cases the outcomes have been less severe, such as the Little Rascals Day Care Center court case in which several adults were given prison sentences. In addition to the witch trials, the cited court case was the result of spurious testimony. In both situations, children provided plausible but false testimony, which Ceci and Bruck (1995) asserted can arise when memories of certain events wind up distorted as a result of external suggestion. Other situations resulted in damaged professional careers. According to Heider in his seminal 1988 article, the Rashômon effect played an essential role in several well-known professional disputes, such as the one that occurred when Derk Freeman (1983) attacked Margaret Mead's well-known interpretation of Samoa's culture, which she presented in her widely influential book *Coming of Age in Samoa* (Mead, 1928). Her book's effect went well beyond the confines of anthropology and motivated a notable range of professional work that was centered on finding answers to questions that pertained to adolescence, gender relationships, social and sexual norms, and uncovering what exactly were the tangible effects of nature and nurture on societal structure (Figure 15.2). Heider (1988) referred to a number of such conflicts in anthropology, but his interest was not who was right. Rather, Heider used these conflicts to highlight the power of the Rashomon effect to foster such conflicts.

According to Heider (1988), "It is only with the assumption of a shared reality ("mundane reasoning") that these disagreements ("reality disjunctures") take on significance as puzzles to be solved; there is a shared reality, true, but differing truths may indeed be said about it" (p. 74). From the described situations it seems that anyone, including those with advanced training and degrees, are susceptible to succumbing to the Rashômon effect, which in the end can lead to the type of historical disagreements that occurred between different theorists and their followers—such disagreements have continued to this day.

What is most important to take from Heider's discussion of the Rashômon effect is that differing truths may indeed be constructed about the exact same phenomena. Therefore, differences that are found among two theoretical counseling explanations do not necessarily prove that one is correct and another false, which is not the same as asserting that any proposed theory that differs from one or more of the long established theories is automatically true on the whole or in part since there are basic ground rules to test the soundness of one theory against others (refer back to the attributes structure integrity, explanatory power, therapeutic scope, and referential integrity discussed in Chapter 1).

Capital *T* Versus Lower Case *t*. We have reached a point in time where capital *T* Truth (i.e., absolute truth) has been relegated to philosophy's trash heap of impossible pursuits. Instead of looking for the Truth, we are now in pursuit of multiple, lower case *t* truths. These are the types of truths that the philosopher Friedrich Nietzsche attributed to *perspektivismus* (perspectivism), which is a concept that relates to the Rashômon effect but possesses a wider and more inclusive impact. Nietzsche's assertion was that reality can only be known relative to the perspectives of individuals, groups, or various cultures at a particular point in time.

An interesting derivative of Nietzsche's position, which occurs fairly often, is when someone decides that a widely admired historical figure said or did something that today would be considered politically incorrect; however, from a historical perspective what had been said or done might have been considered common and benign during that earlier period of time. This conclusion does not mean that all of today's standards of conduct are irrelevant (e.g., today's professional ethical codes are relevant), but it is correct to assert that finding an absolute Truth in today's relativistic world is an *absolute* challenge.

Chopra (2013) offered a succinct summary of the issue when he wrote the following:

In a sense, the modern world was created with a simple editing stroke when Truth lost its capital "T." Instead of pursuing the Truth, along a hundred paths stemming from philosophy and religion, the rise of Newtonian science and the Age of Reason taught us to seek lower-case truth, which consists of a body of verifiable facts. We have inherited a suspicion about absolute Truth that can be heard in everyday speech. How often do people say, "Well, it's all relative" and "There's no such thing as truth with a capital "T." Between them, relativism and the mountain of empirical data assembled by science have suffocated the notion of Truth. (p. 1)

Finally, whereas it appears that the Rashômon effect and the associated concept of perspectivism means no single correct way exists to view the world, this does not mean that all possible perspectives, all possible ways of seeing the world, are equally valid.

The Journey to Find One's Own Theoretical Approach

In writing this textbook, we were not interested in trying to sway readers toward a particular theoretical or therapeutic position, even though we operate from our own beliefs concerning theory and practice. For example, each of us has a personally derived system of theoretical and practice beliefs we call on to structure our professional presentations and to oversee what should be done when fulfilling the role of supervisor for practicums and internships. Most important of all, we agree that constructing a personal theory and approach to therapy is a journey that can be facilitated by others, but ultimately, this journey can only be taken by the individual. This is a journey in which a person must communicate with the inner self and retrieve information about the self while condensing the external information he or she has learned from others to make the approach practical and useful. Each person on such a journey should have an objective in mind from the start. To help readers achieve the purpose of their journey and enable them to arrive at their objective, we have devoted the remainder of this chapter to exploring a few topic areas. These are topic areas that we have found to be helpful to individuals who seek to create their own theoretically based approach to counseling. During your journey to find an answer to the task that has been laid out, we suggest that you remain open to the unexpected because it is not unusual to have an initial thought or prediction concerning what will happen, but, on completing the task, you may discover that something completely different has occurred. The seven topic areas listed next were selected to satisfy our goal of providing sufficient guidance and mentoring to assist readers in completing the task given to them at the start of this chapter.

- Elements That Make a Theory a Theory: A Much Maligned Term Defined
- The Tangible Value of Operating From a Theoretical Position
- Boxing Differences Among the Theories Covered
- Common Factors: Corralling Similarities Among the Theories
- The Master Therapist: A Blending of Science and Art
- Integration's Role in Constructing a Personal Approach
- Future Directions in Counseling and Psychotherapy

These seven areas represent key stopping points that should be considered during your journey to formulate a personal theory of therapy.

Elements That Make a Theory a Theory: A Much Maligned Term Defined

A memorable line spoken in the Japanese movie *Tomie: Replay* is "If you step forward there will be a road" (Higashi & Tsuchikawa, 2000). The line strikes a chord because of the immediacy of truth that it imparts. Almost everyone can recall some anticipated journey (e.g., family vacation to the beach, etc.) that was both pleasantly anticipated and easily planned. An even more interesting aspect of the phrase "If you step forward there will be a road" is what is left out, that is, the potential pitfalls (e.g., the family vacation was booked at the wrong hotel, which is miles from the beach, which incidentally is closed due to anticipated approach of a hurricane). The implication is that if readers want to successfully complete the task of building a personal theory of practice, they must be sure what the final destination traveled to "looks like." (This section serves as a cautionary tale that pertains to terminology, and in this case the question of how we are to define the word *theory*, which ultimately lies at the center, the innermost part of the task that is to be completed by journey's end. Thus, we must know exactly what we mean by the word *theory*.)

Ghose (2013) examined the ways that terms frequently used in the sciences and social sciences are often misunderstood, misused, or wrongly interpreted, not only by readers but also by the professionals who use them. Ghose's list includes terms and phrases such as *natural, organic,* "nature versus nurture," *significance, hypothesis,* and *theory.* Take the term *natural,* which has increasingly been used to refer to products that promote health; however, not all materials that are synthesized in a laboratory are unhealthy for human consumption (e.g., medicines), nor is everything natural healthy (e.g., belladonna, a poisonous plant). Consider the word *hypothesis,* which has a number of different meanings depending on who is speaking. Some citizen scientists and many lay persons who lack a clear understanding of what the word *hypothesis* implies have increasingly come to believe that it means "an educated guess." Clearly, the way in which the term *theory* is applied is of utmost importance to our discussion.

According to Ghose (2013), the phrase "It is just a theory" has been used by deniers of climate change and creationists who use the phrase in a purposeful manner to create uncertainty about scientific conclusions. Ghose quoted Rhett Allain of Southeastern Louisiana University who stated, "It's as though it *weren't true because it's just a theory* [italics added]." Use of the term in this manner downplays the wealth of support that shows a very strong connection exists between climate change and the use of fossil fuels. Ghose also referred to discussion about how further corruption of theory's meaning can be prevented and even reversed. In her article she referred to Rhett Allain, who has advocated replacing terms such as *hypothesis* and *theory* with the term *model* (Ghose, 2013, n.p.). Ghose cogently argued that such a replacement will do little to prevent the misunderstandings of what the term *theory* means. Also, the term *model* already carries with it various connotations (e.g., models who parade the newest French fashions). Ghose concurred with John Hawks, a social scientist at the University of Wisconsin–Madison, who stated, "I don't think that model improves matters. It has an appearance of solidity in physics right now mainly because of the Standard Model. By contrast, in genetics and evolution, models are used very differently" (Ghose, 2013, n.p.).

As a matter of clarification, the term *theory* is used in this and earlier chapters to refer to a set of structured, interrelated ideas that represent a system of postulates, data, and inferences that provide a meaningful description of the human condition that has direct implications for understanding what constitutes mental health and the ways that mental health can be fostered. Thus, a theory has three essential and interrelated components: (1) It is a multifacted idea that is assumed to be true as the basis for reasoning, discussion, or supported beliefs; (2) it represents a combining of facts and statistics for reference or analysis; and (3) it allows for conclusions to be reached on the basis of evidence and reasoning.

The Tangible Value of Operating From a Theoretical Position

When the various theories are viewed along a panoramic perspective, from the abstract to the practical, one can better weigh the real value that they provide for the effective practice of counseling. Examples of the manifold benefits that theory infuses into the therapy process are listed in this section. Although the listed values may not apply in toto to every major theoretical approach covered in this textbook, if weighed as they might generally apply to the theories found in this textbook, they represent how theory-infused practice trumps a nontheoretical, technique-driven approach to working with clients. At its worst, the latter represents a haphazard bundling of skills that misses the mark.

The 20 items listed here are not all-inclusive, nor are they arranged in any particular order of importance. The items represent what one of us, who maintained a private practice for several decades, found to represent the general strengths that are associated with using a theoretically supported approach to working with clients. Readers should keep in mind that these are strengths that are relative depending on the particular theory that is being considered.

Theories provide the following advantages for practitioners:

- Anchor the therapeutic process by providing a form of coherence, a logical and consistent quality, to the special environment that is created through therapy.
- Help the therapist mentally graph out and accurately see how the client's behaviors, emotions, and thought patterns interrelate and overlap to form the client's reality.
- Illuminate important factors that are embedded in the repetitive stories that are told by clients and that can be used to arrive at the goal for therapy.
- Allow for differentiation of a client's ways of distorting thought processes and a type of differentiation that facilitates the successful untwisting of such thinking.
- Enable a therapist to identify the individual, family, societal, and multicultural elements that contribute to a client's problem and, most importantly, a client's strengths that can be used to counteract the client's problem.
- Offer the client a new philosophy of life from which the client can generalize what was learned in therapy, which allows the client to accurately weigh and handle future problems and successes.
- Allow for generating useful and testable in-session hypotheses, which, if refined in terms of research protocol, can often lead to advances in the particular theoretical position that is relied on by the practicing therapist.
- Provide clients with a means to find the normal within the abnormal, the extraordinary in the ordinary, and the difference between potentiality and achievement.
- Allow clients to seek and develop a healthy, improved, and more meaningful version of themselves in concurrence with their particular life stage and unique needs.
- Provide the structure for a therapist to identify what is required to adhere to the most beneficial perspective for understanding a client's concerns—regardless of the exact nature of those concerns, whether idiosyncratic or systemic, trivial or ubiquitous, allegorical or historical.
- Allow the therapist to organize complex or confusing information presented by a client during a session in such a way that the next needed step to take in the therapeutic process comes into focus for the therapist.
- Offer the therapist a basic road map to traverse the complex terrain of the changing and sometimes zig-zagging pathway that is associated with the client–therapist relationship.
- Enable an accurate identification of what is and is not a growth-enhancing response for a client to make in relation to an upcoming situation beyond the confines of a therapy room, which is important for or related directly to the established therapeutic goal.

- Provide a comprehensive guide to carry out the therapeutic process from its start to its successful completion.
- Offer a means to assess whether a client is progressing in therapy as a result of progress markers, which are expected to appear at certain points during the therapy process.
- Provide specific techniques for the therapist to utilize and that are constructed in such a way to provide a logical explanation for how other techniques, those not typically associated with the theory, can fall within the appropriate scope of the selected theory when applied to achieve an established therapy goal.
- Clearly indicate or suggest what types of therapist actions taken in therapy can be expected to foster or hinder desirable client change.
- Possess a body of evidence that supports the approach's use and which can also be called on and utilized to build additional, supportive empirical evidence.
- Can be learned and taught to others and do not rely on a form of metaphysics, which is molded from "realities" assumed to exist but for which there is no proof.
- The scope of a comprehensive theory also provides the means for social justice efforts, such as those found among feminist therapists, who along with others, have sought to change the way women's bodies are portrayed by media outlets. Refer to Figure 15.3 for an example of what such persistent efforts can produce.

▼ FIGURE 15. 3

New Barbie Created Using the Image of the Model Ashley Graham

Matt Winkelmeyer/Stringer/Getty Images Entertainment

Note: Barbie's body image has remained essentially unchanged for over 50 years but was recently changed and now there are four body types to select from: original, petite, tall, and curvy (the figure pictured above).

Boxing Differences Among the Theories Covered

This section provides a truncated, side-by-side comparison of the major theories that are covered in this textbook (Table 15.1). Such boxlike comparisons, with each column of boxes providing salient information for a particular theory, provide a way to globally consider and assess some of the prominent differences among the theories. This type of comparison can be used by readers to help them narrow down the number of theories they would refer to when working to complete the task of establishing their own theoretical position.

Juxtaposing the various major approaches presents both advantages and disadvantages. Even though such a bare bones approach results in a panorama of the major theories, the use of single-sentence summaries can also result in readers misunderstanding

Therapies Compared in Six Areas

Area of Comparison	Psychoanalytic Therapy (Classic)	Adlerian Therapy	Behavioral Therapy	Cognitive Therapy
1. Theoretical perspective used to understand basic human nature	Humans straddle two worlds: the world driven by basic biological urges and the world of rational thought that serves to keep the various urges in check	Humans are largely driven by conscious thoughts and are capable of formulating goals that promote psychological health and are capable of transforming perceived weaknesses into strengths	Humans are essentially the sum of their behavioral responses, and these responses are the result of environmental stimuli that reinforce certain behaviors	Human nature is largely determined by repetitive internal dialogues that clients have constructed and which have gained a strong foothold in the way a client views the world
2. Mental events, processes, or other attributes focused on	A structural explanation for mental functions based on the concepts of id, ego, and superego	Abilities related to goal-directed actions that are positive, helpful, and intended to promote social interactions and friendships	Focusing on internal mental events, processes, or capabilities is not required to change behaviors	Especially focused on the importance of understanding the types of internal self-talk that is maladaptive
3. General explanation given for client problems	Internal, unconscious conflicts traceable to events that occurred during a set of developmental stages	Potential is blocked by misdirected goals that hinder the development of the client's true potential	Reinforcement history and the way the environment reinforces certain reactions	Irrational, dysfunctional thoughts that lead to assessing events in a negative manner
4. Emphasis placed on a client's past, present, or future	Exploration of a client's past is necessary to fully understand problems grounded in the present	Consideration of past events (e.g., parental perceptions of a child) are important, but the approach is largely future driven	Considers which factors lead to the continuation of an effect after its original cause is no longer present	Heavily focused on current dysfunctional thinking rather than on reviewing their relationship in terms of earlier events
5. The role that free agency plays in therapeutic change	Internal forces and early family events are powerful indicators of a client's adult life, but clients are capable of understanding their problems in ways that allow them to change a problem's negative affects	Clients possess the ability to overcome negative past events and utilize their free will in the present to move toward future aims that promote healthy outcomes for them and others	Although determinants of behavior are emphasized, there is recognition that individuals can change maladaptive behavior through strategies, such as modeling and systematic desensitization	Cognitive determinants account for present behavior. and their impact can be lessened or eliminated by changing the present internal dialogue with dialogue that counteracts the effects of maladaptive self-talk
6. Theoretical developments	Numerous and many related theories emerged from the original version of psychoanalysis, e.g., ego psychology, object relations, and self-psychology	Continued to develop in scope and in ways that allowed for wider application, such as working with entire school systems	Ivan Pavlov, widely recognized for his study of the conditioned reflex, had an abiding interest in mental illness that led him to create "experimental neurosis" in animals	Represents a more inclusive version of behavioral theory due to recognition of cognitive involvement in creating a client's problem

Area of Comparison	Gestalt Therapy	Existential Therapy	Person-Centered Therapy	Reality Therapy
1. Theoretical perspective used to understand basic human nature	Humans can only be understood by approaching them in a holistic manner and not by using any sort of reductionist procedure	Humans are destined to be born and die, and in between these two events, they are confronted with the inherent meaningless of life	Reaching human potentiality requires positive, nurturing relationships, which serve to foster reaching one's full potentiality	Humans choose healthy, positive relationships or choose to live a life of irresponsibility and dissatisfaction due to unfilled needs
2. Mental events, processes, or other attributes focused on	Focused on the entirety of being human, including body sensations and feelings along with other qualities	Emphasizes the experience of absolute dread (angst) connected with personal freedom and responsibility	There is a natural tendency in humans to move toward realizing their potential	Attention devoted to acceptance of one's personal responsibility and making appropriate choices
3. General explanation given for client problems	Unfinished gestalts that have resulted in existing problems due to a lack of closure	The result of not dealing with anxiety associated with one's sense of isolation, meaningless existence, and eventual death	The gap between one's self-concept and actual experiences which fail to provide acceptance, respect, and understanding	Mental illness regarded as being a misnomer because it removes the responsibility necessary to make wise choices
4. Emphasis placed on a client's past, present, or future	The *here and now* is the time frame to work out problems that interfere with the client's full experiential existence	Not overly concerned about a client's past; instead, attention is directed toward present and future choices	Present oriented and marked by recognition of the client's inherent ability to solve his or her own problems	The development of current and future means to satisfy basic needs: love and belonging, fun, power, survival, and freedom
5. The role that free agency plays in therapeutic change	Various factors can impinge on living in the present, but humans possess the ability to overcome their inertia	A level of free will that allows for constructing a meaningful life in a cold and uncaring universe	Humans are naturally autonomous beings with the expertise to make correct decisions pertaining to their own lives	Clients' level of free agency is strong enough to move in a direction to remove damaging *DSM* labels
6. Theoretical developments	Later developments focused on the contact between "self and other," the dialogical relationship between the therapist and client, and field theory applications	Owes a great deal to the work of Søren Kierkegaard and Friedrich Nietzsche and others' efforts, which led to various theoretical and therapeutic permutations and combinations	Continues to play a vibrant role in therapy, especially in terms of its relational concepts, such as empathy, which are now widely regarded as important to therapy's success	Evolved continuously through the efforts of its founder and subsequently through the work of those closely associated with this theoretically based approach
Area of Comparison	Feminist Therapy	Postmodern Therapy (Narrative Therapy)	Marriage and Family Therapy	Multicultural/ Cross-Cultural Therapy
1. Theoretical perspective used to understand basic human nature	The interplay of male and female perspectives, biological differences, and social expectations related to gender	Personal "stories" are what define an individual's or group's understanding of reality and the role they play in that reality	The family represents the fulcrum to understand individuals and various groupings of family members	Factors such as racial and ethnic diversity, sexual orientation, disabilities, classism, and the history of marginalized groups

(Continued)

(Continued)

Area of Comparison	Feminist Therapy	Postmodern Therapy (Narrative Therapy)	Marriage and Family Therapy	Multicultural/ Cross-Cultural Therapy
2. Mental events, processes, or other attributes focused on	Prejudice in favor of or against one gender in a way considered to be unfair and detrimental to mental health	Cognitively humans are driven to make meaning of the experiences encountered in their lives	What occurs within and between individuals is related to family dynamics	Factors that contribute to beliefs (positive, negative, or unbiased) about other individuals and groups
3. General explanation given for client problems	Thinking that reflects inherent privilege that leads to systemic gender inequalities within a society or culture	The way clients have interpreted and "written out" the events in their lives can create personal problems	Dysfunctional family systems that originate in many possible ways, but which all have a disruptive impact on family relationships	Attitudes, judgments, and behaviors that reflect prejudice, stereotyping, and discrimination
4. Emphasis placed on client's past, present, or future	Depends on the particular form of feminist therapy; theoretical views overlap and differ	Full range—the past, present, and future can all contribute to the deconstruction and reconstruction of a meaningful narrative	The full range of time periods is utilized, but focus depends largely on the specific family therapy utilized	Full range referred to but can differ as a result of the particular theoretical position and a client's worldview
5. The role that free agency plays in therapeutic change	Self-determination is a key aspect of feminist-oriented therapies in uncovering possible solutions for client concerns	Individuals, couples, and families possess the ability to rescript their lives through reinterpreting events in their lives	Depends on the particular approach referred to since theoretical views differ concerning amount of free agency possessed	In general, the degree of free agency believed to exist allows for changes in the self, others, and systems to occur
6. Theoretical developments	Other forms include Marxist feminism, radical feminism, ecofeminism, erotic feminism, and lesbian feminism	Postmodern theory encompasses several conceptually important additions that continue to remain influential, such as hyperreality	Encompasses earlier approaches and newer approaches that operate from a systems perspective	Theoretical developments include cultural identity development theory, integrative life pattern model, and feminist therapy

exactly how a theory stands on a particular issue. Regardless of the global understanding that such a matrix might provide readers, any insight gained concerning the differences deduced from such comparisons is admittedly limited to the six categories that are used to summarize the various theoretical approaches. Still, it should be apparent to any reader who has reached this point in the textbook that the complexity of each analyzed theory is much greater than what any boxed-in, single-sentence description can provide.

An often overlooked disadvantage of such summary matrixes is the possibility of failing to fully reflect on the implications of the areas that are used to make comparisons. Two of the six areas used in Table 15.1 are briefly discussed to show how a careful consideration of their significance can help readers understand what we are attempting to communicate through the synopses. The area of *temporal focus* (i.e., attention typically devoted to a client's past, present, or future time frame) considers how different therapies apply techniques to impact how clients assimilate their perceptions about past events, current relationships, and possible future expectations and goals. Confusion develops for some readers when a summary statement is taken as being representative of what occurs throughout the course of counseling. Two of the synopses in Table 15.1 illustrate this problem: "Exploration of a client's *past* is necessary to fully understand problems grounded in the present" and "The *here and now* is the time frame to work out problems that interfere with living a full experiential existence" (see Psychoanalytic Therapy [Classic] and Gestalt Therapy). A novice who is studying the field of therapy might misinterpret the foregoing summary statements and conclude that a psychoanalytic therapist is solely interested in probing past life events or interpret the second statement to mean that a gestalt therapist is never concerned with past influences. Neither of these conclusions would be accurate. Finally, we want readers to realize that all therapies, despite their primary temporal focus, are designed to assist clients with *past*, *present*, and *future* concerns even when a therapist does not directly focus on all of these time frames equally. Consider, for example, what is referred to as "classic psychoanalysis," the form developed by and advocated by Sigmund Freud, whose techniques were used to uncover early childhood conflicts. Even Freud always returned to the present time because the present is the only possible time frame to apply a client's insights about past events. It is in the present that therapeutic changes occurred, and such gains were further discussed by Freud and his clients in light of how clients would apply the therapeutic gains achieved to their current and future life.

The concept of *free agency* (i.e., free will) is more complicated than it might seem from the truncated information presented for the 12 theoretical approaches outlined in Table 15.1. The norm for therapy is to consider clients as being responsible for their actions and for the choices they make, but there have been exceptions to this view of personal control. An exemplary example is the position advocated by B. F. Skinner, the renowned behaviorist, social philosopher, and author of widely read works based on his research (e.g., *Walden Two*, in which he described a model for creating a community based on principles of learning), who espoused what he referred to as a radical form of behaviorism in which there was no room for free will (Skinner asserted that free will was an illusion). To be clear, Skinner adhered to a belief that human action can be explained in purely physical, observable terms. His view represented a philosophical position known as *materialism,* which holds that nothing exists except matter and its movements and modifications. Although such a mechanistic worldview as Skinner's may strike some readers as ludicrous, a number of neuroscience researchers have carried out research that is in line with Skinner's belief that free will is an illusion. We admit this is a highly controversial research area, especially considering that a number of investigators in this area have concluded that the empirical evidence supports the conclusion that free will does not exist (Haggard, 2011; Libet, 1985; Soon, Brass, Heinze, & Haynes, 2008).

The good news for therapists and clients is that an indefinite stay of execution has been invoked and free will remains alive for now. Mele (2014), who has written extensively on the topic of free will, has closely examined the studies conducted by neuroscientists and social psychologists—studies that have been used to argue that human decisions are either unconsciously based, not consciously derived, or result from imperceptible factors that have influenced what was decided (this latter explanation applies even to the multitude of comparatively unimportant choices we make daily). Mele's examination of these studies led him to conclude that the findings reported do not negate the existence of free will.

Mele (2014) also has pointed out that scientists and social scientists who strive to prove the nonexistence of free will have often displayed a strong emotional reaction to the term. Mele has contended that their reaction indicates they have failed to understand the full range of meanings associated with free will, especially those meanings that were logically and rationally derived. The misplayed biases held by deniers of free will are exemplified in the following remarks. The first quotation was abstracted by Mele (2014) from an article that Montague wrote for *Current Biology*.

> Free will is the idea that we make choices and have thoughts independent of anything remotely resembling a physical process. Free will is the close cousin to the idea of the soul—the concept that "you," your thoughts and feelings, derived from an entity that is separate and distinct from the physical mechanisms that make up your body. From this perspective, your choices are not caused by physical events, but instead emerge wholly from somewhere indescribable and outside the purview of physical descriptions. This implies that free will cannot have evolved by natural selection, as that would place it directly in a stream of causally connected events. (Montague, 2008, p. 84)

Holding a similar position, Gazzaniga wrote that free will is "some secret stuff that is YOU" (cited in Mele, 2014, p. 85). As these two quotations show, doubters tend to assign free will to a realm that Mele (2014) believed is best described by the words "magical, supernatural, or unnatural" (p. 85). In addition, Mele wholeheartedly agreed with the doubters that any sort of magical, supernatural, or unnatural forms of free will should be rejected, but Mele also pointed out that other forms of free will do exist and do possess such mythic qualities.

So, in what form does free will exist? According to Mele (2014), the "ability to make—and act on the basis of—rational, informed decisions when you're not being subjected to undue force is sufficient for having free will" (p. 78). An example of the "undue force" mentioned by Mele would involve a situation where a gun is pointed at your face while the perpetrator demands you hand over your credit cards. Because space limitations prevent a complete presentation of Mele's thoughts concerning the complexities associated with free will, interested readers should refer directly to Mele's 2014 publication *Free: Why Science Hasn't Disproved Free Will*. Mele purposely wrote this book in a user-friendly style so the current debate about free will could reach a wide professional and public audience.

Common Factors: Corralling Similarities Among the Theories

Before readers can obtain a complete understanding of the major theories that are covered in this textbook, in addition to becoming knowledgeable about theoretical differences, readers must also become aware of what attributes the various theories share. Furthermore, when you start to construct your own personal theory of therapy, most of you will likely discover that completion of this task was made much easier by having knowledge about the shared similarities among the major theories.

The effort to find what commonalities are shared by the theories has a history that predates this textbook by decades. For example, Grencavage and Norcross (1990) reviewed 50 publications to abstract commonalities among different approaches. They identified 89 common factors, 4 of which received the greatest amount of attention across the publications they analyzed. The four theoretical similarities that received widespread support are (1) provision of opportunities for catharsis (i.e., release of emotional tension), (2) the importance of new learning and acquiring new behavioral patterns, (3) the role that clients' positive expectations play in therapy's success, and (4) the importance of the client–therapist relationship that was fostered and maintained throughout the therapeutic process. Grencavage and Norcross's (1990) assessment of the 89 identified commonalities revealed that 41% were tied to change processes, and only 6% were tied to client characteristics. Finally, according to Fischer, Jome, and Atkinson (1998), common factors, such as those discovered by Grencavage and Norcross, have a potential beyond simply revealing the key curative qualities that are shared jointly among the different therapies. Specifically, Fischer et al. (1998) stated that the common factors that are found in psychotherapy and healing across cultures (e.g., intervention by a medicine man or woman) have the potential to bridge the gap between culturally specific and universal approaches to treatment. Thus, according to Fischer et al., a common factors perspective based on empirical support provides mental health professionals with a viable framework to unify the diverse body of multicultural counseling literature, which serves as a means to frame future multicultural research, training, and practice.

Of the four widespread commonalities that were listed by Grencavage and Norcross (1990), the client–therapist relationship has received repeated support for its importance. For example, after conducting a comprehensive review of the professional literature, Russell (1994) found persuasive evidence to conclude that general therapy's success was not dependent on the specific theoretical position that is adhered to by a therapist, nor was success necessarily tied to the type or amount of training a therapist had received; however, they found that success was tied to the level of clinical experience acquired over time by a therapist. In summarizing what was found, Russell (1994) concluded that the differences that were most pronounced among practitioners were differences in the ways they thought about and conceptualized problems rather than how they actually behaved in therapy sessions. Russell (1994) offered the following clarification:

> Therapists behave similarly in many respects and are often influenced by the particular client with whom they are interacting, even though the rationales they give themselves, their patients, and their colleagues may be dissimilar. In other respects, therapists behave dissimilarly in ways that are consonant with their orientation. However, therapists continue to muddy the waters by talking one game and playing another. Many of the advertised contrasts between therapists of various persuasions are just that: advertised, not practiced. (p. 17)

Although no complete agreement exists concerning the exact number of or kinds of common elements that can be found throughout the different therapies, a consensus exists among those who pursue this line of research; that is, they basically agree that interest in this area of study (i.e., common factors) is a logical outgrowth of earlier efforts to find the single most effective therapeutic approach. As pointed out by Leibert and Dunne-Bryant (2015), after many comparisons had been made to find the best single approach across client situations, in the end researchers had to declare a stalemate because no single approach was found to be convincingly superior in all situations, and all the major approaches were found to produce positive results. In addition, a disconcerting realization began to take shape when researchers turned their attention to uncovering what exactly accounted for positive client change. Some found that the specific techniques that are utilized by various theoretical approaches account for a relatively small percentage of the outcome.

A seminal but controversial article by Lambert (1992) proposed that 40% of the change accomplished by a client in therapy is accounted for by *extratherapeutic factors* in the client's life and environment (e.g., family support, involvement in community activities, employment, faith, inner strengths such as persistence, and even chance occurrences in the client's life). *Relationship factors* accounted for 30% of the client's change. This set of factors pertained to the therapeutic relationship that was established between the client and therapist and depended to a large degree on a therapist's ability to be empathic, warm, accepting, and encouraging. The remaining 30% was evenly split between the *model/techniques* used by a therapist and the *hope/expectancy* that the client harbored for a positive outcome. Even though Lambert clearly stated that the percentages in his publication were approximations that were based on the publications he had reviewed, the four percentages that he mentioned were subsequently reported by many others as if they were exact percentages (Leibert & Dunne-Bryant, 2015). As stated by Leibert and Dunne-Bryant, additional research is needed to examine in greater detail each of the four areas that comprise Lambert's proposed *common factor model* (i.e., a theory that accounts for client change through the impactful commonalities between, rather than singularities within, each therapy). Although the percentages that Lambert mentioned do not represent unyielding facts, the weight of value that Lambert attributed to each of the four sets of common factors struck a strong chord of truth among practitioners. Undoubtedly, the important role that the client–therapist alliance plays in effective therapy is well recognized by seasoned therapists and supported by a large number of publications (e.g., Bozarth, Zinring, & Tausch, 2002, Cain & Seeman, 2002; Clark, 2010; Elliott, Bohart, Watson, & Greenberg, 2011). Table 15.2 provides the story of one therapist who realized the healing power of positive relationships through his work with severely traumatized children. Finally, the special client–therapist alliance that is discussed in this section deserves careful consideration when readers reach the end of the current chapter and begin their task of formulating their own approach to rendering effective therapy.

The Master Therapist: A Blending of Science and Art

Bugental (1987) wrote that "the artistry of master therapists shows in their ability selectively to blend the subjective with the objective, their art with their science. . . . Therapeutic goals (e.g., adjustment, symptom reduction) are well served by objective

The Boy Who Was Raised as a Dog

Bruce Perry and Maia Szalavitz's book, *The Boy Who Was Raised as a Dog: And Other Stories from a Child Psychiatrist's Notebook*, was inspired by Perry's realization that traumatized children can teach the rest of us about loss, love, and the natural interpersonal ingredients that support healing. The title of the book was inspired by one of the cases that Perry reported in the book.

Perry, who is internationally recognized for his trauma expertise, was contacted in 1993 to assist with the children who survived the 51-day siege between several government agencies and a religious group known as the Branch Davidians. There were essentially two outcomes for the children who survived. Surviving children who were placed in loving homes fared the best; they adapted, attended colleges, and started families. Children whose lives continued on a chaotic path fared poorly. To Perry the difference appeared to be whether these children had caring, supportive, and loving people in their lives after having been traumatized. Because of such experiences, Perry started to question the general belief that children were naturally resilient and could even recover from trauma independently when their connection to the traumatizing situation was severed. Thus, early in his career Perry questioned the ability of any child to simply bounce back from surviving genocide, being abducted, seeing a murder committed, or experiencing occurrences of extreme family violence. Perry knew that animal studies supported a different conclusion; that is, very young animals that were exposed to stress experienced negative neurobiological outcomes, and such outcomes adversely affected their later behavior. Perry was proven correct; a child's automatic return to normalcy because of innate resilience was a fantasy. Perry eventually created what he called the neurosequential treatment model, whose healing components (neurobiological and interpersonally based) are demonstrated through the cases that he recounted in *The Boy Who Was Raised as a Dog*.

The title of the book refers to a child named Justin, whose 15-year-old mother abandoned him to the care of a loving and attentive grandmother, who died when Justin was 11 months old, which left Justin to be cared for by his grandmother's live-in boyfriend, who was over 60 years old. Perry described the man as having poor cognitive skills and being grossly unaware of how to raise a child. Because of the difficulties that he encountered with Justin's behavior, and because he possessed considerable skill as a dog breeder, when Justin was 2 years old, the man decided to cage Justin as he had done with the dogs that he had successfully raised.

Ironically, when Perry encountered Justin for the first time, he discovered that the hospital staff had confined Justin, who was 6 years old at the time, to a crib with iron bars whose opening at the top had been sealed with plywood that was securely wired to the crib. Perry had been contacted to intervene because the hospital's medical staff did not know how to help Justin, who acted animal-like and threw his feces toward and shrieked at anyone who approached the crib. Perry detailed the steps he took that resulted in Justin's gradual improvement and eventually led to Justin's being able to enjoy a productive life. Perry concluded that recovery from trauma and neglect is all about relationships—rebuilding trust, regaining confidence, returning to a sense of security, and reconnecting to love. Of course, medications can relieve symptoms and talking to a therapist can be incredibly useful. But healing and recovery are impossible—even with the best medications and therapy in the world—without lasting, caring connections to others. Indeed, at heart it is the relationship with the therapist, not primarily his or her methods or words of wisdom, that allows therapy to work.

Source: Perry, B. D., & Szalavitz, M. (2006). *The boy who was raised as a dog: And other stories from a child psychiatrist's notebook.* New York, NY: Basic Books.

means, but life-changing psychotherapy requires major attention to the subjective" (p. ix). The blending of science and art as mentioned by Bugental occurs as a result of experience. *Usus est optimum magister* is from the Roman empire era and means "practice is the best teacher," and even though these words acquired the status of a cliché centuries ago, this once popular saying still retains the truth captured by these four Latin words. Bugental (1987) was correct to insist that it is the "living experiences" amassed by a therapist during years of practice that foster the spot-on, intuitive ability that is the mark of a master therapist.

The psychiatrist Irvin P. Yalom is an example of such a master therapist. Yalom's book *The Gift of Therapy: An Open Letter to a New Generation of Therapists and Their Patients* (2002) comprises 85 short chapters, essentially vignettes describing insights from nearly 50 years of clinical experience. A sample of chapter titles include Empathy—Looking Out the Patient's Window; Create a New Therapy for Each Patient; The Therapeutic Act, Not the Therapeutic Word; Revealing Your Personal

Life—Caveats; Never (Almost Never) Make Decisions for the Patient; Conduct Therapy as a Continuous Session; Therapy as a Dress Rehearsal for Life; Interview the Significant Other; Explore Previous Therapy; and Avoid Diagnosis (Except for Insurance Companies). Readers are encouraged to read Yalom's book to obtain a true appreciation of what this master therapist learned over several decades.

We recognize that even though Yalom used chapter titles that for the most part were self-explanatory in nature, he used some chapter headings that a novice in the field of therapy would probably find confusing (this might even be true in several instances for a seasoned therapist). Consider, for example, the chapter title "Avoid Diagnosis (Except for Insurance Companies)."

Whereas some clients prefer to pay out-of-pocket for their therapy, the majority of clients rely on some form of third-party payment (e.g., a health insurance carrier pays for the therapy services rendered). But before an insurance company pays a therapist, the company expects the therapist to provide a diagnosis (in the United States, this means a diagnosis that can be found in the American Psychiatric Association's *Diagnostic and Statistical Manual of Mental Disorders* [*DSM*]). So the question becomes what exactly did Yalom mean by "Avoid Diagnosis (Except for Insurance Companies)"? According to Yalom (2002),

> Today's psychotherapy students are exposed to too much emphasis on diagnosis. Managed-care administrators demand that therapists arrive quickly at a precise diagnosis and then proceed upon a course of brief, focused therapy that matches that particular diagnosis. Sounds good. Sounds logical and efficient. But it has precious little to do with reality. It represents instead an illusory attempt to legislate scientific precision into being when it is nether possible nor desirable. (p. 4)

(Yalom elaborates that he came to understand that such a diagnostic process can seriously interfere with a therapist's ability to relate to a client because diagnosing reinforces attention to those aspects of a client's life and problems that agree with the diagnostic label given.) Even worse is when a therapist's expectations become so closely aligned with the assigned label that the ultimate effect of such an alignment is that the client's behaviors and ways of thinking change to meet the therapist's expectations. This process amounts to a *DSM*-driven self-fulfilling prophecy or, as the early cartoon character Popeye might have realized after seeing a therapist, "I yam what I yam—diagnosed."

This particular chapter title was also used by Yalom to allude to a common experience that is shared by many veteran counseling practitioners. At some point during the practice of therapy, these practitioners realize "how much easier it is to make a DSM . . . diagnosis following the first interview than much later, let's say, after the tenth session, when we know a great deal more about the individual" (Yalom, 2002, p. 5). Yalom concluded by asserting that the form of diagnostic procedure required by insurance companies has the potential to circumvent what represents the creative and spontaneous qualities of therapy that allow for the client and therapist to connect at a meaningful and therapeutically productive person-to-person level.

One professional who agrees with Yalom's position on the misuse of the *DSM* is Allen Frances, who had worked for 20 years on updating several versions of the *DSM*, including *DSM-III, DSM-III-R,* and *DSM-IV.* In fact, Frances (2013) spearheaded the task force that created *DSM-IV.* This psychiatrist made a number of cogent and worrisome claims concerning the direction that was taken in creating *DSM-V,* which is the most recent version of this diagnostic publication. Of great concern to Frances was the increased number of diagnostic categories that appeared in *DSM-V.* He questioned the justification of adding so many new categories without sound proof of the need to do so. Frances concluded that many psychologically healthy individuals could be misdiagnosed as dysfunctional and prescribed unneeded medications. Frances (2013) claimed that in addition to the countless number of individuals who are now positioned to receive a spurious *DSM* diagnosis, the next big loser due to the recent revamping of the *DSM* is the American Psychiatric Association, which failed to prevent the hyperinflation of diagnostic categories. Other negative consequences predicted by Frances include the misallocation of important mental health resources and the unreasonable financial burden that is placed on families that have to cover the cost of unneeded treatments and medicines. According to Frances, the primary winner from the recent hyperinflation of mental disorders is "Big Pharma" because, collectively, pharmaceutical companies are likely to reap multibillion-dollar gains as a result of an increase in the number of prescriptions being written.

Obviously a need exists to address the problems identified by Frances, but the finding of a solution will not be as easy as it might appear on the surface. One factor that contributes to both the hyperinflation of mental disorder categories and the creation of barriers to reversing this trend is the degree of difficulty mental health professionals have in setting the parameters to determine what is "normal" and what is "abnormal." For example, Frances (2013) asserted that billions of dollars have been spent to find evidence that a particular *DSM* mental disorder takes the form of "a discrete disease entity with a unitary cause," but currently mental disorders characteristically seem to possess too large of a heterogeneous quality to allow us to consider them as representing a simple disease (p. 19). Frances highlighted other inherent problems with the *DSM* system, such as the concerted effort made by its creators to increase the reliability of diagnoses (i.e., the consistency of agreement among diagnosticians) by cataloging the superficial and typical attributes of the various disorders. This approach is certainly a logical goal to achieve, but by pursuing an increase of reliability through such tactics, the authors of the *DSM* might eliminate nuances that accompany a certain mental disorder and in doing so affect the ways that important individual differences within a particular mental disorder might be manifested. Due to these and myriad other weaknesses that accompany use of the *DSM,* Yalom's remarks concerning the drawbacks to using diagnosis are easy to understand.

Integration's Role in Constructing a Personal Approach

Integration is not a haphazard process, nor is it built on the absence of a theoretical foundation because the term *integration* represents a combining and coordinating of separate parts into a unified whole. In many ways integration can be reduced to whether interoperable elements exist between two or more theories. Briefly, the term *interoperable* is applicable when considering the degree of utility for various theoretical systems to work in conjunction with one's own personal approach to counseling or when one abstracts parts (e.g., techniques) from various theories to construct one's own functional approach to therapy.

Forms of Integration

An integrative approach to theory construction can take several pathways, and several of these are briefly discussed and illustrated.

1. *Syncretism* can be thought of as a theoretically sloppy approach to therapy. In its worst form, it is constructed from contradicting belief systems. This form of syncretism occurs when a therapist needlessly tries to forge a unity by forcibly fitting different theoretical worldviews. The end result is a tangle of therapeutic methods for the therapist to follow—methods that create more confusion than clarity for both the client and the therapist. The M. C. Escher image in Figure 15.4 depicts a number of stairways that can be figuratively taken by a therapist, but in the end each stairway leads to a dead end.

2. *Technique Matching* represents a form of integration that matches therapy techniques with both the client and the client's problem. The driving force behind this approach is identifying the best technique(s) to use without aligning one's self with the theoretical position associated with the therapy technique. An example of this is Arnold Lazarus's multimodal therapy (Lazarus, 1981). Multimodal therapists assert that successful treatment requires a therapist to consider seven client dimensions represented by the acronym BASIC I.D. (i.e., Behavior, Affect, Sensation, Imagery, Cognition, Interpersonal relationships, and Drugs and biological functions). Once the primary source(s) for a client's problem is (are) uncovered, it determines the therapy techniques that will be employed.

3. *Theoretical Frames* represents the inclusion of another theory or part of a theory into the whole of one's own approach to working with clients. This can be done in different ways, but it requires the therapist to create an open structure of logical theoretical combinations, such as Marsha M. Linehan's dialectical behavior therapy, which combines principles from behavior therapy, cognitive behavior therapy, and mindfulness while promoting acceptance and client change (Linehan & Dimeff, 2001).

4. *Common Factors Approach* is an approach to theory integration that builds a foundation based on common elements that have been discovered to transcend theoretical barriers. One clear example of such common factors that appear to result in client change across the theories covered in this textbook are those identified by Lambert (1992), which were reviewed in an earlier section of this chapter.

Future Directions in Counseling and Psychotherapy

Benford (2010) assessed the accuracy of hundreds of predictions made by inventors, scientists, and experts in various technological fields that were published from 1903 to 1969 in *Popular Mechanics*. Over 50% of the predictions proved accurate, and the rest never materialized as predicted (e.g., in 1940 biochemists claimed "Ordinary grass gives promise of providing low-income families diets more abundant in vitamins [that] are now enjoyed by the wealthy. Housewives soon may add nourishing powdered grass to recipes" [p. 68]). One of the primary reasons given by Benford for incorrect predictions was an underestimation of the disruptive power of unanticipated broad social changes that altered the course of various technologies and developments. Davidson (2016) wrote, "Forecasting future events is often like searching for a black cat in an unlit room, that may not even be there" (p. 1). This caveat should also be kept in mind when considering any predictions or suggestions about the role that neuroscience, or any other factor, will have on the future practice of counseling.

Recently, the counseling profession has become increasingly interested in the neurosciences (e.g., methodological advances in neuroimaging, neurophysiological methods, and neuromodulation techniques), and some professionals argue for the need to integrate neuroscience in therapy research and practice (Gonçalves & Perrone-McGovern, 2014; Ivey, D'Andrea, & Ivey, 2012; Ivey, Ivey, & Zalaquett, 2013; Ivey & Zalaquett, 2011; Luke, 2016). Neuroscience is now considered to be interdisciplinary, embracing contributions from, for instance, psychology, mathematics, medicine, philosophy, physics, and computer science. In the context of therapy, it has been suggested by Ivey, Ivey, and Zalaquett (2013) that the integration of neuroscience and therapy represents a very important development in the field of mental health.

▼ FIGURE 15.4

Chaotically Constructed Stairs That Lead Nowhere

Title of this 1953 lithograph is *Relativity.*

Note. A frequent theme in Escher's art is an architectural structure or combination of everyday objects that are depicted in a manner to create an impossible but realistic final image.

Evidence is accumulating that suggests that participation in counseling and psychotherapy can modify an individual's brain (Barsaglini, Sartori, Benetti, Pettersson-Yeo, & Mechelli, 2014; Kumari, 2006). In fact, Linden (2006) reported a growing presence in the literature of the idea that a client's brain changes as a result of psychotherapy. Some (Ivey et al., 2013) have even argued that the brain of the counselor changes as well.

To assist comprehension of the benefits of incorporating neuroscience when counseling clients, Gonçalves and Perrone-McGovern (2014) introduced a transdiagnostic developmental perspective. These scholars theorized that interpersonal and environmental factors, such as neurotoxic factors (e.g., emotional stress), positive neurodevelopmental factors (e.g., nurturing and caring), and therapy interventions that impact psychological processes (e.g., reinforcement learning and approach motivation, emotional expression and regulation) in turn affect brain networks (e.g., attention, motivation, social cognition) that then can influence, for instance, social, cognitive, emotional, and vocational development.

Other scholars (Ivey et al., 2013; Luke, 2016) have discussed how various theories of therapy (e.g., psychodynamic, cognitive-behavioral, behavioral, humanistic, constructivist) can be adapted to incorporate findings from neuroscience. Luke's 2006 book is dedicated to this purpose and also to discussion of the role of neuroscience in anxiety, depression, stress, addictions, and substance use disorders.

In the years to come, greater attention will likely be paid to neuroscience by counseling theorists, researchers, practitioners, and educators. Much work remains to validate

THE JOURNEY BEGINS: CREATING A PERSONAL THEORY OF THERAPY

The task of formulating your own personal theory is divided into three parts.

Part I. Using Table 15.3, compare the three theoretical positions that you found most interesting.

Twelve theoretical positions were compared earlier in this chapter using various areas of comparison (see Table 15.1). Although similarities are evident among the 12 therapies, on the whole, the comparisons in Table 15.1 succinctly summarize a number of differences among the major theoretical approaches.

Instructions for Completion of Part I. Starting at the top left side of Table 15.3, write the name of the three theoretical approaches that you have chosen to compare. Next, in the far left column, write in the boxes 1 through 7 the areas you have chosen to make your comparisons (e.g., Role of the Therapist). We suggest that you select your seven comparison areas from those listed in the following paragraph. However, because the listing provided is not all-inclusive, you should feel free to consider other possible areas of comparison.

Possible Comparison Areas. Choose from the following areas to make your comparisons: Philosophical Position Concerning Basic Human Nature, Role of Therapist, Key Concepts, Goals of Therapy, Therapeutic Relationship, Techniques of Therapy, Applications of the Approach, Multicultural Considerations, Social Justice Considerations, General Contributions to the Field, General Limitations, and General Strengths. (Note: The listed areas are essentially the same areas listed in Table 1.2 "Guide for Summarizing the 12 Areas.")

▼ TABLE 15.3

Use for Your Comparisons

Seven Areas Selected for Comparisons
Name of First Theoretical Approach Selected:
Name of Second Theoretical Approach Selected:
Name of Third Theoretical Approach Selected:

Seven Areas Selected for Comparisons	Name of First Theoretical Approach Selected	Name of Second Theoretical Approach Selected	Name of Third Theoretical Approach Selected
Area 1:			
Area 2:			
Area 3:			
Area 4:			
Area 5:			
Area 6:			
Area 7:			

Area 1:

Part II a. Considering what you wrote for Part I, use a single paragraph to *tentatively* describe your personal theoretical position. Provide a name for your position. (Try to create a unique name for your approach that captures its essence.)

Part II b. Answer the following questions.

1. How much of a contribution would each element of Lambert's (1992) common factors model contribute to client healing in your approach?

2. Explain how you would determine whether the theoretical framework that you created would provide effective therapy?

3. Explain the role that choice (free will) would play in your personal form of therapy.

4. Many clients rely on communication patterns that contribute to their problems (problems in cooperating, caring, thinking, and in the gender/cultural interactions that they experience). Explain how such problems would be conceptualized in your approach. (Hint: A person-centered therapist could conceptualize a client's problem in terms of a problem with expressing care for others.)

5. How important would it be to customize the approach that you formulated? That is, to what degree would you change your approach to fit the needs of different clients? Give at least one example of how you might change your approach.

6. The therapeutic relationship is considered very important across many forms of counseling and psychotherapy, but differences concerning its importance exist. To what extent will you emphasize the therapist–client relationship over other aspects of your approach?

▼ FIGURE 15.5

Use of Art to Convey Meaning

Note: Richard Redgrave's *The Outcast* was displayed in the Royal Academy in England during the mid-1850s. The painting shows what happened to a "fallen woman." In the painting a father breaks ties with his daughter, who has had a child without being married. There are areas in the world today where the punishment for having a child outside of marriage would result in strong sanctions or even death.

Source: The Outcast by Richard Redgrave, RA. 1851. Oil on canvas, 31 x 41 inches. Royal Academy of the Arts, London.

7. Find at least one example from art, music, or literature that you can refer to or incorporate into the body of your explanation that would illustrate an aspect of the theoretical approach that you have constructed. See Figure 15.5 below for an example of art that might be used to illustrate one or more concepts that are found in feminist or multicultural therapy.

Part III a. Did your tentatively described position change in light of your answers to the questions posed in Part II? Explain why it did or did not change.

Part III b. Describe your personal theoretical position in detail, and incorporate in your description what you learned by completing Parts I and II.

the complex and intricate relationship between brain behavior, brain networks, and specific methods and strategies that will be employed to conceptualize and treat clients who represent diverse populations and present with a variety of concerns. Furthermore, a need exists for more extensive, elaborate, and longitudinal research to ascertain how and if the integration of neuroscience with specific theories of therapy influences therapist–client interactions and the process and outcome of therapy.

Enders (2015) summarized relatively recent research that examined the intestinal track's (gut's) large matrix of nerves that provide the brain more information than other sensory modalities such as the ears, eyes, nose, or skin. This research found that the gut's matrix of nerves communicate directly to the brain and appear to have a noticeable effect on conditions that traditionally have been associated only with the brain. For example, evidence suggests that depressive disorders, general emotional states, experiences of fear, effectiveness of memory, motivation level, stress reactions, and self-awareness in the present are not just brain-based but are connected to what is occurring in the gut. As a result, the gut has been referred to as the "second brain," which opens up a new avenue to explore in relation to mental health.

CHAPTER REVIEW

SUMMARY AND COMMENTARY ▶▶

Even though we (the authors of this book) have our own personal preferences concerning the theories covered in this textbook, we agree on the importance of "getting out of the way" of readers being introduced to these theoretical approaches. We encourage readers to assess the contributions of each theoretical approach and decide for yourselves what is most meaningful and how to divide the "wheat from the chaff." Of course, this task is not easy for those who are new to the field (even veteran therapists can find such an effort challenging at times).

We made a concerted effort to describe each of the theories and their approaches in a manner that agreed with the facts and that offered a balanced, deliberate, and judicious coverage of the various theoretical approaches. This strategy was purposefully taken, so readers could develop a true appreciation of what each theoretical approach provides to our present understanding of the causes for human difficulties and the numerous ways that are available to overcome such problems or concerns.

We realize that any presentation of the topics covered in this textbook will have limitations. It is impossible to perfectly capture on the pages of any textbook the complete essence or the exactness of any of the theories covered. Nor is it possible to be all inclusive, in part because of space limitations. All textbooks come to an end and as a result some approaches may receive less than desirable coverage, and others are excluded entirely. Sometimes excluding an approach was relatively easy for us to decide due to an inherent weakness, such was the case with neuro-linguistic programming (NLP), which suffers from a serious lack of adequate empirical support for its claims. The dearth of research on this particular approach has led some critics of NLP to conclude that this approach represents a pseudoscience. We encourage users of this textbook to refer to the original works of the theorists who were covered in this textbook and to further explore those approaches we mentioned but did not discuss in depth. We also encourage readers to examine approaches that were excluded, such as NLP, to determine on their own whether any of these approaches should have been included.

This chapter began by stating that by its end readers would be asked to call on their understanding of the various theoretical approaches to construct their own personal theory of therapy. We have reached that point in this textbook. Instructions are provided in Table 15.3 to assist readers in completing this task. Finally, although readers should respond to what has been provided to help guide them in creating their own personal theory of therapy, if a reader wants to venture beyond the guidelines in the box to address an area that is not mentioned but is considered important, readers should feel free to do so.

SUGGESTED READINGS: IMPORTANT PRIMARY SOURCES ▶▶

Fischer, A. R., Jome, L. M., & Atkinson, D. R. (1998). Reconceptualizing multicultural Counseling: Universal healing conditions in a culturally specific context. *Counseling Psychologist, 26*(4), 525–588.

Frances, A. (2013). *Saving normal: An insider's revolt against out-of-control psychiatric diagnosis*, DSM-5, *big pharma, and the medicalization of ordinary life*. New York, NY: HarperCollins.

Gonçalves, Ó. F., & Perrone-McGovern, K. M. (2014). A neuroscience agenda for counseling psychology research. *Journal of Counseling Psychology, 61*, 507–512. doi:10.1037/cou0000026

Haggard, P. (2011). Decision time for free will. *Neuron 69*(3), 404–406.

Ivey, A. E., & Zalaquett, C. J. (2011). Neuroscience and counseling: Central issue for social justice. *Journal for Social Action in Counseling and Psychology, 3,* 103–116.

Luke, C. (2016). *Neuroscience for counselors and therapists: Integrating the sciences of mind and brain.* Thousand Oaks, CA: Sage.

Mele, A. R. (2014). *Free: Why science hasn't disproved free will.* New York, NY: Oxford University Press.

Perry, B. D., & Szalavitz, M. (2006). The boy who was raised as a dog: And other stories from a child psychiatrist's notebook. New York, NY: Basic Books.

Yalom, I. D. (2009). The gift of therapy: An open letter to a new generation of therapists and their patients. New York, NY: Harper Perennial.

REFERENCES

DEDICATION

Vyasa. (1986). *The Bhagavad-Gita* (B. S. Miller, Trans.). New York, NY: Bantam Books.

CHAPTER 1

American Psychological Association Presidential Task Force on Evidence-Based Practice. (2006). Evidence-based practice in psychology. *American Psychologist, 61,* 271–285.

Badri, M. (2013). *Abu Zayd Al-Balkhi's substance of the soul: The cognitive behavior therapy of a ninth century physician.* Markfield, England: International Institute of Islamic Thought.

Bergin, A. E. (1971). The evaluation of therapeutic outcomes. In A. E. Bergin & S. L. Garfield (Eds.), *Handbook of psychotherapy and behavior change* (pp. 217–270). New York, NY: Wiley.

Bergin, L. P., Bigham, L. E., Ginter, E. J., & Scalise, J. J. (2013). *2013 Analysis of marital and family therapy practice.* Colorado Springs, CO: Association of Marital and Family Therapy Regulatory Boards (AMFTRB).

Chant, L. (2003). The Scream *by Edvard Munch—A critical analysis.* Retrieved from http://lukecore.hub-pages.com/hub/The-Scream-by-Edvard-Munch-a-critical-analysis

Corsini, R. J., & Wedding, D. (Eds.). (2000). *Current psychotherapies* (6th ed.). Itasca, IL: Peacock.

De Los Reyes, A., & Kazdin, A. E. (2008). When the evidence says, "Yes, no, and maybe so": Attending to and interpreting inconsistent findings among evidence-based interventions. *Current Directions in Psychological Science, 17,* 47–51.

Devoe, D. (2012). "Viktor Frankl's logotherapy: The search for purpose and meaning." *Inquiries Journal, 4*(07). Retrieved from http://www.student-pulse.com/a?id=660

Dully, H., & Fleming, C. (2008). *My lobotomy.* New York, NY: Crown.

Edson, E., & Savage-Smith, E. (2004). *Medieval views of the cosmos: Picturing the universe in the Christian and Islamic middle ages.* Oxford, England: University of Oxford.

Eysenck, H. J. (1952). The effects of psychotherapy: An evaluation. *Journal of Consulting Psychology, 16,* 319–324.

Eysenck, H. J. (1961). The effects of psychotherapy. In H. J. Eysenck (Ed.), *Handbook of abnormal psychology* (pp. 697–725). New York, NY: Basic Books.

Eysenck, H. J. (1966). *The effects of psychotherapy.* New York, NY: International Science Press.

Fenichel, O. (1930). *Ten years of the Berlin Psychoanalytic Institute, 1920–1930.* Berlin, Germany: Berlin Psychoanalytic Institute.

Foucault, M. (1965). *Madness and civilization: A history of insanity in the age of reason* (R. Howard, Trans.). New York, NY: Pantheon Books.

Garfield, S. L. (1996). Some problems associated with "validated" forms of psychotherapy. *Clinical Psychology: Science and Practice, 3,* 218–229.

Gendlin, E. T. (1962). Client-centered developments and work with schizophrenics. *Journal of Counseling Psychology, 9*(3), 205–212. From http://www.focusing.org/gendlin/docs/gol_2141.html

Gladding, S. T. (2002). *Family therapy: History, theory, and practice* (3rd ed.). Upper Saddle River, NJ: Pearson.

Haque, A. (2004). Psychology from Islamic perspective: Contributions of early Muslim scholars and challenges to contemporary Muslim psychologists. *Journal of Religion and Health, 43*(4), 357–377.

Horvath, A. O., & Bedi, R. P. (2002). The alliance. In J. Norcross (Ed.), *Psychotherapy relationships that work: Therapist contributions and responsiveness to patients* (pp. 37–70). New York, NY: Oxford University Press.

Institute of Medicine. (2001). *Crossing the quality chasm: A new health system for the 21st century.* Washington, DC: National Academy Press.

Ivey, A. E., & Zalaquett, C. P. (2011). Neuroscience and counseling: Central issue for social justice leaders. *Journal for Social Action in Counseling and Psychology, 3*(1), 103–116.

Kakar, S. (1991). *Shamans, mystics, and doctors: A psychological inquiry into India and its healing traditions.* Chicago, IL: University of Chicago Press.

Lambert, M. J. (2011). Psychotherapy research and its achievements. In J. C. Norcross, G. R. VandenBos, & D. K. Freedheim (Eds.), *History of psychotherapy: Continuity and change* (2nd ed., pp. 299–332). Washington, DC: American Psychological Association.

Luborsky, L., Singer, B., & Luborsky, L. (1975.). Comparative studies of psychotherapies: Is it true that "everyone has won and all must have prizes"? *Archives of General Psychiatry, 32,* 995–1008.

McWilliams, N. (2011). *Psychoanalytic diagnosis: Understanding personality structure in the clinical process* (2nd ed.). New York, NY: Guilford Press.

Mercer, J. (2014). *Alternative psychotherapies: Evaluating unconventional mental health treatments.* New York, NY: Rowman & Littlefield.

National Public Radio. (2014). *Sound portraits: My lobotomy.* Retrieved from https://beta.prx.org/stories/7480

Norcross, J. C. (Ed.). (2002). *Psychotherapy relationships that work: Therapist contributions and responsiveness to patients.* New York, NY: Oxford University Press.

Oxford University. (1971). *The compact edition of the Oxford English dictionary* (Vol. I, A-O). Oxford, England: Oxford University Press.

Pickren, W. E. (2014). *The psychology book: From shamanism to cutting-edge neuroscience, 250 milestones in the history of psychology.* New York, NY: Sterling.

Rogers, C. R. (1951). *Client-centered therapy: Its current practice, implications, and theory.* New York, NY: Houghton Mifflin.

Rogers, C. R. (1980). *A way of being.* Boston, MA: Houghton Mifflin.

Rogers, C. R., & Dymond, R. (1954). *Psychotherapy and personality change.* Chicago, IL: University of Chicago Press.

Sackett, D. L., Straus, S. E., Richardson, W. S., Rosenberg, W. M., & Haynes, R. B. (2000). *Evidence based medicine: How to practice and teach EBM.* London, England: Churchill Livingstone.

Sartre, J.-P. (1974). *Being and nothingness* (Abridged ed., H. E. Barnes, Trans.). Secaucus, NJ: Citadel Press. (Original work published 1956)

Sartre, J.-P. (2013). *The Freud scenario* (Q. Hoare, Trans.). Brooklyn, NY: Verso. (Original work published 1984)

Skinner, B. F. (1962). *Walden two.* New York, NY: Macmillan.

Smith, M. L., & Glass, G. V. (1977). Meta-analysis of psychotherapy outcome studies. *American Psychologist, 32,* 752–760.

Task Force on Promotion and Dissemination of Psychological Procedures. (1995). Training in and dissemination of empirically-validated psychological treatment: Report and recommendations. *Clinical Psychologist, 48,* 2–23.

University of Michigan Health System. (2012, June 16). Freud's theory of unconscious conflict linked to anxiety symptoms. *ScienceDaily.* Retrieved from www.sciencedaily.com/releases/2012/06/120616145531.htm

Wampold, B. E. (2001). *The great psychotherapy debate: Models, methods, and findings.* Mahwah, NJ: Erlbaum.

Wampold, B. E. (2010). *The basics of psychotherapy: An introduction to theory and practice.* Washington, DC: American Psychological Association.

Wampold, B. E., Mondin, G. W., Moody, M., Stich, F., Benson, K., & Aim, H. N. (1997). A meta-analysis of outcome studies comparing bona fide psychotherapies: Empirically, "all must have prizes." *Psychological Bulletin, 122,* 203–215.

CHAPTER 2

Ambler, V. M. (2008). Who flourishes? The criteria of complete mental health. In S. J. Lopez (Ed.), *Positive psychology: Exploring the best in people* (pp. 1–20). Westport, CT: Praeger.

American Association of State Counseling Boards (AASCB). (2017). *Licensure & portability.* Retrieved from http://www.aascb.org/aws/AASCB/pt/sp/licensure

American Counseling Association. (2014). *2014 ACA Code of Ethics.* Alexandria, VA: Author. Retrieved from https://www.counseling.org/knowledge-center/ethics

American Counseling Association. (2017). *About us.* Retrieved from http://www.counseling.org/about-us/about-aca

American Psychological Association. (2002). *Ethical principles of psychologists and code of conduct* (including 2010 and 2016 amendments). Washington, DC: Author. Retrieved from http://www.apa.org/ethics/code

American Psychological Association. (2003). Guidelines on multicultural education, training, research, practice, and organizational change for psychologists. *American Psychologist, 58,* 377–402.

American Psychological Association. (2017). *Multicultural guidelines: An ecological approach to context, identity, and intersectionality.* Retrieved from http://www.apa.org/about/policy/multicultural-guidelines.pdf

APA Presidential Task Force on Evidence-Based Practice. (2006). Evidence-based practice in psychology. *American Psychologist, 61,* 271–285.

Barnett, J. E., Baker, E. K., Elman, N. S., & Schoener, G. R. (2007). In pursuit of wellness: The self-care imperative. *Professional Psychology: Research and Practice, 38,* 603–612.

Barnett, J. E., Behnke, S. H., Rosenthal, S. L., & Koocher, G. P. (2007). In case of ethical dilemma, break glass: Commentary on ethical decision-making in practice. *Professional Psychology: Research and Practice, 38,* 7–12.

Bowman, S., & Roysircar, G. (2011). Training and practice in trauma, catastrophes, and disaster counseling. *Counseling Psychologist, 39*(8), 1160–1181.

Bureau of Labor Statistics. (2010–2011). *Occupational outlook handbook.* Washington, DC: Author.

Bylund, C. L., & Duck, S. (2004). The everyday interplay between family relationships and family members' health. *Journal of Social and Personal Relationships, 21*(1), 5–7.

Cameron, L. D., & Leventhal, H. (2003). Self–regulation, health, and illness: An overview. In L. D. Cameron & H. Leventhal (Eds.), *The self-regulation of health and illness behavior* (pp. 1–14). London, UK: Routledge.

Campbell, C. D., & Gordon, M. C. (2003). Acknowledging the inevitable: Understanding multiple relationships in rural practice. *Professional Psychology: Research and Practice, 34*(4), 430–434.

Cashwell, C. S. (2010, March). In CACREP perspective. *Counseling Today, 52*(11), 58–59.

Cloud, H., & Townsend, J. (1992). *Boundaries: When to say yes, how to say no to take control of your life.* Grand Rapids, MI: Zondervan.

Cohen, D. (1993). Occupational hazards of the rural psychologist. *Psychotherapy in Private Practice, 10,* 13–35.

Corey, G. (2017). *Theories and practice of counseling and psychotherapy* (10th ed.). (Boston, MA: Cengage Learning.

Corey, G., Corey, M. S., & Callanan, P. (2007). *Issues and ethics in the helping professions* (7th ed.). Belmont, CA: Thomson Brooks/Cole.

Coster, J. S., & Schwebel, M. (1997). Well-functioning in professional psychologists. *Professional Psychology: Research and Practice, 28,* 5–13.

Council for Training in Evidence-Based Behavioral Practice. (2008). *Definition and competencies for evidence-based behavioral practice (EBBP).* Retrieved from www.ebbp.org/documents/ebbp_competencies.pdf

Cummins, R. A. (2013). Positive psychology and subjective well-being homeostasis: A critical examination of congruence. In A. Efklides and D. Moraitou (Eds.), *A positive psychology perspective on quality of life* (pp. 67–86). New York, NY: Springer.

Diener E., & Lucas, R. E. (1999). Personality and subjective well-being. In D. Kahneman, E. Diener, & N. Schwarz (Eds.), *Well-being: The foundations of hedonic psychology* (pp. 213–229). New York: Russell Sage Foundation.

Erickson, S. H. (2001). Multiple relationships in rural counseling. *Family Journal: Counseling and Therapy for Couples and Families, 9,* 302–304.

Fisher, C. B., & Oransky, M. (2008). *Informed consent to psychotherapy and the American Psychological Association's Code of Ethics.* Washington, DC: National Register for Health Service Psychologists. Retrieved from https://www.nationalregister.org/pub/the-register-report-spring-2008/informed-consent-to-psychotherapy-and-the-american-psychological-associations-ethics-code

Fouad, N. A., Grus, C. L., Hatcher, R. L., Kaslow, N. J., Hutchings, P. S., Madson, M., Collins, Jr., F. L *Fouad, N. A., Grus, C. L., Hatcher, R. L., Kaslow, N. J.; Hutchings, P. S., Madson, M. B.; Collins, Jr., F. L., Crossman, R. E. (2009).* Competency benchmarks: A model for the understanding and measuring of competence in professional psychology across training levels. *Training and Education in Professional Psychology, 3*(4 Suppl.), S5–S26.

Fox, R. (1995). The rape of psychotherapy. *Professional Psychology: Research and Practice, 26,* 147–155.

Fredrickson, B. L. (2000). Cultivating positive emotions to cultivate health and well-being. *Prevention and Treatment, 3,* article 0001a.

Ginter, E. J. (2002). *Journal of Counseling & Development* (JCD) and counseling's interwoven nature: Achieving a more complete understanding of the present through "historization" (Musing of an existing editor - an editorial postscript). *Journal of Counseling & Development, 80,* 85–95.

Gladding, S. T. (2009). *Counseling: A comprehensive profession* (5th ed.). Upper Saddle Hill, NJ: Merrill/Prentice Hall.

Gottlieb, M. C. (1993). Avoiding exploitative dual relationships: A decision-making model. *Psychotherapy, 30,* 41–48.

Gutheil, T. G., & Gabbard, G. O. (1993). The concept of boundaries in clinical practice: Theoretical and risk-management dimensions. *American Journal of Psychiatry, 150*(2), 188–196.

Hargrove, D. S. (1986). Ethical issues in rural mental health practice. *Professional Psychology: Research and Practice, 17,* 20–23.

Harold, M. (1985). Council's history examined after 50 years. *Guidepost, 27*(1), 4.

Helbok, C. M. (2003). The practice of psychology in rural communities: Potential ethical dilemmas. *Ethics and Behavior, 13,* 367–384.

Herlihy, B., & Corey, G. (2006). *Boundary issues in counseling: Multiple roles and responsibilities* (2nd ed.). Alexandria, VA: American Counseling Association.

Hollis, J. W., & Dodson, T. A. (2001). *Counselor preparation 1991–2001: Programs, faculty, trends.* Greensboro, NC: National Board of Certified Counselors.

Hu, F. B., Manson, J. E., Stampfer, M. J., Colditz, G., Liu, S., Solomon, C. G., & Willett, W. C. (2001). Diet, lifestyle, and the risk of type 2 diabetes mellitus in women. *New England Journal of Medicine, 345*(11), 790–797.

Kersting, K. (2003, June). Teaching self-sufficiency for rural practice. *Monitor on Psychology, 34*(6). Retrieved from http://www.apa.org/monitor/jun03/teaching.aspx

Keyes, C. L. M. (2003). Complete mental health: An agenda for the 21st century. In C. L. M. Keyes & J. Haidt (Eds.), *Flourishing: Positive psychology and the life well-lived* (pp. 293–312). Washington, DC: American Psychological Association.

Kitchener, K. S. (1988). Dual role relationships: What makes them so problematic? *Journal of Counseling & Development, 67,* 217–221.

Kocet, M. M. (2006). Ethical challenges in a complex world. Highlights of the 2005 ACA Code of Ethics. *Journal of Counseling & Development, 84*(2), 228–234.

Lichtenberg, J. W., Goodyear, R. K., & Genther, D. Y. (2008). The changing landscape of professional practice in counseling psychology. In S. D. Brown & R. W. Lent (Eds.), *Handbook of counseling psychology* (4th ed., pp. 21–37). New York, NY: Wiley.

Linley, P. A., & Joseph, S. (2007). Therapy work and therapists' positive and negative well-being. *Journal of Social and Clinical Psychology, 26,* 385–403.

Maslach, C. (2003). Job burnout: New directions in research and intervention. *Current Directions in Psychological Science, 12,* 189–192.

Maslach, C., & Goldberg, J. (1998). Prevention of burnout: New perspectives. *Applied and Preventive Psychology, 7,* 63–74.

Maslach, C., Schaufeli, W. B., & Leiter, M. P. (2001). Job burnout. *Annual Review of Psychology, 52,* 397–422.

McCormick, D. W. (1994). Spirituality and management. *Journal of Managerial Psychology, 9*(6), 5–8.

Nagy, T. F. (2011). Essential ethics for psychologists: A primer for understanding and mastering core issues. Washington, DC: American Psychological Association.

National Board for Certified Counselors. (2016). *Certification*. Retrieved from www.nbcc.org/Ourcertifications

National Board for Certified Counselors. (2017). *National Clinical Mental Health Counseling Examination (NCMHCE)*. Retrieved from http://www.nbcc.org/Exams/NCMHCE

National Council on Disability. (2013). *A brief history of managed care*. Washington, DC: Author. Retrieved from http://www.ncd.gov/publications/2013/20130315/20130513_AppendixB

Pope, K. S., & Vasquez, M. J. T. (2016). *Ethics in psychotherapy and counseling: A practical guide* (5th ed.). New York, NY: Wiley & Sons.

Pugh, R. (2007). Dual relationships: Personal and professional boundaries in rural social work. *British Journal of Social Work, 37*, 1405–1423. doi:10.1093/bjsw/bc1088

Rath, T., & Harter, J. (2010). *Well-being: The five essential elements*. New York, NY: Gallup Press.

Remley, T. P., Jr. (1995). A proposed alternative to the licensing of specialties in counseling. *Journal of Counseling & Development, 74*, 126–129.

Remley, T. P., Jr., & Herlihy, B. (2007). *Ethical, legal, and professional issues in counseling* (3rd ed.). Upper Saddle River, NJ: Pearson.

Richards, P. S., Rector, J. M., & Tjeltveit, A. C. (1999). Values, spirituality, and psychotherapy. In W. R. Miller (Ed.), *Integrating spirituality into treatment: Resources for practitioners* (pp. 130–160). Washington, DC: American Psychological Association.

Ridley, C. R., Liddle, M. C., Hill, C. L., & Li, L. (2001). Ethical decision making in multicultural counseling. In J. G. Ponterotto, J. M. Casas, L. A. Suzuki, & C. M. Alexander (Eds.), *Handbook of multicultural counseling* (2nd ed., pp. 165–188). Thousand Oaks, CA: Sage.

Rivas-Vasquez, R. A., Blais, M. A., Rey, G. J., & Rivas-Vasquez, A. A. (2001). A brief reminder about documenting the psychological consultation. *Professional Psychology: Research and Practice, 32*(2), 194–199.

Ross, C. E., & Mirowsky, J. (2002). Family relationships, social support and subjective life expectancy. *Journal of Health & Social Behavior, 43*(4), 469–489.

Roysircar, G. (2003). Counselor awareness of own assumptions, values, and biases. In G. Roysircar, P. Arredondo, J. N. Fuertes, J. G. Ponterotto, & R. L. Toporek (Eds.), *Multicultural competencies, 2003: Association for Multicultural Counseling and Development* (pp. 15–26). Alexandria, VA: American Counseling Association.

Roysircar, G. (2008). *Building community resilience in Mississippi: Self-care for disaster response workers and caregivers* (Grantor Foundation of the Mid-South in partnership with the American Red Cross). Keene, NH: Antioch University New England, Multicultural Center for Research and Practice.

Roysircar, G. (2009a). The big picture of social justice advocacy: Counselor, heal society and thyself. *Journal of Counseling & Development, 87*, 288–295.

Roysircar, G. (2009b). Evidence-based practice and its implications for culturally sensitive treatment. *Journal of Multicultural Counseling and Development, 37*(2), 66–82.

Roysircar, G., Arredondo, P., Fuertes, J. N., Ponterotto, J. G., & Toporek, R. L. (2003). *Multicultural counseling competencies: Association for Multicultural Counseling and Development*. Alexandria, VA: American Counseling Association.

Roysircar, G., Dobbins. J. E., & Malloy, K. (2009). Diversity competence in training and clinical practice. In M. Kenkel & R. Peterson (Eds.), *Competency-based education for professional psychology* (pp. 179–197). Washington, DC: American Psychological Association.

Schank, J. A., & Skovholt, T. M. (1997). Dual-relationship dilemmas of rural and small-community psychologists. *Professional Psychology: Research and Practice, 28*, 44–49.

Schank, J. A., & Skovholt, T. M. (2006). *Ethical practice in small communities: Challenges and rewards for psychologists*. Washington, DC: American Psychological Association.

Seligman, M. E. P. (2011). *Flourish: A visionary new understanding of happiness and well-being*. New York, NY: Free Press.

Shallcross, L. (2011, January 17). Taking care of yourself as a counselor. *Counseling Today*. https://ct.counseling.org/2011/01/taking-care-of-yourself-as-a-counselor

Shedler, J. (2015). Where is the evidence for "evidence-based" therapy? *Journal of Psychological Therapies in Primary Care, 4*, 47–59.

Simon, R. I. (1998). Boundary violations in psychotherapy. In L. E. Lifson & R. I. Simon (Eds.), *The mental health practitioner and the law: A comprehensive handbook* (pp. 195–215). Cambridge, MA: Harvard University Press.

Skovholt, T. (2001). *The resilient practitioner: Burnout prevention and self-care strategies for counselors, therapists, teachers, and health care professionals*. New York, NY: Allyn & Bacon.

Smith, P. L., & Moss, S. B. (2009). Psychological impairment: What is it, how can it be prevented, and what can be done to address it? *Clinical Psychology: Science & Practice, 16*(1), 1–15.

Sobel, S. B. (1992). Small town practice of psychotherapy: Ethical and personal dilemmas. *Psychotherapy in Private Practice, 10*, 61–69.

Sonne, J. L. (2006). *Nonsexual multiple relationships: A practical decision-making model for clinicians*. Retrieved from http://kspope.com/site/multiple-relationships.php

VandenBos, G. R. (Ed.). (2007). *APA dictionary of psychology*. Washington, DC: American Psychological Association.

Wampold, B., & Bhati, K. (2004). Attending to the omissions: A historical examination of evidenced-based practice movements. *Professional Psychology: Research and Practice, 35*(6), 563–570.

Warr, P. (1999). Well-being and the workplace. In D. Kahneman, E. Diener, & N. Schwarz (Eds.), *Well-being: The foundations of hedonic psychology* (pp. 392–412). New York, NY: Russell Sage Foundation.

Weinrach, S. G., & Thomas, K. R. (1993). The National Board for Certified Counselors: The good, the bad and the ugly, *Journal of Counseling & Development, 71*, 105–109.

Werth, J. L., Jr., Hastings, S. L., & Riding-Malon, R. (2010). Ethical challenges of practicing in rural areas. *Journal of Clinical Psychology, 66*, 537–548. doi:10.1002/jclp.20681

Younggren, J. N., & Gottlieb, M. C. (2004). Managing risk when contemplating multiple relationships. *Professional Psychology: Research and Practice, 35*, 255–260. doi:10.1037/0735-7028.35.3.255

Zur, O. (2015). Dual relationships, multiple relationships, boundaries, boundary crossings & boundary violations in psychotherapy, counseling & mental health. Retrieved from http://www.zurinstitute.com/dualrelationships.html

CHAPTER 3

Abbass, A., Kisely, S., & Kroenke, K. (2009). Short-term psychodynamic psychotherapy for somatic disorders: Systematic review and meta-analysis of clinical trials. *Psychotherapy and Psychosomatics, 78*(5), 265–274.

Abbass, A. A., Hancock, J. T., Henderson, J., & Kisely, S. (2006). Short-term psychodynamic psychotherapies for common mental disorders. *Cochrane Database of Systematic Reviews,* Issue 4, Article No. CD004687. doi:10.1002/14651858.CD004687.pub3

Adler, A. (1956). The individual psychology of Alfred Adler: A systematic presentation from his writings (H. L. & R. R. Ansbacher, Eds.). New York, NY: Basic Books.

Akhtar, S. (1995). A third individuation: Immigration, identity, and the psychoanalytic process. *Journal of the American Psychoanalytic Association, 43*(4), 1051–1084.

Alonso, A., & Rutan, J. S. (1984). The impact of object relations theory on psychodynamic group therapy. *American Journal of Psychiatry, 141*, 1376–1380.

American Psychoanalytic Association. (2007). *Principles and standards of ethics for psychoanalysts.* Retrieved from ethics.iit.edu/ecodes/node/3722

Bachrach, H., Galatzer-Levy, R., Skolnikoff, A., & Waldron, S. (1991). On the efficacy of psychoanalysis. *Journal of the American Psychoanalytic Association, 39*, 871–916.

Bauer, G. P., & Kobos, J. C. (1987). *Brief therapy: Short-term psychodynamic intervention.* Northvale, NJ: Aronson.

Bellak, L. (1989). *Ego Function Assessment (EFA): A manual.* Larchmont, NY: Consulting Psychological Services.

Bernard, J. M., & Goodyear, R. K. (20013). *Fundamentals of clinical supervision* (5th ed.). Boston, MA: Merrill.

Blatt, S. J. (1992). The differential effect of psychotherapy and psychoanalysis with anaclitic and introjective patients: The Menninger Research Project revisited. *Journal of the American Psychological Association, 40*(3), 691–724.

Bradshaw, W., Roseborough, D., Pahwa, R., & Jordan, J. (2009). Evaluation of psychodynamic psychotherapy in a community mental health center. *Journal of the American Academy of Psychoanalysis and Dynamic Psychiatry, 37*(4), 665–681.

Brantley, T. (1983). Racism and its impact on psychotherapy. *American Journal of Psychiatry, 140*, 1605–1608.

Brunstetter, R. W. (1998). *Adolescents in psychiatric hospitals: A psychodynamic approach to evaluation and treatment.* Springfield, IL: Thomas.

Burrows, P. B. (1981a). The family connection: Early memories as a measure of transference in a group. *International Journal of Group Psychotherapy, 31*, 3–23.

Burrows, P. B. (1981b). Parent orientation and member-leader behavior: A measure of transference in group. *International Journal of Group Psychotherapy, 31*, 175–191.

Chance, E. (1952). A study of transference in group psychotherapy. *International Journal of Group Psychotherapy, 2*, 40–53.

Cloud, J. (2014). Social sciences. In K. Knauer (Ed.), *Great scientists* (pp. 82–89). New York, NY: Time Books.

Cohen, J. (1988). *Statistical power analysis for the behavioral sciences* (2nd ed.). Abingdon, UK: Routledge.

Cohen, M., & Nagel, E. (1934). *An introduction to logic and scientific method.* New York, NY: Harcourt & Brace.

Colson, D. B. (1985). Transference-countertransference in psycho-analytic group therapy: A family systems view. *International Journal of Group Psychotherapy, 35*, 503–518.

Columbia University Press. (2005, May). Interview with Elizabeth Ann Danto, author of *Freud's free clinics: Psychoanalysis & social justice, 1918–1938.* Retrieved from internationalpsychoanalysis.net/2009/03/10/interview-with-elizabeth-ann-danto/

Comas-Diaz, L., & Minrath, M. (1985). Psychotherapy with ethnic minority borderline clients. *Psychotherapy, 22*, 418–426.

Corbett, S. (2009, September 16). The holy grail of the unconscious. *New York Times Magazine.*

D'Amore, A. R. T., & Eckburg, A. L. (1976). William Alanson *White: The Washington years, 1903–1937: The contributions to psychiatry, psychoanalysis, and mental health by Dr. White while superintendent of Saint Elizabeths Hospital.* Washington, DC: U.S. Department of Health, Education, and Welfare, Public Health Service, Alcohol, Drug Abuse, and Mental Health Administration.

Danto, E. A. (2005). *Freud's free clinics: Psychoanalysis and social justice, 1918–1938.* New York, NY: Columbia University Press.

de Maat, S., de Jonghe, F., de Kraker, R., Leichsenring, F., Abbass, A., Luyten, P., . . . Dekker, J. (2013). The current state of empirical evidence for psychoanalysis: A meta-analytic approach. *Harvard Review of Psychiatry, 21*(3), 107–137.

Eizirik, C. L., & de Armestro, M. S. (2005). Psychoanalysis in Latin America. In E. S. Person, A. M. Cooper, & G. O. Gabbard (Eds.), *Textbook of psychoanalysis* (pp. 335–360). Washington, DC: American Psychiatric Publishing.

Ellman, S. J. (1991). *Freud's technique papers: A contemporary perspective.* New York, NY: Jason Aronson.

Erikson, E. H. (1950a). *Childhood and society.* New York, NY: Norton.

Erikson, E. H. (1950b). Childhood in two American Indian tribes. In E. H. Erikson (Ed.), *Childhood and society* (pp. 109–186). New York, NY: Norton.

Fisher, S., & Greenberg, R. P. (1977). *The scientific credibility of Freud's theories and therapy*. New York, NY: Basic Books.

Foulkes, S. H. (1964). *Therapeutic group analysis*. New York, NY: International Universities Press.

Freud, A. (1966). *The writings of Anna Freud: Vol. 2. The ego and the mechanisms of defense* (C. Baines, Trans.). New York, NY: International Universities Press. (Original work published 1937)

Freud, E., Freud, L., & Grubrich-Simitis, I. (Eds.). (1978). *Sigmund Freud: His life in pictures and words*. London, UK: Harcourt Brace Jovanovich.

Freud, S. (1949). *An outline of psycho-analysis*. New York, NY: Norton. (Original work published 1940) [translated by J. Strachey]

Freud, S. (1953). The interpretation of dreams. In J. Strachey (Ed. & Trans.), *The standard edition of the complete psychological works of Sigmund Freud* (Vols. 4 & 5). London, UK: Hogarth Press. (Original work published 1900)

Freud, S. (1953a). On psychotherapy. In J. Strachey (Ed. & Trans.), *The standard edition of the complete psychological works of Sigmund Freud* (Vol. 7, pp. 255–268). London, UK: Hogarth Press. (Original work published 1905)

Freud, S. (1953b). Three essays on the theory of sexuality. In J. Strachey (Ed. & Trans.), *The standard edition of the complete psychological works of Sigmund Freud* (Vol. 7, pp. 123–247). London, UK: Hogarth Press. (Original work published 1905)

Freud, S. (1957). Instincts and their vicissitudes. In J. Strachey (Ed. & Trans.), *The standard edition of the complete psychological works of Sigmund Freud* (Vol. 14). London, UK: Hogarth Press. (Original work published 1915)

Freud, S. (1958). The dynamics of transference. In J. Strachey (Ed. & Trans.), *The standard edition of the complete psychological works of Sigmund Freud* (Vol. 12, pp. 97–109). London, UK: Hogarth Press. (Original work published 1912)

Freud, S. (1958). Observations on transference love. In J. Strachey (Ed. & Trans.), *The standard edition of the complete psychological works of Sigmund Freud* (Vol. 12, pp. 157–172). London, UK: Hogarth Press. (Original work published 1915)

Freud, S. (1959). Inhibitions, symptoms and anxiety. In J. Strachey (Ed. & Trans.), *The standard edition of the complete psychological works of Sigmund Freud* (Vol. 29). London, UK: Hogarth Press. (Original work published 1926)

Freud, S. (1959). On the history of the psychoanalytic movement. In E. Jones (Ed.) & J. Riviere (Trans.), *Collected papers* (Vol. 1, pp. 287–359). New York, NY: Basic Books. (Original work published 1914)

Freud, S. (1961). The ego and the id. In J. Strachey (Ed. & Trans.), *The standard edition of the complete psychological works of Sigmund Freud* (Vol. 19). London, UK: Hogarth Press. (Original work published 1923)

Gay, P. (1989). Sigmund Freud: A brief life. Introduction to S. Freud, *An outline of psycho-analysis*. New York, NY: Norton. (First German edition, 1940)

Gazda, G. M., Ginter, E. J., & Horne, A. M. (2001). *Group counseling and group psychotherapy: Theory and application*. Needham Heights, MA: Allyn & Bacon.

Gerber, A. J., Kocsis, J. H., Milrod, B. L., Roose, S. P., Barber, J. P., Thase, M. E., . . . Leon, A. C. (2011). A quality-based review of randomized controlled trials of psychodynamic psychotherapy. *American Journal of Psychiatry, 168*, 19–28.

Ginter, E. J. (1988). Stagnation in eclecticism: The need to recommit to a journey. *Journal of Mental Health Counseling, 10*, 3–8.

Ginter, E. J., & Bonney, W. (1993a). Freud, ESP, and interpersonal relationships: Projective identification and the Mobius interaction. *Journal of Mental Health Counseling, 15*, 150–169.

Ginter, E. J., & Bonney, W. (1993b). *Inexplicable classroom behavior. The Mobius interaction*. Paper presented at the annual conference of the American Association for Specialists in Group Counseling, Athens, GA.

Ginter, E. J., & Glauser, A. S. (2008). Assessment and diagnosis: The developmental perspective and its implications. In R. R. Erk (Ed.), *Counseling treatment for children and adolescents with DSM-IV-TR disorders* (2nd ed., pp. 2–36). Upper Saddle River, NJ: Pearson.

Giovacchini, P. L. (1977). Psychoanalysis. In R. J. Corsini (Ed.), *Current personality theories* (pp. 15–43). Itasca, IL: Peacock.

Göttken, T., White, L., Klein, A., & von Klitzing, K. (2014). Short-term psychoanalytic child therapy for anxious children: A pilot study. *Psychotherapy, 51*(1), 148–158.

Greene, L. R., Rosenkrantz, J., & Muth, D. Y. (1985). Splitting dynamics, self-representations and boundary phenomena in the group psychotherapy of borderline personality disorder. *Psychiatry, 48*, 234–245.

Greene, L. R., Rosenkrantz, J., & Muth, D. Y. (1986). Borderline defenses and countertransference: Research findings and implications. *Psychiatry, 49*, 253–264.

Greenspan, S. I., & Shanker, S. G. (2005). Developmental research. In E. S. Person, A. M. Cooper, & G. O. Gabbard (Eds.), *Textbook of psychoanalysis* (pp. 335–360). Washington, DC: American Psychiatric Publishing.

Hart, M. H. (1987). *The 100: A ranking of the most influential persons in history*. Secaucus, NJ: Citadel Press.

Jones, E. (1957). *Sigmund Freud: Life and work* (Vol. 3). London, United Kingdom: Hogarth Press.

Jung, C. G. (2009). *The red book: Liber novus*. (S. Shamdasani, Ed.; M. Kyburz, J. Peck, & S. Shamdasani, Trans.). New York, NY: Norton.

Jung, C. G., & Franz, M.-L. von, Henderson, J. L., Jacobi, J., & Jaffe, A. (1964). *Man and his symbols*. Garden City, NY: Doubleday.

Kahn, M. (2002). *Basic Freud: Psychoanalytic thought for the 21st century*. New York, NY: Basic Books.

Kaplan, J. (Ed.) (2002). *Bartlett's familiar quotations* (17th ed.). New York, NY: Little, Brown.

Keefe, J. R., McCarthy, K. S., Dinger, U., Zilcha-Mano, S., & Barber, J. P. (2014). A meta-analytic review of psychodynamic therapies for anxiety disorders. *Clinical Psychology Review, 34*(4), 309–323.

Kempf, E. J. (1919). The psychoanalytic treatment of dementia praecox: Report of a case. *Psychoanalytic Review, 6*, 15–58.

Kernberg, O. F. (1984). *Severe personality disorders: Psychotherapeutic strategies.* New Haven, CT: Yale University Press.

Kilmann, P. R., Laughlin, J. E., Carranza, L. V., Downer, J. T., Major, S., & Parnell, M. M. (1999). Effects of attachment-focused group preventive intervention on insecure women. *Group Dynamics: Theory, Research, and Practice, 3*, 138–147.

Klein, M. (1946). Notes on some schizoid mechanisms. *International Journal of Psycho-analysis, 27*, 99–110.

Klein, M. (1957). On identification. In M. Klein, P. Heimann, & R. E. Money-Kyrle (Eds.), *New directions in psychoanalysis: The significance of infant conflict in the pattern of adult behavior.* New York, NY: Basic Books.

Klein, M. (1977). Transference in training groups. *Journal of Personality and Social Systems, 1*, 53–64.

Kubie, L. S. (1953). Psychoanalysis as a basic science. In F. Alexander & H. Ross (Eds.), *20 years of psycho-analysis.* New York, NY: Norton.

Leary, T. (1957). *Interpersonal diagnosis of personality: A functional theory and methodology for personality evaluation.* New York, NY: Ronald Press.

Leichsenring, F. (2005). Are psychodynamic and psychoanalytic therapies effective? A review of empirical data. *International Journal of Psychoanalysis, 86*(3), 841–868.

Leichsenring, F., Abbass, A., Luyten, P., Hilsenroth, M., & Rabung, S. (2013). The emerging evidence for long-term psychodynamic therapy. *Psychodynamic Psychiatry, 41*(3), 361–384.

Leichsenring, F., & Leibing, E. (2003). The effectiveness of psychodynamic therapy and cognitive behavior therapy in the treatment of personality disorders: A meta-analysis. *American Journal of Psychiatry, 160*, 1223–1232.

Leichsenring, F., & Rabung, S. (2008). Effectiveness of long-term psychodynamic psychotherapy: A meta-analysis. *Journal of the American Medical Association, 300*, 1551–1565.

Leichsenring, F., Rabung, S., & Leibing, E. (2004). The efficacy of short-term psychodynamic psychotherapy in specific psychiatric disorders: A meta-analysis. *Archives of General Psychiatry, 61*, 1208–1216.

MacKenzie, K. R. (2001). Group psychotherapy. In W. J. Livesley (Ed.), *Handbook of personality disorders* (pp. 497–526). New York, NY: Guilford Press.

MacKenzie, K. R., Dies, R. R., Coché, E., Rutan, J. S., & Stone, W. N. (1987). An analysis of AGPA Institute groups. *International Journal of Group Psychotherapy, 37*(1), 55–74.

Mayes, R., & Horwitz, A. V. (2005). DSM-III and the revolution in the classification of mental illness. *Journal of the History of the Behavioral Sciences, 41*(3), 249–267.

Messer, S. B., & Abbass, A. A. (2010). Evidence-based psychodynamic therapy with personality disorders. Evidence-based treatment of personality dysfunction: Principles, methods, and processes. In J. J. Magnavita (Ed.), *Evidence-based treatment of personality dysfunction: Principles, methods, and processes* (pp. 79–111). Washington, DC: American Psychological Association.

Mitchell, S. A. (1988). *Relational concepts in psychoanalysis: An integration.* Cambridge, MA: Harvard University Press.

Moncayo, R. (1998). Cultural diversity and the cultural and epistemological structure of psychoanalysis: Implications for psychotherapy with Latinos and other minorities. *Psychoanalytic Psychology, 2*(15), 262–286.

Nagel, E. (1959). Methodological issues in psychoanalytic treatment. In S. Hooke (Ed.), *Psychoanalytic; scientific method and philosophy.* New York: New York University Press.

PDM Task Force. (2006). *Psychodynamic diagnostic manual.* Silver Spring, MD: Alliance of Psychoanalytic Organizations.

Person, E. S., Cooper, A. M., & Gabbard, G. O. (Eds.). (2005). *Textbook of psychoanalysis.* Washington, DC: American Psychiatric Publishing.

Robinson, T. L. (1999). The intersections of dominant discourses across race, gender and other identities. *Journal of Counseling and Development, 77*, 73–77.

Robinson, T. L., & Ginter, E. J. (1999). Introduction to the *Journal of Counseling & Development*'s special issue on racism. *Journal of Counseling & Development, 77*, 3.

Santisteban, D. A., Mena, M. P. & Abalo, C. (2013). Bridging diversity and family systems: Culturally informed and flexible family-based treatment for Hispanic adolescents. *Couple and Family Psychology: Research and Practice, 4*(2), 246–263.

Sawilowsky, S (2009). New effect size rules of thumb. *Journal of Modern Applied Statistical Methods, 8*(2), 467–474.

Scharff, J. S. (Ed.) (1989). *Foundations of object relations family therapy.* New York, NY: Aronson.

Serrano, A. C., & Ruiz, E. J. (1991). Transferential and cultural issues in group psychotherapy. In S. Tuttman (Ed.), *Psychoanalytic group theory and therapy: Essays in honor of Saul Scheidlinger.* Madison, CT: International Universities Press.

Shedler, J. (2010). The efficacy of psychodynamic psychotherapy. *American Psychologist, 65*(2), 98–109.

Sifneos, P. E. (1987). *Short-term dynamic psychotherapy: Evaluation and technique* (2nd ed.). New York, NY: Plenum.

Solms, M. (2005). Neuroscience. In E. S. Person, A. M. Cooper, & G. O. Gabbard (Eds.), *Textbook of psychoanalysis* (pp. 335–360). Washington, DC: American Psychiatric Publishing.

St. Clair, M. (1986). *Object relations and self-psychology: An introduction.* Pacific Grove, CA: Brooks/Cole.

Steinberg, R. I., Rosie, J. S., Joyce, A. S., O'Kelly, J. G., Piper, W. E., Lyon, D., . . . Duggal, S. (2004). The psychodynamic psychiatry service of the University of Alberta hospital: A thirty year history. *International Journal of Group Psychotherapy, 54*(4), 521–538.

Tang, N. M., & Gardner, J. (1999). Race, culture, and psychotherapy: Transference to minority therapists. *Psychoanalytic Quarterly, 68*, 1–20.

Vaughan, S. G. (1997). *The talking cure: The science behind psychotherapy.* New York, NY: Putnam.

Wachtel, P. L. (1977). *Psychoanalysis and behavior therapy: Toward an integration.* New York, NY: Basic Books.

Weitkamp, K., Daniels, J., Hofmann, H., Timmermann, H., Romer, G., & Wiegand-Grefe, S. (2014). Psychoanalytic psychotherapy for children and adolescents with severe depressive psychopathology: Preliminary results of an effectiveness trial. *Psychotherapy, 51*(1), 138–147.

Wolf, A., & Schwartz, E. K. (1962). *Psychoanalysis in group.* New York, NY: Grune & Stratton.

Zinner, J., & Shapiro, R. L. (1989). Projective identification as a mode of perception and behavior in families of adolescents. In J. S. Scharff (Ed.), *Foundations of object relations family therapy.* New York, NY: Aronson.

CHAPTER 4

Adler, A. [Alexandra]. (1938). *Guiding human misfits.* New York, NY: Macmillan.

Adler, A. [Alfred]. (1935). Prevention of neuroses. *International Journal of Individual Psychology, 14,* 3–12.

Adler, A. [Alfred]. (1954). *Understanding human nature* (W. B. Wolfe, Trans.). New York, NY: Fawcett Premier. (Original work published 1927)

Adler, A. [Alfred]. (1968). Individual psychology (S. Langer, Trans.). In W. S. Sahakian (Ed.), *History of psychology: A source book in systematic psychology* (pp. 340–347). Itasca, IL: Peacock. (Original work published 1930)

Ambrason, Z. (2007). Adlerian family and couples therapy. *Journal of Individual Psychology, 63,* 371–386.

Amerikaner, M., Elliot, D., & Swank, P. (1988). Social interest as a predictor of vocational satisfaction. *Journal of Individual Psychology, 44,* 316–323.

Ansbacher, H. L. (1974). Goal-oriented individual psychology: Alfred Adler's theory. In A. Burton (Ed.), *Operational theories of personality* (pp. 99–142). New York, NY: Brunner/Mazel.

Ansbacher, H. L. (1977). Individual psychology. In R. J. Corsini (Ed.). *Current personality theory* (pp. 45–82). Itasca, IL: Peacock.

Ansbacher, H. L., & Ansbacher, R. R. (Eds.). (1956). *The individual psychology of Alfred Adler.* New York, NY: Basic Books.

Ansbacher, H. L., & Ansbacher, R. R. (Eds.). (1970). *Superiority and social interest: A collection of later writings.* Evanston, IL: Northwestern University Press.

Arciniega, G. M., & Newlon, B. J. (1999). Counseling and psychotherapy: Multicultural considerations. In D. Capuzzi & D. F. Gross (Eds.), *Counseling and psychotherapy: Theories and interventions* (2nd ed., pp. 435–458). Upper Saddle River, NJ: Merrill/Prentice Hall.

Aronson, L., Tenenbaum, S., & Roures, J. (Producers), & Allen, W. (Director). (2011). *Midnight in Paris* [Motion picture]. United States: Sony Pictures Classics.

Basinger, J. (1999). *Silent stars.* New York, NY: Knopf.

Blackburn, A. B., O'Connell, W. E., & Richman, B. W. (1984). Post-traumatic stress disorder, the Vietman veteran, and Adlerian natural high therapy. *Individual Psychology: Journal of Adlerian Theory, Research & Practice, 40*(3), 317–332.

Bloland, S. E. (2005). *In the shadow of fame: A memoir by the daughter of Erik H. Erikson.* New York, NY: Penguin Books.

Burnett, P. C. (1988). Evaluation of Adlerian parenting programs. *Journal of Individual Psychology, 44,* 63–76.

Campbell, L. F., White, J., & Stewart, A. (1991). The relationship of psychological birth order to actual birth order. *Journal of Individual Psychology, 47,* 382–391.

Carlson, J., Watts, R. E., & Maniacci, M. (2006). *Adlerian therapy: Theory and practice.* Washington, DC: American Psychological Association.

Carlson, J. M., & Carlson, J. D. (2000). The application of Adlerian psychotherapy with Asian-American clients. *Journal of Individual Psychology, 56,* 214–225.

Carmichael, S. (1966, October). *Black power address at UC Berkeley* [Transcribed from recording]. Retrieved from http://www.americanrhetoric.com/speeches/stokely-carmichaelblackpower.html

Corsini, R., & Wedding, D. (2010). *Current psychotherapies.* Florence, KY: Cengage Learning.

Crandall, J. E. (1991). A scale for social interest. *Journal of Individual Psychology, 47,* 106–114.

Croake, J. W., & Myers, K. M. (1985). Goal diagnosis in psychiatric consultation. *Individual Psychology: Journal of Adlerian Theory, Research & Practice, 41*(4), 496–509.

Dagley, J. C., Evans, T. D., & Taylor, P. A. (1992). *The encouragement scale: Research and technical manual.* Athens: University of Georgia.

Dillman-Taylor, D., & Bratton, S. C. (2014). Developmental appropriate practice: Adlerian play therapy with preschool children. *Journal of Individual Psychology, 70*(3), 205–219.

Dinkmeyer, D., Jr., & Sperry, L. (1999). *Counseling and psychotherapy: An integrated individual psychology approach* (3rd ed.). New York, NY: Pearson.

Dinkmeyer, D., Sr., McKay, G. D., & Dinkmeyer, D., Jr. (2008). *The parent's handbook: Systematic training for effective parenting.* Fredericksburg, VA: STEP.

Dinkmeyer, D. C., & Sperry, L. (1987). *Adlerian counseling and psychotherapy.* Columbus, OH: Merrill.

Dreikurs, R. (1973). *Psychodynamic, psychotherapy, and counseling.* Chicago, IL: Alfred Adler Institute. (Original work published 1967)

Ellison, A. M. (2009). *Parent education and the child's perception of parent change* (Unpublished doctoral dissertation). Adler School of Professional Psychology, Chicago, IL.

Emener, W. G., Richard, M. A., & Bosworth, J. J. (2009). *A guidebook to human service professions: Helping college students explore opportunities in the human services field.* Springfield, IL: Thomas.

Fennell, D. C., & Fishel, A. H. (1998). Parent education: An evaluation of STEP on abusive parents' perceptions and abuse potential. *Journal of Child and Adolescent Psychiatric Nursing, 11,* 107–120.

Ferguson, E. D. (2010). Adler's innovative contributions regarding the need to belong. *Journal of Individual Psychology, 66*, 1–7.

Freud, S. (1959). Two encyclopedia articles Psych-analysis. In J. Strachey (Ed. & Trans.), *Sigmund Freud collected papers* (Vol. 5). New York, NY: Basic Books. (Original work published 1922)

Gerstein, L. H., Heppner, P. P., Ægisdóttir, S., Leung, S.-M. A., & Norsworthy, K. L. (Eds.). (2009). *International handbook of cross-cultural counseling: Cultural assumptions and practices worldwide.* Thousand Oaks, CA: Sage.

Herrington, A. N., Matheny, K. B., Curlette, W. L., McCarthy, C. J., & Penick, J. (2005). Lifestyles, coping resources, and negative life events as predictors of emotional distress in university women. *Journal of Individual Psychology, 61*, 341–364.

Hester, R. L. (1987). Memory, myth, parable, and the therapeutic process. *Individual Psychology: Journal of Adlerian Theory, Research & Practice, 43*(4), 444–450.

Ivey, A. E., Ivey, M. B., & D'Andrea, M. J. (2011). *Theories of counseling and psychotherapy: A multicultural perspective.* Thousand Oaks, CA: Sage.

Johansen, T. M. (2005). Applying individual psychology to work with clients of the Islamic faith. *Journal of Individual Psychology, 61*, 174–184.

Jones, J. V., Jr., & Lyddon, W. J. (2003). Adlerian and constructivist psychotherapies: A constructivist perspective. In R. E. Watts (Ed.). *Adlerian, cognitive, and constructivist therapies: An integrative dialogue* (pp. 38–56). New York, NY: Springer.

Manaster, G., Painter, D., Deutsch, J., & Overholt, B. (Eds.). (1977). *Alfred Adler: As we remember him.* Chicago, IL: North American Society of Adlerian Psychology.

Maniacci, M. P. (2002). The *DSM* and individual psychology: A general comparison. *Journal of Individual Psychology, 58*(4), 356–362.

Meany-Walen, K. K., Bratton, S. C., & Kottman, T. (2014). Effects of Adlerian play therapy on reducing students' disruptive behaviors. *Journal of Counseling & Development,*

92(1), 47–56. doi:10.1002/j.1556-6676.2014.00129.x

Milliren, A. P., Evans, T. D., & Newbauer, J. F. (n.d.). *Adlerian theory.* Retrieved from http://carterandevans.com/portal/index.php/adlerian-theory/69-adlerian-theory

Murdock, N. L (2009). *Theories of counseling and psychotherapy: A case approach* (2nd ed.). Upper Saddle River, NJ: Pearson.

NASAP. (n.d.). *The NASAP diplomate in Adlerian psychotherapy: Information sheet.* Retrieved from the North American Society of Adlerian Psychology website: alfredadler.typepad.com/nasap/diplomate/

Newlon, B. J., Borboas, R., & Arciniega, M. (1986). The effects of Adlerian parent study groups upon Mexican mothers' perception of child behavior. *Individual Psychology: Journal of Adlerian Theory, Research & Practice, 42*(1), 107–113.

Newton, B. J., & Mansager, E. (1986). Adlerian life-styles among Catholic priests. *Journal of Individual Psychology, 42*, 367–374.

North American Society of Adlerian Psychology. (2011). *What is an Adlerian?* Fort Wayne, IN: Author.

Perkins-Dock, R. E. (2005). The application of Adler family therapy with African American families. *Journal of Individual Psychology, 61*, 233–249.

Peterson, J. V., & Nisenholz, B. (1999). *Orientation to counseling.* Boston, MA: Allyn & Bacon.

Pfefferle, J., & Mansager, E. (2014). Applying the classical Adlerian family diagnostic process. *Journal of Individual Psychology, 70*(4), 332–378.

Prout, H. T., & Brown, D. T. (2007). *Counseling and psychotherapy with children and adolescents: Theory and practice for school and clinical settings.* New York, NY: Wiley & Sons.

Sawilowsky, S. (2009). New effect size rules of thumb. *Journal of Modern Applied Statistical Methods, 8*(2), 467–474.

Shlien, J. M., Mosak, H. M., & Dreikurs, R. (1962). Effect of time limits: A comparison of two psychotherapies. *Journal of Counseling Psychology, 9*, 31–34.

Smith, M. L., & Glass, G. V. (1977). Meta-analysis of psychotherapy outcome studies. *American Psychologist, 32*, 752–760.

Sperry, L. (2011). Family therapy with personality-disordered individuals and families: Understanding and treating the borderline family. *Journal of Individual Psychology, 67*(3), 222–231.

Sommers-Flanagan, J., & Sommers-Flanagan, R. (2004). *Counseling and psychotherapy theories in context and practice: Skills, strategies, and techniques.* Hoboken, NJ: Wiley & Sons.

Sulliman, J. (1973). The development of a scale for the measurement of social interest. *Dissertation Abstracts International, 34*(6), 567.

Sweeney, T. J. (1998). *Adlerian counseling* (4th ed.). Bristol, PA: Accelerated Development.

U.S. Department of Health and Human Services, Substance Abuse and Mental Health Services Administration. (2010, January). *Intervention summary: Systematic Training for Effective Parenting (STEP).* Retrieved from https://www.samhsa.gov/

Watts, R. E. (2000). Entering the new millennium: Is individual psychology still relevant? *Journal of Individual Psychology, 56*, 21–30.

Watts, R. E. (2003). *Adlerian, cognitive, and constructivist therapies: An integrative dialogue.* New York, NY: Springer.

Watts, R. E., Peluso, P., & Lewis, T. (2008, March). *Adlerian counseling techniques: Beyond the basics.* Paper presented at the American Counseling Association World Conference, Honolulu, HI.

Watts, R. E., & Pietrzak, D. (2000). Adlerian "encouragement" and the therapeutic process of solution-focused brief therapy. *Journal of Counseling and Development, 78*, 442–447.

Watts, R. E., & Shulman, B. H. (2003). Integrating Adlerian and constructive therapies: An Adlerian perspective. In R. E. Watts (Ed.), *Adlerian, cognitive, and constructivist therapies: An integrative dialogue* (pp. 9–37). New York, NY: Springer.

Watts, R. E., Trusty, J., & Lim, M. G. (1996). Characteristics of healthy families as a model of social interest. *Journal of Adlerian Psychology, 26,* 1–12.

Wheeler, M. S., Kern, R. M., & Curlette, W. L. (1993). *BASIS-A inventory (Version 1.3).* Highlands, NC: TRT Associates.

Zarski, J., Sweeney, T. J., & Barcikowski, R. S. (1977). Counseling effectiveness as a function of counselor social interest. *Journal of Counseling Psychology, 24,* 1–5.

Ziomek-Daigle, J., McMahon, G. H., & Paisley, P. O. (2008). Adlerian-based interventions for professional school counselors: Serving as both counselors and educational leaders. *Journal of Individual Psychology, 64,* 450–467.

CHAPTER 5

Altarriba, J., & Santiago-Rivera, A. L. (1994). Current perspectives on using linguistic and cultural factors in counseling the Hispanic client. *Professional Psychology: Research and Practice, 25,* 388–397. doi:10.1037/0735-7028.25.4.388

Bartuska, H., Buchsbaumer, M., Mehta, G., Pawlowsky, G., & Wiesnagrotzki, S. (Eds.). (2008). *Psychotherapeutic diagnosis. Guidelines for the new standard.* New York, NY: Springer.

Basescu, S. (1963). Existential therapy. In A. Deutsch & H. Fishman (Eds.), *The encyclopedia of mental health* (Vol. 2, pp. 583–595). New York, NY: Franklin Watts.

Batthyány, A. (2016). *Logotherapy and existential analysis: Proceedings of the Viktor Frankl Institute Vienna.* Cham, Switzerland: Springer.

Beckett, S. (1982). *Waiting for Godot.* New York, NY: Grove Press.

Boeree, C. G. (2006). *Personality theories: Rollo May.* Shippensburg, PA: Shippensburg University. Retrieved from http://www.ship.edu/%7Ecg-boeree/perscontents.html

Breitbart, W., & Masterson, M. (2016). Meaning-centered psychotherapy in the oncology and palliative case setting. In P. Russo-Netzer, S. E. Schulenberg, & A. Batthyány (Eds.), *Clinical perspectives on meaning* (pp. 245–260). New York, NY: Springer.

Brent, J. S. (1998). A time-sensitive existential method for assisting adults in transition. *Journal of Humanistic Psychology, 38*(4), 7–24. doi:10.1177/00221678980384002

Bronfenbrenner, U., & Ceci, S. J. (1994). Nature–nurture reconceptualized in developmental perspective: A bioecological model. *Psychological Review, 101,* 568–586.

Carroll, L. (1898). *Alice's adventures in wonderland.* New York, NY: The Macmillan Company.

Chochinov, H. M., Kristjanson, L. J., Breitbart, W., McClement, S., Hack, T. F., Hassard, T., & Harlos, M. (2011). Effect of dignity therapy on distress and end-of-life experience in terminally ill patients: A randomized controlled trial. *Lancet, 12,* 753–762.

Classen, C. C., & Spiegel, D. (2011). Supportive-expressive group psychotherapy. In M. Watson & D. Kissane (Eds.), *Handbook of psychotherapy in cancer care* (pp. 107–117). Hoboken, NJ: Wiley-Blackwell.

Cohen, B. N. (2003). Applying existential theory and intervention to career decision-making. *Journal of Career Development, 29,* 195–209.

Comas-Díaz, L. (2006). Latino healing: The integration of ethnic psychology into psychotherapy. *Psychotherapy, 43*(4), 436–453. doi:10.1037/0033-3204.43.4.380

Comas-Díaz, L. (2012). *Multicultural care: A clinician's guide to cultural competence.* Washington, DC: American Psychological Association.

de St. Aubin, E. (1996). Personal ideology polarity: Its emotional foundation and its manifestation in individual value systems, religiosity, political orientation, and assumptions concerning human nature. *Journal of Personality and Social Psychology, 71,* 152–165.

Diamond, S. (1999). Anger, madness, and the daimonic: The psychological genesis of violence, evil, and creativity. Albany: Albany University of New York Press.

Diamond, S. A. (1996). *Anger, madness, and the daimonic: The psychological genesis of violence, evil, and creativity.* Albany, NY: State University of New York Press.

Elliott, R., Greenberg, L. S., & Lietaer, G. (2004). Research on experiential psychotherapies. In M. J. Lambert (Ed.), *Bergin and Garfield's handbook of psychotherapy and behavior change* (5th ed., pp. 493–539). New York, NY: Wiley & Sons.

Fabry, J. B., Bulka, R. P., & Sahakian, W. S. (Eds.). (1996). *Finding meaning in life: Logotherapy.* Northvale, NJ: Jason Aronson.

Fanon, F. (1967). *Black skin, White masks.* New York, NY: Grove Press.

Frankl, V. E. (1967). *Psychotherapy and existentialism: Selected papers on logotherapy.* New York, NY: Simon & Schuster.

Frankl, V. E. (1975). Paradoxical intention and dereflection. *Psychotherapy: Theory, Research & Practice, 12*(3), 226–237.

Frankl, V. E. (1986). *The doctor and the soul* (3rd ed.). New York, NY: Vintage Books.

Frankl, V. E. (1988). *The will to meaning: Foundations and applications of psychotherapy.* New York, NY: Penguin Books.

Frankl, V. E. (1996). *Viktor Frankl—recollections: An autobiography.* New York, NY: Plenum Publishing.

Frankl, V. (1976). *Man's search for ultimate meaning.* New York, NY: Alfred A. Knopf.

Frankl, V. (2004). *On the theory and therapy of mental disorders: An introduction to logotherapy and existential analysis.* New York, NY: Brunner-Routledge (translated by James M. Dubois).

Frankl, V. E. (2006). *Man's search for meaning* (H. Pisano, Trans.). Boston, MA: Beacon Press. (Original work published 1959)

Frankl, V. E. (2008). *Recollections: An autobiography.* New York, NY: Basic Books. [translated by Joesph Farbry and Judith Farbry]

Frey, L. L., & Roysircar, G. (2004). Effects of acculturation and worldview for White American, South American, South Asian, and South East Asian students. *International Journal for the Advancement of Counselling, 26,* 229–248.

Frankl, V. E. (2014). *Man's search for meaning* (H. Pisano, Trans.). Boston, MA: Beacon Press. (Original work published 1959)

Friedman, M. (1962). Existential psychotherapy and the image of man. *New Perspectives for Psychiatry, 4*(2), 285–296.

Ginter, E. J., & Glauser, A. S. (2010). *Lifeskills for college: A curriculum for life.* Dubuque, IA: Kendall Hunt.

Gonzales, N. A., German, M., & Fabritt, F. C. (2012). US Latino youth. In E. Chang & C. Downey (Eds.), *Handbook of race and development in mental health* (pp. 259–278). New York, NY: Springer.

Gurman, A. S., & Messer, S. B. (2003). *Essential psychotherapies: Theory and practice* (2nd ed.). New York, NY: Guilford Press.

Guttmann, D. (1996). *Logotherapy for the helping professional: Meaningful social work.* New York, NY: Springer.

Hwang, K.-K. (2017). The rise of indigenous psychologies: In response to Jahoda's criticism. *Culture & Psychology, 23*(4), 1–15. doi:10.1177/1354067X16680338

Ibrahim, F. A., Roysircar-Sodowsky, G., & Ohnishi, H. (2001). World view: Recent developments and needed directions. In J. G. Ponterotto, M. C. Casas, L. A. Suzuki, & C. M. Alexander (Eds.), *Handbook of multicultural counseling* (2nd ed., pp. 425–455). Thousand Oaks, CA: Sage.

Keshen, A. (2006). A new look at existential psychotherapy. *American Journal of Psychotherapy, 60,* 285–298.

Kluckhohn, C. (1956). Toward a comparison of value-emphasis in different cultures. In L. D. White (Ed.), *The state of the social sciences* (pp. 116–132). Chicago, IL: University of Chicago Press.

Kohatsu, E. L., Concepcion, W. R., & Perez, P. (2010). Incorporating levels of acculturation in counseling practice. In J. G. Ponterotto, J. M. Casas, L. A. Suzuki, & C. M. Alexander (Eds.), *Handbook of multicultural counseling* (3rd ed., pp. 343–356). Thousand Oaks, CA: Sage.

La Roche, M. L. (2013). *Cultural psychotherapy: Theory, methods, and practice.* Thousand Oaks, CA: Sage.

Lakes, K., López, S. R., & Garro, L. C. (2006). Cultural competence and psychotherapy: Applying anthropologically informed conceptions of culture. *Psychotherapy, 43*(4), 380–396. doi:10.1037/0033-3204.43.4.380

Lantz, J. (1993). Countertransference as a corrective emotional experience in existential family therapy. *Contemporary Family Therapy, 15*(3), 209–221. doi:10.1007/BF00894396

Leong, F. T., & Lee, S. H. (2006). A cultural accommodation model for cross-cultural psychotherapy: Illustrated with the case of Asian Americans. *Psychotherapy, 43*(4), 410–423.

Lukas, E. (2014). Meaning in suffering: Comfort in crisis through logotherapy. London, UK: Purpose Research. [translated by Joseph Farbry]

Maisel, E. (2009). *The atheist's way: Living well without gods.* Novato, CA: New World Library.

May, R. (1953). *Man's search for himself.* New York, NY: W. W. Norton.

May, R. (1967). *Psychology and the human dilemma.* New York, NY: W. W. Norton.

May, R. (1969). *Love and will.* New York, NY: Norton.

May, R. (1981). *Freedom and destiny.* New York, NY: Norton.

May, R. (1983). *The discovery of being: Writings in existential psychology.* New York, NY: Norton.

May, R. (1991). *The cry for myth.* New York, NY: Norton.

May, R. (1994). *The courage to create.* New York, NY: W. W. Norton.

May, R., & Yalom, I. D. (1995). Existential psychotherapy. In R. Corsini & D. Wedding (Eds.), *Current psychotherapies* (5th ed., pp. 262–292). Itasca, IL: Peacock.

Messer, S. B., & Gurman, A. S. (2011). *Essential psychotherapies: Theory and practice.* New York, NY: Guilford Press.

Pace, E. (1994, October 4). Dr. Rollo May is dead at 85; Was innovator of psychology. *The New York Times.* Retrieved August 29, 2017, from http://www.nytimes.com/1994/10/24/obituaries/dr-rollo-may-is-dead-at-85-was-innovator-in-psychology.html?pagewanted=print

Padilla, A. M., & Salgado de Snyder, N. (1985). Counseling Hispanics: Strategies for effective intervention. In P. Pedersen (Ed.), *Handbook of cross-cultural counseling and therapy* (pp. 157–164). Westport, CT: Greenwood Press.

Park, C. L. (2010). Making sense of the meaning literature: An integrative review of meaning making and its effects on adjustment to stressful life events. *Psychological Bulletin, 136,* 257–301.

Phrase Finder. (n.d.). *To be, or not to be, that is the question.* Retrieved August 22, 2017 from http://www.phrases.org.uk/mean ings/385300.html

Redsand, A. (2006). *Viktor Frankl: A life worth living.* New York, NY: Houghton Mifflin Harcourt.

Roberts, A. R., & Yeager, K. R. (2009). *Pocket guide to crisis intervention.* New York, NY: Oxford University Press.

Rollo May. (2014, September 27). *New world encyclopedia.* Retrieved August 29, 2017, from http://www.newworldencyclopedia.org/p/index.php?title=Rollo_May&oldid=984604

Roysircar, G. (2009). Evidence-based practice and its implications for culturally sensitive treatment. *Journal of Multicultural Counseling and Development, 37*(2), 66–82.

Roysircar, G. (2012). Foreword: Positive psychology, Eastern religions, and multicultural psychology. In E. Chang & C. Downey (Eds.), *Handbook of race and development in mental health* (pp. vii–xii). New York, NY: Springer.

Roysircar, G., Arredondo, P., Fuertes, J. N., Ponterotto, J. G., & Toporek, R. L. (2003). *Multicultural counseling competencies 2003: Association for Multicultural Counseling and Development.* Alexandria, VA: American Counseling Association.

Roysircar, G., Clarke, B., Love, A., Thomas, S., & Aufiero, J. (2010, January). *Developing multicultural awareness: Using myths to transcend cultural boundaries.* Workshop at the Winter Roundtable, Teachers College, Columbia University, New York.

Roysircar, G., & Mayo, J. (2012). Individual identity, psychosocial conditions, and existential anxiety: Vontress in the context of the U.S.A. In R. Moodley, L. Epp, & H. Yusuf (Eds.), *Counseling across the cultural divide: The Clemmont Vontress reader* (pp. 332–347). Ross-On-Wye, UK: PCCS Books.

Roysircar, G., & Pignatiello, V. (2011). A multicultural-ecological tool: Conceptualization and practice with an Indian immigrant woman. *Journal of Multicultural Counseling and Development, 39*(3), 167–179.

Roysircar, G., & Pignatiello, V. (2015). Counseling and psychotherapy in the United States: Rolando's story. In R. Moodley, M. Lengyell, R. Wu, & U. P. Gielen (Eds.), *Therapy without borders: International and cross-cultural case studies handbook* (pp. 165–172). Alexandria, VA: American Counseling Association.

Roysircar, G., Thompson, A., & Boudreau, M. (2017). Born Black and male: Counseling leaders' self-discovery of strengths. *Counselling Psychology Quarterly, 30*(4), 343–372.

Roysircar-Sodowsky, G., & Frey, L. L. (2003). Children of immigrants: Their worldviews value conflicts. In P. Pedersen & J. C. Carey (Eds.), *Multicultural counseling in schools: A practical handbook* (2nd Ed.) (pp. 61–83). Boston, MA: Allyn & Bacon.

Sartre, J. (1969). *Being and nothingness.* New York, NY: Washington Square Press. (Original work published 1943) [translated by Hazel E. Barnes]

Schneider, K. J. (2011). Existential-humanistic psychotherapies. In S. B. Messer & S. Gurman (Eds.), *Essential psychotherapies: Theory and practice* (pp. 261–294). New York, NY: Guilford Press.

Schneider, K. J., & May, R. (1995). *The psychology of existence: An integrative, clinical perspective.* New York, NY: McGraw-Hill.

Shostrom, E. L. (1964). The Personal Orientation Inventory. *Educational and Psychological Measurement, 24*(2), 207–218. doi:10.1177/001316446402400203

Sodowsky, G. R. (1987). Unfinishing mourning. *Voices: The Art and Science of Psychotherapy, 23,* 72–73.

Sodowsky, G. R., & Sodowsky, R. E. (1991). Different approaches to psychopathology and symbolism in the novel and film "One Flew Over the Cuckoo's Nest." *Literature and Psychology, 37,* 34–42.

Sodowsky, G. R., & Sodowsky, R. E. (1997). Myriad possibilities in Isak Dinesen's "The Dreamers": An existential interpretation. In N. H. Kaylor (Ed.), *Creative and critical approaches to the short story* (pp. 329–340). Lewiston, NY: Edwin Mellen Press.

Spinelli, E. (2006). Existential psychotherapy: An introductory overview. *Analise Psicologica, 3,* 311–321.

Sue, D. W., & Sue, D. (2015). *Counseling the culturally diverse: Theory and practice* (7th ed.). New York, NY: Wiley & Sons.

Tomkins, S. S. (1965). Affect and the psychology of knowledge. In S. S. Tomkins & C. E. Izard (Eds.), *Affect, cognition, and personality: Empirical studies* (pp. 72–97). New York, NY: Springer.

Truscott, D. (2010). Existential. In D. Truscott (Ed.), *Becoming an effective psychotherapist: Adopting a theory of psychotherapy that's right for you and your client* (pp. 53–66). Washington, DC: American Psychological Association.

Tummala-Narra, P. (2016). *Psychoanalytic theory and cultural competence in psychotherapy.* Washington, DC: American Psychological Association.

van Deurzen, E., & Hanaway, M. (2012). *Existential perspectives on coaching.* New York, NY: Palgrave Macmillan.

Viktor Frankl. (2014). Retrieved from Famous Psychologists website: http://www.famouspsychologists.org/viktor-frankl

Vontress, C. E. (1985). Existentialism as a cross-cultural counselling modality. In P. Pederson (Ed.). *Handbook of cross-cultural counseling and therapy* (pp. 207–212). Westport, CT: Greenwood Press.

Walsh, J., & Lantz, J. (2007). *Short-term existential intervention in clinical practice.* Chicago, IL: Lyceum.

Walsh, R. A., & McElwain, B. (2002). Existential psychotherapies. In D. J. Cain & J. Seeman (Eds.), *Humanistic psychotherapies: Handbook of research and practice* (pp. 253–278). American Psychological Association.

Wicks, R. J., Parson, R. D., & Capps, D. (Eds.). (1993). *Clinical handbook of pastoral counseling* (Vol 1, Expanded Edition). New York, NY: Integration Books/Paulist Press.

Wolff, W. (1950). The term "existential." In W. Wolff (Ed.), *Values and personality: An existential psychology of crisis* (pp. 3–7). New York, NY: Grune & Stratton.

Wong, P. T. P. (2010). Meaning therapy: An integrative and positive existential psychology. *Journal of Contemporary Psychotherapy, 40,* 85–99.

Wong, P. T. P. (2014). Frankl's meaning-making model and positive psychology. In A. Batthyány & P. Russo-Netzer (Eds.), *Meaning in positive and existential psychology.* New York, NY: Springer.

Yalom, I. D. (1980). *Existential psychotherapy.* New York, NY: Basic Books.

Yalom, I. D. (n.d.). *Biographical information about Irvin D. Yalom, MD.* Retrieved August 29, 2017, from http://www.yalom.com/pagemaker.php?nav=bio

Young, I. M. (1990). *Justice and the politics of difference.* Princeton, NJ: Princeton University Press.

CHAPTER 6

Axline, V. (1947). *Play therapy.* Boston, MA: Houghton Mifflin.

Bachelor, A. (2013). Clients' and therapists' views of the therapeutic alliance: Similarities, differences and relationship to therapy outcome. *Clinical Psychology and Psychotherapy, 20,* 118–135.

Bell, E. C., Marcus, D. K., & Goodlad, J. K. (2013). Are the parts as good as the whole? A meta-analysis of component treatment studies. *Journal of Consulting and Clinical Psychology, 81,* 722–736.

Bozarth, J. (1998). *Person-centered therapy: A revolutionary paradigm.* Ross-on-Wye, England: PCCS Books.

Bozarth, J. (2000). Person-centered therapy: A revolutionary paradigm. Bath, UK: Bath Press.

Bozarth, J. D., & Brodley, B. T. (1991). Actualization: A functional concept in client-centered psychotherapy: A statement. *Journal of Social Behavior and Personality, 6*(5), 45–59.

Bratton, S. C., Ray, D., Edwards, N. A., & Landreth, G. (2009). Child-centered play therapy (CCPT): Theory, research, and practice. *Person-Centered and Experiential Psychotherapies, 8*(4), 266–281.

Bratton, S. C., Ray, D., Rhine, T., & Jones, L. (2005). The efficacy of play therapy with children: A meta-analytic review of treatment outcomes. *Professional Psychology: Research and Practice, 36*(4), 376–390.

Brodley, B. T. (1994). Some observations of Carl Rogers' behavior in therapy interviews. *Person-Centered Journal, 1*, 37–48.

Brodley, B. T. (2005). About the nondirective attitude. In B. E. Levitt (Ed.). *Embracing nondirectivity: Reassessing person-centered theory and practice in the 21st century* (pp. 1–4). Ross-on-Wye, UK: PCCS Books.

Bugental, J. F. T. (1964). The third force in psychology. *Journal of Humanistic Psychology, 4*(1), 19–25.

Carkhuff, R. R. (1969). *Helping and human relations: 2 vols.* New York, NY: Holt, Rinehart & Winston.

Cornelius-White, J. H. D. (2002). The phoenix of empirically supported therapy relationships: The overlooked person-centered foundation. *Psychotherapy: Theory, Research, Practice, Training, 39*, 219–222.

Cornelius-White, J. H. D. (2003). Person-centered multicultural counseling: Rebutted critiques and revisited goals. *Person-Centered Practice, 11*(1), 3–11.

Cornelius-White, J. H. D. (2007). The actualizing and formative tendencies: Prioritizing the motivational constructs of the person-centered approach. *Person-Centered and Experiential Psychotherapies, 6*, 129–140.

Cornelius-White, J. H. D. (Ed.). (2012). *Carl Rogers: The China diary.* Ross-on-Wye, UK: PCCS Books.

Cornelius-White, J. H. D., Motschnig-Pitrik, R., & Lux, M. (Eds.). (2013). *Interdisciplinary handbook of the person-centered approach: Research and theory.* New York, NY: Springer.

deCarvalho, R. J. (1999). Otto Rank, the Rankian circle in Philadelphia, and the origins of Carl Rogers' person-centered psychotherapy. *History of Psychology, 2*(2), 132–148.

Duncan, B., & Miller, S. (2000). The client's theory of change. *Journal of Psychotherapy Integration, 10*, 169–187.

Elliott, R., & Freire, B. (2008). *Person-centred/experiential therapies are highly effective: Summary of the 2008 meta-analysis.* Retrieved from http://www.pce-world.org/images/stories/meta-analysis_effectiveness_of_pce_therapies.pdf

Elliott, R., Watson, J., Goldman, R., & Greenberg, L. (2003). *Learning emotion-focused therapy: The process-experiential approach to change.* Washington, DC: American Psychological Association.

Evans, R. I. (1975). *Carl Rogers: The man and his ideas.* New York: E.P. Dutton.

Freire, E. S., Koller, S. H., Silva, R. B., & Piason, A. (2005). Person-centered therapy with impoverished, maltreated and neglected children and adolescents in Brazil. *Journal of Mental Health Counseling, 35*(3), 135–158.

Freire, P. (2009). *Pedagogy of hope.* New York: Continuum

Gendlin, E. T. (1962). *Experiencing and the creation of meaning.* New York, NY: Free Press.

Gendlin, E. T. (1996). *Focusing-oriented psychotherapy.* New York, NY: Guilford Press.

Ginsberg, B. G. (2012, March). *Filial therapy: An attachment based, emotion focused, and skill training approach.* Paper presented at the 2012 American Counseling Association's annual conference, San Francisco, CA.

Glauser, A. S., & Bozarth, J. D. (2001). Person-centered counseling: The culture within. *Journal of Counseling and Development, 79*(2), 142–147.

Gordon, T. (2000). *Parent effectiveness training: The proven program for raising responsible children.* New York, NY: Three Rivers Press.

Guerney, B. G. (1964). Filial therapy: Description and rationale. *Journal of Consulting Psychology, 28*, 303–310.

Kirschenbaum, H. (1979). *On becoming Carl Rogers.* New York, NY: Delacorte Press.

Kirschenbaum, H. (2009). *Life and work of Carl Rogers.* Washington, DC: American Counseling Association.

Kriz, J. (2006). *Self-actualization.* Norderstedt, Germany: BoD.

Kriz, J. (2007). Actualizing tendency—the link between person-centered and experiential psychotherapy and interdisciplinary systems theory. *Person-Centered and Experiential Psychotherapies, 6*(1), 30–44.

Kriz, J. (2013). Person-centered approach and systems theory. In J. H. D. Cornelius-White, R. Motschnig-Pitrik, & M. Lux (Eds.), *Interdisciplinary handbook of the person-centered approach: Research and theory* (pp. 261–275). New York, NY: Springer.

Lambert, M. J., & Barley, D. E. (2001). Research summary on therapeutic relationship and psychotherapy outcome. *Psychotherapy: Theory, Research, Practice, Training, 38*, 357–361.

Lewis, J., & Bradley, L. (Eds.). (2000). *Advocacy in counseling: Counselors, clients, and community.* Greensboro, NC: ERIC Clearinghouse on Counseling and Student Services.

Lin, Y., & Bratton, S. C. (2015). A meta-analytic review of child-centered play therapy approaches. *Journal of Counseling and Development, 93*(1), 45–58.

MacDougall, C. (2002). Rogers's person-centered approach: Consideration for use in multicultural counseling. *Journal of Humanistic Psychology, 42*(2), 48–65.

Martin, D. G. (2011). *Counseling and therapy skills* (3rd ed.). Long Grove, IL: Waveland.

Maslow, A. H. (1968). *Toward a psychology of being.* New York, NY: Van Nostrand Reinhold.

McCulloch, L. (2001). A person-centered approach to antisocial personality disorder. *Dissertation Abstracts International: Section A. Humanities and Social Sciences, 61*(9A), 3475.

Moon, K., Witty, M., Grant, B., & Rice, B. (2013). *Practicing client-centered therapy: Selected writings of Barbara Temaner-Brodley.* Ross-on-Wye: PCCS Books.

Norcross, J. C. (Ed.). (2001). Empirically supported therapy relationships: Summary of report of the Division 29 Task Force. *Psychotherapy, 38*(4).

Patterson, C. H. (1984). Empathy, warmth, and genuineness in psychotherapy: A review of reviews. *Psychotherapy, 21*, 431–438.

Prouty, G. (1994). *Theoretical evolutions in person-centered/experiential therapy: Applications to schizophrenic and retarded psychoses.* Westport, CT: Praeger.

Remley, T. P., Jr., & Herlihy, B. (2015). *Ethical, legal, and professional issues in counseling 5th* (ed.). Upper Saddle River, NJ: Pearson.

Rice, L. N. (1974). The evocative function of the therapist. In D. A. Wexler & L. N. Rice (Eds.), *Innovations in client-centered therapy* (pp. 289–311). New York, NY: Wiley.

Rogers, C. R. (1942). *Counseling and psychotherapy: Newer concepts in practice.* Boston, MA: Houghton Mifflin.

Rogers, C. R. (1951). *Client-centered therapy: Its current practice, implications, and theory.* Boston, MA: Houghton Mifflin.

Rogers, C. R. (1957). The necessary and sufficient conditions of therapeutic personality change. *Journal of Consulting Psychology, 21,* 95–103.

Rogers, C. R. (1959). A theory of therapy, personality, and interpersonal relationships, as developed in the client-centered framework. In S. Koch (Ed.), *Psychology: A study of science* (Vol. 3). New York, NY: McGraw-Hill.

Rogers, C. R. (1961). On becoming a person: A therapist's view of psychotherapy. Boston, MA: Houghton Mifflin.

Rogers, C. R. (1967a). Autobiography. In E. Boring & G. Lindzey (Eds.), *A history of psychology in autobiography* (Vol. 5). New York, NY: Appleton, Century, & Crofts.

Rogers, C. R. (1967b). *On becoming a person.* London, UK: Constable.

Rogers, C. R. (1969). *Freedom to learn: A view of what education might become.* Columbus, OH: Merrill.

Rogers, C. R. (1970). *On encounter groups.* New York, NY: Harper & Row.

Rogers, C. R. (1975). Empathic: An unappreciated way of being. *Counseling Psychologist, 5,* 2–9.

Rogers, C. R. (1977). *Carl Rogers on personal power: Inner strength and its revolutionary impact.* New York, NY: Dell.

Rogers, C. R. (1980). *A way of being.* Boston, MA: Houghton Mifflin.

Rogers, C. R. (1987). Journal of South-African trip. January 14 - March 1. *Counseling and Values* (Special issue on Carl Rogers and the Person-Centered Approach to Peace), *32*(1), 21–37.

Rogers, C. R., Lyon, H. C., Jr., & Tausch, R. (2013). *On becoming an effective teacher: Person-centered teaching, psychology, philosophy, and dialogues with Carl R. Rogers.* New York, NY: Routledge.

Rogers, C. R., & Russell, D. (2002). *Carl Rogers: The quiet revolutionary: An oral history.* Roseville, CA: Penmarin Books.

Stiles, W. B., Barkham, M., Mellor-Clark, J., & Connell, J. (2008). Effectiveness of cognitive-behavioural, person-centered, and psychodynamic therapies in UK primary care routine practice: Replication with a larger sample. *Psychological Medicine, 38,* 677–688.

Swan, L. K., & Heesacker, M. (2013). Evidence of a pronounced preference for therapy guided by common factors. *Journal of Clinical Psychology, 69,* 869–879.

Thorne, B. (2003). *Carl Rogers* (2nd ed.). London, UK: Sage.

Wagner, C. C. (2013). Motivational interviewing and client-centered therapy. In J. H. D. Cornelius-White, R. Motschnig-Pitrik, & M. Lux (Eds.), *Interdisciplinary applications of the person-centered approach* (pp. 44–47). New York, NY: Springer.

Wagner, C. C., & Ingersoll, K. S. (2012). *Motivational interviewing in groups.* New York, NY: Guilford Press.

Wampold, B. E. (2001). *The great psychotherapy debate: Models, methods, and findings.* Mahwah, NJ: Erlbaum.

CHAPTER 7

Aleksandrov, A. A. (1997). Combining psychodynamic and phenomenological approaches in psychotherapy: Ways to improve effectiveness. *International Journal of Mental Health, 26,* 21–29.

Clarkson, P., & Mackewn, J. (1993). *Fritz Perls.* London, UK: Sage.

Eid, M., & Diener, E. (2001). Norms for experiencing emotions in different cultures: Inter- and intranational differences. *Journal of Personality and Social Psychology, 81,* 869–885.

Ellison, J., Greenberg, L., Goldman, R., Angus, L. (2009). Maintenance of gains following experiential therapies for depression. *Journal of Consulting and Clinical Psychology, 77*(1), 103–112.

Fagan, J. (1992). The importance of Fritz Perls having been. In E. W. L. Smith (Ed.), *Gestalt voices* (pp. 331–333). Norwood, NJ: Ablex.

Fagan, J., & Shepherd, I. L. (Eds.). (1970). *Gestalt therapy now: Theory, techniques, & applications.* Palo Alto, CA: Science and Behavior Books.

Frew, J. (2008). Gestalt therapy. In J. Frew & M. Spiegler (Eds.), *Contemporary psychotherapies for a diverse world* (pp. 228–274). New York, NY: Lahaska Press.

Frew, J. (2013). Gestalt therapy. In J. Frew & M. D. Spiegler (Eds.). *Contemporary psychotherapies for a diverse world* (pp. 215–257). Boston, MA: Lahaska Press.

Gaines, J. (1979). *Fritz Perls, here and now.* Millbrae, CA: Celestial Arts.

Gazda, G. M, Ginter, E. J., & Horne, A. H. (2001). *Group counseling and group psychotherapy: Theory and application.* Needham Heights, MA: Allyn & Bacon.

Greenberg, L. (1980). The intensive analysis of recurring events form the practice of gestalt therapy. *Psychotherapy: Theory, Research & Practice, 17,* 143–152.

Greenberg, L., Elliot, R. & Lietaer, G. (1994). Research on experiential psychotherapies. In A. Bergin & S. Garfield (Eds.), *Handbook of psychotherapy and behavior change* (pp. 509–539). New York, NY: Wiley.

Greenberg, L., & Rice, L. (1981). The specific effects of a gestalt intervention. *Psychotherapy: Theory, Research & Practice, 18*(1), 31–37.

Greenberg, L., Warwar, S., & Malcom, W. (2008). Differential effects of emotion-focused therapy and psychoeducation in facilitating forgiveness and letting go of emotional injuries. *Journal of Counseling Psychology, 55*(2), 185–196.

Hardy, R. E. (1991). *Gestalt psychotherapy: Concepts and demonstrations in stress, relationships, hypnosis and addiction.* Springfield, IL: Thomas.

Harman, R. L. (1984). Recent developments in gestalt group therapy. *International Journal of Group Psychotherapy, 34,* 473–483.

Harman, R. L. (1989). *Gestalt therapy with groups, couples, sexually dysfunctional men, and dreams.* Springfield, IL: Thomas.

Houston, G. (2003). *Brief gestalt therapy.* Thousand Oaks, CA: Sage.

Human Rights and Social Responsibility Committee. (2006). Retrieved from www.eagt.org/joomla/index .php/eagt-home

Ivey, A. E., Ivey, M. B., & Simek-Morgan, L. (1980). *Counseling and psychotherapy: A multicultural perspective.* Boston, MA: Allyn & Bacon.

Johnson, S. M., & Greenberg, L. S. (1985). Differential effects of experiential and problem-solving interventions in resolving marital conflict. *Journal of Consulting and Clinical Psychology, 53,* 175–184.

Joyce, P., & Sills, C. (2009). *Skills in gestalt counseling & psychotherapy* (2nd ed.). London, UK: Sage.

Katz, J. (1985). The sociopolitical nature of counseling. *Counseling Psychologist, 13,* 615–624.

Korb, M. P., Gorrell, J., & Van De Riet, V. (1989). *Gestalt therapy: Practice and theory* (2nd ed.). New York, NY: Pergamon Press.

Latner, J. (1973). *The gestalt therapy book: A holistic guide to theory, principles, and techniques of gestalt therapy developed by Frederick S. Perls and others.* New York, NY: Julian Press.

Litt, S. (2000). Laura Perls (1905–1990): Co-founder of gestalt therapy. Retrieved from http://www .positivehealth.com/article/psychology/laura-perls-1905-1990-co-founder-of-gestalt therapy.

Matsumoto, D., Yoo, S. H., Fontaine, A., Anguas-Wong, A. M., Arriola, M., Ataca, B., . . . Granskaya, J. V. (2008). Mapping expressive differences around the world: The relationship between emotional display rules and individualism versus collectivism. *Journal of Cross-Cultural Psychology, 39,* 55–74.

Melnick, J. (1980). Gestalt group process therapy. *Gestalt Journal, 3,* 86–96.

Mocan-Aydin, G. (2000). Western models of counseling and psychotherapy within Turkey: Crossing cultural boundaries. *Counseling Psychologist, 28,* 281–298.

Niedenthal, P. M., Krauth-Gruber, S., & Ric, R. (2006). *Psychology of emotion: Interpersonal, experiential and cognitive approaches.* New York, NY: Psychology Press.

Norcross, J. C., & Lambert, M. J. (2005). The therapy relationship. In J. Norcross, L. Beutler, & R. Levant (Eds.), *Evidence-based practices in mental health: Debate and dialogue on fundamental questions* (pp. 208–218). Washington, DC: American Psychological Association.

Perls, F. S. (1947). *Ego, hunger and aggression.* London, UK: Allen & Unwin.

Perls, F. S. (1969). *Gestalt therapy verbatim.* Lafayette, CO: Real People Press.

Perls, F. S. (1970). Dream seminars. In J. Fagan & I. L. Shepherd (Eds.), *Life techniques in gestalt therapy* (pp. 69–76). New York, NY: Perennial Library.

Perls, F. S. (2012). *An autobiography.* Retrieved from http//www.fritz perls.com/autobiography/

Perls, F. S., Hefferline, R., & Goodman, P. (1951). *Gestalt therapy: Excitement and growth in the human personality.* New York, NY: Gestalt Journal Press.

Perls, L. (1970). One gestalt therapist's approach. In J. Fagan & I. L. Shepherd (Eds.), *Life techniques in gestalt therapy* (pp. 125–129). New York, NY: Perennial Library.

Perls, L. (1992). Concepts and misconceptions of gestalt therapy. *Journal of Humanistic Psychology, 32*(3), 50–56.

Polster, E., & Polster, M. (1973). *Gestalt therapy integrated: Contours of theory and practice.* New York, NY: Brunner/Mazel.

Rong, X. L., & Preissle, J. (2009). *Educating immigrant students in the 21st century: What educators need to know* (2nd ed.). Thousand Oaks, CA: Sage.

Rosanes-Berrett, M. B. (1993). Reflections on Fritz Perls: A response to Laura Perls and Ilene Serlin. *Journal of Humanistic Psychology, 93*(1), 106–109.

Rosenblatt, D. (1975). *Opening doors: What happens in gestalt therapy.* New York, NY: Harper & Row.

Rosenfeld, E. (1977). *An oral history of gestalt therapy—An interview with Laura Perls.* Obtained on October 30, 2012 at www.awaken.com/.../ an-oral-history-of-gestalt-therapy-an-interview-with-laura-perls//

Shepard, M. (1975). *Fritz: An intimate portrait of Fritz Perls and gestalt therapy.* New York, NY: Bantam.

Sinay, S. (1997). *Gestalt for beginners.* New York, NY: Writers and Readers Publishing.

Smith, E. W. L. (Ed.). (1992). *Gestalt voices.* Norwood, NJ: Ablex.

Smith, M. L., & Glass, G. V. (1977). Meta-analysis of psychotherapy outcome studies. *American Psychologist, 32*(9), 752–760. doi:10.1037/0003-066X.32.9.752

Stoehr, T. (1994). *Here now next: Paul Goodman and the origins of gestalt therapy.* San Francisco, CA: Jossey-Bass.

Strümpfel, U. (2004). Research on gestalt therapy. *International Gestalt Journal, 27,* 9–54.

Strümpfel, U. (2006). *Therapie der Gefühle: Forschungsbefunde zur Gestalttherapie.* Cologne, Germany: Edition Humanistische Psychologie. (Part translation into English: http:// www.therapie-der-gefuehle.de/.

Ting-Toomey, S., Yee-Jung, K. K., Shapiro, R. B., Garcia, W., Wright, T. J., & Oetzel, J. G. (2000). Ethnic/ cultural identity salience and conflict styles in four US ethnic groups. *International Journal of Intercultural Relations, (1)*24, 47–81.

Tsunetomo, Y. (1979). *Hagakure: The book of the samurai* (W. S. Wilson, Trans.). Tokyo, Japan: Kodansha International. (Original work published 1716)

Wagner-Moore, L. E. (2004). Gestalt therapy: Past, present, theory, and research. *Psychotherapy: Theory, Research, Practice, Training, 41*(2), 180–189. doi:10.1037/0033-3204.41.2.180

Wheeler, G. (2013). *Gestalt reconsidered: A new approach to contact and resistance.* New York, NY: Taylor & Francis.

Yontef, G. M. (1971). *A review of the practice of gestalt therapy.* Los Angeles: California State University, Trident Shop.

Yontef, G. M. (1993). *Awareness, dialogue and process: Essays on gestalt therapy.* New York, NY: Gestalt Journal Press.

Yontef, G. M., & Jacobs, J. (2011). Gestalt therapy. In R. Corsini & D. Wedding (Eds.), *Current psychotherapies*

(342–382). Belmont, CA: Brooks/Cole.

Yontef, G. M., & Simkin, J. S. (1989). Gestalt therapy. In R. J. Corsini & D. Wedding (Eds.), *Current psychotherapies* (pp. 323–361). New York, NY: Peacock.

CHAPTER 8

Abramowitz, J. S., Whiteside, S. P., & Deacon, B. J. (2005). The effectiveness of treatment for pediatric obsessive-compulsive disorder: A meta-analysis. *Behavior Therapy, 36*(1), 55–63.

American Psychological Association. (2017). *Health disparities & mental/behavioral health workforce.* Washington, DC: Author.

Asnaani, A., & Hofmann, S. G. (2012). Collaboration in culturally responsive therapy: Establishing a strong therapeutic alliance across cultural lines. *Journal of Clinical Psychology, 68*(2), 187–197.

Babkin, B. P. (1971). *Pavlov: A biography.* Chicago, IL: University of Chicago Press.

Bach, P., Hayes, S. C., & Gallop, R. (2012). Long-term effects of brief acceptance and commitment therapy for psychosis. *Behavior Modification, 36,* 165–181.

Bandura, A. (1977). *Social learning theory.* Englewood Cliffs, NJ: Prentice Hall.

Bandura, A. (1986). *Social foundations of thought and action: A social cognitive theory.* Englewood Cliffs, NJ: Prentice Hall.

Barraca, M. J. (2012). Mental control from a third-wave behavior therapy perspective. *International Journal of Clinical and Health Psychology, 12*(1), 109–121.

Berkowitz, R. I., Wadden, T. A., Tershakovec, A. M., & Cronquist, J. L. (2003). Behavior therapy and sibutramine for treatment of adolescent obesity, *JAMA, 289,* 1805–1812.

Butler, A. C., Chapman, J. E., Forman, E. M., & Beck, A. T. (2006). The empirical status of cognitive-behavioral therapy: A review of meta-analyses. *Clinical Psychology Review, 26,* 17–31.

Christensen, A., Atkins, D. C., Yi, J., Baucom, D. H., & George, W. H. (2006). Couple and individual adjustment for two years following a randomized clinical trial comparing traditional versus integrative behavioral couple therapy. *Journal of Consulting and Clinical Psychology, 74,* 1180–1191.

Cone, D. J. (1997). Issues in functional analysis in behavioral assessment. *Behavior Research and Therapy, 35,* 259–275.

Constantino, G., Malgady, R. G., & Rogler, L. H. (1986). Cuento therapy: A culturally sensitive modality for Puerto Rican children. *Journal of Consulting and Clinical Psychology, 54,* 639–645.

Doss, B. D., Rowe, L. S., Morrison, K. R., Libet, J., Birchler, G. R., Madsen, J. W., & McQuaid, J. R. (2012). Couple therapy for military veterans: Overall effectiveness and predictors of response. *Behavior Therapy, 43,* 216–227.

Emmelkamp, P. M. (2004). Behavior therapy with adults. In M. J. Lambert (Ed.), *Bergin and Garfield's handbook of psychotherapy and behavior change* (5th ed., pp. 393–446). New York, NY: Wiley.

Feske, U., & Chambless, D. L. (1995). Cognitive behavioral versus exposure only treatment for social phobia: A meta-analysis. *Behavior Therapy, 26,* 695–720.

Foa, E., Hembree, E., & Rothbaum, B. (2007). *Prolonged exposure therapy for PTSD: Emotional processing of traumatic experiences: Therapist guide.* New York, NY: Oxford University Press.

Forman, E. M., Herbert, J. D., Moitra, E., Yeomans, P. D., & Geller, P. A. (2007). A randomized controlled effectiveness trial of acceptance and commitment therapy and cognitive therapy for anxiety and depression. *Behavior Modification, 31,* 772–799.

Freud, S. (1955). Analysis of a phobia in a five-year-old boy. In J. Strachey (Ed. & Trans.), *The standard edition of the complete psychological works of Sigmund Freud* (Vol. 10, pp. 3–149). London, UK: Hogarth Press. (Original work published 1909)

Freud, S. (1989). *An outline of psychoanalysis.* (J. Strachey, Ed. & Trans).

New York, NY: Norton. (Original work published 1949)

Hayes, S. C. (2004). Acceptance and commitment therapy, relational frame theory, and the third wave of behavioral and cognitive therapies. *Behavior Therapy, 35*(4), 639–665.

Hayes, S. C., Luoma, J. B., Bond, F. W., Masuda, A., & Lillis, J. (2006). Acceptance and commitment therapy: Model, processes and outcomes. *Behaviour Research and Therapy, 44,* 1–25.

Hayes, S. C., & Pierson, H. (2005). Acceptance and commitment therapy. *Behaviour Research and Therapy, 44,* 1–25.

Hayes, S. C., Pistorello, J., & Levin, M. E. (2012). Acceptance and commitment therapy as a unified model of behavior change. *Counseling Psychologist, 40*(7), 976–1002.

Hayes, S. C., Strosahl, K. D., & Wilson, K. G. (1999). *Acceptance and commitment therapy: An experiential approach to behavior change.* New York, NY: Guilford Press.

Hays, P. A. (2009). Integrating evidence-based practice, cognitive-behavior therapy, and multicultural therapy: Ten steps for culturally competent practice. *Professional Psychology: Research and Practice, 40*(4), 354–360. doi:10.1037/a0016250

Hubble, M. A., Duncan, B. L., Miller, S. D., & Wampold, B. E. (2010). Introduction. In B. L. Duncan, S. D. Miller, B. E. Wampold, & M. A. Hubble (Eds.), *The heart and soul of change: Delivering what works in therapy* (2nd ed., pp. 23–46). Washington, DC: American Psychological Association.

Iacoboni, M., Molnar-Szakacs, I., Gallese, V., Buccino, G., & Mazziotta, J. C. (2005). Grasping the intentions of others with one's own mirror neuron system. *PLOS Biology, 3,* e79. doi:10.1371/journal.pbi0.0030079

Ivanoff, A., & Schmidt, H. (2010). Functional assessment in forensic settings: A valuable tool for preventing and treating egregious behavior. *Journal of Cognitive Psychotherapy: An International Quarterly, 24*(2), 81–91. doi:10.1891/0889-8391.24.2.81

Iwamasa, G. Y. (1997). Behavior therapy and a culturally diverse society: Forging an alliance. *Behavior Therapy, 28,* 347–358.

Jones, M. C. (1924). A laboratory study of fear: The case of Peter. *Pedagogical Seminary, 31,* 308–315.

Kliem, S., Kröger, C., & Kosfelder, J. (2010). Dialectical behavior therapy for borderline personality disorder: A meta-analysis using mixed-effects modeling. *Journal of Consulting and Clinical Psychology, 78*(6), 936–951.

Kopelowicz, A., Liberman, R.P., & Zarate, R. (2006). Recent advances in social skills training for schizophrenia. *Schizophrenia Bulletin, 32,* S12–S23.

Lambert, M. J., & Ogles, B. M. (2004). The efficacy and effectiveness of psychotherapy. In M. J. Lambert (Ed.), *Bergin and Garfield's handbook of psychotherapy and behavior change* (5th ed., pp. 139–193). New York, NY: Wiley.

Lazarus, A. A. (1971). *Behavior therapy and beyond.* New York, NY: McGraw-Hill.

Lazarus, A. A. (1976). *Multimodal behavior therapy.* New York, NY: Springer.

Lejuez, C. W., & Hopko, D. R. (2006). The therapeutic alliance in behavior therapy. *Psychotherapy: Theory, Research, Practice, Training, 42,* 456–468.

Linehan, M. M. (1993). Cognitive-behavioral treatment of borderline personality disorder. New York, NY: Guilford Press.

Linehan, M. M., Comtois, K. A., Murray, A. M., Brown, M. Z., Gallop, R. J., Heard, H. L., . . . Linenboim, N. (2006). Two-year randomized controlled trial and follow-up of dialectical behavior therapy vs. therapy by experts for suicidal behaviors and borderline personality disorder. *Archives of General Psychiatry, 63,* 757–766.

Matthews, L. (1997). Culturally competent models in human service organizations. *Journal of Multicultural Social Work, 4*(4), 131–135.

McCrady, B. S., Epstein, E. E., Cook, S., Jensen, N. K., & Hildebrandt, T. (2009). A randomized trial of individual and couple behavioral alcohol treatment for women. *Journal of Consulting and Clinical Psychology, 77,* 243–256.

Miller, S. D., Hubble, M. A., Duncan, B. L., & Wampold, B. E. (2010). Delivering what works. In B. L. Duncan, S. D. Miller, B. E. Wampold, & M. A. Hubble (Eds.), *The heart and soul of change: Delivering what works in therapy* (2nd ed., pp. 421–429). Washington, DC: American Psychological Association.

Morin, C., Bootzin, R., Buysse, D., Edinger, J., Espie, C., & Lichstein, K. (2006). Psychological and behavioral treatment of insomnia: Update of the recent evidence (1998–2004). *Sleep, 29,* 1398–1414.

Murdock, N. L., Duan, C., & Nilsson, J. E. (2012). Emerging approaches to counseling intervention theory, research, practice, and training. *Counseling Psychologist, 40*(7), 966–975.

Neacsiu, A. D., Ward-Ciesielski, E. F., & Linehan, M. M. (2012). Emerging approaches to counseling intervention: Dialectical behavior therapy. *Counseling Psychologist 40*(7), 1003–1032.

Neukrug, E. S. (2011). *Counseling theory and practice.* Belmont, CA: Brooks/Cole.

Öst, L. G. (2007). Efficacy of the third wave of behavioral therapies: A systematic review and meta-analysis. *Behavior Research and Therapy, 46*(3), 296–321.

Pavlov, I. P. (1927). *Conditioned reflexes: An investigation of the physiological activity of the cerebral cortex.* Oxford, UK: Oxford University Press.

Rizzolatti, G., & Craighero, L. (2004). The mirror-neuron system. *Annual Review of Neuroscience, 27,* 169–192. doi:10.1146/annurev. neuro.27.070203.144230

Rose, A. J. (2002). Co-rumination in the friendship of girls and boys. *Child Development, 73,* 1830–1843.

Segal, Z. V., Williams, J. M. G., & Teasdale, J. D. (2012). *Mindfulness-based cognitive therapy for depression.* New York, NY: Guilford Press.

Sharf, R. S. (2012). *Theories of psychotherapy and counseling: Concepts and cases* (5th ed.). Belmont, CA: Brooks/Cole.

Sipe, W. E., & Eisendrath, S. J. (2012). Mindfulness-based cognitive therapy: Theory and practice. *Canadian Journal of Psychiatry. Revue Canadienne de Psychiatrie, 57*(2), 63.

Skinner, B. F. (1938). *The behavior of organisms. An experimental analysis,* New York, NY: Appleton-Century-Crofts.

Skinner, B. F. (1974). *About behaviorism.* New York, NY: Knopf.

Skinner, B. F. (1989). *Recent issues in the analysis of behavior.* Columbus, OH: Merrill.

Spiegler, M. D., & Guevremont, D. C. (2010). *Contemporary behavior therapy* (5th ed.). Belmont, CA: Wadsworth/Cengage.

Sue, D. W. (2004). Whiteness and ethnocentric monoculturalism: Making the "invisible" visible. *American Psychologist, 59,* 761–769.

Sue, D. W., & Sue, D. (2008). *Counseling the culturally diverse: Theory and practice.* (5th ed.). Hoboken, NJ: Wiley.

Tanaka-Matsumi, J., Seiden, D. Y., & Lam, K. N. (1996). The culturally informed functional assessment (CIFA) interview: A strategy for cross-cultural behavioral practice. *Cognitive and Behavioral Practice, 3,* 215–233.

U.S. Department of Veterans Affairs, Veterans Health Administration, Office of Patient Care Services, Mental Health Services. (2012). *Guide to VA mental health services for veterans & families.* Washington, DC: Author.

Watson, J. B. (1924). *Behaviorism.* New York, NY: People's Institute.

Weaver, H. N. (1999). Indigenous people and social work profession: Defining culturally competent services. *Social Work, 44*(3), 217–225.

Weiner, B. (1986). An *attributional theory of motivation and emotion.* New York, NY: Springer.

Wetherell, J. L., Afari, N., Rutledge, T., Sorrell, J. T., Stoddard, J. A., Petkus, A. J., . . . Atkinson, J. H. (2011). A randomized, controlled trial of acceptance and commitment therapy and cognitive-behavioral therapy for chronic pain. *Pain, 152,* 2098–2107.

Wilson, G. T. (2008). Behavior therapy. In R. J. Corsini & D. Wedding (Eds.), *Current psychotherapies* (pp. 223–262). Belmont, CA: Thompson.

Wolpe, J. (1958). *Psychotherapy by reciprocal inhibition*. Redwood City, CA: Stanford University Press.

Wolpe, J. (1969). *The practice of behavior therapy*. New York, NY: Pergamon Press.

Wolpe, J. (1973). *The practice of behavior therapy* (2nd Ed.). New York, NY: Pergamon Press.

Wolpe, J., & Rachman, S. (1960). Psychoanalytic "evidence": A critique based on Freud's case of Little Hans. *Journal of Nervous and Mental Disease, 131*, 135–148.

CHAPTER 9

Academy of Cognitive Therapy. (2018). Certification in cognitive therapy. Retrieved from http://www.acade myofct.org/page/Certification

Achenbach, T. M. (1991). *Manual for the Child Behavior Checklist/4-18 and 1991 profile*. Burlington: University of Vermont, Department of Psychiatry.

ALGBTIC LGBQQIA Competencies Taskforce. (2013). Association for Lesbian, Gay, Bisexual, and Transgender Issues in Counseling Competencies for counseling with lesbian, gay, bisexual, queer, questioning, intersex, and ally individuals. *Journal of LGBT Issues in Counseling, 7*(1), 2–43.

American Psychiatric Association. (2013). *Diagnostic and statistical manual of mental disorders* (5th ed.). Washington, DC: Author.

American Psychological Association. (2012). Guidelines for psychological therapy with lesbian, gay, and bisexual clients. *American Psychologist, 67*(1), 10–42.

Antony, M. M., & Roemer, L. (2011). Behavior therapy: Traditional approaches. In S. B. Messer & A. S. Gurman (Eds.), *Psychotherapies: Theory and practice* (3rd ed., pp. 107–142). New York, NY: Guilford Press.

Aponte, J. F. (2004). The role of culture in the treatment of culturally diverse populations. In U. P. Gielen, J. M. Fish, & J. G. Draguns (Eds.), *Handbook of culture, therapy, and healing* (pp. 103–120). Mahwah, NJ: Erlbaum.

Aaron T. Beck Psychopathology Research Center. (n.d.). Retrieved from https://aaronbeckcenter.org/beck/

Ball, J. R., Mitchell, P. B., Corry, J. C., Skillecorn, A., Smith, M., & Malhi, G. S. (2006). A randomized controlled trial of cognitive therapy for bipolar disorder: Focus on long-term change. *Journal of Clinical Psychiatry, 67*, 277–286. doi:10.4088/JCP.v67n0215

Bandura, A. (1965). Vicarious processes: A case of no-trial learning. In L. Berkowitz (Ed.), *Advances in experimental social psychology* (Vol. 2, pp. 1–55). New York, NY: Academic Press.

Bandura, A. (1977). *Social learning theory*. Englewood Cliffs, NJ: Prentice Hall.

Bandura, A. (1986). Social foundations of thought and action: A social cognitive theory. Englewood Cliffs, NJ: Prentice Hall.

Bandura, A. (1997). *Self-efficacy: The exercise of control*. New York, NY: Freeman.

Bandura, A. Ross, D., & Ross, S. A. (1961). Transmission of aggression through the imitation of aggressive models. *Journal of Abnormal and Social Psychology, 63*, 575–582

Basco, M. R., Glickman, M., Weatherford, P., & Ryser, N. (2000). Cognitive-behavioral therapy for anxiety disorders: Why and how it works. *Bulletin of the Menninger Clinic, 64*, A52–A70.

Baucom, D. H., Shoham, V., Mueser, K. T., Daiuto, A. D., & Stickle, T. R. (1998). Empirically supported couple and family interventions for marital distress and adult mental health problems. *Journal of Consulting and Clinical Psychology, 66*(1), 53–88.

Beck, A. T. (1967). *Depression: Clinical, experimental, and theoretical aspects*. New York, NY: Harper & Row.

Beck, A. T. (1976). *Cognitive therapy and the emotional disorders*. New York, NY: International Universities Press.

Beck, A. T. (1988). Love is never enough. New York, NY: Harper & Row.

Beck, A. T. (2005). The current state of cognitive therapy: A 40-year retrospective. *Archives of General Psychiatry, 62*, 953–959.

Beck Institute for CBT. (2016). *Beck scales*. Retrieved from https://www .beckinstitute.org/get-informed/ tools-and-resources/professionals/ patient-assessment-tools

Bisson, J., & Cohen, J. (2006). Disseminating early interventions following trauma. *Journal of Traumatic Stress, 19*, 583–595.

Bos, H. M. W., van Balen, F., & van den Boom, D. C. (2005). Lesbian families and family functioning: An overview. *Patient Education and Counseling, 59*, 263–275.

Bradley, R., Greene, J., Russ, E., Dutra, L., & Westen, D. (2005). A multidimensional meta-analysis of psychotherapy for PTSD. *American Journal of Psychiatry, 162*, 214–227.

Brown, G. K., Tenhave, T., Xie, S., Henriques, G. R., Xie, S. X., Hollander, J. E., & Beck, A. T. (2005). Cognitive therapy for the prevention of suicide attempts: A randomized controlled trial. *Journal of the American Medical Association, 5*, 563–570.

Burlingame, G. M., MacKenzie, K. R., & Strauss, B. (2004). Small group treatment: Evidence for effectiveness and mechanisms of change. In M. J. Lambert (Ed.), *Bergin and Garfield's handbook of psychotherapy and behavior change* (5th ed., pp. 647–696). New York, NY: Wiley.

Center for the Prevention of Suicide, The Trustees of the University of Pennsylvania. (n.d.). A biography of Aaron T. Beck, M.D. Retrieved from http://www.med.upenn.edu/suicide/ beck/biography.html

Chambless, D. L., Baker, M. J., Baucom, D. H., Beutler, L. E., Calhoun, K. S., Crits-Christoph, P., . . . Woody, S. R. (1998). Update on empirically-validated therapies, II. *Clinical Psychologist, 51*, 3–16.

Chambless, D. L., Sanderson, W. C., Shoham, V., Bennett Johnson, S., Pope, K. S., Crits-Christoph, P., . . . McCurry, S. (1996). An update on empirically validated therapies. *Clinical Psychologist, 49*, 5–18.

Cherry, K. (2017, June 6). *Aaron Beck and cognitive therapy: Brief profile of the founder of cognitive therapy*. Retrieved from https://www.verywell.com/ aaron-beck-biography-2795492

Cherry, K. (2017, June 15 [updated]). *Albert Ellis biography*. Retrieved from https://www.verywell.com/ albert-ellis-biography-2795493

Choy, Y., Fyer, A. J., & Lipsitz, J. D. (2007). Treatment of specific phobia in adults. *Clinical Psychology Review, 27*, 266–286.

Cohen, J. A. (2005). Treating traumatized children: Current status and future directions. *Journal of Trauma & Dissociation, 6*, 109–121.

Coleman, H. L. K. (2003). Culturally relevant empirically supported treatments. In G. Roysircar, P. Arredondo, J. Fuertes, J. Ponterotto, & R. Toporek (Eds.), *Multicultural counseling competencies (2003): Association for Multicultural Counseling and Development* (pp. 79–86). Alexandria, VA: American Counseling Association.

Constantine, M. G. (2007). Racial micro aggressions against African American clients in cross-racial counseling relationship. *Journal of Counseling Psychology, 54*(1), 1–16.

Craighead, L. W., Craighead, W. E., Kazdin, A. E., & Mahoney, M. J. (1994). *Cognitive and behavioral interventions: An empirical approach to mental health problems.* Needham Heights, MA: Allyn & Bacon.

Craske, M. G., Niles, A. N., Burklund, L. J., Wolitzky-Taylor, K. B., P. Vilardaga, J. C. P., Arch, J. J., . . . Lieberman, M. D. (2014). Randomized controlled trial of cognitive behavioral therapy and acceptance and commitment therapy for social phobia: Outcomes and moderators. *Journal of Consulting and Clinical Psychology, 82*, 1034–1048. doi:10.1037/a0037212

Crawley, S. A., Podell, J. L., Beidas, R. S., Braswell, L., & Kendall, P. C. (2010). Cognitive behavioral therapy with youth. In K. S. Dobson (Ed.), *Handbook of cognitive-behavioral therapies* (3rd ed., pp. 375–410). New York, NY: Guilford Press.

Cuijpers, P., Berking, M., Andersson, G., Quigley, L., Kleiboer, A., & Dobson, K. S. (2013). A meta-analysis of cognitive-behavioural therapy for adult depression, alone and in comparison with other treatments. *Canadian Journal of Psychiatry, 58*, 376–385.

Davis, M. L., Powers, M. B., Handelsman, P., Medina, J. L., Zvolensky, M., & Smits, J. J. (2015). Behavioral therapies for treatment-seeking cannabis users: A meta-analysis of randomized controlled trials. *Evaluation & the Health Professions, 38*(1), 94–114. doi:10.1177/0163278714529970

Day, A., Howells, K., Mohr, P., Schall, E., & Gerace, A. (2008). The development of CBT programs for anger: The role of interventions to promote perspective-taking skills. *Behavioural and Cognitive Psychotherapy, 36*(3), 299–312.

DeGruy, J. (2005). *Post traumatic slave syndrome: America's legacy of enduring injury and healing.* Milwaukie, OR: Uptone Press.

Denis, C., Lavie, E., Fatseas, M., & Auriacombe, M. (2007). Psychotherapeutic interventions for cannabis abuse and/or dependence in outpatient settings. *Cochrane Database of Systematic Reviews, 3*, CD005336.

Department of Veterans Affairs & Department of Defense (VA/DoD). (2010). *VA/DoD clinical practice guideline for management of post-traumatic stress: VA/DoD evidence based practice* (Version 2.0). Retrieved from http://www.healthquality.va.gov/PTSD-Full-2010c.pdf

Dimeff, L. A., Baer, J. S., Kivlahan, D. R., & Marlatt, G. A. (1999). *Brief alcohol screening and intervention for college students (BASICS): A harm reduction approach.* New York, NY: Guilford Press.

Dobson, D. J. G., & Dobson, K. S. (2009). *Evidence-based practice of cognitive behavior therapy.* New York, NY: Guilford Press.

Dobson, K. S., & Block, L. (1988). Historical and philosophical bases of the cognitive-behavioral therapies. In K. S. Dobson (Ed.), *Handbook of cognitive-behavioral therapies* (pp. 3–38). New York, NY: Guilford Press.

Draper, C., & Ghiglieri, M. (2011). Post-traumatic stress disorder. Computer-based stepped care; Practical applications to clinical problems. In C. Draper & W. O'Donahue (Eds.), *Stepped care and e-health: Practical applications to behavioral disorders* (pp. 77–97). New York, NY: Springer.

Editors @ TheFamousPeople (2013, November 21). *Albert Ellis biography.* Retrieved from http://www.thefamouspeople.com/profiles/albert-ellis-642.php

Ellis, A. (1962). *Reason and emotion in psychotherapy.* Secaucus, NJ: Lyle Stuart.

Ellis, A. (1994). Reason and emotion in psychotherapy. *British Journal of Psychiatry, 165*(1), 131–135.

Ellis, A. (1996). *Better, deeper, and more enduring brief therapy: The rational emotive behavior therapy approach.* New York, NY: Brunner/Mazel.

Epp, A. M., & Dobson, K. S. (2010). The evidence base for cognitive-behavioral therapy. In K. S. Dobson (Ed.), *Handbook of cognitive-behavioral therapies* (pp. 39–73). New York, NY: Guilford Press.

Epstein, R. (2001, January 1). The prince of reason. *Psychology Today.* Retrieved from https://www.psychologytoday.com/articles/200101/the-prince-reason

Freeman, A., Simon, K. M., Beutler, L. E., & Arkowitz, H. (Eds.). (1989). *Comprehensive handbook of cognitive therapy.* New York, NY: Plenum Press.

Fischer, H. (2015, August 7). *A guide to U.S. military casualty statistics: Operation Freedom's Sentinel, Operation Inherent Resolve, Operation New Dawn, Operation Iraqi Freedom, and Operation Enduring Freedom* (CRS Report No. RS22452). Washington, DC: Congressional Research Service.

Foy, D. W., Ruzek, J. I., Glynn, S. M., Riney, S. J., & Gusman, F. D. (2002). Trauma focus group therapy for combat-related PTSD: An update. *Journal of Clinical Psychology, 58*, 907–918.

Fuertes, J. N., Mueller, L. N., Chauhan, R. V., Walker, J. A., & Ladany, N. (2002). An investigation of European American therapists' approach to counseling African American clients. *Counseling Psychologist, 30*(5), 763–788.

Fuertes, J. N., & Ponterotto, J. G. (2003). Culturally appropriate intervention strategies. In G. Roysircar, P. Arredondo, J. N. Fuertes, J. G. Ponterotto, & R. L. Toporek (Eds.), *Multicultural counseling competencies: Association for Multicultural*

Counseling and Development (pp. 51–58). Alexandria, VA: American Counseling Association.

Gazda, G. M., Ginter, E. J., & Horne, A. M. (2001). Group counseling and group psychotherapy. Boston, MA: Allyn & Bacon.

Gibson, L. E. (n.d.). Acute stress disorder. Retrieved from PSTD: National Center for PTSD website: https://www.ptsd.va.gov/professional/treatment/early/acute-stress-disorder.asp)

Gonzales, N. A., Germán, M., & Fabrett, F. C. (2012). US Latino youth. In E. C. Chang & C. A. Downey (Eds.), Handbook of race and development in mental health (pp. 259–278). New York, NY: Springer.

GoodTherapy. (2007-2017). Albert Ellis (1913-2007). Retrieved from http://www.goodtherapy.org/famous-psychologists/albert-ellis.html

Griffin, J. (2007, September). Trauma focused cognitive behavioral therapy. Paper presented at Beck Institute of Assumption College, Worcester, MA.

Gurman, A. S. (2008). Clinical handbook of couple therapy (4th ed.). New York, NY: Guilford Press.

Haldeman, D. C. (1994). The practice and ethics of sexual orientation conversion therapy. Journal of Consulting and Clinical Psychology, 62, 221–227.

Harrell, S. P. (2000). A multidimensional conceptualization of racism-related stress: Implications for the well-being of people of color. American Journal of Orthopsychiatry, 70(1), 42–57.

Hay, P. P. J., Bacaltchuk, J., Stefano, S., & Kashyap, P. (2009). Psychological treatments for bulimia nervosa and binging. Cochrane Database of Systematic Reviews, 4, CD000562.

Hayes, S. C. (2004). Acceptance and commitment therapy and the new behavior therapies: Mindfulness, acceptance, and relationship. In S. C. Hayes, V. M. Follette, & M. M. Linehan (Eds.), Mindfulness and acceptance: Expanding the cognitive behavioral tradition (pp. 1–29). New York, NY: Guilford Press.

Hayes, S. C., Follette, V. M., & Linehan, M. M. (2011). Mindfulness and acceptance: Expanding the cognitive-behavioral tradition. New York: Guilford Press.

Hayes, S. C., Strosahl, K. D., & Wilson, K. G. (2016). Acceptance and commitment therapy: The process and practice of mindful change (2nd ed.). New York: Guilford Press.

Hayes, S.C., Villatte, M., Levin, M. & Hildebrandt, M. (2011). Open, aware, and active: Contextual approaches as an emerging trend in the behavioral and cognitive therapies. Annual Review of Clinical Psychology, 7, 141–168.

Hays, P. A. (1995). Multicultural applications of cognitive-behavioral therapy. Professional Psychology: Research and Practice, 26, 309–315.

Heimberg, R. G. (2002). Cognitive-behavioral therapy for social anxiety disorder: Current status and future directions. Biological Psychiatry, 51, 101–108.

Hofmann, S., Asnaani, A., Vonk, I., Sawyer, A., & Fang, A. (2012). The efficacy of cognitive behavioral therapy: A review of meta-analyses. Cognitive Therapy and Research, 36(5), 427–440. doi:10.1007/s10608-012-9476-1

Kanter, J. W., Manos, R. C., Busch, A. M., & Rusch, L. C. (2008). Making behavioral activation more behavioral. Behavioral Modification, 32(6), 780–803. doi:10.1177/0145445508317265

Kaufman, M. T. (2007, July 25). Albert Ellis, 93, influential psychologist, dies. The New York Times, p. A1.

Kelly, G. A. (1955). The psychology of personal constructs (2 vols.). New York, NY: Norton.

Kelly, G. A. (1991). The psychology of personal constructs: Vol. 2. Clinical diagnosis & psychotherapy. New York, NY: Routledge.

Kendall, P. C., Hudson, J. L., Gosch, E., Flannery-Schroeder, E., & Suveg, C. (2008). Cognitive-behavioral therapy for anxiety disordered youth: A randomized clinical trial evaluating child and family modalities. Journal of Consulting and Clinical Psychology, 76(2), 282–297. doi:10.1037/0022-006X.76.2.282

Kendall, P. C., & Southam-Gerow, M. A. (1996). Long-term follow-up of a cognitive–behavioral therapy for anxiety-disordered youth. Journal of Consulting and Clinical Psychology, 64(4), 724–730.

Ladouceur, R., Sylvain, C., Boutin, C., Lachance, S., Doucet, C., Leblond, J., & Jacques, C. (2001). Cognitive treatment of pathological gambling. Journal of Nervous and Mental Disease, 189(11), 774–780. doi:10.1097/00005053-200111000-00007

Lam, D. H., Watkins, E. R., Hayward, P., Bright, J., Wright, K., Kerr, N., . . . Sham, P. (2003). A randomized controlled study of cognitive therapy for relapse prevention for bipolar affective disorder: Outcome of the first year. Archives of General Psychiatry, 60, 45–152.

Lawless, L. L., Ginter, E. J., & Kelly, K. (1999). Managed care: What mental health counselors need to know. Journal of Mental Health Counseling, 21, 50–66.

Lawrence, R., Bradshaw, T., & Mairs, H. (2006). Group cognitive behavioural therapy for schizophrenia: A systematic review of the literature. Journal of Psychiatric and Mental Health Nursing, 13, 673–681.

Leichsenring, F., Hiller, W., Weissberg, M., & Leibing, E. (2006). Cognitive-behavioral therapy and psychodynamic psychotherapy: Techniques, efficacy, and indications. American Journal of Psychotherapy, 60(3), 233–259.

Leichsenring, F., & Leibing, E. (2003). The effectiveness of psychodynamic therapy and cognitive behavior therapy in the treatment of personality disorders: A meta-analysis. American Journal of Psychiatry, 160(7), 1223–1232. doi:10.1176/appi.ajp.160.7.1223

Linehan, M. M. (1993). Cognitive-behavioral treatment of borderline personality disorder. New York, NY: Guilford Press.

Manos, R. C., Kanter, J. W., & Busch, A. M. (2010). A critical review of assessment strategies to measure the behavioral activation model of depression. Clinical Psychology Review, 30, 547–561.

March, J. S., Amaya-Jackson, L., Murray, M. C., & Schulte, A. (1998). Cognitive-behavioral psychotherapy for children and adolescents with posttraumatic stress disorder after a single-incident stressor. *Journal of American Academy of Child and Adolescent Psychiatry, 37*(6), 585–593.

Meichenbaum, D. (2009, May). *Psychocultural assessment and interventions: The need for a case conceptualization model.* Paper presented at the 13th annual Melissa Institute Conference on Race, Ethnicity and Mental Health, Miami, FL.

Meichenbaum, D. H. (1995). Cognitive-behavioral therapy in historical perspective. In B. Bongar & L. E. Beutler (Eds.), *Comprehensive textbook of psychotherapy: Theory and practice* (pp. 140–158). New York, NY: Oxford University Press.

Miller, R. B. (2004). *Facing human suffering: Psychology and psychotherapy as moral engagement.* Washington, DC: American Psychological Association.

Miller, W. R., & Rollnick, S. (2002). *Motivational interviewing* (2nd ed.). New York, NY: Guilford Press.

Morrison, A. P., Bentall, R. P., French, P., Kilcommons, A., Green, J., Walford, L., & Lewis, S. W. (2003). Cognitive therapy in ultra-high risk individuals for psychosis: Randomized controlled trial. *Schizophrenia Research, 60,* 326.

Morrison, A. P., French, P., Lewis, S. W., Roberts, M., Raja, S., Neil, S. T., . . . Bentall, R. P. (2006). Psychological factors in people at ultra-high risk of psychosis: Comparisons with non-patients and associations with symptoms. *Psychological Medicine, 36*(10), 1395–1404.

National Association of Cognitive-Behavioral Therapists. (2018). Promoting, supporting, and furthering the practice of CBT. Retrieved from www.nacbt.org/

Neuner, F., Schauer, M., Roth, W. T., & Elbert, T. (2002). A narrative exposure treatment as intervention in a refugee camp: A case report. *Behavioral Cognitive Psychotherapy, 30*(2), 205–209. doi:10.1017/S1352465802002072

Norcross, J. C., Karg, R., & Prochaska, J. O. (1997). Clinical psychologists in the 1990's, Part II. *Clinical Psychologist, 50,* 4–11.

O'Callaghan, P., McMullen, J., Shannon, C., Rafferty, H., & Block, A. (2013). A randomized controlled trial of trauma focused cognitive therapy for sexually exploited, war-affected Congolese girls. *Journal of American Academy of Child and Adolescent Psychiatry, 52*(4), 539–569.

Okajima, I., Komada, Y., & Inoue, Y. (2011). A meta-analysis on the treatment effectiveness of cognitive behavioral therapy for primary insomnia. *Sleep and Biological Rhythms, 9*(1), 24–34. doi:10.1111/j.1479-8425.2010.00481.x

Okun, B. (1990). Evolution and key concepts. In B. Okun, *Seeking connections in psychotherapy* (pp. 115–146). San Francisco, CA: Jossey-Bass.

Onyut, L. P., Neuner, F., Schauer, E., Ertl, V., Odenwald, M., Schauer, M., & Elbert, T. (2005, February). Narrative exposure therapy as a treatment for child war survivors with posttraumatic stress disorder: Two case reports and a pilot study in an African refugee settlement. *BMC Psychiatry, 5,* 7. doi:10.1186/1471-244X-5-7

Organista, K. C. (2006). Cognitive-behavioral therapy with Latinos and Latinas. In P. A. Hays & G. Y. Iwamasa (Eds.), *Culturally responsive cognitive-behavioral therapy: Assessment, practice, and supervision* (pp. 73–96). Washington, DC: American Psychological Association. doi:10.1037/11433-003

Otto, M. W., Pollack, M. H., & Maki, K. M. (2000). Empirically supported treatments for panic disorder: Costs, benefits, and stepped care. *Journal of Consulting and Clinical Psychology, 68*(4), 556–563.

Pantalone, D. W., Iwamasa, G. Y., & Martell, C. R. (2010). Cognitive-behavioral therapy with diverse populations. In K. S. Dobson (Ed.), *Handbook of cognitive-behavioral therapies* (3rd ed., pp. 445–464). New York, NY: Guilford Press.

Parrott, L. (2003). *Counseling and psychotherapy* (2nd ed.). Pacific Grove, CA: Thomson.

Ponniah, K., & Hollon, S. D. (2009). Empirically supported psychological treatments for adult stress disorder and posttraumatic stress disorder: A review. *Depression and Anxiety, 26*(12), 1086–1109.

Prochaska, J. O., DiClemente, C. C., & Norcross, J. C. (1992). In search of how people change: Applications to the addictive behaviors. *American Psychologist, 47,* 1102–1114.

Proctor, G. (2008). Cognitive behavioral therapy: The obscuring of power in the name of science. *European Journal of Psychotherapy and Counseling, 10*(3), 231–245.

Purcell, D. W., Campos, P. E., & Perilla, J. L. (1996). Therapy with lesbians and gay men: A cognitive behavioral perspective. *Cognitive and Behavioral Practice, 3*(2), 391–415.

Reinecke, M. A., & Freeman, A. (2003). Cognitive therapy. In A. Gurman & S. Messer (Eds.), *Essential psychotherapies* (pp. 224–271). New York, NY: Guilford Press.

Reinecke, M. A., Ryan, N. E., & DuBois, D. L. (1998). Cognitive-behavioral therapy of depression and depressive symptoms during adolescence: A review and meta-analysis. *Journal of the American Academy of Child & Adolescent Psychiatry, 37*(1), 26–34.

Rosenblum, J., & Forman, S. (2002). Evidence-based treatment of eating disorders. *Current Opinion in Pediatrics, 14,* 379–383.

Rossello, J., & Bernal, G. (1996). Adapting cognitive-behavioral and interpersonal treatments for depressed Puerto Rican adolescents. In E. D. Hibbs & P. S. Jensen (Eds.), *Psychosocial treatments for child and adolescent disorders: Empirically based strategies for clinical practice* (pp. 157–185). Washington, DC: American Psychological Association.

Rousmaniere, T. (2013). *Steven Hayes on acceptance and commitment therapy (ACT).* Retrieved from Psychotherapy.net website: https://www.psychotherapy.net/interview/acceptance-commitment-therapy-ACT-steven-hayes-interview

Roysircar, G. (2009). Evidence-based practice and its implications for culturally sensitive treatment. *Journal of Multicultural Counseling and Development, 37*(2), 66–82.

Safren, S. A., & Rogers, T. (2001). Cognitive-behavioral therapy with gay, lesbian, and bisexual clients. *Journal of Clinical Psychology, 57*(5), 629–643.

Seligman, L. (2006). *Theories of counseling and psychotherapy; Systems, strategies, and skills* (2nd ed.). Columbus, OH: Allyn & Bacon.

Steketee, G., Frost, R. O., Tolin, D. F., Rasmussen, J., & Brown, T. A. (2010). Waitlist-controlled trial of cognitive behavior therapy for hoarding disorder. *Depression & Anxiety, 27*(5), 476–484. doi:10.1002/da.20673

Steketee, G., Frost, R. O., Wincze, Greene, K., & Douglass, H. (2000). Group and individual treatment of compulsive hoarding: A pilot study. *Behavioural and Cognitive Psychotherapy, 28,* 259–268.

Sylvain, C., Ladouceur R., & Boisvert, J.-M. (1997). Cognitive and behavioral treatment of pathological gambling: A controlled study. *Journal of Consulting and Clinical Psychology, 65,* 727–732.

Taraborrelli, R. (Ed.) (2012, Spring). Our distinguished faculty: Awards and honors. *Penn Psychiatry Perspective, 11,* 9.

The Albert Ellis Institute. (2014). *About Albert Ellis, PhD.* Retrieved from http://albertellis.org/about-albert-ellis-phd/

Toporek, R. L. (2003). Counselor awareness of client's worldview. In G. Roysircar, P. Arredondo, J. N. Fuertes, J. G. Ponterotto, & R. L. Toporek, *Multicultural counseling competencies: Association for Multicultural Counseling and Development* (pp. 39–50). Alexandria, VA: American Counseling Association.

Van Etten, M., & Taylor, S. (1998). Comparative efficacy of treatments for post-traumatic stress disorder: A meta-analysis. *Clinical Psychology and Psychotherapy, 5,* 126–145.

Wampold, B. E., Minami, T., Baskin, T. W., & Tierney, S. C. (2002). A meta-(re) analysis of the effects of cognitive therapy versus "other therapies" for depression. *Journal of Affective Disorders, 68,* 159–165.

Wang, M.-Y., Wang, S.-Y., & Tsai, P.-S. (2005). Cognitive behavioural therapy for primary insomnia: A systematic review. *Journal of Advanced Nursing, 50,* 553–564.

Watkins, C. E., Jr., & Terrell, F. (1988). Mistrust level and its effects on counseling expectations in Black client-White counselor relationships: An analogue study. *Journal of Counseling Psychology, 35,* 194–197.

Wilfley, D. E., Agras, W. S., Telch, C. F., Rossiter, E. M., Schneider, J. A., Cole, A. G., . . . Raeburn, S. D. (1993). Group cognitive-behavioural therapy and group interpersonal psychotherapy for the nonpurging bulimic individual: A controlled comparison. *Journal of Consulting and Clinical Psychology, 61,* 296–305.

Wood, J. J., Piacentini, J. C., Southam-Gerow, M., Chu, B. C., & Sigman, M. (2006). Family cognitive behavioral therapy for child anxiety disorders. *Journal of the American Academy of Child and Adolescent Psychiatry, 45*(3), 314–321.

Xiaomin, Z., & Palmer, M. (2000). *Chinese fortune sticks.* New York, NY: Metro Books.

Yarhouse, M. (1998). When clients seek treatment for same-sex attractions: Ethical issues in the "right to choose" debate. *Psychotherapy: Theory, Research, Practice, Training, 35*(2), 248–259.

Young, J. E., Weinberger, A. D., & Beck, A. T. (2001). *Cognitive therapy for depression.* In D. H. Barlow (Ed.), *Clinical handbook of psychological disorders* (3rd ed., pp. 264–308). New York, NY: Guilford Press.

CHAPTER 10

Brinson, J., & Kottler, J. (1995). Minorities' underutilization of counseling centers' mental health services: A case for outreach and consultation. *Journal of Mental Health Counseling, 17*(4), 371–385.

Carbo, B. C. (2006). *The behavioral effects of group therapy on at-risk middle school students* (Unpublished master's thesis). University of South Alabama, Mobile.

Edens, R., & Smyrl, T. (1994). Reducing classroom behaviors in physical education: A pilot study. *Journal of Reality Therapy, 13*(2), 40–44.

Edens, R. M. (1995). *Effects of teaching control theory and reality therapy as an approach to reducing disruptive behavior in school physical education* (Unpublished doctoral dissertation). University of North Carolina at Greensboro.

European Association for Reality Therapy. (2012a). *Choice theory.* Retrieved from https://wgii.ie/wgii/european-association-for-reality-therapy/

European Association for Reality Therapy. (2012b). *Reality therapy.* Retrieved from https://wgii.ie/wgii/europe-an-association-for-reality-therapy/

Fry, S. (n.d.). *Quotes about self-help.* Retrieved from www.goodreads.com/quotes/tag/self-help

Glasser, W. (1960). *Mental health or mental illness? Psychiatry for practical action.* New York, NY: Harper & Brothers.

Glasser, W. (1965). *Reality therapy: A new approach to psychiatry.* New York, NY: Harper & Row.

Glasser, W. (1972). *The identity society.* New York, NY: Harper & Row.

Glasser, W. (1976). *Positive addiction.* New York, NY: Harper & Row.

Glasser, W. (1984). *Take effective control of your life.* New York, NY: Harper & Row.

Glasser, W. (1985). *Control theory: A new explanation of how we control our lives.* New York, NY: Harper & Row.

Glasser, W. (1994). *The control theory manager.* New York. NY: HarperCollins.

Glasser, W. (1998). *Choice theory: A new psychology of personal freedom.* New York, NY: Harper & Row.

Glasser, W. (2003). *Warning: Psychiatry can be hazardous to your mental health.* New York, NY: HarperCollins.

Glasser, W. (2005). *Treating mental health as a public health problem.* Chatsworth, CA: William Glasser Institute.

Glasser, W. (2010). My vision for the *International Journal of Choice Theory and Reality Therapy. International Journal of Choice Theory and Reality Therapy, 24*(2), 12.

Glasser, W., & Glasser, C. (1999). *The language of choice theory.* New York, NY: HarperCollins.

Ingram, J., & Hinkle, S. (1990). Reality therapy and the scientist-practitioner approach: A case study. *Journal of Reality Therapy, 10*(1), 54–58.

Jusoh, A. J., & Ahmad, R. (2009). The practice of reality therapy from the Islamic perspective in Malaysia and variety of custom in Asia. *International Journal of Reality Therapy, 28*(2), 3–8.

Kaplan, J. (Ed.). (2002). *Bartlett's familiar quotations* (17th ed.). New York, NY: Little, Brown.

Kim, J.-U. (2008). The effect of an R/T group counseling program on the Internet addiction level and self-esteem of Internet addiction university students. *International Journal of Reality Therapy, 27*(2), 4–12.

Loyd, B. D. (2005). The effects of reality therapy/choice theory principles on high school students' perception of needs satisfaction and behavioral change. *International Journal of Reality Therapy, 25*(1), 5–9.

Maisiak, R., Austin, J., & Heck, L. (1995). Health outcomes of two telephone interventions for patients with rheumatoid arthritis or osteoarthritis. *Arthritis and Rheumatism, 39*(8), 1391–1399.

Mathieson, E., & Tapies, X. A. (2011). *Street artists: The complete guide.* London, UK: Graffito Books.

Morgareidge, C. (2005). *Hell is other people, but must other people be hell?* Retrieved from https://books.google.com/books?isbn=073917486X

Mower, O. H. (1965). Foreword. In W. Glasser, *Reality therapy: A new approach to psychiatry* (pp. vii–xviii). New York, NY: Harper & Row.

Owens, C. (2002). *Group methods of increasing self-esteem in learning disabled students* (Unpublished master's thesis). Salisbury University, Salisbury, MD.

Parish, T. S. (2010). Be all that you can be by efficiently implementing choice theory and reality therapy. *International Journal of Choice Theory and Reality Therapy, 29*(2), 10.

Peterson, A., Chang, C., & Collins, P. (1998). Taiwanese University students meet their basic needs through studying choice theory/reality therapy. *International Journal of Reality Therapy, 17*(2), 27–29.

Posada, P. E. (1991). *A descriptive study of the therapeutic use of humor by professional social workers* (Unpublished master's thesis). California State University at Long Beach.

Prenzlau, S. (2006). Using reality therapy to reduce PTSD-related symptoms. *International Journal of Reality Therapy, 25*(2), 23–29.

Rachor, R. (1995). An evaluation of the first step PASSAGES domestic violence program. *Journal of Reality Therapy, 14*(2), 29–36.

Radtke, L., Sapp, M., & Farrell, W. (1997). Reality therapy: A meta-analysis. *International Journal of Reality Therapy, 17*(1), 4–9.

Vitello, P. (2013, September 4). William Glasser, 88, Doctor Who Said One Could Choose Happiness, Is Dead. *The New York Times.* Retrieved from http://www.nytimes.com/2013/09/05/us/william-glasser-88-psychiatrist-who-promoted-mental-health-as-a-choice-dies.html

Wesley, J. (1988). Group therapy intervention for substance abuse with the severely and chronically mental ill. *Masters Abstract International (59),* 2701.

Wicker, C. W. (1999). *The use of reality therapy group counseling with African-American high school students who claim to be suffering from premenstrual syndrome* (Unpublished doctoral dissertation). Mississippi State University.

William Glasser Institute. (2012a). *Choice theory.* Retrieved from http://www.wglasser.com/choice-theory

William Glasser Institute. (2012b). *Development of the ideas.* Retrieved http://www.wglasser.com/the-glasser-approach/development-of-ideas

William Glasser Institute. (2012c). *The Glasser approach.* Retrieved from http://www.wglasser.com/the-glasser-approach/development-of-ideas

William Glasser Institute. (2012d). *Who we are.* Retrieved from http://www.wglasser.com

William Glasser Institute Ireland. (2009). *WGII code of ethics.* Meath, Ireland: Author. Retrieved http://www.wgii.ie

Wilson, L., & Stith, S. (1991). Culturally sensitive therapy with Black clients. *Journal of Multicultural Counseling and Development, 19*(1), 32–43.

Woo, E. (2013, August). OBITUARIES: Dr. William Glasser, 1925–2013. "Reality Therapy" psychiatrist. *Los Angeles Times.* Retrieved from *www.latimes.com/about/la-contact-us-htmlstory.html*

Wubbolding, R. E. (2000). *Reality therapy for the 21st century.* Philadelphia, PA: Brunner-Routledge.

Wubbolding, R. E. (2003). Reality therapy theory. In D. Capuzzi & D. R. Gross. (Eds.), *Counseling and psychotherapy: Theories and interventions* (3rd ed., pp. 255–282). Upper Saddle River, NJ: Pearson.

Wubbolding, R. E. (2007). Glasser quality school. *Group Dynamics: Theory, Research and Practice, 11*(4), 253–261. doi:10.1037/1089-2699.11.4.253

Wubbolding, R. E. (2008). Reality therapy. In J. Frew & M. D. Spiegler (Eds.), *Contemporary psychotherapies for a diverse world* (pp. 360–396). Boston, MA: Houghton Mifflin.

Wubbolding, R. E. (2011). *Reality therapy.* Washington, DC: American Psychological Association.

Wubbolding, R. E., Brickell, J., Imhof, L., Kim, R. I., Lojk, L., & Al-Rashidi, B. (2004). Reality therapy: A global perspective. *International Journal for the Advancement of Counselling, 26*(3), 219–228.

CHAPTER 11

Algeria, M., Mulvaney-Day, N., Woo, M., & Viruell-Fuentes, E. A. (2011). Psychology of Latino adults: Challenges and an agenda for action. In E. Chang & C. Downey (Eds.), *Handbook of race and development in mental health* (pp. 279–306). New York, NY: Springer.

Altarriba, J., & Santiago-Rivera, A. L. (1994). Current perspectives on using linguistic and cultural factors in counseling the Hispanic client. *Professional Psychology: Research and Practice, 25*(4), 388–397.

American Psychiatric Association. (2001). *Diagnostic and statistical manual of mental disorders* (4th ed., text rev.). Washington, DC: Author.

American Psychiatric Association. (2013). *Diagnostic and statistical manual of mental disorders* (5th ed.). Washington, DC: Author.

American Psychological Association. (2011). *Definitions Related to Sexual*

Orientation and Gender Diversity in APA Documents Retrieved from http://www.apa.org/pi/lgbt/resources/sexuality-definitions.pdf

American Psychological Association. (2015). *Guidelines for psychological practice with transgender and gender nonconforming people*. Washington DC: Author. Retrieved from https://www.apa.org/pi/lgbt/resources/policy/gender-identity-report.pdf

American Psychological Association Task Force on Gender Identity and Gender Variance. (2009). *Report of the APA Task Force on Gender Identity and Gender Variance*. Washington, DC: Author. Retrieved from http://www.apa.org/pi/lgbt/resources/policy/gender-identity-report.pdf

Baldwin, R. (2013). *Know your rights: Transgender people and the law*. Retrieved from https://www.aclu.org/lgbt-rights/know-your-rights-transgender-people-and-law

Ballou, M., & Hill, M. (2008). The context of therapy: Theory. In M. Ballou, M. Hill, & C. West (Eds.), *Feminist therapy theory and practice* (pp. 1–8). New York, NY: Springer.

Banks, M. E. (2013). *35 IS 35! The past, present, and future of feminist psychology*. Retrieved from http://www.apadivisions.org/division-35/about/heritage/division-35-is-35.pdf

Baumgold-Land, J. (2010). Still feminist/together/growing . . . After all these years. *Women & Therapy, 34*(1–2), 159–177. doi:org/10.1080/02703149.2010.532686

Bess, J., & Stabb, S. D. (2009). The experiences of transgendered persons in psychotherapy: Voices and recommendations. *Journal of Mental Health Counseling, 31*(3), 264–282.

Bohart, A. C. (2005). The active client. In J. Norcross, L. Beutler, & R. Levant (Eds.), *Evidence-based practices in mental health: Debate and dialogue on fundamental questions* (pp. 218–226). Washington, DC: American Psychological Association.

Bornstein, K. (1994). *Gender outlaw: On men, women, and the rest of us*. New York, NY: Random House.

Brown, L. (n.d.). *About Laura*. Retrieved January 19, 2018, from http://www.drlaurabrown.com/

Brown, L. S. (2006). Still subversive after all these years: The relevance of feminist therapy in the age of evidence-based practice. *Psychology of Women Quarterly, 30*, 15–24.

Brown, L. S. (2008). Feminist therapy. In J. Lebox (Ed.), *Twenty-first century psychotherapies: Contemporary approaches to theory and practice* (pp. 277–306). Hoboken, NJ: Wiley.

Brown, L. S. (2010). *Feminist therapy*. Washington, DC: American Psychological Association.

Bucholtz, M., Liang, A. C., & Sutton, L. A. (1999). *Reinventing identities: The gendered self in discourse*. New York, NY: Oxford University Press.

Carroll, L., Gilroy, P. J., & Ryan, J. (2002). Counseling transgender, transsexual, and gender-variant clients. *Journal of Counseling and Development, 80*(2), 131–140.

Chandler, R., Worell, J., Johnson, D., Blount, A., & Lusk, M. (1999, August). *Measuring long-term outcomes of feminist counseling and psychotherapy*. Paper presented at the annual convention of the American Psychological Association, Boston, MA.

Coleman, H. L. K. (1998). General and multicultural counseling competency: Apples and oranges? *Journal of Multicultural Counseling and Development, 26*, 147–156.

Comas-Diaz, L. (1987). Feminist therapy with mainland Puerto Rican women. *Psychology of Women Quarterly, 11*, 461–474.

Comas-Diaz, L. (2006). Latino healing: The integration of ethnic psychology into psychotherapy. *Psychotherapy: Theory, Research, Training, 43*(4), 397–453.

Comas-Diaz, L., & Jacobsen, F. M. (1991). Ethnocultural transference and countertransference in the therapeutic dyad. *American Journal of Orthopsychiatry, 61*(3), 392–402.

Crenshaw, K. W. (1989). Demarginalizing the intersections of race and sex: A Black feminist critique of antidiscrimination doctrine, feminist theory, and antiracist politics. *University of Chicago Legal Forum, 140*, 139–167.

Diaz-Lazaro, C. M., Verdinelly, S., & Cohen, B. (2012). Empowerment feminist therapy with Latina immigrants: Honoring the complexity and socio-cultural contexts of clients' lives. *Women & Therapy, 35*(1–2), 80–92.

Eagly, A. H., Eaton, A., Rose, S. M., Riger, S., & McHugh, M. C. (2012). Feminism and psychology: Analysis of a half-century of research on women and gender. *American Psychologist, 67*(3), 211–230.

Enns, C. Z., Sinacore, A. L., Ancis, J. R., & Phillips, J. (2004). Toward integrating feminist and multicultural pedagogies. *Journal of Multicultural Counseling and Development, 32*, pp. 414–427.

Evans, K. M., Kincade, E. A., & Seem, S. R. (2011). *Introduction to feminist therapy: Strategies for social and individual change*. Thousand Oaks, CA: Sage.

Fee, E., Brown, T. M., & Laylor, J. (2003). One size does not fit all in the transgender community. *American Journal of Public Health, 93*(6), 899–900.

Fine, M. (2010). The breast and the state: An analysis of good and bad nipples by gender, race, and class. *Studies in Gender and Sexuality, 11*(1), 24–32.

Frey, L. L. (2013). Relational–cultural therapy: Theory, research and application to counseling competencies. *Professional Psychology: Research and Practice, 44*(5), 177–185. doi:10.1037/a0033121

Friedan, B. (1963). *The feminine mystique*. New York, NY: Norton.

Gonzales, N. A., German, M., & Fabrett, F. C. (2011). US Latino youth. In E. Chang & C. Downey (Eds.), *Handbook of race and development in mental health* (pp. 259–278). New York, NY: Springer.

Greene, B. (2010). 2009 Carolyn Wood Sherif Award Address: Riding trojan horses from symbolism to structural change: In feminist psychology, context matters. *Psychology of Women Quarterly, 34*(4), 443–457. doi:10.1111/j.1471-6402.2010.01594.x

Haas, A., Rodgers, P., & Herman, J. (2014). *Suicide attempts among transgender and gender-nonconforming adults: Findings of the National Transgender Discrimination Survey*.

Retrieved from http://williamsinstitute.law.ucla.edu/wp-content/uploads/AFSP-Williams-Suicide-Report-Final.pdf

Hartling, L. M., Rosen, W. B., Walker, M., & Jordan, J. V. (2004). Shame and humiliation: From isolation to relational transformation. In J. Jordan, M. Walker, & L. Hartling (Eds.), *The complexity of connection* (pp. 103–129). Washington, DC: American Psychological Association.

hooks, b. (1984). *Feminist theory: From margin to center.* Boston, MA: South End Press.

Hwang, W. C. (2006). Acculturative family distancing. *Psychotherapy: Theory, Research, Training, 43*(4), 397–409.

Jean Baker Miller Training Institute. (2017). *Jean Baker Miller, M.D.* Wellesley, MA: Author. Retrieved January 19, 2018, from //www.jbmti.org/Founding-Scholars/jean-baker-miller

Jensvold, M. F., Halbreich, U., & Hamilton, J. A. (Eds.). (1996). *Psychopharmacology and women: Sex, gender, and hormones.* Washington, DC: American Psychological Association.

Jordan, J. V. (2004). Relational resilience. In J. Jordan, M. Walker, & I. Hartling (Eds.), *The complexity of connection* (pp. 28–46). New York, NY: Guilford Press.

Jordan, J. V. (2009). *Relational–cultural therapy.* Washington, DC: American Psychological Association.

Jordan, J. V., & Hartling, L. M. (2002). New developments in relational–cultural theory. In M. Ballou & L. S. Brown (Eds.), *Rethinking mental health and disorders: Feminist perspectives* (pp. 48–70). New York, NY: Guilford Press.

Jordan, J. V., Kaplan, A. G., Miller, J. B., Stiver, I. P., & Surrey, J. L. (1991). *Women's growth and connection: Writings from the Stone Center.* New York, NY: Guilford Press.

Korell, S. C., & Lorah, P. (2006). An overview of affirmative psychotherapy and counseling with transgender clients. In K. L. Bieschke, R. M. Perez, & K. A. DeBord (Eds.), *Handbook of counseling and psychotherapy with lesbian, gay, bisexual, and transgender clients* (2nd ed., pp. 271–287).

Washington, DC: American Psychological Association.

Langer, S. S. (2011). Gender (dis)agreement: A dialogue on the clinical implications of gendered language. *Journal of Gay & Lesbian Mental Health, 15*(3), 300–307. doi:10.1080/19359705.2011.581194

Lev, A. I. (2004). *Transgender emergence: Therapeutic guidelines for working with gender-variant people and their families.* New York, NY: Haworth Clinical Practice Press.

Litosseliti, L., & Sunderland, J. (2002). *Gender identity and discourse analysis.* Philadelphia, PA: John Benjamins.

Livingston, J. (Director & Producer). (1991, August 16). *Paris is burning* [Documentary]. United States: Academy Entertainment, Off White Productions. (Available from Miramax Film Corp., Watergarden Complex, Ste. 2000, 1601 Cloverfield Blvd., Santa Monica, CA 90404, United States)

Lombardi, E. (2001). Enhancing transgender health care. *American Journal of Public Health, 91,* 869–872.

Maguen, S., Shipherd, J. C., & Harris, H. N. (2005). Providing culturally sensitive care for transgender patients. *Cognitive and behavioral practice, 12,* 479–490.

Marcus-Mendoza, S. T. (2004). Feminist therapy behind bars: Women, crime, and the criminal justice system. *Women's Studies Quarterly, 32*(3/4), 49–60.

Miller, J. B. (2003). *Introducing relational–cultural theory: A new model of development.* Retrieved from http://www.tribal-institute.org/2004/download/ppppresentations/C10%20-%20Pamela%20Burgess-Responding%20to%20Violence%20Against%20Native%20LGBT-Handouts.pdf

Miller, J. B., & Stiver, I. P. (1997). *The healing connection: How women form relationships in therapy and in life.* Boston, MA: Beacon Press.

Munoz-Plaza, C., Quinn, S. C., & Rounds, K. A. (2002). Lesbian, gay, bisexual, and transgender students: Perceived social support in the high school environment. *High School Journal, 85*(4), 52–63.

Norcross, J. C. (Ed.). (2002). *Psychotherapy relationships that work.* New York, NY: Oxford University Press.

Norcross, J. C., Beutler, L., & Levant, R. (Eds.). (2005). *Evidence-based practices in mental health: Debate and dialogue on fundamental questions.* Washington, DC: American Psychological Association.

Nova Southeastern University. (2017). *Lenore Walker, Ed.D., ABPP.* Fort Lauderdale, FL: Author. Retrieved January 19, 2018, from http://psychology.nova.edu/faculty/profile/walker.html

Pfäfflin, F. (2011). Remarks on the history of the terms *identity* and *gender identity. International Journal of Transgenderism, 13*(1), 13–25. doi:10.1080/15532739.2011.608014

Prochaska, J. O., & Norcross, J C. (2002). *Systems of psychotherapy: A transtheoretical analysis.* Belmont, CA: Brooks/Cole.

Roysircar, G. (2003a). Counselor awareness of own assumptions, values, and biases. In G. Roysircar, P. Arredondo, J. N. Fuertes, J. G. Ponterotto, & R. L. Toporek. (Eds.), *Multicultural Competencies 2003: Association for Multicultural Counseling and Development* (pp. 15–26). Alexandria, VA: Association for Multicultural Counseling and Development.

Roysircar, G. (2003b). Understanding immigrants: Acculturation theory and research. In F. D. Harper & J. McFadden (Eds.), *Culture and counseling: New approaches* (pp. 164–185). Boston, MA: Allyn & Bacon.

Roysircar, G. (2004). Counseling and psychotherapy for acculturation and ethnic identity concerns with immigrants and international student clients. In T. B. Smith (Ed.), *Practicing multiculturalism: Affirming diversity in counseling and psychology* (pp. 248–268). Boston, MA: Allyn & Bacon.

Roysircar, G. (2012). Foreword: Positive psychology, Eastern religions, and multicultural psychology. In E. Chang & C. Downey (Eds.), *Mental health across racial groups: Lifespan perspectives* (pp. vii–xii). New York, NY: Springer.

Roysircar-Sodowsky, G., & Frey, L. L. (2003). Children of immigrants: Their worldviews value conflicts. In P. Pedersen & J. C. Carey (Eds.),

Multicultural counseling in schools: A practical handbook (pp. 61–83). Boston, MA: Allyn & Bacon.

Roysircar-Sodowsky, G., & Maestas, M. (2000). Acculturation, ethnic identity, and acculturative stress: Evidence and measurement. In R. H. Dana (Ed.), *Handbook of cross-cultural and multicultural personality assessment* (pp. 131–172). Mahwah, NJ: Erlbaum.

Sehgal, P., & Genzlinger, N. (2017, September 8). Kate Millett, whose "Sexual Politics" became a bible of feminism, dies at 82. *The New York Times*, p. B13.

Sheehy, G. (2013, February 26). The new feminists: Young, multicultural, strategic, and looking out for each other. *The Daily Beast*. Retrieved from https://www.thedailybeast.com/new-feminists-young-multicultural-strategic-and-looking-out-for-each-other

Shipherd, J. C., Green, K. E., & Abramovitz, S. (2010). Transgender clients: Identifying and minimizing barriers to mental health treatment. *Journal of Gay & Lesbian Mental Health, 14*(2), 94–108. doi:10.1080/1935970100 3622875

Singh, A. A., Meng, S. E., & Hansen, A. W. (2014). "I am my own gender": Resilience strategies of trans youth. *Journal of Counseling & Development, 92*(2), 208–218. doi:10.1002/j.1556-6676.2014.00150.x

Smith, A. J., & Douglas, M. A. (1990). Empowerment as an ethical imperative. In H. Lerman & N. Porter (Eds.), *Feminist ethics in psychotherapy* (pp. 43–50). New York, NY: Springer.

Sussman, L. K. (2004). The role of culture in definitions, interpretations, and management of illness. In U. P. Gielen, J. M. Fish, & J. G. Draguns (Eds.), *Handbook of culture, therapy, and healing*. Mahwah, NJ: Erlbaum.

State of New Hampshire, Governor's Commission on Domestic and Sexual Violence. (2012, June). *Eighth report of the Domestic Violence Fatality Review Committee*. Retrieved from doj.nh.gov/criminal/victim-assistance/documents/domestic-violence-report-2011.pdf

University of Oxford. (2017). *Women at Oxford: The history of women at Oxford*. Retrieved from http://www.ox.ac.uk/about/oxford-people/women-at-oxford

U.S. National Library of Medicine. (2015). *Biography: Dr. Jean Baker Miller*. Bethesda, MD: Author. Retrieved January 19, 2018, from https://cfmedicine.nlm.nih.gov/physicians/biography_225.html

Vanderburgh, R. (2007). *Transition and beyond: Observations on gender identity*. Portland, OR: Q Press.

Walker, M., & Miller, J. B. (2001). *Racial images and relational possibilities* (Talking Paper No. 2). Wellesley, MA: Wellesley College, Stone Center.

Whitehead, J., Thomas, J., Forkner, B., & LaMonica, D. (2012). Reluctant gatekeepers: "Trans-positive" practitioners and the social construction of sex and gender. *Journal of Gender Studies, 21*(4), 387–400. doi:10.1080/09589236.2012.68118

Worell, J., & Remer, P. (2002). *Feminist perspectives in therapy: Empowering diverse women* (2nd ed.). New York, NY: Wiley & Sons.

CHAPTER 12

Ahearn, L. M. (2001). Language and agency. *Annual Review of Anthropology, 30*, 109–137. doi:10.1146/annurev.anthr0.30.1.109

Barber, M. (1993). *Guardian of dialogue. Max Scheler's phenomenology, sociology and philosophy of love*. Lewisburg, PA: Bucknell University Press.

Brabender, B., & Fallon, A. (2009). Group development in practice: Guidance for clinicians and researchers on stages and dynamics of change. Washington, DC: American Psychological Association.

Bruner, J. (2004). The narrative creation of self. In L. E. Angus & J. McLeod (Eds.), *The handbook of narrative and psychotherapy: Practice, theory, and research* (pp. 3–14). Thousand Oaks, CA: Sage.

Carr, A. (1998). Michael White's narrative therapy. *Contemporary Family Therapy, 20*, 485–503.

Charmaz, K. (2009). Shifting the grounds: Constructivist grounded theory methods. In J. M. Morse, P. N. Stern, J. Corbin, B. Bowers, K. Charmaz, & A. E. Clarke (Eds.), *Developing ground theory: The second generation* (pp. 127–154). Walnut Creek: Left Coast Press.

Charmaz, K. (2012). The power and potential of grounded theory. *Medical Sociology Online, 6*(3), 2–15.

Crossley, M. L. (2003). Formulating narrative psychology: The limitations of contemporary social constructionism. *Narrative Inquiry, 13*(2), 287–300.

Currier, J. M., Neimeyer, R. A., & Berman, J. S. (2008). The effectiveness of psychotherapeutic interventions for bereaved persons: A comprehensive quantitative review. *Psychological Bulletin, 134*, 648–661.

D'Cruz, H., Gillingham, P., & Melendez, S. (2007). Reflexivity: A concept and its meanings for practitioners working with children and families. *Critical Social Work, 8*(1), 1–18.

Feixas, G., & Villegas, M. (1991). Personal construct analysis of autobiographical texts: A method representation and case illustration. *International Journal of Personal Construct Psychology, 4*, 51–84.

Fuertes, J. N., & Ponterotto, J. G. (2003). Culturally appropriate intervention strategies. In G. Roysircar, P. Arredondo, J. N. Fuertes, J. G. Ponterotto, & R. L. Toporek (Eds.), *Multicultural Counseling Competencies: Association for Multicultural Counseling and Development* (pp. 51–58). Alexandria, VA: AMCD.

Therapist multicultural competency: A study of therapy dyads. *Psychotherapy: Theory, Research, Practice, Training, 43*(4), 480–490.

Genovese, F., & Atwood, J. D. (2014). *Therapy with single parents: A social constructionist approach*. Abingdon-on-Thames, UK: Taylor & Francis.

Gergen, K. J. (1991). *The saturated self: Dilemmas of identity in contemporary life*. New York, NY: Basic Books.

Gergen, K. J. (2001). Psychological science in a postmodern context. *American Psychologist, 56*(10), 803–813. doi:10.1037//0003-066X.56.10.803

Gergen, K. J. (2006). *Therapeutic realities: Collaboration, oppression and relational flow.* Chagrin Falls, OH: Taos Institute.

Gergen, K. J. (2009). *An invitation to social construction* (2nd ed.). London, UK: Sage.

Gergen, K. J. (2009). *Relational being: Beyond self and community.* New York, NY: Oxford University Press.

Gergen, K. J. (2011). The self as social construction. *Psychological Studies, 56*(1), 108–116.

Gergen, K. J., & Gergen, M. M. (1991). Toward reflexive methodologies. In F. Steier (Ed.), *Research and reflexivity* (pp. 76–95). Newbury Park, CA: Sage.

Gergen, K., & Graumann, C. F. (Eds.). (1996). *Psychological discourse in historical perspective.* New York, NY: Cambridge University Press.

Gergen, K. J., Schrader, S., & Gergen, M. (Eds.). (2008). *Constructing worlds together: Interpersonal communication as relational process.* Boston: Pearson.

Gergen, K., Stam, H. J., & Rogers, T. B. (1987). *Metapsychology: The analysis of psychological theory.* New York, NY: Praeger.

Gonzales, N. A., German, M., & Fabrett, F. C. (2011). U.S. Latino youth. In E. C. Chang & C. A. Downey (Eds.), *Handbook of race and development in mental health* (pp. 259–278). New York, NY: Springer.

Guidano, V. F. (1995). Constructivist psychotherapy: A theoretical framework. In R. A. Neimeyer & M. J. Mahoney (Eds.), *Constructivism in psychotherapy* (pp. 93–108). Washington, DC: American Psychological Association.

Haggbloom, S. J., Warnick, R., Warnick, J. E., Jones, V. K., Yarbrough, G. L., Russell, T. M., . . . Monte, E. (2002). The 100 most eminent psychologists of the 20th century. *Review of General Psychology, 6*(2), 139–152.

Hoffman, L. (1992). A reflexive stance for family therapy. In S. McNamee & K. J. Gergen (Eds.), *Therapy as social construction* (pp. 7–24). London, UK: Sage.

Hoshmond, L. T. (1989). An alternate research paradigm: A review and teaching proposal. *Counseling Psychologist, 17,* 3–79.

Howard, G. S. (1986). The scientist-practitioner in counseling psychology: Toward a deeper integration of theory, research, and practice. *Counseling Psychologist, 14*(1), 61–105.

Hruby, G. G. (2001). Sociological, postmodern, and new realism perspectives in social constructionism: Implications for literacy research. *Reading Research Quarterly, 36*(1), 48–62.

Hwang, W. (2006). Acculturative family distancing. *Psychotherapy: Theory, Research, Practice, Training, 43*(4), 397–409.

Jaipal, R. (2004). Indian conceptions of mental health, healing, and the individual. In U. P. Gielen, J. M. Fish, & J. G. Draguns (Eds.), *Handbook of culture, therapy, and healing* (293–308). Mahwah, NJ: Erlbaum.

Karácsony, A. (2008). Soul–life–knowledge: The young Mannheim's way to sociology. *Studies in East European Thought, 60*(1/2), 97–115.

Lakes, K., López, S. R., & Garro, L. C. (2006). Cultural competence and psychotherapy: Applying anthropologically informed conceptions of culture. *Psychotherapy: Theory, Research, Practice, Training, 43,* 380–396.

Lax, W. D. (1992). Postmodern thinking in clinical practice. In S. McNamee & K. J. Gergen (Eds.), *Therapy as social construction* (pp. 69–85). Thousand Oaks, CA: Sage.

Legowski, T., & Brownlee, K. (2001). Working with metaphor in narrative therapy. *Journal of Family Psychotherapy, 12,* 19–28. doi:10.1300/J085v12n01_02

Mahoney, M. J. (1974). *Cognition and behavior modification.* Cambridge, MA: Ballinger.

Mahoney, M. J. (1991). *Human change processes.* New York, NY: Basic Books.

Mahoney, M. J. (1995). The psychological demands of being a constructive psychotherapist. In R. A. Neimeyer & M. J. Mahoney (Eds.), *Constructivism in psychotherapy* (pp. 385–399). Washington, DC: American Psychological Association.

Mahoney, M. J. (2000). Behaviorism, cognitivism, and constructivism: Reflections on persons and patterns in my intellectual development. In M. R. Goldfried (Ed.), *How therapists change: Personal and professional reflections* (pp. 183–200). Washington, DC: American Psychological Association. Retrieved from https://sites.google.com/site/drmichaelmahoney/autobiography

Mahoney, M. J. (2003). *Constructive psychotherapy: A practical guide.* New York, NY: Guilford Press.

Mahoney, M. J. (2004). *Scientist as subject: The psychological imperative.* Clinton Corners, NY: Percheron Press.

Mahoney, M. J. (2008a). Behaviorism, cognitivism, and constructivism: Reflections on persons and patterns in my intellectual development. In M. R. Goldfried (Ed.), *How therapists change: Personal and professional reflections* (pp. 183–200). Washington, DC: American Psychological Association. Retrieved July 28, 2017, from ttps://sites.google.com/site/drmichaelmahoney/autobiography

Mahoney, M. J. (2008b). Power, politics, and psychotherapy: A constructive caution on unification. *Journal of Psychotherapy Integration, 18,* 367–376.

Marquis, A., Warren, E. S., & Arnkoff, D. (2009). Michael J. Mahoney: A Retrospective. *Journal of Psychotherapy Integration, 19*(4), 402–418.

McLeod, J. (2004). The significance of narrative and storytelling in post psychological counseling and psychotherapy. In A. Lieblich, D. P. McTomás, & R. Josselson (Eds.), *Healing plots: The narrative basis of psychotherapy* (pp. 11–27). Washington, DC: American Psychological Association.

Milgram, S. (1963). Behavioral study of obedience. *Journal of Abnormal and Social Psychology, 67*(4), 371–378.

Moskowitz, C. (2016). Are we living in a computer simulation? *Scientific American, 25*(5), 84–85.

Murdock, N. L. (2009). *Theories of counseling and psychotherapy: A case approach* (2nd ed.). Upper Saddle River, NJ: Pearson.

Nagayama-Hall, G. C. (2001). Psychotherapy research with ethnic minorities: Empirical, ethical, and conceptual issues. *Journal of*

Consulting and Clinical Psychology, 64, 502–510.

Neimeyer, G. J., & Neimeyer, R. A. (1994). Constructivist methods of marital and family therapy: A practical precis. *Journal of Mental Health Counseling, 16,* 85–104.

Neimeyer, R. A. (1993). An appraisal of constructivist psychotherapies. *Journal of Consulting and Clinical Psychology, 61,* 221–234.

Neimeyer, R. A. (1995). Constructivist psychotherapies: Features, foundations, and future directions. In R. A Neimeyer & M. J. Mahoney (Eds.), *Constructivism in psychotherapy* (pp. 11–38). Washington, DC: American Psychological Association.

Neimeyer, R. A. (2000). *Constructions of disorder: Meaning making frameworks for psychotherapy.* Washington, DC: American Psychological Association.

Neimeyer, R. A. (2004). Constructions of death and loss: Evolution of a research program. *Personal Construct Theory & Practice, 1,* 8–20.

Neimeyer, R. A. (2006). Complicated grief and the reconstruction of meaning: Conceptual and empirical contributions to a cognitive-constructivist model. *Clinical Psychology: Science and Practice, 13*(2), 141–145.

Neimeyer, R. A. (2009). *Art of longing: Selected poems.* North Charleston, SC: BookSurge.

Neimeyer, R. A. (2012). *Techniques of grief therapy: Creative practices for counseling the bereaved.* New York, NY: Routledge.

Neimeyer, R. A., & Bridges, S. (2003). Postmodern approaches to psychotherapy. In A. Gurman & S. Messer (Eds.), *Essential psychotherapies* (pp. 272–316). New York, NY: Guilford Press.

Neimeyer, R. A., & Epting, F. R. (1992). Measuring personal meanings of death: 20 years of research using the Threat Index. In R. A. Neimeyer & G. J. Neimeyer (Eds.), *Advances in personal construct psychology* (Vol. 2, pp. 121–147). Greenwich, CT: JAI Press.

Neimeyer, R. A., & Mahoney, M. J. (Eds.). (1995). *Constructivism in psychotherapy.* Washington, DC: APA Books.

Neimeyer. R. A., Winokuer, H. R., Harris, D. L., & Thornton, G. F. (Eds.). (2011). *Grief and bereavement in contemporary society: Bridging research and practice.* New York, NY: Routledge.

Orwell, G. (1949). *Nineteen eighty-four: A novel.* London, United Kingdom: Secker & Warburg.

Parton, N. (2003). Rethinking professional practice: The contributions of social constructionism and the feminist "ethics of care." *British Journal of Social Work, 33*(1), 1–16.

Peterson, D. R., & Peterson, R. L. (1997). Ways of knowing in a profession: Toward an epistemology for the education of professional psychologists. In D. R. Peterson (Ed.), *Educating professional psychologists: History and guiding conception* (pp. 193–219). Washington, DC: American Psychological Association.

Polkinghorne, D. E. (1992). Postmodern epistemology of practice. In S. Kvale (Ed.), *Psychology and postmodernism* (pp. 146–165). London, UK: Sage.

Polkinghorne, D. E. (2000). Psychological inquiry and the pragmatic and hermeneutic traditions. *Theory & Psychology, 10*(4), 453–479.

Polkinghorne, D. E. (2004). Narrative therapy and postmodernism. In L. E. Angus & J. McLeod (Eds.), *The handbook of narrative and psychotherapy: Practice, theory, and research* (pp. 53–67). Thousand Oaks, CA: Sage.

Raffee, J. A. (2016). Rhetoric, Aboriginal Australians and Northern Territory intervention: A socio-legal investigation into pre-legislative argumentation. *International Journal of Crime, Justice and Social Democracy, 5*(1), 131–147.

Raskin, J. D., & Bridges, S. K. (Eds.). (2002). *Studies in meaning: Exploring constructivist psychology.* New York, NY: Pace University Press.

Roysircar, G. (2004). Cultural self-awareness assessment: Practice examples from psychology training. *Professional Psychology: Research and Practice, 35,* 658–666.

Roysircar, G. (2005). Culturally sensitive assessment, diagnosis, and guidelines. In M. G. Constantine & D. W. Sue (Eds.), *Strategies for building multicultural competence in mental health and educational settings* (pp. 19–38). Hoboken, NJ: Wiley & Sons.

Roysircar, G. (2009). Evidence-based practice and its implications for culturally sensitive treatment. *Journal of Multicultural Counseling and Development, 37*(2), 66–82.

Roysircar, G. (2012). Foreword: Positive psychology, Eastern religions, and multicultural psychology. In E. Chang & C. Downey (Eds.), *Handbook of race and development in mental health* (pp. vii–xi). New York, NY: Springer.

Roysircar, G. (2013). Multicultural assessment: Individual and contextual dynamic sizing. In F. T. L. Leong & J. Trimble (Eds.), *APA handbook of multicultural psychology: Vol 1. Theory & Research* (pp. 141–160). Washington, DC: American Psychological Association.

Roysircar, G., Carey, J. C., & Koroma, S. (2010). Asian Indian college students' science and math references: Influences of cultural contexts. *Journal of Career Development, 36*(10), 324–347.

Roysircar, G., & Gill, P. (2009). Cultural encapsulation and decapsulation of therapist trainees. In M. M. Leach & J. Aten (Eds.), *Culture and the therapeutic process: A guide for mental health professionals* (pp. 157–180). New York, NY: Routledge.

Roysircar, G., & Lee-Barber, J. (in press). *Multicultural relationship competency: Managing client-therapist cultural divide.*

Roysircar, G., & Pignatiello, V. (2011). A multicultural-ecological tool: Conceptualization and practice with an Indian immigrant woman. *Journal of Multicultural Counseling and Development, 39*(3), 167–179.

Roysircar, G., & Pimpinella, E. (2008). Second culture acquisition. In F. T. L. Leong (Ed.), *Encyclopedia of counseling* (Vol. 4, pp. 1309–1313). Thousand Oaks, CA: Sage.

Sarbin, T. R. (1986). The narrative as a root metaphor for psychology. In T. R. Sarbin (Ed.), *Narrative psychology* (pp. 3–21). New York, NY: Praeger.

Schrader, S., & Gergen, M. (Eds.). (2008). *Constructing worlds together: Interpersonal communication as relational process.* Boston: Pearson.

Schreiber, R.S. (2001). The "how to" of grounded theory: Avoiding the pitfalls. In R.S. Schreiber and P. Noerager Stern (Eds.). *Using* grounded theory in nursing (pp. 55–83). New York, N.Y.: Springer Publishing Company, Inc.

Seligman, M. E. P. (2002). *Using the new positive psychology to realize your potential for lasting fulfillment*: Authentic happiness. New York, NY: Free Press.

Shmoop Editorial Team. (2008, November 11). *1984 Power quotes.* Retrieved from http://www.shmoop.com/1984/power-quotes-5.html

Thornberg, R., & Charmaz, K. (2012). Grounded theory. In S. D. Lapan, M. Quartartaroli, & F. J. Reimer (Eds.), *Qualitative research: An introduction to methods and designs* (pp. 41–67). San Francisco, CA: Jossey-Bass.

Urmson, J. O., & Rée, J. (1989). *The concise encyclopedia of western philosophy & philosophers.* New York, NY: Routledge.

VandenBos, G. R. (Ed.). (2007). *APA dictionary of psychology.* Washington, DC: American Psychological Association.

Viney, L. L. (1987). *Interpreting the interpreters: Towards a science of construing people.* Malabar, FL: Krieger.

Watts, R. E. (2003). Adlerian therapy as a relational constructivist approach. *Family Journal, 11*(2), 139–147.

White, M., & Epston, D. (1989). *Literate means to therapeutic ends.* Adelaide, South Australia: Dulwich Centre Publications.

White, M., & Epston, D. (1990). *Narrative means to therapeutic ends.* New York, NY: Norton.

Wickman, S. A., Daniels, M. H., White, L. J., & Fesmire, S. A. (1999). A "primer" in conceptual metaphor for counselors. *Journal of Counseling and Development, 77,* 389–394. doi:10.1002/j.1556-6676.1999.tb02464.x

Wong, Y. J. (2006). Strength-centered therapy: A social constructionist, virtues-based psychotherapy. *Psychotherapy: Theory, Research, Practice, Training, 43*(2), 133–146.

CHAPTER 13

Alexander, P. C. (2003). Parent–child role reversal: Development of a measure and test of an attachment theory model. *Journal of Systemic Therapies, 22,* 31–43.

Baxter, L. A., Braithwaite, D. O., & Bryant, L. E. (2006). Types of communication triads perceived by young-adult stepchildren in established stepfamilies. *Communication Studies, 57,* 381–400.

Beck, A. T. (1979). *Cognitive therapy and the emotional disorders.* New York, NY: Meridian.

Bergen, L. P., Bigham, L. E., Ginter, E. J., & Scalise, J. J. (2013). *2013 Analysis of marital and family therapy practice.* Colorado Springs, CO: Association of Marital and Family Therapy Regulatory Boards (AMFTRB).

Biblarz, T. J., & Gottainer, G. (2000). Family structure and children's success: A comparison of widowed and divorced single-mother families. *Journal of Marriage and Family, 54,* 570–581.

Bitter, J. R. (2009). *Theory and practice of family therapy and counseling.* Belmont, CA: Brooks/Cole.

Bowen, M. (1978). *Family therapy in clinical practice.* New York, NY: Jason Aronson.

Bradley, P. D., Bergen, L. P., Ginter, E. J., Williams, L. M., & Scalise, J. J. (2010). A survey of North American Marriage and Family Therapy Practitioners: A role delineation study. *American Journal of Family Therapy, 348,* 281–291.

Carlson, J., Watts, R. E., & Maniacci, M. (2006). *Adlerian therapy: Theory and practice.* Washington, DC: American Psychological Association.

Coleman, M., Fine, M. A., Ganong, L. H., Downs, K. J. M., & Pauk, N. (2001). When you're not the Brady bunch: Identifying perceived conflicts and resolution strategies in stepfamilies. *Personal Relationships, 8,* 55–73.

Cowan, P. A., & Cowan, C. P. (2002). Interventions as tests of family systems theories: Marital and family relationships in children's development, and psychopathology [Special issue]. *Development and Psychopathology, 14,* 731–760.

Davies, P. T., Forman, E. M., Rasi, J. A., & Stevens, K. (2002). Children's emotional security in the marital subsystem: Psychometric properties for a new measure. *Child Development, 73,* 544–562.

De Shazer, S. (1982). Patterns of brief family therapy: An ecosystemic approach. New York, NY: Guilford Press.

De Shazer, S., & Berg, I. (1988). Doing therapy: A post-structural revision. *Journal of Marital and Family Therapy, 18,* 71–81.

De Shazer, S., & Molnar, A. (1984). Four useful interventions in brief family therapy. *Journal of Marriage and Family Therapy, 10,* 297–304.

Dreikurs, R. (1968). *Psychology in the classroom* (2nd ed.). New York, NY: Harper & Row.

Dupree, W. J., Bhakta, K. A, Patel, P. S., & Dupree, D. G. (2013). Developing culturally competent marriage and family therapists: Guidelines for working with Asian Indian American couples. *American Journal of Family Therapy, 41,* 311–329.

Ellis, A. (2001). *Overcoming destructive beliefs, feelings, and behaviors: New directions for rational emotive behavior therapy.* New York, NY: Prometheus Books.

Fine, M. A., & Fincham, F. D. (2013). *Handbook of family theories: A content-based approach.* New York, NY: Routledge.

Gerard, J. M., Buehler, C., Frank, K., & Anderson, O. (2005). In the eyes of the beholder: Cognitive appraisals as mediators of the association between interparental conflict and youth maladjustment. *Journal of Family Psychology, 19,* 376–384.

Grych, J. H., Raynor, S. R., & Focco, G. M. (2004). Family processes that shape the impact of interparental conflict on adolescents. *Development and Psychopathology, 16,* 649–665.

Hampden-Turner, C. (1981). *Maps of the mind: Charts and concepts of the mind and its labyrinths.* New York, NY: Macmillan.

Hanna, S. M., & Brown, J. H. (1995). *The practice of family therapy: Key elements across models.* New York, NY: Brooks/Cole.

Hoffman, L. (1981). *Foundations of family therapy: A conceptual framework for systems change.* New York, NY: Basic Books.

Jurkovic, G. J., Thirkeild, A., & Morrell, R. (2001). Parentification of adult children of divorce: A multidimensional analysis. *Journal of Youth and Adolescence, 30,* 245–258.

Kaplan, D. M. (2000). Who are our giants? *Family Digest, 12*(4), 1, 6.

Kosutic, I., & McDowell, T. (2008). Diversity and social justice issues in family therapy literature: A decade review. *Journal of Feminist Family Therapy, 20*(2), 142–165.

Loving v. Virginia, 388 U.S. 1 (1967).

McGoldrick, M., & Hardy, K. V. (2008). *Re-visioning family therapy: Race, culture, and gender in clinical practice* (2nd ed.). New York, NY: Guilford Press.

Minuchin, S. (1974). *Families and family therapy.* Cambridge, MA: Harvard University Press.

Minuchin, S., Nichols, M. P., & Lee, W.-Y. (2007). *Assessing families and couples: From symptom to system.* Boston, MA: Allyn and Bacon.

Obergefell et al. v. Hodges, Director, Ohio Department of Health, et al., 14–556 U.S. (2015).

Poulsen, S. S., & Thomas, V. (2007). Cultural issues in couple therapy. *Journal of Couple & Relationship Therapy, 6,* 141–152.

Richmond, R., Gimple, S. M., McCann, J. L., Seghers, C., & Bates, J. W. (Eds.). (2010). *Simpsons world: The ultimate episode guide* (Seasons 1–20). New York, NY: HarperCollins.

Santisteban, D. A., Mena, M. P., & Abalo, C. (2013). Bridging diversity and family systems: Culturally informed and flexible family-based treatment for Hispanic adolescents. *Couple and Family Psychology: Research and Practice, 2,* 246–263.

Satir, V. (1964). *Conjoint family therapy: A guide to theory and technique* (Rev. ed.). Palo Alto, CA: Science and Behavior Books.

Schwab, J. (1990). *A resource handbook for Satir concepts.* Palo Alto, CA: Science and Behavior Books.

Sharry, J. (2007). *Solution-focused groupwork.* Thousand Oaks, CA: Sage.

Skopp, N. A., McDonald, R., Manke, B., & Jouriles, E. N. (2005). Siblings in domestically violent families: Experiences of interparent conflict and adjustment problems. *Journal of Family Psychology, 17,* 324–333.

Thompson, J. (Director). (1999). *The Mexican celebration of the days of the dead: Food for the ancestors* [DVD]. Alexandria, VA: Public Broadcasting Service. Available from www.pbs.org

Turkle, S. (2011). *Alone together: Why we expect more from technology and less from each other.* New York, NY: Basic Books.

VandenBos, G. R. (Ed.). (2007). *APA dictionary of psychology.* Washington, DC: American Psychological Association.

Watzlawick, P., Beavin, J. H., & Jackson, D. D. (1967). *Pragmatics of human communication: A study of interactional patterns, pathologies, and paradoxes.* New York, NY: Norton.

Wolfe, J. L. (2007). Rational emotive behavior therapy (REBT). In A. Rochlen (Ed.), *Applying counseling theories: An online case-based approach* (pp. 177–191). Upper Saddle River, NJ: Prentice Hall.

CHAPTER 14

Ægisdóttir, S., & Gerstein, L. (2010). International counseling competencies. In J. G. Ponterotto, J. M. Casas, L. A. Suzuki, & C. M. Alexander (Eds.), *Handbook of multicultural counseling* (3rd ed., pp. 175–188). Thousand Oaks, CA: Sage.

Aguilera, A., Miranda, J., Aguilar-Gaxiola, S., Organista, K. C., González, G. M., Kohn-Wood, L P., Le, H., Ghosh-Ippen, C., Urizar, G. G., Soto, J., Mendelson, T., Barrera, A. Z., Torres, L. D., Leykin, Y., Schueller, S., Liu, N., & Muñoz, R. F. (2016). Depression prevention and treatment interventions: Evolution of the San Francisco Latino Mental Health Research Program. In N. Zane, G. Bernal, & F. T. L. Leong (Eds.), *Evidence-based psychological practice with ethnic minorities: Culturally informed research and clinical practices* (pp. 247–271). Washington, DC: American Psychological Association. doi: org/10.1037/14940-012

Akinyela, M. M. (2005). Testimony of hope: African centered praxis for therapeutic ends. *Journal of Systemic Therapies, 24,* 5–18.

Aklin, W. M., & Turner, S. M. (2006). Toward understanding ethnic and cultural factors in the interviewing process. *Psychotherapy: Theory, Research, Practice, Training, 43*(1), 50–64. doi: org/10.1037/0033-3204.43.1.50

Albee, G. W. (1986). Toward a just society: Lessons from observations on the primary prevention of psychopathology. *American Psychologist, 41,* 891–897.

Aldarondo, E. (2007). *Advancing social justice through clinical practice.* New York, NY: Routledge.

American Educational Research Association, American Psychological Association, & National Council on Measurement in Education. (2014). *Standards for educational and psychological testing* (3rd ed.). Washington, DC: American Educational Research Association.

American Psychiatric Association. (2013a). *Diagnostic and statistical manual of mental disorders* (5th ed.). Washington, DC: Author.

American Psychiatric Association. (2013b). *American Psychiatric Association's cultural formulation interview.* Washington, DC: Author.

American Psychological Association. (2002). Guidelines on multicultural education, training, research, practice, and organizational change for psychologists. *American Psychologist, 58,* 377–402.

American Psychological Association, Presidential Task Force on Evidence-Based Practice. (2006). Evidence-based practice in psychology. *American Psychologist, 61,* 271–285.

American Psychological Association, Task Force on Resilience and Strength in Black Children and Adolescents. (2008). *Resilience in African American children and adolescents: A vision for optimal development* (Executive summary). Washington, DC: Author. Retrieved September 1, 2017, from http://www.apa.org/pi/cyf/resilience.html

American Psychological Association. (2010). 2010 amendments to the 2002 ethical principles of psychologists and code of conduct. *American Psychologist, 65*(5), 493.

America Psychological Association. (2012). Guidelines for psychological practice with lesbian, gay, and bisexual clients. *American Psychologist, 67*(1), 10–42.

American Psychological Association. (2017). *Multicultural guidelines: An ecological approach to context, identity, and intersectionality.* Washington, DC: Author.

Atkinson, D. R., Thompson, C. E., & Grant, S. K. (1993). A three-dimensional model for counseling racial/ethnic minorities. *The Counseling Psychologist, 21*(2): 257–277. doi: 10.1177/0011000093212010

American Psychological Association. (2017). *Multicultural Guidelines: An Ecological Approach to Context, Identity, and Intersectionality.* Retrieved from: http://www.apa.org/about/policy/multicultural-guidelines.pdfpson, C. E., & Grant, S. K. (1993). A three-dimensional model for counseling racial/ethnic minorities. *The Counseling Psychologist, 21,* 257–277.

Bean, R. B. (1906). Some racial peculiarities of the Negro brain. *American Journal of Anatomy, 5,* 353–415.

Berry, J. (2001). A psychology of immigration. *Journal of Social Issues, 57,* 615–631.

Black, E. (2003, November 9). Eugenics and the Nazis—the California connection. *San Francisco Chronicle.* Retrieved January 5, 2018, from http://www.sfgate.com/opinion/article/Eugenics-and-the-Nazis-the-California-2549771.php

Bradford, P. V., & Blume, H. (1992). *Ota Benga: The pygmy in the zoo.* New York, NY: St. Martin Press.

Clark, K. B., & Clark, M. K. (1940). Skin color as a factor in racial identification of Negro preschool children. *Journal of Social Psychology, 11*(S.P.S.S.I. Bulletin), 159–169.

Clauss-Ehlers, C. S., & Weist, M. D. (Eds.). (2004). *Community planning to foster resilience in children.* New York, NY: Kluwer Academic.

Cofresi, N. I., & Gorman A. A. (2004). Testing and assessment issues with Spanish-English bilingual Latinos. *Journal of Counseling and Development, 82,* 99–106.

Cokley, K. O. (2002). Testing Cross's revised racial identity model: An examination of the relationship between racial identity and internalized racialism. *Journal of Counseling Psychology, 49,* 476–483.

Colby, S. L., & Ortman, J. M. (2014). Projection of the size and composition of the U.S. population: 2014 to 2060 (Current Population Reports, P25–1143). Washington, DC: U.S. Census Bureau.

Comas-Díaz, L. (2000). An ethnopolitical approach to working with people of color. *American Psychologist, 55*(11), 1319–1325. doi: 10.1037/0003-066X.55.11.1319

Comas-Díaz, L. (2006). Latino healing: The integration of ethnic psychology into psychotherapy. *Psychotherapy: Theory, Research, Training, 43*(4), 436–453. doi: 10.1037/0033-3204.43.4.380

Comas-Díaz, L. (2012). *Multicultural care: A clinician's guide to cultural competence.* Washington, DC: American Psychological Association.

Constantine, M. G. (2007). Racial microaggressions against African American clients in cross-racial counseling relationships. *Journal of Counseling Psychology, 54,* 1–16.

Costantino, G., Malgady, R. G., & Rogler, L. H. (1986). Cuento therapy: A culturally sensitive modality for Puerto Rican children. *Journal of Consulting and Clinical Psychology, 54*(5), 639–645.

Cook, D. A., & Wiley, C. Y. (2014). Psychotherapy with members of African American churches and spiritual traditions. In P. S. Richards & A. E. Bergin (Eds.), *Handbook of psychotherapy and religious diversity* (pp. 369–396). Washington, DC: American Psychological Association.

Cross, W., Jr. (1971). The negro-to-black conversion experience. *Black World, 20*(9), 13–27.

Cross, W. E., Jr. (1995). The psychology of nigrescence: Revising the Cross model. In J. G. Ponterotto, J. M. Casas, L. A. Suzuki, & C. M. Alexander (Eds.), *Handbook of multicultural counseling* (pp. 93–122). Thousand Oaks, CA: Sage.

Darwin, C. (1859). *The origin of species by means of natural selection.* London, UK: Murray.

Darwin, C. (1871). *The descent of man, and selection in relation to sex* (Vol. 1). London, United Kingdom: John Murray.

Dovidio, J. F., Gaertner, S. L., Kawakami, K., & Hodson, G. (2002). Why can't we just get along? Interpersonal biases and interracial distrust. *Cultural Diversity & Ethnic Minority Psychology, 8,* 88–102.

Dovidio, J. F., Kawakami, K., & Gaertner, S. L. (2002). Implicit and explicit prejudice and interracial interaction. *Journal of Personality and Social Psychology, 82,* 62–68.

Draguns, J. G. (1996). Multicultural and cross-cultural assessment: Dilemmas and decisions. In G. Roysircar & J. C. Impara (Eds.), *Multicultural assessment in counseling and clinical psychology.* Lincoln, NE: Buros Institute of Mental Measures.

Draguns, J. G. (2001). Toward a truly international psychology: Beyond English only. *American Psychologist, 56*(11), 1019. doi: org/10.1037/0003-066X.56.11.1019

Drasgow, F., & Probst, T. M. (2005). The psychometrics of adaptation: Evaluating measurement equivalence across languages and cultures. In R. K. Hambleton, P. F. Merenda, & C. D. Spielberger (Eds.), *Adapting educational and psychological tests for cross-cultural assessment* (pp. 265–296). Mahwah, NJ: Erlbaum.

Dyche, L., & Zayas, L. H. (2001). Cross-cultural empathy and training the contemporary psychotherapist. *Clinical Social Work Journal, 29*(3), 245–258. doi. org/10.1023/A:1010407728614

Espelage, D. L., & Poteat, P. V. (2012). Counseling psychologists in schools. In N. A. Fouad, J. A. Carter, & L. M. Subich (Eds.), *APA handbook of counseling psychology: Practice, interventions, and applications* (Vol. 2, pp. 541–566). Washington, DC: American Psychological Association.

Falicov, C.J. (1998). The cultural meaning of family triangles. In M. McGoldrick (Ed.), *Revisioning family therapy: Race, culture, and gender in clinical practice* (pp. 37–49). New York, NY: Guilford Press.

Frey, M., & Roysircar, G. (2006). South and East Asian international students' perceived prejudice, acculturation, and frequency of help resource utilization. *Journal of Multicultural Counseling and Development, 34,* 208–222.

Frisby, C. L., & Henry, B. (2016). Science, politics, and best practices: 35 years after Larry P. *Contemporary School Psychology, 20*(1), 46–62.

Fuertes, J. N., Mueller, L. N., Chauhan, R. V., Walker, J. A., & Ladany, N. (2002). An investigation of Euro-American therapists' approach to counseling African-American clients. *The Counseling Psychologist, 30*, 763–788.

Fuertes, J. N., & Ponterotto, J. G. (2003). Culturally appropriate intervention strategies. In G. Roysircar (Ed.), *Multicultural counseling competencies: Association for Multicultural Counseling and Development* (pp. 51–58). Alexandria, VA: Association for Multicultural Counseling and Development.

Fuertes, J. N., Stracuzzi, T. I., Bennett, J., Scheinholtz, J., Mislowack, A., Hersh, M., & Cheng, D. (2006). Therapist multicultural competency: A study of therapy dyads. *Psychotherapy: Theory, Research, Practice, Training, 43*, 480–490.

Galton, S. F. (1870). *Hereditary genius: An inquiry into its laws and consequences.* New York, NY: Appleton.

Gardner, M. R. (2002). *Harry Truman and civil rights: Moral courage and political risks.* Carbondale: Southern Illinois University Press.

Gauchet, M., & Swain, G. (1999). *Madness and democracy: The modern psychiatric universe* (C. Porter, Trans.). Princeton, NJ: Princeton University Press.

Gerber, D. A. (2011). *American immigration: A very short introduction.* New York, NY: Oxford University Press.

Gerstein, L. H., & Ægisdóttir, S. (2007). Training international social change agents: Transcending a U.S. counseling paradigm. *Counselor Education and Supervision, 47*(2), 123–139.

Gerstein, L. H., Heppner, P. P., Stockton, R., Leong, F. T., & AEgisdottir, S. (2009). The counseling profession in- and outside the United States. In L. H. Gerstein, P. P. Heppner, S. AEgisdottir, S.-M. A. Leung, & K. L. Norsworthy (Eds.). *International handbook of cross-cultural counseling: Cultural assumptions and practices worldwide* (pp. 53–67). Thousand Oaks, CA: Sage.

Gerstein, L. H., Hurley, E., & Hutchison, A. (2015). The

dynamic-systemic-process model of international competencies for psychologists and trainees. *Revista de Cercetare si Interventie Sociala, 50*, 239–261.

Gonzales, N. A., Germán, M., & Fabrett, F. C. (2012). US Latino youth. In E. C. Chang & C. A. Downey (Eds.), *Handbook of race and development in mental health* (pp. 259–278). New York, NY: Springer Science.

González, R. C., Biever, J. L., & Gardner, G. T. (1994). The multicultural perspective in therapy: A social constructionist approach. *Psychotherapy: Theory, Research, Practice, Training, 31*(3), 515–524. doi: org/10.1037/0033-3204.31.3.515

Goodman, L. A., Liang, B. Helms, J. E., Latta, R. E., Sparks, E., & Weintraub, S. R. (2004). Training counseling psychologists as social justice agents: Feminist and multicultural principles in action. *The Counseling Psychologist, 32*(6), 793–836.

Griner, D., & Smith, T. B. (2006). Culturally adapted mental health interventions: A meta-analytic review. *Psychotherapy: Theory, Research, Practice, Training, 43*(4), 531–548.

Grzanka, P. R. (2014). Intersectionality: A foundations and frontiers reader. Boulder, CO: Westview Press.

Guthrie, R. V. (1998). *Even the rat was white: A historical view of psychology.* Boston, MA: Allyn & Bacon.

Hardtke, K. K., & Angus, L. E. (2004). The narrative assessment interview: Assessing self-change in psychotherapy. In L. Angus & J. McLeod (Eds.), *The handbook of narrative psychotherapy: Practice, theory and research* (pp. 247–262). Thousand Oaks, CA: Sage. doi: org/10.4135/9781412973496.d19

Hays, P. A. (2016). Understanding clients' identities and contexts. Addressing cultural complexities in practice: Assessment, diagnosis, and therapy (3rd ed.). Washington, DC: American Psychological Association. doi: 10.1037/14801-005

Helms, J. E. (1990). An overview of Black racial identity theory. In J. Helms (Ed.), *Black and White racial identity: Theory, research, and practice* (pp. 3–8). New York, NY: Greenwood.

Helms, J. E. (1995). An update on Helms's White and people of color racial identity models. In J. G. Ponterotto, J. M. Casas, L. A. Suzuki, & C M. Alexander (Eds.), *Handbook of multicultural counseling* (2nd ed., pp. 143–192). Thousand Oaks, CA: Sage.

Helms, J. E., & Cook, D. A. (1999). *Using race and culture in counseling and psychotherapy: Theory and process.* Boston, MA: Allyn & Bacon.

Helms, J. E., Jernigan, M., & Mascher, J. (2005). The meaning of race in psychology and how to change it: A methodological perspective. *American Psychologist, 60*, 27–36.

Heppner, P. P., Leong, F. T. L., & Gerstein, L. H. (2008). Counseling within a changing world: Meeting the psychological needs of societies and the world. In W. B. Walsh (Ed.), *Biennial review of counseling psychology* (pp. 231–258). New York, NY: Taylor & Francis.

Heppner, P. P., Wang, K. T., Heppner, M. J., & Wang, L. F. (2012). From cultural encapsulation to cultural competence: The cross-national cultural competence model. In N. A. Fouad (Ed.), *APA handbook of counseling psychology: Practice, interventions, and applications* (Vol. 2, pp. 433–471). Washington, DC: American Psychological Association.

Herzig, B. A., Roysircar, G., Kosyluk, K. A., & Corrigan, P. W. (2013). American Muslim college students: The impact of religiousness and stigma on active coping. *Journal of Muslim Mental Health, 7*(1), 33–42.

Hollingshead, A. B., & Redlich, G. C. (1958). *Social class and mental illness: A community study.* New York, NY: Wiley & Sons.

Howard, J. A., & Renfrow, D. G. (2014). Intersectionality. In J. D. McLeod, E. J. Lawler, & M. Schwalbe (Eds.), *Handbook of the social psychology of inequality* (pp. 95–121). Netherlands, Holland: Springer. doi: org/10.1007/978-94-017-9002-4_5

Hwang, W. C. (2006). Acculturative family distancing: Theory, research, and clinical practice. *Psychotherapy: Theory, Research, Training, 43*(4), 397–409. doi: 10.1037/0033-3204.43.4.380

Hwang, W. C. (2016). Culturally adapting evidence-based practices for ethnic minorities and immigrant families. In N. Zane, G. Bernal, & F. T. Leong (Eds.), *Evidence-based psychological practice with ethnic minorities: Culturally informed research and clinical strategie*s (pp. 289–309). Washington, DC: American Psychological Association. doi: org/10.1037/14940-011

Ibrahim, F. A., & Dykeman, C. (2011). Counseling Muslim Americans: Cultural and spiritual assessments. *Journal of Counseling & Development, 89*, 387–396.

Institute for the Study and Promotion of Race and Culture. (2011). *Life questions.* Retrieved September 1, 2017, from http://www.bc.edu/content/bc/schools/lsoe/isprc/staff/helms/lifequestions.html

Institute for the Study and Promotion of Race and Culture. (2012). *Meet the staff: Dr. Janet E. Helms.* Retrieved from http://www.bc.edu/content/bc/schools/lsoe/isprc/staff/helms.html

Jensen, A. R. (1969). How much can we boost IQ and scholastic achievement? *Harvard Educational Review, 39*, 1–123.

Jensen, J. (2012). An interview with Dr. Paul B. Pedersen. *Church and Life.* Retrieved from http://www.churchandlife.org/Pedersen%20Interview.htm

Jones, W. J. P. (2013). *The march on Washington: Jobs, freedom, and the forgotten history of civil rights* (1st ed.). New York, NY: Norton.

Journal of Multicultural Counseling and Development. (2010). Interviews with African American male past presidents of AMCD. Journal of Multicultural Counseling and Development, 38(4), 193–255.

Kesselman, L. C. (1946). The fair employment practice committee movement in perspective. *Journal of Negro History, 31*(1), 30–46.

Khanna, N., & Johnson, C. (2010). Passing as Black: Racial identity work among biracial Americans. *Social Psychology Quarterly, 73*(4), 380–397.

Kim, B. S. K., & Omizo, M. M. (2006). Behavioral acculturation and enculturation and psychological functioning among Asian American college students. *Cultural Diversity and Ethnic Minority Psychology, 12*, 245–258.

Kleijin, W. C., Hovens, J. E., & Rodenburg, J. J. (2001). Posttraumatic stress symptoms in refugees: Assessments with the Harvard Trauma Questionnaire and the Hopkins Symptoms Checklist-25 in different languages. *Psychological Reports, 88*, 527–532.

Klineberg, O. (1965). *The human dimension in international relations.* New York, NY: Holt, Rinehart and Winston.

Kluchin, R. M. (2009). *Fit to be tied: Sterilization and reproductive rights in America 1950–1980.* New Brunswick, NJ: Rutgers University Press.

Kuo, B. C. H., Roysircar, G., & Newby-Clark, I. R. (2006). Development of the Cross-Cultural Coping Scale: Collective, avoidance, and engagement coping. *Measurement and Evaluation in Counseling and Development, 39*,161–181.

LaFromboise, T., Coleman, H., & Gerton, J. (1993). Psychological impact of biculturalism: Evidence and theory. *Psychology Bulletin, 114*(3), 395–412.

LaFromboise, T. D., & Malik, S. S. (2016). A culturally informed approach to American Indian/Alaska Native youth suicide prevention. In N. Zane, G. Bernal, & F. T. Leong (Eds.), Evidence-based psychological practice with ethnic minorities: Culturally informed research and clinical strategies (pp. 223–245). Washington, DC: American Psychological Association. doi: org/10.1037/14940-011

Lakes, K., López, S. R., & Garro, L. C (2006). Cultural competence and psychotherapy: Applying anthropologically informed conceptions of culture. *Psychotherapy: Theory, Research, Practice, Training, 43*, 380–396.

Lal, S. (2002). Giving children security: Mamie Phipps Clark and the racialization of child psychology. *American Psychologist, 57*, 20–28.

Lambert, B. (1992). Otto Klineberg, who helped win '54 desegregation case, dies at 92. *The New York Times.* Retrieved January 6, 2018, from http://www.nytimes.com/1992/03/10/obituaries/otto-klineberg-who-helped-win-54-de-segregation-case-dies-at-92.html

LaRoche, M. L. (2013). *Cultural psychotherapy: Theory, methods, and practice.* Thousand Oaks, CA: Sage.

LaRoche, M. J., D'Angelo, E., Gualdron, L., & Leavell, J. (2006). Culturally sensitive guided imagery for allocentric Latinos: A pilot study. *Psychotherapy: Theory, Research, Training, 43*(4), 555–560. doi: 10.1037/0033-3204.43.4.380

Laughin, H. H. (1920, April 16). *Biological aspects of immigration: Harry H. Laughlin testimony before the House Committee on Immigration and Naturalization.* Washington, DC: House of Representatives.

Leary, J. D. (2005). Posttraumatic slave syndrome: America's legacy of enduring injury and healing. Milwaukie, OR: Uptone Press.

Lee, C. C. (Ed.). (2007). *Counseling for social justice* (2nd ed.). Alexandria, VA: American Counseling Association.

Leong, F. T., & Lee, S.-H. (2006). A cultural accommodation model for cross-cultural psychotherapy: Illustrated with the case of Asian Americans. *Psychotherapy: Theory, Research, Training, 43*(4), 410–423. doi: 10.1037/0033-3204.43.4.380

Leong, F. T. L., Leung, K., & Cheung, F. M. (2010). Integrating cross-cultural psychology: Research methods into ethnic minority psychology. *Cultural Diversity and Ethnic Minority Psychology, 16*, 590–597.

Leong, F. T. L, Pickren, W. E., & Tang, L. C. (2012). A history of cross-cultural clinical psychology, and its importance to mental health today. In E. Chang & A. C. Downey (Eds.), *Handbook of race and development in mental health* (Chapter 1). New York, NY: Springer. http://dx.doi.org/10.1007/978-1-4614-0424-8_15

Malgady, R. G. (2010). Treating Hispanic children and adolescents using narrative therapy. In J. R. Weisz & A. E. Kazdin (Eds.), *Evidence-based psychotherapies for children and adolescents* (2nd ed., pp. 391–400). New York, NY: Guilford.

Martinez-Taboas, A. (2005). Psychogenic seizures in an *espiritismo* context: The role of culturally sensitive psychotherapy. *Psychotherapy: Theory,*

Research, Practice, Training, 42(1), 6–13.

McCabe, P. C., & Rubinson, F. (2008). Committing to social justice: The behavioral intention of school psychology and education trainees to advocate for lesbian, gay, bisexual, and transgendered youth. *School Psychology Review, 37*(4), 469–486.

Milburn, N. G., & Lightfoot, M. (2016). Improving participation of families of color in evidence-based interventions: Challenges and lessons learned. In N. Zane, G. Bernal, & F.T. L. Leong (Eds.), *Evidence-based psychological practice with ethnic minorities: Culturally informed research and clinical strategies* (pp. 273–287). Washington, DC: American Psychological Association.

Moodley, R., Lengyell, M., Wu, R., & Gielen, U. P. (Eds.) (2015). *International counseling: Case studies handbook*. Alexandria, VA: American Counseling Association.

Nelson-Jones, R. (2002). Diverse goals for multicultural counselling and therapy. *Counselling Psychology Quarterly, 15*(2), 133–143.

Padilla, A. M., & Ruiz, R. A. (1973). *Latino mental health: A review of the literature*. Washington, DC: Superintendent of Documents: U.S. Printing Office (Stock # 1724-00317).

Pedersen, P. B. (2002). The making of a culturally competent counselor. *Online Readings in Psychology and Culture, 10*(3). Retreived from https://doi .org/10.9707/2307-0919.1093

Ponterotto, J. G., Casas, J. M., Suzuki, L. A., & Alexander, C. M. (2010). *Handbook of multicultural counseling* (3rd ed.). Thousand Oaks, CA: Sage.

Pope-Davis, D. B., Toporek, R. L., Ortega-Villalobos, L., Ligiero, D. P., Brittan-Powell, C. S., Liu, W. M., & Liang, C. T. H. (2002). Client perspectives of multicultural counseling competence: A qualitative examination. *The Counseling Psychologist, 30*, 355–393.

Poyrazili, S., & Thompson, C. (Eds.) (2013). *International case studies in mental health*. Thousand Oaks, CA: Sage.

Raimundo Oda, A. M. G., Banzato, C. E. M., & Dalgalarrondo, P. (2005).

Some origins of cross-cultural psychiatry. *History of Psychiatry, 16*(2), 155–169.

Ratts, M. J., & Hutchins, A. M. (2009). ACA advocacy competencies: Social justice advocacy at the client/ student level. *Journal of Counseling and Development, 87*(3), 269–275. doi: org/10.1002/j.1556-6678.2009. tb00106.x

Reed, J. (1987). Robert M. Yerkes and the mental testing movement. In M. M. Sokal (Ed.), *Psychological testing and American society* (pp. 75–94). New Brunswick, NJ: Rutgers University Press.

Reissman, F. (1962). *The culturally deprived child and his education*. New York, NY: Harper and Brothers.

Richards, P. S., & Bergin, A. E. (2014). Toward religious and spiritual competency for mental health professionals. In P. S. Richards & A. E. Bergin (Eds.), *Handbook of psychotherapy and religious diversity* (pp. 3–26). Washington, DC: American Psychological Association.

Roland, A. (2006). Across civilizations: Psychoanalytic therapy with Asians and Asian American. *Psychotherapy: Theory, Research, Practice and Training, 43*(4), 454–463.

Rosenthal, R., & Jacobson, L. (1968). *Pygmalion in the classroom*. New York, NY: Holt, Rinehart, & Winston.

Roysircar, G. (2003a). Religious differences: Psychological and sociopolitical aspects of counseling. *International Journal for the Advancement of Counselling, 25*, 255–267.

Roysircar, G. (2003b). Counselor awareness of own assumptions, values, and biases. In G. Roysircar, P. Arredondo, J. N. Fuertes, J. G. Ponterotto, & R. L. Taporek (Eds.), *Multicultural counseling competencies: Association for Multicultural Counseling and Development* (pp. 17–38). Alexandria, VA: Association for Multicultural Counseling and Development.

Roysircar, G. (2004a). Counseling and psychotherapy for acculturation and ethnic identity concerns with immigrants and international student clients. In T. B. Smith (Ed.),

Practicing multiculturalism: Affirming diversity in counseling and psychology (pp. 248–268). Boston, MA: Allyn & Bacon.

Roysircar, G. (2004b). Cultural self-awareness assessment: Practice examples from psychology training. *Professional Psychology: Research and Practice, 35*, 658–666.

Roysircar, G. (2005). Culturally sensitive assessment, diagnosis, and guidelines. In M. G. Constantine & D. W. Sue (Eds.), *Strategies for building multicultural competence in mental health and educational settings* (pp. 19–38). Hoboken, NJ: Wiley & Sons.

Roysircar, G (2006). Prevention work in schools and with youth: Promoting competence and reducing risks. In R. Toporek, L. H. Gerstein, N. A. Fouad, G. Roysircar, & T. Israel (Eds.), *Handbook for social justice in counseling psychology* (pp. 77–85). Thousand Oaks, CA: Sage.

Roysircar, G. (2009a). Evidence-based practice and its implications for culturally sensitive treatment. *Journal of Multicultural Counseling and Development, 37*(2), 66–82.

Roysircar, G. (2009b). The big picture of social justice advocacy: Counselor, heal society and thyself. *Journal of Counseling and Development, 87*, 288–295.

Roysircar, G. (2013). Multicultural assessment: Individual and contextual dynamic sizing. In F. T. L. Leong & J. Trimble (Eds.), *APA handbook of multicultural psychology: Theory & Research* (Vol 1., pp. 141–160). Washington, DC: American Psychological Association.

Roysircar, G., Arredondo, P., Fuertes, J. N., Ponterotto, J. G., & Toporek, R. L. (2003). *Multicultural counseling competencies 2003: Association for Multicultural Counseling and Development*. Alexandria, VA: Association for Multicultural Counseling and Development.

Roysircar, G., Carey, J. C., & Koroma, S. (2010). Asian Indian college students' science and math preferences: Influences of cultural contexts. *Journal of Career Development, 36*(4), 324–346.

Roysircar, G., Colvin, K. F., Afolayan, A. G., Thompson, A., & Robertson, T.

W. (2017). Haitian children's resilience and vulnerability assessed with House-Tree-Person (HTP) drawings. *Traumatology, 23*(1), 68–81. doi: org/10.1037//trm0000090

Roysircar, G., Dobbins, J. E., & Malloy, K. A. (2010). Diversity competence in training and clinical practice. In M. B. Kenkel & R. L. Peterson (Eds.), *Competency-based education for professional psychology* (pp. 179–197). Washington, DC: American Psychological Association.

Roysircar, G., & Krishnamurthy, R. (2018). Nationality and assessment. In S. Smith & R. Krishnamurthy (Eds.), *Diversity sensitive personality assessment* (pp.151–178). New York, NY: Taylor Francis/Routledge.

Roysircar, G., & Pimpinella, E. (2008). Immigrants. In F. T. L. Leong (Ed.), *Encyclopedia of counseling* (Vol. 4). Thousand Oaks, CA: Sage.

Roysircar, G., Thompson, A., & Boudreau, M. (2017). "Born Black and male": Counseling leaders' self-discovery of strengths. *Counselling Psychology Quarterly.* doi: org/10.1080/095150 70.2016.1172204

Roysircar-Sodowsky, G., & Maestas, M. (2000). Acculturation, ethnic identity, and acculturative stress: Evidence and measurement. In R. H. Dana (Ed.), *Handbook of cross-cultural and multicultural personality assessment* (pp. 131–172). Mahwah, NJ: Erlbaum.

Sanchez, G. I. (1932). Scores of Spanish-speaking children on repeated tests. *Journal of Genetic Psychology, 40*, 223–231.

Schlosser, L. Z. (2006). Affirmative psychotherapy for American Jews. *Psychotherapy: Theory, Research, Training, 43*(4), 424–435. doi: 10.1037/0033-3204.43.4.380

Selden, S. (2005, June). Transforming better babies into fitter families: Archival resources and the history of American eugenics movement, 1908–1930. *Proceedings of the American Philosophical Society, 149*, 199–225.

Sellers, R. M., & Shelton, J. N. (2003). The role of racial identity in perceived racial discrimination. *Journal of Personality and Social Psychology, 84*, 1079–1092.

Sellers, R. M., Smith, M. A., Shelton, J. N., Rowley, S. A. J., & Chavous, T. M. (1998). Multidimensional model of racial identity: A reconceptualization of African American racial identity. *Personality and Social Psychology Review, 2*, 18–39.

Shin, R. Q. (2015). The application of critical consciousness and intersectionality as tools for decolonizing racial/ethnic identity development models in the fields of counseling and psychology. In D. R. Goodman & C. P Gorski (Eds.), *Decolonizing "multicultural" counseling through social justice* (pp. 11–22). New York, NY: Springer.

Shonfeld-Ringel, S. (2000). Dimensions of cross-cultural treatment with late adolescent college students. *Child and Adolescent Social Work Journal, 17*(6), 443–454.

Smith, T. B., Constantine, M. G., Dunn, T. W., Dinehart, J. M., & Montoya, J. A. (2006). Multicultural education in the mental health professions: A meta-analytic review. *Journal of Counseling Psychology, 53*, 132–145.

Sodowsky, G. R. (1991). Effects of culturally consistent counseling tasks on American and international student observers' perception of therapist credibility. *Journal of Counseling and Development, 69*, 253–256.

Sodowsky, G. R., Lai, E. W. M., & Plake, B. (1991). Moderating effects of sociocultural variables on acculturation attitudes of Hispanics and Asian Americans. *Journal of Counseling and Development, 70*, 194–204.

Sokal. M. M. (1987). James McKeen Cattell and mental anthropometry: Nineteenth-century science and reform and the origins of psychological testing. In M. Sokal (Ed.), *Psychological testing and American society, 1890–1930* (pp. 21–45). New Brunswick, NJ: Rutgers University Press.

Spengler, P. M., Strohmer, D. C., Dixon, D. N., & Shivy, V. A. (1995). A scientist-practitioner model of psychological assessment: Implications for training, practice, and research. *The Counseling Psychologist, 23*(3), 506–534.

Starr, A., & Adams, J. (2003). Anti-globalization: The global fight for local autonomy. *New Political Science, 25*(1), 19–42.

Steele, C. M. (1997). A threat in the air: How stereotypes shape intellectual identity and performance. *American Psychologist, 52*, 613–629.

Steele, C. M., & Aronson, J. (1995). Stereotype threat and the intellectual test performance of African Americans, *Journal of Personality and Social Psychology, 69*, 797–811.

Sue, D. W. (1981). *Counseling the culturally different: Theory and practice.* New York, NY: Wiley & Sons.

Sue, D. W. (2010). Racial microaggressions in everyday life. *Psychology Today.* Retrieved from https://www.psychologytoday.com/blog/microaggressions-in-everyday-life/201010/racial-microaggressions-in-every-day-life

Sue, D. W., Arredondo, P., & McDavis, R. J. (1992). Multicultural counseling competencies and standards: A call to the profession. *Journal of Counseling & Development, 70*, 477–486.

Sue, D. W., Bernier, J. E., Durran, A., Feinberg, L., Pedersen, P., Smith, E. J., & Vasquez-Nuttall, E. (1982). Position paper: Cross-cultural counseling competencies. *The Counseling Psychologist, 10*, 45–52.

Sue, D. W., Capodilupo, C. M., Torino, G. C., Bucceri, J. M., Holder, A. M. B., Nadal, K. L., & Esquilin, M. E. (2007). Racial microaggressions in everyday life: Implications for clinical practice. *American Psychologist, 62*(4), 271–286.

Sue, S. (1998). In search of cultural competence in psychotherapy and counseling. *American Psychologist, 53*, 440–448.

Sue, S. (1999). Science, ethnicity, and bias: Where have we gone wrong? *American Psychologist, 54*, 1070–1077.

Sue, S., Fujino, D., Hu, L., Takeuchi, D., & Zane N. (1991). Community mental health services for ethnic minority groups: A test of the cultural responsiveness hypothesis. *Journal of Consulting Clinical Psychology, 59*, 533–540.

Sue, S., & Zane, N. (1987). The role of culture and cultural techniques in psychotherapy: A reformulation. *American Psychologist, 42*, 37–45.

Thakore, R. V., Apfeld, J. C., Johnson, R. K., Sathiyakumar, V., Jahangir, A. A., & Sethi, M. K. (2015). School-based violence prevention strategy: A pilot evaluation. *Journal of Injury and Violence Research, 7*(2), 45–53.

Thompson, C. E., Alfred, D. M., Edwards, S, L., & Garcia, P. G. (2006). Transformative endeavors: Implementing Helms's racial identity theory to a school-based heritage project. In R. L. Toporek, L. H. Gerstein, N. A. Fouad, G. Roysircar, & T. Israel (Eds.), *Handbook for social justice in counseling psychology: Leadership, vision, and action* (pp. 100–116). Thousand Oaks, CA: Sage.

Toporek, R. L. (2003). Counselor awareness of client's worldview. In G. Roysircar, P. Arredondo, J. N. Fuertes, J. G. Ponterotto, & R. L Toporek (2003), *Multicultural counseling competencies 2003: Association for Multicultural Counseling and Development* (pp. 39–50). Alexandria, VA: Association for Multicultural Counseling and Development.

Toporek, R. L., Gerstein, L., Fouad, N. A., Roysircar, G., & Israel, T. (Eds.). (2006). *Handbook for social justice in counseling psychology: Leadership, vision and action.* Thousand Oaks, CA: Sage.

Toporek, R. L., Lewis, J., & Crether, H. C. (2009). Promoting systemic change through ACA advocacy competencies, *Journal of Counseling & Development, 87*, 260–268.

Trickett, E. J., Watts, R. J., & Birman, D. (Eds.). (1994). *Human diversity: Perspectives on people in context.* San Francisco, CA: Jossey-Bass.

Trimble, J. E. (1981). Value differences and their importance in counseling American Indians. In P. B. Pedersen, J. G. Draguns, W. J. Lonner, & J. E. Trimble (Eds.), *Counseling across cultures* (2nd ed.). Honolulu: University Press of Hawaii.

Tummala-Narra, P. (2016). *Psychoanalytic theory and cultural competence in psychotherapy.* Washington, DC: American Psychological Association.

Turner, S., & Pope, M. (2009). Counseling with North America's native peoples: A social justice and trauma counseling approach. *Journal of Multicultural Counseling and Development, 37*, 194–205. doi: org/10.1002/j.2161-1912.2009.tb00102.x

Utsey, S. O., Bolden, M. A., & Brown, A. L. (2001). Visions of revolution from the spirit of Frantz Fanon: Psychotherapy of liberation for confronting societal racism and oppression. In J. G. Ponterotto, J. M. Casas, L. A. Suzuki, & C. M. Alexander (Eds.), *Handbook of multicultural counseling* (2nd ed., pp. 311–336). Thousand Oaks, CA: Sage.

Valencia, R. R., & Suzuki, L. A. (2001). *Intelligence testing and minority students: Foundations, performance factors, and assessment issues.* Thousand Oaks, CA: Sage.

VandenBos, G, R. (Ed.). (2007). *APA dictionary of psychology.* Washington, DC: American Psychological Association.

Vasquez, M. J. T. (2014). Speak up and speak out: Why psychologists should take up John Lewis' call for immigration reform. *Psychology Benefits.* Retrieved from https://psychologybenefits.org/2014/11/12/speak-up-and-speak-out-why-psychologists-should-take-up-john-lewis-call-for-immigration-reform/

Vontress, C. E., & Epp, L. R. (1997). Historical hostility in the African American client: Implications for counseling. *Journal of Multicultural Counseling and Development, 25*(3), 170–184.

Whaley, A. L. (1998). Cross-cultural perspective on paranoia: A focus on the Black American experience. *Psychiatric Quarterly, 69*(4), 325–343.

White, J. L. (1972). Toward a black psychology. In R. L. Jones (Ed.), *Black psychology* (pp. 43–50). New York, NY: Harper & Row. (An early version appeared in *Black Scholar* and a popular version in *Ebony* magazine, 1970)

White, J. L. (2004, October). *Oral history interview with Wade E. Pickren.* Washington, DC: American Psychological Assiociation [Archives].

White, J. L., & Cones, J. H., III (1999). *Black man emerging: Facing the past and seizing a future in America.* New York, NY: Routledge.

Whitaker, R. (2002). *Mad in America: Bad science, bad medicine, and the enduring mistreatment of the mentally ill.* Cambridge, MA: Perseus.

Wijeyesinghe, C., & Jackson, B. W. (Eds.). (2012). *New perspectives on racial identity development: Integrating emerging frameworks.* New York: New York University Press.

Williams, R. (1974). A history of the Association of Black Psychologists: Early formation and development. *Journal of Black Psychology, 1*, 9–24.

Wrenn, G. (1962). The culturally encapsulated therapist. *Harvard Educational Review, 32*, 444–449.

Yeh, C. J., & Inose, M. (2002). Difficulties and coping strategies of Chinese, Japanese, and Korean immigrant students. *Adolescence, 37*, 69–82.

Young, R. A., & Collin, A. (2004). Introduction: Constructivism and social constructionism in the career field. *Journal of Vocational Behavior, 64*(3), 373–388. doi: org/10.1016/j.jvb.2003.12.005

Zalaquett, C. (n.d.a) *Interview with Derald Wing Sue.* Microtraining: An imprint of Alexander Street Press. Retrieved September 1, 2007, from http//www.academicvideostore.com/

Zalaquett, C. (n.d.b). *The person and the professional in counseling and therapy: Paul Bodholt Pedersen.* Retrieved September 1, 2007, from http://www.coedu.usf.edu/zalaquett/mt/pp.htm

CHAPTER 15

Alia, V. (2004). *Media ethics and social change.* Edinburgh, UK: Edinburgh University Press.

Anderson, L. W., & Krathwohl, D. R. (Eds.). (2001). *A taxonomy for learning, teaching, and assessing: A revision of Bloom's taxonomy of educational objectives.* Boston, MA: Allyn & Bacon.

Barsaglini, A., Sartori, G., Benetti, S., Pettersson-Yeo, W., & Mechelli, A. (2014). The effects of psychotherapy on brain function: A systematic and critical review. *Progresses in Neurobiology, 114*, 1–14. doi:10.1016/j.pneurobi0.2013.10.006

Benford, G. (2010). *The wonderful future that never was: Flying cars, mail delivery by parachute, and other predictions from the past.* New York, NY: Hearst Books.

Bloom, B. S., Engelhart, M. D., Furst, E. J., Hill, W. H., & Krathwohl, D. R. (1956). *Taxonomy of educational objectives: The classification of educational goals: Handbook I. Cognitive domain.* New York, NY: David McKay.

Bozarth, J. D., Zimring, F. M., & Tausch, R. (2002). Client-centered therapy: The evolution of a revolution. In D. J. Cain (Ed.), *Humanistic psychotherapies: Handbook of research and practice* (pp. 147–188). Washington, DC: American Psychological Association.

Bugental, J. F. T. (1987). *The art of the psychotherapist.* New York, NY: Norton.

Cain, D. J., & Seeman, J. (Eds.). (2002). *Humanistic psychotherapies: Handbook of research and practice.* American Psychological Association: Washington. DC.

Ceci, S. J., & Bruck, M. (1995). *Jeopardy in the courtroom: A scientific analysis of children's testimony.* Washington, DC: American Psychological Association.

Chopra, D. (2013, July 8). Can the truth come back with a capital "T"? *Huffington Post.* Retrieved from http://www.huffingtonpost.com/deepak-chopra/can-the-truth-come-back-w_b_3561406.html

Clark, A. J. (2010). Empathy: An integral model in the counseling process. *Journal of Counseling & Development, 88,* 348-356.

Davidson, S. (2016). Black cat quotes and sayings. *MediaCet Ltd.* Retrieved from https://mysmelly.com/content/cats/black-cat-quotes-and-sayings.htm

Enders, G. (2015). *Gut: The inside story of our body's most underrated organ.* Vancouver, Canada: Greystone Books.

Ernst, B., & Escher, M. C. (2002). *Impossible worlds.* Cologne, Germany: Taschen.

Eysenck, H. J. (1952). The effects of psychotherapy: An evaluation. *Journal of Consulting Psychology, 16,* 319–324.

Eysenck, H. J. (1965). *Fact and fiction in psychology.* Baltimore, MD: Penguin Books.

Frances, A. (2013). *Saving normal: An insider's revolt against out-of-control psychiatric diagnosis, DSM-5, big pharma, and the medicalization of ordinary life.* New York, NY: HarperCollins.

Freeman, D. (1983). *Margaret Mead and Samoa: The making and unmaking of an anthropological myth.* Cambridge, MA: Harvard University Press.

Fischer, A. R., Jome, L. M., & Atkinson, D. R. (1998). Reconceptualizing multicultural counseling: Universal healing conditions in a culturally specific context. *Counseling Psychologist, 26*(4), 525–588.

Elliott, R., Bohart, A. C., Watson, J. C., Greenberg, L. S. (2011). Empathy. In J. Norcross (Ed.), *Psychotherapy relationships that work* (2nd ed., pp 132–152). New York, NY: Oxford University Press.

Eysenck, H. J. (1952). The effects of psychotherapy: An evaluation. *Journal of Consulting Psychology, 16,* 319–324.

Ghose, T. (2013, April 2). "Just a theory": 7 misused science words. *Scientific American.* Retrieved from https://www.scientificamerican.com/article/just-a-theory-7-misused-science-words

Ginter, E. J., & Glauser, A. S. (2010). *Life-skills for the university and beyond* (4th ed.). Dubuque, IA: Kendall/Hunt.

Glass, G. V., & Smith, M. L. (1978). A reply to Eysenck. *American Psychologist, 33,* 517–519.

Gonçalves, Ó. F., & Perrone-McGovern, K. M. (2014). A neuroscience agenda for counseling psychology research. *Journal of Counseling Psychology, 61,* 507–512. doi:10.1037/cou0000026

Grencavage, L. M., & Norcross, J. C. (1990). Where are the commonalities among the therapeutic common factors? *Professional Psychology: Research and Practice, 21*(5), 372–378.

Haggard, P. (2011). Decision time for free will. *Neuron 69*(3), 404–406.

Heider, K. G. (1988). The Rashomon effect: When ethnographers disagree. *American Anthropologist, 90*(1), 73–81.

Higashi, Y., & Tsuchikawa, T. (Producers). (2000). *Tomie: Replay* (富江) [Motion picture]. Tokyo, Japan: Art Port.

Ivey, A. E., D'Andrea, M. J., & Ivey, M. B. (2012). *Theories of counseling and psychotherapy: A multicultural perspective* (7th ed.). Thousand Oaks, CA: Sage.

Ivey, A. E., Ivey, M. B., & Zalaquett, C. (2013). *Intentional interviewing and counseling: Facilitating client development in a multicultural world* (7th ed.). Belmont, CA: Brooks/Cole.

Ivey, A. E., & Zalaquett, C. J. (2011). Neuroscience and counseling: Central issue for social justice. *Journal for Social Action in Counseling and Psychology, 3,* 103–116.

Kumari, V. (2006). Do psychotherapies produce neurobiological effects? *Acta Neuropsychiatrica, 18,* 61–70. doi:10.1111/j.1601-5215.2006.00127.x

Lambert, M. J. (1992). Psychotherapy outcome research: Implications for integrative and eclectic therapists. In J. C. Norcross, C. John, & M. R. Goldfried (Eds.), *Handbook of psychotherapy integration* (pp. 94–129). New York, NY: Basic Books.

Lazarus, A. (1981). *The practice of multimodal therapy.* New York, NY: McGraw-Hill.

Leibert, T. W., & Dunne-Bryant, A. (2015). Do common factors account for counseling outcome? *Journal of Counseling & Development, 93,* 225–235.

Libet, B. (1985). Unconscious cerebral initiative and the role of conscious will in voluntary action. *Behavioral and Brain Sciences, 8,* 529–566.

Linden, D. E. J. (2006). How psychotherapy changes the brain: The contribution of functional neuroimaging. *Molecular Psychiatry, 11,* 528–538. doi:10.1038/sj.mp.4001816

Linehan, M. M., & Dimeff, L. (2001). Dialectical behavior therapy in a nutshell. *California Psychologist, 34,* 10–13.

Luke, C. (2016). *Neuroscience for counselors and therapist: Integrating the sciences of mind and brain.* Thousand Oaks, CA: Sage.

Mead, M. (1928). *Coming of age in Samoa: A psychological study of primitive youth for western civilisation*. New York, NY: William Morrow.

Mele, A. R. (2014). *Free:Why science hasn't disproved free will*. New York, NY: Oxford University Press.

Montague, P. R. (2008). Free will. *Current Biology, 18*, 584–585.

Perry, B. D., & Szalavitz, M. (2006). *The boy who was raised as a dog:And other stories from a child psychiatrist's notebook*. New York, NY: Basic Books.

Russell, R. L. (Ed.). (1994). *Reassessing psychotherapy research*. New York, NY: Guilford Press.

Smith, M. L., & Glass, G. V. (1977). Meta-analysis of psychotherapy outcome studies. *American Psychologist, 32*, 752–760.

Soon, C. S., Brass, M., Heinze, H.-J., Haynes, J.-D. (2008). Unconscious determinants of free decisions in the human brain. *Nature Neuroscience, 11*(5), 543–545.

Yalom, I. D. (2002). *The gift of therapy:An open letter to a new generation of therapists and their patients*. New York, NY: Harper Perennial.

INDEX

Dream work:
    gestalt therapy, 232–233, 234*t*
    individual psychology, 114
    psychoanalytic theory, 53,
        71–73, 77
Dreikurs, Rudolf, 99, 122
Drive perspective, 59–60, 72
Dual relationships, 31–33, 35–36
Dully, Howard, 6*f*
Dynamic unconscious, 56–57,
    58–59

Eastern perspective:
    cognitive-behavioral theory, 296
    existentialism, 158
    gestalt therapy, 208–209
    person-centered theory,
        184–185
Eastman, Sylvester, 208
Egalitarianism, 367
Ego, 58–59, 60, 70–71, 72
Ego, Hunger and Aggression (Perls &
    Perls), 211, 212*t*
Ego assessment, 68
Ego defense mechanisms, 7, 60–63
Ego Function Assessment (Bellak), 68
Ego-ideal, 59
Egotism, 228
Eight Lessons for a Happier Marriage
    (Glasser), 325, 343*t*
Ellis, Albert:
    cognitive-behavioral theory,
        281–282
    personal background, 279,
        281–282, 444*f*
    publications, 444
    quotes from, 283*t*, 461*t*
    rational emotive behavior
        therapy (REBT), 55, 443,
        444–445
Emic (multicultural) approach, 499
Emotional cutoff, 469
Emotional exhaustion, 41–42
Emotionally-based reasoning, 292
Emotional self-care, 43–44, 48*t*
Emotion-focused therapy, 186, 193
Empathetic-following technique, 185
Empathy, 176, 177*t*
Empirically supported treatment
    (EST), 10, 266, 510
Empirically validated treatment,
    9–10
Empowerment, 366, 372
Empty-chair technique, 231, 238
Enactment technique, 457
Encounter group movement, 173
Encouragement Scale, 121
End of The Story, The (Davis),
    420–421
England, 2
Enmeshed family structure, 456
Epstein, Timofeyewna, 98
Epston, David, 410–411
Erickson, Milton H., 394

Erikson, Erik, 77–78, 81, 95
Esalen Institute (California), 213
Escher, M. C., 546, 547*f*
Essence of Psychotherapy, The
    (Rogers), 177*t*
Essentialism, 406
Ethics:
    American Counseling
        Association, 30–33, 37–38
    American Psychoanalytic
        Association, 86–87
    American Psychological
        Association, 33–38
    behavioral theory, 269
    boundary crossing, 32
    boundary violation, 32
    cognitive-behavioral theory,
        304–305
    confidentiality, 30–31, 34–35
    constructivism, 419
    counselor competence, 33,
        36–37
    counselor motivation, 28
    counselor values, 29
    decision-making, 37–39
    in existentialism, 155
    family therapy, 463–464
    feminist therapy, 374–378
    gestalt therapy, 240
    in individual psychology, 125
    informed consent, 29
    legal issues, 39
    multicultural therapy, 510–511
    multiple role relationships,
        31–33, 35–36
    online counseling, 39
    person-centered theory,
        189–190
    professional guidelines, 28–39
    record keeping, 29–30
    sexual client relationships, 32
Ethnicity, 496
Etic (cross-cultural) approach, 499
Eugenics, 483
European Association of Gestalt
    Therapy (EAGT), 237
Every Day Gets a Littler Closer
    (Yalom), 141
Every Student Can Succeed
    (Glasser), 343*t*
Evidence-Based Medicine Working
    Group, 10
Evidence-based practice (EBP), 10,
    26, 266
Evocative-response technique, 186
Existence (May), 139
Existential Analysis, 158
Existential-humanistic theory, 217
Existentialism:
    aloneness, 144–145
    anxiety, 145
    bandwagon effect, 146
    basic concepts, 143–145
    case illustration, 134, 158–161

change process, 147
client assessment, 148–151
client role, 146–147
contemporary research
    support, 156
courage, 139
cultural example, 133, 144–145
death, 145
dereflection technique, 135
destiny, 139
developmental stages of, 139
diagnostic criteria, 157
Eastern perspective, 158
ethics, 155
existential analytic diagnosis,
    150–151
freedom, 143–144
free will, 14–15
historical context, 142–143
humanist orientation, 150
identity, 144–145
insurance reimbursement, 157
internalized marginalization, 154
life, 145
logotherapy, 14, 136–138.152
love, 140
meaning-making, 133, 145
meaning of the moment,
    151–152
meaning-triangle technique,
    151–152
multicultural case illustration,
    161–164
multicultural perspective,
    153–155
myths, 140–141
normative orientation, 150
paradoxical-intention
    technique, 152
physical dimension, 148
psychological dimension, 149
relatedness, 144–145
responsibility, 143–144
self-awareness, 143–144
social dimension, 148
social justice perspective,
    153–155
Socratic dialogue technique, 152
spiritual dimension, 149–150
study guide, 165–166
Sunday neurosis, 137
systemic impacts, 156–157
techniques and strategies,
    151–153
theoretical comparison, 537*t*
theoretical limitations, 156–157
theoretical relevance, 157–158
theorist background, 135–136,
    138–139, 141
theorist contribution, 14–15,
    136–138, 139–141,
    143–153
theorist quotes, 142*t*
therapeutic goals, 146

therapeutic process, 145–153
therapist role, 146
training programs, 157–158
ultimate life meaning, 151–152
will, 140
worldview, 145, 148, 150
Existential Psychotherapy (Yalom), 141
Experiential family therapy,
    458–460
    change process, 460
    client assessment, 459
    family dynamics, 458
    family-life chronology, 459
    family role, 459
    I-message technique, 459
    sculpting technique, 460
    stress-response technique,
        459–460
    techniques and strategies,
        459–460
    termination phase, 460
    theorist background, 458
    therapeutic goal, 459
    therapist role, 458–459
Experimentation, 229
Explanatory power of theory, 7
Explicit racism, 498
Exposure therapy, 294–295
Extinction strategy, 259–260

Failure identity, 331
Families and Family Therapy
    (Minuchin), 455
Families of the Slums (Minuchin), 455
Family constellation relationships,
    108–110, 440
Family council, 440
Family-life chronology, 459
Family of origin, 435
Family secrets, 463–464
Family systems therapy, 452–455
    change process, 455
    client assessment, 453–454
    coaching technique, 454
    de-triangulation technique,
        454–455
    differentiation assessment, 453
    family dynamics, 453
    family role, 453
    fused assessment, 453–454
    techniques and strategies,
        454–455
    termination phase, 455
    therapeutic goal, 454
    therapist role, 453
Family therapy:
    ABCDE technique, 447
    accreditation programs, 460–461
    appropriate client populations,
        460–462
    basic concepts, 439–440
    binuclear families, 436
    blended family, 435
    case illustration, 437, 466–468